DEFINING DANGER

Books by James W. Clarke

American Assassins:
The Darker Side of Politics

Last Rampage:
The Escape of Gary Tison

On Being Mad or Merely Angry:
John W. Hinckley, Jr. and Other Dangerous People

The Lineaments of Wrath:
Race, Violent Crime, and American Culture

Defining Danger:
American Assassins and the New Domestic Terrorists

American Assassins and the New Domestic Terrorists

DEFINING DANGER

James W. Clarke

Transaction Publishers
New Brunswick (U.S.A.) and London (U.K.)

New material this edition copyright © 2012 by Transaction Publishers, New Brunswick, New Jersey. Originally published in 2006 by Transaction Publishers.

All rights reserved under International and Pan-American Copyright Conventions. No part of this book may be reproduced or transmitted in any form or by any means, electronic or mechanical, including photocopy, recording, or any information storage and retrieval system, without prior permission in writing from the publisher. All inquiries should be addressed to Transaction Publishers, Rutgers—The State University of New Jersey, 35 Berrue Circle, Piscataway, New Jersey 08854-8042. www.transactionpub.com

This book is printed on acid-free paper that meets the American National Standard for Permanence of Paper for Printed Library Materials.

Library of Congress Catalog Number: 2011030475
ISBN:978-0-7658-0341-2 (cloth); 978-1-4128-4590-8 (paper)
Printed in the United States of America

Library of Congress Cataloging-in-Publication Data

Clarke, James W., 1937-
   Defining danger : American assassins and the new domestic terrorists / James W. Clarke ; with a new epilogue by the author.
      p. cm.
   Includes bibliographical references and index.
   ISBN 978-1-4128-4590-8
    1. Assassins--United States--Biography. 2. Assassination--United States. 3. Terrorists--United States--Biography. 4. Domestic terrorism--United States. I. Title.

HV6285.C53 2012
364.152'4092273--dc23

2011030475

For

Betty, Don, Mary and Steve

Contents

Acknowledgments	ix
Prologue	xi
1. On Being Mad or Merely Angry	1

Part 1: Type I

2. Type I—Region and Class: John Wilkes Booth and Leon F. Czolgosz	11
3. Type I—Nationalism: Oscar Collazo, Griselio Torresola, and Sirhan Bishara Sirhan	57

Part 2: Type II

4. Type II—Rejection: Lee Harvey Oswald and Samuel Joseph Byck	103
5. Type II—The Feminine Dimension: Lynette Alice Fromme and Sara Jane Moore	145

Part 3: Type III

6. Type III—Nihilism: Giuseppe Zangara and Arthur Herman Bremer	171
7. Type III—Nihilism: John W. Hinckley, Jr. and Francisco Martin Duran	201

Part 4: Type IV and Atypical

8. Type IV—The Psychotics: Richard Lawrence, Charles J. Guiteau, and John Schrank	235
9. The Atypicals—Family and Money: Carl Austin Weiss and James Earl Ray	267

Part 5: Domestic Terrorists

10.	Industrial Society: Theodore John Kaczynski	309
11.	Ruby Ridge, Waco, and Roe. v. Wade: Timothy James McVeigh and Eric Robert Rudolph	335

Part 6: Conclusion

12.	Criminal Responsibility and Risk	373

Epilogue   385

Selected Bibliography   393

Index   409

Acknowledgments

I first became interested in the subject of assassination in 1968 in the wake of the assassinations of Martin Luther King, Jr. and Robert Kennedy. Since then I have spent a good part of my academic career researching, lecturing, and writing about that subject. Along the way, I am grateful to a number of people who helped, but let me emphasize, bear no responsibility for any mistakes and the conclusions, which are mine alone.

The *British Journal of Political Science* led the way in publishing this research, which many considered controversial in the early 1980s, because it challenged conventional wisdom on the subject. I remain indebted to Ivor Crewe who, as editor, published the first article on the now accepted general typology of assassins and would-be assassins. For the same reasons, I also remain indebted to Sandy Thatcher, former director of Princeton University Press, which published my first two books on the subject: *American Assassins: The Darker Side of Politics* (1982), and *On Being Mad or Merely Angry: John W. Hinckley, Jr. and Other Dangerous People* (1990).

I was fortunate to attract the attention of the U.S. Secret Service. Ken Baker, former agent and director of research at that time, gave me the opportunity to lecture, discuss, and exchange insights on the subject with him and others at Secret Service headquarters in Washington. On one of those trips I began to research John Hinckley's attempted assassination of President Reagan. Roger Adelman and Dick Chapman, of the U.S. Attorneys Office in Washington, were most helpful to my gaining access to the voluminous transcripts and documents associated with that landmark case.

As my research continued after Hinckley, Captain Seth Lucente, U.S. Army Special Forces and former student at the University of Arizona, helped me research President Clinton's would-be assassin, Francisco Martin Duran. The paper we wrote was published, again, in the *British Journal of Political Science*, thanks to the sterling editorial judgment of Albert Weale. Seth also assisted on the Timothy McVeigh case, providing important insights from a soldier's perspective. Another University of Arizona student, Courtney Hartstein, wrote an interesting paper on Ted Kaczynski, the so-called

"Unabomber," which I found useful in developing my own thoughts about that case. In the course of my research on Kaczynski, I spent a rewarding afternoon in Lincoln, Montana, talking with Sherri Wood. Mrs. Wood probably knew this strange, interesting man better than anyone outside his family.

As I began to put this book together, the College of Social and Behavioral Sciences at the University of Arizona kindly approved a Research Professorship for a semester, during which a portion of this work was done. Vickie Healey and Pat Rhyner, of the Department of Political Science, deserve many thanks for all their help – and the time they saved me – in organizing the vast amount of documentation that went into this project.

Once again, it is an honor and pleasure to have this work published under the editorial direction of Irving Louis Horowitz and Mary E. Curtis of Transaction Publishers. As always, I am grateful to my wife, Jeanne Nienaber Clarke, who patiently watched and listened as this project evolved, and never once doubted that it was important to do.

Prologue

It was March 30, 1981 and President Ronald Reagan had just completed a speech he had given to thirty-five hundred AFL-CIO delegates who were meeting in Washington at the Hilton Hotel on Connecticut Avenue. Moments later as the applause receded there was a stirring in the lobby as the president emerged from the ballroom surrounded by his aides and Secret Service detail. They walked briskly through the lobby and outside to the limousine waiting at the curb.

On the sidewalk cameramen and reporters jostled spectators and one another to get closer to the president. "Press, press," a reporter said as he tried to elbow his way toward the Secret Service agents who marked the president's exit route. "No way," a fair-haired young man replied stubbornly, "we were here first."[1]

Moments later that same young man aimed a .22 caliber pistol at the president. Six shots exploded in less than three seconds, fired from a crouched position, pistol held professionally with both hands, moving methodically right to left as he tracked the president's movement toward the waiting limousine. Secret Service agents reacted instantly, pushing through the crowd to pounce on the shooter who was already in a bystander's grasp, and then wrenching the weapon from his hands and forcing him to the ground.

As the first shots exploded, Secret Service agent Tim McCarthy leaped between the president and the source of the gunfire, arms spread wide, providing a human shield. Suddenly he stiffened, then dropped as the fourth bullet caught him in the stomach. In another swift movement, agent Jerry Parr, who was walking at Reagan's side, grabbed the startled president's shoulders and forced him down behind the armored rear door of the limousine only milliseconds before Hinckley's fifth bullet smashed into its bulletproof window. The shot was well aimed. Without the window the bullet would probably have struck the left side of the president's head.

Had it not been for that sixth bullet, the president would have been spared entirely due to the quick and courageous actions of McCarthy and Parr. As Reagan was leaning into the limousine, the last bullet hit the rear fender and glanced forward and upward behind the open door, striking the president's left armpit. Reagan groaned when Parr pushed him inside to the floor and dove on top of him.² Not yet aware that he had been shot, Reagan attributed the sharp pain that flashed through his chest – "like someone hitting me with a hammer as hard as they could" – to Parr's rough handling. "You sonofabitch, you broke my rib," the president moaned half jokingly as the limousine lurched away from the curb, its tires squealing against the wet pavement.³

The scene they left behind was bedlam. Amid the hysterical screams of bystanders, wailing sirens, and shouts of Secret Service agents and police attempting to gain control of the situation, Tim McCarthy lay doubled up on the sidewalk, hands clutching the bullet wound in his stomach; a few feet away police officer Tom Delahanty writhed in agony from a neck wound; next to him lay presidential press secretary Jim Brady, the first to fall, his face flattened against the sidewalk, arms twitching convulsively at his sides as blood trickled from a pea-sized bullet hole over his left eye. Another bullet had narrowly missed the head of presidential aide Michael Deaver before striking a building across the street. Out of six shots it was the only clean miss.⁴

***

First reports of the president's condition, and subsequent White House press releases about his supposed rapid recovery, attempted to conceal the critical nature of his wound. Despite public statements that the president was "A-OK" after having "sailed through surgery," and a hospital spokesman's assurance that he would "be able to make decisions by tomorrow, certainly," persons who saw the president knew differently. Except for an informed snap judgment by Secret Service agent Jerry Parr, the fortuitous presence that afternoon of a very competent trauma team and two highly skilled thoracic surgeons who just happened to be on duty at George Washington University Hospital, President Reagan would have surely become the fifth president of the United States to die from an assassin's bullet.

Jerry Parr, like Reagan himself, was at first unaware that the president had been hit. In Washington normal procedure in such emergencies is to return directly to the White House, the most secure area in the city. Had that procedure been followed in this instance, Ronald Reagan would have died there. It was only when Reagan turned to speak that Parr noticed the bright-red oxygenated blood flecking the president's lips and filling the corners of his mouth. He knew at once that the seventy-year-old president had been shot, and that it was a life-threatening lung wound. Parr immediately ordered the driver, Drew Unrue, to head for the Emergency Room of the George Washington University Hospital. Unrue changed routes and radioed ahead to alert the Emergency Room staff.⁵

By the time they arrived, the color had drained from Reagan's normally ruddy complexion; Parr could tell he was in pain, and then Reagan complained that he was having difficulty breathing. Strangely, a stretcher was not waiting for the stricken president. With Parr's support Reagan tried to walk. He almost made it through the doors before he staggered and dropped to one knee. "I can't breathe," he gasped, fear for the first time flickering in his eyes. Parr was afraid they were going to lose him. It was 2:35 P.M.[6]

Within moments the president was wheeled into the trauma room, nurses cut and stripped his clothes away, as doctors rushed to begin their examination. They found only an entry wound, a gash under his left arm. The bullet was still inside. Reagan was now coughing blood, his complexion gray, his breathing labored, coming in gasps. His diastolic blood pressure had dropped to seventy-five. Fearing a collapsed lung and other damage to the president's heart or major blood vessels, Dr. Joseph M. Giardano, chief of the trauma team, ordered a chest tube inserted at once and also began a transfusion of five units of blood to replace the frightening two-and-a-half quarts the president had already lost. Mrs. Reagan arrived and rushed to her husband's side as he was being prepared for surgery. "Honey," he whispered as she bent over him, "I forgot to duck."

As he was wheeled to surgery, the president, still conscious but growing weaker, tried to keep up a good front. "All in all, I'd rather be in Philadelphia," he mumbled through the tubes in his mouth. Then noticing the masked faces backlit by bright surgical lights suddenly surrounding him in the operating room, he whispered, "Please tell me you're Republicans." Those were the last words he spoke before he lost consciousness.[7] The president's courage was remarkable.

It was a complicated and dangerous three-and-a-half-hour operation. Dr. Benjamin Aaron, assisted by Dr. Kathleen Cheyney, finally discovered the bullet "flattened almost as thin as a dime," embedded in the president's lung. It had splintered the seventh rib and ricocheted past the heart before coming to rest in the lung. Miraculously the devastator bullet had not exploded inside the president's chest, probably because it had hit the limousine first. A fraction of an inch either way, or a larger caliber bullet, would have been fatal.[8]

Two of the other victims, Tom Delahanty and Tim McCarthy, were seriously wounded, but they would recover. There were grave doubts about Jim Brady. Doctors recognized that even if they were able to save Brady's life, the devastator bullet that penetrated his brain caused serious and irreversible damage. Life as the gregarious Jim Brady had known it was forever changed.

***

"I remember waking up early in the morning, seven or eight, and thinking why I couldn't get to sleep," John Hinckley said, recalling the morning of

March 30, 1981. He got out of bed, snapped on the *Today Show* – or maybe it was *Good Morning America,* he wasn't sure – on the way to the bathroom. He looked out the window of his Park Central Hotel room, two blocks from the White House, to the busy street below. It was gray and drizzling in Washington that morning, gloomy like his mood. He dressed and, about nine o'clock left the room he had checked into the night before and walked up K Street to the Crown Bookstore.[9]

Hinckley's tastes in reading ran toward the lives of violent people. Not ordinary street crime, but books and articles about people whose crimes had, in some sense, achieved celebrity status for them – mass and serial murderers, skyjackers – and it was difficult to name a book he hadn't read about assassins. Occasionally he also read political biographies, most recently books about Ronald Reagan and Senator Edward Kennedy. But John Lennon was his hero. He had read every book and had clipped every article he could find about the slain Beatles superstar, all of whose albums he had collected since childhood.[10] That morning nothing in the bookstore caught his eye, and he left after half an hour without buying anything. He walked across the street to a McDonald's, where he ordered an Egg McMuffin, and as he sat in a booth eating, he contemplated what to do with the rest of his day.[11]

One thing that John Hinckley always had plenty of was time. Lots of time to think or brood, and scheme, often about money. The thing that annoyed him about money was that although there was lots of it in the Hinckley family, he always had a problem prying it loose from his father. Jack Hinckley counted every dollar he gave to his youngest son and was notably disappointed with the way John Jr. had been squandering it for the past seven years. That morning John was down close to the end of the last installment his father had sent; he had somewhere between $130 and $150 left. The question he was pondering was whether to spend it on a trip to New Haven in the hope of maybe catching a glimpse of someone very special on the Yale campus, or whether to remain in Washington where he had been considering assassinating some prominent figure. Senator Edward Kennedy was among the options he had been considering or, possibly, blasting away randomly in the chambers of the United States Senate, or if he really got lucky, which is to say within range, maybe taking out the president himself. All these ideas had been running through his mind for months.[12]

He was still thinking about the possibilities when he got back to the hotel about 11:30 A.M., bought a *Washington Star,* and took the elevator up to his room. He opened the paper to page A–4, the schedule of congressional activities for the day, scanned it, then turned to the "President's Schedule." President Reagan was scheduled to make a luncheon speech at the Washington Hilton, just a short distance up Connecticut Avenue.[13]

Still undecided, he decided that in any case he should take a shower and clean up a bit. "It was in the shower," he said, "that I debated whether to detour to the Hilton or go up to New Haven. I was thinking, should I go over to the Hilton and take my little pistol and see how close I could...well, see what the scene was like." As he dressed, he decided that's what he would do.[14]

Why New Haven? In addition to President Reagan, the person who occupied a large place in John Hinckley's thoughts and fantasies was a pretty college freshman at Yale University. Hinckley had been infatuated with the actress Jodie Foster ever since he had seen her in the film *Taxi Driver*. He had written to her, even talked with her briefly on the telephone a couple of times when he called her Yale dormitory. He had traveled back and forth to New Haven repeatedly, since September, in vain attempts to see her. Disappointed but hardly surprised, he realized that a young woman as appealing as Jodie Foster would be surrounded by attentive males who were better looking than he, more sophisticated, and probably from families at least as wealthy as his. If he had learned anything during high school and his six years at Texas Tech, it was that he was not a ladies' man. And that was confirmed, once again, in New Haven.

He decided to write a last letter to her anyway. As he sat down at the small desk in his room, he wanted to be sure that he didn't say anything stupid, or something that would offend her. His carefully worded sentiments were something he wanted her to remember. "Dear Jodie," he began. "There is a definite possibility that I will be killed in my attempt to get Reagan. It is for this reason that I am writing you this letter now." Thirty minutes later he closed with, "I love you forever, John Hinckley." He dated the letter, including the time (12:45 P.M.), folded it neatly into an envelope, and placed it in his suitcase.[15]

He then put on his coat and removed a .22 caliber pistol and several boxes of ammunition from one of his two suitcases. He shook out a couple of handfuls of bullets, loaded the pistol, and pocketed the rest. "I had a whole bunch of ammunition with me," he explained later, "cheap ammo, expensive ammo. They all look the same to me."[16]

But that was a lie. Hinckley carefully chose the most lethal ammunition, deadly "devastator" bullets, which explode a second time on impact, inside the victim. There were only six devastators among the forty-three bullets he had, and he selected those six when he loaded the pistol.[17] Leaving his luggage behind, he exited the hotel, the pistol concealed in his jacket pocket, and hailed a cab. As the driver headed north on busy Connecticut Avenue to the Hilton, about nine minutes away, Hinckley was nervous and suddenly aware that he should have used the bathroom before he left his room. He asked the driver to stop at the Holiday Inn just short of his destination. After paying the fare, he dashed inside to the rest room. When he emerged, he could see television crews and a crowd gathering across the street at the T Street side entrance of the Hilton. He walked over and joined the crowd. A few minutes later the presidential entourage arrived.[18]

Hinckley was impressed when he saw the president, and excited. "He waved to us," he recalled later, "me and other people where I was, and the cameramen and all....And when he waved to us, he was looking right at me and I waved back. I was kind of startled, but maybe it was just my imagination."[19]

A few minutes after Reagan entered the hotel, Hinckley followed, walking into the lobby where he sat to wait for the president to finish his speech. A half hour later he got up and walked outside. He was having second thoughts. "Should I? Should I?" he wondered to himself. Then he decided to set a deadline. "If I was going to have to wait more than five or ten minutes, I was going to go back to the hotel. I just wasn't that desperate about it. I just wasn't that desperate to act that afternoon.... Also it was raining and I wasn't going to stand around in the rain."[20]

"I didn't even see him at first," Hinckley said, describing his first view of the president. "I just saw Secret Service and police.... Then I saw him. He was in the midst, of course, waving across the street first, then he turned toward us again, or was in the motion of turning. I never let him get all the way around. That's when I pulled out the gun and started firing."[21]

"I remember an impulse," he said afterward, "put the gun back." But it was too late. "The reporters had already seen the gun."[22] It was 2:25 P.M.

***

After his arrest, John Hinckley was subdued but responsive as he was processed and interrogated in the Central Cell Block of the Metropolitan Police Department. Eddie Meyers, a fourteen-year veteran homicide detective who looked and talked like a character in an Elmore Leonard novel, sat across from Hinckley, while FBI and Secret Service agents hovered in the background. Meyers had questioned a lot of sleazy people over the years; he knew that he couldn't let what people had done bother him if he wanted information. So when he began to question the sullen, chubby sandy-haired suspect before him, he was friendly.

"I want to hear your side of the story," he said reassuringly. Hinckley had been roughed up a little as he was disarmed and forced to the pavement after the shooting. The result was a minor scrape on one hand, but it was enough to intimidate a young man unaccustomed to scrapes and bruises. "It's okay," Meyers assured him. "You're perfectly safe here."

Hinckley hesitated before he spoke. "I don't know anything about the shooting," he said finally.

"Come on now, John. You must be a Democrat," Meyers said with a smile, hinting at Hinckley's motive.

Hinckley's mouth cracked into a grin. He couldn't help chuckling. No one had joked with him like that in a long, long time.

Later, as Meyers was completing his paperwork on Hinckley's charges, he called to another officer and asked how to spell "assassinate."

Hinckley looked up with a smirk. "I'll spell it for you," he volunteered before the officer could reply. "A-s-s-a-s-s-i-n-a-t-e."

"Thank you," Meyers replied as he typed the word on the form.

Hinckley smiled again. He seemed to be relaxing.

John Hinckley appeared to be in complete control of himself when Dr. William Brownley came in to give him a physical examination. When Brownley finished, noting no abnormalities, an FBI agent who was present during the examination asked Brownley to remove a sample of Hinckley's pubic hair.

"Pubic hair?" Meyers called from across the room in disbelief. "George, for Chrissakes, he didn't fuck Reagan, he shot him."

Hinckley couldn't restrain himself. He doubled over, shaking with laughter. Eddie Meyers was a funny guy. Hinckley liked his sense of humor.[23]

It seemed to everyone who observed John Hinckley those first few hours after his arrest that he was very aware of his situation and in control of himself. Whatever one may think of Eddie Meyer's sense of humor, Hinckley was not the only one who laughed there, or later, when the story was recounted, as it often was. Hinckley experienced, and expressed, a normal range of emotions in an appropriate manner throughout the period immediately following his arrest. He was serious when the conversation was serious; and he laughed and traded quips when it wasn't.

He was also quite aware of what he had done and its significance. During his interrogation he asked Secret Service agent Steve Colo and FBI agent George Chmiel whether his assassination attempt had been taped by television crews on the scene. When Chmiel replied that it was, Hinckley then asked if its showing was going to preempt the Academy Award presentations that evening. Both Chmiel and Colo could tell that Hinckley was hoping that it would. He was, they observed, "very concerned about the media exposure affecting other people."[24]

***

At his trial, John Hinckley's attorneys entered a plea of *Not Guilty by Reason of Insanity*. Months later, when a jury announced its verdict, acquitting Hinckley on all counts, public outrage spilled across editorial pages around the nation. It was a controversial verdict based on often confusing and conflicting psychiatric testimony.

John W. Hinckley, Jr.'s nearly successful assassination of President Reagan marked the fifteenth time serious attempts have been made to end the lives of American presidents and presidential candidates. More would follow. But why in what may be the world's most successful democracy are such events so common? What motivated this unlikely would-be assassin, the pampered son of wealthy and devoted parents? Was he really mad, acting out in the grip of some severe mental disorder, as a jury later concluded, or was he merely angry? But, if so, with whom? President Reagan, a man his father admired and had so enthusiastically supported? What was going on in John Hinckley's mind when he began squeezing the trigger?

As we will see, questions like these have been raised about almost every one of the twenty-one American assassins, would-be assassins and domestic terrorists who are the subjects of this book. Its objective is to answer them.

Notes

1. *United States v. John W. Hinckley, Jr.* Cr. No. 81-3-306 (1981); Hinckley as quoted by Dr. Park Dietz, p. 6524. Hereafter cited as Trial Transcripts.
2. The account of the shooting is drawn from FBI File No. 175-601, "John W. Hinckley, Jr." (1981), pp. 1-626. Hereafter cited as FBI Files.
3. Reagan as quoted in the *Washington Post,* April 5, 1981, p. A12.
4. FBI Files, p. 227. The sequence of Hinckley's shots was as follows: the first hit Brady; the second struck Delahanty; the third narrowly missed Deaver; the fourth hit McCarthy; the fifth stuck the limousine window; the sixth ricocheted off the fender and wounded the president.
5. Ibid., pp. 519-521.
6. Ibid., "Evidence from Hospitals;" Reagan quoted in *Washington Post,* April 5, 1981, A12.
7. Reagan as quoted in the *Washington Post,* April 5, 1981, A12; and *Time Magazine,* April 13, 1981, p. 30.
8. *Washington Post,* April 5, 1981, A12.
9. FBI Files.
10. Ibid., "Evidence from Evergreen, Colorado," pp. H29-H33, H565-H566, H1022.
11. Trial Transcripts, Dietz testimony, pp. 6520-6521.
12. FBI Files, pp. H29, H31, H33; Trial Transcripts, Dietz testimony, p.6522.
13. Ibid., "Evidence from the Park Central Hotel," pp. H15-H26.
14. Trial Transcripts, Dietz quoting Hinckley, p. 6522.
15. FBI Files, "Evidence from the Park Central Hotel;" Trial Transcripts, Government Document N-15.
16. Trial Transcripts, Dietz quoting Hinckley, pp. 6522-6523.
17. FBI Files, p. 626.
18. Trial Transcripts, Dietz testimony, pp. 6522-6523.
19. Ibid., pp. 6524-6524.

20. Ibid., Dietz quoting Hinckley remarks to Dr. Sally Johnson, p.6539; and Dietz quoting Hinckley, p. 6528.
21. Ibid., Dietz quoting Hinckley, pp. 6524-6525.
22. Ibid., Dietz quoting Hinckley remarks to Dr. Sally Johnson, p. 6539.
23. FBI Files, "Arrest and Interview Log, John W. Hinckley, Jr.," March 30, 1981, pp. 1042-1044; "Evidence from the Person of John Hinckley," pp. H1-H5; Trial Transcripts, Meyers testimony, pp. 5852-5873.
24. Ibid., pp. 175, A-311.

1

On Being Mad or Merely Angry

The title of this book, *Defining Danger,* conveys its two central themes. The first is that a sustained pattern of *individual* acts of violence directed toward America's democratically elected leaders represents a defining element of American politics that sets it apart from the rest of the modern world. The second theme addresses the issue of how that danger is defined and may be confronted through an analysis of the motives and characteristics of twenty American assassins, would-be assassins, and domestic terrorists.

Assassination is the premeditated murder of a political figure for reasons associated with the victim's prominence, or perspective, or some combination of both. In the 211 years between 1789, when George Washington became the first president of the United States and the conclusion of Bill Clinton's second term in 2001, forty-two men have held the nation's highest office. Four of them were killed by assassins,[1] and serious attempts were made on the lives of seven others.[2] Thus approximately one in four presidents was the target of violence. Furthermore, the political careers of four presidential candidates were interrupted, or ended, by violence.[3] Add to that list of casualties the names of Black Muslim leader Malcolm X, who was murdered by members of his own sect in 1965, civil rights leader Martin Luther King, Jr., shot to death three years later by a contract killer, and the murders in 1998 of two Capitol security guards at the hands of a gunman intent on killing members of Congress, and it is reasonable to conclude that political prominence in the United States entails grave risks that exceed those faced by leaders in every other modern nation.

This is especially the case since 1963. In the thirty-seven years from the first Kennedy assassination and the end of the century, there were ten assassination attempts on the lives of nationally prominent political leaders. That is one more than the nine presidential elections during the same period. That's two more assassination attempts in this recent period than the eight recorded

2   Defining Danger

in the previous 174 years of the nation's presidential history. New elements of domestic terror in American life were introduced in the 1980s and 1990s by Ted Kaczynski, the "Unabomber," Timothy McVeigh, the "Oklahoma City Bomber," and Eric Rudolph, the Summer Olympics and abortion clinic bomber. All were politically motivated; their crimes unprecedented. The twenty-one subjects — assassins, would-be assassins, and domestic terrorists — their victims, actual or intended, and the dates of their attacks are presented in table 1.1.

Criminal Responsibility

Standards of criminal responsibility have evolved over the years and remain fluid. In one of the first cases to establish a standard which recognized mental illness as a mitigating factor in a defendant's guilt, an English court in 1843 established what has since become known as the M'Naghten Rule.[4] M'Naghten was based on the answers to two questions: Did the defendant know what he/she was doing at the time the crime was committed? Did the defendant know that his/her actions were in violation of the law? This was the standard adopted and followed in American courts until the 1950s when

Figure 1.1
American Assassins, Would-be Assassins, and Domestic Terrorists and Their Victims

1835	Richard Lawrence	Andrew Jackson
1865	John Wilkes Booth	Abraham Lincoln
1881	Charles Guiteau	James Garfield
1901	Leon Czolgosz	William McKinley
1912	John Schrank	Theodore Roosevelt
1933	Giuseppe Zangara	Franklin D. Roosevelt
1935	Carl Weiss	Huey Long
1950	Oscar Collazo Griselio Torresola	Harry S Truman
1963	Lee Harvey Oswald	John F. Kennedy
1968	James Earl Ray	Martin Luther King, Jr.
1968	Sirhan Sirhan	Robert F. Kennedy
1972	Arthur Bremer	George Wallace
1974	Samuel Byck	Richard Nixon
1975	Lynette Alice Fromme	Gerald Ford
1975	Sara Jane Moore	Gerald Ford
1981	John W. Hinckley, Jr.	Ronald Reagan
1994	Francisco Martin Duran	Bill Clinton
1978–1996	Theodore Kaczynski	American scientists and businessmen
1995	Timothy McVeigh	Federal Building, Oklahoma City
1996–1998	Eric Robert Rudolph	Summer Olympics and Abortion Clinics

modifications began to be introduced to take into account expanding knowledge of mental illness and its effects on behavior. In 1962, the American Law Institute drafted what it called a Model Penal Code to incorporate these developments in the science of mental health. The code stated in part that:

A person is not responsible for criminal conduct if at the time of such conduct, as a result of mental disease or defect, he lacks substantial capacity either to appreciate the criminality of his conduct or to conform his conduct to the requirements of the law.[5]

This new approach to assessing criminal responsibility, sometimes referred to as the diminished capacity standard, stripped to its essentials, asks two questions: Did the defendant have a mental disease or defect? If so, was that mental disease or defect the cause of his criminal act? If both questions were answered in the affirmative, the defendant could not be held accountable for his crime.

Many states incorporated the concept of diminished capacity into state law during the 1960s and 1970s, setting aside the earlier M'Naghten Rule as being too insensitive to modern medical science and the complexities of mental illness. But that trend ended in reaction to the public outcry that followed the lenient sentences and acquittals handed down to defendants who the public believed were fully accountable for their crimes. Perhaps the best known of these cases was the acquittal by reason of insanity of President Ronald Reagan's would-be assassin, John W. Hinckley, Jr., in 1981. In direct response to that unpopular verdict, Congress enacted the Insanity Defense Reform Act in 1984 and many state legislatures followed its lead. Among the key changes in these new laws, was a return to standards of criminal responsibility resembling the more restrictive M'Naghten Rule. Many also included provisions which shifted the burden of proof from the prosecution to the defense, placing the difficult task of erasing "reasonable doubt" squarely on the defendant rather than the state. In the chapters that follow, we will see how important these changes have been in determining the degree to which some defendants are held accountable for their crimes.

Defining Danger

For some time, at least until the early 1980s, the psychological literature on American assassins mistakenly labeled them all "paranoid schizophrenics," describing them as short, loner, white males, acting in the grip of delusions of persecution and grandeur.[6] In similar fashion, historical accounts of American assassinations usually described the perpetrators of these unfortunate events as mentally disordered subjects driven by irrational or irresistible impulses. Subsequent research by the author challenged the medical/psychiatric model, suggesting, instead, that there is no single type of assassin in the

4   Defining Danger

American context. Moreover, fully a third of these subjects were primarily motivated by political ideals rather than personal deficits as the stereotype claims. Instead of a single "type," four distinct motivational patterns are identified. The patterns are derived from an assessment of dispositional *and* contextual factors which describe the mental states and motivations of all but three of the twenty-one American assassins, would-be assassins, and domestic terrorists who are the subjects of this book. The typology presented in table 1.2 spans a motivational range from rational political extremism (Type I) through two shades of mental and emotional disturbance (Type II and Type III), to those who are truly mentally disordered (Type IV). This contextual perspective has, since then, informed the revised assessment strategies of the U.S. Secret Service.[7]

- *Type I* subjects — be they assassins or domestic terrorists — are primarily motivated by political issues. They view their actions as a probable sacrifice of self for some important political purpose. They are fully aware of what they are doing and the consequences of their actions. Such persons may or may not attempt to escape, but the sacrificial theme that characterizes their zeal suggests that capture and punishment, like death, is an acceptable risk. If apprehended, a Type I subject does not recant on his political principles, or seek clemency. While seeking to publicize the injustice that motivates him or her, purely personal motives, such as a quest for recognition or notoriety, are absent. Type I assassins are political extremists whose actions, within the context of their political beliefs, are rational and principled.
- *Type II* subjects are primarily motivated by profound, seemingly unresolvable, personal problems. They are persons with overwhelming unmet needs for acceptance, recognition, and status. Almost always their difficulties are linked to failed relationships and/or careers that fuel their anger and deepen their depression, in some cases, to suicidal levels. What distinguishes

Figure 1.2
Types of American Assassins, Would-be Assassins, and Domestic Terrorists

Characteristics:	Type I	Type II	Type III	Type IV
Emotional distortion	Mild	Moderate	Severe	Severe
Cognitive distortion	Absent	Absent	Absent	Severe
Hallucinations	Absent	Absent	Absent	Present
Delusions	Absent	Absent	Absent	Present
Reality contact	Clear	Clear	Clear	Poor
Social relations	Varied	Disturbed	Absent	Absent
Primary motive	Political	Personal/ Compensatory	Personal/ Provocation	Irrational

them from other assassins is their "political personalities," that is, their inclination to blame personal difficulties on their political victims and to *rationalize* their violent acts in terms of some larger political ideals.[8] In this sense, they displace or redirect their anger, striking out at a prominent political figure who becomes a scapegoat for their personal problems. The notoriety that accompanies their acts generates the public attention and notoriety they desire. Type II subjects may or may not be self-destructive, but either way, their acts are intended to advance very personal concerns in a public manner. In some cases, their acts may serve as a form of *vengeance,* placing the burden of guilt for what they have done on those persons in their personal lives whose rejection is the real cause of their unhappiness. In others, the same acts may be intended to advance some highly *personal* — not political — concerns. But Type II subjects are not mentally disordered in the sense that they are fully aware of their actions and the consequences.

• *Type III* subjects differ only in degree from the Type II. They also are angry, depressed but, unlike Type II subjects, they are always suicidal, having slipped further over the edge into perversity in an obsessive desire for revenge and recognition. Cut off and isolated from persons in their personal lives who once mattered to them, their anger and resentment spills over and spreads out to society *at large.* Unlike the Type II assassin, the Type III subject makes *no* attempt to rationalize his actions in terms of political ideals. This is the essential difference between the two types. Political purpose, in any sense, has *nothing* to do with the deliberate, calculating, nihilistic plans of Type III assassins. Their objective is to strike out in the most perverse, outrageous way to show their contempt for a society that has no place for them. Revenge and notoriety are their *only* goals. Thus their victims may be selected for their *prominence,* such as a political figure or a celebrity, or for their *number,* such as a sufficiently large gathering of ordinary people who are killed in a public setting like a workplace, a restaurant, or a school. Either scenario — assassination or mass murder — ensures the page-one notoriety and media attention that the Type III subject desires for his final act of revenge.

• *Type IV* subjects are the only ones who fit the earlier stereotype of severe mental derangement. Unlike the others, Type IV subjects are afflicted with serious disorders that are reflected in delusional thinking and bizarre behavior. With only a tenuous and discontinuous grasp of reality, Type IV subjects act in the grip of delusions, of imaginary grievances, with only an incomplete sense of what they are doing and no awareness at all that it is wrong to do it.

Although this typology accurately describes the basic characteristics of all but the three atypical subjects in this research, it does not presume the purity of the four classifications. Human behavior is much too complex for that. The rationalizations of Type II subjects and the delusions of Type IVs, for example, may be couched in the ideological language of the politically motivated Type I. And the violent and perverse rage of the Type III subjects may be confused with the psychotic acts of Type IVs if the reasoned and controlled manner in which that rage is expressed is overlooked.

The lethally aggressive actions of all but one of the subjects in this book can be understood as responses to some *frustration*. The pattern — frustration which builds into anger, which is, in turn, expressed aggressively — is a familiar one in the social and behavioral sciences.[9] It is the frustrating object which varies in the accounts that follow. The primary source of frustration may be political (Type I), personal (Types II and III, and one of the Atypical subjects), or purely imaginary (Type IV). The only exception is James Earl Ray who killed Martin Luther King, Jr. for money he never received. The distribution of subjects is presented in table 1.3.

My Approach

There are risks in writing a book about twenty-one complicated people. Given the scope of the study, no attempt is made to write complete biographies of each. My purpose is to focus on only those details of each subject's life that lend the most complete understanding of his or her violent act. My hope is that such comparisons across cases yield insights about the assassination and domestic terrorism phenomenon in America that are missing in case studies of particular individuals. Chapters 2 through 10 are stories about these men and women. The stories are presented in typological, rather than in chronological, order, moving from Types I through IV, and ending with the two

Table 1.3
A Typology of American Assassins, Would-Be Assassins, and Domestic Terrorists (1835–1996)

Rational———	———Disturbed———		———Irrational
Type I	Type II	Type III	Type IV
Booth	Oswald	Zangara	Lawrence
Czolgosz	Byck	Bremer	Guiteau
Collazo	Fromme	Hinckley	Schrank
Torresola	Moore	Duran	
Sirhan			
McVeigh			
Rudolph			
	Atypical		
	Weiss		
	Ray		
	Kaczynski		

domestic terrorists. As much as possible I have tried to let the facts speak for themselves. I have also tried to do the same for the subjects, so that their words, and not only my analyses and interpretations of them, are an important part of understanding each. The research relies as much as possible on primary sources, but the existence, quality, and availability of information spanning two centuries varies. In some cases it is voluminous; in others it is scant. Working within these constraints, I sought not only to present facts but also to convey moods, and feelings that pervaded these dark events. Put differently, I tried to see the world as these subjects saw it and to explain their behavior with that perspective always in mind.

To understand violence, it is essential to understand not only the personality of the perpetrator, but also the *context* in which the behavior occurs. In the rush to analyze personalities, context is sometimes ignored. By context I mean the array of cultural, political, economic, and social forces that mold and channel human behavior over time, as well as the immediate *situational* factors that often precipitate the actions in question. Without taking into account the context of behavior, it is virtually impossible to understand the motives behind it. For the same reason, an understanding of context provides the best clues yet known concerning the potential *dangerousness* of suspects who come to the attention of the Secret Service and other security agencies. These potentially lethal patterns of behavior that often precede assassination attempts and mass murder, and the broader implications of this research, are described in a concluding chapter.

Empathy often follows understanding, and a few of these stories may be disturbing in that sense. If some of these subjects seem more human that they have been depicted in the past, it is because they are, and not because I made them that way. My purpose is to present accurate information — not apologies or excuses — that enhances our understanding of the reasons for these sad events and, maybe, even our ability to anticipate and prevent them from happening. Almost all assassins are "troubled" in some sense. That is not the issue. It is *how* and *why* they are troubled that this book seeks to explain.

Notes

1. They were Abraham Lincoln in 1865, James Garfield in 1881, William McKinley in 1901, and John F. Kennedy in 1963.
2. They were Andrew Jackson in 1835, Franklin Roosevelt in 1933, Harry Truman in 1950, Richard Nixon in 1974, Gerald Ford (twice) in 1975, Ronald Reagan in 1981, and Bill Clinton in 1994.
3. They were Theodore Roosevelt in 1912, Huey Long in 1935, Robert Kennedy in 1968, and George Wallace in 1972. Although Senator Long was not a formally declared presidential candidate at the time of his death, there is little doubt that he was actively campaigning for that office.

8   Defining Danger

4. *Daniel M'Naghten's Case*, 10 Clark and Fin. 200, 8 Eng. Rep. 718 (1843). See, also, W.C. Townsend, *Modern State Trials* (London: Longman, Brown, 1850).
5. Model Penal Code 4.01 (American Law Institute, P.O.D. 1962)
6. See, for example, R.J. Donovan, *The Assassins* (New York: Harper & Brothers, 1952); D.W. Hastings, "The Psychiatry of Presidential Assassination, Part I: Jackson and Lincoln," *The Journal-Lancet* 85 (March 1965), 95–100; "Part II: Garfield and McKinley, *The Journal-Lancet* 85 (April 1965): 157–162; "Part III: The Roosevelts," *The Journal-Lancet* 85 (May 1965), 189–192; L.Z Freedman, ""Assassination: Psychopathology and Social Pathology," *Postgraduate Medicine* 37 (June 1965), 650–658; S.J. Slomich and R.E. Kantor, "Social Psychopathology of Political Assassination," *Bulletin of Atomic Scientists* 25 (March 1969), pp. 9–17; A.E. Weisz and R.L. Taylor, "American Presidential Assassinations," *Diseases of the Nervous System* 30 (October 1969), pp. 658–659; J.F. Kirkham, S.G. Levy, and W.J. Crotty, *Assassination and Political Violence: A Report to the National Commission on the Causes and Prevention of Violence* (New York: Praeger and the New York Times, 1970); C.V. Hassel, "The Political Assassin," *Journal of Police Science and Administration* 4 (December 1974), 399–403; and J. Takeuchi, F. Solomon, and W. W. Menninger (eds.), *Behavioral Science and the Secret Service: Toward the Prevention of Assassination* (Washington, DC: Institute of Medicine/National Academy Press, 1981).
7. J. W. Clarke, *American Assassins: The Darker Side of Politics* (Princeton, NJ: Princeton University Press, 1982). For a sense of the impact of this book and another, *On Being Mad Or Merely Angry: John W. Hinckley and Other Dangerous People* (Princeton NJ: Princeton University Press, 1990) have had on the threat assessment strategies of the U.S. Secret Service, compare the perspectives offered in 1981 in J. Takeuchi, F. Solomon, and W.W. Menninger (eds.), *Behavioral Science and the Secret Service: Toward the Prevention of Assassination* (Washington, DC: National Academy Press) to the revised perspective released three years later in a report by the Institute of Medicine, *Research and Training for the Secret Service: Behavioral Science and Mental Health Perspectives* (Washington, DC: National Academy Press, February 1984); and more recently in another report by the Secret Service, R.A. Fein and B. Vossekuil, *Protective Intelligence and Threat Assessment Investigations: A Guide for State and Local Law Enforcement Officials* (Washington, DC: U.S. Department of Justice Office of Justice Programs, July 1998).
8. H. D. Lasswell, *Power and Personality* (New York: Viking Press, 1948), ch. 3.
9. The classic exposition of the frustration-aggression hypothesis is J. Dollard, L. Doob, N. Miller, O. Mowrer, and R. Sears, *Frustration and Aggression* (New Haven: Yale University Press, 1939). Its basic tenets have been refined as a result of subsequent research, but remain essentially unchanged.

Part 1

Type I

2

Type I—Region and Class:
John Wilkes Booth and Leon F. Czolgosz

> *"I know how foolish I shall be deemed for undertaking such a step as this, where on one side I have my friends and every thing to make me happy, where my profession alone has gained me an income of more than twenty thousand dollars a year, and where my great personal ambition in my profession has such a great field of labor."*—John Wilkes Booth

> *"I killed the President because he was the enemy of the good people—the good working people. I am not sorry for my crime."*—Leon Czolgosz

The actions of the two Type I assassins discussed in this chapter, John Wilkes Booth and Leon Czolgosz, can be understood only in the context of the political events that defined their motives; neither was mentally disordered. The assassination of Abraham Lincoln in 1865 was a direct result of the regional conflict that had taken such a terrible toll of American lives from 1861 to 1865. William McKinley's death in 1901 was expressly linked to the bitter class struggle that characterized a major segment of American politics during the last quarter of the nineteenth century. Yet most accounts of both assassinations have little to say about how these eras of conflict might have stirred the passions of the two assassins John Wilkes Booth and Leon Czolgosz. Instead we are led to believe, incorrectly, that both assassinations were the result of acts of irrational men who killed only to satisfy their warped, egocentric needs for acclaim and notoriety. As the following accounts demonstrate, each acted, instead, on the basis of political principles they maintained to their dying breaths.

* * *

JOHN WILKES BOOTH (1838–1865)

For some time it was commonly assumed that President Lincoln's assassin, John Wilkes Booth, killed to achieve the fame that had eluded him in a floundering career as an actor. Booth's stage career, it was reasoned, had never achieved the distinction of his famous father, the English-born tragedian Junius Brutus Booth, or his older brother Edwin. Realizing this in 1864, and confronted with a bronchial condition that threatened his ability to perform, Booth, in a classically compensatory manner, supposedly decided to resolve his personal disappointments and failures and achieve lasting fame by striking a dramatic political blow for the Confederate cause. Probably the most widely respected and quoted proponent of this view is Stanley Kimmel's *The Mad Booths of Maryland*.[1] Drawing upon Kimmel, Booth has been dismissed elsewhere in even less qualified language as merely a self-absorbed, acrobatic, and noisy alcoholic with limited acting ability.[2] Other secondary work has imposed a rather strained psychoanalytic interpretation on this general explanation that goes even further in stressing Booth's neurotic motives.[3] Yet even in Kimmel's carefully researched work, numerous facts appear that raise doubts about his interpretation.

The most important weakness in Kimmel's explanation, however, is that it virtually ignores the political context of the assassination: facts such as Lincoln's unpopularity in the North as well as the South, the vicious opposition within his cabinet and the Congress, and the controversy surrounding his reelection in 1864. To ignore the political circumstances and events of the Civil War era is to miss the most important element in Booth's motives. And virtually every account of the assassination that shares Kimmel's conclusion about Booth does just that.

In most cases, the omission is a result of the erroneous assumption that the nation's esteem and affection for Lincoln preceded his death. The fact is that until Appomattox, a week before his death, Lincoln was one of the most criticized and vilified presidents in American history, commonly referred to as "the baboon, the imbecile, the wet rag, the Kentucky mule."[4] Although winning reelection in 1864 by a convincing margin (55 percent of the popular vote), that victory can be best understood, not in terms of Lincoln's personal popularity, but rather in terms of the ineffectiveness and confusion of the opposition — both within his own party as well as among his Democratic opponents — and a final reluctant resignation of party leaders to the principle that in time of a war close to being won it is best not to change horses in midstream. When considered in this political context, the facts of Booth's life — both his upbringing and his career — suggest a different view of the man and his motives.

Youth and Career

John Wilkes Booth was born on May 10, 1838 near Baltimore. He was almost twenty-seven years of age when he probably shot himself[5] in a burning barn surrounded by soldiers on April 26, 1865. Of the ten children born to Junius Brutus Booth and his second wife, Mary Ann Holmes Booth, John Wilkes, or "Johnny" as he was called, was their favorite. A beautiful child with shiny black hair and classically sculpted features, he exuded the brightness and exuberance of a happy childhood. His mother and his older sister Asia adored his kind and gentle ways, while his tempestuous but doting father admired his fiery spirit and athletic ability. As we will see, this positive view of Booth was shared by virtually everyone who ever knew him.[6] He made friends easily and was loyal and generous to a fault.[7] Even after he had achieved fame as an actor, Booth did not forget his childhood friends. Throughout his life his friendships endured, uncontaminated by his success, and they would span a sociological range from stable boys and clerks to debutantes and high-ranking public officials.

As a youth, Booth attended private schools where he studied history and the classics, reading Milton, Byron, and Shakespeare, and committing much of the latter to memory in preparation for a stage career virtually assured by family tradition. He also played the flute.[8] He learned to ride early and well, and his sister later remembered fondly their spirited gallops together chasing imaginary villains through the wooded Maryland countryside.[9] A lover of the outdoors, Booth's respect for living creatures prevented him from becoming the hunter and angler so encouraged by the frontier culture of nineteenth-century America. His sister described him as "very tender of flowers, and of insects and butterflies; lightning bugs," she said, "he considered as `bearers of sacred torches' and would go out of his way to avoid injuring them."[10]

Booth's gaiety and exuberance for life had a contagious quality that partly explains his popularity with those who knew him. Often his activities were punctuated with melodramatic exclamations that delighted his friends. His sister recorded one occasion where he exclaimed,

> Heaven and Earth! How glorious it is to live! how divine! to breathe this breath of life with a clear mind and healthy lungs! Don't let us be sad. Life is so short-and the world is so beautiful. Just to breathe is delicious.[11]

Booth was fourteen when his father died in 1852. During a long and distinguished career, the elder Booth had become the most acclaimed Shakespearean actor in America. Although his career kept him away from home frequently during his son's formative years, there was no question of his love for the handsome boy who displayed so much of the old man's spirit and flamboyance. Edwin, Booth's talented but more taciturn older brother, had studied as an apprentice with his father and thus logically assumed many of the roles and much of the acclaim associated with the Booth name. The oldest brother, Junius Brutus, Jr., was also an actor, but being some seventeen years older than John Wilkes, a sibling rivalry, which often placed strains on the relationship between the two younger brothers, never developed between them.

When Booth began his acting career at the age of seventeen, three years after his father's death, there is little doubt that a keen rivalry developed between him and the better known Edwin. Both were intent on carrying on the proud tradition established by their father. What is less clear, however, is the familiar contention that John Wilkes fared less well with audiences and critics than did Edwin, thus contributing to the younger brother's alleged sense of inferiority.

A careful evaluation of the evidence suggests that Booth labored in the shadow of his late father and older brother only for the first three years of his career, a period when his inexperience was acknowledged in a number of reviews. But the fact that he had himself billed as "J. Wilkes" suggests his desire to make a reputation on his own merits rather than capitalizing on the fame of his father and brother. Determined in this respect, Booth learned from the criticism he absorbed as an obscure "J. Wilkes" before emerging triumphantly on the Richmond stage in the autumn of 1858 where he delighted audiences. From that time until his death he was widely acclaimed for his talent but also as "the handsomest actor on the American stage."[12]

Moreover, the argument that Booth's sympathies for the Confederacy had their origins in the applause of Southern audiences and the critical disdain he received in the North has no basis in fact. After his first three apprenticeship years, Booth was never to receive a bad review — North or South. He was a star, a matinee idol whose talents approximated those of Edwin, while his physical attractiveness and flair on stage exceeded his older brother's and placed him in a position of undeniable ascendancy in the American theater. In fact, the only reservations about his abilities cited by Kimmel are those expressed by Edwin in private correspondence.[13] Edwin's reservations, however, were not widely shared. Consider the following representative observations taken from Booth's reviews: "An artist of the highest order [*Richard III*, New York, January,1862]"; " . . . the most brilliant [Richard III] ever played in the city [Chicago, January-February, 1862]."

In Baltimore, for example, his performances were thought superior to

Edwin's. Even in New York where Edwin was a special favorite of theater audiences, complementary comparisons were made. Critical praise could also be observed in the typically restrained Boston *Daily Advertiser*, which allowed that with some reservations about "proper treatment of the voice," it was "greatly pleased" by his Richard III.[14] When he returned to Boston in January 1863 for an appearance in *The Apostate* with brother Edwin in the audience, he was "wildly cheered."[15]

In February of the same year, Booth played Macbeth at the Arch Street Theater in Philadelphia where one of his early appearances as a fledgling actor had been poorly received. Nearby at the Chestnut Street Theater, Edwin Forrest, perhaps America's first matinee idol, was performing in the same role. In a convincing demonstration of his great appeal, audiences ignored Forrest and lined up to see the handsome new star of the American stage John Wilkes Booth. And reviews indicate that they were not disappointed."[16] Advanced billings for Booth's April appearance as Richard III in Washington described him as "a star of the first magnitude."[17] Reviewers later gushed that he had established himself as a reigning favorite in the capital. Attracted by such reviews, President Lincoln saw Booth perform in *The Marble Heart* on November 9, 1863.[18] Later that month, the Washington *Daily National Intelligencer* praised his performance of Romeo in the Shakespearean drama as "the most satisfactory of all renderings of that fine character."[19]

Recognition of Booth's talents was not limited to audiences and critics. Established professionals in the theater acknowledged his superior talents. John Ellsler, for example, director of the Cleveland Academy of Music, who knew and admired all the Booths, observed that John Wilkes had "more of [his famous father's] power in one performance than Edwin can show in a year." He went on to predict that John Wilkes Booth would become "as great an actor as America can produce."[20]

Such appraisals were recorded wherever, and for as long as, Booth performed. At a March 1864 appearance in New Orleans, for example, he gave an emotional performance in the same role and on the same stage where his father last appeared before his death. Sustained applause followed.[21] Similar praise followed his engagements in Boston later that year, where crowds waited after the performance outside the stage exit, straining for one more glimpse of the handsome young actor.[22] On November 25, 1864, he appeared in New York for the first and last time with his brothers Edwin and Junius in *Julius Caesar*. An enthusiastic audience of over two thousand crowded the Winter Garden Theater and cheered a command performance.[23] Again, it should be emphasized that there is *no* evidence that Booth received other than the most complimentary reviews of his work from 1858 through his last performance at Ford's Theater less than a month before the assassination.

In view of such resounding success, it may be surprising that he remained so well-liked by his peers in the acting profession. Although numerous young women succumbed to Booth's dashing good looks and personal charm, he remained kind and discreet. Such refinement set him apart from many men of this period. Women, regardless of age and background, found him irresistible. Clara Morris, for example, a well-known actress of the period, described him as "so young, so bright, so gay, so kind." Recalling an incident where Booth, hurrying from the stage door of the theater, inadvertently knocked over a small child, the actress described how Booth stooped to pick up the little boy, carefully wiping the tears from his grimy face. Then satisfied that the child was not injured, Booth kissed him and pressed a pocketful of change into his hand before dashing off. The significance of the act was that it was so characteristic of Booth. "He knew of no witness to the act," she said:

> To kiss a pretty clean child under the approving eyes of mamma might mean nothing but politeness, but surely it required the prompting of a warm and tender heart to make a young and thoughtful man feel for and caress such a dirty, forlorn bit of babyhood as that.[24]

Nor was Booth's kindness and generosity confined to star-struck young women and children. He remained a close and devoted son and brother to his mother and sister Asia.[25] More interesting, however, is that men from seemingly all walks of life valued the friendship of the engaging young actor. Even male peers within a profession known for its jealous rivalries genuinely liked and admired Booth. A fellow actor, Sir Charles Wyndham, described him as "a man of flashing wit and magnetic manner. He was one of the best raconteurs to whom I ever listened."[26] Another actor who knew Booth explained that he was liked because of his quick good humor, his love of fun, and his unassuming ease with people regardless of social rank. He never permitted his celebrity status to become a barrier to old friends. He was also generous with his money.[27]

Thus an accurate view of John Wilkes Booth — the view of his contemporaries — represents a stark contrast to the image of a frustrated, self-absorbed actor obsessed with achieving fame. Booth's character emerged out of a childhood of great love and affection. All accounts indicate that he was a beautiful, self-confident child who never knew unkindness or hardship. Raised in the cultured, if eccentric environment of a theatrical aristocracy, his transition to the stage was swift, smooth, and highly successful. The acclaim denied to so many in the acting profession was well within grasp by his twenty-first year. By the time of his death, some six years later, his reputation as a fine actor and matinee idol was established. Booth's popularity and success were reflected in his income: in 1862, he wrote that he was averaging $650 per week for his performances — an extraordinary sum for that period.[28] At the time of his death, even after he had cut his performances drastically because of his war-related activities, he wrote that he was earning "more than twenty-thousand dollars a year."[29]

If professional jealousy and an obsessive "greed for fame" are eliminated as motives, what about the alleged bronchial condition that threatened to cut short his career?[30] Was political notoriety and extremism viewed by Booth as the only means left to him to eclipse a loathsome brother's theatrical ascendancy, as some have claimed? While this argument cannot be substantiated or denied in the absence of medical evidence, it is true that Booth's sixth performance in New Orleans in March, 1864 was cancelled because of a "cold."[31] But there is simply no other evidence to support Kimmel's suggestion of the alleged seriousness or chronic nature of a medical condition that threatened to end Booth's career. The claim that the onset of this alleged disability heightened Booth's alleged "neurotic sense of inferiority"[32] is without merit.

The Political Context

Political events in 1864, rather than assumptions about chronic laryngitis and sibling rivalry, provide a more accurate context in which to assess Booth's motives. Nearing the completion of his first term in office, Abraham Lincoln enjoyed none of the esteem accorded to him after his death. Lincoln had been elected president, a minority candidate of an upstart new party, with less than 40 percent of the popular vote. He had won only because the Democratic party had divided ranks with two candidates, J. C. Breckenridge and Stephen A. Douglas, splitting 47.5 percent of the vote while the remaining 12.6 percent went to Constitutional Union party candidate John Bell. Undaunted by his lack of a popular mandate, Lincoln quickly embarked upon a course of action with a single overriding purpose in mind — the restoration of the Union between the North and South. All other issues — most notably, slavery, for example — were secondary to that goal.

Needless to say, Lincoln was hated in the rebellious states. Not so obvious in history texts, however, was his unpopularity in the North where growing opposition to the war required drastic — some would say unconstitutional — executive actions to control the festering and volatile dissent. Lincoln quickly, and on his own initiative, suspended the constitutionally guaranteed writ of habeas corpus and authorized the arbitrary arrest of any suspected opponents of his war policies. In 1863, for example, some 38,000 persons were arrested in the North and imprisoned without trial for suspected anti-war activities. Soon after the first shots were fired at Fort Sumter, he had called up the militia and expanded the size of the regular army without Congressional approval. He arbitrarily, and again without congressional approval, transferred some two million dollars to Union agents in New York to assist their efforts in stifling the anti-war movement. Ignoring Congress, he instituted unpopular conscription in 1862 by executive order. He aggressively appointed and removed a succession of politically ambitious Union generals before finding a satisfactory commander in Ulysses S. Grant. He issued the Emancipation Proclamation, freeing slaves in the rebellious states *only* without consulting Congress. He issued executive orders establishing provisional courts in conquered states and appointed military governors in Arkansas, Louisiana and Tennessee without Congressional approval or clear constitutional authority. In general, President Lincoln ignored the Congress and strained Constitutional limits as he dramatically exploited his executive authority to wage war during his first term in office.

A nation averse to strong central government, sympathetic to states' rights, and imbued with notions of Jacksonian democracy did not respond kindly to this unimpressive-looking, obscure mid-westerner who was presiding over the bloodiest war in American history. It was an unpopular war that would kill and maim over a million American men, many of them drafted as reluctant participants in war to free slaves few cared about.[33] Criticism was reflected most vigorously in the Congress, where Lincoln was especially reviled by members of his own party. It was criticism shared by members of his own cabinet. Prominent and influential newspaper editors charged him with abuses ranging from incompetence to war profiteering. On one side, Democrats blasted him for waging an unconstitutional war against political self-determination; on the other, radical Republicans condemned his restraint in prosecuting the war. By 1864, it was difficult to identify any important segment of support for the president.[34]

Opposition to the war, Lincoln, and his draft policy was particularly vigorous in New York City and Philadelphia, as well as smaller towns on the eastern seaboard. Lincoln's unpopularity was also evident in Ohio and Wisconsin in the Midwest, not to mention the marginally loyal border states like Maryland and Kentucky. Following on the heels of New York Governor Horatio Seymour's denunciation of Lincoln in a July Fourth speech in 1863, draft resisters rioted in New York City, attacking blacks and abolitionists in a three-day rampage of brutal assaults, murder, and arson.[35]

By early 1864, many prominent Union supporters considered Lincoln's presidency an unqualified failure[36] it was certain that his re-nomination would be challenged. As the anti-war movement grew that year, influential newspapers in New York and Philadelphia criticized the propriety of encouraging the enlistment of some 179,000 black soldiers in the Union Army. Moreover, Lincoln's vilification was evident even in the European press. Newspapers in London, for example, sneered at his manners and ridiculed his homeliness while condemning his policies.[37] But probably Lincoln's most unpopular act occurred earlier on January 1, 1863, when he issued the Emancipation Proclamation.[38]

A discouraged Lincoln anticipated defeat in 1864 and prepared a memorandum on the transition of power to his successor. Salmon P. Chase, his treasury secretary, as well as two former generals, the "Great Pathfinder" John C. Fremont, and Benjamin Butler mounted serious challenges to his renomination.[39] Largely as a result of the fragmented quality of his opposition, rather than his own popularity, Lincoln was re-nominated in Baltimore by an unenthusiastic party amid feelings of sullen resentment.[40] Former supporters of the president such as William Cullen Bryant, Theodore Tilton, and Horace Greeley now considered his administration a failure but saw no acceptable alternative.

Undoubtedly, the curious nomination and an incongruous party platform of opposition Democrats contributed importantly to the beleaguered Lincoln's subsequent reelection. Democrats nominated another former general, George McClellan, as a candidate committed, like Lincoln, to an uncompromising military solution to the war. They then saddled the general with an incongruous peace platform written by chief antiwar advocate and vice-presidential nominee Clement L. Vallandigham — a man who had been arrested and deported to the South by a military court for his treasonous Confederate sympathies.[41] Confronted with a choice between such a contradiction or the unpopular Lincoln, the electorate held its nose and voted for the incumbent. The recent military successes of General William Tecumseh Sherman made that decision easier than it would have been otherwise. Throughout the weeks preceding the election, news of Sherman's army cutting a devastating swath across the Southern heartland, burning not only Atlanta but, also, the capital in Columbia, South Carolina, gave the president an electoral boost when he most needed it. In the view of many war-weary Northern voters a successful end of an unpopular war seemed at hand. Except for Sherman's triumphant campaign in the South in the weeks preceding the election, this unpopular president almost certainly would not have been reelected.[42]

Sherman's successful campaign in September and October and Lincoln's convincing reelection in November signaled an ominous message for the South. Until his reelection, Lincoln's unpopularity in the North and the growing anti-war sentiment in that part of the country provided a ray of hope for many war-weary Southerners who anticipated his defeat and a negotiated end to the war. The hope was that such negotiations would recognize, as many Northern papers advocated, an independent Confederacy.[43] The loss of life on both sides during Grant's Wilderness Campaign in May and June 1864 was staggering — an estimated 90,000 casualties. Lincoln, like another president a hundred years and a different war later, was widely blamed for this carnage that many, anticipating a shorter, less costly war, now considered unnecessary. For the South, his reelection meant that the destructive war of attrition Grant's and Sherman's armies were now conducting would grind on toward its humiliating ultimate objective — unconditional surrender. It was a time of desperation. Lincoln, as Commander in Chief of the Union armies now intent on destroying men and property, not merely capturing territory, was intensely hated by southerners. As the *Richmond Examiner* editorialized, "What shall we call him? Coward, assassin, savage, murderer of women and babies? Or shall we consider them all embodied in the word of fiend, and call him Lincoln the Fiend."[44]

Booth's Politics and Plan

Few persons loved the South and hated Abraham Lincoln more than John Wilkes Booth. From the beginning of the war, Booth had made his Southern sympathies clear in the most outspoken and unequivocal manner. His hatred for the president was both personal and political, and it grew more intense as the conflict dragged on. He held Lincoln responsible for a bloody and unnecessary war and, as a man of some refinement, he was contemptuous of what he saw as Lincoln's personal coarseness of style and manner. In Booth's eyes, Lincoln was not qualified by birth or training to be president.[45]

As a performer, Booth was permitted to travel throughout the country — North and South — during the war. He used this privilege to smuggle quinine and other war-related material, as well as information, into the South at every opportunity.[46] As prospects for a Southern victory began to dim after Lee's defeat at Gettysburg in 1863, Booth's activities intensified. By 1864, he was preoccupied with the war effort, severely curtailing his professional commitments — not because of bad reviews or throat problems — but because his priorities were now elsewhere.

Booth's theatrical tours regularly took him to areas of the most intense opposition to the president. In addition to Southern cities, Booth regularly toured New York, Philadelphia, and Baltimore, not to mention the capital itself where the anti-war movement was very strong. It is little wonder that he correctly viewed himself as participating in a widely popular cause.

In September 1864, the same month that Lincoln was re-nominated for a second term, Sherman's forces swept through Atlanta burning and pillaging as they went. To the north, Lee's army was being forced into a last stand outside Richmond. The situation for the Confederates was desperate. It was at this time that Booth became part of a plan to abduct the president. Once captive, Lincoln could then be ransomed for the release of Confederate prisoners of war who were sorely needed to restore Lee's badly depleted ranks. In October, Booth went to Montreal on the first of many trips he would make across the Canadian border over the next few months to meet with Confederate agents.[47] While there, he opened a bank account. He also packed his theatrical wardrobe and paraphernalia in a trunk for future shipment back to Richmond. Any doubts about moving forward with the plan were put aside with Lincoln's triumphant November reelection. It was now evident that drastic measures would be required to cut Southern losses and avoid complete defeat.

Various alternatives were discussed by Confederate agents: plots to sabotage government ships and buildings; raids from Canada on cities such as Buffalo and Detroit; attacks on prisoner of war camps to release Confederate soldiers; a plot to burn New York City; and a plan to distribute clothing and blankets infested with yellow fever, smallpox, and other contagious diseases in Washington — all desperate measures to stem the tide of a war ebbing badly for the South.[48]

In this context, the plan to abduct the president seems less bizarre. Earlier in April 1864, General Grant had refused a Confederate proposal for a prisoner exchange; a successful abduction of the president could possibly accomplish the same purpose. Presidential security — basically consisting of a personal bodyguard — was not a major concern. In any case, it was worth the gamble. In November, Booth initiated preparations to carry out the abduction. He began to recruit among old friends and acquaintances for persons willing to assist in the operation. He also made trips into southern Maryland to plan the route by which the manacled president would be transported across Southern lines. During the year, Booth had spent large sums of his own money on such espionage activities.

Intent on having the purpose of the plan and his motives clearly understood, Booth drafted a sealed letter of explanation and left it with his sister Asia's husband, John Sleeper Clarke, for safekeeping. The letter, which remained unopened until it was discovered after the assassination, reveals the scope and depth of Booth's feeling and his rationale for his anticipated crime:

My Dear Sir:
You may use this as you think best. But as some may wish to know when, who and why, and as I know not how to direct, I give it (in the words of your master).
   To whom it may concern,
   Right or wrong, God judge me, not man. For be my motive good or bad, of one thing I am sure, the lasting condemnation of the North.
   I love peace more than life. Have loved the Union beyond expression. For four years I have waited, hoped and prayed for the dark clouds to break, and for the restoration of our former sunshine. To wait longer would be a crime. All hope for peace is dead. My prayers have proved as

idle as my hopes. God's will be done. I go to see and share the bitter end. I have ever held the South were right. The very nomination of Abraham Lincoln, four years ago, spoke plainly war — war upon Southern rights and institutions. His election proved it. Await an overt act. Yet, till you are bound and plundered. What folly! The South was wise. Who thinks of argument or patience when the finger of his enemy presses the trigger? In a foreign war, I too, could say, country right or wrong. But in a struggle such as ours where the brother tries to pierce the brother's heart, for God's sake, choose the right. When a country like this spurns justice for her side, she forfeits the allegiance of every honest free man, and should leave him untrammeled by any fealty soever, to act as his own conscience may approve.

People of the North, to hate tyranny, to love liberty and justice, to strike at wrong and oppression, was the teaching of our fathers. The study of our early history will not let me forget it and may it never.

This country was formed for the white man and not for the black. And looking upon African slavery from the same stand point as held by the noble framers of our Constitution, I, for one, have ever considered it one of the greatest blessings for themselves and for us that God ever bestowed upon a favored nation. Witness heretofore our wealth and power; witness their elevation and enlightenment above their race elsewhere. I have lived among it most of my life, and have seen less harsh treatment from master to man than I have beheld in the North from father to son. Yet heaven knows that no one would be more willing to do more for the negro race than I, could I but see a way to still better their condition.

But Lincoln's policy is only preparing the way to their total annihilation. The South are not nor have they been fighting for the continuance of slavery. The first battle of Bull Run did away with that idea. The causes since for war have been as noble, and greater far than those that urged our fathers on. Even though we should allow that they were wrong at the beginning of this contest, cruelty and injustice have made the wrong become the right, and they now stand before the wonder and admiration of the world, as a noble band of patriotic heroes. Hereafter reading of their deeds, Thermopylae will be forgotten.

When I aided in the capture and execution of John Brown who was a murderer on our western border, who was fairly tried and convicted before an impartial judge and jury, of treason, and who by the way, has since been made a god, I was proud of my little share in the transaction, for I deemed it my duty, and that I was helping our common country to perform an act of justice. But what was a crime in poor John Brown is now considered by themselves as the greatest and only virtue of the Republican party. Strange transmigration. Vice is to become a virtue, simply because more indulge in it.

I thought then, as now, that the Abolitionists were the only traitors in the land, and that the entire party deserved the same fate as poor old Brown, not because they wish to abolish slavery, but on account of the means they have endeavored to use to effect that abolition. If Brown were living, I doubt whether he himself would set slavery against the Union. Most, or many in the North do, and openly curse the Union, if the South are to return and attain a single right guaranteed to them by every tie which we once revered as sacred. The South can make no choice. It is either extermination or slavery for themselves worse than death to draw from. I know my choice.

I have also studied hard to discover upon what grounds the right of a state to secede has been denied, when our name, United States and Declaration of Independence, both provide for secession. But this is no time for words. I write in haste. I know how foolish I shall be deemed for undertaking such a step as this, where on one side I have my friends and every thing to make me happy, where my profession alone has gained me an income of more than twenty thousand dollars a year, and where my great personal ambition in my profession has such a great field of labor. On the other hand the South have never bestowed upon me one kind word, a place where I have no friends except beneath the sod: a place where I must either become a private soldier or a beggar.

To give up all the former for the latter, besides my mother and sisters whom I love so dearly, although they differ so widely in opinion, seems insane; but God is my judge. I love justice more than a country that disowns it; more than fame and wealth; heaven pardon me, if wrong, more than a happy home. I have never been upon the battle field, but, O my countrymen, could all but see the reality or effects of this horrid war, as I have seen them in every state save Virginia, I know you would think like me, and would pray the Almighty to create in the Northern mind a sense of right and justice even should it possess no seasoning of mercy, and then he would dry up this sea of blood between us, which is daily growing wider. Alas, poor country, is she to meet her threatened doom? Four years ago I would have given a thousand lives to see her as I have always known her, powerful and unbroken. And even now I would hold my life as naught, to see her what she was. O, my friends, if the fearful scenes of the past four years had never been enacted or if what had been done were but a frightful dream from which we could now awake with over-flowing hearts, we could bless our God and pray for his continued favor. How I have loved the old flag can never be known.

A few years since the world could boast of none so pure and spotless. But of late I have been seeing and hearing of the bloody deeds of which she has been made the emblem, and would shudder to think how changed she has grown. Oh, how I have longed to see her break from the midst of blood and death that circles round her folds, spoiling her beauty and tarnishing her honor! But no: day by day she has been dragged deeper into cruelty and oppression, till now in my eyes her once bright red striped look [like] bloody gashes on the face of heaven.

I look now upon my early admiration of her glories as a dream.

My love as things stand today is for the South alone. Nor do I deem it a dishonor in attempting to make for her a prisoner of this man to whom she owes so much misery. If success attends me, I go penniless to her side. They say she has found that last ditch which the North has so long derided and been endeavoring to force her in, forgetting they are our brothers, and it is impolite to goad an enemy to madness. Should I reach her in safety and find it true, I will proudly beg permission to triumph or die in that same ditch by her side.

A Confederate doing duty on his own responsibility,
J. Wilkes Booth[49]

Booth carefully recruited five men (all of whom he had known earlier) to assist him: John Surratt, a Confederate spy and a person well acquainted with the roads, trails, and geography of southern Maryland; David Herold, a simpleminded but extremely loyal person; George Atzerodt, an experienced boatman who was familiar with the river crossings that would be required; Lewis Payne,[50] a burly, physically powerful ex-Confederate soldier familiar with firearms; and finally, another ex-Confederate soldier and boyhood friend, Samuel Arnold. The qualifications of all but possibly Herold, who had only his loyalty to recommend him, suggest Booth's choices were not as poorly considered as some have made them out to be. A number of other persons were indirectly involved in the conspiracy (and theories abound about those who were not involved but were aware of the plot), but these were the main actors.[51]

The plan was to abduct Lincoln on his way to the play, *Still Waters Run Deep*, which was being performed at the Soldier's Home on what was then the outskirts of Washington. On either March 16 or 20,[52] 1865, the conspirators prepared for the abduction. They hoped to stop the president's carriage, overpower him and any aides (he was rarely escorted by more than one), then take the bound chief executive south of the city to a rendezvous where fresh horses would be waiting to carry the group beyond to the protection of the Confederate lines.

The plan only failed for one reason: Lincoln did not appear as scheduled. Rather, he had asked Treasury Secretary and political adversary Salmon P.

Chase to go in his place. The carriage of a startled Chase was stopped by a group of riders who, upon seeing the president was not on board, then galloped off.[53]

Military events soon made it clear that abduction was no longer a viable strategy. Lee's army could not hold its positions at Petersburg much longer without elevating the already enormous sacrifice of life. Surrender or defeat was inevitable. But on April 4, Confederate President Jefferson Davis, fearing the terms of surrender, urged a continuation of the war as a guerrilla campaign "operating in the interior . . . where supplies are more accessible, and where the foe will be far removed from his own base." He went on to ask the South for a renewed commitment to "render our triumph certain."[54]

Lee, closer to the bloodshed and suffering than the truculent Davis, saw no reason to continue a senseless slaughter. On April 7, he asked for terms, and two days later he formally surrendered his army. Desperate, Davis continued to press for a continuation of the war west of the Mississippi. With General Joe Johnston's Confederate army still in the field and able to slow Sherman's movement north through the Carolinas, he reasoned, perhaps there was a way out yet. Davis, the Southern zealot, was grasping for straws. So was Booth.

The Assassination

After the abduction plot had failed, Booth began to consider other more drastic measures that could throw the Union war effort into disarray long enough to enable the South to regroup militarily. The goal was, again, not victory, but only to raise the possibility of a negotiated settlement rather than an unconditional surrender which seemed certain otherwise — a surrender dictated by the man who had given the infamous Sherman his marching orders. The plan that evolved was to assassinate simultaneously the government's formal political and military leadership, thus producing complete chaos in Washington. The targets: the president, Vice President Andrew Johnson, Secretary of State William H. Seward (who would become President in the event of the death of a succeeding vice president), and commander of the Union Army, General Ulysses S. Grant.

On April 14, after learning of the president's plans to attend a play at Ford's Theater with General Grant, a determined Booth decided that this was the opportunity he had been awaiting. Further delay and the opportunity would be lost. He again wrote a letter to explain what he was about to do and gave it to a fellow actor, John Matthews, in a sealed envelope. He asked Matthews to deliver it personally to the publisher of the *National Intelligencer* the next day. An unnerved Matthews tore open the letter after the assassination, then fearing the consequences of having it in his possession, destroyed it. He recalled the closing paragraph, however:

The moment has at length arrived when my plans [to abduct] must be changed. The world may censure me for what I am about to do, but I am sure posterity will justify me.[55]

To this Booth signed his name and those of fellow conspirators Payne, Atzerodt, and Herold. Booth assigned Atzerodt to kill Vice President Johnson and Payne to kill Secretary of State Seward with Herold's assistance. He personally would kill the president and General Grant.

That evening as the president, Mrs. Lincoln, and two guests sat in the president's box at Ford's Theater, eyes fixed on the performers below and to their right, Booth quietly eased the door open behind them, stepped quickly inside and fired the fatal shot from a pistol he held just inches from the president's ear. Lincoln's head recoiled slightly then dropped to his chest. As Mrs. Lincoln screamed in terror, Booth leaped over the railing, the spur on his boot catching a banner that adorned the president's box. As he landed clumsily on the stage, breaking his leg, he turned toward the audience, shouting, "sic semper tyrannous," before limping out a rear stage door to the horse that waited in the darkness. Chaos followed as the stunned audience grasped what had happened.

Why did Booth choose a public theater for the act? And why the leap to the stage after the fatal shot, unless it was for recognition and the notoriety? Booth's choice of Ford's Theater was in part fortuitous, but it was also a rational, carefully considered decision. As a famous actor, he had unlimited access to Ford's. This meant that he could enter and leave the theater when and where he pleased without questions. Thus, he could enter and climb the stairs to the president's box without suspicion. He was, after all, a celebrity who might have been invited to join the president. He leaped to the stage after the shooting because that was the quickest, most direct way out of the crowded theater. To go back down the narrow stairwell and through the cramped lobby into a street clogged with carriages and people would have meant almost certain capture. This is not to suggest that Booth was averse to the publicity. As his letters and diaries indicate, he was convinced that what he was doing was right and he hoped that public opinion would ultimately share that view. But the desire for notoriety, in Booth's case, was a distinctly secondary consideration — neither necessary nor sufficient as a motive for his act.

Except for whatever fleeting personal satisfaction Booth may have derived from Lincoln's death, the plan was a failure: Payne's attempt to kill Seward ended bloodily but unsuccessfully, Seward, gravely injured from stab wounds, survived. Atzerodt could not bring himself to execute a drunken man he did not know, and so Vice President Johnson's life was spared.[56] Grant, who had declined the president's theater invitation, was on a train to New Jersey to visit a daughter when the president was shot. Except for the president, all the intended victims survived.

If it hadn't been for the broken leg Booth sustained in his leap to the stage, he and his faithful companion, Davy Herold, who accompanied him on his flight toward an anticipated sanctuary in Virginia, might have escaped. Booth's diary records his despair after the event as he realized that his act was poorly timed and widely condemned. The nation was tired of killing after four long years of war. North and South, a nation sick of bloodshed welcomed Appomattox. A year earlier, the result may have been different, but except for zealots like Jefferson Davis and Booth, most Americans were ready to lay down their arms and return to their homes and farms. Now in great pain, making his way through the Maryland swamps, Booth wrote:

> Ides   April, 13, 14, Friday, The
> Until today nothing was ever thought of sacrificing to our country's wrongs. For six months we have worked to capture [and abduct the president unharmed]. But our cause being almost lost, something decisive and great must be done. But its failure was owing to others [his co-conspirators] who did not strike for their country with a heart. I struck boldly, and not as the papers say. I walked with a firm step through a thousand of his friends, was stopped but pushed on. A colonel was at his side. I shouted Sic semper before I fired. In jumping I broke my leg. I passed all his pickets. Rode sixty miles that night, with the bone of my leg tearing the flesh at every jump.
>
> I can .never repent it, though we hated to kill. Our country owed all our troubles to him, and God simply made me the instrument of his punishment.[57]
>
> The country is not what it was. This forced union is not what I have loved. I care not what becomes of me. I have no desire to outlive my country. This night [before the deed] I wrote a long article and left it for one of the editors of the National Intelligencer, in which I fully set forth our reasons for our proceedings. He or the Gov't [58] . . . . [the entry ends][59]

A week later, a depressed Booth laments that his act has been misunderstood:

> Friday 21
> After being hunted like a dog through swamps, woods, and last night being chased by gunboats till I was forced to return wet, cold, and starving, with every man's hand against me, I am here in despair. And why? For doing what Brutus was honored for — what made Tell a hero. And yet I, for striking down a greater tyrant than they ever knew, am looked upon

as a common cutthroat. My action was purer than either of theirs. One hoped to be great.[60] The other had not only his country's, but his own, wrongs to avenge. I hoped for no gain. I knew no private wrong. I struck for my country and that alone. A country that groaned beneath this tyranny, and prayed for this end, and yet now behold the cold hand they extend me. God cannot pardon me if I have done wrong. Yet I cannot see my wrong, except in serving a degenerate people. The little, the very little, I left behind to clear my name, the government will not allow to be printed [the letter he had left with John Matthews]. So ends all. For my country I have given up all that makes life sweet and holy, brought misery upon my family, and am sure there is no pardon in the Heaven for me, since man condemns me so. I have only heard of what has been done (except what I did myself), and it fills me with horror. God, try and forgive me, and bless my mother. Tonight I will once more try the river with the intent to cross. Though I have a greater desire and almost a mind to return to Washington, and in a measure clear my name — which I feel I can do. I do not repent the blow I struck. I may before my God, but not to man. I think I have done well. Though I am abandoned, with the curse of Cain upon me, when, if the world knew my heart, that one blow would have made me great, though I did desire no greatness. Tonight I try to escape these bloodhounds once more. Who, who can read his fate? God's will be done. I have too great a soul to die like a criminal. O, may He, may He spare me that, and let me die bravely.

I bless the entire world. Have never hated or wronged anyone. This last was not a wrong, unless God deems it so, and it's with Him to damn or bless me. And for this brave boy [Davy Herold] with me, who often prays (yes, before and since) with a true and sincere heart, was it crime in him? If so, why can he pray the same?

I do not wish to shed a drop of blood, but "I must fight the course." Tis all that's left me.[61]

Given the tone and intensity of Booth's remarks, it is difficult to take seriously an often-quoted subsequent remark he allegedly made to a farm girl, who, unaware of who he was, said to him that she thought Lincoln's assassin had killed for money. Booth was said to have replied that in his opinion "he wasn't paid a cent, but did it for notoriety's sake."[62]

Had Booth been seeking more fame than he already possessed, it is likely that he would have welcomed a well-publicized trial where he could have spoken with the dramatic persuasiveness of the skilled actor he was in his own defense. He could have given expression to the many eloquent political statements he had penned in letters and diary. Rather, he chose to die alone "bravely." With that in mind, as he leaned heavily on a crutch, surrounded by

Union troops who had encircled his refuge in a barn, he shouted back when asked to surrender:

> Captain, I know you to be a brave man, and I believe you to be honorable: I am a cripple. I have got but one leg; if you withdraw your men in "line" one hundred yards from the door, I will come out and fight you.[63]

When the officer-in-charge replied that it was his intention to take him and Herold alive, as prisoners, Booth shouted back: "Well, my brave boys, prepare a stretcher for me."[64] He then negotiated with the soldiers to permit his panicked companion to surrender alone. Soon after Herold left the barn, it was set afire by the soldiers. Seeing no other honorable alternative, Booth most likely raised his pistol and fired a shot behind his right ear, smashing instead his spinal column and leaving him paralyzed but conscious to die a slow agonizing death. Throughout an ordeal so painful that he pleaded to be killed, he did not recant on his principles. Shortly before he died, he whispered to a soldier bending over him, "Tell mother I die for my country."[65]

Booth's co-conspirators, except for John Surratt, were quickly arrested.[66] Considerable controversy about the conspiracy and who else might have been involved, remained after Booth's death. David Herold, George Atzerodt, Lewis Payne, and Mary Surratt (the latter in a highly questionable judgment) were tried and found guilty. All were hanged on July 7, 1865. Other alleged conspirators who were not directly involved — Samuel Arnold, Samuel Mudd, Edward Spangler, and Michael O'Laughlin — were also convicted and given long prison sentences.

Conclusions

Much of the misunderstanding about Booth and his motives has been the result of the failure to consider the political context of his actions. It has been assumed that Lincoln was the revered leader in life that he became after his death: the fact that his assassination is frequently referred to as a martyrdom attests to this point. Thus, it has been further assumed that only a deranged person could have killed so noble a human being. Just as Lincoln's alleged liabilities in life — his humble beginnings and lack of formal education, for example — were transformed into *virtues* after his death, so were Booth's accomplishments in life diminished after his death. Thus politics, in all its dimensions, dictates the historical legacy of both men.

And there can be little doubt that politics — not notoriety — was what motivated Booth. He was wrong, obviously, on moral grounds. Can assassination ever be justified in a democracy? Moreover, he was wrong politically, as subsequent events illustrated.[67] But he was not deranged, nor was he mentally disordered. His motives were more akin to those of the German officers who conspired and attempted to kill Hitler to end the horrors of World War II than they were to a deranged person. Such a conclusion is difficult to accept because it conflicts so sharply with the mythology surrounding a slain national hero. But during most of his presidency, Abraham Lincoln was viewed by many Americans, especially in the South, as a cruel, heartless man. As a more restrained but still bitter Jefferson Davis wrote some years later about Lincoln, "[The South] could not be expected to mourn" an enemy who had presided over such misery.[68]

* * *

LEON CZOLGOSZ (1873–1901)

On September 6, 1901, Leon Czolgosz shot and fatally wounded President William McKinley as the latter stood greeting a line of well wishers at the Pan-American Exposition in Buffalo, New York. The President died eight days later. Czolgosz, who was arrested at the scene, was tried and convicted of first degree murder and executed forty-four days later on October 29. His trial had lasted less than eight hours. Czolgosz freely acknowledged his guilt and expressed no remorse. He refused to cooperate with his court-appointed attorneys and offered no defense after his guilty plea was denied."[69]

When the calm and composed assassin was strapped into the electric chair at New York's Auburn Prison he turned to the grim-faced witnesses and "in a clear distinct voice" repeated the explanation he had given since his arrest: "I killed the President because he was the enemy of the good people — the good working people. I am not sorry for my crime. I am sorry I could not see my father."[70]

Problems of Past Research

Before his execution, Czolgosz had been examined by five psychiatrists, or alienists as they were then called at that time. All concluded that they could find no evidence of mental disorder.[71]

After the execution, two other alienists/psychiatrists became interested in the case. Walter Channing and his assistant L. Vernon Briggs were skeptical about the official conclusion that Czolgosz was sane. Then citing the fact that the five doctors who actually examined Czolgosz did not carefully consider his personal history, the two began an investigation of Czolgosz's family and past.

In October 1902, Channing published an article in the *American Journal of Insanity* disputing the earlier conclusion that Czolgosz was without mental defect.[72] Channing made much of the fact that as a child Leon was "quiet and retired" and only played with "a few" other children. Channing also thought it was significant that as Leon grew older lie spent a lot of time alone reading. Odd also, he argued, that Czolgosz apparently only had one girlfriend but she had broken off the relationship. After that, Channing claimed, he had difficulty even speaking to women. Strange, Channing thought, that Czolgosz especially did not like his stepmother and refused to eat his meals with her, preferring instead to cook his own food or simply to drink milk and eat bread alone. He also slept a lot, Channing noted. Channing considered these characteristics to be of great "pathological significance." Of special importance in Channing's view was the "nervous breakdown" Leon appeared to have in 1897 when he became ill and depressed before quitting his job in a wire mill a year later. Czolgosz refused to work after that — a fact Channing also considered of major significance in his diagnosis of the assassin's mental condition.[73]

Nineteen years later, Dr. Channing's associate, Dr. L. Vernon Briggs, presented these same facts in a book entitled *The Manner of Man that* Kills.[74] Like his late associate, Briggs also concluded that Czolgosz was mentally ill when he killed the president, afflicted with paranoid schizophrenia or "dementia praecox" as it was called then.

The Channing and Briggs interpretation and conclusion soon became the most widely known and accepted assessment of Czolgosz's life and motives in the McKinley assassination. Robert Donovan's influential book on assassins relies on Briggs.[75] Donald Hastings' later article draws heavily on both Donovan and Briggs.[76] Virtually all the work written on Czolgosz since Briggs' book has accepted his analysis as truth.[77]

But there are fundamental problems in the conclusions advanced in the Channing and Briggs analyses. Missing is the political context of Czolgosz's life and, without that, we are left with a highly questionable interpretation of alleged motives that is not supported by any of the evidence they themselves report.

In his book, Dr. Briggs attempted to bolster his diagnostic conclusions about Czolgosz by citing the opinions of other authorities who, without having examined Czolgosz or his life history in any systematic manner, agreed with his diagnosis. For example, Briggs quoted Dr. Allan McLane Hamilton, who in 1881 was convinced that Charles Guiteau was not mentally ill when he shot President James A. Garfield. Hamilton later was equally convinced that Czolgosz suffered from a severe mental condition. Citing the assassin's "prepossessing personality," Hamilton concluded that Czolgosz was "clearly demented" because "[he] seemed to take little or no interest in his trial." Additionally, Hamilton viewed Czolgosz's final statement that President McKinley was "the enemy of working people" as evidence of mental "delusions." Following Channing, Hamilton proposed that Czolgosz's refusal to eat his stepmother's food, as well as his refusal to work, were evidence of paranoia.[78] Briggs also cites approvingly another mental health authority of the day, Dr. Sanderson Christieson, who offers the following insights concerning Czolgosz:

> Such a monstrous conception and impulse as the wanton murder of the President of the United States, arising in the mind of so insignificant a citizen, without his being either insane or degenerate could be nothing short of a miracle, for the reason that we require like causes to explain like results. To assume that he was sane, is to assume that he did a sane act, i.e., one based upon facts and for a rational purpose."[79]

Dr. Christieson agreed with Hamilton's diagnosis that Czolgosz's critical beliefs about the slain president were evidence of "insane egotism." In this back-and-forth exercise, Briggs then quotes Dr. Christieson's list of other symptoms of the assassin's alleged mental disorder as supporting evidence. These include his reticence, alleged hypochondria, the fact that "he was notoriously prone to fall asleep in a chair at any hour of the day," and his decision to quit his job and subsequent refusal to seek another.[80]

Moreover, Briggs contends that Czolgosz's anarchist sympathies were probably delusional. This conclusion is based on a survey of anarchist publications after the assassination which revealed a diversity of views concerning the McKinley assassination that ranged from approval to condemnation. Such lack of agreement, Briggs implies, suggests Czolgosz must have imagined that his act was consistent with anarchist beliefs. To support this assertion, Briggs cites the reluctance of anarchists he contacted after the assassination to acknowledge any support for Czolgosz's act.[81] Briggs' insensitivity and failure to comprehend the political context of the assassination is remarkable. Given the mood of hostility in the government toward any socialist, and especially toward anarchist groups, it is little wonder that some reticence was observed among the anarchist groups he contacted.

Leon Czolgosz's decision to assassinate William McKinley on that warm late afternoon in September 1901 can be understood only if analyzed in the context of the economic and political circumstances of American society in the last quarter of the nineteenth century.

The Context: 1873–1901

Leon Czolgosz was twenty-eight years of age when he was executed. Conceived in what is now Czechoslovakia, he was born in Alpena, Michigan, near Detroit, within a month of his mother's arrival in the United States. Leon was her fourth child. She would have five more children before she died twelve years later after childbirth at the age of forty-two. Before she slipped into a final coma from the internal hemorrhaging and inadequate medical care that claimed her life, she was frequently delirious. Her husband recalled that she often repeated this statement to the children she loved and knew she was leaving: "My children, the time will come when you will have greater understanding and be more learned."[82] After the assassination, Emma Goldman, the well-known anarchist and feminist who was a contemporary of Czolgosz, would contend that it was what Czolgosz had learned from experience about the realities of American society that motivated him to act.[83] Earlier attempts notwithstanding, it is difficult to challenge that conclusion.

When Leon Czolgosz was born in 1873, the American industrial revolution was underway. Society was changing rapidly as the economy began to shift from a predominantly agricultural base to one of heavy industrialization. Hard times in Eastern and Southern Europe and a demand for industrial labor were the reasons for the successive waves of immigrants, like the Czolgosz family, who came impoverished to America seeking a better life. While there is no question that opportunity existed in America to a greater degree than on the Continent, the last quarter of the nineteenth century remains one of the most exploitative and oppressive periods in American history.

The country was run by men of enormous wealth and limited perspectives, industrialists such as Vanderbilt, Rockefeller, Carnegie, and Frick; masters of capital like Morgan and Gould, and their spokesmen in government with names like Blaine and Aldrich and Hanna, and every president elected since Lincoln — all eminently forgettable men because of their personal insignificance in office. Like the Congress, most served simply to ratify and forward the policies advocated by big banks, big railroads, big oil, and big iron and steel. The policies advanced by industrial capital during this period were remarkably indifferent to human concerns.

In the name of progress, treaties were broken and American Indians were being systematically exterminated by rank-seeking commanders in massacres at places like Sand Creek, Aravaipa Creek, the Big Hole and Wounded Knee. Buffalo herds, upon which many tribes depended for food, shelter, and clothing, virtually disappeared as hundreds of thousands of these great beasts were wantonly slaughtered and left to rot on the plains. The decimated remnants of a once proud and colorful people were herded onto disease-ridden reservations as the railroads and speculators took over their land and water.

In the South, the marginal gains made by former slaves during a brief period of "radical" reconstruction quickly disappeared after 1877 as black men and women were again, as a matter of public policy, stripped of their constitutional rights guaranteed by the Fourteenth and Fifteenth Amendments. And even the Thirteenth Amendment, which had freed them from slavery, was effectively neutralized by the imposition of an exploitative system of sharecropping, and debt peonage that soon had blacks bound again by shackles of economic indenture. Convict labor or lynch mobs awaited those who challenged the system.

In the growing cities of the industrial Northeast and Midwest and the coalfields of Pennsylvania, Ohio, West Virginia, and Kentucky, workers — a large proportion of them eastern and southern Europeans who did not yet speak English — labored under intolerable circumstances. Wages low, hours long, safety ignored, and rights nonexistent, the life of the American worker was difficult, dirty, dangerous, and, all too frequently, short. It was such a life that Leon Czolgosz and others like him lived in the grimy steel and glass industries that lined the riverbanks in eastern Ohio and western Pennsylvania.

Discontent grew as poorly paid men labored in often brutal and dangerous conditions. When the economy slipped into a depression in 1873, the year of Czolgosz's birth, wages were cut back. Unions, weak as they were at that time, fought back. Unionized workers went on strike in textile mills, coalfields, and foundries from Chicago to New York, but the strikes were quickly broken by the overwhelming economic and political strength of industry. Striking unionists were fired and replaced with non-unionists. Blacklisting was common so that future employment for strikers would be difficult to find. Legal harassment with political backing followed for those who fought back. With approximately 60 percent of the average workingman's pay going for food alone, most families did not have enough for adequate housing or medical care. For American labor, there was little to celebrate in 1876 when the nation observed its first one hundred years of freedom and independence.

A year later, when Leon Czolgosz was four, railroad workers walked off their jobs in Pennsylvania to protest a scheduled 10 percent reduction in their wages. The walk-off marked the beginning of a chain-reaction strike that eventually consumed the major railroads of the nation. The strike lasted from May 15 until August 1 when federal and state troops subdued the last remaining strikers in Scranton, Pennsylvania. There were casualties. The first striker was killed on July 17 in Martinsburg, West Virginia by the state militia. Three days later, the Maryland militia shot and killed eleven unarmed persons in Baltimore. On July 22, the Pennsylvania militia shot and killed twenty strikers in Pittsburgh while sustaining the loss of several of their own killed and wounded as workers lashed back. The next day in Pittsburgh, the National Guard shot into a crowd of unarmed demonstrators killing eleven more. On July 25, more died in Chicago, as police fired into crowds of strikers. The killing continued in Chicago for another day.[84] The response dictated by industrial and political leaders and carried out by private "coal and iron police" and state militias was vicious.

In 1879, at the age of six, Leon Czolgosz began to shine shoes and sell papers on the streets of Detroit to supplement his father's meager income. After an uneven five years of schooling in Polish parochial and public schools, he was forced to quit and work full time. He was twelve years of age in 1885 when he began to work long hours for little pay in a Michigan factory. That same year his mother died.[85]

The following year, on May 4, 1886, a bomb exploded during a labor rally of some 1,500 people who had gathered in Chicago's Haymarket Square. The bomb killed eleven persons, including seven policemen, and more than one hundred persons were injured. Eight anarchists were arrested for the crime. All were tried and convicted, despite the prosecutions failure to produce any evidence linking them to the crime. Five were sentenced to die. The Haymarket Square affair and its aftermath remained as a major news story for nearly a year, providing a catalyst for the bitter continuing disputes that divided capital and labor.

The day before their scheduled hanging, one of the condemned men committed suicide in his cell. The next day, November 11, 1887, the remaining four — Spies, Fischer, Engel, and Parsons — died bravely on the gallows, proclaiming the justice of their cause to the last breath. "There will come a time when our silence will be more powerful than the voices you strangle today," Spies shouted to the crowd. "Hurrah for anarchy," Fisher yelled out. "Hurrah for anarchy," Engel echoed, adding, "This is the happiest moment of my life." "Let the voice of the people be heard," Parsons said moments before they dropped to their death, becoming martyrs of the American labor movement.[86]

Leon Czolgosz was an impressionable fourteen-year-old when news of this gross injustice reverberated through the labor movement. The executions also made a lasting impression on a teen-aged Emma Goldman. Her autobiography written years later would recall with reverence the inspiration provided by Haymarket Square martyrs.[87]

The Czolgosz family moved to Natrona, Pennsylvania, near Pittsburgh in 1889. Leon found work there in a glass factory. Leon was sixteen, earning seventy-five cents a day. For ten to twelve hours per shift, he carried red hot glass from the ovens to cooling racks.[88] The heat was intense. Two suits of long woolen underwear were worn beneath an outer layer of clothing to provide some insulation from the searing temperatures. But even so, workers frequently developed severe abdominal pains and muscle cramps from dehydration. Often bent over with pain by the time their shifts ended, wives and mothers kept salty pickle brine on hand which husbands and sons drank for relief.

Slavic immigrants confronted other difficulties in the western Pennsylvania. Thomas Bell (Tomas Belejcak), a Slavic-American writer who grew up in Braddock, Pennsylvania (near Natrona), describes the impressions of his youth in these gray turn-of-the-century steel towns and explains his reasons for writing about them:

> I saw a people brought here by steel magnates from the old country and then exploited, ridiculed, and oppressed. . . . The life of a Slovak boy in Braddock 30–40 years ago was a bitter one. As a small boy I could not understand why I should be ashamed of the fact that I was Slovak. While Irish and German kids could boast of the history of their ancestors, I did not know anything about the history of my people. I made up my mind to write a history of the Braddock Slovaks. . . . I wanted to make sure that the hardships my grandfather, my father, my mother, and my brother, sisters, and other relatives lived through would not be forgotten.[89]

In 1892, the Czolgosz family moved back to the Cleveland area just before the Homestead strike broke near Pittsburgh on June 29. Steel workers, a large number of them Slavic, had limits on their ability to control the resentment Thomas Bell described. When the Carnegie Steel Company arbitrarily decided to reduce the meager wages these workers received, their anger boiled to the surface. Workers walked off their jobs in protest and blocked the entrances to the Homestead plant.

Rather than negotiate, company manager Henry Clay Frick hired some two hundred Pinkerton detectives to disperse the mob and break the strike. Outraged by Frick's callousness, the strikers refused to leave the scene. Bloodshed followed on July 6 as Pinkerton agents fired into a crowd killing sixteen and wounding many others. Overwhelmed by the brutal response, workers gave up on the strike. On July 23, an outraged anarchist, Alexander Berkman, failed in an attempt to assassinate Frick in his Pittsburgh offices. The loss of the Homestead strike was a severe blow to the cause of American labor, demonstrating the lengths to which industrialists like Frick were willing to go to deny workers decent wages and working conditions.[90]

Back in Cleveland, Leon went to work at the Newberg Wire Mills. Working conditions were primitive and dangerous. Menacing hot steel wire was stretched under pressure, leaving unprotected workers exposed to a potentially lethal whiplash if the steel broke, as it frequently did. Leon was lucky. When the wire broke once on his shift, he survived with only a bloody gash that scarred his cheek. The six-day work week and hours remained the same as his previous jobs, but the wages were better — twenty-six cents per hour for the ten-hour day shift. The twelve-hour night shift was difficult but paid better at thirty-three cents per hour. Also, it was a relief not to have to contend with the enervating heat of the glass factory. As a result, he was less tired than he had been and was able to spend more of his time doing what he enjoyed most — following his late mother's admonition to read and learn. Leon's love of learning was no surprise to his brother Waldek who considered him "the best scholar of them all" before he was forced to drop out of school.[91]

When the depression of 1893 hit, the wire mill announced a cut in wages. The workers, including Leon, went on strike and were promptly fired. Six months later, he used an alias, Fred C. Nieman, to avoid the company blacklist and successfully regained a job at the same mill.

It was during this period of labor strife that he began to question his Roman Catholicism. The teachings of the church and the advice of the priests did not square with the radical papers and pamphlets he had been spending increasing amounts of time reading. Both he and his brother, Waldek, had prayed for help during the difficult period they had been on strike, but their prayers had gone unanswered. Moreover, they felt the priests they knew were fairly comfortable men who were largely indifferent to the economic difficulties of their parishioners. The two brothers decided "the priests' trade was the same as the shoemaker's or any other." Priests, they decided, were primarily interested in money — not the welfare of their parishioners.[92] For this reason, they broke with the Church and focused on the radical political literature of the day for guidance. It was the socialists and anarchists, it seemed to them, who honestly addressed the basic contradictions they observed in American society. Moreover, unlike the conservatism they observed at Mass, the socialists and anarchists offered solutions in this world, not the next. Leon's brother-in-law, Frank Bandowski, who had been an officer in a socialist organization for some time, joined the two brothers in their study and discussion sessions. Leon and Waldek eventually joined Bandowski's group and attended meetings with him. Before long, however, disagreements between members who supported Eugene Debs and others who did not split the organization. But Leon, Waldek, and Frank continued to read and study together.

One of their favorite books was Edward Bellamy's *Looking Backward 2000–1887*. Published in 1888, Bellamy's book envisioned a utopian society of state socialism by the year 2000. Next to the Bible, which he continued to read, it was Leon's favorite book. Waldek and Frank recalled that he studied it as one might study a textbook, marking passages, writing comments in the margins. After his arrest, both men demonstrated considerable affection and courage, given the hostility that prevailed, by visiting him in prison.[93]

About the time Leon and his brother left the Church and were heavily involved in what might be considered their political self-education, another great labor uprising occurred. The Pullman strike of 1894 was a bitter strike, accompanied by the worst kind of nineteenth-century corporate brutality. The driving force for that brutality was the principle "that property was the highest good and the chief end of society . . . that social justice and human rights should remain forever subordinate to considerations of property."[94] With railroad tycoons George Pullman and Richard Olney embracing that creed, the battle lines were drawn when the fiery Eugene Debs, leader of the American Railway Union, challenged the Pullman Company's right to use economic coercion to force its workers to rent company-owned housing. Wages had been arbitrarily reduced to compensate the company for the housing it was attempting to force its employees to rent.[95]

President Grover Cleveland, siding with the company, brought the full force of federal troops in to prevent what he feared would be the destruction of railroad property. Debs was quickly jailed. Frustrated with industry and disillusioned with a government that responded to every dispute as an arm of industry, Debs, like Czolgosz, found inspiration in the radical literature he read and studied during his confinement. Debs went on to lead the largest Socialist movement in American history. Probably no other strike had a greater radicalizing influence on the American working class than the Pullman strike of 1894. During this time, the issues between industry and labor were starkly defined in word and deed for not only Eugene Debs, but men like Leon Czolgosz as well.

The injustice, corruption, and brutality of this "Gilded Age" of powerful "trusts and combinations" were apparent and fueling the resentments, as well, of the farmers and small businessmen who were now swelling the ranks of the newly emerging Populist party. A genuine grass-roots movement succeeded in nominating the Populist William Jennings Bryan to head the Democratic ticket in the presidential election of 1896. With the support of individuals like Tom Watson of Georgia, a compelling advocate for poor Southern farmers, and Eugene Debs, by then the most prominent spokesman for the industrial working class, Bryan's candidacy posed a major challenge to the economic status quo.

That challenge resulted in the most massively organized and hugely financed Republican campaign ever waged until that time. Closely managed by the Ohio industrialist-politician Marcus Hanna, the comfortable and agreeable Republican nominee, William McKinley, ran on a platform that proclaimed with religious solemnity the "sanctity of contracts," "national honor," and "peace, progress, patriotism and prosperity." Worried by the Democratic/Populist definition of the issues as "the people" versus "the great trusts and combinations," Wall Street was willing to reach deep into its bulging coffers to aid Mark Hanna's Republican cause of silencing this ominous threat from the Left. The nation's largest corporations rallied to the call. Firms such as Rockefeller's Standard Oil, J. P. Morgan's banking empire, New York Life, as well as the Pennsylvania and New York Central railroads contributed unprecedented amounts to McKinley's campaign.[96]

The purple platitudes about God, country, and the virtues of American life that the carefully managed candidate proclaimed were designed to appeal to the well-dressed, churchgoing, Protestant mainstream of American life. And these same values of Protestantism, corporatism, and Americanism became one and the same in Hanna's astutely programmed campaign advertising.

The more subtle message of the campaign spoke to the issue of political power in America — who should exercise it and why? The McKinley victory of 1896 stands as the indisputable triumph of nineteenth-century industrial capitalism, or as historian Lawrence Goodwyn has described the election, "the conclusive triumph of the corporate ethos."[97] Hanna's skillful campaign had succeeded in isolating on the Left the poor, immigrant, and largely Catholic, working class. Many Democrats, for example, in the industrial Northeast, who sought to distance themselves from this segment of the party, voted Republican as an affirmation of their belief in truly *American* "values" and "progress." The result was a major realignment in the electorate that left American labor politically weakened and dormant until it was mobilized by Franklin Delano Roosevelt in his successful campaign of 1932.[98]

It was a disheartening election for the radical American Left from which it would never truly recover. For Leon Czolgosz, the election was a confirmation of what he, Waldek, and Frank had been discussing and reading in the anarchist journals and pamphlets that were stacked in his bedroom — that the oppressive corporate structure in America could only be changed through revolution.

The Lattimer Mines Massacre

In 1897,[99] Leon contributed four hundred dollars to the family's purchase of a farm outside of Cleveland.[100] His father had remarried and although Leon did not like his domineering stepmother and tried to avoid her as much as possible, he did enjoy the farm. Owning a farm represented a big step toward the self-sufficiency, freedom, and financial independence virtually every immigrant hoped to find in America. For Leon, the farm was a pastoral escape from the noise, ugliness, and danger of the wire mill.

Across the Allegheny Mountains near Hazleton, Pennsylvania, Slavic coal miners lived much the same way as the Czolgosz family. Isolated by language, culture, and poverty in the rural setting of the anthracite coalfields, the life of the Slavic worker was bleak regardless of whether he worked in the hillside mines or the iron and steel mills on the rivers. Eastern and southern Europeans were invariably relegated to the least desirable jobs. Lacking the gregarious qualities of the Italians and Irish, Slavic workers seemed to their employers especially foreign and difficult to understand. Michael Novak's perceptive account of Slavic workers of that period explains why:

In the gregarious, informal, quick-talking America described by Tocqueville, the Slavs were not as articulate and sociable as many other immigrants. As their clothes were dark and their demeanor dour, so their manners were also somewhat forbidding. As newcomers, they were strange enough. Their personal style was stiff, formal, distant. Their languages were more distant from English than were Latin or Germanic tongues. Taught by life to be thoroughly suspicious of authorities but outwardly deferential, they were hard to flatter, cajole, amuse, or kid.

The wit of the Irish did not penetrate their defenses. The wink and elbow of the con man and the regular guy made those defenses tighten. The signals they received and those they gave were not easy to recognize. They lived in poverty so extreme it scandalized their neighbors. Their capacity for saving was prodigious.

These immigrants were not, then, a wholly attractive people. If one places oneself in the shoes of those who experienced their coming, one sees how frictions and misunderstandings must have festered. Sheer verbal communication was, for the most part, out of the question, and the rituals and gestures of nonverbal expression must have been so skewed that great feelings of hopelessness and frustration had to well up. Among some of the Slavs, it was considered rude and impolite to smile on formal occasions or in the presence of superiors. Even to look superiors straight in the eye was considered an impudent and rebellious act. On this point alone, conflict with Anglo-American mores was assured.[101]

In September 1897, Slavic miners at the Lattimer Mines near Hazleton walked off their jobs to protest an "alien tax" on their wages that the Pennsylvania legislature had just passed. Since most were only working at half-time already because of earlier cutbacks, the new tax meant practically all their remaining wages would be siphoned off for rents, groceries, and medical care at company-owned enterprises. With the new tax, virtually nothing would be left to save in order to bring other members of their families to this country, or, as many planned to do, to return to Europe someday.[102]

On September 10, over four hundred miners began a protest march that would cover the six miles from Hazleton to the Lattimer Mines. Unarmed and orderly, the march was conceived as a peaceful protest against company wage policies and the new state tax. At about 3:00 in the afternoon, the marchers were intercepted by the Hazleton sheriff and some one hundred fifty armed deputies who took up positions along the road leading to the mine superintendent's office. As the miners approached, the sheriff, revolver drawn, walked toward the front rank of the shuffling column and ordered them to stop and disperse. When the marchers ignored his command and continued to file silently by, the sheriff grabbed one and thrust his pistol into the man's chest. A second miner pulled the sheriff's arm away from the first. At that point, the sheriff raised his pistol to the second man's forehead and pulled the trigger. But the gun misfired. The panicked sheriff looked toward his deputies and shouted "Fire." A murderous fusillade exploded from the muzzles of their rifles and shotguns. Amid cries of "shoot the sons of bitches," witnesses recalled that the shooting continued for one to five minutes. As the workers scattered, they were chased and shot in the back by their relentless attackers. When the firing began to slacken, the groans and cries of the wounded filled the dusty, smoke-filled air. Angry deputies walked among the bodies and answered the pleas for water with, "We'll give you hell, not water, hunkies!" Nineteen miners died and some thirty-nine others were wounded.[103]

The enormity of this massacre shocked even radicals who were by then conditioned to the excesses of corporate violence. There can be little doubt that Leon Czolgosz was aware of the event, and even less that he followed the trial that began the following February to determine the guilt of the sheriff and his deputies.

The atrocity assumed national significance as protest rallies were held in Slavic settlements throughout the country. A "National Prosecuting and Welfare Committee of the Lattimer Victims" was formed by Slavic groups to handle court and relief costs.[104] But the trial was a sham. On March 9, 1898, the all-male, Protestant, and Republican jury brought in its verdict of not guilty on all counts.[105] The Slavic community was outraged.

The Nervous Breakdown

In the fall of 1897, in the wake of the Lattimer Mines Massacre, Leon Czolgosz became ill from what appeared to be an emotional and physical breakdown. His brother Waldek said that he just seemed "gone to pieces like."[106] His symptoms? Shortness of breath, fatigue, heart palpitations, stomach discomfort, insomnia, and loss of appetite — the well-known symptoms of clinical depression. Leon refused to seek hospital admittance and — given the quality of medical care available to his mother before her death — had little confidence in doctors. After his mother died, he said, "There is no place in the hospital for poor people; [only] if you have lots of money you will get well taken care of." So Leon suffered alone, without medical care, in silence.[107] Although possibly unaware of the link between his mental state and its physical symptoms, he was quite aware of the reason for his depression — the intolerable injustice of industrial employment epitomized by events such as the unpunished atrocity at Lattimer Mines. He refused to return to his job at the wire mill. As he explained to his brother, "I can't stand it any longer."[108]

A secondary source of continuing irritation was his domineering stepmother, whom he had always resented as she did him. He now refused to take his meals with the family when the "old woman," as he called her, was present, preferring instead to eat alone in his room. Moreover, he even refused to eat the food she prepared. It is important to note, however, that he did eat with the family when she was absent, and he frequently prepared the family meals himself.[109] His refusal to eat with this woman had nothing to do with paranoia, an unfounded fear that she would poison his food as others have alleged. He simply could not bear to be around her.

Except for Waldek and Frank, Leon had little to say to anyone during the period of his depression. Although he did occasionally play with his sister's children, most of his time was spent reading and sleeping. According to his brother, Leon was aware that his family was, as he put it, "uneducated" and did not understand him, so he made no effort to explain his feelings to them.[110]

Waldek, concerned about his brother's health and his need for future employment, insisted that Leon see a doctor. But the several doctors Leon eventually saw could find no physical cause for his problems.[111] Once more, it seems certain that Leon understood that the causes of his problems were *external,* not internal. During this period he continued to read voraciously, and the substance of his reading was invariably political. He consumed all the anarchist and socialist literature he could get his hands on. Periodically, he would travel the five miles into Cleveland where he would purchase newspapers, journals, and books. On some of these trips he also made discrete visits to houses of prostitution.[112] He also became a casual visitor at political rallies and meetings where he picked up any pamphlets that might be available. Returning to the farm he would read and study until he had exhausted his supply before returning again to replenish his growing political library and, sometimes, to satisfy his sexual desire. His collection consisted of virtually "everything pertaining to working men, strikes, etc."[113] He was obsessed with the need for radical social change in America.

On August 29, 1898, he formally quit the wire mill job, which as a practical matter he had avoided for nearly a year. But in spite of his bitterness, Czolgosz had never expressed any hostility on the job. Except for his participation in the strike of 1893, he was a cooperative, reliable, and skilled worker. His foreman said there was none better on his shift.[114]

But this was typical, as Novak has suggested, of the Slavic workers of his day. Quiet and obedient, even to the point of being obsequious to persons who did not understand their culture; resentments were most often expressed away from their employers. Domestic quarrels, such as Leon had with his stepmother, sullen moodiness, and explosive outbursts of temper characterized Slavic neighborhoods of that period. So also did a pattern of heavy drinking, which Novak describes as "a ransom paid to demons," that stirred the reservoirs of resentment deep within.[115]

Czolgosz was typical of this culture in most respects, except that he controlled his anger better than most. His intellectual curiosity, fed by extensive reading and increasing attendance at anarchist and socialist meetings, provided him with a more sophisticated grasp of the predicament the immigrant working class in America confronted. He understood that the familiar eddies of domestic violence and melancholy, swirling in the tides of alcoholism that characterized immigrant populations of the day, were symptoms of political and economic oppression and not, as Protestant ministers proclaimed from their pulpits, moral weakness. It was this realization and not "dementia praecox" that was at the core of Leon Czolgosz's "breakdown" following the Lattimer Mines incident.

Prelude

For the next year and a half, Czolgosz's life continued much as it had after he quit work. His major activity was reading. Occasionally he hunted rabbits, entertained his sister's children, and sometimes prepared evening meals for the family — if his stepmother was absent.[116] Apart from his continuing political discussions with Waldek and Frank, he had little to say beyond functional conversations to anyone else in the family. On his trips to Cleveland, however, he did go to the theater on occasion with a friend, Walter Nowak, who also attended the same political meetings. But eventually Nowak stopped attending because the meetings had become too radical, he said, for his tastes.[117]

This angered Czolgosz. He was contemptuous of his faint-hearted former friend. He believed in revolution. The assassination of King Humbert I of Italy on July 29, 1900 greatly interested him.[118] The king had been killed by the Italian-American anarchist, Gaetano Bresci, who was praised in anarchist publications around the world. It was praise Czolgosz shared.

In the spring of 1901, Leon announced to his family that he had decided to relocate, perhaps to Chicago or further west to look for different kinds of employment. He told his brother that he could not bear to return to the kind of factory work he had left. Perhaps in the West, he said, he could find a job "binding wheat or fixing machines or something."[119] With that in mind, he asked the family to return his share of the farm investment. It took a while, but that summer his father finally agreed and returned a first installment of seventy dollars from the four hundred dollars he had contributed.

In the meantime, Czolgosz had heard for the first time the fiery anarchist crusader Emma Goldman when she spoke at a meeting in Cleveland on May 6, 1901. Czolgosz was impressed.[120] On May 19, he returned to the anarchist headquarters on 4 Elivell Street and talked with Emil Shilling the association's treasurer. Schilling later reported that they discussed class and revolutionary aspects of the labor movement. He recalled that he gave Czolgosz a book about the Haymarket Square martyrs and invited the young man home to dinner where their conversation continued. One of the issues discussed was whether King Humbert's assassination had been a result of a conspiracy or simply that of an individual acting alone.[121]

But Schilling did not care for Czolgosz, believing him to be arrogant and poorly informed about the theoretical aspects of anarchism. The feeling was mutual. Czolgosz found Schilling to be condescending and patronizing. On his second visit, Czolgosz returned the book he had been loaned with the curt explanation that he did not have time to read it. It is virtually certain that Czolgosz already had read as much as there was to read about the Haymarket affair and considered the loan an insult. When Schilling offered him a beer, Czolgosz refused and countered by offering Schilling a cigar. Miffed, Schilling "told him to smoke it himself."[122] Czolgosz did not observe in Schilling the revolutionary vision and charisma he so admired in Emma Goldman. Cautious and suspicious, Schilling carefully weighed every answer he gave to Czolgosz's very direct inquiries. And to that extent he aroused the contempt of the idealistic Czolgosz just as did his condescending offer of a book whose contents were well-known to every literate radical.

Sometime in late May or early June, Czolgosz visited Schilling again. This time he talked at length about Goldman and how impressed he had been when he had heard her speak. During the intermission of her talk, he had spoken with her briefly to inquire about reading material she would recommend; she had treated him kindly.[123] He asked Schilling how he could meet her again. Schilling explained that Goldman was in Chicago and advised him simply to introduce himself to her there.

On July 11, he caught a westbound train in Cleveland, repeating to his family before leaving that his purpose was to look for work. He wrote to them from Fort Wayne, Indiana on July 14 to say he was continuing west and would write again later.[124] This was to be the last contact he had with his family until after the assassination.

Czolgosz's precise movements and activities after this point are difficult to pinpoint with any certainty. The pattern, however, is fairly clear. His objective had nothing to do with finding work in the West, as he told his family. Rather he intended to become actively involved in the anarchist movement. He had spent the last few years in study and reflection about the need for radical political change in America, now he was prepared to act. All he needed was more direction and support. Thus, for the next six weeks he traveled between Cleveland, Chicago, and Buffalo, establishing contacts with anarchist groups and volunteering his services. In the brief meeting he eventually had with Emma Goldman in Chicago, he asked her to introduce him to other activists. Similarly, in Cleveland and Buffalo he made the same kind of inquiries, so often, in fact, that it led to suspicions that he might be a government infiltrator. The intensity of his manner, the probing nature of his questions, and, especially, his insistence that violence must be a necessary component of the class struggle alarmed many party functionaries (or so they claimed after the assassination).

He was an enigma to most of the persons he met. His basic reticence and lack of verbal sophistication, so characteristic of Slavic men of his day, was punctuated with intense questions and ideological statements. This unfamiliar style was misunderstood by the doctrinaire leftist intellectuals he talked with. Abe Isaak, for example, editor of the Chicago-based anarchist publication, *Free Society,* became convinced that this strange, intense young man was really a government agent. In the September 1, 1901 issue of *Free Society,* he published an alert:

ATTENTION

The attention of the comrades is called to another spy. He is well dressed, of medium height, rather narrow-shouldered, blond and about twenty-five years of age. Up to the present he has made his appearance in Chicago and Cleveland. In the former place he remained but a short time, while in Cleveland he disappeared when the comrades had confirmed themselves of his identity & were on the point of exposing him. His demeanor is of the usual sort, pretending to be greatly interested in the cause, asking for names or soliciting aid for acts of contemplated violence. If this same individual makes his appearance elsewhere, the comrades are warned in advance and can act accordingly.[125]

By this time, Czolgosz — who had been using his wire-mill alias, Fred C. Nieman, since he left Cleveland — had left Chicago and had checked into a room above John Nowak's saloon in downtown Buffalo.[126] A day or two later, he purchased a new .32 caliber Iver Johnson revolver for $4.50 at a hardware store.[127] He had given his old pistol, the one he had used to hunt rabbits on the farm, to a previous landlord in lieu of the $1.75 rent he had owed.[128]

It is possible that Czolgosz's decision to kill the president may have been prompted by the Free Society notice questioning his purpose. He did say after his arrest that "something I read in Free Society suggested the idea," but he never identified what it was. Nor did he ever comment on the *Free Society* allegation that he was a spy.[129] Emma Goldman, for example, was concerned that the unsubstantiated charge may have prompted Czolgosz to demonstrate the sincerity of his commitment by assassinating the president.[130] It is a question that will, unfortunately, remain unanswered. But the overall pattern of his behavior suggests that he had the assassination in mind long before Abe Isaak questioned his integrity.

The Assassination

President McKinley, accompanied by his wife, arrived in Buffalo on the evening of September 4, 1901 aboard a special Lake Shore & Michigan Southern Railway train. The Pan-American Exposition was being held in Buffalo that year, and the president was making a first official visit. It was hard not to like the president. A large affable individual with a penchant for speeches presented in the most florid patriotic prose, he was a man of the times. McKinley was happily oblivious to the circumstances of life for the working masses whose labor, under intolerable conditions, provided the soft cushion of affluence that he and men of his class so much enjoyed. He epitomized the small-town, well-dressed, churchgoing values of protestant turn-of-the-century America. This portly, tuxedoed, socially insulated, Christian man, so solicitous of the frail wife who accompanied him, had no idea of the danger that lurked in the shuffling, shabbily dressed masses of American life he understood no better than the strange languages they spoke.

Thursday, September 5, had been proclaimed President's Day, and the president and his entourage toured the Exposition grounds accompanied by a detail of mounted National Guardsmen, bands, and city police. McKinley was scheduled to address an immense crowd of Exposition visitors. Leon Czolgosz was among the cheering throng, attempting to edge closer to the speaker's platform, but the press of the crowd made it impossible. Czolgosz stood frustrated and anxious as the president, surrounded by local and foreign dignitaries, colorfully dressed Marines, and the parasols of wealthy women, began his speech by extolling the virtues of progress and prosperity.

"Expositions are the timekeepers of progress," he boomed. "They record the world's advancement." He went on to describe the nation's "unexampled prosperity." And then to deafening applause, "We hope that all that are representatives here may be moved to higher and nobler efforts for their own and the world's good . . . " He went on to urge "greater commerce and trades." He closed his speech with ministerial solemnity in this benediction:

> Our earnest prayer is that God will graciously vouchsafe prosperity, happiness, and peace to all our neighbors and like blessings to all the people and powers of earth.[131]

Then amid the sounds of a military band and the cheers of his enthusiastic audience, the president, wearing a tall silk hat and black frock coat, nodded and smiled benignly to the applauding dignitaries as his doting wife moved to his side. He exuded the good will of the self-satisfied and comfortable man that he was as he accompanied her to an awaiting carriage. One can imagine Czolgosz's resentment as he witnessed this spectacle of privilege that was so far beyond the grasp of the weary masses he knew.

On Friday, September 6, the president was scheduled to appear at a public reception in the ornate Temple of Music on the Exposition grounds. Before the afternoon reception, he and his party boarded a special train for a short sightseeing trip to Niagara Falls. Czolgosz followed but was frustrated again in his attempt to get close enough for a shot. He returned to the Exposition by streetcar and was one of the first in the lengthening reception line that was forming inside the Temple. The president returned shortly after 4 P.M. and was escorted to the position of honor amidst potted palms and bay trees.[132]

The first man to shake the president's hand looked intently into his eyes and said dramatically "George Washington, Abraham Lincoln and President McKinley."[133] The president smiled approvingly and eased the admirer on with the pleasant indifference of a man accustomed to such praise.

As the line shuffled toward the president, Czolgosz carefully removed the pistol from his pocket, concealing it in his handkerchief-wrapped hand. The white cloth looked like a bandage and did not arouse the curiosity of the security guards who casually scrutinized the line of well-wishers. The President was flanked by his personal secretary, George B. Cortelyou, on his right and the director of the Pan-American Exposition, John G. Milburn, to his left. As Czolgosz approached, the president extended his hand. Czolgosz casually extended his left hand as if to greet the president, then suddenly pushed the president's hand aside as he stepped forward and fired two fatal shots through the tuxedo vest and bloused white shirt while smiling directly into the president's face.[134] The startled McKinley stiffened, then staggered backward, but remained on his feet as soldiers swarmed over his assailant. Dazed, McKinley murmured "Be easy with him, boys."[135] It was almost four years to the day after the Lattimer Mines Massacre.

At the police station, a badly beaten Czolgosz was questioned as the wounded president was rushed to the Exposition Hospital and prepared for emergency surgery. The hastily assembled doctors were hampered by confusion, inadequate surgical instruments and, ironically, poor lighting.[136] The president died of a gangrenous infection eight days later. His physicians were never able to locate the fatal bullet even after a four-hour search during the autopsy.[137] His doctors claimed that the president's chances for recovery had been seriously limited by his obesity (as had their search for the bullet) and "a rather low vitality" that was characteristic of his sedentary lifestyle.[138]

Retribution

Czolgosz was arraigned on first-degree murder charges on September 23. When the judge asked for his plea, he uttered the only word he would speak in the courtroom during his brief trial: "guilty." The judge explained that a guilty plea could not be entered and instructed the clerk to enter a plea of not guilty. Czolgosz tried unsuccessfully to dismiss his court-appointed attorneys; failing that, he refused to participate in his own defense. The trial was a farce. His attorneys spent more time apologizing for the onerous task they had been assigned than they did defending the silent defendant. In fairness, there was little to defend. The trial was swift and to the point. Within eight hours it was over, and Czolgosz was sentenced to die, as he expected.

Before the trial began, however, Czolgosz did make several statements concerning his motives; he went to his execution without deviating from them. Immediately after the shooting he told his interrogators that he shot the president because he felt it was his "duty" to do so. He said he resented the president's indifference and hostility toward the "working people." "I didn't believe," he continued, "[that] one man should have so much and another should have none." He added that he understood and accepted the consequences of his act.[139]

The day after the shooting he was questioned by several doctors. He repeated essentially the same explanation:

> I don't believe in the Republican form of government and I don't believe we should have any rulers. It is right to kill them.

On another occasion, he mentioned how he was offended by the slain President's speeches:

> McKinley was going around the country shouting prosperity when there was no prosperity for the poor man. I am not afraid to die. We all have to die sometime.[140]

Then explaining that he was an anarchist, he added:

> I fully understood what I was doing when I shot the President. I realized I was sacrificing my life. I am willing to take the consequences.[141]

Czolgosz remained calm, polite, and remorseless while awaiting his execution.[142] Witnesses testified that he maintained his principles and composure to the end. They reported that as he entered the execution chamber, "he appeared calm and self-possessed, his head was erect and his face bore an expression of defiant determination."[143] He died a few minutes after 7 A.M. on October 29, 1901 in what one observer described as a "cool and courageous manner."[144] An autopsy revealed nothing more than a "good-looking, youthful" corpse. There were no organic abnormalities.[145]

When Waldek asked to claim his dead brother's body for burial, prison authorities denied the request. Instead the body of Leon Czolgosz was lowered casket less into a prison grave bubbling with the contents of "six barrels of quicklime and a carboy of sulphuric acid."[146]

Conclusions

Following the assassination, some anarchists — then under siege from a government committed to the eradication of the "social disease" that resulted in the president's death — condemned Czolgosz's act and labeled him a "lunatic."[147] Others, less timid, viewed him as a courageous martyr in the fight against political and economic oppression.[148] One who shared the latter opinion was Emma Goldman, who viewed the assassin in the same way she viewed the Haymarket martyrs. She endorsed the "social necessity" and selflessness of his act, saying at the time:

> The boy in Buffalo is a creature at bay. . . . He committed the act for no personal reasons or gain. He did it for what is his ideal: the good of the people. That is why my sympathies are with him.[149]

Writing years after the event, Goldman explained the controversy over Czolgosz as one that divided American-born and Jewish anarchists, who condemned the assassination, and their European-born comrades, who considered it a meaningful act of political significance.[150] It was such ethnic and cultural differences that accounted, in part, for the lack of cohesiveness that continued to weaken leftist movements in the United States.

Much of what has been written about the assassination since those troubled times has discounted the rationality and political motive of Leon Czolgosz. Rather than examining the political context of Czolgosz's act, purportedly significant details of his life have been sifted out to support the claim that he was mentally ill. For such observers, the extraordinary nature of the crime itself provided sufficient evidence of mental disorder.

Typical of such reasoning are Drs. Channing and Briggs, whose collaborative observations were outlined earlier. Both doctors based their conclusion that Czolgosz was mentally ill on the assertion that his belief that President McKinley was an "enemy of the working people" was the "essence of his delusion."[151] Moreover, his other anarchist beliefs — for example, the rejection of organized religion and marriage — were considered evidence of the "moral chaos" of mentally deranged persons. Further, based on the denials of acquaintanceship with Czolgosz and the reluctance to endorse his act that Briggs observed in his post-assassination interviews with known anarchists, both doctors concluded that Czolgosz's anarchism was also a "delusion."[152] Channing also dismissed the absence in Czolgosz of any evidence of "divine" inspiration or spiritual "mission" associated with two earlier psychotic assassins, Lawrence and Guiteau, suggesting that Czolgosz undoubtedly shared such a delusion in spite of his denials. Channing explained:

> We must remember that this man was an ignorant Pole [sic], who spoke his own language most of the time, and it would have been quite impossible for him to have made use of words that a man like Guiteau, who had a great facility of speech, might have used.[153]

Even respected historians such as McKinley biographer Margaret Leech slipped into such glib and inaccurate generalizations. Ignoring the fact that Czolgosz refused to make any public statements about the crime or to seek notoriety of any kind, Leech concludes that he killed McKinley to "attract attention." To support her conclusion, she makes much of Czolgosz's choice of the alias "Nieman":

> There was bleak self-revelation in the alias which he often used, and which he would use again when the time came for the police to question him: Fred Nieman, Fred Nobody (Nieman in German means Nobody). But on this September afternoon, for the first time in his thwarted twenty-eight years, Czolgosz was going to be somebody.[154]

Interesting speculation, but the fact is that Czolgosz used the alias Nieman because, as he explained, it was the English derivation of his mother's maiden name, Nebock — not because he felt like a nobody.[155]

The other associated so-called "symptoms"[156] of Czolgosz's alleged mental disorder also fade under close examination: For example, his eating alone (he resented his domineering stepmother and refused to share the table with her), his fatigue (he worked a seventy-two hour work week most of his life), his reticence (Slavic culture), and his social isolation (but he was close to his brother and brother-in-law and he did have other friends in Cleveland).[157]

A leading publisher of the day, Henry Holt,[158] apparently not completely convinced that Czolgosz was as mentally disturbed as so many wanted to believe, grappled with the disturbing implications of a politically inspired assassination:

> We are left sitting in the dark, still wondering how such a deed could have been done by a man in his sound and sober senses in fair and free America and appalled at the possibility of a sane man murdering an American President.[159]

There were a number of realities in nineteenth-century America. There was a black reality of servitude in the segregated Deep South, a red reality of segregation on reservations or extermination west of the Mississippi, a working-class reality of hardship and economic exploitation in the industrial centers of the East and Midwest, and the comfortable reality of "greater commerce," "happiness" and "vouch-safe[d] prosperity" of William McKinley and the American mainstream. All were valid perspectives, none more so than any other. Commenting on this point in the February 14, 1902 issue of *Free Society,* Abe Isaak argued that if Czolgosz's anti-establishment views were, in fact, symptomatic of the "moral chaos" of insanity, as some authorities claimed, then all anarchists must be insane.

Like John Wilkes Booth, Leon Czolgosz was a politically motivated Type I assassin. As in Booth's case the effort to attribute the McKinley assassination to the actions of a mentally disordered individual is without any convincing empirical support. What we see in Leon Czolgosz is not a psychotic, deranged killer, but a young man who was as much a product of the times as William McKinley. A man whose beliefs, considered in the context of the life he knew, were no less removed from reality than the platitudes of the president he killed.

Notes

1. S. Kimmel, *The Mad Booths of Maryland* (1940; reprinted., New York: Dover, 1969).
2. E. Hyams, *Killing No Murder* (Camden, N.J.: Thomas Nelson & Sons, 1969), pp. 69–70.
3. See, for example, G. W. Wilson, "John Wilkes Booth: Father Murderer," *The American IMAGO 1* (June 1940): 49–60; P.Weissman, "Why Booth Shot Lincoln," in *Psychoanalysis and the Social Sciences* (New York: International Universities Press, 1958), 5:99–115.
4. J. G. Randall, *The Civil War and Reconstruction* (Boston and New York: D. C. Heath, 1937), p. 65.
5. At least one of his captors claimed to have shot Booth but, given the nature of his wound, suicide seems more likely.
6. E.V. Mahoney, *Sketches of Tudor Hall and the Booth Family* (Belair, Md.: Ella V. Mahoney, 1925), p. 33.
7. Kimmel, *The Mad Booths, pp.* 66-78.
8. A. Booth Clarke, *The Unlocked Book* (New York: G. P. Putnam's Sons, 1938), pp. 74, 91; Kimmel, *The Mad Booths, p.* 70.
9. Kimmel, *The Mad Booths, pp.* 341–342.
10. Booth Clarke, *The Unlocked Book, pp.* 73–74.
11. Ibid., pp. 72–73.
12. Kimmel, *The Mad Booths, pp.* 150–153, 158.
13. Ibid., p. 153.
14. Ibid., p. 168.
15. Ibid., p. 170.

16. Ibid., p. 172.
17. Ibid.
18. Ibid., p. 173.
19. Ibid., p. 177.
20. C. Morris, *Life on the Stage* (New York: McClure, Phillips & Co., 1901), p. 103.
21. Kimmel, *The Mad Booths, p.* 180.
22. L. J. Weichmann, *A True History of the Assassination of Abraham Lincoln and the Conspiracy of* 1865, ed. F. E. Risvold (New York: Vintage Books, 1975; written in the 1890s), p. 42.
23. A. Booth Clarke, *The Elder and the Younger Booth* (Boston: James R, Osgood & Co., 1882), pp. 66–67.
24. Morris, *Life on Stage, p.* 103.
25. F. Wilson, *John Wilkes Booth* (New York: Benjamin Bloom, Inc., 1929, 1972), pp. 7, 10.
26. Ibid., pp. 15–16.
27. Ibid., pp. 11–12, 16.
28. Quoted in Kimmel, *The Mad Booths, p.* 169.
29. Quoted in the Washington *Evening Star,* April 20, 1865; also Weichmann, A True History, pp. 49–52; and Wilson, *Booth, pp.* 50–54..
30. Kimmel, *The Mad Booths, pp.* 179–181, 184–185, 187, 204.
31. New Orleans *Times,* March 17, 1864; cited in Kimmel, *The Mad Booths, p.* 180.
32. Kimmel, *The Mad Booths, p.* 187.
33. D. Donald, *Lincoln Reconsidered* (New York: Vintage Books, 1961), pp.188–196; C. A. and M. R. Beard, *The Rise of American Civilization* (New York: Macmillan & Co., 1927), pp. 94–97.
34. Randall, *The Civil War, pp.* 222–223, 597, 602.
35. J. T. Headley, *The Great Riots of New York, 1712 to 1873* (New York: Dover, 1971; orig., 1873).
36. Randall, *The Civil War, pp.* 412–414.
37. Wilson, *Booth, pp.* 117–118.
38. W. Dusinbeere, Civil *War Issues in Pennsylvania* (Philadelphia: University of Pennsylvania Press, 1965), p. 157; Randall, *The Civil War, pp.* 643–645.
39. Randall, *The Civil War, p.* 620.
40. T. H. Williams, *Lincoln and the Radicals* (Madison: University of Wisconsin Press, 1941), pp. 316–333.
41. Williams, *Lincoln, pp.* 328–329; W. R. Brock, *Conflict and Transformation: The United States, 1844–1877* (New York: Penguin Books, 1973), pp. 280, 294.
42. For example, the *Chicago Times* panned the President's brilliant second inaugural speech as being so bad that it did not "conceive it possible that even Mr. Lincoln could produce a paper so slipshod, . . . so puerile, not alone in literary construction, but in its ideas, its sentiments, its grasp . . . . By the side of it, mediocrity is superb" (*Chicago Times,* March 6, 1865; quoted in Randall, The Civil War, p. 644). For a detailed discussion of Lincoln's unpopularity, see also Randall's *Lincoln the Liberal Statesman* (New York: Dodd, Mead & Co., 1947), esp. ch. 3. For the political significance of Sherman's campaign, see, C. Royster, *The Destructive War* (New York: Alfred A. Knopf, 1991).

Type I—Region and Class 53

43. Randall, *The Civil War*, pp. 642–645; Brock, *Conflict and Transformation*, pp. 292–293.
44. Quoted in J. Cottrell, *Anatomy of an Assassination* (London: Frederick Muller, 1966), p. 35.
45. Booth Clarke, *The Elder*, pp. 123–124.
46. Ibid., pp. 115–117, 119; Kimmel, *The Mad Booths, p.* 179.
47. B. Pitman, *The Assassination of President Lincoln and the Trial of the Conspirators: The Courtroom Testimony* (New York: Funk & Wagnalls, 1954; orig., 1865).
48. Ibid., pp. 47–57.
49. *Letters of John Wilkes Booth*, Attorney General's Papers, Lincoln Assassination, RG No. 60, National Archives.
50. He was variously known as Lewis Powell or Lewis Paine.
51. For example, see O. Eisenschiml, *Why Was Lincoln Murdered?* (Boston: Little, Brown, 1937).
52. The exact date remains uncertain.
53. Weichmann, *A True History, p.* 137; Wilson, *Booth, pp.* 70–71.
54. Randall, *The Civil War, p.* 683.
55. Kimmel, *The Mad Booths, p.* 218.
56. Pitman, *Courtroom Testimony, pp.* 154–168, 144–153.
57. The final phrase of this sentence is often cited out of context as evidence of Booth's alleged delusion of divine inspiration.
58. In the last incomplete sentence, Booth probably intended to express his frustration that "he [John Matthews] or the Govt" suppressed his letter of explanation.
59. *Diary of John Wilkes Booth*, Attorney General's Papers, Lincoln Assassination, RG No. 60, National Archives.
60. The phrase "one hoped to be great" is also cited out of context as evidence of Booth's alleged desire for fame, despite the fact that the reference is clearly to another earlier assassin.
61. Ibid.
62. Kimmel, *The Mad Booths, p.* 249.
63. Pitman, *Courtroom Testimony, p.* 92.
64. Ibid.
65. Ibid., p. 93.
66. John Surratt escaped to Europe. He was arrested in Cairo, Egypt in November 1866 and brought back to the United States for trial. He was released in August 1867 after a jury failed to reach a verdict.
67. Lincoln's reconstruction policies for the South, which were implemented by his successor, were much more benevolent than Southerners might have imagined during the last year of the war.
68. J. Davis, *The Rise and Fall of the Confederate Government* (South Brunswick, N.J.: Thomas Yoseloff, 1958; orig., 1881).
69. *People v. Leon F. Czolgosz* (1901), Courthouse Archives, Erie County, Buffalo, New York. Reprinted in *American State Trials,* ed. J.D. Lawson (St. Louis: Thomas Law Book Co., 1923), 14: 169–170. Hereafter cited as *Trial Transcripts.*

54 Defining Danger

70. C. F. MacDonald, "The Trial, Execution, Autopsy, and Mental Status of Leon F. Czolgosz, Alias Fred Nieman, the Assassin of President McKinley," *The American Journal of Insanity* 58 (January 1902): 375; W. Channing, "The Mental State of Czolgosz, the Assassin of President McKinley," *The American Journal of Insanity* 59 (October 1902): 274.
71. J. Fowler, F. S. Crego, and J. W. Putnam, "Official Report of the Experts for the People in the Case of the People v. Leon F. Czolgosz" (1901). Reprinted in *American State Trials*, ed. John D. Lawson (St. Louis: Thomas Law Book Co., 1923), 14: 195-199. Hereafter cited as *Fowler Report*. "Report of Dr. Carlos F. McDonald and Dr. Arthur.Hurd, Experts for the Prisoner" (1901), in Lawson, ed., *American State Trials*, 14: 196-203. Hereafter cited as *McDonald/Hurd Report*.
72. Channing, "The Mental State."
73. Ibid., pp. 261–266.
74. L. V. Briggs, *The Manner of Man that Kills* (Boston: The Gorham Press, 1921).
75. R. J. Donovan, *The Assassins* (New York: Harper & Bro:hers, 1952).
76. D.W. Hastings, "The Psychiatry of Presidential Assassination, Part II: Garfield and McKinley," *The Journal-Lancet* 85 (April 1965):157–162.
77. See, for example, J. McKinley, *Assassination in America* (New York: Harper & Row, 1977).
78. A, M. Hamilton, *Recollections of an Alienist* (New York: George H. Dolan, 1916), pp. 363, 365–366; Briggs, *The Manner of Man that Kills*, pp. 252–253.
79. Briggs, *The Manner of Man that Kills, p.* 338.
80. Ibid.
81. Ibid., pp. 321–331.
82. Ibid., p. 290.
83. E. Goldman, *Living My Life* (Garden City, N.Y.: Garden City Publishing Co., 1931), p. 355.
84. R. V. Bruce, *1877: Year of Violence* (Chicago: Quadrangle Books, 1959); P. S. Foner, *The Great Labor Uprising of 1877* (New York: Monad Press, 1977), pp. 231–240.
85. Goldman, *Living My Life*, pp. 355–356; Briggs, *The Manner of Man that Kills,* p. 290.
86. H. David, *The History of the Haymarket Affair,* 2d ed. (New York: Russell & Russell, 1958), p. 463.
87. Goldman, *Living My Life, p.* 304.
88. Briggs, *The Manner of Man that Kills, p.* 303.
89. T. Bell, *Out of the Furnace* (Pittsburgh: University of Pittsburgh Press, 1976; orig., 1941), p. 418.
90. J. G. Rayback, *A History of American Labor* (New York: The Free Press, 1959, 1966), pp. 194–197.
91. Briggs, *The Manner of Man that Kills, p.* 302.
92. Ibid., pp. 279, 304–305.
93. Ibid., pp. 260, 305.
94. A. Lindsey, *The Pullman Strike* (Chicago: The University of Chicago Press, 1942), p. 359.

95. Ibid., pp. 90–95.
96. L. Goodwyn, *Democratic Promise: The Populist Movement in America* (New York: Oxford University Press, 1976).
97. Ibid., p. 555.
98. V. O. Key, "A Theory of Critical Elections," *The Journal of Politics* 17 (February 1955): 3–18.
99. Various dates have been suggested for the farm purchase, ranging from 1892 to 1897, The date is not of great significance.
100. Briggs, *The Manner of Man that Kills*, p. 306.
101. M. Novak, *The Guns of Lattimer* (New York: Basic Books, 1978), p. xvi.
102. Ibid., pp. 18–19, 111–112.
103. Ibid., pp. 125-134.
104. V. R. Greene, *The Slavic Community on Strike* (Notre Dame, Ind.: University of Notre Dame Press, 1968), pp. 141–142.
105. Novak, *The Guns of Lattimer*, pp. 201, 235–236.
106. Channing, "The Mental State," p. 239.
107. Briggs, *The Manner of Man that Kills*, p. 307.
108. Channing, "The Mental State," p. 241; Briggs, *The Manner of Man that Kills*, p. 308.
109. Channing, "The Mental State," pp. 241–242; Briggs, *The Manner of Man that Kills*, pp. 293–294, 306, 313.
110. Briggs, *The Manner of Man that Kills*, p. 311.
111. Ibid., p. 300.
112. He acknowledged that he had contracted gonorrhea once as a result of these visits (MacDonald, 1902, p. 379).
113. Ibid., p. 306.
114. Ibid., pp. 313-314.
115. Novak, *The Guns of Lattimer*, pp. xv–xvi.
116. Briggs, *The Manner of Man that Kills*, p. 313.
117. *Trial Transcripts*, p. 194.
118. Channing, "The Mental State," p. 263.
119. Briggs, *The Manner of Man that Kills*, p. 308.
120. Ibid., p. 321; *Cleveland Plain Dealer,* May 6, 1901, p. 8.
121. Briggs, *The Manner of Man that Kills*, p. 317.
122. Ibid.
123. R. Drinnon, *Rebel in Paradise: A Biography of Emma Goldman* (Chicago: The University of Chicago Press, 1961), p. 68.
124. Briggs, *The Manner of Man that Kills*, pp. 274, 309.
125. Ibid., pp. 321–322.
126. Ibid., p. 278.
127. *Fowler Report*, p. 196.
128. Briggs, *The Manner of Man that Kills*, p. 277.
129. Ibid.
130. Drinnon, *Rebel in Paradise*, p. 69.
131. A. W. Johns, *The Man Who Shot McKinley* (South Brunswick and New York: A. S. Barnes, 1970), p. 60.

56   Defining Danger

132. *Trial Transcripts, pp.* 184–185.
133. Johns, *The Man Who Shot McKinley, p.* 91.
134. *Trial Transcripts, p.* 179.
135. Ibid., p. 191.
136. The insufficient lighting was ironic because the main features of the Exposition were extravagant electrical displays, announcing the technological advances of a new century. The central attraction, for example, was a 389-foot Electric Tower with a 2500 pound gilded "Goddess of Light" glowing from her perch at the top.
137. Ibid., pp. 175–176.
138. Ibid., pp. 175, 178. See, also, S. Adler, "The Operation on President McKinley," *Scientific American* 208 (March 1963): 118–130.
139. *Trial Transcripts, pp.* 184, 186.
140. MacDonald, "The Trial, Execution, Autopsy," p. 384.
141. *Fowler Report,* p. 196.
142. Ibid., p. 198.
143. MacDonald, "The Trial, Execution, Autopsy," p. 375.
144. Ibid., p. 386.
145. E. A. Spitzka, "The Post-Mortem Examination of Leon F. Czolgosz, the Assassin of President McKinley," *American Journal of Insanity* 58 (January 1902): 386-387.
146. *Trial Transcripts, pp.* 163–164.
147. Briggs, *The Manner of Man that Kills, p.* 327.
148. Ibid., pp. 322–323.
149. Goldman, *Living My Life, pp.* 306, 324–325; see also, her, "The Tragedy at Buffalo," *Mother Earth 1* (October 1906): 11–16.
150. Goldman, *Living My Life, pp.* 316–317.
151. Channing, "The Mental State," p. 271; Briggs, *The Manner of Man that Kills, pp.* 336–343.
152. Briggs, *The Manner of Man that Kills, pp.* 331, 337.
153. Channing, "The Mental State," p. 272. In his *Recollections,* Hamilton argues the same totally unsubstantiated position.
154. M. Leech, *In the Days of McKinley* (New York: Harper & Row, 1959), p. 594.
155. Briggs, *The Manner of Man that Kills, p.* 259.
156. Czolgosz's father had heard that one of Leon's maternal aunts in Europe was "crazy." Leon claimed no knowledge of this. If true this represents the only potentially significant evidence of the Czolgosz alleged mental illness. It was discounted by the doctors who later wrote about the case.
157. After the execution Waldek wore a button picture of his dead brother on his coat lapel. Frank Bandowski kept Leon's political library as a fond remembrance of his old friend.
158. Holt was the founder of the publishing house, Holt, Rinehart & Winston.
159. Ibid., p. 343.

3

Type I—Nationalism: Oscar Collazo, Griselio Torresola, and Sirhan Bishara Sirhan

> *"I intend to continue where I left off, to keep on fighting for Puerto Rico's independence until I die."*—Oscar Collazo *(after his release from prison, September 1979)*
>
> *"Kennedy got what was coming to him."*—Sirhan Sirhan *(March 1969)*

Like their nineteenth-century counterparts, Oscar Collazo, Griselio Torresola, and Sirhan Sirhan can only be understood within a political context. In the case of the two Puerto Rican would-be assassins of President Truman, Collazo and Torresola, there has been less disagreement about their motives than there has been with other subjects. This is largely due to the fact that the intensity of support aroused by Puerto Rican nationalism is so well know that it is difficult to dismiss the positions of an entire political movement as some form of mental illness.

Such is not the case for Arab terrorist Sirhan Sirhan, who for some time after his crime was viewed as yet another disturbed young man who killed Robert Kennedy for personal rather than political reasons. Some suggested he did it for fame and notoriety; others of the psychoanalytic persuasion were convinced that he was the victim of an unresolved oedipal conflict and, as a consequence, viewed Kennedy as a hated father surrogate. In this chapter, evidence is presented that clearly defines Sirhan's calculating political motives. Had such an event occurred in Europe, there would have been little question that it was a terrorist act. Since then as Americans have become sensitized to the bitter and seemingly intractable hostility that runs through politics and toward America in the Middle East, Sirhan's political motives are less subject to dispute.

In both the Truman and Kennedy attacks, the primary motives were nationalism. Each was an expression of resentment about the foreign policies of the United States. Consider first the case of the Puerto Ricans.

* * *

Oscar Collazo (1915-1998) and Griselio Torresola (1927-1950)

Near dawn on October 30, 1950, five days before Puerto Ricans were to vote on a new home-rule constitution, members of the Nationalist Party of Puerto Rico quietly took up positions around the Insular Police Headquarters at Bario Mucana, Penuelas, Puerto Rico. Twenty-six police officers were on duty. At 4:00 A.M., the Nationalists opened fire wounding six of them. Five hours later, at 9:00 A.M., a policeman was shot and killed in the town of Ponce on the southern coast of the island. Shortly after, at 10:30 A.M., Nationalist guerrillas attacked the police station in the northern coastal town of Arecibo. An hour later, Nationalists fought Insular Police and National Guard troops from houses they had barricaded in the town of Utuado in the island interior. At noon, they attacked the governor's mansion and the general post office in San Juan killing a policeman and losing four of their own members in the ensuing exchange of gunfire. Police counterattacked, and a sustained battle developed at the home and party headquarters of Pedro Albizu Campos, the Harvard-educated leader of the Nationalist movement. While the siege continued at Campos' home, Nationalists bombed the police station in the interior town of Jayuya later that night and shot down six policemen as they ran from the burning building. The guerrillas then set fire to most of the town before National Guardsmen arrived and drove them off.[1] The siege at Campos' headquarters would continue three more days.

The Backgrounds of Collazo and Torresola

The next day, American newspapers carried news of the insurrection. In the Spanish Harlem section of New York City, members of the Nationalist Party followed the papers and discussed developments. Two were particularly concerned, Oscar Collazo and Griselio Torresola, both committed Nationalists active in party affairs. Torresola had been born and raised in Jayuya, one of the towns under siege, and Collazo had spent a good part of his youth there. Although Collazo was nearly thirty-seven years of age — twelve years older than Torresola — they had known each other as youths in Jayuya and had both joined the Nationalist Party in the 1930s. Since then each had served in various leadership positions within the party. Griselio's brother, Elio, was also active in the Nationalist movement and was later arrested for his role in the October 30 insurrection.[2]

Both Torresola and Collazo knew Albizu Campos personally. Collazo first met the fiery Puerto Rican leader in 1932; their friendship and cooperative political activity never ceased after that. Virtually the entire Torresola family was involved in the Nationalist movement and was even closer to Campos and his family.[3] Torresola's sister Doris worked directly with Campos as his personal secretary and was severely wounded during the battle at the party headquarters.

Campos's rise to prominence in the Nationalist movement began at a mass rally in San Juan on April 16, 1925 when he tore an American flag from a speaker's stand and denounced U.S. colonialism. His activism continued until 1936 when he was arrested and convicted of conspiracy to overthrow United States rule in Puerto Rico. He was imprisoned for his earlier involvement in the bloody Rio Piedras riots on October 24, 1935 and his role in the assassination of a government police chief in 1936. When he was released from the federal penitentiary in Atlanta in 1943, he traveled to New York where he lived until 1947 in the same tenement building as Oscar Collazo. Part of this time he was hospitalized for a heart condition and a paralytic condition in one arm. A close friend and admirer, Collazo was a regular visitor during these periods.[4] In December 1947, Campos returned to Puerto Rico where he resumed his activities as leader of the movement. He played a key role in establishing an official party headquarters in San Juan.[5]

Unlike their well-educated leader, neither Collazo nor Torresola had much formal education; both came from impoverished backgrounds. Collazo left school after completing the eighth grade; Torresola left after two years of high school. But both were intelligent men who read widely and kept themselves informed. Collazo especially was a voracious reader of newspapers, history, and political biography. Each had married young, as was the custom, and had fathered a daughter before their first marriages ended in divorce.

Collazo left Puerto Rico for New York in 1937 to look for work. His father had been a small sugar-cane farmer who had been wiped out by failing health and, in Collazo's opinion, an American embargo on Puerto Rican sugar in the 1920s; he died shortly afterward.

Collazo remained in the United States, except for periodic stays in Puerto Rico. He worked in a variety of menial jobs in New York. He was always considered a competent, cooperative, and well-liked worker by his employers and fellow employees.[6]

Throughout these early years in the United States, his activities in the Nationalist party continued. He served as head of the Manhattan junta of the party from 1940 to 1943; from 1944 to 1946, he was editor of the party magazine, *Puerto Rico;* and in 1949, he was elected secretary of the Nationalist party board in New York City.[7]

In 1939, Collazo met Rosa Mercado at a political meeting. Rosa was a forty-year-old divorcee with two daughters. She was also a committed Puerto Rican Nationalist. As their friendship developed, Rosa managed to get Oscar a job as a polisher in the metal products company she worked for in Connecticut. A month later they were married on August 3, 1940. It was to be a close and good marriage. Oscar became a devoted father to his two stepdaughters who adored him; Rosa soon loved his daughter as her own. Not long after their marriage, they moved to a small apartment in the Puerto Rican section of New York. They were a close-knit family bound by their love and respect for each other and also their unwavering commitment to the Nationalist cause. By November 1950, the Collazos had been happily married for ten years.[8]

On August 21, 1948, Griselio Torresola first stepped onto American soil at the airport in Teterboro, New Jersey. He left behind him in Puerto Rico a wife he thought he had divorced[9] and an infant daughter. Unlike Collazo, Torresola did not actively seek employment. He signed up for government relief and immediately became involved in Nationalist party politics in New York. His party activities brought him into contact with a young strikingly attractive Puerto Rican woman, Carmen Dolores. Well-educated by the standards of the time for women, she had completed two years at the University of Puerto Rico before leaving for New York in November 1948. Carmen said she married Griselio in an unofficial ceremony shortly after they met. They moved into a couple of rooms at the Hotel Clendenning at 202 West 103rd Street. Her husband worked briefly at a store on Fifth Avenue called El Sigho but soon quit and applied again for relief in order to devote all of his time to politics. In May 1950, she bore his second daughter. Like Griselio, she was a committed Nationalist.[10]

The October Insurrection

On Wednesday, September 20, 1950, Torresola flew to Puerto Rico to meet with Albizu Campos in San Juan.[11] The next day he talked with Campos, leaving afterward with two notes of instructions signed by the party leader. The first is dated September 21, 1950 and reads as follows:

My dear Griselio:
  If by some circumstance it may become necessary that you assume leadership of the Movement in the United States, you will do it without any kind of qualms. We leave everything concerning this affair to your high patriotism and sound discretion.

> I embrace you
> [signed] Albizu Campos[12]

The second note read:

> Griselio will draw the funds which he deems necessary to attend to the supreme necessities of the cause. He will be responsible directly to the Treasurer General. The Delegate will lend him all the cooperation necessary that his mission may be a triumph.
>
> [signed] Albizu Campos[13]

Torresola returned to New York on Friday, September 22, on an American World Airways flight.[14] For the next month or so, his activities continued much as they had before his visit with Campos. Almost all of his and his wife's social life was associated with political activities of the Nationalist party. He remained unemployed, managing to support his wife and baby on the $129-a-month relief check he received.

Toward the end of October, the pattern of activity changed. Increasing numbers of visitors began to come to the Torresola's Hotel Clendenning rooms. Arriving in twos and threes, both men and women would enter, stay for a short time, and leave. All were associated with the Nationalist party.[15] One can assume that the primary subject of these meetings was the information Torresola had received from Campos. There is little question that he confided to his fellow Nationalists that a revolt was planned prior to the home-rule referendum in Puerto Rico set for November 4. To the Nationalists, the advantages of "home rule" were illusory; the referendum was simply another attempt to siphon off growing Puerto Rican discontent with the colonial domination exercised by the United States.

October 29-31

Although Torresola and Collazo had known each other from their early days in Jayuya, they were not close personal friends; they saw each other only at political meetings. Thus it was somewhat surprising when Torresola knocked on the door of the Collazo's Bronx apartment at 173 Brook Avenue at about 9:00 P.M. on October 29. Earlier that evening, he had met with a small group of party activists at his hotel room.[16]

Torresola had a copy of the Puerto Rican newspaper *El Diario de Nueva York* in his hand and said he wanted to talk with Collazo alone about the political situation in Puerto Rico. Keep in mind that this was hours before the first shots were fired in Penuelas. The two left together and walked four blocks to the Willis Avenue Bridge where they stopped and talked for "almost two hours." It is not certain whether Collazo knew about the planned revolt, but it is probable that he did, given his involvement in the higher levels of party leadership. He may not have known, however, that the insurrection was planned for the next day. In any event, Torresola proposed that they both go to Puerto Rico to aid in the revolution. After more discussion about the historical context of the situation — for example, Collazo reminded Torresola of past failures at places like Ponce and Rio Piedras where government police had killed a number of Nationalist demonstrators — Collazo agreed to go with him. Then, almost as an afterthought, he told Torresola that he had no weapon. Torresola replied that if Collazo could give him some money, he could quickly pick up a gun. Collazo gave him fifty dollars and they parted close to midnight, agreeing that they would fly to Puerto Rico to join the fight as quickly as they could make arrangements.[17]

The next day, October 30, news of the insurrection was broadcast on radio reports and splashed across the front pages of the afternoon newspapers in New York. That evening, some twenty to twenty-five persons filed in and out of the Torresola's hotel rooms. According to one of those present, all the visitors had family members involved in the revolution and had come for any additional information that Torresola might have on their welfare and other developments.[18]

Earlier that evening, Torresola had walked a few doors down West 103rd Street to the apartment of Manuel Lopez. Lopez later reported that Torresola was very excited about news of the revolt and asked him to return to Puerto Rico with him to join in the fight. Lopez declined, saying he could not leave his pregnant wife, but he did accompany Torresola back to his apartment. At the apartment, the phone rang continuously as a steady stream of Puerto Rican males arrived.[19] Presumably, Torresola made similar proposals to each. Then shortly before 9:00 P.M. he left the hotel and walked to meet Collazo, as planned, at the Willis Street Bridge.

Torresola's optimism about the revolt was diminished somewhat when he met with Collazo. Collazo had worked as usual that day but had listened to radio reports on the revolt and read the newspapers when he returned home that evening. He was upset because the news reports made it appear that the conflict was between the Puerto Rican government and the Nationalist party only — omitting the important fact that American domination was the fundamental issue in the hostilities. He went on to explain to the less sophisticated Torresola how crucial this omission was to the success of the Nationalist cause. Most Americans, he explained, did not know where Puerto Rico was located, let alone understand anything about the political history of the island. Until the American public understood, he continued, how Puerto Rico was seized as a result of the Spanish-American War and forced to submit to the colonial domination and economic exploitation of the United States government, there would be no sympathy and support in America for the Nationalist cause.

With that in mind, Collazo suggested that they could accomplish more by going to Washington rather than San Juan. As he explained later:

> I told him that a better idea would be to come to Washington; as long as the American people didn't know what Puerto Rico was, or where Puerto Rico was, or which was the real Government of Puerto Rico, they would never care what was happening in Puerto Rico; that by coming to Washington and making some kind of demonstration in the capital of this nation, we would be in a better situation to make the American people understand the real situation in Puerto Rico; that Puerto Rico has no government; there is no Government of Puerto Rico.[20]

After more discussion, Torresola, who had been anxious to return to Puerto Rico, reluctantly agreed that Washington would better serve their purposes. They decided that the best way to get the publicity they needed was to attack the president just as their compatriots had attacked the governor's mansion that day in San Juan. But since neither one had ever been to Washington, they were unable to plan their venture beyond agreeing to buy new clothes for the occasion the next morning and to take an afternoon train to the capital.[21]

Sometime during the day, Torresola had purchased a Walther P-38 pistol for thirty-five dollars. After their discussion, and, again, almost as an afterthought, he gave Collazo the gun and fifteen dollars change. Collazo was unfamiliar with guns, but Torresola assured him that he would show him how to use it later.[22]

Both men had told their wives the previous day that they were considering leaving for Puerto Rico to fight if the revolt continued. That night when they returned to their respective apartments they lied to their anxious wives, saying that they would be leaving the next day for Puerto Rico. Both wives later substantiated Collazo's claim that he and Torresola did not reveal their change of plans. Neither was aware that their husbands were going to Washington instead of San Juan. It would have been too upsetting, Collazo explained later, since both he and his companion recognized their chances for survival would be slim.[23]

The next morning, Rosa Collazo called her husband's employer, the Gainer Corporation in New Rochelle, and told them that Oscar was ill and would not be coming to work that day. Collazo then asked her to go to the post office and withdraw one hundred dollars from their postal savings account. When she returned, Collazo took the money and left at about 9:00 A.M. He returned a few hours later with a new pinstripe suit, shirt, underwear, and a small valise he had bought for the trip. He didn't reveal that he had also purchased two one-way train tickets at the Pennsylvania Station. Still thinking he was bound for San Juan, his wife cried and pleaded with him not to go as he packed his things. At 2:00 P.M. the Collazos left the apartment together and walked to 138th Street near Brook Avenue and Bronx Place where he hailed a cab. He kissed his wife saying, "Good bye, pray for me."[24]

Torresola had much the same kind of morning. He arose early and went to sign for a relief check he was to receive on November 6. He returned at about 10:30 A.M., also with a new pinstripe suit. He and his wife then left with the baby and walked to various stores buying a blue valise, two white shirts, and a light gray necktie. They returned home about noon. Carmen carefully pressed the new suit, packed his suitcase, and prepared lunch for her husband.

Meanwhile he dressed and then stood at a bureau writing. He told Carmen to mail one of the notes to his daughter by his first marriage in Puerto Rico. The second note was for their infant daughter, Rebecca. Both notes were dated October 31, 1950 and said "Remembrances of your Daddy [signed] Griselio." After eating, he left some money with Carmen, kissed her and his daughter good-bye, and left.[25]

The two short, slightly built men met at Pennsylvania Station and caught the 3:30 P.M. train for Washington. On the trip, they read accounts of the fighting in Puerto Rico in the *New York Times* and also in the Philadelphia papers they purchased when the train stopped there.[26] They arrived at Union Station at about 7:30 P.M. and walked along Massachusetts Avenue looking for a place to stay. It didn't take long, choosing the Harris Hotel at 17 Massachusetts Avenue, N.W., the first one they saw. They entered separately, each using an alias to register. Collazo signed in as Anthony de Silva of 150 Aldridge Drive, Aldridge Village, Connecticut, and Torresola used the name Charles Gonzalez of 167 Ponce de Leon Avenue, Miami, Florida.[27]

By chance, they were given adjoining rooms. Both men were unfamiliar with Washington, but were aware that the president was living temporarily at the Blair House while the White House was undergoing repairs. They had no idea where that was, so they decided to take a cab tour of the area to find out. On that tour the cab driver, at their request, pointed out the Blair House.[28] They then returned to their hotel and went to bed.

The Attack

The next morning, the two had breakfast together and decided over coffee that they had best take another look at the Blair House in the daylight. They hailed another taxi and were driven down Pennsylvania Avenue to Lafayette Square across from the White House, just a short stroll from the Blair House. The next hour was spent walking around as inconspicuously as possible, making mental notes of the security guards and the location of the two sentry boxes that stood at either end of the large Georgian-style mansion. The small leafless trees along the sidewalk permitted an unobstructed view of the four story building and the canopied front entrance. The house was separated from the sidewalk by only a small hedge and a thin patch of grass.

Although neither of the two knew it, the president's unprotected bedroom window was located directly above the main entrance, a very short distance from the sidewalk where hundreds of sightseers like themselves strolled in the November sunshine. An American president had not been attacked since 1933 when Giuseppe Zangara tried unsuccessfully to kill President Truman's predecessor, Franklin D. Roosevelt, and security was remarkably lax by present standards. It would have been very easy for anyone on the sidewalk to hurl a grenade or bomb through the window into the bedroom where the president, like most people, spent some seven to nine hours a day.

But Collazo and Torresola had not had the time to plan that carefully. In fact neither was even sure the president was at the Blair House that day.[29] But it didn't matter. Their primary purpose was to awaken the American public to conditions in Puerto Rico. They believed the only way that could be accomplished was to sacrifice *themselves* in some dramatic fashion. Americans did not care about Puerto Ricans, Collazo said later, but maybe they would change if they realized Puerto Ricans were willing to die for their cause. Neither one disliked Mr. Truman personally. As Collazo explained later: "I never had any feeling of hatred or dislike for Mr. Truman or any other American or anybody else for that matter · · · [30]

> Our intentions were to make a demonstration on the steps of the Blair House. In the Blair House was the residence of the President of the United States and we wanted the American people and the people of the world to know that Puerto Rico was a possession of the United States and at that time, particularly, the Puerto Rican people were being murdered by the American authorities in Puerto Rico, we wanted them to realize that . . . we figured out that a demonstration would never be serious enough . . . to attract the attention of the American people if we were not hurt or wounded or killed in some way . . . especially if two Puerto Ricans were killed in front of his [the president's] residence.[31]

After their reconnaissance, they had lunch and returned to the hotel. As yet Collazo did not know how to use his semi-automatic pistol. For the next two hours Torresola first oiled their weapons and then showed Collazo how to load and fire his. They also planned their attack.[32] With these preliminaries out of the way, they called another cab and rode downtown, getting out on Pennsylvania Avenue near Lafayette Square, as they had the night before, a short block from the Blair House. After a quick conversation, they took one more casual walk past their target and returned to the corner of 15th Street and Pennsylvania Avenue. Pausing there, they decided to approach the Blair House entrance from opposite directions in order to appear less suspicious. Torresola crossed Pennsylvania Avenue and walked down the sidewalk across from and past the Blair House where he re-crossed the street and began his approach from the west. Meanwhile, Collazo walked slowly east along Lafayette, timing his pace to give his partner time to make his return.[33]

It was approximately 2:15 P.M. and unbeknownst to the two would-be assassins, President Truman had just stretched out for his customary afternoon nap in the front bedroom. Oddly enough, as Collazo approached the east sentry box, he was not wearing the glasses his weak eyesight required. They were in his pocket.[34] As he closed to within a few yards of security guard Donald T. Birdzell, Collazo drew his pistol from the waistband of his trousers, aimed, and pulled the trigger but he had failed to release the safety. In a frantic movement, he fumbled with the weapon, attempting to release the safety lever. Suddenly the safety snapped off and the pistol discharged accidentally striking the startled Birdzell in the knee and knocking him to the pavement. As the wounded security guard began to crawl away from his attacker out into the street, Collazo fired off the remaining eight shots in the clip at the other security guards now converging on him. But he hit no one else as he moved toward the front steps of Blair House in a hail of bullets now aimed at him. Missing death by fractions of inches from bullets that cut his nostril, right ear and tore a hole in his hat, he paused on the steps to reload.

Meanwhile Torresola opened fire with deadly accuracy, fatally wounding guard Leslie Coffelt with three shots, then whirling around, he hit another guard, Joseph H. Downs, with three more shots. As he paused to reload near a hedge separating him from the building, the dying Coffelt was able to fire a last shot that struck Torresola in the right ear. He died instantly, falling, hands clasped together, head bowed, knees drawn up in the fetal position, next to the hedge.

Moments later, Secret Service Agent Vincent P. Mroz stopped Collazo on the entrance steps with a single shot to the chest. Collazo fell unconscious face-down with his hat still on, blood trickling down the side of his face from his bullet-nicked ear.

Three days later, on November 4, the siege ended in San Juan with the surrender of Albizu Campos. Some twenty-eight persons had been killed, a score wounded, and hundreds arrested.[35] But the movement would continue.

The Trial

Collazo's chest wound proved to be not as serious as it first appeared, and his life was saved. He was charged with four counts of homicide (in the death of Officer Coffelt) and assault. His trial ended on March 7, 1951 convicted on all counts. He was sentenced to die.

During the trial, an unidentified attorney had contacted Collazo's court-appointed counsel and offered him five hundred dollars to permit him to take over the assassin's defense. His intention was to enter a plea of temporary insanity — a strategy Collazo had earlier rejected.[36] When Collazo learned of this, he was furious. Convinced that the attorney was an agent of the loyalist Puerto Rican government, Collazo repeated his position to the court that he "would not accept any insanity plea, either temporary or any kind of insanity plea."[37] The purpose of such a plea, he said, was not to save his life but only to "discredit my cause."[38] Collazo said he would rather die. His position was vindicated when a court-appointed psychiatrist found no evidence of mental disorder.

But Collazo's life once again was spared, this time by his intended victim. On July 24, 1951 President Truman commuted Collazo's death sentence to life imprisonment. The president granted the clemency this Type I assassin refused to request for the same reasons he had rejected the insanity plea at his trial.

The Aftermath

Throughout his trial and his long subsequent confinement, Collazo never recanted from the principles that brought him to the steps of the Blair House on that warm November afternoon in 1950. Just three years after Collazo was found guilty of attempting to assassinate the president, four Puerto Rican Nationalists, and former associates, attacked the U.S. House of Representatives. On March 1, 1954, Lolita Lebron, Rafael Cancel-Miranda, Irving Flores-Rodriguez, and Andres Figuero-Cordero opened fire from House Gallery 11, shouting Nationalist slogans and wounding five congressmen before they were overpowered. Each was tried and, like Collazo, remained adamant in maintaining the principle of Puerto Rican independence as their only defense. And, accordingly, each was convicted and sentenced to long prison terms. Like Collazo, the four refused during the long years of imprisonment to petition for clemency, maintaining throughout that they were political prisoners.[39]

The Release

Twenty-five years later, on September 10, 1979, in a surprise move, President Carter commuted their sentences to the time already served. Carter commuted the sentence, as well, in the twenty-ninth year of his confinement, of the balding, white-haired, would-be assassin, Oscar Collazo. A jubilant but remorseless Collazo was joined by Cancel-Miranda, Flores-Rodriguez, and Lolita Lebronc as all were hailed after their release as heroes at a packed rally at Roberto Clemente High School in Chicago.[40] Cancel-Miranda defiantly tore up his clemency papers before the crowd; Mrs. Lebron shouted into the microphone that their release "was done for political expediency and not because of a concern for human rights." A happy but more subdued Oscar Collazo, now sixty-four, told the cheering throng of Hispanics: "The fight for freedom is always a long fight and always a hard fight. I have nothing to be disappointed about."[41]

Later in New York City, where they were scheduled to appear (strangely enough, given the nature of their crimes) before the United Nations on September 11, they told another throng of cheering Puerto Ricans that they would fight to their "last breath" for "the liberation and freedom of Puerto Rico."[42]

Then before boarding a plane for their return to Puerto Rico, Oscar Collazo, small and frail, wearing glasses like the ones he had forgotten many years before, said this to the New York crowd:

> Repression brought about the violence. Not the aggressiveness of the Nationalist Parry but the aggressiveness of the United States Government." And he concluded: "I intend to continue where I left off, to keep on fighting for Puerto Rico's independence until I die.[43]

An estimated crowd of five thousand people greeted the triumphant foursome when they landed in San Juan on September 12. Refusing to renounce violence, the four vowed the movement would continue until independence was won.[44]

A few months later, on December 3, 1979, Puerto Rican Nationalists ambushed a U.S. Navy bus outside of San Juan, killing two sailors and wounding ten others—two critically with automatic weapons fire. It was the first attack on American military personnel in Puerto Rico in nearly ten years.[45]

Conclusions

During his trial, the prosecuting attorney asked Collazo, "What, if anything, had Birdzell [the security guard], done to you, sir, to warrant your shooting at him?"

Collazo replied, "Just the same thing, what did the Puerto Ricans ever do to the Americans either, but they were shot at by the Americans and killed."

The attorney countered, "You had never seen him before?"

Collazo responded, "No, sir, and the Puerto Ricans had never seen the Americans either, but they were shot at by the Americans and killed."[46]

Oscar Collazo never expressed any doubts or remorse about what he attempted to do on November 1, 1950. As his answers illustrate, it all made sense, given his values and priorities. He believed completely in the morality of his cause and was willing to die or spend the rest of his life in prison for it. And his values and priorities were shared not only by his slain associate Griselio Torresola but by those who fought for Albizu Campos in Puerto Rico during the insurrection, the four who attacked Congress three years later, and the guerrillas who ambushed the naval personnel in San Juan in December 1979.

As Type I subjects, Collazo and Torresola were political zealots set apart from the Types II, III, and IV assassins by their very clearly defined political motives. They were hardly the "couple of lame-brained New York Puerto Ricans" they had been labeled the day after the attack.[47] There was no evidence of emotional or cognitive distortion in either. Neither suffered from delusions or hallucinations, or imagined themselves divinely inspired. And both enjoyed normal social relations and strong family loyalties and confidence. Nor was there suggestion of compensatory personal motives in their act. Collazo, for example, shunned personal publicity, rejected an insanity plea, refused to request clemency, and remained true to his principles during his long silent years of imprisonment. He spent his remaining years in his beloved Puerto Rican where he died in 1998.

Both Collazo nor Torresola recognized the limits of their action. Each realized that the most they could accomplish was the creation of greater awareness among Americans about the conditions they opposed in Puerto Rico. There was no thought that independence would be won as a result of their act. Collazo always recognized, as he said after his release, that "the fight for freedom is always a long fight." He was well aware that the Blair House attack was only one symbolic step toward their objective. Feeling no specific hostility toward Mr. Truman, their act was simply a powerful statement against what they considered oppression by a colonial government. As Collazo later explained, the success of their act did not hinge at all on the president's death but rather their own. The cause was paramount, the ideological theme unmistakable.

Sirhan Bishara Sirhan (1944–)

Of all the assassins considered in this study, Sirhan Sirhan stands out as possibly the shrewdest, most devious, and remorseless of the lot. Unlike Oscar Collazo and Griselio Torresola, Sirhan hated his victim. Probably no other assassin, with the possible exceptions of John Wilkes Booth and Carl Weiss, hated the person they killed more. But he is hardly the mentally unbalanced paranoid schizophrenic that his defense attorneys and some psychiatrists claimed. The Sirhan trial provides an example of attempts to implement the so-called "diminished capacity" standard described in chapter 1. Stripped of complex and sometimes confusing legal and clinical terms, the standard in its various manifestations in state law essentially poses two questions: Did the defendant have a mental disease or defect at the time the crime was committed? And, was that disease or defect the reason for the crime? The standard reflects a significant departure from the earlier M'Naghten Rule whose equivalent questions are: Did the defendant understand what he was doing when he committed the crime? Did he understand that it was wrong? One of the central figures in the evolution of this doctrine in the 1960s was Dr. Bernard L. Diamond, an attorney and psychiatrist at the University of California, Berkeley, who participated in Sirhan's defense.

Another participant in Sirhan's defense was the well-known New York attorney Emile Zola Berman. Berman volunteered his services free of charge, eliciting praise from many who viewed the Jewish attorney's willingness to defend a Palestinian Arab — whose hatred of Jews was, by his own admission, the reason he shot his victim — an extraordinary act of humanitarianism. But Berman's willingness to assist in the trial may not have been merely an act of good will because it hinged upon offering the insanity defense. Berman strongly opposed any attempt to address or air Sirhan's political motives in the trial. It was imperative in his view to deny a rational political motive, to portray Sirhan as "mentally ill," and to keep the Arab-Israeli issue out of the trial.[48] Despite Sirhan's strong objections, this was the strategy selected after the judge rejected an initial attempt to plea-bargain a second degree murder conviction with a life sentence.

In addition to the trial testimony and documents, the most interesting and useful source of information on the Sirhan case is Robert Blair Kaiser's book *"R.F.K. Must Die!" A History of the Robert Kennedy Assassination and Its Aftermath*.[49] Kaiser worked as an assistant to Sirhan's legal defense and, for that reason, had access to information on many facets of the case unknown to outsiders. Especially important are Sirhan's off-the-record statements about the assassination and the trial, as well as conversations among his attorneys and psychiatrists. While some of my interpretations and basic conclusions do not always agree with Kaiser's, his excellent book remains an informative and truly unique contribution to the literature on assassins.

The Event

Shortly after midnight on June 5, 1968, a weary but happy Robert Kennedy stepped to the podium in the Embassy Ballroom of the Ambassador Hotel in Los Angeles to acknowledge his victory in the California presidential primary election. Moments later, his speech finished, he made his way through a dimly lit food service corridor in order to avoid an onslaught of cheering well-wishers. Anticipating this move, Sirhan Bisbara Sirhan had positioned himself behind a food tray rack in the corridor. As the Senator approached, Sirhan stepped from behind the rack snarling, "Kennedy you son of a bitch,"[50] as he raised his .22 caliber Iver Johnson revolver to within an inch of the forty two-year-old New York senator's head and fired. The fatal first hollow-point bullet exploded through the right mastoid bone, disintegrating into the right hemisphere of Kennedy's brain. Two more shots struck the Senator's right armpit as he fell to the floor.[51] His relentless attacker continued to fire five more shots that struck and wounded five other persons as he was being wrestled onto a steam table where he was held until police arrived. Moments later, police officers Travis White and Art Placentia pushed the handcuffed assassin into their patrol car as a hysterical mob clamored for vengeance. Jesse Unruh, leader of Kennedy's California campaign, accompanied the two officers, concerned that nothing happen to prevent the senator's attacker from standing trial, as had been the case nearly five years before when President Kennedy was slain in Dallas.

Once in the car Unruh asked Sirhan why he had done it. Sirhan's reply, "I did it for my country,"[52] was the same comment he had made earlier at the scene of the crime according to an eye witness, Dr. Marcus McBroom. Both the Unruh and McBroom accounts of Sirhan's statement were reported by United Press and the Associated Press but denied by the *New York Times*. Later both police officers denied hearing Sirhan make the statement, and Unruh claimed he could not remember. In his book *Why Robert Kennedy Was Killed,* Godfrey Jansen cites this as evidence that a systematic attempt was made to deny Sirhan's political motive from the beginning.[53]

Whether or not Sirhan made the statements on June 5, the record shows that he offered the same explanation repeatedly during the months before and during his trial. Moreover, the same explanation is implicit in the notebooks Sirhan kept prior to the assassination. The record also reveals that an attempt was made to present Sirhan's pre-assassination political writings as evidence of his alleged paranoia rather than as they were — rational expressions of political anxiety and a consuming hatred based on Senator Kennedy's pro-Israeli stance. To understand the source and intensity of Sirhan's political views, it is necessary to review his experiences as a Palestinian child living in Jerusalem during the period of brutal conflict in early 1948.

Childhood and Identity

Sirhan Bishara Sirhan was born on March 19, 1944 in Jerusalem. His father had a comfortable job with the city water department, and the family — six brothers and a sister — lived in an attractive stone house in the

Musrara section of the city. In December 1947, the undeclared prelude to the first Arab-Israeli war broke out. Although armed conflict had been common in the region since 1920, when Great Britain had assumed the League of Nations mandate for Palestine, it intensified in the period 1945 to 1948 as Zionist guerrilla forces fought both British and Palestinian Arab troops to establish a new state of Israel in what was, at that time, Palestinian territory. In 1947, Zionist pressures continued to build with the realization that their objective was within reach: Palestine would soon cease to exist, being transformed into a new sovereign, independent nation, the homeland for tens of thousands of Jewish refugees from postwar Europe. By December of that year, the conflict intensified as snipers monitored and controlled movement on the streets and terrorist bombs made any public assembly exceedingly dangerous. Shouts and machine gun fire regularly shattered the barbed-wire tension of Jerusalem nights. The air reeked of fire, smoke, and death as the battle for a homeland locked the inhabitants of that ancient city in the cold terror and brutality of a religious war.

Sirhan Sirhan had just turned four in the midst of this period, but the terror he witnessed with childish bewilderment remained with him, as such traumas invariably do, etched in his memory like painful scars that never quite heal and are easily reopened. Much violence occurred in the contested section of the city where the Sirhans lived among both Jews and Arabs. In late December or early January 1948, the perplexed child witnessed a bomb explosion at the Damascus gate that left the street strewn with the bloody, mutilated bodies of Arab victims. Later, as he played with one of his older brothers, gunfire rattled when a Zionist truck rumbled down the street. The driver swerved to avoid the sniper's bullets, running over and killing the older child as Sirhan screamed in horror and disbelief. It would be months before he could accept the finality of his brother's death. The horror was unrelenting. On another occasion, he was the first to discover the corpse of an Arab neighbor lying in a pool of blood along the same street. Later he and his family observed portions of a British soldier's body that dangled from a church tower after being blown to pieces by a terrorist bomb; a finger was found in the Sirhan's yard. On yet another occasion, he was among those who fled in panic as a driverless, bomb-laden truck rolled silently down a street to explode on impact; the deafening blast destroyed three buildings.[54]

Such experiences were not uncommon in Jerusalem, as the Zionist Stern Gang and the Irgun terrorists systematically attacked Arab resistance forces with the efficiency and heartless resolve of persons who had survived the holocaust and now vowed never again to seek quarter or grant it to their enemies. It was a war of survival as a people.[55]

In this context, the words Deir Yassin have the same significance for Palestinian Arabs as does Buchenwald for Jews, Sand Creek and Wounded

Knee for American Indians, and My Lai for the Vietnamese. Deir Yassin is the name of a small Arab village where some 250 old men, women, and children were massacred by Zionist attackers on April 10, 1948. For Arabs, Deir Yassin remains a symbol of Zionist brutality as immoral and evil as the atrocities the Zionists themselves had fled in Europe.[56] It is not surprising that Sirhan Sirhan's political hostility is so easily traced to this formative period of his life.

Shortly after the Deir Yassin massacre and the declaration of Israel's independence on May 14, 1948, the Sirhan family was forced to flee their home in the middle of the night, leaving all their possessions behind. This marked the beginning of a nine-year period during which Sirhan and his family lived as poverty-stricken refugees on the fringes of a hostile Israeli society, on land that was no longer theirs.

An uneasy armed truce was declared between Israel and the Arab states in 1949. Hostile feelings between Jews and Arabs continued to grow, however, and the truce was frequently broken by raids and reprisals. Some forty thousand displaced Palestinian refugees lived in camps along Israel's contested borders, contributing to the tensions. During this period, the Sirhan family lived in a fifteen-by-thirty-foot dome-ceilinged room, without furniture, lighted by a single kerosene lamp in the Old Walled City section of Jerusalem. The building also housed two other Arab families who had been forced to abandon their homes in the conquered part of the city the Zionists now controlled. An Arab friend who lived in the same building confirmed the ugly circumstances of their lives.[57]

Sirhan's mother, Mary, found solace from the family's hardships in religion.[58] An intensely religious Christian convert, she raised her children in the Lutheran faith. Fearing for her children's safety following the death of her oldest son, she kept them indoors much of the time, refusing to permit them to play in the street with other children. The unrelieved stresses of a large family living in such small quarters and Mary Sirhan's preoccupation with her children's safety began to take a toll on the marriage. The constant stress, combined with the generalized frustration and outrage over their situation, soon were reflected in Sirhan's father's hostility toward his wife and children.[59] Bishara Sirhan's fits of temper and harsh beatings led to the estrangement of his two oldest sons, Sharif and Saidallah, and a cowering obsequiousness in the younger children. Mary Sirhan increasingly withdrew into her messianic Christian beliefs, obsessed with the safety of her children. Under normal circumstances she might have been considered overprotective — but not in Jerusalem during those dangerous years.

From 1951 to 1956, Sirhan attended kindergarten through the fifth grade in a Lutheran school, compiling an overall "C" average in the fifth grade in spite of a demanding curriculum that included English as well as Arabic, geometry, arithmetic, science, geography, history, and religion. His best subject was religion, his worst, arithmetic.[60] Sirhan got along well in school. According to his teachers and classmates, he was mature beyond his years — possibly a reflection of the various crises he had survived — possessed a quiet engaging sense of humor for his age, and was well-liked.[61]

On October 29, 1956, Israeli troops launched a successful attack, advancing into the Egyptian Sinai Peninsula; the armed conflict that had been smoldering beneath the surface since the 1949 cease-fire quickly followed. Although another cease-fire was declared on November 6 and Israel eventually relinquished its captured territory, including the Gaza Strip, to a United Nations emergency force, it was clear that any hope the Palestinian refugees might have had of regaining their homeland was now fading.

For that reason, Mary and Bisbara Sirhan sought financial assistance to emigrate to the United States. With the aid of Lutheran missionaries and the United Nations Relief and Works Agency, the family, without the two eldest sons, left Jerusalem on December 14, 1956. Sirhan was twelve years old.[62]

After arriving in New York, the Sirhans traveled to Pasadena, California, where the missionaries had suggested they relocate. They moved into a modest three-bedroom frame house on Howard Street, a shaded, respectable, lower middle-class neighborhood. The stresses within the family did not ease, however, and before the year ended, Bisbara left his family and returned to Jordan. In one sense, his departure was a relief. According to those who knew him, he was a mean, self-centered man who treated his family badly. But his absence also added a sense of abandonment to the feelings of isolation the family already was experiencing in a totally new and alien environment.

Senator Kennedy's Political Career

In May 1948, Robert Kennedy completed his studies at Harvard and flew to Israel to cover the establishment of the new state of Israel as a reporter for the *Boston Globe*. While there, an associate filmed him thoughtfully surveying the war-ravaged scene. Twenty years later clips from that film would be shown in a television campaign documentary shortly before the June 4 California primary. The film, which Sirhan viewed in Los Angeles, would have a decidedly unsettling effect on him.[63]

After his trip to Israel, Robert Kennedy returned home and enrolled in law school at the University of Virginia. In 1951, the year Sirhan began kindergarten in Jerusalem, he graduated and immediately went to work managing his older brother John's successful Massachusetts campaign for the U.S. Senate in 1952. A year later, he became counsel, along with Roy Cohn, to the Senate Permanent Investigations Subcommittee chaired by Wisconsin Senator Joseph R. McCarthy, a close friend of his father.

In 1950 McCarthy had launched the most callous and virulent anti-communist crusade in American history.[64] Through the use of unsubstantiated public statements, indiscriminate accusations, and publicized hearings, McCarthy used his committee to destroy the careers of numerous persons in public and private life, for no other reason than to advance his own. McCarthy pursued this vicious course, which many considered an outrage to public decency, before he was formally "condemned" by the Senate for his activities in December 1954. Nevertheless, Robert Kennedy remained loyal and continued to serve on the subcommittee until 1956. His affiliation with McCarthy together with his older brother's seeming senatorial indifference[65] to McCarthy's excesses were to become an issue of some concern to liberals whose support the Kennedy family would seek for John Kennedy's presidential bids in 1956 and 1960 respectively.

As the Kennedy brothers moved onto the national political scene, older liberals would also recall Joseph P. Kennedy's non-interventionist position toward Germany when he was ambassador to Great Britain from 1937 until his resignation in November 1940. Kennedy had consistently supported the Chamberlain government's overtures to Adolph Hitler.

Memories of these controversial pages in the Kennedy family's political history would remain fresh even as late as 1964 when, in the melancholy last light of Camelot, Robert Kennedy mounted his senatorial campaign in New York. Liberals in that state — many of them Jewish, with family and friends who had been victims of Hitler and/or McCarthy — would feel uneasy about the rash, but now seemingly mellowed, younger brother's bid for the U.S. Senate. On the positive side was his sometimes sympathetic support for minorities as attorney general in his brother's administration. But offsetting that was his relentless investigation and prosecution of Teamster president James Hoffa, which was, for some civil libertarians, a chilling reminder of the "McCarthyism" of the previous decade.

Others also criticized Kennedy's abrupt move from Massachusetts to New York, for no other reason than to establish residency for his Senate campaign, as yet another Machiavellian move made possible only by the wealth and power of the Kennedy family. And to challenge whom but Kenneth Keating — a liberal and also a strong and consistent supporter of Israel in the U.S. Senate. Then in 1968, Kennedy's decision to challenge President Johnson's renomination was made only after anti-war candidate Eugene McCarthy had demonstrated the strength of anti-war sentiment by running a very strong campaign against Johnson in the New Hampshire primary. Gene McCarthy's supporters were dismayed and angered when Kennedy announced his candidacy on March 16, 1968. And it was difficult, even for Kennedy supporters, to deny the opportunistic nature of his announcement. Thus in spite of his recent strong support for social reform and civil rights and his eventual opposition to the Vietnam War, Robert Kennedy still would find it necessary to deny that he was as "ruthless" as his political past seemed to indicate.

In addition to his liberal positions on minorities and his opposition to the war, another issue Kennedy had used to win the confidence and support of the wealthy and influential New York Jewish community was his strong advocacy of Israeli interests in the Middle East. In part, the senator's strong unequivocal support for Israel can be understood as compensatory politics. The checkered Kennedy political history required such a commitment to allay a generation of fears and resentments among many American Jews. Jewish support was absolutely essential in New York and also vital to his presidential campaign in 1968.

Sirhan in America

Adjustments to life in America were difficult for the Sirhan family. Many of their problems were a result of cultural and language barriers. One brother, for example, had difficulty finding employment because he could not speak English. Another was arrested for threatening the life of an American girl whose friendship he had misunderstood. A sister, who had secretly married an American, died of leukemia in 1964. Another brother was arrested for drug dealing. Only Sirhan and his brother Adel seemed to avoid any major difficulties during this period, although they, too, found life in America considerably more difficult than they had been led to believe.

A major element in their difficult adjustment was the fact that they had come to the United States reluctantly, and only as a last resort. Their true home was Palestine, and they had been forced to leave. Thus they were more resistant to American acculturation than they might have been otherwise, and continued to speak Arabic, listen to Arabic music, read Arabic newspapers, and observe Arabic customs, all in the hope that someday they could return to their homeland.[66]

Given the fact that Sirhan arrived in the United States at the brink of that most difficult time of life — adolescence — his adjustment during this stressful period is remarkable. While maintaining a strong Arab identity in music, language, and politics — for example, he would listen to the poetic Arabic music of vocalist Umm Kulthum for hours — he also seemed to adjust easier and better than his brothers to American life. He learned English quickly and successfully completed the elementary grades at Pasadena's Longfellow Elementary School before entering John Muir High School. There he accumulated a record of mostly above average grades and graduated 558th in a competitive class of 829 students on June 13, 1963.[67] It was a respectable record, especially given his unusual background and the difficulties he had to overcome.

While at Muir he got along well, as he always had, with his teachers and classmates. Never a social recluse, he joined the officer cadet corps and was elected to the student council both his junior and senior years.[68] Fellow members of the council recalled him as a cooperative and enthusiastic person.[69]

After graduating from high school, Sirhan entered Pasadena City College for the fall 1963 semester. There was, however, a notable change in his scholastic performance. In four semesters, he accumulated grades of mostly D's and F's, primarily because he did not attend classes. As a consequence, he was dismissed in May 1964.[70] His dearly beloved sister's sudden illness and death during this period account for his distracted behavior. He had been very close to her, much closer than he had been to any of his brothers.[71]

After losing his sister and dropping out of college, Sirhan was at loose ends. He worked as a gas station attendant and then as a landscaper for the next year. Both his employers spoke well of him. He liked horses and decided to become a jockey. It was a possibility, given his small size and light weight — five-feet-five-inches and about 120 pounds. An apprenticeship was required. Late in 1965, he got a job as a stable boy and "hot-walker" at the race track in Santa Anita. He gradually worked his way up to a job as an exercise boy. This was a huge promotion, meaning that he would actually ride rather than walk and clean up after the horses. In the summer of 1966, he left Santa Anita to work in the same capacity at the Granja Vista Del Rio Ranch in Corona. Then during a fog-shrouded morning workout in September 1966, his ambitions were cut short when he suffered a bad spill at full gallop. He was taken to Corona Community Hospital where an examination revealed no serious injuries. Almost immediately, however, Sirhan began to complain of blurred vision and pain. In July 1967, he filed a workman's compensation complaint. The following February, he was paid a two thousand-dollar settlement. In the meantime, Sirhan had gotten a two-dollar-an-hour job at a health food store in Pasadena. The owner knew his mother. By the time he got the settlement, however, he was growing tired of menial work; with cash now in hand, he quit his job in March 1968.[72] But by this time, Sirhan had decided life in the United States was a huge disappointment.[73]

The Motive

Sirhan had always been well-informed about politics, especially on the subject of the Middle East. He was an avid reader of newspapers — both Arab and American — and his library card provided evidence of his preoccupation with books on this topic.[74] A college friend reported that Sirhan used to talk with him at length about the Middle East situation. It was his passion. He said that his goal was to return to Jordan someday. His future, he insisted, was there — not the United States.[75] As a consequence, he faithfully monitored political developments in that part of the world. And, unsurprisingly, his abiding hatred of Jews and Israel was passionate — the deep, smoldering, unforgiving hatred of the persecuted and dispossessed that could ignite with even a casual remark. Anyone who ever discussed politics with him at anytime in his life quickly observed his hostility toward Israel.

Sometime during high school he had underlined passages in two history books that described the assassinations of Archduke Ferdinand and President McKinley. The last underlined sentence in the McKinley passage reads: "After a week of patient suffering the President died, the third victim of an assassin's bullet since the Civil War." In the margin, Sirhan wrote, "many more will come."[76] Although it is unlikely that he had anything definite in mind at that point in his life, his past experiences had prepared him to think along those lines.

After high school he began to attend regular meetings of the Organization of Arab Students, where members recalled his strident Arab nationalism and his hatred of Zionists. He equated Zionists with Nazis in their cruelty and immorality.[77] Thus it was with intense anger that Sirhan read, listened to, and watched reports on Israel's invasion of the Sinai on June 5, 1967. His political hero was Egyptian President Nasser,[78] but Nasser's forces were defeated with shocking swiftness by the Israeli army and air force. Israeli units gained total control of the Sinai in only three days. Then in three more days, they turned toward the Jordanian frontier to capture the Old City of Jerusalem (where Sirhan had spent part of his childhood) and the strategically important Golan Heights. The brief but devastating engagement that ended on June 10 became known as the Six Day War. It was a humiliating defeat complete with reports of the cowardice and ineptitude of Egyptian units. For Arabs like Sirhan, it meant that prospects of ever regaining their homeland were now more remote than they had ever been.

Sirhan's frustrations during this period were expressed in his frequent political arguments and eventual difficulties with his last employer, John Weidner, before he angrily quit his job at the health food store. He angrily told Weidner, for example, that he had no intention of ever becoming an American citizen. He condemned the United States as a supporter of Zionist terrorism. Sirhan insisted that wealthy American Jews controlled politicians and the media to ensure the continuation of policies favorable to Israel. Zionists, Sirhan claimed, were as wicked as the Nazis Weidner had fought in World War II.[79]

Earlier, before his injury at the racetrack in Corona, he became interested in occult sciences and mind control. He subscribed to the belief advanced by some that mental mastery of a subject would enable him to achieve his personal and political objectives.[80] Early in 1968, he joined the Ancient Mystical Order of the Rosae Crucis, a San Jose-based organization that promised self-improvement through control of the mind.[81] His interest intensified as he began both to read books on mind control and to practice prescribed exercises in his room. The exercises ranged from self-hypnosis to attempts to exert subconscious control over others.[82]

Thus from the Six Day War to the end of 1967, two major concerns seemed to weigh on Sirhan's mind: his disappointment with life in the United States and the realization that his dream of ever returning to Jordan was effectively ended unless something unforeseen happened. Arab newspapers, which he continued faithfully to read,[83] daily reported Israel's increasing power and expanding military presence in the Middle East.

With such events paramount in Sirhan's thoughts, there can be little doubt that he read in the Arab papers that the *New York Times* reported on January 9 and 10, 1968, Senator Kennedy's proposed sale of fifty Phantom jet bombers to Israel.[84] Sirhan was enraged when he learned of the proposal. He had been an admirer of President Kennedy and thought of him as a reasonable person who had attempted to understand the Arab position. He had had similar hopes for his younger brother. His disappointment was profound.[85]

Sirhan kept a notebook in which he recorded his hopes and disappointments; he also used it to practice his mind control exercises. The two activities became inseparable. The entries were often seemingly incoherent, sometimes disjointed, often repetitious statements. The idea behind this approach was that once the expressed objective became imprinted on the subconscious, commitment and success in attaining the objective were virtually assured. On Friday, January 31, 1968, Sirhan scrawled what was the first of a series of trance-like notebook entries declaring repeatedly that "RFK must die."[86] From this point on, Sirhan Sirhan began to prepare himself psychologically to assassinate Robert Kennedy. Fate would determine whether he got the chance. On January 31, 1968 Robert Kennedy was only, however, a senator from New York — not yet a presidential candidate — and it must have seemed unlikely, even to Sirhan, that such an opportunity would arise.

The probabilities changed suddenly on March 16, however, with the senator's announcement of his candidacy for the Democratic presidential nomination. Just two weeks later, on March 31, President Johnson announced his stunning decision not to seek reelection. With a familiar California loser, Richard M. Nixon, virtually assured the Republican nomination, and only the phlegmatic Eugene McCarthy and the Johnson-tainted Hubert Humphrey to defeat for the Democratic nomination, it seemed obvious to Sirhan that the popular, suddenly charismatic pro-Israeli senator from New York would be the next president of the United States. Already on record supporting the sale of more bombers to Israel, Kennedy's election, in Sirhan's view, would have devastating consequences for the Palestinian Arabs struggling to survive on the Israeli border. Kennedy had to be stopped.[87]

Preparations

Sirhan's notebook entries during this period reveal a rather well-defined plan of preparation for the assassination. Much like the ancient sect of Arabs from whom the term "assassin" is derived,[88] and with whom Sirhan identified, he began to ready himself for his challenging task. His preparations were based on the Rosecrucian assumption that one can accomplish any objective by writing it down over and over while in deep concentration on its realization. Sirhan explained the process as " . . . how you can install a thought in your mind and how you can have it work and become a reality if you want it to."[89] Sirhan began to record his intent to assassinate Robert Kennedy and to establish his own defense after the deed was committed by claiming that he could not remember what he had done.

Sirhan's notes during this period anticipate in remarkable detail his behavior immediately preceding and following the assassination. Before he shot Kennedy, Sirhan had had four drinks — Tom Collinses. He then was seen drinking coffee with a young woman. After the shooting, he claimed no memory of the event — although it is significant that he never asked why he had been arrested.[90]

On February 1, 1969, while under hypnosis, Sirhan recalled and recorded his thoughts of the year before when, on January 31, 1968, he had made his decision to kill Senator Kennedy. After writing over and over "RFK must die," "Robert Kennedy must die," "Robert Kennedy is going to die," he then shifted to what would become his defense: "Who Killed Kennedy? I don't know I don't know I don't know." This was followed with these words:

> girl the girl the girl no no no no no practice practice practice practice practice Mind Control mind control mind control
> 1234 1234 1234 1234 give me a Tom Collins were you drunk yes yes yes where is the [girl or gun][91] I don't know go home go hom home car car car car car I want coffee cofee cofee at theparty at the party [illegible]

And then:

> Kathleen Kathleen Kathleen Kathleen NO [illegible] NO Kathleen She did not tell me her name NO NO I don't know she wanted she wanted coffee NO NO NO NO"[92]

While the identity of "Kathleen" remains a mystery,[93] Sirhan's recall of his feelings under hypnosis strongly suggests that the notebook contained not the incoherent writings of a paranoid schizophrenic, as some psychiatrists claimed but, possibly, the efforts of a determined assassin to prepare himself psychologically for an assassination as well as for his anticipated capture and defense if he survived.

Elsewhere in the diary the entries vary from statements of political belief to more trance-like writings — sometimes in English, sometimes in Arabic — that reflect objectives Sirhan hoped, in this manner, to achieve. Although political objectives were paramount to him, the notebook reveals his desire for money, two particular women he had met briefly,[94] and "a new Mustang."[95] His political entries did not vary too much. A sampling:

> Ambassador Goldberg must die-Goldberg must be eliminated[96]
> Sirhan is an Arab
> American capitalism will fall an[d] give way to the worker's dictatorship.
> Long live Nasser

Taking note of President Kennedy's assassination he wrote:

> I believe that the U.S. is ready to start declining, not that it hasn't began in Nov. 23, 63.

And he had particular contempt for American politicians:

> I advocate the overthrow of the current president of the fucken United States of America.
> The American politician leads his people through any course that he wants them to — this is possible because the people lack the initiative or are indifferent to the actions of their leaders. Their leaders say: You have the right to speak against your government and support its Changeover — but remember — through Democratic means Only — if otherwise we will blast the hell out of you-and besides, you wouldn't want to do anything like that, it is stupid, costly and wasteful. Just let us run the country, hire our relatives to work for us-and earn fat checks . . . . Well my solution to this type of government is to do away with its leaders . . . . The President-elect is your best friend until he gets into power then he suck[s] every drop of blood out of you — and if he doesn't like you — you're dead.[97]

The persistent theme of his writings, however, was his obsession with Senator Kennedy's assassination:

> Kennedy must fall.
> Robert F. Kennedy must be sacrificed for the cause of poor exploited people.
> Kennedy must die.[98]

Activities: March to May 18, 1968

An attempt was made during the trial to dismiss the notebooks as further evidence of Sirhan's sick mind — his paranoid delusions.[99] But considered in the context of his experiences in Palestine and the very clear positive slant of United States foreign policy toward Israel, the evidence of paranoia seems much less convincing. These issues were not imagined.

He shared these concerns not only with fellow Arab students at the meetings of the Organization of Arab Students, but he also voiced them in informal conversations he had with other political friends. One of these was Walter Crowe, a high-school friend who went on to attend Pasadena City College with Sirhan. Crowe appears to have been a typical campus radical of the period. In 1965, he had organized an ad hoc committee for black civil rights. That was followed by an unsuccessful attempt to establish a chapter of the Students for Democratic Society). In 1966, he joined the W.E.B. DuBois Club, and the following year he was one of the founders of an eight-member Communist Party at UCLA where he had since transferred.

In March 1968, he spent an evening bar hopping with Sirhan, talking politics and watching topless dancers. They discussed Mideast politics—the Six Day War, the loss of Arab territory, the predicament of the Palestinians, and the activities of Al Fatah, the Arab terrorist organization — but without much intensity, according to Crowe.[100] Sirhan's notebook entries during the period reveal a great deal of intensity on these issues, however. And his abundant anger was focused on Robert Kennedy, especially after Kennedy announced his candidacy for the Democratic presidential nomination. It was also at this time that Sirhan began to practice shooting with what was to be the murder weapon, a .22 caliber revolver that had been purchased for unrelated reasons in February by Sirhan's brother, Munir.[101]

A few days after the assassination of Martin Luther King, Jr. on April 4, Sirhan discussed the event with an acquaintance, Alvin Clark, a black trash collector in Pasadena. According to Clark, Sirhan was angry about King's death and asked him if he thought black people would retaliate. Clark replied that he didn't know what blacks could do even if they wanted to strike back. Then Sirhan asked Clark how he was going to vote in the California primary. When Clark replied that he was going to vote for Senator Kennedy, Sirhan expressed surprise and anger and asked why Clark would vote for that "son of a bitch." He told Clark that his vote would be wasted "because I'm planning on shooting him."[102]

Later, on May 2, Sirhan met once again with his friend Walter Crowe. Crowe told Sirhan about his Communist party activities at UCLA. He went on to explain to Sirhan that the Arab-Israeli conflict was actually a war of national liberation — an internal struggle by Palestinians against the Israeli oppressors that could be best understood in terms of Marxist theory. He added that the terrorist activities of Al Fatah had boosted the morale and self-respect of Arabs everywhere. Sirhan agreed, emphasizing that the revolutionary objectives of Al Fatah required total commitment.[103]

After the assassination, an anguished Walter Crowe would wonder whether his discussion of the strategic and tactical importance of terrorism had influenced Sirhan.[104] Only after the trial began would he realize that Sirhan's thoughts about assassinating Robert Kennedy were first recorded in January when he learned of the senator's endorsement of the bomber sale to Israel — some two months before their first conversation together in March and five months before their second in May.

The Stalk

At 9:45 A.M. on May 18, 1968, Sirhan wrote these words in his notebook:[105]

My determination to eliminate RFK is becoming . . . more of an unshakeable obsession.

Following below in his trance-inspired mechanical scrawl he had written over and over again:

R.F.K. must die — RFK must be killed — Robert F. Kennedy must be assassinated

And then, most significantly, he set the date:

Robert F. Kennedy must be assassinated before 5 June 68.

Why June 5, 1968? It was the first anniversary of the humiliating Six Day War. It also just happened to be the day after the California presidential primary, which was central to the Senator's presidential aspirations. As Sirhan later explained to author Robert Kaiser: "June 5 stood out for me, sir, more than my own birth date. I felt Robert Kennedy was coinciding his own appeal for votes with the anniversary of the Six Day War."[106]

Any lingering doubts Sirhan might have had about Kennedy's Israeli commitment were removed two days later, on May 20, when the senator's campaign documentary "The Story of Robert Kennedy" was televised in Los Angeles. Midway through the film, a voice described Kennedy's 1948 visit to Israel as battle scenes and milling crowds of frightened refugees were shown. Noting that Kennedy had lived with Israeli troops and witnessed war firsthand, the narrator added that, as a young man, the senator had joined in to "celebrate" Israel's independence. It was during this experience in Israel, the narrator intoned, Kennedy had made a decision. And then with the Israeli flag waving in the background, the decision was announced: "Bob Kennedy decided his future lay in the affairs of men and nations." Innocuous, perhaps, but not to persons with intense Palestinian sympathies like Sirhan Sirhan. To him the message was clear — Kennedy's future was tied to the *Israeli* cause. He could remember little else about the film.[107]

But, in fact, Sirhan's course was already set. The film simply reinforced his determination to end the senator's life. Earlier that same day, Senator Kennedy had made a campaign appearance before a group assembled in the banquet room of Robbie's Restaurant in Pomona. A bartender who was acting as a security check at a stairway leading to the room stopped a young man and woman who claimed they were with the Kennedy party.[108] The young man, if not Sirhan, looked very much like him, carried a coat over his right arm and became very angry when their explanation was challenged. But the couple left without further discussion. The incident and resemblance were verified by two other onlookers.[109] This was probably the first in a series of documented attempts Sirhan would make to get within striking distance of Kennedy.

On Sunday, May 24, Sirhan continued his stalk of the candidate at a political rally in the Los Angeles Sports Arena. He was later identified as moving about the fringes of the crowd as the rally ended. But, once more, the opportunity did not develop and Kennedy was spared.[110]

On May 26, a column by political commentator David Lawrence appeared in the Pasadena *Independent Star-News*. The title of the column was "Paradoxical Bob" and went on to criticize what Lawrence considered to be Kennedy's inconsistency in opposing the war in Vietnam while advocating military aid for Israel. Sirhan clipped out the column and carried it with him. It was found in his pocket after his arrest.[111]

That same evening, May 26, an Associated Press wire reported that Kennedy had again advocated the sale of fifty jet bombers to Israel in a speech he had made earlier that day in Portland, Oregon. Sirhan later that night heard on radio station KFWB "All News Radio" that Kennedy had promised a Zionist audience in Beverly Hills that he would send jet bombers to Israel.[112] Such reports only strengthened Sirhan's resolve.

Kennedy's pro-Israeli position and his connections with wealthy Jewish liberals in the film industry were hardly obscure facts in his California campaign. He regularly made well-publicized appearances in synagogues, and photographs often appeared of him wearing a yarmulke when he addressed Jewish audiences. All this was obvious, even without the explicit Jewish appeal presented in his televised campaign film.

Two days later, on May 28, Sirhan attended an uneventful meeting of the

Rosecrucian Society in Pasadena.[113] Then on Saturday, June 1, he drove to the Lock, Stock, and Barrel Gun Shop in San Gabriel and purchased two boxes of .22 caliber hollow-point high velocity ammunition and drove to a pistol range in Corona to practice. He had practiced with the gun maybe half a dozen times since he first shot it in March after hearing the announcement of Kennedy's presidential candidacy.[114]

The next day, Sunday, June 2, after again practicing at the Corona range, he went to a Kennedy campaign rally at the Ambassador Hotel in Los Angeles. Sirhan stalked the lobbies and banquet rooms of the Ambassador but without success.[115] Time was growing short. Sirhan was committed to the June 5 deadline he had set and then programmed himself to meet.

On Monday, June 3, the day before the primary, Kennedy was scheduled to speak in San Diego at a rally at the El Cortez Hotel. Sirhan made the two-hour trip to San Diego[116] in his battered 1956 De Soto and then returned that evening to Pasadena — once more without success.[117]

The next day, Tuesday, June 4, was crucial for both Kennedy and Sirhan. The outcome in the June 4 California primary was a critical event in Kennedy's quest for the presidential nomination. For Sirhan, who was convinced that Kennedy would win, it meant he had only twenty-four hours left to meet the objective he had been preparing himself for at least since March, and thinking about since January.

The day of the election Sirhan drove to the San Gabriel Valley Gun Club where he again spent the afternoon practicing rapid-fire shooting. He left the range when it closed at 5 P.M. and went to a Bob's Big Boy restaurant where he ate a hamburger.[118] Then he drove into Los Angeles to the Ambassador Hotel at 3400 Wilshire Boulevard where Kennedy and his supporters had gathered to await the election results. After parking his car, he wandered around the hotel visiting at least one other political gathering. He also downed the first two of his four Tom Collinses in the process — just as he may have prepared himself to do in the self-induced trances he recorded in his notebook. He then walked to the second floor banquet area where excited, anxious Kennedy supporters crowded in to await the results. There he had two more Tom Collinses. A little later, Sirhan left the hotel briefly, walked to his car, and got the pistol he had left there, tucked it into the waistband of his trousers beneath his jacket and returned to the hotel where he began to drink coffee and talk with an unidentified woman.[119]

At about 10:00 P.M. Sirhan walked over to a hotel electrician, Hans Bidstrup, and asked him how long the senator would be staying at the hotel. He then inquired whether Kennedy's bodyguards remained with him all the time.[120] Bidstrup wasn't sure. Sometime during this period, Enrique Rabago, an unemployed auto mechanic began to small talk with Sirhan. He had come to celebrate Kennedy's anticipated victory with a friend, Humphrey Cordero.

When Rabago expressed that hope and his enthusiasm for the candidate, Sirhan replied, "Don't worry if Senator Kennedy doesn't win. That son of a bitch is a millionaire. Even if he wins, he won't do anything for you or me or the poor people."[121]

About 11:45 P.M., Sirhan approached Jesus Perez, a kitchen helper, and Martin Patrusky, a waiter, and asked if Kennedy would be coming through the kitchen. They told him they didn't know. While talking with the two, Sirhan looked around the kitchen area.[122] He then made a calculated guess that altered political history. Given the size of the crowd assembling, he reasoned, Kennedy would probably leave the Embassy Room by way of the pantry to avoid the crush. He positioned himself by the tray rack and waited.

Arrest and Trial

After his arrest Sirhan claimed he could not remember the shooting and refused to give his name or reveal any information about himself. At the police station, he seemed calm, careful, especially lucid, and quite glib about subjects *he* wanted to discuss. Two of these, for example, were the trial of a Los Angeles district attorney, Jack Kirschke, who had killed his wife and her lover, and the Boston strangler case.[123] The fact that both defendants got lighter sentences than had been anticipated for double and multiple murders may have had something to do with his interest and familiarity with these cases. But his other actions and words reveal that he was lying about his alleged memory loss.

There was a pattern to his deceit from the first words he uttered as he pulled the trigger — "Kennedy, you son of a bitch" — to his reply to Jesse Unruh's question in the police car — "I did it for my country." Both statements leave little doubt that Sirhan was in control of his thoughts and actions. He also knew why he had been arrested. That's why he didn't ask.[124] When a police officer asked him if he was ashamed of what he had done, he replied angrily, "Hell no!"[125]

Other evidence supports the same conclusion. Although he refused to ask the police anything about the crime, he was very anxious to see the newspapers the following day.[126] Concerned that drugs might be used to elicit information from him, Sirhan refused to drink coffee or water until someone else first took a drink.[127] Probably the most telling evidence of his total awareness of what he had done was his concern about the police finding the incriminating notebooks he had left in his bedroom.[128]

When a representative from the American Civil Liberties Union met with him the day after the shooting to arrange for legal counsel, Sirhan, in what under the circumstances seemed to be a totally bizarre command, said "Tell my mother to clean up my room. It's a mess."[129] His hope was that his mother would find the notebooks and destroy them. But it was too late. Sirhan's brothers had already identified him, and police had quickly discovered the notebooks when they searched the house.[130] Sirhan correctly recognized that the notebooks would provide indisputable evidence of premeditation. Indeed the notebooks provide the best evidence Sirhan's political motive.

Psychiatrists disagreed. The battery of mental health professionals that had been assembled by Sirhan's attorneys viewed the notebooks as further evidence of the paranoid schizophrenia that they believed their extensive testing of Sirhan had revealed.[131] The testing had been conducted by Dr. Martin M. Schorr, a clinical psychologist from San Diego who had volunteered to assist in Sirhan's defense. It was a curious arrangement. Before Sirhan's trial, in a July 10, 1968 letter addressed to Russell E. Parson, one of Sirhan's attorneys, Schorr wrote:

> I would like to help you very much in the matter of pre-planning jury selection on the basis of the personality dynamics of the client, since so many headaches can be avoided if proper jury selection tuned to the emotional needs of Sirhan can be trial.[132]

After Dr. Schorr had signed on to the case, he was given the permission he so anxiously sought to administer a battery of psychological tests to Sirhan on November 25 and 26, 1968. On the basis of his interpretation of Sirhan's responses on the Rorschach Inkblot Test, the Bender-Gestalt Test of Intelligence, the Thematic Apperception Test, the Minnesota Multiphasic Personality Inventory, and his answers during an interview, Dr. Schorr diagnosed Sirhan's mental condition as "paranoid psychosis, paranoid state."[133]

Dr. Schorr explained the psycho-dynamics of the condition in the somewhat strained language of unresolved *oedipal* conflict. Sirhan didn't really want to kill Kennedy, Schorr claimed, rather he wanted to kill his father for whom he felt "strong antagonism." Consequently, Sirhan generalized this hostility to all "men in authority, of persecutors, of all that is unjust in Israel."[134] Sirhan, Schorr insisted, "had never advanced beyond the primitive stages of love for his mother — a common pattern in paranoia." Then he offered this conclusion:

> By killing Kennedy, Sirhan kills his father, takes his father's place as the heir to his mother. The process of acting out this problem can only be achieved in a psychotic, insane state of mind.[135]

Even Sirhan's attorneys had trouble with this explanation, but accepted it with head-scratching amusement. In their situation, any evidence of Sirhan's "diminished responsibility" was welcome. An insanity defense was their only hope, if they were to avoid a first degree murder conviction and a probable death sentence. The most they could expect from a jury was some form of institutionalization, medical or penal, for life.

The circumstances of Sirhan's crowded cell where the tests were conducted were alone enough to raise questions about the scientific basis of the testing.[136] Dr. Schorr administered his tests and conducted his interviews with Sirhan in the presence of a team of security guards, one of Sirhan's attorneys, Russell Parsons, and a legal assistant, in addition to author Robert Kaiser. All were assembled in the midst of the most elaborate and intimidating security arrangements. According to Kaiser, Sirhan's attorney and he — neither of whom had the greatest confidence in Schorr — laughed and wisecracked about the tests as they were being administered. At one point Parsons broke into laughter and said to Schorr, "I don't know who is crazier, you or Sirhan."[137]

It is hardly surprising that Sirhan's anxiety about his situation was translated into "paranoid" responses on the tests he took. Imagine the situation: confined in a small windowless cell with a multiple twenty-four-hour guard, every move monitored, and facing a murder charge that could carry the death penalty; add to this his alien status as an Arab whose victim was a very prominent American — a man adored by many. Who in such circumstances would not feel depressed, threatened, and anxious?[138] Indeed, the absence of such emotions would appear more bizarre. But Dr. Schorr labeled it paranoia — or the presence of persecutory delusions. To compound the difficulties in this questionable diagnosis, it was subsequently revealed during the trial that Dr. Schorr had plagiarized much of his explanation from A *Case Book of a Crime Psychiatrist* by James A. Brussel, a book about another killer.[139]

Unfortunately, in spite of the difficulties in Dr. Schorr's testing procedures and his diagnosis, as well as those of other psychologists called into the case, whose examinations were conducted under similar circumstances, such evidence provided the basis for much of the psychiatric testimony that was to follow.[140] It also set the tone of this testimony. Few persons were convinced that Sirhan was as sick and mentally disordered as the psychiatrists and clinical psychologists who were summoned to his defense said he was. According to Kaiser, even Sirhan's attorneys privately rejected the notion of his insanity.[141]

Foremost among those rejecting this diagnosis was Sirhan himself. Although maintaining his claim that he had no memory of the shooting, he consistently stated that his primary motive was political. Rather than subject himself to a demeaning defense based on his alleged "diminished responsibility," Sirhan, like Leon Czolgosz and Oscar Collazo, preferred to plead guilty. After Schorr had examined him, Sirhan angrily told his attorneys, "I don't want a trial. I don't want doctors proving I'm insane."[142] He maintained this position throughout his trial, frequently objecting strenuously to the psychiatric testimony intended to save his life.[143]

His family as well as other Arab observers also objected to the attempt to develop a defense based on Sirhan's mental state rather than on the Arab-Israeli conflict which, they insisted, provided a political understanding for his actions.[144] But the battery of expert witnesses who testified in his behalf rejected Sirhan's own explanation that he hated Robert Kennedy, saw him as a friend of the Zionists, and the next president of the United States, and killed him for those reasons. This in spite of Sirhan's surprisingly articulate discussion[145] on the witness stand of the history of Zionism, the Arab-Israeli conflict, and the atrocities he had witnessed.[146] Nevertheless, most of the doctors continued to cling to the oedipal theme, bolstered with some rather questionable test results, that Sirhan was actually lashing out at one or the other of his parents when he shot Kennedy.[147] All refused to acknowledge that, given the political context of Sirhan's life and what Kennedy represented within that context, his motives and actions could have been as rational as those of any political terrorist. The only reason Sirhan reluctantly agreed to go along with the diminished responsibility defense (only after a fashion — he continued to object to suggestions of mental illness throughout the trial) was that he hoped that he might become part of a future prisoner exchange if he was able to avoid the death sentence.[148] This had been an important element in his plan all along. Or, as he had whispered to Robert Kaiser in court, "Better a live dog than a dead lion."[149]

It was not a hope without basis. In 1962, there had been such an exchange. An American spy, Francis Gary Powers, had been captured by the Soviet Union when his U2 spy plane was shot down over Russian territory. As a result of negotiations between Washington and Moscow, Powers was exchanged for the release of Rudolph Abel, a Soviet spy who had been imprisoned in the United States. But that was not to be in this case. Sirhan was not merely a spy, he was an assassin.

Of the psychiatrists testifying for the defense, only Bernard Diamond seemed close to an understanding of Sirhan, but he, too, dismissed Sirhan's political motive. Rejecting the oedipal theme advanced by others, Diamond testified that Sirhan had killed Kennedy irrationally in a self-induced trance brought on by the mirrors and lights in the hotel lobby. In Diamond's view, the killing was virtually accidental and was due solely to Sirhan's "dissociated" mental state. According to Diamond, had the mirrors and lights not been present, Sirhan would not have gone into his trance, and the assassination would not have occurred.[150] He described the defendant this way:

> I see Sirhan as small and helpless, pitifully ill with a demented, *psychotic* rage, out of control of his own consciousness and his own actions, subject

to bizarre dissociated trances in some of which he *programmed himself* to be the instrument of assassination, and then in an almost accidentally induced twilight state he actually executed the crime, knowing next to nothing what was happening.[151]

Diamond rejected the possibility that all this could have been deliberate. He dismissed Sirhan's political views as "delusional fantasies." He also denied that the mind control exercises could have been part of a plan to prepare for a difficult and dangerous task. Sirhan practiced mind control, according to Diamond, merely to "improve his mind."[152]

During cross-examination, prosecuting attorney David Fitts asked how Sirhan's April conversation with Alvin Clark could be explained if the assassination was the unplanned accident Diamond insisted that it was (recall that in April Sirhan had told Clark that he was planning to shoot Kennedy):

DIAMOND: I don't believe he [Sirhan] said that, sir.
FITTS: Well the witness testified to it from the stand.
DIAMOND: I think the witness was incorrect.
FITTS: Is that a polite word for saying the witness was lying?
DIAMOND: No. It's just that he was incorrect.
FITTS: And the basis for your belief — you didn't see the witness on the stand?
DIAMOND: No.
FITTS: You don't know anything about the witness except for the statement you read?
DIAMOND: No.
FITTS: You were not here when he was present?
DIAMOND: I prefer to believe Sirhan.[153]

Only one psychiatrist, Seymour Pollack for the prosecution, was willing to accept Sirhan's own explanation for his crime. In his report to the district attorney, Pollack concluded that although Sirhan may have been, in some sense, a troubled individual, "[his] motivation in killing Senator Kennedy was entirely political, and was not related to bizarre or psychotic motivation or accompanied by peculiar or highly idiosyncratic reasoning."[154]

Of the nine psychiatrists and psychologists who testified during the trial, the jury believed Pollack. One probable reason for the jury's rejection of opposing testimony was that in spite of the diagnostic agreement among the others — that is, Sirhan was schizophrenic — their explanations were often contradictory, poorly defended during cross-examination, and unconvincing. Only Diamond, for example, attempted to explain how the alleged paranoid schizophrenia caused the assassination in other than strained language of

Type I—Nationalism

unresolved oedipal conflict. But his admission that he found his own explanation "an absurd and preposterous story, unlikely and incredible" did little to add to its credibility.[155]

On April 17, 1969, twelve jurors found Sirhan guilty of the first degree murder of Senator Kennedy. In so doing, they endorsed Sirhan's own explanation that his motives were political. Six days later, on April 23, they agreed with the assessment of prosecuting attorney John E. Howard who urged the jury "to apply the only proper penalty for political assassination in the United States of America":

> You may eliminate Sirhan from society altogether or merely eliminate him from your society. This defendant will regard permission to live as a further triumph of imprisonment, for life imprisonment is an entry into a form of custodial society that can only suffer by the inclusion of this defendant.[156]

Sirhan was sentenced to die in the gas chamber in spite of a handwritten plea for clemency made by the late senator's brother, Senator Edward Kennedy.[157] His sentence was later reduced to life imprisonment when the United States Supreme Court halted all executions in 1972.

Conclusions

Sirhan Sirhan possesses all the characteristics of a Type I assassin. He was not, as his attorney Emile Zola Berman told reporters, "obviously mad."[158] He remains satisfied and confident that his act was justified. His intent was to deny the presidency to a powerful pro-Israeli politician on the brink of the American presidency. In that most powerful position in the world, Sirhan believed that Arabs everywhere would have suffered as a result. The only emotional and cognitive distortion present was self-induced in order to carry out his plan. To that extent, his "mind control" exercises served the same function as hashish did for the first Arab assassins centuries ago. There was no credible evidence of mental disorder. For example, when Robert Kaiser asked him if he saw himself as "an instrument of divine wrath," he shook his head and said smiling, "God didn't tell me to shoot Kennedy."[159] He understood completely what he had done — and why. He also had weighed the consequences should he survive the attack. He had read extensively about previous assassins. Even his alleged loss of memory was part of a carefully calculated plan to avoid the death sentence. And his hope to become part of a future prisoner exchange was not only based on precedent but was substantiated on September 6, 1970 when Arab terrorists in Europe hijacked four commercial jetliners bound for the United States and forced them to fly to the

Middle East. The hijackers reportedly sought to exchange their captives for the release of Sirhan.[160]

Moreover, Sirhan has not yet given up the idea of a prisoner exchange. In a 1978 article in *Playboy* magazine, a former cellmate of Sirhan's at Soledad Prison is quoted as saying that Sirhan told him that he was still hopeful that Arab terrorists would be successful in arranging circumstances to facilitate his release.[161] Sirhan recognizes correctly that he is a hero to many Arabs. In 1980 there was a report that. The Arab-American Relations Committee was seeking his release, having made arrangements for his return to any one of five Arab countries should he ever be paroled.[162] And on February 4, 1981, the Associated Press reported that friends of Sirhan Sirhan have appealed to Senator Edward M. Kennedy to support the early release of the man who assassinated his brother, Robert."[163]

Since then, an aging and bitter Sirhan appears regularly before the California Parole Board seeking his release. He claims that, except for the prominence of his victim, his appeals would have been granted long ago. He remains remorseless; he has never once expressed sorrow or regret, except for himself as he languishes in a maximum security prison. His most common references to his victim are illustrative:

Kennedy, you son-of-a-bitch. (June 5, 1968)

The bastard isn't worth the bullets. (October 1968)

... a fuckin' politician, who would have been a killer if he had been elected, he would have sent those fuckin' jets, I don't think I should be convicted at all. (December 1968)

That bastard is not worth my life. (January 1969)

Kennedy got what was coming to him. (March 1969)

In the first place, Robert Kennedy was a Fascist pig. Eldridge Cleaver said so. (May 1969)

Every morning when I get up, sir, I say I wish that son of a gun were alive, because I wouldn't have to be here now. (May 1969)[164]

In a rare interview in 1979, Sirhan discussed the assassination a decade later. Although attempting to project the image of a completely changed, now patriotic, and born-again Christian hoping for parole or deportation, the theme persists. In words eerily similar to those he first recorded in his notebook in early 1968, his contempt for his victim remains as stark as his political motive:

> As far as the loss of a human being, loved by his family and all that, loved by his children-on that basis my action was undefensible (sic). I acknowledge that. And I am willing to pay the price. But as far as a politician, a self-seeker, getting votes and preferring one ethnic group against another in this great democracy, for personal interest, I have no — what's the word? I don't feel that he was even fair in that respect.[165]

In a flash of anger, he noted that former San Francisco supervisor Dan White received only a seven-year, eight-month sentence for his 1979 slaying of San Francisco mayor George Moscone and supervisor Harvey Milk. "Who was Robert Kennedy?" he demanded. "Was he a greater creation of God? Was he more loved by God than, say, Moscone or Milk? . . . I have been victimized by this country, deprived of my homeland, dispossessed."[166]

In addition to his enduring anger and remorseless reflections on the assassination, there are other aspects of Sirhan's behavior that also support his Type I classification. With rare exceptions, such as his 1979 interview, Sirhan has consistently shunned publicity. Had he killed for the neurotic compensatory reasons of seeking fame and glory, as some have suggested, it is certain he would have sought rather than avoided public attention. In 1969, for example, he was extremely upset when he learned that Robert Kaiser was going to write a book about him; at his request, his attorneys sought to prevent its publication. And that basic reclusive pattern continues into a new century.

Similarly there is no evidence to support the "loner, white male with sexual problems" stereotype of assassins. All the known facts reveal a basically quiet, but friendly and conversant person who got along well with most people and especially enjoyed the companionship of women right up through the evening of the assassination.

In the final analysis, what we see in Sirhan is a calculating, determined, and remorseless assassin who killed for political reasons — reasons that were difficult for many to grasp or accept in 1968 and 1969. But now with the increased awareness of the intensity of feelings and the divergence of values in the Middle East, Sirhan's motives, no matter how objectionable and deplorable, cannot be dismissed as irrational — not when they are shared by so many others in that part of the world.

Sirhan's crime on June 5, 1968 was no different than the atrocities of numerous Palestinian terrorists who continue to bomb and assassinate in attempts to reach their political objectives. He is no more irrational than the young Palestinians who continue to express their anger and frustration in

94   Defining Danger

Israel as human bombs, or the Black September terrorists who murdered the Israeli athletes at the 1972 Munich Olympics, or the Zionists who participated in the Deir Yassin massacre in 1948, or the two Zionist assassins who killed Lord Moyne in 1944. Sirhan was mad or irrational only to the extent that war and intense nationalism are mad or irrational.

Notes

1. "Incidents Preceding November 1, 1950, Attempted Assassination of President Truman," Federal Bureau of Investigation, File No. 62–7721–1695, p. 17. Hereafter cited as *FBI Document 62-7721-1695*.
2. Ibid., p. 32.
3. "Origin of Nationalist Party of Puerto Rico (NPPR), Including the Rise of Pedro Albizu Campos," Federal Bureau of Investigation, Document 9450590–2, p. 10. Hereafter cited as *FBI Document 94-50590-2*.
4. *United States v. Oscar Collazo* (1951), United States District Court for the District of Columbia), Collazo testimony, vol. 8, p. 745. Hereafter cited as *Trial Transcripts*.
5. *FBI Document 94-50590-2*, pp. 1–7.
6. "Nationalist Party of Puerto Rico," Federal Bureau of Investigation, File No. 100–7689, pp. 35–36. Hereafter cited as *FBI Document 100-7689*.
7. *FBI Document 94-50590-2*, p. 9.
8. Puerto Rican Nationalists, Oscar Collazo, Federal Bureau of Investigation, File No. 3–36–A, November-December 1950. Hereafter cited as *FBI Document 3-36-A*.
9. The divorce was contested and had not been granted at the time of his death.
10. *FBI Documents 3-36-A, 94-50590-2, and 100-7689*, p. 21.
11. *FBI Document 100-7689*.
12. Ibid., pp. 7–8
13. Ibid., p.8
14. Ibid., p. 7
15. Ibid., pp. 9–10
16. Ibid., p. 10
17. *Trial Transcripts*, Collazo testimony, vol. 7, pp. 702–704
18. *FBI Document 100-7869*, p.11.
19. Ibid., pp. 10–11
20. *Trial Transcripts*, Collazo testimony, vol. 7, p. 711.
21. Ibid., pp. 711–712.
22. Ibid., p. 712.
23. *FBI Document* 100–7689, pp. 14, 21.
24. Ibid., p. 15; *Trial Transcripts*, Collazo testimony, vol 7, pp. 714–716.
25. *FBI Document* 100–7689, pp. 12–13.
26. *Trial Transcripts*, Collazo testimony, vol. 8, p. 752.
27. *FBI Document* 100–7689, p. 17;,*Trial Transcripts*, Collazo testimony, vol. 7, p. 717.

28. *Trial Transcripts*, Collazo testimony, vol. 7, p. 718.
29. Ibid., vol. 7, p. 719.
30. Ibid., vol. 7, p. 719.
31. Ibid., vol. 7, pp. 717, 722; vol. 8, p. 740.
32. Ibid., vol. 7, p. 720.
33. Ibid., pp. 722–723.
34. Ibid., p. 724.
35. *FBI Document* 94–50590–2, p. 8.
36. *Trial Transcripts*, Rover testimony, vol. 7, pp. 725–726.
37. *Trial Transcripts*, Collazo testimony, vol. 7, p. 726.
38. Ibid., p. 727.
39. *New York Times,* September 11, 1979, A16.
40. Figuero-Cordero, dying of cancer, was freed in 1977. He died shortly thereafter.
41. Ibid.
42. Ibid., September 12, 1979, A1, A14.
43. Ibid.
44. Ibid., September 13, 1979, B23.
45. Ibid., December 4, 1979, A1.
46. *Trial Transcripts*, Collazo testimony, vol. 8, p. 766.
47. *Chicago Daily News,* November 1, 1950, A1.
48. R. B. Kaiser, *"RFK Must Die!" A History of the Robert Kennedy Assassination and its Aftermath* (New York: Dutton, 1970), pp. 419–422, 425.
49. Ibid.
50. *State of California v. Sirhan Bisbara Sirhan* (1969), Superior Court, Crim. Case No. 14026, Lubic testimony, vol. 19, p. 5525. Hereafter cited as *Trial Transcripts.*
51. *Trial Transcripts*, People's Exhibit 78, Autopsy Report.
52. *Trial Transcripts,* Unruh testimony, vol. 12, pp. 3283, 3291; S. Sirhan testimony, vol. 18, p. 5217.
53. G. Jansen, *Why Robert Kennedy Was Killed* (New York: The Third Press, 1970), ch. 11.
54. *Trial Transcripts,* M. Sirhan testimony, Mary Sirhan, vol. 16, pp. 4671–4729; Hashimeh testimony, vol. 16, pp. 4591–4622; S. Sirhan testimony, vol. 17, pp. 4810–4833.
55. *Trial Transcripts*, Nahas testimony, vol. 16, pp. 4575–4588.
56. *Trial Transcripts*, M. Sirhan testimony, vol. 16, pp. 4704–4707; Sirhan, vol. 17, pp. 4815, 4832–4833.
57. *Trial Transcripts,* Hashimeh testimony, vol. 16, pp. 4599–4607.
58. Ibid., p. 4621.
59. Ibid., p. 4616.
60. Ibid., S. Sirhan testimony, vol. 17, p. 4869.
61. Ibid., Hashimeh testimony, vol. 16, pp. 4591–4622.
62. Ibid., M. Sirhan testimony, vol. 16, pp. 4712–4713.
63. Ibid., S. Sirhan testimony, vol. 17, pp. 4970–4971.
64. For a discussion of this period, see R. H. Rovere, *Senator Joe McCarthy* (New York: World Publishing, 1960).

96   Defining Danger

65. Senator John F. Kennedy did not vote on McCarthy's condemnation.
66. *Trial Transcripts*, S. Sirhan testimony, vol. 17, pp. 4856, 4937.
67. *Trial Transcripts,* Defendant's Exhibit D.
68. Ibid.
69. Ibid., Harris testimony, vol. 16, pp. 4625–4644.
70. Ibid., Lewis testimony, vol. 17, pp. 4787–4802; Defendant's Exhibit G.
71. Ibid., Weidner testimony, vol. 19, pp. 5427–5445; S. Sirhan testimony, vol. 17, p. 4878.
72. Trial testimony, Weidner, vol. 19, pp. 5427–5445.
73. Ibid., Strathman testimony, vol. *9*, pp. 5381–5406.
74. Ibid., S. Sirhan testimony, vol. 17, p. 4898.
75. Ibid., S. Sirhan testimony, p. 4937; Strathman testimony, vol. 19, pp. 5381–5406.
76. Ibid., Defendant's Exhibits II and JJ.
77. Ibid., S. Sirhan testimony, vol. 17, pp. 4924–4937.
78. Ibid., p. 5026.
79. Ibid., Weidner testimony, vol. 19, pp. 5431–5434; S. Sirhan testimony, vol. 18, pp. 5236–5254.
80. Ibid., Sirhan testimony, vol. 17, pp. 4905–4924.
81. Ibid., Defendant's Exhibit J.
82. Ibid., pp. 4919–4920; Defendant's Exhibits H and I.
83. Sirhan was also a regular reader of the *B'nai B'rith Messenger*. His purpose, he explained, was to, "know what the Zionists are up to" (*Trial Transcripts*, Sirhan testimony, vol. 17, pp. 4896-4897).
84. On January 9, the *New York Times* reported that Israeli jets had knocked out Jordanian artillery positions on the east bank of the Jordan River (p. 12). In another article by Max Frankel, President Johnson was quoted as promising visiting Israeli Premier Levi Eshkol that the United States would sell Israel "planes and other weapons." Because Israel had lost forty planes in the Six Day War, it sought a replacement purchase of fifty Phantom Jet fighter-bombers from the United States. Forty-eight A-4 Skyhawks had already been ordered before the Six Day War. Thus Israel was hoping to add nearly one hundred new jet bombers to its air force.

    In a related article in the same newspaper concerning an address Senator Kennedy made before faculty and students at Manhattan Community College, Richard Witkin wrote: "Mr. Kennedy said he thought the United States should supply Israel whatever weapons it needed to offset whatever Russia was supplying the Arabs so that Israel can protect itself. *He specifically included the 50 supersonic jets the Israelis have been seeking*" (January 9, 1968, p. 25; emphasis added).

    The next day, January 10, the *Times* reported that Senator Kennedy had met privately with Premier Eshkol at the Premier's suite in the Plaza Hotel and had assured him that "he favored supplying Israel with `whatever assistance is necessary to preserve Israel's borders and protect the integrity of its people' " (January 10, 1968, p. 14). It is most unlikely that news of this importance would have been overlooked in the Arab papers Sirhan faithfully read.

85. Ibid., Sirhan testimony, vol. 17, pp. 4931, 4971, 4977.
86. Ibid., Defendant's Exhibit RR; see, also, Kaiser, *"RFK Must Die,"* pp. 364–369, and Appendix D.
87. *Trial Transcripts*, S. Sirhan testimony, vol. 17, pp. 4969, 4971.
88. Assassin or "hashshashin" in Arabic means user of hashish which was smoked by a secret order of the Ismaili sect (c. 1090) of Islam to prepare themselves to commit politically inspired murders.
89. Ibid., p, 4905.
90. Ibid., Sirhan tapes, *vol.* 21, pp, 5948–5961.
91. Nearly illegible, but could be either word.
92. Ibid., Defendant's Exhibit RR; see, also, Kaiser, *"RFK Must Die,"* p. 369, and Appendix D.
93. He may have been referring to a former high-school classmate, Kathleen Rafferty, who had no connection to the assassination.
94. There is ample evidence that Sirhan liked women, found them easy to talk with, and enjoyed a normal sex life that probably compared well with most young men of his age and circumstances.
95. *Trial Transcripts,* People's Exhibit 71.
96. Sirhan's specific hatred for Goldberg began when he saw the U.N. ambassador in a televised United Nations debate on the Arab-Israeli conflict in 1967 (Trial Transcripts, Sirhan testimony, vol. 17, pp. 5019-5020).
97. Ibid.
98. Ibid.
99. Ibid., Defendant's Exhibit HH.
100. Kaiser, *"RFK Must Die," pp.* 111–112.
101. *Trial Transcripts*, S. Sirhan testimony, vol. 18, p. 5125; Erhard testimony, vol. 13, pp. 3747–3755.
102. Ibid., Clark testimony, vol. 14, pp. 4010–4017.
103. Kaiser, *"RFK Must Die,"* pp. 164–165.
104. Ibid., pp. 163–164, 228–229.
105. Ibid., People's Exhibit 71.
106. Kaiser, *"RFK Must Die," p.* 219.
107. *Trial Transcripts*, S. Sirhan testimony, vol. 17, pp. 4970–4971.
108. Police could not identify or locate the female suspect.
109. Kaiser, *"RFK Must Die,"* p. 533.
110. Ibid., p. 534.
111. *Trial Transcripts*, Placentia testimony, vol. 12, pp. 3482–3511; White testimony, vol. 13, pp. 3810–3832.
112. Ibid., S. Sirhan testimony, vol. 17, pp. 4977–4978.
113. Ibid., Bryan testimony, vol. 19, pp. 5459–5464.
114. Ibid., S. Sirhan testimony, vol. 18, pp. S 125–5126; Erhard testimony, vol. 13, pp. 3747–3755; People's Exhibits 22–23.
115. Ibid., S. Sirhan testimony, vol. 18, pp. 5131–5143.
116. Although Sirhan denied this, it is almost certain that he did follow Kennedy to San Diego.
117. Kaiser, *"RFK Must Die," p.* 534.
118. *Trial Transcripts,* S. Sirhan testimony, vol. 18, pp. 5152–5171.

119. Ibid, pp. 5182–5187, 5200–5202, 5214–5215.
120. Ibid., Bidstrup testimony, vol. 19, pp, 5465–5484.
121. Ibid., Rabago testimony, vol. 19, pp. 5490–5491; Cordero testimony, vol. 19, pp. 5499–5505.
122. Ibid., Perez testimony, vol. 12, pp. 3374–3375; Patrusky testimony, vol. 19, p. 3881.
123. Ibid., Jordon testimony, Jordan, vol. 16, p. 4448; Sirhan tapes, vol. 21 pp. 5971–6011.
124. Ibid., Sirhan tapes, vol. 21, pp. 5971–6170.
125. Ibid, pp. 5971–6170; Kaiser, *"RFK Must Die," p.* 56.
126. *Trial Transcripts*, Sirhan tapes, vol. 21, pp. 5971–6170.
127. Ibid., Jordan testimony, vol. 16, pp. 4430–4434.
128. Ibid., Sirhan tapes, vol. 21, pp. 5985–5986.
129. Kaiser, *"RFK Must Die," p.* 94.
130. *Trial Transcripts,* Evans testimony, vol. 15, pp. 4317–4326.
131. Ibid., Defendant's Exhibits H, S, T, U, R.
132. Ibid., People's Exhibit 99.
133. Ibid., Defendant's Exhibit U.
134. Ibid., People's Exhibit 102.
135. Ibid.
136. When questioned about the testing situation during the cross-examination, Schorr claimed that the tapes of his interviews with Sirhan had been accidentally destroyed.
137. Kaiser, *"RFK Must Die," pp.* 242–243, 293; see, also, *Trial Transcripts*, Schorr testimony, vol. 19, p. 5547.
138. *Trial Transcripts,* Defendant's Exhibit T.
139. Ibid., People's Exhibit 102.
140. Ibid., Diamond testimony, vol. 25, p. 7197.
141. Kaiser, *"RFK Must Die," p.* 388.
142. Ibid., pp. 243, 343–345.
143. Trial Transcripts, S. Sirhan testimony, vol. 16, pp. 4646–4650; Cooper statement, vol. 16, p. 4645; Berman statement, vol. 15, pp. 4381–4384.
144. Ibid., S. Sirhan testimony, vol. 17, pp. 4931–4937.
145/ Some tests had also supposedly revealed a below average IQ of 89 — thus the surprise.
146. Ibid., vol. 17, pp. 4931–4937.
147. Ibid., Defendant's Exhibit H; People's Exhibit 102.
148. Kaiser, *"RFK Must Die," pp.* 218–219.
149. Ibid., p. 440.
150. Ibid.
151. Ibid., Diamond testimony, vol. 24, p. 6998; emphasis added.
152. Ibid., p. 6994.
153. Ibid., Diamond testimony, vol. 24, pp. 7099–7100.
154. Ibid., People's Exhibit 111.
155. Ibid., Diamond testimony, vol. 24, p. 6998.
156. Ibid., Howard statement, vol. 31, pp. 8887–8888.

157. Kaiser, *"RFK Must Die,"* Appendix H.
158. Ibid., p. 422.
159. Ibid., p. 466.
160. The passengers were later released. The Palestine Liberation Organization denied that Sirhan was part of the attempted exchange (*New York Times*, September 8, 1970, A1).
161. J. McKinley, "Inside Sirhan," *Playboy,* April 1978, p. 96.
162. *Arizona Daily Star,* September 27, 1980, A2.
163. *Tucson Daily Citizen,* February 4, 1981, A1.
164. Kaiser, "*RFK Must Die*", pp. 26, 230, 265, 294, 466, 514, 524.
165. C. Gorney, "Sirhan," *Washington Post,* Aug. 21, 1979, B3.
166. Ibid.

Part 2

Type II

4

Type II—Rejection
Lee Harvey Oswald and Samuel Joseph Byck

> *"There is no borderline between one's personal world and the world in general."*—Lee Harvey Oswald
>
> *"I think this all begins with a lack of respect."* —Samuel Byck

The primary characteristic of the Type II subjects of this chapter and the next is what Harold Lasswell has called a "political personality."[1] According to Lasswell, such persons seek power in order to compensate for low estimates of self. The low estimates of self, he contends, are most frequently a consequence of a deprivation of affection experienced in the individual's personal life — for example, the denial of love or rejection by a parent, spouse, one's children, or some other loved one. The exercise of power in a public manner generates the attention and, occasionally, the affection, that otherwise are denied in their private lives. Lasswell had in mind specifically persons like politicians who seek positions of authority where, for example, the deference one receives and/or the roar of the crowd may compensate for an unhappy childhood, a failed career, or a loveless marriage.[2]

But the same explanation can be applied to some similarly frustrated persons who, lacking the skills or other personal attributes, or opportunities, necessary for conventional political success, choose another more spectacular and tragic alternative — namely, assassination — to launch themselves into the public eye, compensating for their disappointments and obtaining the attention that has eluded them all their lives. But Type II subjects want to be perceived as selfless, even heroic figures, willing to die for a cause, rather than the losers they know they are. For that reason, they do not acknowledge the very real personal reasons behind their actions. Instead they rationalize their crimes, falsely claiming to be sacrificing themselves for some higher public purpose. Thus their true motives are very different from the politically motivated Type I subjects. As we will see, a reconciliation with their estranged wives, for example, probably would have deterred the violent actions of the two killers discussed in this chapter.

Type II subjects are depressed, angry, and may be suicidal but they are not psychotic as are their Type IV counterparts; they know exactly what they are doing and fully appreciate the consequences. Additionally, a number of other important qualities differentiate between the Type II and the severely disordered Type IV subjects. Unlike the Type IV subjects, the Type II assassins and would-be assassins do not suffer from delusions or hallucinations. Type II assassins maintain their grip on reality. They are not confused by events they cause or encounter; their personalities remain intact. The tensions and anxieties generated in their personal lives may produce a tendency toward paranoia. But, as we will see, their suspicions and fears are, more often than not, firmly grounded in the objective circumstances of their lives. Ruled by anxiety, anger, and depression, they ultimately become self-destructive. Eventually, as one coping strategy after another failed, each of the Type II subjects turned to desperate acts seeking to demonstrate in death their importance to an indifferent world.

Two of the four subjects fit this basic description: Lee Harvey Oswald and Samuel Byck. As the first women in American history who attempted to assassinate a president, Lynette Fromme and Sara Jane Moore illustrate interesting variations on this theme. For that reason they are considered separately in chapter 5.

Volumes have been written and continue to be written about the assassination of President John F. Kennedy in 1963 and the man who, alone, killed him, Lee Oswald. But most people still have not heard of Samuel Byck who, on February 22, 1974, died in his attempt to hijack and crash dive, kamikaze style, a Delta jetliner into the White House. His target? President Nixon and the White House staff. Both men illustrate the basic compensatory motives of Type II assassins. Consider first the case of Lee Harvey Oswald.

* * *

LEE HARVEY OSWALD (1939–1963)

The skies were blue and the sun was shining brightly in Dallas on November 22, 1963. President John F. Kennedy and his Secret Service detail decided it was a perfect day to ride past the cheering crowds that lined the streets without the top on the presidential limousine. And so it was until half past noon. The president's car had just made a sharp left turn from Houston Street onto Elm Street at Dealey Plaza when rifle fire exploded from a sixth floor window of the Texas School Book Depository. The first shot missed, probably deflected by a tree branch. The second shot hit the president in the upper back, exited through his throat and struck Texas governor John Connally who was sitting immediately in front of the president. The bullet passed though Connally's right shoulder and wrist before spending itself as a flesh wound in the governor's left thigh. As the president lurched, raising both hands to his throat, a third bullet struck him in the back of the head, ending a life of great promise in a pink cloud of blood and brain tissue.

There can be little doubt that Lee Harvey Oswald fired fatal shots that killed the president. Whether one or more other gunmen were also involved remains a subject of much speculation, but after more than four decades of contentious debate no other shooter has been identified or linked by evidence to Oswald. The evidence pointing to Oswald, however, is overwhelming.

Oswald, an employee at the Depository, left the murder weapon poorly hidden at the scene and made good his escape from the front entrance of the building at approximately 12:33 P.M. A bus ride and about forty-five minutes later, Oswald was stopped for questioning by a Dallas police officer as he was walking along Tenth Street in Oak Cliff, a residential neighborhood. When J.D. Tippit got out of his patrol car, Oswald shot him four times with a .38 caliber pistol, killing him instantly. Tippit didn't have a chance; he died with his gun still in his holster. At approximately 1:45 P.M., police responded to a call that Oswald was spotted entering the Texas Theatre on West Jefferson Avenue, a short distance from the murder scene. After a brief but vigorous scuffle, during which Oswald tried to shoot another policeman, he was arrested at the theatre and taken to the Dallas city jail. It seemed as though he did not expect to get far; he had only $13.87 in his pocket.

And he didn't. Less than forty-eight hours later, on Sunday, November 24, Lee Harvey Oswald was shot and killed by a Dallas nightclub owner as he was being transferred from the Dallas jail to another more secure facility.

Childhood

Lee Harvey Oswald was born in New Orleans on October 18, 1939, the third of Marguerite Oswald's three sons. His father had died two months before. The death forced his mother to seek employment and, as a result, his brothers were placed in an orphanage where he joined them two years later.[3] When he was four years of age, he was withdrawn from the orphanage and taken by his mother to Dallas where she remarried five months before Lee's fifth birthday. After her marriage, the older brothers were sent to a military academy and Lee lived with his mother and new stepfather, who, according to his half-brother, John Pic, Lee loved as a father. But the marriage soon deteriorated and his parents were divorced in 1948.[4] This brief period between his fifth and eighth birthdays — when his parents' marriage was breaking up — was to be the closest Lee Oswald was to come to an ordinary family experience.

After the divorce, Marguerite and the boys moved back and forth between Dallas and New Orleans as she worked and quit a variety of unskilled jobs. As soon as they were old enough, the two older boys, John and Robert, enlisted in the military. Lee was left behind with the unhappy, self-absorbed woman his brothers had escaped. When he was not in school, he was often alone. Still, he didn't do badly in school, compiling an "average" record with little support or encouragement at home.

The first serious evidence of the effect that his unpleasant childhood was having on him came in August 1952 when, shortly before school started, Marguerite abruptly decided to move to New York. There they lived briefly with her oldest son, John, before eventually moving to a rundown apartment in the Bronx. Missing friends and familiar surroundings, Lee found himself thrust into an alien urban culture where his new seventh-grade classmates ridiculed his unfashionable clothes, peculiar mannerisms, and Southern accent. Confronted with such daily harassment, Lee withdrew and began to spend more and more time away from his classes, watching television and reading magazines alone in the seedy apartment. His poor school attendance resulted in truancy charges. He was subsequently sent for psychiatric observation to determine the cause of his increasing psychological as well as social withdrawal. In the post-examination report, the thirteen-year-old boy's problems were diagnosed as "intense anxiety, shyness, feelings of awkwardness and insecurity." It concluded that:

> Lee has to be seen as an emotionally, quite disturbed youngster who suffers under the impact of really existing emotional isolation and deprivation, lack of affection, absence of family life and rejection by a self-involved and conflicted mother.[5]

Likable and even charming when he wanted to be, this bright, good-looking, and very troubled, youngster was elected president of his eighth grade class when he returned to school in the fall of 1953. But he soon became distracted, once more, then surly, and, at times, disruptive. According to reports prepared by his probation officer, he refused to do his assignments and frequently disobeyed his teachers; among other things, for example, he refused to salute the flag with his classmates.[6]

Although doing little in school beyond attending in order to avoid probation problems, Lee had become an avid reader. During this period, a major political issue was the controversial Rosenberg case. Julian and Ethel Rosenberg had been tried, convicted, and sentenced to death for spying for the Russians. Their eventual execution on June 19, 1953 was nowhere more vigorously and emotionally contested than in New York City. It was during this time that someone handed Lee a Marxist pamphlet protesting the injustices of that trial and the impending execution. Oswald was later to say that this event in his troubled fourteenth year first stirred his interest in Marxism. From this point on, he began to develop through his voracious reading and new Marxist perspective the idea that the unhappiness and difficulties of his life were not unique. Like the Rosenbergs and the innocent people who were to fall victim the following year to the indiscriminate attacks of U.S. Senator Joseph R. McCarthy, Lee Harvey Oswald began to see himself as a victim of capitalist oppression. Even his hostility or, at best, ambivalence toward his mother — "well I've got to live with her. I guess I love her"[7] — could be rationalized this way; for in Lee's view, she, too, was a victim — as she, in less doctrinaire fashion, constantly complained — of the same oppressive system.[8]

Indeed, it is interesting to observe the striking similarity between the personality of Marguerite Oswald and the evolving personality of her son. She was described by the psychologists who were treating Lee in 1953 as "very self-possessed and alert," with a "superficial" affability that did not quite conceal "a defensive, rigid, self-involved person who had real difficulty in accepting and relating to people."[9] Essentially the same words would be used to describe her son by virtually everyone who knew him. Lee was in every sense his mother's son. The stamp of her personality on his was undeniable.

It was in the midst of these difficulties with the New York public school authorities that Marguerite, with Lee in tow, moved again. Back to New Orleans, where Lee finished the ninth grade, and where he was once again looked upon as an outsider.

Thus, with no family life to speak of, isolated and frequently harassed in school, and having few, if any, close friends, Lee Oswald was to make the first of series of major decisions designed to alter the dismal circumstances of his life: he would join the Marines. Following in the footsteps of his older brother Robert, he hoped to find the adventure, recognition, pride, and self-respect portrayed in Marine Corps recruitment posters, not to mention the escape he sought from his mother and school authorities.

The Marines (October 1956 to September 1959)

Soon after enlisting in the Marines in October of 1956 he realized he had made a mistake. His fellow Marines were no more tolerant of his reclusiveness and surliness than his schoolmates in New York and New Orleans. Nor were

Marine officers any more inclined to ignore his indiscretions than his teachers were. Moreover, they were perhaps even less inclined to acknowledge what he considered to be his superior abilities.[10]

In the barracks, this slightly built, intense little guy with the pinched, unsmiling little mouth was soon dubbed "Ozzie the Rabbit."[11] Oswald didn't fit in. Ignoring the sex and violence that typify the reading material in most barracks, Oswald read instead poetry like Whitman's *Leaves of Grass* and serious novels like Orwell's *1984*.[12] At the height of the Cold War, he also began to study Russian and even read a Russian newspaper.[13] Although he had his first sexual experiences with Japanese prostitutes and drank a little beer in the local "slop-chutes," Oswald was not a typical hell-raising Marine. Unhappy with barracks life and military discipline, his resentment began to surface in disputes with superiors that resulted in two court-martial convictions and twenty-eight days in the brig. One of the convictions was for the unauthorized possession of a pistol with which he had accidentally shot himself in the arm.[14]

Four weeks in a Marine brig, at that time, was a personally degrading, emotionally searing, and embittering experience. Prisoners were forced to do trivial and repetitive tasks, often required to stand at attention when not working or doing physical exercise, forbidden all but task-related conversations with fellow prisoners, required to ask permission to relieve themselves, and were frequently harangued and ridiculed in humiliating boot-camp fashion. This totally punitive experience was designed to minimize recidivism. Few prisoners left Marine brigs without a great deal of resentment.

Lee Oswald was no exception. For him the experience was a confirmation of all he hated about the military as well as the wisdom of the plans he had been considering to defect to the Soviet Union. There was a direct relationship between his difficulties in the Marines, his interest in the Soviet Union, and the intensity with which he pursued his study of the Russian language.

The Soviet Union (1959–1962)

Securing an early discharge, falsely claiming in order to care for his allegedly disabled mother, Lee instead left almost immediately for the Soviet Union, using money he had saved for that purpose during his enlistment. Denouncing the United States in the most unqualified terms, he anticipated a warm reception in the nation that had become his political ideal.[15] Instead, he was crushed by the indifference and skepticism of the Soviet bureaucracy when informed immediately after his arrival that he was not welcome to remain.

On October 21, 1959, Oswald attempted suicide by drawing a razor through the flesh and tendons of his left wrist, but not before he recorded his disappointment in his own badly misspelled — Oswald was dyslexic — "Historic Diary":

> I am shocked!! My dreams! . . . I have waited for 2 years to be accepted. My fondes dreams are shattered because of a peety offial, . . . I decide to end it. Soak rist in cold water to numb the pain, Than slash my left wrist. Than plaug wrist into bathtum of hot water. . . . Somewhere, a violin plays, as I wacth my life whirl away. I think to myself "How easy to Die" and "A Sweet Death, (to violins) . . . "[16]

Although Soviet officials eventually agreed to let him remain, there is no evidence that Oswald completely recovered from this disillusioning first experience in what he hoped would be his new homeland. It was unrequited love and it left him bitter. His disillusionment would be complete some four years later when he was again rebuffed by yet another nation that had become his revolutionary ideal and new best hope for a new life.

Although his life in the Soviet Union was to take on novel and appealing social dimensions for a lonely young man — he made friends, dated attractive young women who found him interesting, and eventually married one of them — the drab, daily routine of Soviet life soon began to wear on him. And there were other disappointments. He was denied admission to a university in Moscow and, instead, was given an assembly line job at a radio and television factory in dreary Minsk. Even the generous allowance that supplemented his factory salary and an unusually commodious apartment were not enough to compensate for the obscurity of his position and the daily boredom of Soviet life; nor were an attractive Russian wife and baby.[17] In January of 1961, he wrote in his diary:

> I am stating to reconsider my disire about staying the work is drab the money I get has nowhere to be spent. No night clubs or bowling allys no places of recreation acept the trade union dances I have had enough.[18]

Disillusionment

In June 1962, he returned to the United States with his wife Marina and their infant daughter June. Earlier in a preface he had written to *The Collective*,[19] a manuscript about his Soviet experience, he presented a brief autobiographical assessment of his own life at that point:

> Lee Harvey Oswald was born in Oct 1939 in New Orleans La. the son of a Insuaen Salesmen whose early death left a far mean streak of indepence brought on by negleck. entering the US Marine corp at 17 this streak of

independence was strengthened by exotic journeys to Japan the Philipines and the scores of odd Islands in the Pacific immianly after serving out his 3 years in the USMC he abonded his american life to seek a new life in the USSR. full of optimism and hope he stood in red square in the fall of 1959 vowing to see his chosen course through, after, however, two years and alot of growing up I decided to return to the USA.[20]

But it was not a joyous return. Even though his illusions about the Soviet Union had been shattered, his hostility toward his own government remained as intense as before. His great adventure had been a failure, and now he was returning to an unhappy past he had hoped to forget.

A brief and clearly strained reunion with his mother and brother Robert in Texas followed the Oswald's arrival in June 1962. After that Lee and his wife saw very little of his mother and brothers. The pattern his life soon assumed was familiar: the self-imposed isolation, the transience — moving from one dead-end job and shabbily furnished apartment to another — and the ever-deepening alienation from all things American.[21]

His frustration and anger were reflected in his deteriorating marriage. Domestic violence, or its threat, were a daily reality for Marina. She lived in fear, never knowing when her verbally and sexually abusive husband might strike her for some real or imagined provocation; his verbal tirades were, in some respects, worse.[22] His abusive ways, however, only deepened his own depression, adding further to the already heavy strains on the marriage. The future looked grim. Disillusioned with the bureaucratization and betrayal of Marxism in the Soviet Union and confronted with the dismal realities of life on the edge of a Fort Worth slum, he wasn't sure where to turn when he wrote in despair:

> No man, having known, having lived, under the Russian Communist and American capitalist system, could possibly make a choice between them. there is no choice, one offers oppresstion the other poverty. Both offer imperilistic injustice, tinted with two brands of slavery. But no rational man can take the attitude of "a curse on both your house's."

There *are* two world systems, one twisted beyond recognition by its misuse, the other decadent and dying in its final evolution.[23]

Marina Oswald's biographer, Priscilla Johnson McMillan, attributes great significance to this document, suggesting that "it gives a better idea than anything else he wrote of what appears to have been his conscious purpose in killing President Kennedy, and of the resigned, stoical and yet exalted spirit in which he went about it."[24]

Although Oswald does anticipate that "a coming economic, political or military crisis, internal or external, will bring about the final destruction of the capitalist system,"[25] this statement would appear to be nothing more than a familiar Marxist assessment of the end of capitalism rather than a revelation of what motivated him to kill the president. Indeed, as a doctrinaire Marxist, his stoical belief in the historical inevitability of the collapse of capitalism denies the utility of individual violence in precipitating the final "crisis." He mentions this fact repeatedly in his manuscript. On pages four and five he writes,

> We have no interest in violently opposing the U. S. Government, why should we manifest opposition when there are far greater forces at work, to bring-about the fall of the United States Government than we could ever possibly muster.

And later, on page five, he states,

> Resoufullniss and patient working towards aforesaid goal's, are prefered rather than loud and useless manifestations of protest.

Further on he writes that failure to work and organize to prepare for the crisis would be as big a mistake "as trying to use force now to knock down the door." And in the next sentence, he declares, "Armed Defenses of our ideals must be an accepted doctrine after the crisis, just as refrointing [refraining] from any demonstrations of force must be our doctrine in the mean time."

Thus, his anticipation of an impending "crisis" would appear to be nothing more or less than a statement of Marxist doctrine. There is little in this essay that sheds any light on his reasons for the subsequent attacks on General Edwin A. Walker and President Kennedy. Indeed, the utility of violence, as we have seen, is repeatedly denied. His philosophical musings are important, however, to the extent that they reveal his disillusionment with the Soviet Union and the United States and the enormous personal and political importance he was to attach to a Cuban alternative.

General Walker and the Cuban Alternative

By March 1963, Oswald's political interest had begun to shift to the Third World, and he renewed a particularly abiding interest in Cuba. With that shift, his depression began to lift. Long an admirer of Fidel Castro, he began to formulate a plan that would prepare the way for a new life in a truly revolutionary society. In Oswald's mind Castro's Cuba represented a fresh, shimmering revolutionary ideal — a country uncontaminated by the stultifying, gray bureaucracy of the Kremlin or the materialism and greed of the United States. He believed that it was a country that would recognize and appreciate a fellow revolutionary like himself. In Cuba, he could imagine assuming a leadership role in society — certainly, he would be taken seriously and not relegated to the obscurity of an assembly plant as he had been in the Soviet Union or the menial, low-wage work that was his lot in Texas. But first he had to establish his political credentials in a way that would impress a revolutionary military government that had seized power after years of skillfully directed guerrilla warfare.

Living in Dallas at the time was retired Army Major General Edwin A. Walker. Walker had recently gained national attention as the result of his right-wing political activities. A militant anti-communist of paranoid proportions, Walker urged an invasion of Cuba and the overthrow of its "Communist regime" in the most unqualified terms. He condemned the Kennedy administration for its restraint in dealing with a Communist threat only ninety miles from American beaches. Walker was also an outspoken racist and a vigorous opponent of the civil rights movement. His extremism led to his forced resignation from the Army. There could be no doubt about it: Walker was high profile. No one represented America's international imperialism and racism better, in Oswald's mind, than the general; no one, therefore, offered a more convenient symbol at whom to strike a blow for Cuba; and, in so doing, establish the revolutionary credentials Lee Harvey Oswald desperately needed to legitimize his anticipated appeal for Cuban citizenship.

Early in March, Oswald decided he would assassinate Walker. He began to make preparations for the assassination, taking care to document his actions with photographs of Walker's home, supplemented with elaborately drafted plans that could subsequently be shown to Cuban officials to substantiate his claims. On March 12, he ordered the intended murder weapon from a Chicago mail-order house. It was a real bargain at $19.95 — an Italian made, World War II vintage, 6.5 millimeter Mannlicher-Carcano rifle with a 4X telescopic sight.

Shortly after the rifle arrived, Oswald posed for the now-famous photographs of himself dressed in black, holding the rifle and copies of *The Militant* and *The Worker*, with his holstered .38 on his hip.[26] He made prints of the photo for posterity. One for his daughter June; as he told Marina, it would be something "to remember Papa by sometime."[27] He inscribed another with the statement, "Ready for anything," hoping that it would be published in *The Militant*.[28] He also signed a third for his friend George de Mohrenschildt, who shared Oswald's contempt for Walker: "For George, Lee Harvey Oswald," dating it "5–IV–63" (meaning April 5, 1963).[29] By this time, he had begun practicing with the rifle.[30]

The events that follow from this point in his life are important because they provide some insight into Oswald's motives and his behavior leading up to his attack on President Kennedy. On Saturday, April 6, Oswald was fired from his job with a commercial photography firm. He was terribly disappointed because it was probably the only job he had ever held that, in his fashion, he had liked. He had learned of his impending dismissal earlier that week, but embarrassed and hurt, he had not told his wife.[31]

By the time of his actual dismissal, Oswald had made a detailed study of bus schedules and routes in Walker's neighborhood. On Sunday, he left the apartment with the rifle. When he returned later that afternoon, he did not have the rifle; he had buried it near Walker's home.[32] After supper, he left again and did not return until later that evening. Presumably, he was making further preparations. On Monday, April 8, General Walker returned from a cross-country speaking tour. On Wednesday, April 10, Oswald tearfully admitted to his wife that he had lost his job, largely he felt, because of FBI harassment.[33] Probably as important as the FBI's inquiries about him as a security risk, was the fact that Oswald reinforced whatever suspicions might have been raised in his employer's mind by reading Russian language newspapers during his breaks.

In any case, his course of action was set, losing his job only reinforced his decision to get Walker. Soon after, he prepared written instructions in Russian for Marina in the event he was arrested or killed in the attempt.[34] She found the note when he did not return for supper that Wednesday evening:

1. This is the key to the mailbox which is located in the mainpost office in the city on Ervay Street. This is the same street where the drugstore, in which you always waited is located. You will find the mailbox in the post office which is located 4 blocks from the drugstore on that street. I paid for the box last month so don't worry about it.
2. Send the information as to what happened to me to the Embassy and include newspaper clippings (should there be anything about me in the newspapers). I believe that the Embassy will come quickly to your assistance on learning everything.
3. I paid the house rent on the 2d so don't worry about it.
4. Recently I paid for water and gas.
5. The money from work will possibly be coming. The money will be sent to our post office box. Go to the bank and cash the check.
6. You can either throw out or give my clothing etc. away. Do not keep these. However, I prefer that you hold on to my personal papers (military, civil, etc.).
7. Certain of my documents are in the small blue valise.
8. The address book can be found on my table in the study should you need same.

9. We have friends here. The Red Cross also will help you.
10. I left you as much money as I could. $60 on the second of the month. You and the baby [illegible-possibly baby's name] can live for another 2 months using $10 per week.
11. If I am alive and taken prisoner, the city jail is located at the end of the bridge through which we always passed on going to the city (right in the beginning of the city after crossing the bridge).[35]

At approximately 9 P.M on Wednesday evening, he shot and barely missed Walker as the latter worked at a desk in his study. The bullet was deflected by a window pane, otherwise Walker would have probably died. Oswald had planned the attack to coincide with the conclusion of evening services at a Mormon church near Walker's home. As churchgoers flooding the street added to the confusion, Oswald placed the rifle back where he had buried it near the scene, boarded a bus amid the departing Mormons, and returned home flushed with excitement.[36] When he told his wife, she was distraught. The next morning, greatly disappointed to learn on the news that he had missed, he explained to his distressed wife that he wanted to kill Walker because he was a dangerous "Fascist" like Hitler had been; he said Walker had the same potential for human destruction.[37]

Later as he read accounts of the police investigation into the incident, he ridiculed their incompetence, laughing aloud about their inability to identify the bullet and their presumption that he had fled in a car. The simplicity and success of his escape plan confirmed his opinion that the Dallas police were, as he explained to his wife, "fools."[38] As if to confirm his contempt, Oswald was on the streets a few days later with a "Hands Off Cuba! Viva Fidel" placard hanging from his neck handing out pro-Castro pamphlets.[39]

On April 21, he alarmed his wife once more when he abruptly bolted from his reading of the *Dallas Morning News,* quickly dressed, and slipped his .38 under his belt, announcing that Nixon was coming to town. "I am going to have a look," he said excitedly. The headline in the paper read "Nixon Calls for Decision to Force Reds Out of Cuba."[40]

In fact, Nixon was not coming to town. Oswald had been bluffing simply to provoke his terrified wife. In any event, it did not matter since, by this time, Marina was convinced her husband was on the verge of a mental breakdown. Unaware of his long-range Cuban plans, his attack on Walker and the disturbing Nixon bluff convinced her that he was coming unhinged. She urged him to get out of town before he was arrested and to look for work elsewhere. She reassured him that she and the baby would join him as soon as he found another job. In the meantime, she said she would remain in Dallas, staying with friends. Much to her relief, he agreed, and on the night of April 24 he boarded a bus for the city of his birth, New Orleans.

Fair Play for Cuba

After the Walker incident, Oswald's interest in Cuba continued to grow. In his mind, it was his last best hope. He had first become interested in Cuba as a Marine. As many young Marines did during the period, he talked of joining Fidel Castro's guerrilla forces in the Sierra Maestre Mountains, a grand adventure to be sure.[41] Now that Castro was in power — and an avowed Communist — he was viewed as a real threat by the United States. That, of course, heightened his appeal to Oswald. Oswald's concern centered on the Kennedy administration's hostile policies toward the new revolutionary government — first the Bay of Pigs invasion in 1961 and then, a year later, the Cuban missile crisis. There could be little doubt in anyone's mind — let alone Oswald's — that the Kennedy administration wanted to bring down the Castro regime.

Soon after Oswald arrived in New Orleans, he obtained a job as a greaser and oiler in a coffee processing plant. It was dirty, uninteresting work, but it paid the rent and, besides, he was focused on other concerns. Within a month after his arrival, he wrote to the national headquarters of the Fair Play for Cuba Committee to request literature and instructions for establishing a chapter in New Orleans.[42]

In the meantime, his pregnant wife and infant daughter had arrived; they settled into yet another rundown apartment on Magazine Street. Oswald's indifference on the job caught up with him on July 19, when he was fired.[43] Now without a job and living only on unemployment compensation, political activities consumed his free time. He had "Hands Off Cuba!" handbills printed and by August 9 was on the streets, dressed in a white shirt and tie, distributing them. His activities were calculated to attract as much attention as possible. Twice, once on August 9th and again on the 16th he was arrested when disputes developed between himself and anti-Castro Cuban exiles who objected to his demonstrations. Shortly after, he appeared on two radio programs where he discussed and debated, in a very knowledgeable manner, his objections to the Kennedy administration's Cuban policy.[44] As a voracious reader of newspapers and radical publications such as *The Militant* and *The Worker,* Oswald had become an informed and formidable debater on the Cuban issue.

All the publicity he was receiving as a result of his public political activities and his bogus Fair Play For Cuba chapter (he was its only member) prepared the way for his next move. Rumors had been circulating for weeks of an American plot to assassinate Fidel Castro. On September 9, it is virtually certain that Oswald read in the New Orleans *Times-Picayune* that Fidel Castro had announced that if CIA plots to assassinate him and other Cuban leaders continued, Cuba would respond in kind: "United States leaders should

116 Defining Danger

think that if they are aiding terrorist plans to eliminate Cuban leaders," Castro warned, "they themselves will not be safe."[45] Eight days later on September 17, Oswald applied for a Mexican visa as a first step in going to Cuba, he hoped, to join the revolution.

During this same period, August to September 1963, it is probable that Oswald had contact with any number of persons in New Orleans on both sides of the Cuban issue. One such person was probably David Ferrie, a former flight instructor in the New Orleans chapter of the Civil Air Patrol. As a youth, Oswald was a CAP member in 1954 and 1955. Although Ferrie was an ardent anti-Castro activist with Mafia connections, Oswald's attempts to infiltrate such groups raises the probability that the two did meet, as witnesses testified, in Clinton, Louisiana, early in September 1963. It is also probable that both were trying to use each other for their own political purposes, since it is as likely that Oswald knew of Ferrie's anti-Castro activities as it is that the latter was well aware of his former student's well-publicized Fair Play for Cuba efforts.[46] Thus Oswald was probably in contact with Ferrie in an attempt to obtain information on anti-Castro activities that he hoped to relay to the Castro government.[47]

Having failed that summer to complete arrangements for Marina and the baby to return to Russia where he had promised to join her later, he told her to return to Texas with family friend Ruth Paine who had come to see them in New Orleans. A day or two later, Oswald left by bus, also for Dallas, but for different reasons. After arriving in Dallas, Oswald immediately made contact with two pro-Castro Cubans for assistance in obtaining a visa. They, in turn, took him to the apartment of a young Cuban exile, Silvia Odio. Odio was a member of the anti-Castro Cuban Revolutionary Junta. Her parents, wealthy Cuban aristocrats, had opposed Castro and were subsequently imprisoned in Cuba for their activities. The purpose of the meeting was, in all probability, to gain more information about anti-Castro activities that would be useful in advancing his case for a visa. Ms. Odio, however, was suspicious of the three visitors, and the short meeting was concluded inconclusively.[48] Afterwards Oswald boarded a bus for Mexico City confident that, in spite of this minor disappointment, his record of pro-Castro activity was sufficiently impressive that his request for a Cuban visa would be quickly approved. In addition to his near miss on General Walker, he had succeeded in compiling a well-documented record of public activity in behalf of the Castro regime.

On Friday, September 27, Oswald walked into the Cuban Embassy in Mexico City and requested an in-transit visa to Cuba for a trip that would eventually take him, he falsely claimed, back to the Soviet Union. Then announcing that he was a friend of the Cuban revolution, he produced a fistful of documents attesting to the fact: a Fair Play for Cuba Committee membership card, a newspaper photograph and clippings describing his political activities and arrest in New Orleans, letters to the Communist party, a labor card and marriage license from the Soviet Union. When he told the secretary, Sylvia Duran, that he was a member of the Communist Party, she asked why the Party had not arranged for his visa. He replied that he had not had time to do that. He added that he had brought the odd assortment of documents to prove that he was a friend and supporter of Cuba. Pleasantly unimpressed, she told Oswald that it was more complicated than that and suggested that he go down the street to have the necessary photographs taken while she checked with the Russian Embassy. Greatly dismayed, Oswald rushed out to get the photographs.

When he returned an hour or so later with the photographs, he was told that he must first have a Russian visa before an in-transit visa to Cuba could be approved. Oswald again bolted out and rushed down the street to the Russian Embassy where he was informed that it would be three or four months before a Russian visa could be approved. Oswald was seething at this point, probably recalling his first crushing encounter with the Soviet bureaucracy in Moscow. But instead of suicide, this time he lied, returning to the Cuban Embassy and saying he had been granted the Russian visa. Sylvia Duran didn't believe him; she called the Soviet Embassy and learned the truth. Oswald was enraged. Angrily waving his membership cards and clippings, his face flushed, he shouted that he had been jailed for his activities in behalf of the Cuban revolution. What's wrong with you, he wanted to know. His credentials were beyond question, he cried, demanding the visa.

Duran said that she realized the exchange was escalating out of her control so she asked the Cuban Consul, Eusebio Azcue, to try to reason with this irate American. When Azcue tried again to explain the Cuban policy on visas, a flushed and crying Oswald screamed that he deserved better treatment for all that he had done for Cuba. It was during this incident that Oswald probably made threatening remarks about President Kennedy.[49] Offended, Azcue shouted back that the revolution *didn't need* friends like Oswald and threatened to throw him out of the office if he didn't leave immediately. A wild-eyed and "desperate" looking Oswald stormed out, devastated by the insult.[50]

A Warning to the FBI

Oswald arrived back in Dallas on October 3 after a long and frustrating bus trip from Mexico City. His hopes shattered in a humiliating rebuke, low on money, and having suffered a final indignity of being harassed by Mexican customs officials at the border, one can only imagine how discouraged and depressed Oswald must have been when he stepped off the bus in Dallas.[51] He went immediately to file a claim for unemployment compensation and to register for employment with the Texas Employment commission. After that, probably too drained and depressed to face his wife, he spent the night at the only place he could afford, the Dallas YMCA.[52] The next day, after some unsuccessful job hunting, he hitchhiked to Irving where Marina was living with the Paines, empty-handed after yet another misspent political venture. Cuban bureaucrats, he complained to Marina after he arrived, were as stupid and ugly as the Russians. In this time of crisis and desperation, Oswald drew closer to his pregnant wife. For the next few weeks, his family would be uppermost in his mind.[53]

With the second baby due anytime, Oswald and Marina decided it would be best for her to stay on with Ruth and Michael Paine in Irving, at least until the baby was born. Oswald planned to get a cheap room in Dallas and look for a job. Two weeks later, on October 14, Ruth Paine told him of an opening at the Texas School Book Depository. He got the $1.25–an-hour job and began work on October 16.[54] Two days later, Marina and the Paines presented him with a surprise birthday cake. It was his twenty-fourth. He broke down and wept when they sang "Happy Birthday."[55] A few days later, he would weep again when his second daughter was born. Chastened by months of disappointment, Oswald was for this brief October interlude kinder and more considerate toward Marina than he had been at any time since the early days of their marriage.

But resentments linger and there was an edge beneath this facade of family contentment, and it cut through the surface again just before the birth of his second child. The insensitive and often abusive way Oswald had treated his wife since their arrival from Russia had been aggravated by the difficult circumstances they faced in America. The employment difficulties, poverty, and transience had created a chronic state of bitterness in Marina that, even in the best of times, lapped at the edges of her relationship with her husband. With no other resources at her disposal, Marina expressed her resentment with the only means available to her — ridicule and indifference.

Often such ridicule was sexual where it hurt an insecure young man the most. Friends reported that Marina sometimes made invidious comparisons of Oswald to other idealized males and unflattering remarks about the quality of their sex life.[56] For example, the evening after his birthday, which had been spent pleasantly together; he had held her close and they had talked quietly about their affection for one another. Then Marina shattered the mood with a revelation that she had had an erotic dream about a former lover:

"And what did you dream?" he asked.
"We kissed, as we always did. Anatoly kissed so well it made me dizzy. No one ever kissed me like that."
"I wish I did," he replied.

"It would take you your whole life to learn."[57]

Remarks like that would probably hurt any young husband; Oswald was no exception. Having endured the rejection of Cuban officials only a few weeks before in Mexico City, Marina's remark that he was a disappointing lover had to be especially damaging. It was to be the last time he would approach his wife sexually.

But in his case, it would rekindle the desire to demonstrate that he was not the failure all indicators in his life suggested he was. His attention again turned to politics. It was as though he decided that if he could not change the circumstances of his personal life, he would concentrate on changing the world. Only two nights after his second daughter was born, he sought out a familiar figure, attending a political rally that featured as its speaker, General Edwin A. Walker. But the evening ended uneventfully.[58]

By the end of October, Oswald was fast withdrawing into a familiar pattern of isolation, depression, and smoldering anger. Still living alone in Dallas and commuting to Irving on the weekends to see his family, the only warmth evident in this frustrated man was his undeniable love for his children. All others, according to Michael Paine who observed him during this period, were once again "cardboard."[59]

Even Oswald's renewed political activity could not fill the emptiness of his life. He lived in a starkly furnished single room at 1026 North Beckley, usually ate packaged food alone in his room, and endured long evenings alone in his room, broken only by occasional trips to a coin laundry or a nearby Dobb's House Restaurant for a hot meal. He missed his children and the wife who had shown little interest in rejoining him in Dallas. He called them everyday, but the hollowness in Marina's responses remained.[60]

On Friday, November 1, the FBI sent special agent James Hosty to Irving to interview Marina. The FBI had kept a file on Oswald since his defection and return from Russia. Now, aware of his political activities in New Orleans and his recent trip and activities in Mexico, a routine check on his whereabouts was considered in order. The same day, Oswald resumed his political activities. He applied for membership in the American Civil Liberties Union, then mailed a letter to the Communist Party describing the political situation in Dallas. Later he went to the post office and opened a post office box.[61] Earlier in October, he had been evicted from a room he had rented and blamed the eviction on a by-now-familiar pattern of FBI harassment. He subsequently registered for the room on North Beckley using an alias unknown to Marina, "O. H. Lee." His resentment of the FBI's compromising presence in his life was now an obsession. When Oswald arrived in Irving later that Friday afternoon for the weekend, Ruth Paine related the matter of Agent Hosty's visit. Oswald, she said, became quiet and visibly angry.

On November 5, James Hosty returned again and this time talked only with Ruth Paine. Oswald began to call each day to inquire whether the agent had been there. Afraid to upset him, Ruth and Marina decided to wait until the weekend before telling him about the second visit. When they did, he was irate.[62] Early the next morning — Saturday, November 9 — he hand drafted and then typed a letter to the Soviet Embassy in Washington, describing his difficulties in Mexico City and his recent harassment by what he called "the notorious FBI."[63] On Tuesday, November 12, after brooding alone over a long Armistice Day weekend, he mailed the letter, probably on the way to work. Sometime during the weekend, or perhaps on Tuesday morning, he had written another much more significant note. During his lunch break, he walked to the Dallas FBI office and delivered it personally. Oswald took the elevator up to the FBI suite at 1114 Commerce Street and stalked over to the desk of receptionist Nancy Lee Fenner. "S. A. Hosty, please," he announced angrily, eyes flashing, nervously fingering the contents of the unsealed envelope in his hands. After a quick check, Ms. Fenner informed Oswald that Hosty was not in. Whereupon Oswald threw the envelope on her desk saying, "Well get this to him." Then he turned and left.[64]

A somewhat shaken Ms. Fenner noticed when she reached for the envelope that a portion of the letter was exposed. According to Ms. Fenner, it said, in effect: "Let this be a warning. I will blow up the FBI and the Dallas Police Department if you don't stop bothering my wife."[65] Despite its threatening message, the note was ignored until *after* the assassination when it was quickly destroyed by Agent Hosty.[66]

Three days later Marina telephoned her husband to say that it would probably be better if he remained in Dallas that weekend instead of coming to Irving for the customary weekend with her and the children. The reason, she explained, was that the Paines were planning a birthday party for one of their children and, since Lee did not care for Michael Paine, it would be less awkward if he did not attend. She went on to suggest that it might also be easier for everyone concerned if he did not visit every weekend as he had been doing. "As you wish," he said. "If you don't want me to come, I won't."[67] Except for a brief trip to a laundromat, he remained alone in his room the entire weekend. On Sunday he did not call as he usually did.[68]

Perhaps feeling a little guilty about her remarks and the thought of her husband spending a lonely weekend in a rooming house, Marina, who had trouble dialing the phone, asked Ruth Paine to call him. But when she asked for Lee Oswald, the voice at the other end informed her that no one by that name lived there. The next day when Lee finally called, Marina asked him about the incident. When he told her that he was now using an alias to avoid FBI harassment, she became furious. He lashed back. His lonely weekend of resentment boiling to the surface, he angrily explained once more that he had lost jobs and been evicted from a rented room the previous month because of the FBI's activities. He was enraged that his wife was so insensitive that she could not, or would not, recognize the difficulties he faced because of the FBI, an organization whose Dallas offices he had, unbeknownst to her, threatened to destroy only a week earlier.[69]

The President's Visit

From the second week of September, the Dallas newspapers had carried articles anticipating President Kennedy's scheduled November visit. The weekend of November 15 to 17 that Oswald had spent alone brooding and reading in his room, the papers revealed that the president's motorcade would travel through the downtown area on its way to a luncheon address at the Trade Mart on November 22. Oswald would have known there was a high probability that it would pass the Texas School Book Depository. On Tuesday, November 19, the probability was confirmed with the announcement of the president's specific route.[70]

With Oswald's personal frustrations peaking, another plan to resolve the difficulties of his life began to emerge. If this one worked, he would be able to accomplish several of what had recently become all-consuming goals: even the score with the FBI, prove his mettle and revolutionary credentials to the Cubans who had humiliated him, and assert his manhood to an increasingly hostile and indifferent wife who had belittled him. It would be fairly easy; he had done it before — the rifle and scope, an unwary victim, a virtual replay of his failed attempt on General Walker. He would follow the same successful escape plan: leave the rifle at the scene, walk calmly away in the confusion, and take a bus home. There would be one difference this time, however, and he knew it: he would not escape for long. But that didn't matter to a young man who felt he had nothing much to live for anymore. Besides, he wanted everyone — and especially Marina — to know that *he* did it.

Unlike his feelings toward General Walker, Oswald had no known personal animosity toward the president. But Kennedy was *the* president, the chief architect of the government's hostile policies toward Cuba, and symbolized a capitalist society which Oswald despised. Moreover, the FBI was at the forefront of presidential security; to humiliate the organization that had brought so much distress into his life would be sweet revenge.

On Thursday morning, the day before President Kennedy's visit, Oswald asked a fellow worker who lived near the Paines if he could ride to Irving with him that afternoon after work. He said he wanted to get some "curtain rods" for his "apartment."[71] His real purpose was to retrieve the rifle that he would use the next day to kill the president.

Still Oswald had second thoughts about his wife and the two children he adored. This was his last chance to hold on to his family, for tomorrow and the calamitous situation he would precipitate if he went through with his plan would end any hope he had of ever being with them. He decided to surprise them with a visit. If it went well as he hoped — if Marina welcomed him home, if they could put the bitterness and disappointments behind them, if they could start a new life together with the children — it is virtually certain that he would have set aside his self-destructive plan to assassinate the president.

But when he got home, Marina was having none of it. Still angry and resentful about his use of an alias and what that implied about his activities, she greeted his unexpected arrival after a two week absence coldly. Stiffening in his embrace and turning away from his kisses, she asked why he had come. When he told her he was lonely and missed her and the children, she looked at him indifferently and suggested that he "wash up."[72]

Throughout the evening, she treated him with the same toneless indifference. He told her that he was lonely, that he loved her, that he needed her and the children; he promised a washing machine, a modern apartment; he begged her repeatedly to come live with him again as a family in Dallas. It didn't work. Marina listened then told him she would be happier and the children would be better off if they remained apart for the time being. That was it for Oswald. The die was cast. He dropped the subject and spent the rest of the evening playing quietly with his oldest daughter. Then, after tucking her into bed and kissing the baby, he turned to Marina, who hadn't spoken more than a few words all evening,

> "I'm going to bed," he said. "I probably won't be out this weekend."
> "Why not?" she asked as she stood at the sink with her back toward him.
> "It's too often. I was here today."
> "Okay," she replied airily over her shoulder.[73]

After a restless night, Oswald arose early on November 22 and prepared for what would be the second most momentous day of his life; the other would follow two days later. Without kissing his wife goodbye as he usually did, he told her that he would prepare his own breakfast. He always did anyhow, but this morning he chose to tell her that he would. After kissing the two sleeping children, he discretely removed his wedding ring and placed it in the delicate demitasse cup Marina's grandmother had given her. Then turning to his drowsy wife he announced that he had placed some money for her in the bureau. "Take it and buy everything you and Junie and Rachel need," he said as he left.[74] He left $170 — virtually all the money he had, in effect their life savings — keeping less than $15 for himself. Oswald did not expect to get far on that.

Conclusions

President Kennedy's assassination has generated more controversy than any assassination in American history. Even the Lincoln assassination which remains the only presidential assassination with indisputable evidence of a conspiracy — ranks a distant second. Yet the weight of evidence leaves little doubt who killed the president. The psychology of the assassin, his actions before, during, and after the fatal shots were fired, combined with the physical evidence left at the scene provide compelling proof of Oswald's guilt.

Oswald fits the pattern of a Type II assassin who was motivated primarily by personal problems that throughout his brief life he tried to resolve *politically*. Consider the psychological evidence, the low points of his life that stand as markers on a road to self destruction: the neglected childhood; the dashed expectations in the Marine Corps; the disillusionment in the Soviet Union; the marginality of his life in the United States after his return and the flowering hostility, especially toward the FBI, that accompanied it; the Cuban rejection of his overtures that he probably saw as his last hope of redemption; and, finally, his deteriorating marriage and, as the last straw, his wife's rejection on November 21, 1963. The cumulative effect was a depression of suicidal proportions accompanied by anger, a compelling need to get even — with his wife, the FBI, the Cuban government, and America.

Was there a political purpose as one observes in his Type I counterparts? Hardly. Oswald, for example, didn't expect to change American foreign policy toward Cuba when he fired the shot that killed President Kennedy; instead he wanted to demonstrate to Cuba that he was undeserving of its disdainful and humiliating treatment of him in Mexico City; so he, Lee Harvey Oswald would single-handedly destroy the man who had ordered the Bay of Pigs invasion and approved the CIA's plots to assassinate Fidel Castro. Similarly, his earlier attempt on the life of General Walker (the tactics of which he followed again in Dealey Plaza) was not intended to advance any political agenda. Walker, considered unfit for military service, had zero influence on American foreign policy. Rather it was to establish the credentials he felt he needed to advance his *personal* goal of getting to Cuba to start what he hoped would be a new life with his wife and children.

But if he was suicidal and expected to be caught, why did he kill Officer Tippit and try to kill a second officer in the theater? Probably rage. At this point, time was running out; Oswald had nothing to lose and he knew it. Tippit and, later, the officers who arrested him were law enforcement, an extension of James Hosty and the FBI that had compromised his employment and, in his mind, wrecked his marriage; Oswald surely wanted these police officers to pay, probably for what they symbolized in a troubled, unhappy life.

Additionally, the physical evidence supports the lone assassin conclusion that was first put forward by the Warren Commission in 1964 and this author in 1982. Since then, Gerald Posner has done the most thorough reexamination of the original Commission Report as well as of new physical evidence which has appeared in the interim.[75] His conclusions support the Commission's finding that Lee Harvey Oswald acted alone.

Probably the most controversial evidence in Warren Commission Report was its conclusion that the second bullet fired by Oswald struck the president, caused serious injuries to Governor John Connally, and emerged in remarkably "pristine" condition. Highly sophisticated ballistics research done by Failure Analysis Associates in 1992 supports the Commission's "single-bullet" theory. Additionally, computer simulations of the shooting indicate not only that it was possible for Oswald — who qualified as a "sharpshooter" with the M1 rifle in the Marines — to fire three shots, two of them accurately, in the critical time frame, but that he fired the fatal third bullet which struck the back of the president's head.[76] With a 4X scope, Kennedy's head would have appeared about the size of an apple. Still controversy continues, based on acoustical evidence, that a fourth shot may have been fired from the grassy knoll in front of the president's car by a co-conspirator.[77] But physical evidence of the alleged shooter does not exist.

Similarly, attempts to link Oswald's killer, Jack Ruby, to co-conspirators have been unsuccessful. Ruby was not a hit man for the Mafia or any other organization. Like Oswald, all the evidence indicates that he was singularly motivated by highly personal considerations. Still periodic and unsatisfying allusions to the motives of as yet unnamed co-conspirators are likely to continue as long as there is money to be made advancing conspiracy theories. In the absence of any credible evidence of conspiracy, too many extraordinary assumptions are required, not only about the mysterious identities and motives of other conspirators and about such issues as: Oswald's chance employment in a tall building on the president's route before the president's Dallas itinerary was drawn up; about why Oswald, as part of a conspiracy, would have blown his cover by threatening the FBI just ten days before he planned to kill the president;[78] or why the president's devoted brother, Attorney General Robert Kennedy — the most powerful figure in American law enforcement and a relentless prosecutor, a man described at the time as "ruthless" by his detractors — chose not to pursue an investigation into a possible conspiracy. Conspiracy theories have to ignore such disconfirming evidence. Finally, the alleged conspirators would have had to depend on a mercurial, anxiety-ridden young man who, the facts suggest, should have been in custody on November 22, and could have been turned away from his deadly plan had he been able to envision a future with his wife and children.

SAMUEL JOSEPH BYCK (1930–1974)

A little after 7 a.m. on February 22, 1974, sleepy-eyed passengers shuffled into a line waiting at Gate C at Baltimore-Washington International Airport to board Delta DC9 Flight 523 for Atlanta. It was a cold, gray drizzling winter morning in Baltimore. A jowly heavy-set man walked up behind the security guard and, suddenly drawing a .22 caliber pistol from beneath his dark raincoat, fired two shots. One of the shots tore through the officer's back, severing the main aorta, killing him instantly. As shocked passengers recoiled in terror, the man, with the lumbering agility and swiftness of a bear, leaped over the security chain, ran down the boarding ramp, and boarded the plane.

Confronting the crew in the cockpit, the perspiring and winded assailant fired a warning shot into the floor. "Fly this plane out of here," he gasped. Then, following a second command to close the door, the flight attendants seized the opportunity to leave the plane. A shot was fired as they fled.

Turning again to the pilot and co-pilot, the man repeated his command to "take off." The pilot responded that he could not do anything until the wheel blocks were removed. Enraged, the man fired a shot that struck the co-pilot in the stomach screaming, "The next one will be in the head." He then grabbed a passenger and shoved her toward the control panel. "Help this man fly this plane," he shouted. Just then shots were heard from outside the plane. An off-duty policeman, Charles Troyer, had taken a 357 magnum from the holster of the slain security guard and running across the tarmac to the plane, tried unsuccessfully to shoot out its tires. Pushing the passenger back toward her seat, the man whirled and fired two shots, one hitting the already wounded co-pilot above the left eye, killing him; the other struck the pilot in the shoulder. Desperate, the wounded pilot called Ground Control:

> PILOT: *Ah, ground, this is . . . ah . Delta at the ramp C8 . . . do you read?*
> GC: *Delta C, go ahead.*
> PILOT: *Do you read?*
> GC: *I cut Delta out. Go ahead, Delta.*
> PILOT: *Emergency, emergency, we're all shot . . . ah . . . can you get another pilot here to the airplane . . . ah . . . this fellow he shot us both. Ground . . . I need ground . . . ah . . . this is a state of emergency. Get a hold of our ramp and ask the people to come on out to unhook the tug.*

The pilot lost consciousness.[79]

Turning again toward the first-class cabin, the gunman reloaded his pistol and then seized another passenger by the hair and dragged her forward to the entrance of the cockpit where he again shot the wounded pilot and the dead co-pilot as they slumped over the controls.

Just then a bullet smashed through the window in the plane's door, splattering glass throughout the cabin and cutting the panic-stricken woman on the thigh. As Charles Troyer maneuvered for another shot, the assailant released his grip on his hostage, pushing her toward a seat. At that instant, Troyer fired two well-aimed shots through the broken window, striking the would-be hijacker in the lower chest and stomach. Clutching his chest with both hands, he staggered and dropped to the floor. Then reaching for his pistol, he rested the barrel against his right temple and squeezed the trigger. Authorities later found a crude gasoline bomb inside the briefcase under his body.

An Unlikely Killer

Who was this man who had killed two innocent victims and critically wounded a third before taking his own life? Where did he so desperately want to take the plane? Who was Samuel Joseph Byck? As we will see, in a very real sense, he was a Willy Loman gone haywire.

Sam Byck was born on January 30, 1930 and raised in Philadelphia, the eldest of three brothers. Byck's father was a kindly, well-meaning man who, Sam recalled fondly, liked to play pinochle in the evenings with his sons. Unfortunately, to the disappointment of everyone in this Jewish family — especially his wife — Dad never made much money. As a result of the financial difficulties the family had to endure, Sam seemed to feel a certain amount of ambivalence about him.

Sam attended Olney High School in Philadelphia, but did not graduate. After bumming around in various jobs, he entered the army in 1954 at the age of twenty-four. He served uneventfully except for one AWOL scrape, received training in firearms and explosives, and was honorably discharged in 1956. By the time his father died in 1957, Sam's girlfriend, Arline, was pregnant. In an act either of urgency or insensitivity, Sam and Arline married within a month of the funeral while the rest of the Byck family was still in formal mourning.[80]

After his marriage, he seemed to enjoy his new role as husband and father to the three daughters and a son who arrived in regular two-year intervals. And he succeeded in most respects, except one: like his father, he just didn't make enough money to support his family the way he wanted and his wife expected. Outshone by his two younger brothers—one a successful businessman, the other a dentist—Sam's lack of success as a breadwinner began to place strains on his marriage and growing family. A fifth pregnancy was aborted in 1966. It was a difficult decision, but they simply could not afford another child. Now more than ever, the disturbing realization that he was just like his father was reflected in his periodic and deepening depressions.[81]

As he failed in one job and business venture after another, his jealousy and resentment of his brothers' success grew, as did the emerging rifts in his marriage. Finally, he severed all relations with his brothers, even to the extent of formally mourning them, according to Jewish custom, as if they had died.

Sam turned briefly to petty crime as an alternative. Even that didn't work. In November 1968, he was arrested for receiving stolen goods. The case was dismissed the following May. About this time, Byck decided to start his own business. He decided he just wasn't cut out to work for other people. President Nixon had just announced a new program to assist small businesses with start-up loans administered by the Small Business Administration. So Sam applied for one for twenty thousand dollars. His plan was to restructure his life on the basis of a rather novel scheme for retailing automobile tires in a brightly painted and remodeled school bus that he intended to park at various shopping centers. Low overhead, no rent, cheap operating expenses meant low prices and lots of customers. Or so Sam thought. In any case he was unhappy with his job at Korvette's Tire City, his last employer, and the marginal income he was paid as a tire salesman. Also in the back of his mind was drawing business away from with his greatly resented younger brother who was also in the tire business.[82]

Politics

But loan applications took time and the financial stress took its toll. On November 12, 1969, Sam had himself admitted to the Friends Psychiatric Hospital for in-patient treatment for anxiety and depression. Two weeks later, he received a letter from the Small Business Administration informing him of its rejection of his loan application.[83] He was very disappointed and remained in the hospital until the Christmas holidays. Diagnosed as having a "manic-depressive illness," he continued in out-patient care for the rest of his life.[84]

But Byck did not believe his problems were the result of mental "illness." He had real problems: no job and, now, a troubled marriage. Increasingly he began to rationalize his mounting marital and employment problems as being symptomatic not of personal inadequacies but of political corruption and oppression that afflicted others as well. In March 1972, he established contact with the Black Liberation Army and later contributed some five hundred dollars he couldn't afford and a couple of truck tires to the organization.[85] Like the blacks, the poor, and other casualties of political oppression he now identified with, Sam Byck believed he too was a victim. Only people who sold out to the system — grasping self-seekers like his brothers — could make it. But Sam Byck was different; he had principles.

By this time, the marriage was spiraling toward separation. Byck's wife asked him to move out during the summer of 1972. The separation was hard on him. He claimed that he was permitted to see his children for only an hour on Sundays. Whether those very punitive terms are accurate or not is not certain, but that's the way Byck saw it and he was angry.

The angrier he got the more he began to focus it on the Nixon administration. If he had gotten that loan, he could have held the marriage together. When George McGovern announced his candidacy for the Democratic presidential nomination, Byck became a strong McGovern supporter and an outspoken critic of the policies of Richard Nixon. And it wasn't as if he was alone. In October, stories began to appear in the *Washington Post* and *Philadelphia Inquirer* about what would eventually become known as the Watergate scandal. One evening after a few drinks in a Philadelphia bar, Sam suggested to no one in particular that someone ought to shoot the president. A few days later, on October 16, 1972, a couple of Secret Service agents knocked on his door. They wanted to inquire about the threatening remark he had made about President Nixon. But Sam handled it well. Described in the Secret Service report as "quite intelligent and well read," Byck jovially denied he had made such a statement. A psychiatrist who had treated Byck told the Secret Service that he did not consider Byck a threat to himself or others. He described Byck as "a big talker who makes verbal threats and never acts on them."[86]

In November, President Nixon was reelected, to Sam's dismay, in a landslide of epoch proportions. As the Christmas holidays approached, Sam made every effort to salvage the marriage. But his pleas for reconciliation were rejected. The loneliness of the Christmas holidays, which the Bycks customarily celebrated, were almost unbearable. Nothing had worked out. His life was a bust. At least his own father had been a good father, if not a successful breadwinner. Now with the separation, Sam was denied the opportunity to be even that. Without his children, there was nothing to live for. But his death had to mean something; it was obvious to him that his life had not.

On January 12, 1973, a black man, Mark "Jimmy" Essex, armed with a high-powered rifle, killed six persons from his sniper's nest on the roof of the Howard Johnson's hotel in New Orleans before he was gunned down by police. Sam was fascinated by the story. He clipped newspaper accounts of the incident and underlined the descriptions of slogans authorities found on the walls of the slain killer's apartment. The slogans — "The quest for freedom is death. Then by death I shall escape to freedom"; "Political power comes from the barrel of a gun"; and most significantly: "Kill pig Nixon and all his running dogs" — held great meaning for Sam. He taped them to the walls of his own rooms.

It was then that he decided what he wanted to do. Above the byline on an Essex article, he wrote in large letters:

I'LL MEET YOU IN VALHALLA,[87] MARK ESSEX—OK!
SAM BYCK [88]

For months certainly, and possibly years, Byck had contemplated suicide. But it is almost certain that the Essex incident triggered the idea of combining his own suicide with President Nixon's assassination. On January 16, he went to his estranged wife's residence. She wasn't home. He took her car, leaving a note saying he would be away for awhile. He then drove directly to Washington to attend the Nixon inauguration on January 20.

Once in Washington, he visited the inauguration site and talked casually with police and laborers about preparations. But then he apparently decided that an attempt on President Nixon's life wasn't feasible at that time due to the tight security. Instead, he left Washington and drove on to North Carolina, perhaps on his way to Florida to visit his mother, before looping back north to Long Island where he visited relatives there. His wife notified authorities. By January 22, he was back in Philadelphia. Police found him sitting in the waiting room of his friend Boney Jones' tire store in Bristol. When questioned a second time by the Secret Service, Byck again denied that he had entertained any designs on the president's life. Rather, he explained, he was very lonely without his family and took the trip impulsively only to meet and talk with someone. He explained that he had a new mission in life to establish lines of communication "between the races and peoples of the world." When Secret Service agents searched his car they found "many 3 x 5 index cards containing threatening statements authored by Byck," many concerning "violent behavior, including suicide," but agents were unable to find any that specifically referred to the President. As a consequence, the U.S. Attorney's office "declined to authorize prosecution due to lack of physical evidence." On January 30, a Secret Service agent testified "during a commitment procedure pertaining to Byck." The court ordered Byck to undergo thirty days of observation at Philadelphia General Hospital after which he was "released to the custody of his mother."[89]

By the end of January 1973, Sam Byck was set on a destructive course in which his problems were, in his mind, rapidly becoming every man's problems: if he could not communicate with his family, he would tackle the communications problems of the world; if he could not salvage his failed marriage, he would save a deteriorating society from the government that, in his view, caused it. The cards were stacked against him, and his only recourse — the only way to salvage a degree of self-respect and release his terrible frustration and anger — was to get the dealer, the nefarious Richard M. Nixon.

Consumed with futile attempts to save his marriage, financial pressures, and acutely depressed, Byck did not surface again politically until August 1973. That's when his wife filed for divorce — the inevitable was happening as he watched helplessly. Someone had to pay.

Nearly four years had passed since his loan application had been denied by the Small Business Administration, and he had never formally responded. Now he wrote angrily to Connecticut Senator Lowell Weicker to complain about the denial, alleging corrupt practices of the SBA were the reason.[90] That same month, August 1973, he wrote another irate letter to the Federal Communications Commission, protesting a radio editorial that endorsed capital punishment.[91] A week or so later, he wrote to the Israeli Consulate, enclosing a map of Egypt on which he had circled the Sinai Peninsula. Above the circled area he had written, "Israelis go home and let my brothers alone." This was reported to the Secret Service. When they questioned him, Byck denied any malign intent, explaining that he felt it was important for him, as a Jew, to let the Israelis know that he wanted peace in the Middle East and that "he cared."[92]

The divorce decree was granted sometime that September. On September 6, Byck was arrested for picketing without a permit in front of the White House. His placard said "Slow down inflation" and called for Nixon's impeachment. After Byck posted a $25 bond, Secret Service agents put him on a bus to Philadelphia. In October and November, Byck submitted numerous applications to the National Park Service requesting permission to demonstrate in front of the White House, but he appeared only on November 26 and 30. During the same period, he was again interviewed by the Secret Service "on several occasions."[93]

In December, he wrote again to Senator Weicker requesting the names and offenses of persons granted executive clemency by President Nixon.[94] During this period, he also wrote to Senator McGovern to protest the senator's vote for Gerald Ford's confirmation as vice president:

> How come you voted to confirm Gerald Ford when you and I both know Ford is Nixon's Echo-ooo-ooo-oo. P.S. From the mind of Ford came Edsels.

Other letters were also written protesting the actions of Philadelphia Mayor Frank Rizzo and the City Council.[95]

On Christmas Eve, apart from his children, Sam Byck played Santa Claus instead to the nation. A lonely, pathetic figure in a Santa Claus costume, he paraded up and down in front of the White House, stopping to ask passing children for their Christmas wishes. He carried a huge placard with the words, "Santa sez," and in bold letters,

ALL I WANT FOR CHRISTMAS IS MY CONSTITUTIONAL RIGHT TO PEACEABLY PETITION MY GOVERNMENT FOR A REDRESS OF GRIEVANCES.

The other side called for the President's impeachment.[96]

Pandora's Box

Another Christmas alone, his forty-fourth birthday looming in another month, Byck began to make specific plans for his own death and the assassination, and the political rationale for both. Isolated except for his tire store friend, Boney, and Boney's family, and frustrated in his attempts to see his children, Byck began to confide in his Sony tape recorder as he paced his apartment late into the winter nights. The tapes ramble as he talked about his love for his children, the unwanted divorce, the fuel shortage, his weight problem (5' 9", 225 pounds) and bad back, his loss of jobs, the racism of the Philadelphia Phillies, his admiration for the late baseball player Roberto Clemente (who had died in a plane crash while working to aid hurricane victims in Puerto Rico), and so forth. Most pathetic was the heartbreaking loss of contact with his children. When he was denied the opportunity to attend his daughter's birthday party due to the presence of his ex-wife's new companion, he hired an airplane to pull a "Happy Birthday" streamer over the neighborhood.

But blame for all that misfortune continued to be redirected into his obsession with the corruption in Washington. Hardly any portion of the federal bureaucracy was spared as he lashed out at the SBA for denying his loan application, the Department of the Interior, the Justice Department, and the Federal Communication Commission for a variety of grievances. But Byck placed most of the blame for the rampant corruption being revealed daily in the Watergate investigation squarely on the shoulders of President Nixon. It was almost as if Nixon had personally denied his loan application. The dingy 1967 Buick he now drove was plastered with "Impeach Nixon" stickers when he picketed the White House for the last time on February 4, 1974.[97]

With Mark Jimmy Essex as his hero, Byck also read about other assassins (he had photocopied a chronology of assassinations from the pages of the *Report to the National Commission on the Causes and Prevention of Violence*), and was intent on making his own death and, simultaneously, the President's, in his words, a "smashing success."[98]

The plan that evolved was, indeed, spectacular, anticipating in chilling detail the September 11 attacks on the World Trade Center and the Pentagon twenty-seven years later. Rather than using the conventional firearms of past assassins, Byck planned to destroy not only the president, but to incinerate a good portion of his entire administration by crashing a fuel-laden commercial jetliner directly into the White House. Byck was not stupid. He understood that a jetliner loaded with fuel could easily become a flying bomb, against which there was no defense if one was willing to die in the process as he was. And he knew it was possible: a week before, an Army private in a stolen helicopter had flown directly onto the White House grounds before being stopped in a hail of gunfire by uniformed Secret Service officers just short of the structure itself. He explained his terrifying plan — that he called "Operation Pandora's Box" — in a calm voice on tape the day before:

> I will try to get the plane aloft and fly it towards the target area, which will be Washington, D.C., the capitol of the most powerful wealthiest nation of the world.... By guise, threats or trickery, I hope to force the pilot to buzz the White House — I mean, sort of dive towards the White House. When the plane is in this position, I will shoot the pilot and then in the last few minutes try to steer the plane into the target, which is the White House.... Whoever dies in Project Pandora Box will be directly attributable to the Watergate scandals ....[99]

Concerned that his actions not be misunderstood, Byck sent copies of the tape to a number of prominent people — for example, the noted conductor Leonard Bernstein, Nobel Prize winner Dr. Jonas Salk, columnist Jack Anderson, Connecticut Senator Abraham Ribicoff, and other well-known persons. He also sent letters to the *Detroit Free Press, Miami News, Atlanta Journal,* and the *Toledo Blade*. Denying that he was a "maniac or a madman," Byck went on to explain that he viewed himself as a political terrorist, like those in Northern Ireland and the Middle East.[100]

Although most of the last tapes he made contain only oblique references to his personal problems, there can be little doubt that those problems propelled him toward his tragic end.[101] On January 30, his birthday, he insisted that he had been a good father and stated resentfully that his ex-wife and lately estranged children — all of whom ignored his birthday — were partially responsible for the action he was about to take.[102] Five days after that, he acknowledged that he had no reason to live now that his family had deserted him.[103] On February 8, he angrily denounced his mother, with whom he had been staying, because she had gone to Florida, adding that she would be returning soon "in a damn hurry."[104]

In his handwritten and unfiled "Last Will," dated February 20, two days before his death, Byck left everything he owned to his only friend Boney

Jones and Boney's wife Ruby. At the bottom of the document he wrote bitterly, "I will each of my children [names deleted] the sum of one dollar each. They have each other and they deserve each other."

His Last Tapes

But what does a man think about, knowing that he has just a few more hours to live? As Byck drove from Philadelphia to Baltimore in the early morning hours of February 22, he talked into his tape recorder. He ruminates about the gas shortage and Nixon's responsibility for it, and worries that he might run out before he reaches his destination, smiling to himself about a newspaper account of "hitchhiker hijacks an airliner." But, more importantly, these melancholy reflections, made lonelier somehow by the thumping windshield wipers in the background, illustrate how the threads of Sam Byck's personal tragedy have been woven into a tapestry of political justification for what he was about to do. "I don't feel as nervous as I thought I should feel," he begins,

> This is the last day of my life, if all goes as according to plan. . . . my watch says 12:30 [A.M.]. . . . I went to Boney's house this evening . . . and, eh, I brought some books over for a couple of the six sick kids, Richard and Sharon. I was very very touched because Richard came over and gave me a hug. I felt very touched. . . . [that] family is one of the most beautiful families I have ever seen, if not the most beautiful family. Having a family like that really makes life worth living and they have shown me the only real kindness that anybody has for years now and what can I say, I will miss them very, very dearly [voice trails off].
>
> Wouldn't that be something if the so-called would-be assassin ran out of gas. Some people would have their lives to congratulate for the energy crisis, including my life. . . . It's now 1:15 A.M., February 22, 1974. Today is Friday, Washington's Birthday . . .
>
> I suspect the way people are acting towards each other with this energy crisis . . . crisis, that's a big joke that, eh, they're acting very mean and rotten towards each other. And, eh, as far as I'm concerned, I would rather try to do something about the world I've lived in then just to try to hang around and . . . and . . . and tolerate some of the injustices and the indignities that I have seen. I don't know if I can live, or if I want to live in the type of world that I see developing with the type of people's emotions and bitterness that I see developing. . . .
>
> I was thinking, of course this is ridiculous, if I really had a choice about life or death, I guess I do have a choice, I'm choosing death. Nobody is forcing me to do it and it's not like that , you know, eh, I don't have any

choice you know, it's going to be either die or I can face, I could face doing it . . . eh . . . I don't have to die right now it's not necessary, but, eh, I don't know if I could go through life, eh, and then when I'm about to die whether it's in an accident or natural you know, from heart attack or, eh, cancer or something like that and I, and I would be a nothing because 1 don't think 1 would amount to anything in this life. I'm not willing to pay the kind of price that you have to pay to be successful without being ambitious and screwing your fellow workers and being a fink and kissing ass and everything like that, I'm not willing to pay that price for success.

But, if I had sort of an after wish I would like to be alive, after I'm dead, I would like to be alive you know, for about a week afterward to see what, eh, what people say and think, not that it makes any difference, I, eh, what they say or think about me, I mean they'll have their own opinions, but I want to see who sheds an honest sincere tear, who's really gonna miss me. I'll tell you something, I'm gonna miss myself. Yeah, I'm not looking forward to dying. I'm gonna miss myself, that's for damn sure. But as Caesar said when he crossed, crossed the Rubicon, "The die is cast." It's not really cast, I mean I can go back very easily. I could probably even, eh, finagle the gun back into Boney's cabinet without him missing it and if not I could always tell him that I was fixin on killing myself and I, eh, got cold feet. He's quite a lovable guy, I'm sure he would understand and wouldn't make too much of a stink about it. It's just a shame there aren't more people like him. If there were, I don't think I, I know I wouldn't be doing what I'm planning to do. . . . I would like to say it's like a horrible nightmare and that, eh, things are happening and, eh, it's just like a average thing here I'm just riding and riding.

Maybe in my own mind I don't believe that I'm gonna go ahead with what I think that I'm gonna go ahead with. That could be you know. I think well, I'll get all the way down here and I'll turn around but I don't know . . . I'll probably go ahead with it. Ain't that awful to talk about killing people and myself dying and just by saying I'll go ahead with it. No, I have many reasons for going ahead with it . . . .

How 'bout that. We're gonna make it in with the needle touching empty, I guess. It would be a hell of a thing if they didn't have any gas and I'd have to wind up hitchhiking, eh, hitchhiking to the airport and attempting to, eh, hijack an airliner. Hitchhiker, a hitchhiker hijacks an airliner. That would be beautiful . . . .

I don't think I'm gonna turn back and I don't feel like you know my life is passing before me, you know, like the drowning man and all that jazz. I'm, eh, just riding and looking at the trucks and everything and reading the signs. I was thinking really that for all intents and purposes I'm not gonna be around too much longer.

Type II—Rejection 135

I've got another half a dozen hours or so, something like that. But it all boils down to about a half a dozen hours right now. It'll boil down to a lot less in the, you know as time goes by, but right now I hold forty-four illustrious years that have boiled down to about the next half a dozen hours.

The sign just said Baltimore twenty-eight miles. I wonder, I wonder how far the airport is? . . .

. . . I just feel, eh, resigned to what's going to happen. I think I feel that way. I really don't understand my emotions completely. I don't say I'm confused or mixed up. I just am going through this thing just like there is no tomorrow, or at least there'll be, eh, no there'll be no tomorrow because it's after twelve, after midnight. So, everything that's happening will be and, eh, this is the last time, it's almost two o'clock [a.m.] I guess or it's a little after two o'clock. And I'm gonna do this thing step by step and find out just how far I'm gonna get along with it, but eh, there's no malice in my heart. I feel that I'm doing something that just has to be *done for,* eh . . . for, eh . . . if it doesn't we're in an awful shape. I don't know. It's just I can't see the world that . . . eh . . . is going on around me. So . . . eh, that's that.

Now I'm going into the Maryland House [a restaurant] and . . . eh . . . have what should be my last meal. The condemned man's meal. The food in this place stinks anyhow. Oh, well, talk to you in a minute.

After paying for his food, Byck had only $1.90 in loose change left. He continues:

I suspect there will be some people that will say oh my, if I had done this and this wouldn't have happened and all the regrets and the remorse. I guess there will be some that will feel that way. Well, I don't know for sure whether it will have happened or not. All I know is that I'm a rather determined fellow and that I hold and prize things more dearly than the things that most people hold and prize dearly. Like, eh, the tangible things that they care about, eh, so-called good things that make up the good life. I think . . . eh . . . this is nice it's nice to have a good life since I really believe that you only go around once and that there is no hereafter for me or anybody for that matter. So, I feel that you should have a good life, but what price are you willing to pay? Are you willing to pay for these so-called good things with, eh, your dignity and your honor and your liberty? I . . . eh . . . I am not willing to pay this price and so I do what I am afraid to do but I do what I know must be done by somebody, and if not me, who could that somebody be?

His thoughts then turned to his one true friend:

I only feel sorry for Boney because I know that when he gets over being angry at me for not confiding in him or not saying anything, he'll say to himself that he probably thought that he could have stopped me. But that's not really true because you see there's no way of knowing, at least there wasn't for me, I didn't get that cruel smirk on my lips and that dark look in my eyes and do all kinds of weirdo type of things. No, I was just feeling fairly well-resigned, I guess is the word, and I just . . . eh . . . went ahead and did it and there were no outward signs or any inward signs, you know, such as those and tapping of the toes or tapping of the fingers or what have you. . . . must be almost three o'clock [a.m.]. So, there is no way of . . . eh . . . doing anything about it. There's no way of looking at a man's face and looking and seeing what he has in his mind.

So my dear friend, Boney, you're all right. I don't know if you're all right, but you're as right as anybody I've ever met in this world and if I live to be a thousand I don't think I'll ever meet anybody quite as all right as you are. So, don't feel sorry that you think that there was anybody that could have foreseen what I was gonna do. Most of all myself . . . don't fret. . . .

Then his thoughts turn to his innocent victims:

I . . . eh . . . suspect I'll just go ahead and do it even if it means my self-destruction and unfortunately, the destruction of innocent people who I don't even know. Maybe it's just as well that I don't, and this to me is the real tragedy of this adventure or mission or project or whatever you want to call it. But I guess in just about everything whether it's war or any sort of struggle that the innocent not only die, but in most cases, a lot of the innocent. . . . Well, in this case I'm trying to do the best I can to prevent as many deaths as I can.

It's three-thirty [a.m.], I'm in Baltimore and you wouldn't believe it, but people are lined up in front of the gas pumps now. . . . It's unbelievable

. . . It's, eh, now a quarter after four. Airport areas. This used to be Friendship Airport. That's one thing this world doesn't have enough of or much of, that is friendship. Very unfortunate that a good wholesome guy like me has to kill himself or get himself killed to try to make a point, but if I make the point and if I can show you the futility or show the people the futility of this stupid greed when we live in a world that could be plentiful for everybody. If I could show you that millionaires do not have to be billionaires to be happy, they should not have to be, while other people do without. If that lesson can be learned, and I doubt if it can, it hasn't been learned for thousands of years, but somebody has to resist just somebody has to resist or else there is no end to tyranny.

I'm ending this tape right here. It's, eh, almost five o'clock and I'm parked at the airport and, eh, I think I lost my wallet. So, this really looks like a one-way street now. Maybe there was an element that I would chicken out. So, here I am, almost five o'clock

[Voice trails off in a lengthy pause.]

This will be the last tape that I will make for [unintelligible]. It's now after five o'clock at, eh, Washington Baltimore Airport and I'm trying to get some sleep, would you believe it. I am very tired. I hope if this cannon goes off that I wake up cause I'm sleepy. I didn't sleep all night. Just made it in here without too much gas to spare. Lost my wallet on the way, all I had in there I think was maybe about ten dollars and my drivers license... and my drivers license... and my registration card. I had a hole in my pocket and it went through it. Oh, well, I'm so punchy that I was about to say I'll be glad when this day is over, this night is over... I guess I will.

Someday men will learn to walk upright, someday other men might, might be aware that these people, their brothers have feelings. They don't like to be squeezed, they like to be respected. Someday this may happen; of course I'll never live to see it happen and neither will many, many people that will follow me....

This will be actually the next to the last tape. The other one has just oh, I don't know ... a ... eh ... a couple hundred feet which will be instructions ... eh ... of no, what I want done if possible, if I'm dead, and I suspect I will be, eh, I'd like to be ... eh ... well Boney has everything anyhow. I'm sending him the title to the car and the keys ....

I wonder if they'll [the Secret Service and FBI] figure that I'm a product of these two plots that are going on. One in California with Patricia Hearst and the other in Atlanta with the editor. I wonder if they'll think that all this crap triggered me off. If they do, they're a bunch of damm fools because I've been planning this thing for well over a year. Planning it, thinking about it, trying not to think about it and I realized that at once I had conceived it, once I had conceived the Pandora Box, the Mission Pandora Box that it would be the downfall of me. And so it shall be. It's the end.[105]

Then sitting in his white and beige 1967 Buick in the airport parking lot, Byck records his last tape in a drizzling rain less than an hour before his death. In it he dwells on his political rationale:

It's a quarter to six and I'll be moving toward the airport ... uh ... one hour. If there is a moral to this madness I suspect it may be the expression,

"Am I my brother's keeper?" And the answer would have to be, positively, yes. For we are all brothers and if any one of us is hurting, then we all stand to get hurt.

I've never owned a pistol or even fired a pistol. It's rather strange. I'm not possessed by guns . . . only when I realize[d] it that killing and being killed may have to be done before men begin to respect other men. I think this all begins with the lack of respect. So I've got the gun and the time is beginning to run out on me for it's five of six now. If that flight is ready, it should moving be departing at 7:15. . . . One man's terrorist is another man's patriot. See what happens in Ireland. Who's the patriot and who's the terrorist? It all depends on which side of the fence you happen to be on at the time. Of course, the Israelis call the Arabs terrorists but they forget about [an] organization called the Stern Gang and the IRGUN and that's the way it is when a man has to fight a greater force, and would be ridiculous for him to meet that force head on and have himself destroyed uselessly.

Then he becomes a terrorist. He acts clandestine secret acts and he strikes dirty. And that's what it is about being a terrorist . . . .

I feel not like a hero but like a terrorist. . . . I don't know what they call it when they burn you up — cremated. I think a tombstone that I would like to have is that "He didn't like what he saw and he decided to do something about it." I just wish that I don't get to be known as a . . . uh . . . maniac or a madman. There are a lot of things I am, but these are two things that I'm not, a maniac or a madman.

He concludes with a very revealing explanation of his motive:

It's always easy for a . . . huh . . . the authorities to look outward for the causes, say . . . uh . . . this guy acted as a madman, a mad dog, and this guy acted like a maniac, when basically these hostile actions, or at least my hostile actions, are inward, that of being robbed and cheated out of my dignity . . . .

And then follows the projection from personal to political:

. . . and seeing my country being raped and ravished almost before my very eyes. And I won't stand idly by and allow it to happen. They can call me misguided, if they like, but of course being misguided or being guided is only a matter of again, of who is interpreting the action and what side of the fence you are sitting on. I feel that I am guided, that I have a purpose, and I think that I have made it abundantly clear what I think my purpose is. It's always easy for a . . . uh [and the tape ends].[106]

Conclusions

If Samuel Byck had had other options in his personal life, he almost certainly would not have chosen to die as he did. He acknowledged as much when this lonely, unloved man said, "It's just a shame there aren't more people like Boney. . . . if there were. . . . I know I wouldn't be doing what I'm planning to do." He was looking for a way out, a reason to keep living, but was unable to find one. In his view, others had failed him and now they would have to live with horror of what he was about to do.

Byck decided that he had nothing left to live for. So in death he tried to establish his personal worth — a new legacy in death to compensate for his failures and the respect he had been denied in life — through an elaborate political rationalization of his attempt to kill an unpopular and corrupt president. Byck wanted to see himself as a selfless martyr. And like another Type II assassin, Lee Harvey Oswald, he hoped to place the burden of guilt for his actions on the real *personal* sources of his unhappiness — the wife who divorced him, the children who now refused to see him, and an indifferent mother who had deserted him in his time of need for a Florida vacation.

In this context, the anger he directed toward the Small Business Administration, other government agencies, and the president was a symptomatic, rather than a causal, factor in his attempt on the President Nixon's life. This is not to suggest that his political resentments were imagined or delusional, for they were shared by a majority of Americans who applauded Richard Nixon's impending impeachment and his resignation less than six months later. But like Oswald's politics, the intensity of these resentments and the self-destructive way Byck acted upon them reveals the compensatory motives of an angry, depressed and suicidal Type II would-be assassin. But, except for the bravery of the pilot and co-pilot and an off-duty policeman, Byck's plan might have worked and, as he hoped, he would have altered the course of American history.

Notes

1. H. D. Lasswell, *Power and Personality* (1948; reprinted. New York: The Viking Press, 1962).
2. *Ibid.,* pp. 39–58.
3. President's Commission on the Assassination of President Kennedy, *Hearings on the Investigation of the Assassination of President John F. Kennedy* (Washington, DC: U.S. Government Printing Office, 1964), vols. 1–26: testimonies of J. Pic, vols. 11, 12; and Marguerite Oswald, vol. 1, p. 254. Hereafter cited as *Hearings 1964.*
4. *Hearings 1964,* testimonies of Marguerite Oswald, vol. 1, pp. 250–252; and John Pic, vol. 11, pp. 27–29.

5. *Hearings 1964,* R. Hartogs, Deposition (Dep.) 1.
6. *Hearings 1964,* J. Carro, Dep. 1, pp. 3, 6; E. Siegel, Dep. 1, p. 3.
7. *Hearings 1964,* J. Carro, Dep. 1, p. 2.
8. *Hearings 1964,* testimony of J. Pic, vol. 11, p. 809.
9. *Hearings 1964,* E. Siegel, Dep. 1, pp. 2, 3.
10. *Hearings 1964,* testimonies of K. Thornley, vol. 11, pp. 89, 101; A. D. Graef, vol. 8, p. 318; J. R. Heindell, vol. 8, p. 318; M. Osborne, vol. 8, p. 321; and J. E. Donovan, vol. 8, pp. 292–293.
11. *Hearings 1964,* testimony of D. Powers, vol. 8, pp. 270, 287.
12. *Hearings 1964,* testimonies of D. Powers, vol. 8, p. 277; and K. Thornley, vol. 11, pp. 93-94.
13. *Hearings 1964,* testimonies of D. Murray, vol. 8, p. 319; J. Botelho, vol. 8, p. 315; and M. Osborne, vol. 8, p. 321.
14. *Hearings 1964,* A. Folsom, Dep. 1, pp. 31–34, and vol. 8, p. 308.
15. President's Commission on the Assassination of President Kennedy, *Report of the President's Commission on the Assassination of President John F. Kennedy* (Washington, DC: U.S. Government Printing Office, 1964,1967), Commission Exhibit 295, pp. 4, 7, 8; Commission Exhibit 294, p. 1. Hereafter cited *Report 1964.*
16. *Report 1964,* CE 24, 1964, pp. 1–2; CE 985.
17. *Report 1964,* CE 985; CE 24; CE 25; and *Hearings 1964,* testimony of Marina Oswald, vol. 5, p. 589.
18. *Report 1964,* CE 24, p. 9.
19. *Report 1964,* CE 92.
20. *Report 1964,* CE 94, p. 1.
21. *Hearings 1964,* testimonies of Marina Oswald, vol. 1, pp. 5–7; and A. D. Graef, vol. 10, pp. 186–189.
22. P. J. McMillan, *Marina and Lee* (New York: Bantam, 1978), pp. 341–342, 350–355, 426, 452–453.
23. *Report 1964,* CE 97, 1964.
24. McMillan, *Marina and Lee, p.* 646, n. 17.
25. *Report 1964,* CE 97.
26. *Report 1964,* CE 133, 134.
27. McMillan, *Marina, p.* 367.
28. *Hearings 1964,* testimony of Marina Oswald, vol. 1, pp. 15–16.
29. U.S. Congress, House, Select Committee on Assassinations, *Hearings on the Investigation of the Assassination of President John F. Kennedy,* 95th Cong., 2d Sess., 1978, vol. 2, pp. 242–249. Hereafter cited as *Hearings 1978.*
30. McMillan, *Marina and Lee, pp.* 373–375.
31. Ibid., pp. 368–369, 376.
32. Ibid., p. 384.
33. Ibid., p. 378.
34. The, improved spelling and writing observed in this note is due to the fact that this is a translation from Oswald's original Russian version.
35. *Report 1964,* CE 1, 1964.
36. McMillan, *Marina and Lee, p.* 380.

37. Ibid., p. 383.
38. Ibid., p. 384.
39. Ibid., p. 394.
40. Ibid., pp. 395–396.
41. *Hearings 1964*, testimony of N. Delgado, vol. 8, pp. 233, 240.
42. *Hearings 1978*, vol. 4, p. 480; Appendix, vol. 10, pp. 123-136.
43. *Hearings 1964*, testimony of A. Alba, vol. 19, p. 220.
44. *Hearings 1964,* testimony of W. Stuckey, vol. 11, pp. 165–166.
45. *Report 1964,* CE 1349, 1964; *Hearings 1978*, statement of G. R. Blakey, vol. 3, p. 3.
46. *Hearings 1978,* statement of G. R. Blakey, vol. 4, pp. 484–485; and vol. 10, pp. 131–132.
47. It has been suggested that during this time in New Orleans, Oswald may have come into contact with other Mafia functionaries through his uncle "Dutz" Murret. Mutter was a bookmaker and was acquainted with a number of persons, such as Ferrie, who were associated with Mafia-related gambling operations in New Orleans. This, combined with organized crime's well-documented antipathy for the Kennedy administration, has led to the speculation that such persons may have conspired with Oswald to kill the president. Although intriguing and seemingly unanswerable questions remain, it is my contention that the circumstances of the assassination do not bear out this claim. For a discussion of the issue see the appendix to *Hearings on the Investigation of the Assassination of President John F. Kennedy* (vol. 9 and vol. 5, 1–471).
48. *Hearings 1978*, vol. 19, pp. 5–35.
49. In his book *Clearing the Air,* Daniel Schorr describes an interview that Fidel Castro granted to a British journalist in July 1967. In that conversation, Castro is quoted as saying that Oswald had made a threat against President Kennedy's life on his second visit to the Cuban Embassy. In particular, Oswald allegedly had said that "someone ought to shoot" the President, adding "maybe I'll try to do it" (Schorr, 1977, p. 177). In April 1978, Castro denied that he made this statement (Hearings, 1978, vol. 3, pp. 273–274). Two months later, Sylvia Duran claimed that she could not remember Oswald's threat but acknowledged that he might have made it because he was extremely angry (Hearings, 1978, vol. 3, pp. 53–54).
50. Ibid., vol. 3, pp. 33–60, 130–147.
51. McMillan, *Marina and Lee, p.* 504.
52. *Hearings 1964,* vol. 25, pp. 768–769.
53. McMillan, *Marina and Lee, pp.* 505–506.
54. *Hearings 1964*, testimony of R. Truly, vol. 3, pp. 216–218.
55. McMillan, *Marina and Lee, p.* 509.
56. *Hearings 1964*, testimonies of George and Jeanne de Mohrenschildt, vol. 9, pp. 233, 309–314; and Ruth Paine, vol. 11, p. 396.
57. McMillan, *Marina and Lee, p.* 511.
58. Ibid., p. 517.
59. Ibid.
60. Ibid., pp. 514–515.

61. Ibid., p. 529.
62. Ibid., pp. 535–537. See also U.S. Congress, House, Subcommittee on Civil and Constitutional Rights of the Committee of the Judiciary, *Hearings on Federal Bureau of Investigation,* 94th Cong., 2d Sess., 1975-1976, serial no. 2, pt. 3: testimony of J. P. Hosty, pt. 3, pp. 124–129. Hereafter cited as *Hearings 1975–1976.*
63. *Report 1964,* CE 103.
64. *Hearings 1975–1976*: testimony of N. L. Fenner, pt. 3, p. 37
65. Ibid.
66. James Hosty later admitted that he saw the note, but recalled it stating, in effect: "If you don't cease bothering my wife I will take appropriate action and report this to proper authorities." Hosty destroyed the note approximately two hours after Oswald's death on November 24. He claimed his superior instructed him to do so. Hosty was quietly disciplined by FBI Director J. Edgar Hoover, but the note was not reported to the Warren Commission and knowledge of it did not become public until July 1975 (Hearings, 1975–1976: testimonies of James B. Adams, pt. 3, pp. 2–5; James P. Hosty, pt. 3, pp. 130–148; Kenneth Howe, pt. 3, pp. 179-180).
67. *Hearings 1964,* testimony of Marina Oswald, vol. 1, pp. 54, 63.
68. *Hearings 1964,* testimony of A. C. Johnson, vol. 10, pp. 297–298.
69. *Hearings 1964,* testimony of Marina Oswald, vol. 1, pp. 46, 63, 65
70. *Report 1964,* CE 1361–1380.
71. *Hearings 1964,* testimony of B. W. Frazier, vol. 2, p. 222.
72. McMillan, *Marina and Lee, pp.* 559–560.
73. Ibid., pp. 562–563.
74. Ibid., p. 564.
75. G. Posner, *Case Closed: Lee Harvey Oswald and the Assassination of JFK* (New York: Random House, 1993).
76. Posner, *Case Closed,* Appendix A, pp. 473–482.
77. U.S. Congress, House, Select Committee on Assassinations, *Report on Findings and Recommendations,* 1979, 95th Cong., 2d Sess., 1979, HR 951828, pt. 2, pp. 6593; D.B. Thomas, *Science and Justice* (March 2001).
78. Had the FBI responded appropriately to the threat, Oswald would have been arrested and either been in custody or under surveillance when the president came to Dallas.
79. Documents, Samuel Byck, Department of Transportation Federal Aviation Administration, *Security Summary* (SE-1600-20) ASE-74-4.
80. Telephone interview [name withheld], March 12, 1979,
81. Ibid.
82. Ibid.; and *Philadelphia Inquirer,* February 23, 1974, A3.
83. Documents, Samuel Byck, Small Business Administration, 1973. Hereafter cited as *SBA Documents.*
84. Letter dated October 22, 1972, Documents, Samuel Byck, United States Secret Service, 1972-1974. Hereafter cited as *Secret Service Documents.*
85. Samuel Byck, Recorded Tapes, Federal Bureau of Investigation, February 21, 1974. Hereafter cited as *Byck tapes.*

86. *Secret Service Documents,* earlier incident described in report of November 21, 1973.
87. According to Norse mythology, Valhalla is the Hall of Odin, where warriors who have died bravely in battle are received.
88. Documents, Samuel Byck, Federal Bureau of Investigation, File No. BA 164170. Hereafter cited as *FBI Documents.*
89. *Secret Service Documents,* report of January 26, 1973.
90. *SBA Documents,* February 8, 1979.
91. Documents, Samuel Byck, Federal Communications Commission, File No. 8310100, C6-1833, August 8, 1973.
92. *Secret Service Documents,* October 12, 1973.
93. *Secret Service Documents,* report of November 21, 1973.
94. Documents, Samuel Byck, Office of Pardon Attorney, U.S. Department of Justice, January 9, 1974.
95. *FBI Documents.*
96. *Secret Service Documents.*
97. *FBI and Secret Service Documents.*
98. *Byck tapes,* February 5, 1974.
99. Ibid., February 21, 1974
100. *FBI Documents.*
101. Ibid., February 5, 1974.
102. Ibid., January 30, 1974.
103. Ibid., February 5, 1974.
104. Ibid., February 8, 1974.
105. Ibid., February 22, 1974.
106. Ibid.

5

Type II—The Feminine Dimension
Lynette Alice Fromme and Sara Jane Moore

> *"Well you know when people around you treat you like a child and pay no attention to the things you say you have to do something."*
> —Lynette Fromme

> *"I did not want to kill somebody, but there comes a point when the only way you can make a statement is to pick up a gun . . . "*—Sara Jane Moore

In 1975, for the first time in American history, two serious attempts were made on a president's life in less than three weeks. Moreover, the attempts were made — again for the first time in American history — by two women. Although classified as Type II subjects, both Lynette Fromme and Sara Jane Moore reveal important distinctions from their male counterparts. Oswald and Byck closely resemble Harold Lasswell's description of the "political personality." Of the two women, only Moore comes close to that description, and then only with some qualifications. Fromme represents a more complex variation of compensatory behavior.

The major dimension of Fromme's behavior is revealed in what some would describe as her obsessive/compulsive commitment to cult leader Charles Manson. Unlike the Type II males, her motive in attacking President Ford was not to attract attention to herself or to make anyone else feel guilty for what she had done. Rather she wanted to be arrested and tried so that Manson could be called as a witness in her defense. With the media attention such a trial would command, Fromme reasoned, Manson's message would, at long last, reach the ears of the world. She viewed him as a Christ figure with a solution for the world's problems. A false belief? Undoubtedly, but as the evidence will show, her misplaced confidence in Manson is well within the range of behavior often observed in persons with strong moral convictions.

Lasswell's "political personality" hypothesis comes closer to explaining the actions of Sara Jane Moore, for she did use a political act to resolve her personal dilemma; she also offered a political rationale for her actions. Moore differs from Oswald and Byck, however, in one important respect: Whereas Oswald and Byck acted, in large part, to place guilt on significant *others* in their lives — specifically the spouses who had rejected them — Moore acted to resolve her *own* guilt stemming from her betrayal of the radical friends she had made while serving as an FBI informant.

Thus there is an important quality that separates these two female subjects from their Type II male counterparts: the *personal* motives of the women are less ego-defensive and more selfless (if one can describe such violent acts as selfless). Fromme wanted to help Manson — the one person who had ever taken her seriously — get the new trial he had been denied; she was convinced that he could clear himself. Similarly, Moore sought the forgiveness of perhaps the first group of people in her life who had ever taken her seriously. In this sense, both women shot at the president as a result of a warped sense of *love* and *concern* — not vindictiveness — for significant others in their lives. It is highly improbable they would have attacked a president neither took very seriously for political reasons. Moore, for example, considered President Ford "a nebbish,"[1] and Fromme viewed him in much the same way — as merely an amiable puppet of the Nixon regime she despised. Each acknowledged the existence of worthier political targets, but it was the assault on the *presidency* — not Gerald Ford — that was required to meet their primary personal objectives.

The one striking similarity between the male and female counterparts is that neither was taken seriously by authorities. Like Oswald and Byck, both Fromme and Moore had provided rather pointed warnings of their potential for violence that were either dismissed or ignored.

* * *

LYNETTE ALICE FROMME (1948–)

In an untitled manuscript, Lynette Fromme describes her introduction to Charles Manson on the beach in Venice, California. Earlier the same day, after an argument, her father had ordered her out of "his" house with instructions "never to come back." Alone and frightened, she sat on a bench clutching her books and her eye makeup, not knowing what to do or where to go. As she sat staring at the ocean through her tears, suddenly, she wrote, "an elfish, dirty-looking creature," flashing a smile "that went from warm daddy to twinkley devil" startled her with, "so your father kicked you out." He talked with her, making her laugh and feel relaxed — strange emotions for this troubled young girl — and then he invited her to go with him:

> He smiled a soft feeling and was on his way. I grabbed my books, running to catch up with him. I didn't know why—I didn't care and I never left.[2]

This episode marks the psychological and spiritual conversion of Lynette Fromme and the beginning of a journey that led through the formation of the Manson "family," the ghoulish Tate-LaBianca murders two years later, and the trial and conviction of Manson and four followers for those murders. The journey ends when a federal judge sentence the twenty-six-year-old Manson disciple to life in prison for the attempted assassination of President Gerald R. Ford on September 5, 1975.

Losing and Finding Daddy

On the surface, Lynette Fromme appears to have had an unremarkable American childhood in the middle-class Los Angeles suburbs of Santa Monica, Westchester, and Redondo Beach. Ballet lessons, baton twirling, cheerleading, beach parties, and the Beach Boys — all are childhood memories. And, like many of her middle-class friends, she graduated from high school in 1967 without any clear idea of who she was or what she wanted to do.

But this typical teenage ambivalence was translated into political terms as the placidity of the 1950s was disrupted by the jarring events of the following decade. Lynette Fromme's generation — the first to be socialized in a television-dominated era of "Howdy Doody" and the "Mouseketeers" — also witnessed on the same flickering black and white screens new and unsettling events. The 1960s of Fromme's youth witnessed unprecedented challenges to authority and the political status quo in American society. For example, she grew up watching scenes on the evening news that, by then, followed these children's programs, of Southern lawmen with snarling dogs beating and fire-hosing civil rights demonstrators. In 1963, when she was fourteen, Martin Luther King, Jr. gave his stirring "I Have A Dream" speech before tens of thousands at the Washington Monument; a few months later President Kennedy was assassinated in Dallas; the following year heavy-handed university officials precipitated a "free-speech movement" at Berkeley that evolved into a nationwide mass protest against the escalating Vietnam War; the same year, 1964, South Central Los Angeles was in flames as blacks rioted against police brutality. By the time she graduated from high school, racial rioting had reached epidemic proportions in Detroit, Newark and other American cities.

It was a period of turmoil and profound moral ambiguity, especially for Fromme's generation. Religion was divided. Most established faiths, with historical predictability, ducked the moral issues and held to a defense of the status quo; others declared God dead but offered no alternative. In this context, it is not surprising that the parents of Lynette Fromme, as the parents of many teenagers of that period, found themselves at odds with their daughter's increasingly independent spirit. It was especially difficult for them because she was a daughter, and the usual sex-related concerns of parents of teenage daughters were aggravated by the new ideological challenges to all authority, including their own.

The disputes between Lynette and her father became particularly bitter. A no-nonsense aeronautical engineer, her father did not adjust easily to change. Moreover, it was difficult for him to take Lynette seriously. A delicate, freckled-faced little girl with big wide eyes and fluffy auburn hair, Lynette always seemed like the cute little baton twirler she no longer was, nor wanted to be. Her more important problem was that she had no idea what she wanted to be, or do, except find acceptance and understanding. After a brief enrollment at El Camino Junior College and a final explosive argument with her father, the saga described at the beginning of this chapter began.

In the bizarre life she was to live with Manson, Fromme's commitment to the bearded, sparkling-eyed guru was complete. In Manson, she found the father she always wanted, one who loved and accepted her; he was also a spiritual force who explained and made sense of a very confusing world. These were the qualities that were much more important than the sexual relationship that aroused the curiosity of so many commentators of that period. Even in the sexual context, Lynette seems to have viewed Manson always more as a father figure than a lover: "I felt so close to him and layed my head on his shoulder, wanting a daddy to hold me . . . " she wrote later. "As all daughters I had wanted all the attention I could get from my daddy."[3]

Nor was Manson the only beneficiary of her need for fatherly acceptance. Prior to the Tate-LaBianca murders, when the Manson family lived at a vacated movie ranch, east of Los Angeles in the California desert, Lynette established a close relationship with the eighty-one-year-old owner of the ranch, George Spahn. Later, before the assassination attempt in Sacramento, she had an ongoing friendship with Harold Boro, a retired man of sixty-five who had befriended her. Boro loaned her money, his car and, unwittingly, the .45 caliber pistol she used to threaten the President's life. In the documentary film, *Manson,* Fromme states: "Every girl should have a daddy just like Charlie."

Manson's Influence

Closely related to Manson's importance as a stabilizing influence in her chaotic life was her belief that he literally represented Jesus Christ. Manson grew up in the hell-fire-and-hallelujah fundamentalism the West Virginia-southern Ohio Bible Belt. Before drifting west, he was well acquainted with the significance of the prophesied Second Coming of Christ. According to these prophecies, those who had accepted Christ as their personal Savior were, so to speak, "born again" and Heaven bound. They would live with Christ in a paradise created when Satan was destroyed at the cataclysmic Battle of Armageddon. But for Lynette, Christ had already returned for the second time in the form of Manson; the battle against evil — as defined by Charlie — was about to begin. Manson's bearded Christ-like appearance, piercing eyes, and mystical utterances added to this captivating aura of spiritual authenticity.

Thus, Manson's family struck at the decadence of Hollywood affluence in the Tate-LaBianca murder spree hoping to precipitate a racial Armageddon of whites against blacks that Manson envisioned. Evidence was planted at the murder scene suggesting the crime was committed by blacks. In response, Manson predicted that a race war would break out in America that blacks would win. Manson said that he would quickly fill a leadership vacuum created by the triumphant, but racially inferior, blacks' inability to govern.[4] The scenario unraveled for Manson, however, when he was arrested and convicted for the Tate-LaBianca murders even though he did not participate directly in them. That fact — that Manson actually killed no one — was the reason Fromme believed he was being unjustly tried for a crime he did not commit.

Mourning his anticipated fate, Fromme and other followers, at times with heads shaved, sat outside the courthouse in Los Angeles during the entire lengthy trial, their foreheads scarred with X's they had sliced into their flesh.[5] Nor would the mourners ever forget that during this time, President Nixon, like the Pharisees of old, publicly declared his belief in Manson's guilt. In Fromme's mind the injustice of it all held the same significance as the Crucifixion.

Her Mission

After Manson's conviction and incarceration, Lynette Fromme's mission in life was set: she was to resurrect Charlie as the Christ figure who could save the world from the destructive course it was on. Moving to the state capital in Sacramento, she shared an apartment at 1725 P Street, near the capital complex, with two other Manson disciples, Sandra Good and Susan

Murphy. The women lived quietly, eschewing the drugs, alcohol, and free-wheeling sex of an earlier period for an ascetic life of meditation, organic gardening, and vegetarian food. They were described by their landlord as "model tenants."[6] With a small income based on Sandra Good's trust fund and handouts from various friends around the country, they threw themselves into plans to combat the destructive influences that Charlie had warned about, in particular, the choking industrial pollution in American cities, the clear-cutting of national forests, and, especially, the logging of the irreplaceable redwood forests of northern California.

With such concerns in mind, the three set up among themselves a self-styled "International People's Court of Retribution" whose purpose was to begin to kill and terrorize polluters until their destructive activities ceased.[7] The initial targets were selected corporate executives and their wives. To carry out this planned terrorist campaign, they sought support from people they knew around the country. For example, in a tape sent to a friend, Edward Vandervort, in Pennsylvania, Fromme instructed him on how to make a terrorist phone call:

> Muster up your meanest voice, think of your dying world, and call. Speak slowly and precisely and clearly and as mean and frightening as you can.... I know you'll do it good.... Tell them the following:
>
> "Your product or activity (or you may mention the name of it) is killing, poisoning the world. There is no excuse for it. (Now say this slowly): If you do not stop killing us, Manson will send for your heart. If the company pollutes the air (you may say lungs) close the shop. Flee the country. Or watch your own blood spell out your crime on the wall. Remember Sharon Tate."[8]

In a follow-up letter postmarked June 17, 1975, Lynette wrote, in part, to the same party:

> Ed,
> I just sent you a list of corporations to call. This one is to take care of NOW. William Roesch — President of Kaiser Company, makers of more forms of pollution than I can count — sellers of lives and souls-killers of U.S. more than anyone.
> William Roesch.
> With an address in Bridgeville, Pennsylvania. Do not threaten him first. Here's How.
> 1. Case it out. Check for kids. We want to avoid hurting any kids. But get him and the wife however you can. Use gloves. Be careful and sly. Could wear paint clothes. Take with you an aerosol can of BAN deodor-

ant. Take also a can of pink paint and a large paint brush. When bodies are dead, paint as much as you can of them with PINK paint. (faces, arms, etc.) Put the aerosol can in the man's mouth.[9]

Then in a departure from the earlier taped instruction in which she mentioned Sharon Tate, Fromme now advised: "Do not write anything about *Helter Skelter* or any other words you got out of that book. Or anything about Manson."[10]

Thus a plan for a terrorist campaign directed at corporate executives, which would follow the European terrorist model being implemented at that time in Germany and Italy, began to unfold. Government leaders were curiously excluded from the hit list of top executives and their wives. Politicians were viewed as merely the lackeys of the corporate elite that ruled the country. This conception of political power was hardly novel in its Marxist perspective. Indeed, it was one shared by the radical Symbionese Liberation Army was holding Patty Hearst captive at this time — although there was no evidence linking Fromme or her associates with the SLA — and the "Unabomber," Ted Kaczynski..

But her Pennsylvania collaborator proved reluctant to implement this scheme. Frustrated, Fromme came to the conclusion that such plans could not be implemented without Manson. Only he could command the kind of commitment necessary for a true revolution.

With that in mind, she wrote sometime during June 1975 to Los Angeles Supreme Court Judge Raymond Choate who was the presiding judge at Manson's trial. She told the judge that Manson, with whom she maintained a regular correspondence, had asked her to visit the judge to request that he reduce the convicted killer's sentence. Fromme went on to say that she had failed to do that and apologized. The judge thought little about the letter until a month later when he received an unsettling phone call from Lynette. In this conversation, he reported that she inquired about him and his four children and then went on in a sinister voice to ask about how he felt about all the killing in Vietnam and the "killing of the ecology" in this country and the rest of the world. "She said she wanted to talk to me," he said, "because she was going to do something desperate. At first I thought she meant she was going to kill herself, but she specifically said she didn't mean suicide." Choate told police he thought she might have been threatening him and his family but could not be sure.[11] She was, of course.

Still nothing actually happened. Her threats were dismissed by authorities. As Fromme explained later, no one would take her seriously, no one would listen.

About this time, Lynette and her roommate Sandra Good began to wear red robes to draw attention to their concerns and tried without much success to get stories about their mission in the press. The red attire, Lynette explained, was to signify a new religious order that would pray for Manson's release/resurrection from prison. "We're nuns now," she explained,

> and we wear red robes. We're waiting for our Lord [Manson] and there's only one thing to do before he comes off the cross [prison], and that's clean up the earth. Our red robes are an example of new morality. We must clean up the air, the water and the land. They're red with sacrifice, the blood of sacrifice.[12]

Fromme and Good, with missionary zeal, hoped to save as much of the world as possible in order to hasten the Second Coming of Christ, who, they insisted, was the imprisoned Manson. In their minds salvation was possible only through the shed blood of Christ and His resurrection from the tomb of San Quentin. Still the press's interest in their bizarre attire and curious purpose was short-lived, and within a day or two, the two proselytizers found themselves in the same shaded obscurity of the white frame tenement house on P Street.

In July, after a sharp increase in correspondence from Manson,[13] Lynette asked a Sacramento reporter to do a story on a "press release" she claimed Manson had sent her. The thrust of the letter was an attack on President Nixon. It read in part:

> Nixon declared the Manson family guilty before the trial was over, leaving them no defense. All laws were broken to put Manson in prison.
>
> If Nixon's reality wearing a Ford face continues to run this country against the law without any real truth, trust and faith if Manson is not allowed to explain what you are too sheltered to face, your homes will be bloodier than the Tate-LaBianca houses and My Lai put together.

The last line proved to be significant: *"It will take a courtroom to explain it"* (emphasis added).[14] When the reporter refused to do the story, Fromme angrily warned him, "It's your life that's on the line — that message has got to go out."[15]

Shortly after this incident, on August 2, 1975, Lynette wrote to a writer. Charles Rossie had sought an interview with Manson the year before but was refused. Manson sent the request to Fromme and now, with his permission, she wrote to Rossie. The letter is important because it provides much insight into what was motivating Lynette throughout the summer of 1975. Her hope was that Rossie, as a last resort, would provide the media exposure for Manson's ideas. Her hope was such exposure would generate popular support for a new trial for the convicted killer. She wrote in part:

Type II—The Feminine Dimension 153

I am enclosing a double sided statement concerning both Nixon and what will happen to Los Angeles, even as I find it unlikely that you will use or pass this grim warning.[16]

In an obvious reference to Jesus Christ, she went on to describe Manson's qualities and the hope he held out to a troubled world:

I am certain that you could find in history men with as strange and mystical, individual and yet all-encompassing qualities as Manson, if one could only think to compare. A braver (real) man would take a good long look at a phenomenon to see not what others think or fear about it — but WHAT IS. This is difficult for the schooled mind to see. . . . the American mind is left blocked by dozens of already tried solutions, to the OVERALL problems, that have fizzled.[17]

Then she exhorted Rossie with these words:

As a member of the media it is your responsibility to take into consideration the thought that the Man Family has presented. [On other occasions, Fromme had attached great spiritual significance to Manson's name — Man's Son.]

She continued with a condemnation of the "old school of thought" and the decadence of American life style represented in Tennessee Williams' plays. But, she contended, there is hope:

There is around the corner of evolution a new experience, awareness and perception beyond anything we have yet experienced and this itself is so feared that it has been locked up [by the ruling corporate elite]. The death of an old thought is the completion of a long line of grandmother's ways, and hard for most to let go of.[18]

"The media CAN be used," she continued,

"to unwind the tangles of a world running in circles toward what it fears most. Manson can *explain* the self-destructive thought. He can *explain* the Christ thought" (emphasis added). But he must have the opportunity to bring this message of salvation to the world, she continued, otherwise human lives will terminate in the "drug store[s], booze bottles and morgues" of a decadent, materialistic society.[19]

The first step in removing the "concrete billboard cancer reality killing the world," according to Fromme, was to put Nixon and the Pope in a *courtroom with Manson and family* and we will see what has been running our ignorances, what truth has been kept in closets, and who are the real servants of the people and earth. . . . Manson can explain it. . . . It is an exceptional man who tells the truth others do not want to hear. Those of us not exceptional, caught up in foolish formalities signifying nothing, may learn to face ourselves through him-but only while he lives. If he dies *[or remains silenced behind bars],* the truth along with him dies.

The urgency of her appeal was conveyed in a threat: "If [Manson is] not allowed to explain, there will be many more young murderers, beginning with the person typing this letter." In a postscript, Fromme expressed her desire to debate Vincent Bugliosi, Manson's prosecutor and the author of the book, *Helter Skelter.* Bugliosis, she claimed, lied during the trial and grossly misrepresented Manson and the family. She went on to suggest that Rossie arrange a talk show appearance with Bugliosi, Sandra Good, and herself on CBS.[20]

Targeting President Ford

Before Rossie could respond, a frustrated and very discouraged Lynette Fromme learned that President Ford would be visiting Sacramento. All other means of obtaining the sought-after forum for Manson had failed. But the president's arrival presented a new opportunity. As the president and his entourage checked into the Senator Hotel adjacent to the Capitol Complex, Lynette Fromme, with her borrowed .45 caliber automatic and red robe, prepared for their anticipated rendezvous the next day.

After a breakfast meeting the following morning, the President left the hotel at 9:55 A.M. to walk across the attractively landscaped Capitol grounds to meet California governor Jerry Brown. As the affable Ford smiled and waved at onlookers, he noticed a small childlike woman standing to his left. The president noticed her red dress and turban before she reached under the robe and quickly leveled the ugly looking weapon directly at his genitals. She was, he estimated, "approximately two feet from me" when a bodyguard grabbed the weapon, wrenching the would-be assassin to the ground. Surrounded by a flying wedge of Secret Service agents, Ford was hustled out of danger toward the Capitol.[21]

It is questionable whether Fromme intended to kill the president. Her frustration had never been directed specifically at Ford except to acknowledge that he was simply another willing instrument of the ruling corporate elite. All her efforts over the past few months had been directed toward gaining the kind of exposure that would, she hoped, lead to a new trial for

Type II—The Feminine Dimension

Manson. There was little to be gained in killing the president even in retribution — except perhaps in the sense that he was a Nixon surrogate who had pardoned the widely condemned former president. The hatred for Nixon among Manson followers was highly personalized. Ford was no Nixon, but he would serve the purpose.

Fromme aimed a loaded weapon at the president in order to focus the nation's attention on her subsequent trial. As she explained the day after her arrest: "Well you know when people around you treat you like a child and pay no attention to the things you say you have to do something."[22] A major witness in her defense, she assumed, would be Charles Manson, with the forum he needed to gain his pardon and save the world. In a pre-trial interview with the press, Lynette explained once more that the world would continue on its destructive course "until our Christ is taken off the cross." She added that Charlie "could do a lot" for the world if given the chance.[23]

The Trial

Lynette Fromme wanted a political trial on the order of the Chicago Seven. She intended to represent herself, call her own witnesses, and say whatever she had on her mind. That didn't work. U.S. District Court Judge Thomas J. McBride denied her request and ordered that she be represented by a court-appointed attorney. Fromme responded angrily by dismissing the appointed attorney. It was only with great reluctance that she accepted another. After repeated and disruptive attempts to speak in her own behalf, she was finally ordered removed from the courtroom.

At that point, she tried unsuccessfully to plead guilty; when that motion was denied, she announced that she refused to participate in the trial. She watched most of the proceedings in a cell on closed-circuit television. This, of course, made her defense most difficult. Repeated opportunities were provided for her to testify, but she refused unless she could do so on her terms. The following was typical of the exchanges that occurred throughout the trial:

JUDGE MCBRIDE: "Good morning, Miss Fromme. Do you wish to participate in the trial today?"
MISS FROMME: "No."
On this occasion, the judge inquired whether she intended to waive her right to confront witnesses who testified against her:
MISS FROMME: "Your Honor, I feel all the laws were broken when Manson was put in prison."
JUDGE MCBRIDE: "All right, thank you."

Whereupon the defendant would be escorted from the courtroom.[24]

Fromme's defense was based on the argument that she did not intend to harm the President. Rather her purpose was only to provoke arrest for an incident that would guarantee the widest possible publicity for her cause. The fact that there was no bullet in the chamber of the weapon was cited by her attorney as evidence that her objective was not to harm the president. Similarly, there were arguments back and forth about whether she had actually squeezed the trigger. Witnesses such as William Melcher, assistant district attorney for Los Angeles County, found it difficult to believe that Fromme wanted to kill Ford. Melcher, who had known the defendant since the Manson trial five years earlier, stated in a pretrial hearing that, in his opinion, there was little risk in reducing the $1 million bail to $350,000 because Lynette had what she wanted in the trial — in his words, "the ears of the world." From the moment she was pushed to the ground and disarmed, she kept repeating to her captors, "It didn't go off." Whether she said this defensively as a statement of fact, hoping to avoid further rough treatment, or as an expression of surprise, was a key point of contention in the trial. Soon after her arrest she had explained: "I wasn't going to shoot him. I just wanted to get some attention for a new trial for Charlie and the girls."[25]

That may have been true, but the jury didn't believe her. Fromme was found guilty of attempting to assassinate the president and was sentenced to life in prison just like Charlie.

Conclusions

Whether Lynette Fromme was guilty of attempting to kill the president, as the jury decided, or only was seeking publicity in a terrifying bluff, her fanatical commitment to Charles Manson cannot be questioned. But her view of the decadence, waste, and pollution of modern society could be considered well within the mainstream of social criticism at that time. Her solution, a bizarre version of fundamentalist Christianity to which she was totally committed, is extreme but no more so perhaps than the beliefs of millions of others who live their lives on the basis of some equally curious interpretations of myth and reality extending from the Old Testament to Jonestown and Waco.

Lynette Fromme was a true believer — a person who put nothing above her faith. She would do virtually anything to spread the gospel according to Manson, even if it meant symbolic acts such as the Tate-LaBianca murders or the attempted assassination of a president. To this extent, she possesses some of the qualities of Type I subjects. The major difference between Fromme and the Type I subjects was her uncritical acceptance of the bizarre views of Charles Manson. Her commitment to the bearded-guru-as-savior was something more personal than political, different in degree than the ideologies that motivate and define Type I subjects; it accounts for her highly neurotic emotional dependency on him — a dependency that was, as we have seen, a major unyielding component in virtually all aspects of her life. In this sense Manson defined reality for his followers; his views were accepted as an article of faith, not reason. But that difference can be a fine line, to be sure.

Was such dependency the result of the delusions that characterize Type IV subjects? Hardly, unless we are willing to label all religious and political fanatics who embrace strange beliefs that are without firm empirical support delusional. Are Muslim terrorists delusional, for example, those young boys who blow themselves and their victims to pieces in Israel in the belief that they will be rewarded unlimited sex with virgins in an afterlife?

One is reminded of the sad tale of Nicholas II and Alexandra and how the destruction of Czarist Russia was hastened by Alexandra's total — some would say, irrational — reliance on the Manson-like Rasputin. Like Alexandra, Lynette's religious beliefs imposed a highly selective perceptual screen that enabled her to dismiss or rationalize the evil concealed in the devious mysticism and strange, seemingly supernatural, prescience of her Rasputin. Manson's strange grip on not only Fromme, but on his other disciples, defied logic and common sense. But like the early Christians who died rather than renounce their belief in another bearded vagabond who claimed he was the Son of God, the scorn of the world only strengthened her commitment and, indeed, prompted her to await the president beneath the shade trees in Sacramento.

* * *

SARA JANE MOORE (1930–)

Two and a half weeks after Lynette Fromme leveled a pistol at President Ford in Sacramento, a second attempt was made on his life in San Francisco. As the president, amid heavy security, left the St. Francis Hotel and walked quickly toward his waiting limousine, a shot exploded from across the street. Ford flinched, clutched his chest, and was immediately pushed down and into the back seat of the limousine by his Secret Service detail. Tires squealed as it sped away with the ashen-faced but unharmed president.

Across the street, police had pounced on a heavy-set, middle-aged woman, knocking her to the ground and twisting a .38 caliber revolver from her grasp. It was difficult to believe: another woman, but this time hardly a flower-child.

Growing Up in West Virginia

Sara Jane Kahn was born in Charleston, West Virginia, on February 15, 1930. Her father, Olaf, an engineer, worked for DuPont, one of the many chemical plants that border the Kanahwa River that flows north through the Charleston valley to the Ohio River. Although hardly the lumber and coal baron Sara was later to suggest, her father did provide a comfortable middle-class home for his wife and five children. Her mother Ruth found time, even with five children, to play the violin in the Charleston Chamber Music Society.[26] As a result, the family attended many concerts and other cultural events.

Sally, as she preferred to be called, played the flute in the Stonewall Jackson High School band and was an active member of the school's drama program. Her mother was delighted when she was selected to play the lead in the senior play. Her photograph — that of a slim and pretty, dark-haired girl — appeared in the 1947 high school yearbook in a melodramatic pose from the production. Her childhood dream was to become a famous actress.[27]

Described by her high school friends as quiet and bookish, Sally was a serious student who brought home A's on her report card. She was not drawn toward boys or the frivolities of high school social life. Nonetheless, strains began to develop between her and her father who was, like Lynette Fromme's father, another no-nonsense disciplinarian who regularly attended the Randolph Street Baptist Church with the family. Much to the annoyance of her father, Sally developed an interest in the occult and read widely on the subject during her teenage years.

Van Watson, who owned a neighborhood grocery store — Van's Never Closed Market — recalled that Sally, always with a couple of books tucked under her arm, used to stop by on her way to and from school to buy candy. Unlike another regular at Van's at that time, young Charles Manson, whose mother clerked for Van, Sally seemed serious and responsible to everyone but her father.[28] Finally, completely frustrated with his stern looks and disapproval, Sally ran away from home briefly at the age of sixteen. When she returned, she struck back in a way sure to displease, announcing that she was leaving the fundamentalist confines of the Baptist congregation for the modernist pews of the Episcopalians. It was an act verging on heresy for a fundamentalist Baptist of that time and region and one viewed by her father as being directly associated with her continuing interest in the occult.

Immediately after her high school graduation in 1947, Sally entered nurse's training at St. Francis Hospital, a Roman Catholic institution in Charleston. Although nursing was one of the few professions readily accessible to women at that time, the Catholic affiliation again jarred the exasperated Olaf.

But finding the punitive and unyielding rules of Catholic nuns no easier to bear than her father's, Sally deliberately arranged to have herself expelled before the end of her first year. She accomplished this, according to a source close to the situation, by "doing something that was very indiscreet and uncouth, then telling about it — the sort of thing that was taboo in a Catholic nursing school."[29] The act itself was not revealed.

Type II—The Feminine Dimension 159

Love and Marriage

Next she enlisted in the Women's Army Corps and was serving in Washington, D.C. where she met and impulsively married a young Marine. The marriage ended within a month. For some reason, perhaps the trauma of the experience, she was found wandering about the Capitol, apparently suffering from amnesia. After treatment at Walter Reed Hospital, she was released. This was to be the first of her five tempestuous and unsuccessful marriages.

In 1950, within a week after her first marriage was annulled, she married an Air Force officer and bore him a son and a daughter before a divorce in 1953. A month later, they remarried. Two years and another son later, Sally once again filed for divorce.[30]

In 1958, now living in California, Sally remarried — this time an older, minor executive in the motion picture industry. Finding the care of her three children cumbersome in her new marriage, Sally arranged with her former husband to have them sent to her parents back in Charleston. As part of the arrangement, she promised to send twenty dollars a month to help with the additional expenses. Her payments, always erratic, finally stopped; soon after her ex-husband disappeared.

Overwhelmed with the responsibility of caring for three small children, Olaf Kahn secured a warrant for his daughter's arrest. Still Sally wouldn't help. Finally, weary with attempts to force her cooperation, the Kahns adopted their grandchildren, with Sally's consent, in 1963. Shortly thereafter, Olaf Kahn died. Sally was notified of his death but did not attend the funeral. That was the last her family was to hear of her until her attack on President Ford some twelve years later.[31]

Once free of the maternal responsibilities she never accepted, the ambitious and intelligent Sally studied and soon passed the rigorous examination to become a certified public accountant. The years of intense study had taken their toll, however, and her fourth marriage was deteriorating. Then either through fate or, paradoxically, design, Sally bore a fourth child, a son, just three years after giving up her other children. If the little boy, named for his father, was to mark a new beginning, it failed. Within a year, his parents had separated and his mother, in her haste to wed a prosperous Bay Area physician, had remarried on December 22, 1967 and, unbeknownst to her new husband, without benefit of a divorce from his predecessor.

Now comfortably ensconced in an expensive home in the East Bay suburb of Danville, Sally, putting aside her interest in a fifty-thousand dollar-a-year accounting career, quickly settled into the middle-class vacuity of country club activity.[32] But the reality of the utter purposelessness of this materially comfortable lifestyle began to trouble her. The club and candy-striper mentality of her neighbors bored her; the bridge parties and lunches didn't interest her; and how many San Francisco art shows could a person attend before the clichés, both verbal and on canvas, became unendurable? Feeling her life was without meaning, she became very depressed, separated in 1971, and, in 1973 her fifth marriage was annulled (on the grounds that she had failed to obtain a divorce from her previous husband before she had remarried).

Radical Politics

On her own again, but now—for the first time—with no marriage prospects in sight, Sally used her generous child support payments to put her son in a private school while she took a job as head of the accounting department at a country club in Alamo, California. Withdrawal symptoms soon set in, however, as the day-to-day routine of an accounting department began to wear on her. Failing to open mail, working in the dining room instead of her office, hating the job but refusing to acknowledge it, Sally took out her frustrations on subordinates. Finally it worked. She was fired.

Completely soured on the status-seeking pursuits that had consumed most of her adult life and were reflected most clearly in the occupational hierarchy of her many marriages — enlisted man, officer (twice), business executive, physician — Sally did an about-face, turning now away from men to the street scene of Bay Area radical politics. Searching for a new and different identity and life, she was eventually to discard her pant suits and wedgies, bridge clubs and art shows, for jeans, boots, and leftist politics.

She began a hesitant exploration of this new world that contrasted so starkly with the life she had known. When Patricia Hearst was kidnapped by members of the Symbionese Liberation Army and a ransom was demanded, Sally — who by this time had assumed her mother's maiden name, Moore — volunteered her accounting skills to the "People In Need" organization, a privately funded welfare program for disadvantaged people set up by Randolph Hearst. The program was established in response to the ransom demand of his daughter's kidnappers.[33]

As a result of her work for PIN and her intense curiosity, she met different, fascinating people like ex-convicts — one of them a man called "Popeye" Jackson. She became intrigued with people like Jackson and cultivated his friendship. She had never known anyone like him. A black, streetwise ex-convict with a political perspective, if not ideology, Jackson introduced the sheltered middle-aged woman to, as she described it,

> this murky world of drugs, of wholesale screwing, of filthy language. Frequently, I was the only person at parties who did not openly use drugs. This was the fringes of the [radical] movement and it was really a shock to see how they lived.[34]

Type II—The Feminine Dimension   161

Moore began to attend political rallies and listened intently as radicals such as Kathy Soliah spoke in behalf of the SLA and the need for revolutionary social change in America. She was intrigued as she became aware of the variety of groups that made up the movement, for example, the October League, the Communist Labor Party, the Prairie Fire Organizing Committee, the May First Movement. As she became exposed to the intellectual side of the movement, Sally recalled: "I was learning that there was a whole . . . left movement that had been around all the time, that I lived right here and knew nothing about."[35]

It was during this period of infatuation that she was approached by the FBI. Having observed her contacts with the radicals as a result of her PIN activities, the Bureau asked her to work for it as an informant in April 1974. Moore was flattered, excited by the importance of her task, and not a little amused by the cloak and dagger antics of the agents — "just like a very bad movie script," she said.[36] After forty-four years of middle-class, soap-opera tedium, Sara Jane Moore embarked on a true adventure — a mission of some significance. She recalled her induction: "The picture they [the FBI] painted was the very thing designed to make a nice, middle-class lady go off and save the country."[37]

The FBI gave her instructions to establish contact with and observe the activities of a young man named "Tom" who was suspected of having SLA contacts. They were also interested in any information she could provide on her friend Popeye Jackson, although Jackson was a person they did not take too seriously.

Acceptance and Conversion

Several things occurred as a result of her involvement with the ideologically committed activists (as opposed to ordinary street people). Before long, her view of the groups she was infiltrating began to change as she learned more about them: she began to respect and then even to like them. They accepted her as a human being — not merely a dumpy, middle-aged divorcee — and for perhaps the first time in her life, she was taken seriously. In addition, she began to understand and appreciate that real political radicalism was not based on the drugs and recreational sex of Popeye Jackson's world. In her words:

> I began to see that the leftist people I was working with were not enemies of this country — they were dedicated people working for qualitative change. They were not evil. Yes, they recognized revolution, they were dedicated to the armed overthrow of the Government — because they did not think there was any other way to do it.[38]

She found herself drawn to these people she admired. Moreover, they became her friends.

As her view of the radicals changed, she also became aware, for the first time, of the very real risks involved in what she was doing. She realized that what had begun as a naive little adventure was much more serious:

> I became aware of how dangerous it was in terms of those people [the radicals]. I was looking at people getting arrested on the basis of information like that which I was telling the FBI — I was looking at people getting killed. . . . I was afraid of the Bureau. It kills people.[39]

Rejection, Fear, and Guilt

More important than her fear was the *guilt* she now felt about being an informer, being paid to betray people she genuinely liked and respected. In July 1974, after only three months with the FBI, Sally could take it no more. She confessed to the young man whose activities she had been observing that she was an FBI informant. He found it hard to believe, but after conferring with others, she was condemned and ostracized with the words, "Go make your own way." Cut off from the group, Moore was distraught, realizing now how very dependent upon these people she had become:

> I didn't realize how thoroughly I was going to be isolated. When you're in a group, you're getting mailings, you're talking to people, you're going to meetings. . . . When they cut you off, you're really cut off.[40]

Isolated in what had suddenly become an even more alien and threatening environment, Moore was afraid. And there was some basis for her fear: in a matter of months, school principal Marcus Foster' had been murdered in Oakland by political terrorists, Patty Hearst had been kidnapped, and six SLA members had been shot down in a flaming gun battle in Los Angeles. By this time, Sally had moved into a flat on Guerrero Street in San Francisco's tough Mission District, far from her familiar digs in the suburbs. For a while, she didn't know where to turn. Slipping back into a familiar mode, she even placed an advertisement with a dating service describing herself as a woman who "enjoyed opera, theater, needlework, backpacking, entertaining, a lovely home, her art collection, her wonderful little son and pleasant work." She hoped to attract a "well-educated man who can be comfortable in any atmosphere, who can laugh and be enthusiastic, with a sense of curiosity and wonder at the world."[41]

Her real need, unstated, was rescue from the terrifying world in which she now found herself. Then lonely, depressed, and fearing retribution from the radicals she had betrayed, she chose what, at the time, appeared to be her only option: she went back to the FBI.

When the FBI learned she had blown her cover, she was told that she was no longer of use as an informant and was advised, for her own safety, to remove herself from all contacts with the movement. Now threatened with complete isolation, Sara desperately sought to demonstrate that she was still of some value to the Bureau's surveillance operations. In October 1974, as William and Emily Harris traveled from Pennsylvania back to the Bay Area with Patty Hearst in tow, the FBI decided to recycle Moore as an informant on a limited basis.[42]

But guilt once again began to weigh heavily because her sympathy and loyalty remained with her friends in the radical movement, friends she now both missed and feared. In January 1974, she sought out attorney Charles Garry, who was representing the San Quentin Six, black inmates who had killed prison guards in a failed prison escape. Relating her dilemma, she asked for his advice. According to Moore, Garry suggested that the only way she could possibly regain the confidence of the Left was to confess her sins — not just to the group she had associated with most closely, as she had already done — but to everyone who might have been adversely affected. Moore accepted the advice, contacted various leaders within the movement and, with some shading of detail, made her confession.[43]

The result was predictable: the leadership was somewhat sympathetic, tending to accept the sincerity of her conversion to the faith, but the rank and file was angry — so angry, that they scared poor frightened Sally right back to the unpleasant but better-than-nothing security of the FBI. No longer able to endure the dissonance created by her conflicting emotions, she began to rationalize her FBI affiliation. "I began to see," she explained, "that [keeping up her association with the FBI] was really the only way I could serve the left." Thus this unlikely refugee from East Bay bridge parties became a double agent, informing both the FBI and the radicals of the other's activities. Did this duplicity bother her? Sure, but she said,

> nobody knew I was doubling. There were not two but three Sally Moores operating at that point: one the Sally Moore moving toward armed protest and starting to work with people dedicated to violence, telling no one — not the FBI, not friends on the left; two, the Sally Moore, converted informant, struggling to find acceptance with the theoreticians and "respectable" Communists; and, three, Sally Moore, FBI informant, reporting on who was asking me what about my "past," as well as on the new groups and people I was meeting.[44]

It is clear, however, that the intense conflicts described in this statement could not be endured for long. Pressure at any point would destroy the precarious balance upon which her life now literally depended.

The pressure was to come from the radicals. They demanded that she put her confession in writing. She sought the advice of the FBI, then complied. Ironically, the document, which was read by six movement people, was considered too revealing, and therefore dangerous, and was destroyed to keep it out of the hands of authorities. Shortly afterward, on June 8, 1975, Sally's friend Popeye and his girlfriend were shot and killed as they sat in a car near her apartment. She was distraught and terribly frightened. Although unnamed in her confession, Popeye's identity was apparent to anyone familiar with the movement. Was she responsible? A few nights later, her question was answered when she picked up her telephone to hear an ominous, "You're next." The balance was destroyed; her life was on the line. Accused by the Left, too hot for the FBI (they referred her to the San Francisco police for protection), and aware that accepting police protection was tantamount to an admission of her guilt, Sally was desperately in need of some way to dramatize an undeniable break with the FBI and her true loyalties to the Left. Cut loose from everyone and everything she had identified with, something had to be done to end the terrifying fear, rejection, and isolation of her personal life.[45]

Penance

On September 5, Lynette Fromme had attacked President Ford in Sacramento. By the time the president's San Francisco visit on September 21 and 22 was announced, Sally had decided what she had to do, or so she thought. She had purchased a lethal .44 caliber pistol and practiced with it at a shooting range; the stage was set for the fateful September weekend. When she was finished, she reasoned, no one — not even the most committed ideologue — could ever again question the loyalty and sincerity of her commitment.[46]

As the weekend approached, her anxiety grew. In a surprise raid on Thursday morning, September 18, the FBI had arrested Patty Hearst in the San Francisco apartment of Steve Soliah and Wendy Yoshimura. Moore was in a state of panic, fearing that she would be blamed for the arrest. Two days later, unable to cope with the stress, she called the San Francisco police to say that she was considering a "test" of the presidential security system. She told the police she carried a gun.[47] Her hope, obviously, was to be taken into protective custody — not for the president but for *herself*.

The next morning, Sunday, a policeman interviewed her, confiscated her .44 caliber pistol, and alerted the Secret Service.[48] Late that night, she was interviewed by two Secret Service agents. They incorrectly concluded that she was psychologically incapable of assassination, adding "that she was not of sufficient protective importance to warrant surveillance during the president's visit."[49] She was distraught. They wouldn't take her seriously. One by one her options were being closed; she was desperate. She felt that she had to do something at once to protect herself.

After a sleepless night, she arose on Monday morning, pulled on a pair of yellow polka-dot slacks and cowboy boots, took her nine-year-old son to school, and drove out to her old haunts in middle-class Danville to purchase a .38 caliber Smith and Wesson revolver from a right-wing gun dealer named Mark Fernwood.[50] Still apprehensive and ambivalent about what she planned to do, Sally drove recklessly at excessive speeds back to the city while loading the gun, hoping to attract attention and arrest. But it didn't work. She arrived in the city, parked her car, and walked to the St. Francis Hotel. Asked about her thoughts while she stood waiting for the president to appear, Moore described her continuing ambivalence:

> There was a point when anything could have stopped me and almost did. The most trivial little thing and I would have said, "Oh this is ludicrous. What am I doing standing here?" ... There was a point whe[n] I was trapped.... I was actually up on the ropes, my hand in my purse, my finger on the trigger and the hammer back on the gun. I couldn't move, even if I had wanted to leave. I did try to leave once, but the crowd was just so tight.... There was a point where I thought, "This has to be the most ridiculous thing I have done in my entire life. What the hell am I doing here, getting ready to shoot the President?" I turned around to leave. Couldn't get through the crowds.[51]

Moore stood for three hours outside the St. Francis Hotel waiting for the president to emerge. After a luncheon speech to the World Affairs Council. Ford finally appeared at 3:30 P.M. — shortly before the time Sally had decided to leave to pick up her son after school. She raised the pistol and fired in what was less an attempt to kill than an act of contrition. Her aim was spoiled by a disabled Vietnam veteran who grabbed her arm.

Conclusions

It was such ambivalence that seemed to have been the most distinguishing characteristic of Sally Moore's life. It was reflected in her family relationships, her marriages, her lifestyles, and finally her politics. Although stoutly and consistently asserting her political motive after her arrest, the circumstances of her life reveal that her act was, instead, a means of regaining the personal acceptance she so badly needed from those who had rejected her.

In an almost allegorical explanation of her actions after the arrest, Moore alluded to her personal dilemma and frustration: "It [the assassination attempt] was a kind of ultimate protest against the system. I did not want to kill somebody, but there comes a point when *the only way you can make a statement* is to pick up a gun" (emphasis added).[52] The "statement" Sara Jane Moore wanted to make was not really against the corrupt "system" that Gerald Ford represented (although she undoubtedly shared that opinion). Rather, politics was merely the vehicle for the more important *personal plea* for forgiveness she was making to her radical friends. Having failed in all previous efforts, Moore felt that she had reached the point where only political extremism and personal sacrifice could convey the sincerity of her contrition. To that extent her crime was the compensatory act of a Type II would-be assassin.

Consistent with such reasoning, Moore entered a plea of guilty to the charge of attempted assassination after a psychiatric examination confirmed her competence. Like Fromme, she was given a life sentence. Things had worked out fairly well for her. Satisfied that she had been forgiven, relieved that the shot she fired had missed, Sara Jane Moore serenely began a new phase of her life in prison — a certified revolutionary with impeccable credentials.

Notes

1. Sara Jane Moore, "Playboy Interview," *Playboy,* June 1976, p. 70. Hereafter cited as *Moore interview.*
2. Lynette Fromme, untitled manuscript, *Time,* September 15, 1975, p. 12. Hereafter referred to as *Fromme manuscript.*
3. Ibid.
4. Vincent Bugliosi, with Curt Gentry, *Helter Skelter* (New York: W. W. Norton & Co., 1974).
5. The forehead scars recall another familiar prophecy from the Book of Revelation. In the "last days" before Christ's return — the mark of the "beast" or Antichrist would determine one's fate. Those who accepted the mark became the doomed followers of Satan. It is not clear whether Manson considered himself Christ or the Antichrist. It is certain that, whatever his conception of himself, it was viewed positively by his followers.
6. *Sacramento Bee,* September 17, 1975, B1.
7. *Ibid,* September 12, 1975, A3.
8. *United States v. Lynette Alice Fromme* [November-December 1975], United States District Court for the Eastern District of California, CR. No. 5–75451, vols. 1–10), Exhibit No. 24. Hereafter cited as *Trial Transcripts.*
9. Ibid., pp. 1899–1900.
10. Ibid.
11. *Sacramento Bee,* September 10, 1975, A14.
12. *Fromme manuscript,* p. 17.
13. *Sacramento Bee,* September 7, 1975, A20.

Type II—The Feminine Dimension 167

14. *Trial Transcripts*, p. 1631.
15. Ibid. See also *Fromme manuscript*, p. 17.
16. *Trial Transcripts*, p. 1622.
17. Ibid., pp. 1622–1623.
18. Ibid., pp. 1623–1624.
19. Ibid., p. 1624–1625.
20. Ibid., pp. 1626–1628.
21. Ibid., pp. 2250–2258.
22. *Sacramento Bee,* September 7, 1975, A20.
23. Ibid., September 9, 1975, A3.
24. *Trial Transcripts*, p. 2365.
25. *Sacramento Bee,* September 10, 1975, Al.
26. *Charleston Gazette,* September 24, 1975, A1, B1.
27. Ibid., p. A16.
28. Ibid., September 25, 1975, A1.
29. Ibid., p. A2.
30. Ibid., September 24, 1975, A3.
31. Ibid., September 24–25, 1975, Al, A3.
32. *Los Angeles Times,* September 23, 1975, 1–3.
33. Ibid., p. I–1.
34. Ibid.
35. Ibid.
36. *Moore interview,* p. 78.
37. *Los Angeles Times,* September 23, 1975, I–19.
38. *Moore, interview,* p. 80.
39. Ibid., pp. 80–81.
40. Ibid., p. 82.
41. *Newsweek,* October 6, 1975, 24.
42. *Moore interview*, p. 82.
43. Ibid., p. 82.
44. Ibid., p. 84.
45. Ibid., pp. 84–86.
46. Ibid., p. 72.
47. *Los Angeles Times,* September 25, 1975, I–3, I–29; *Moore interview*, p. 77.
48. Ibid., September 24, 1975, I–1.
49. Ibid., p. 1–18; and September 25, 1975, I–29.
50. Ibid., September 23–24, 1975, I–1, I–3.
51. *Moore interview,* pp. 70–71.
52. Los *Angeles Times,* September 25, 1975, 1–1.

Part 3

Type III

6

Type III—Nihilism
Giuseppe Zangara and
Arthur Herman Bremer

> *"I reached the point where I felt some kind of secret, abnormal, base gratification when I returned to my corner on some awful Petersburg night and felt intensely conscious that again that day I had committed another vile act, that what was done could never be undone again, and then inwardly, secretly I would gnaw, gnaw at myself for it, pestering and sucking the life out of myself until the bitterness eventually turned into some kind of shameful, damned sweetness and finally into a real definite pleasure."*
> —Fyodor Dostoyevsky, Notes from Underground

> *"I don't believe in nothing."*—Giuseppe Zangara

> *"Ask me why I did it and I'd say 'I don't know,' or 'Nothing else to do,' or 'Why not,' or 'I have to kill somebody.'"*—Arthur Bremer

The Type III subjects of this chapter and the next reflect a special kind of psychopathology. What sets them apart from other psychopathic killers such as Theodore Bundy, John Wayne Gacy, and Jeffrey Dahmer is that Bundy, Gacy, and Dahmer were serial killers who directed their very controlled but perverse rage selectively over time at victims who happened to represent some *segment* of society that each hated for reasons that remain obscure.

Bundy chose young women and Gacy and Dahmer killed young men each had seduced. Serial killers enjoy what they do and avoid capture as long as they can.

The rage of the Type III subject is more generalized, more inclusive of the *whole* society from which they are alienated, and it is expressed episodically in one explosive event in which they expect to die with their victims. Unlike serial killers, they are suicidal; also, their victims are selected because they symbolize, or are representative of, a cross-section of society rather than a specific segment. Their victims may be the anonymous randomly selected targets of a sniper, such as Charles Whitman in the clock tower on the University of Texas campus in 1966; Mark Essex on the roof of a New Orleans hotel in 1973; James Huberty who killed men, women, and children at a restaurant in San Ysidro, California in 1983; or they may select well-known political figures who, in their minds, symbolize the society they hate, such as the two politicians selected by the subjects of this chapter, Giuseppe Zangara and Arthur Bremer.

Type III subjects like Zangara and Bremer differ from other assassins and would-be assassins primarily in their perversity. Unlike the truly mentally disordered Type IV subjects discussed in a later chapter, their cognitive processes, their ability to perceive and reason, remained unimpaired. There were fantasies to be sure, but no evidence of the delusions and hallucinations that complicate the lives of those who are truly psychotic. Both Zangara and Bremer were completely aware of what they were doing and understood the consequences of their actions. They expected — indeed wanted — to die with their victims.

Type III subjects led the most isolated lives of all the subjects considered in these pages. They hated society; they were close to no one, and were totally alienated from life. It was from this alienation that their perversity and hostility were nourished and grew into the flowering pathology that defined their existence. So complete was their self-estrangement that their capacity for love or empathy for anyone or anything had simply drained away. Zangara and Bremer knew only what they hated: there was nothing they loved, including themselves. It was this amorphous suicidal rage that was released when they opened fire on their victims. Their actions had no political purpose. Rather, their motives were highly personal: to end their own lives in an outrageous display of nihilistic contempt for a society they hated. *Any* prominent political/ authority figure — regardless of political persuasion — would serve their purposes.

* * *
GIUSEPPE ZANGARA (1900–1933)

The evening of February 15, 1933 was as moonlit and balmy as winter tourists expect February nights in Miami to be. At a little after 9 P.M., president-elect Franklin Delano Roosevelt arrived at an outdoor rally in a light blue Buick touring car that sparkled in the floodlights as it rolled toward the bandstand in Bay Front Park. Roosevelt, speaking from his open car, gave a brief statement about how pleased he was with the warm weather and reception of the Miami crowd. He was finished before a short, swarthy, would-be assassin could position himself in an opening among the taller bystanders to fire the bullets he hoped would end Roosevelt's life.

As Chicago mayor Anton Cermak and other officials moved toward the car to greet Roosevelt, the would-be assassin, still unable to see his smiling and waving intended victim, commandeered a rickety wooden folding chair and from this tottering perch opened fire. A brave woman pushed his arm, spoiling his aim, but five of the deflected bullets tore into the flesh of as many bystanders — striking three in the head, another in the stomach. One of the six bullets struck Mayor Cermak, smashing through his rib cage and tearing into his right lung, Cermak staggered, falling against the president-elect's car, before slipping to the pavement. A stunned Roosevelt miraculously escaped injury. The shooter was immediately mobbed by bystanders before being rescued by the police and hauled off to jail. Cermak died three weeks later.[1]

Two days earlier, on Monday, February 13, Giuseppe Zangara left his hotel room and walked to Davis's Pawn Shop on Miami Avenue and purchased a .32 caliber pistol for eight dollars with the thought that he would take a bus to Washington to assassinate the out-going President Herbert Hoover. The next morning on a walk around the docks, he happened to pick up a newspaper and read that President-elect Franklin D. Roosevelt would arrive in Miami the next day and was scheduled to make a speech that evening at Bay Front Park.[2] Washington is cold and wet in February, he reasoned, so why not remain in balmy Miami and shoot the president-elect instead. Besides, as he observed later, either would due, "Hoover and Roosevelt — everybody the same."[3]

An Unhappy Life

Not much is known about Giuseppe Zangara except what he volunteered after his arrest. He had no friends. Even his uncle, with whom he lived for a year, knew little about him and was unable to add much to the scant details that Zangara had volunteered about himself. He was born in Ferruzzano in southern Italy on September 7, 1900, and lived there until August 18, 1923, when he sailed with his uncle, Vincent Cafaro, for the United States on the ship *Martha Washington.*

The seeds of his alienation and self-imposed isolation that characterized Zangara's life were probably sown when his mother died when he was only two years old. His father soon remarried a widow with six daughters. Giuseppe was, from that point, the outsider in a large peasant family scratching out a difficult existence in rural southern Italy.

At the age of six, Giuseppe's father put him to work to help support the family. Years later, after his arrest, he gave this bitter description of the event in broken English:

> I was two months in school. My father came and take me out like this [makes a rough gesture] and say "You don't need no school. You need to work." He take me out of school. Lawyers ought to punish him — that's the trouble — he send me to school and [then] I don't have this trouble. Government!

Asked if he hated government, Zangara replied "yes" through clenched teeth.[4]

The association between the hostility he felt toward his father and all authority figures provides the clearest indication of Zangara's motives when he opened fire during the political rally at the Bay Front Park in Miami. The "trouble" that Zangara referred to was not his arrest but the stomach pain that had plagued him for as long as he could remember. The chronic condition, Zangara was convinced, was a direct result of being forced to carry heavy bricks and tile as a child. Zangara blamed his condition not only on his father, but seemingly all authority figures, especially wealthy capitalists and heads of state who exploited and made life so difficult for people like himself. So closely entwined were these elements in Zangara's thinking that it was often difficult to determine to whom or to what authorities he was referring in his tirades. For example, after his arrest Zangara was asked why he hated the rich and powerful:

> ZANGARA: Because rich people make me suffer and do this [stomach pain] to me. My father he sent me to school and then make me work.
> QUESTION: Joe, the rich man make you suffer? Since you were how old?
> ZANGARA: Six years old.
> QUESTION: Six years old?
> ZANGARA: Yes, since they sent me to work in a big job.
> QUESTION: What makes your belly burn?
> ZANGARA: Because when I did tile work it hurt me there. It all spoil my machinery. My stomach—all my insides. Everything inside no good.
> QUESTION: All because you worked when you were too young?

ZANGARA: Doctor say so. My father bring me to Doctor. Doctor told my father it spoil me.
QUESTION: The Doctor told your father it would spoil you [or] hurt you?
ZANGARA: Yes.
QUESTION: What did your father say?
ZANGARA: He said nothing because he say he have to send me to work.
QUESTION: Joe, do you like your father or do you hate him? [Do] you love your father?
ZANGARA: I don't know much.
QUESTION: He make you work?
ZANGARA: He didn't have no brains-no-no.[5]

The authoritarian patriarchal culture of rural southern Italy and perhaps his small size — he was barely five feet tall and weighed only 105 pounds — probably prevented him from expressing his resentment directly toward his father. Escape seemed his only option. So at the age of sixteen or seventeen (the records are unclear), he left home to join the Italian army. The discipline and drudgery of soldiering did nothing to diminish his deepening resentment of authority, but it did expand his perspective. The real causes of misery in the world — and the incessant burning in his stomach — were, he now believed, political leaders — those who ruled the system and set the terms of exploitation of little people like himself. Thus, near the end of his enlistment, he decided he would assassinate King Victor Emmanuel III of Italy; but he never got the opportunity.[6]

America

In 1923, Zangara emigrated to the United States, arriving in Philadelphia on September 2". He soon found employment as a bricklayer in Paterson, New Jersey, where he shared a room with his uncle. Making as much as fourteen dollars a day, Zangara lived frugally and saved his money.[7] After a year — what proved to be his last year of any sustained social contact — his uncle decided to marry. Josephine, the new bride, didn't care for her moody little nephew any more than he did her.[8] He moved out and from that time on he lived in almost complete isolation, an irritable recluse who took no part in the boisterous social life of the Italian neighborhood. He didn't smoke, drink red wine, play cards, or seek the company of women like so many men of his age. Nor was he religious; for this atheist, the Pope was just another corrupt man in power. Except for functional conversations, such as those he had with the men he occasionally hired to do subcontract construction work with him, he seems to have hardly spoken to anyone.

His whole life was structured around a hypochondriac's obsession with his health. In 1926, he had his appendix removed after doctors suggested that it might be the source of his stomach problem, but it didn't help. By 1927, he had saved enough money to permit some leisure, and he traveled to New Orleans, hoping the warmer southern climate would ease his pain. It didn't. So he returned to New Jersey and moved in with his uncle again, briefly, at 138 Jersey Street in Paterson. But that didn't work either. He hadn't changed and neither had Josephine. He was asked to leave and did. At that point, he began to work occasionally in Hackensack. His goal was to compile a solid record of employment to present at his upcoming naturalization hearing, and the extra money helped. It worked. Zangara became a naturalized citizen on September 11, 1929 in the common pleas court in Paterson.

After the stock market crash of 1929, jobs were hard to find and wages were low. But Zangara wasn't especially concerned. He knew that industrious and competent bricklayers like himself could usually find work when he needed money. But he hated to work and did as little as possible. Moreover, he had saved enough to live and travel if he lived frugally. He liked to travel, especially to warmer climates. In 1930, he took a ship from New York through the Panama Canal to Los Angeles. But California was a disappointment. Less than a year later, he returned by rail to Miami. After a brief stay there in 1931, he left again for another short visit to Panama. It is likely that he lived no differently on the road than he did in New Jersey. Which is to say he spent much time in his room, leaving only to take brief strolls and occasionally place a bet. He ate at diners and cafeterias — always alone — carefully choosing economical meals. When he returned from Panama, he went back to New Jersey, once more, where he rented two ten-dollar-a-month rooms at 100 Green Street in Hackensack — one to live in, the other he left empty to prevent anyone from moving in next to him.[9]

But he didn't stay long. He returned to Florida by bus in August of 1932, and rented a room at the shabby Colonial Hotel in downtown Miami. In December, he left the hotel to avoid the higher winter rates and moved into a single room at a house on 126 N.E. 5th Street. He ate fifteen-cent meals at Murphy's restaurant a few blocks away. In New Jersey, Zangara had been getting by on about one hundred dollars a month, which he withdrew at regular intervals from a postal savings account he had in Paterson. After arriving in Miami, he tried to supplement his declining savings with a little judicious betting at horse and dog tracks. If his withdrawals are any indication, he seemed to do fairly well. On August 23, 1932, he withdrew two hundred dollars and lived on that and his winnings, presumably, until the end of the year. Then his luck must have changed. On December 30, he withdrew another two hundred dollars. But within a few weeks, he was broke again, and on January 20, he was forced to make another two hundred dollar withdrawal. His last deposit had been made on July 1, 1932.[10] The stomach and now money, Zangara was more frustrated and angrier than usual.

By the second week of February, with less than a hundred dollars left and a stomach that permitted no rest, Zangara decided he was going to get even. He would shoot that "no good capitalist," Herbert Hoover, in Washington. Everybody was saying Hoover was the cause of the unemployment and the soup lines. Moreover, in his present state Zangara was even more convinced that it was because of men like Hoover that he had to endure the constant misery of his burning stomach.

Trial and Execution

After the assassination attempt, Mayor Cermak lingered in the hospital another three weeks in a deteriorating condition. During that time Zangara was tried and convicted on four counts of assault with intent to kill. Five days after the attack, he was sentenced to four consecutive twenty-year terms in prison. He had pleaded guilty, stating that his only regret was that he had missed Roosevelt.[11] His attorney let him testify in his own behalf. It was not a wise move. On the stand, Zangara was at times matter-of-fact and at others defiant. Complaining of his chronic stomach problems, he explained in his broken English, "I decided to kill ... and make him [Roosevelt] suffer. I want to make it fifty-fifty since my stomach hurt I get even with capitalists by kill the President. My stomach hurt long time."[12]

When Judge E. C. Collins asked if he wanted to live or die, Zangara, who was still awaiting a possible second trial for murder depending upon the fate of his victims, replied: "I no care. I sick all time. I just think maybe cops kill me if I kill President. Somebody hit my arm when I try it."[13] The judge asked if he knew what he was doing when he shot at Roosevelt. Scoffing at the idea that he was insane, Zangara answered:

> Sure I know. I gonna kill President. I take picture of President in my pocket. I no want to shoot Cermak or anybody except Roosevelt. I aimed at him. I shoot at him. But somebody move my arm. They fools. They should let me kill him.[14]

Attempting to get at the roots of Zangara's hostility, the judge asked:
"Have the American people been kind to you?"
"No," Zanagara replied.
"Have they mistreated you?"
"Yes. *Everybody*" (emphasis added).
Then his defense attorney asked him if he was sorry for what he did.
"Sure," Zangara replied, "Sorry I no kill him."[15]

On March 6, 1933, Mayor Cermak died and Zangara was immediately indicted for first degree murder. Again, he entered a second remorseless guilty plea. As he stood before Circuit Judge Ely O. Thompson, Zangara, his dark eyes glittering with anger, shouted to the judge: "You give me electric chair. I'm no afraid that chair. You're one of capitalists. You is crook man too. Put me in electric chair. I no care." The judge did. Zangara was sentenced to die in "Old Sparky," the electric chair at the Florida State Penitentiary in Raiford on March 20, only two weeks after his victim died.[16]

On that day, Zangara walked unaided to the electric chair, sat down without assistance, then spotting observers in the witness chamber, shouted, "Lousy capitalists . . . no pictures!" A few moments later, after the shroud was placed over his head, a muffled shout was heard seconds before the first charge burned through his body: "Go ahead. Push the button." With relatives who disavowed him and not a single friend, Zangara's unclaimed remains were buried in an unmarked prison grave.[17]

Conclusions

Zangara's lack of remorse and angry response, "Yes. Everybody," when he was asked if had been mistreated provides the most succinct evidence supporting his Type III classification. Except for the rage within, he was without emotion. Mean, friendless, estranged from all family ties, he was a man who lived in almost complete isolation, angry, depressed, ultimately suicidal, a nihilist brooding over the real and imagined injustices done to him. Unlike the neurotic Type II subjects, there was no love or anxiety-laden emotional attachment to anyone in his lonely, unhappy life. He never dated a woman, never made a friend, and belonged to a union he disliked only in order to work.[18]

Unlike Type I subjects, he embraced no political ideology. When asked about his political beliefs, he stated that he had none. He went on to say that he thought anarchism, socialism, communism, and fascism were all "foolish." In further questioning, he rejected all religious beliefs and the existence of anything resembling an immortal soul. When asked if he believed anything he read, he replied, "I don't believe in nothing. I don't believe in reading books because I don't think [and] I don't like it. . . . I got everything in my mind."[19]

A very troubled man, obviously, but was he insane? A psychiatrist who headed the state sanity commission that examined him concluded there was no evidence of insanity as that term was understood at the time: He intended to kill the president and he understood that doing so was a crime for which he would be punished. His conduct before and after his arrest supported that conclusion. There was also no history of mental illness in his family. The commission concluded that he was a "psychopathic personality" with at least average intelligence. Intrigued by what this angry little man did not believe, his interrogators asked what, if anything, he *did* believe. His reply was, "The land, the sky, the moon — what I see."[20]

Giuseppe Zangara died indifferently, angry only because witnesses were given what he considered to be the privilege of watching. There was nothing inside but his hatred for a world that he believed had mistreated him and the disappointment that his intended victim had survived. Except, perhaps, a perverse satisfaction in the vile act he had committed and the contempt he knew he had stirred in others "until the bitterness eventually turned into some kind of shameful, damned sweetness and finally into a real definite pleasure" — in his own execution.[21]

* * *

ARTHUR HERMAN BREMER (1950–)

In the cold, dismal Milwaukee January of 1972, a marginally-employed young man began what was to be a deadly odyssey that would end some four months and many miles later in a steamy sun-drenched asphalt parking lot in Laurel, Maryland. His victim, Alabama governor and presidential candidate, George Wallace, would recover but would remain paralyzed from the waist down. The bullet that struck his spine and left him a cripple and in constant pain the rest of his life, effectively ended George Wallace's controversial and highly successful political career.[22] As a result, the unlikely George McGovern was able to win the Democratic presidential nomination, setting the stage for the 1972 Democratic equivalent of the Republican debacle of 1964; the incumbent, Richard M. Nixon, was swept into a second term in a major political landslide. Nixon's impressive victory provided the foundation for a fatal arrogance that would, as it had for his predecessor Lyndon Johnson in 1964, lead to Nixon's own self-destructive political downfall in 1974 when he was forced to resign the presidency. President Nixon would learn later that he had, as Wallace's attacker's first choice for assassination, narrowly missed being shot at on an April presidential visit to Canada.

Frustrated in his attempts to kill the president, the would-be assassin later turned his attention, with some reluctance, to the more accessible presidential candidate, George Wallace. Arthur Herman Bremer was an intelligent, at times even thoughtful, occasionally humorous would-be assassin who knew exactly what he was doing and why — and it had nothing to do with the politics of his two intended victims. On a cognitive level, Bremer was as rational as the doctors who later examined him, but his emotions were stunted, leaving him an unfeeling and suicidal person, intent on mass murder or assassination. Like Dostoyevsky's narrator in *Notes From Underground,* and his

Type III predecessor, Giuseppe Zangara, morbid thoughts and acts triggered pleasurable emotions to define the perversity of his life. Distinctions — pleasure and pain, life and death, love and hate — became blurred in Bremer's mind. The origins of Bremer's perversity can be traced to that icy "Petersburg night" of emotional neglect that characterized his childhood.

The Wallace Attack

On the warm, humid Monday afternoon of May 15, 1972, George Wallace, governor of Alabama and presidential candidate, walked to his special bullet-proof podium to address an open-air rally at a Laurel, Maryland shopping center. The Governor's talks followed a well-established format: before he would appear, a country western band would "warm up" the audience as surly and conspicuous security personnel in dark suits — the Secret Service as well as Wallace's personal cadre of Alabama State Troopers scrutinized the shuffling, clapping crowds from behind dark sunglasses; then Wallace would appear and deliver well-rehearsed remarks about the abuses of the "government in Washington,"a Supreme Court that was usurping the powers of the states, and desegregation. Wallace had sanitized his racist appeals since his first national campaign in 1968, but there was no doubt in voters' minds about his hostility toward blacks and the threat of "bloc" voting. Nor was there much doubt among pollsters that he was the most popular Democrat running in the 1972 presidential campaign.

Perhaps, for that reason, the controversial governor was worried about attempts on his life. Earlier in Wheaton, Maryland, he had been heckled badly and afterward he expressed his concern, as he had on numerous other occasions, about the possibility of an assassination attempt. As a precaution, Wallace usually spoke from behind the bullet-proof podium and often wore a bullet-proof vest. That afternoon, the heat and humidity were particularly oppressive, especially on the asphalt parking area where he was to speak, and the Governor decided he would forego the vest. Like the open car in Dallas in 1963, it was a fateful decision.

When Wallace appeared shortly before 4 p.m., the crowd cheered and clapped. Unlike the Wheaton Plaza crowd, there was no noticeable heckling. He launched into the familiar law and order theme that had produced surprisingly strong victories or showings in primary elections in Florida, Pennsylvania, Michigan and Indiana, as well as several deep-South states he had been expected to win easily. The Wallace campaign was rolling, and the fact that he appeared to be the strongest contender on the Democratic ticket was viewed with alarm by liberal Democrats, which, in this case, included most of the party establishment. And with President Nixon's popularity pegged at only 43 percent, even the incumbent recognized that he was vulnerable to the appeals of the pugnacious little governor from Montgomery. George Wallace had become a much more important figure in the 1972 presidential election than many observers, including his would-be assassin, thought possible.

Shortly before the Governor's speech, a pleasant-looking young man sporting a blond crew cut parked his 1967 Rambler Rebel in the shopping center lot and joined the gathering crowd. Arthur Bremer had become a familiar face at recent Wallace rallies. Dressed in red, white, and blue combinations of blazer, shirt, and tie, adorned with huge Wallace campaign buttons, and always smiling beneath silvery sunglasses, Bremer appeared to be one of the Governor's most loyal and enthusiastic supporters — a male Wallace groupie of sorts.[23] Applauding, whistling, and shouting enthusiastically, even in indifferent crowds, Bremer was hard to miss.

When the perspiring candidate concluded his speech, he turned to leave. Then drawn by the shouts of the crowd, he hesitated, then turned back, took off his suit jacket, rolled up his sleeves, and walked toward the cheering throng. As he approached, Bremer shouted, "Over here. Over here." Then as Wallace reached for one out-stretched hand after another, one of those hands suddenly exploded sending a .38 caliber bullet smashing through his midsection. As he fell backward, the explosions continued amid screams of terror as the now grim-faced Bremer continued to fire four more shots hitting his victim in the right arm, shoulder, and chest. One of Wallaces bodyguards reeled sideways and clutching his throat as blood flowed out between his fingers. Another bodyguard and a woman bystander were also wounded before Bremer was wrestled to the ground.[24]

At the arraignment on May 30, Bremer's attorney entered a plea of *Not Guilty by Reason of Insanity* plea to multiple counts of assault with intent to kill and lesser charges.[25] His victims all survived, but the Governor would never walk again. After jury selection and other legal preliminaries, Bremer's trial began on July 31 in the county courthouse in tiny Upper Marlboro, Maryland. Federal charges were also filed against Bremer in Baltimore.

Under Maryland law, the legal standard of "diminished responsibility" was recognized in such crimes. In other words, the prosecution was required to prove that the defendant — in this case, Bremer — did *not* lack "substantial capacity" to appreciate the criminality of his act or to "conform his conduct" to the law and was, therefore, legally sane and responsible for his actions when he shot the governor.[26] If a defendant lacks such capacity, he is considered legally insane and cannot, as a consequence, be held responsible for his crime.

Coming of Age in Milwaukee

Arthur Herman Bremer was born on August 21, 1950, the fourth of five children. A social worker described Arthur's parents as "an amiable, bland, white unsophisticated couple in their late fifties, of modest height, from a low socioeconomic background, with minimal education, born, raised and now living in Milwaukee, Wisconsin."[27] His mother, Sylvia, had a particularly difficult life, and it showed. Abandoned to a foundling home by her unwed mother, and raised under trying circumstances in a threatening and uncertain world, the very real difficulties she experienced as a youngster produced a suspicious, withdrawn woman who was given to erratic hostile outbursts at both her husband and her children. Her husband insulated himself from these attacks with alcohol, which would, in a seemingly never-ending pattern of conflict, result in more hostility from his wife. It was common, for example, for her to lock him out of the house, refuse to prepare meals, and so forth.[28] All this had a marked impact on the children. The older two sons and daughter fled to the streets as soon as possible, and their mistakes and misfortunes are recorded in a long history of difficulties with juvenile authorities in Milwaukee.[29] Each of the three older children had minimal contact with the family after adolescence.

Bill Bremer, Arthur's father, was a well-meaning man who worked regularly and tried in his way to be a good father. He took his boys to parades and once on a vacation to a lake, but the overall atmosphere of the family was either one of conflict or passive resignation to an unhappy situation.

Unlike his older brothers and sister, Arthur did not take to the streets, perhaps because his mother took a special interest in this pretty blond little boy. Seemingly intent on proving to herself that she was a good mother with her fourth child, she subjected him to ritualistic forms of attention that were also completely lacking in warmth and communication. He was toilet-trained, for example, very early by placing him on the toilet every half hour. Thus he was always, in her words, "clean" and, to that extent, proof that she was a good mother.[30] He became a very compliant little boy who "never cried," but also didn't talk until he was four years of age. A caseworker wrote that he was "fed, toileted, clothed on some impersonal, extraneous schedule and never fondled or talked to." His infancy and childhood were characterized by a "gross lack of inter-personal stimulation."[31]

When Sylvia was questioned about events in Arthur's life, the caseworker noted that "she knew more about the condition [and] cleanliness of Arthur's underwear than she did about his age, or whether he had ever had a friend, a toy, an interest, or even a nightmare." Arthur's mother was also very proud that he never asked about sex or masturbated — seemingly unaware of the significance of the long hours Arthur spent alone locked in the bathroom during his adolescence.[32]

There was also little communication of any sort with his father. Bill appeared to be nothing more than a benign nonentity who went to work, brought home his pay, skirmished regularly with his wife over money, and got drunk regularly, to relieve his frustrations. He didn't think much beyond the day-to-day realities of earning a living and getting by. One day was pretty much like the next for Bill, with little prospect of change, so his grasp of things beyond this limited perspective was quite tenuous. He did not understand his children, but, more importantly, he did not seem aware until after Arthur's arrest that there was much to understand. Usually befuddled by outside events when they impinged on his life, he took life a day at a time, passively resigned to the fact that whatever happened, things would go on much as they had before. He speculated after the event that his son's attack on Wallace might not have occurred if the law providing eighteen-year-olds with the vote had been passed earlier.[33]

One consequence of this unreflective, uncommunicative and divisive family was a very withdrawn and emotionally repressed and depressed child who concealed his anxiety under a smiling facade of compliant behavior. By the age of eight or nine, Arthur was beginning to have suicide fantasies, among them, dying under the wheels of a train on the railroad tracks near his home. About this time, he seemed to find solace in a neighborhood church and thought for a time that he would become a Catholic priest. But the family moved, and he never returned to church. As he told a psychiatrist after his arrest, if the family had not moved, "maybe I would have been a priest by now."[34] Whether he would have or not, the move meant the end of perhaps the first positive experience in his life.

The move was unsettling and he had difficult time adjusting to the new school. He failed the fifth grade, but he didn't offer excuses. He failed, he said, because "I did failing work." He blamed himself for most things that went wrong and decided that he would end his life before the age of thirteen.[35] But he didn't. Instead, he entered South Division High School and his years there passed uneventfully. He had few friends, did not date, and, except for a year as a second-string member of the football team, engaged in no school activities.[36] An average student who did not apply his above-average intelligence,[37] Arthur received his diploma in 1968, registering the only known accomplishment in his life.

During his senior year of high school, his parents noticed a marked change in Arthur's passive and compliant behavior. He became, for the first time in his life, irritable and verbally aggressive, complaining about his mother's cooking and making insulting remarks to her about it. A compulsively neat person up until this time, he now refused to keep his room clean. Yet, he demanded clean wash cloths, towels, and bedding two and three times a week. He also became extravagant in his dress, choosing odd colors and outrageous styles. He began to argue with his father over which television programs to watch. It was during this period that Arthur became obsessed with pornography, deliberately leaving pornographic materials scattered about his room to embarrass and anger the mother who still liked to inspect his underwear.[38]

After graduation, he worked at various menial jobs: as a busboy at the Milwaukee Athletic Club and at the swank Pieces of Eight restaurant. In all of these jobs, fellow workers reported that they knew little about him except that he did his job and kept to himself. No one could recall more than a brief conversation with him. One co-worker recalled that Arthur liked to antagonize a supervisor at one of the restaurants by pouring water into glasses from eye level.[39]

But he was bored, much too intelligent to find such jobs fulfilling. So in September 1970, Arthur enrolled at the Milwaukee Technical College. He took courses in psychology, art, writing, and photography, but his grades reflect indifferent performances.[40] His teachers and fellow students recalled little about him. He made no impression on anyone and dropped out after a year.

Falling in Love

While working and taking courses in his indifferent way, Arthur's behavior at home continued its disruptive course with he and his father shouting at one another and, at times, nearly coming to blows during their many arguments. Then it happened; he struck his father and announced that he was moving out.[41] By this time, October 1971, Arthur found a new job as a janitor at the Story Elementary School. The same month, he met his first love, a fifteen-year-old sophomore at West Division High School who worked at Story Elementary as a hall monitor. Arthur was euphoric about the possibilities. He found a cheap apartment he could afford, and began to chart the course for his first romantic adventure.

After a few weeks of furtive meetings in the halls, Arthur, who was twenty-one, worked up the courage to ask the fifteen-year-old hall monitor, Joan Pembrick, for a date — his first — on November 19, 1971. The next day, Saturday, they went to an art museum after missing a movie, then walked around the Lake Michigan shore before going to a restaurant. He was enthralled with her. She was less so with him, mainly because she was annoyed by his prying questions about her personal life. She was also offended by his suggestion that her friends really didn't like her. He urged her to confide in him because, as he explained, he knew a good deal about psychology and psychiatry and would help her get over her "hang ups.".[42]

Joan Pembrick wasn't sure what to make of Arthur, but she was flattered by the attention of this older and presumably more mature man. The attraction was fleeting, however, for she quickly realized that Arthur was not only terribly immature, he was also rude and unmannered. Not only were ordinary table manners missing, this formerly quiet and withdrawn young man now seemed to imagine himself a sex machine, or so he suggested to his young date.

Arthur's clumsy and inane sexual overtures remind one of a comedy routine. His sexual socialization seemed to be based on what he could glean from the "sex comics" pornography that he collected — and it showed. He thought the way to a girl's heart was to show her an arousing display of cartoon characters engaged in a variety of sexual acts. This was accompanied with vulgar language describing the acts with unsubtle references to his own sexual prowess. On one date, for example, at Ms. Pembrick's home, she introduced him to a cousin about her own age. Bremer, who knew neither of the girls very well, began to make what he considered amusing and sexually stimulating remarks about the cousin's "big ass and boobs."[43]

A few days before Christmas 1971, Arthur took his date to a concert featuring the rock group, *Blood, Sweat, and Tears*. He was elated and could hardly contain his excitement. While they were standing in line outside the concert hall, the once painfully shy janitor swept an unknown girl into his arms and kissed her passionately. He was promptly reported to a policeman, who warned him to control himself. Only momentarily chastened, Arthur's attempts to impress his date and her friends continued during the concert as he repeatedly jumped from his seat, swaying back and forth to the music. He shouted his approval and applauded enthusiastically, often at inappropriate times. His date's young friends, who sat in front of the couple, thought Arthur Bremer was the most ridiculous person they had ever met.[44] She was mortified.

Unaware of such appraisals, Arthur's buoyancy continued after the concert when he slyly complained that he could barely walk because of discomfort in the area of his genitals. He went on to explain to his disbelieving companion that he had to take medication to prevent his hugely distended organ from "rupturing." And then he whispered in plaintive tones that he had forgotten to take his pills. The relationship ended abruptly.[45]

These episodes are reminiscent of the film *Taxi Driver* in which Robert DeNiro's superbly acted character, a would-be assassin named Travis Bickle, ineptly attempts to develop a relationship with an attractive political campaign worker.[46] The young woman, with some hesitation, finally agrees to go out with the shy young man and is appalled when he escorts her with prom-night innocence to view a grainy porno film.

Bremer, like his *Taxi Driver* counterpart, was perplexed when the young woman he had tried so hard to impress, refused to see him again. After some five dates and numerous phone conversations, on January 13, 1972, Joan's mother confirmed to Arthur her daughter's wish that he not bother her again.[47]

That same day he went to Casanova Guns and purchased the .38 caliber pistol he would use four months and two days later.[48]

The breakup was devastating for Arthur. The relationship had been, he said, "the happiest time of my life."[49] For young Joan Pembrick, the brief friendship was an embarassing experience best forgotten. Unable to call as a result of her mother's injunction, Arthur decided on a last desperate scheme to get her attention. On January 15, he shaved his head bald except for his sideburns. Then confronting the startled teenager at the high school, he jerked off a knit cap exposing the incongruous bald head gleaming above bushy sideburns and a wide smile. It was shocking, even scary. She hurried past him without a word, convinced more than ever that he was as weird as he looked. It was a different realization for Bremer. At that moment, he realized that the first and only person who had ever meant anything in his empty, unhappy life was gone.[50] He quit his job at the school and retreated like a wounded animal to his drab apartment. There he brooded, starring at a black and white tv, living on cold cereal, bread and peanut butter, and whatever he could scrounge, once again working as a busboy at the Athletic Club to pay the rent. The middle of February he quit he quit his job.[51] His mood was as bleak as the dark Wisconsin winter.

Despair, Perversity, and the Political Targets

During this time, Bremer became preoccupied, once again, with the vivid suicidal fantasies of his youth. On one cold evening, he decided the time had come to act. He attached a noose around his neck and scrawled "KILLER" across his forehead with a blue felt marker. Then pulling his knit cap down to conceal his forehead and buttoning his heavy coat over the noose he proceeded to a Milwaukee diner for a last meal. His plan was to tie the rope to a cross girder of a busy midtown bridge, then shoot himself while perched on the girder so that he would drop to hang as a grisly spectacle for passing commuters. He wanted a public death in a manner that would shock and disgust.

His life was spared by the kindness of a stranger. A waitress smiled and talked easily with this strange young man who ate while perspiring heavily in his knit cap and tightly buttoned winter coat. Moved by her attention, he left a generous tip. Shortly after, as he stood in the middle of the bridge about to get on with his plan, the now off-duty waitress walked by and smiled at him again. Arthur decided not to go through with it.[52]

But the relief was brief and the depression settled back, now accompanied by anger. Suicide wasn't enough. He wanted revenge. A desire to inflict on someone else the pain he had endured for years began to crowd his thoughts.

For what seems to have been the first time, he contemplated a mass murder to accompany his suicide. He thought about hijacking an armored car, and then with a hostage to hold the police at bay, he planned to park the vehicle in a busy intersection and kill as many people as possible with rifle fire through the vehicle's slit windows. This and similar ideas were considered as he brooded in his apartment. Then he decided to broaden his horizons. Instead of a mass killing of ordinary people — after all that waitress had been kind to him — why not kill a celebrity who would ensure even greater notoriety. On March 1, 1972, Arthur Bremer decided he would kill the most prominent person in America, President Richard M. Nixon.[53]

Bremer was not more or less angry with President Nixon than he was with the anonymous pedestrians on the streets of Milwaukee who he had earlier considered killing; nor were Nixon's policies any more offensive to him than the behavior of the Viet Nam war protestors who denounced those policies. He could kill some of them, but who would notice or, more importantly, care? They were marginal to society just as he was. It was only Nixon's *prominence* that made him a preferred victim. A president — any president — symbolized the society he had come to hate, a society that had no place for a loser like Arthur Bremer. He needed an audience for his perversity, and a celebrity like the president would ensure that. Who could remember Charles Whitman's name or even that he had killed and wounded a lot of people at the University of Texas in 1966? But who could forget Lee Harvey Oswald and Sirhan Sirhan? He had read about each of them. Someday, he hoped, people would read about him. It was during this period, that Bremer began to keep a diary to record his thoughts and feelings as he began an odyssey that would crisscross through Michigan, Ontario, and New York as he stalked first the president and then the governor; it would end forty-two days later at the shopping center in Laurel, Maryland.

The Diary

Bremer's diary is important because it provides a first-hand view of what he was thinking about during this period and what were the driving forces behind his actions. Some critics have questioned whether he actually wrote the diary, largely because it was widely believed that he was not that intelligent.[54] Sometime after his trial, a second portion of the diary was found, removing all doubt about its authenticity. Moreover, virtually all the pretrial psychological testing revealed an intelligent, if disturbed, young man who had literary aspirations.[55]

The entire diary was read in court by Bremer's court-appointed attorney with the intent that it would convince the jury that the defendant was mentally ill. But the strategy backfired because what the diary reveals is that its author's frustration and anger were reasoned, controlled, and focused: psychopathological, antisocial, to be sure, but not psychotic.

What also emerges from its pages is a person contemptuous of life, but one who is, at the same time, able to make sophisticated distinctions when humor and irony, rather than hostility, provide a more effective vehicle for his contempt. The diary leaves little doubt that Bremer had carefully considered what he was about to do and completely understood the consequences.

The diary begins on April 4, 1972 and describes his thoughts and experiences as he pursued President Nixon in Canada where the president was making a state visit. Driving from one location to another, the stalker never got the chance he needed to carry through with his plans. His random thoughts provide glimpses of a complex, alienated but reflective person who was in complete control of his actions. His frequently misspelled diary reveals a universal contempt for himself and society, a well-developed, if bizarre, sense of humor and irony, and the deep frustrations of an empty, joyless life.

For example, Bremer was disdainful of the Nixon protestors in Canada who were milling around waving placards and chanting slogans and, not incidentally, frustrating his efforts to get close to the president when he wrote,

> They'se nothing. There the new establishmen. To be a rebel today you have to keep a job, wear a suit [as he was] & stay apolitical. Now THAT'S REBELLION!"[56]

Later he recorded these observations about a demonstration leader:

> Mr. Bull Horn bounced his voice off the building with a couple of dozen "Nixon Go Home's." He turned to address the crowd. Some other guys spoke to. A wild shouting idiot shouted some senseless phrases. [He was] The kind of guy Hollywood hires to play the wagon train attacking Indian.[57]

Bremer's contempt was often expressed humorously. Concerned that Canadian customs officials might detect his two concealed pistols and ammunition, he took elaborate precautions before crossing the Canadian border. Later he recorded his thoughts as he anxiously drove up to the border station only to be alternately relieved and disappointed by the cursory inspection he received:

> I slowed down to be inspected. Canada had crooked teeth and a moustach. He asked where I was from, where I wanted to go, for how long I wanted to go, for how long and if I had anything to declare. (I was prepared for

Type III—Nihilism 189

this last question, I was going to say, "I declair its a nice day." But I just asked, "What should I declair?").[58]

Once in Ottawa, Bremer had difficulty finding lodging. He had hoped to stay in the same hotel as the press corps so that it would be easier to learn the president's whereabouts and schedule. Finding the press corps hotel full, Bremer had to settle for only a drink at the hotel bar. Already frustrated, he was further annoyed by a bartender who failed to serve the Manhattan he ordered on ice. Dubbing the unfriendly bartender "Ice-less," Bremer describes an incident that occurred moments later when a reporter asked the same bartender for a drink to take back to the press room:

> Ice-less said it was against the rules. A short argument. The reporter lost.
> "That's Canada for you," I said.
> "It's not Canada, it's just this (points to the bar-keeper) fucking cant!" (Reporter replies) Walks quickly away
> "A fucking cant is the best kind of cant to be," I say to the amusement of a fat man in glasses.[59]

In other entries his frustration and anger is expressed directly.. On April 24, 1972, after failing in his plan to kill the president, he scrawled angrily:

> Shit! I am thruerly pissed off. About a million things. Was pissed off befor I couldn't find a pen to write this down. This will be one of the most closely read pages since the [Dead Sea] Scrolls in those caves. And I couldn't find a pen for 40 seconds & went mad. My fuse about burnt. There's gona be an explosion soon. I had it. I want something to happen. I was sopposed to be Dead a week & a day ago. Or at least in a few hours. FUCKING tens-of–1,000's of people & tens-of-millions of $. I'd just like to take some of them with me & Nixy.

Then scrawled in huge letters:

ALL MY EFFORTS & NOTHING CHANGED.

And on the next page:

Just another god Damn failure

He continues:

> But I want em all to know. I want a big shot and not a little fat noise [the

mayor of Milwaukee] I want that god damn [Nixon] tired of writtmg about it. About what I was gonna do about what I failed to do. About what I failed to do again and again. Traveling around like a hobo or some kind of comical character. I'm as important as the start of WWI [the assassin of Archduke Ferdinand]. I just need the little opening & a second of time. Nothing has happened for so long. 3 months [since his girlfriend broke off their relationship]. the 1st person I held a conversation with in 3 months was a near naked girl rubbing my erect penis & she wouldn't let me put it thru her [the reference is to an expensive and unrewarding experience in a New York massage parlor].

Then in large letters:

FAILURES .[60]

By the time of his next entry some ten days later on May 4, 1972, he has seen the film "Clockwork Orange" (and notes that he was "Fantasizing myself as the Alek on the screen . . . "), traveled back to Milwaukee, taken long walks to think and get himself settled down, and decided that he would kill presidential candidate George C. Wallace because the governor was the leading challenger in the polls. He guessed correctly that Wallace would be a more accessible target than the president.[61]

After his Milwaukee respite, the humor reappears as he confidently awaits an opportunity to shoot the Alabama governor on a forthcoming Michigan speaking tour. In the following entry, he laments his new intended victim's lack of international visibility, compares Wallace disparagingly to the late FBI director, J. Edgar Hoover, and mentions other possible more newsworthy events that could push his actions from the front page:

It seems I would of done better for myself to kill the old G-man Hoover, In death, he lays with Presidents. Who the hell ever got buried in "Bama" for being great? He certainly won't be buryed with the snobs in Washington. SHIT! I won't even rate a T.V. enterobtion in Russia or Europe when the news breaks-they never heard of Wallace. If something big in Nam flares up I'll end up at the bottom of the 1st page in America. The editors will say-"Wallace dead? Who cares." He won't get more than 3 minutes on network T.V. news. I don't expect anybody to get a big thobbing erection from the news. You know, a storm in some country we never heard of kills 10,000 people-big deal-pass the beer and what's on T.V. tonight.[62]

A few days later, on May 7, he mockingly speculates about the publicity problem and muses about organizing assassins:

It bothers me that there are about 30 guys in prison now who threatened the Pres & we never heard a thing about 'em. Except that they're in prison.

Maybe what they need is organization. "Make the First Lady a Widow, Inc." "Chicken in Every Pot and Bullet in Every Head, Com., Inc."

They'll hold a national convention every 4 years to pick the exacutioner. A winner will be chosen from the best entry in 40,000 words or less (preferably less) upon the theame "How to Do a Bang-Up Job of Getting People to Notice You" or "Get It Off Your Chest; Make Your Problems Everybody's."[63]

In Dearborn, Michigan, where he stalked Wallace, Bremer describes an amusing scene that occurred when he was hurriedly changing into a suit and tie at a gas station on his way to a Wallace rally. In his haste, he can't find his belt and then speculates about the problem this presents because he has nowhere to hide his pistol. He imagines entering the hall beltless, amid security guards, and having one guard return the pistol that has just dropped down his trouser leg, landing with a thud on the floor with a polite, "Excuse me sir, is this your gun?"[64]

After his arrest, Bremer's humor appeared to escape two doctors who examined him. When one asked him to explain the meaning of the proverb "people who live in glass houses shouldn't throw stones," Arthur dead-panned, "People who live in glass houses shouldn't." The psychiatrist later cited this as an example of "parahumor" or, as he explained, "verbal behavior with some of the form but without the feeling of ordinary jokes or humorous remarks." He claimed it was symptomatic of Bremer's "schizophrenia."[65]

Later a clinical psychologist viewed Bremer's use of irony and self-deprecating humor as evidence of "his egocentricity and grandiosity." Bremer's habit of mockingly referring to his guards as his "entourage" was cited corroborating evidence. On other occasions, confined in his cell, facing a hopeless trial on very serious charges, the curious doctors would comment that he seemed depressed and inquire why. Bremers replies — "It's not easy being a star," or "it's lonely at the top"– were interpreted as further evidence of his "delusions of grandeur."[66]

The Motive

Bremer's primary purpose was to get even, to show his contempt for a society he did not fit into and therefore hated by striking down one of its best known political leaders. But he had no political agenda. Thus, at one point he wrote:

> Ask me why I did it & I'd say 'I don't know,' or 'Nothing else to do,' or 'Why not' or 'I have to kill somebody.'[67]

But Bremer's seeming indifference in these laconic responses is meant to provoke. Here is a man who is about to commit a calculating, cowardly, and vile act for no reason other than he felt like it. That's his point. His act becomes, therefore, that much more outrageous and perverse. His was not the existential estrangement of Albert Camus's murderer, Meursault in *The Stranger*.[68] Not only did Bremer intend to offend and outrage, he wanted the world to witness it and pay for the privilege:

> Hey world! Come here! I wanna talk to ya!
> If I don't kill-if I don't kill myself I want you to pay thru the nose, ears, & belly button for the beginning of this manuscript. The 1st pages are hidden & will preserve a long time. If you don't pay me for them, I got no reason to turn 'em over-understand punk!? One of the reasons for this action is money and you the American (is there another culture in the free world?) public will pay me. The silent majority will be my benifactor in the biggest hijack ever!

Then predicting — or more accurately, hoping — his act would have a contagion effect, causing an epidemic of assassinations, he writes:

> It was kidnapping in the early part of this century. Then hijacking] became popular.... I'm gonna start the next crime binge! HA. HA. And the silent majority will back me all IRONY!! The Way! IRONY!!

Thus in selecting first Nixon and then Wallace as targets, Bremer was in a very real sense aiming at the values — showing his contempt for — of what both men referred to as the "silent majority" of American society.. He recognized that the success of his act hinged on the accuracy of his presumption that Nixon and Wallace were the two most popular leaders in the eyes of most Americans. On one occasion, observing that Democratic candidate George McGovern had moved up in the polls, he expressed some misgivings. "The whole country's going liberal," he wrote.

> You known my biggest failure may be when I kill Wallace. I hope everone screams & hollers and everything!! I hope the rally goes mad!!![69]

The Sanity Question

But was Bremer mad, as his attorney claimed, or was he merely angry? This was the question before the jury at the courthouse in the sleepy, summer heat of tiny Upper Marlboro, Maryland, in July and August 1972. More specifically, was Arthur Bremer mentally ill and, if so, was the illness the reason for his crime? As might have been predicted, the eight psychiatrists and two clinical psychologists who testified at the trial divided on the issue according to whether their testimony was called by the defense or prosecution. All agreed on the symptoms, but disagreed on whether Bremer should be held accountable for his act.

The prosecution argued that Bremer was not only completely aware of what he was doing but that he had thoughtfully weighed the various consequences for himself in the most calculating manner. His methodical planning, adjustment to change, and ability to exercise appropriate restraint throughout the period he stalked Nixon, and then Wallace, were apparent in his own words. Describing one of his several attempts to shoot Nixon in Ottawa, he wrote:

> I didn't want to attrack too much attention standing near the barracade for so long waiting for Nixon. And I was concerned with my appearance [he wore a black business suit and conservative tie] & composure after the bang bangs. I wanted to shock the shit out of the SS [Secret Service] men with my calmness. A little something to be remmened [remembered] by.[70]

Later in Michigan as he stalked Wallace, he speculates about the consequences of his crime and his future:

> Really would feel better if Michigan had a death penalty. The trial might be interesting but after visits from the attorneys... how will I spend my time in my little cell? You know, suicide is a birth right.[71]

The same day he had written, "I am one sick assissin. Pun! Pun!."[72] But was he too "sick" to control his behavior? Hardly. He was calculating, very deliberate in his actions, and on one occasion, at least, compassionate. Following the ranting frustration precipitated by his failure to get close enough to get a shot at President Nixon in Ottawa, Bremer's heart raced with excitement as he stood watching his new alternate, George Wallace, walk toward him after a May 13 rally in Dearborn, Michigan. As Wallace, waving goodbyes to the cheering crowd, walked to within fifteen feet and a pane of glass from Bremer, the would-be assassin was again frustrated but well under control. He described what happened:

> Two fifteen year old girls had gotten in front of me. Their faces were 1 inch from the glass I would shutter with a blunt-nosed bullet. They [would be] blinded and disfigured. I let Wallace go only to spare these 2 stupid

innocent delighted kids. We pounded on the window together at the governor. [There would] be other times.[73]

Throughout the period he stalked Wallace, Bremer frequently reflected on whether he would be killed in the planned attack. On May 8, one week before the shooting, he wrote:

> Gotta leave [Milwaukee] soon. I'll stay here long enought to eat all the food up. Still know weather its trail [trial] & prison for me or bye bye brains. I'll just have to decide that at the last few seconds. Must seceed. Gota.[74]

Then he speculates about the future value of the diary he is keeping and reaches a typical self-deprecating conclusion. Note that his flights of fancy were always well-grounded in a keen sense of reality and irony. First the fancy:

> As late as yesterday I had thought of burying this whole paper [the diary] & reading it after I had gone to Hollywood (I KNOW IT SOUNDS INSANE SO DON'T THINK IT) & making my fortune on the old silver screen.

Then the reality:

> Sure! The same way I was gonna fuck 4 million of New York's finest."

Also, it is important to observe his awareness of the histories of past assassins and their fates — particularly Sirhan Sirhan's. On May 5, he had checked out two books on Robert Kennedy's assassin: Robert Blair Kaiser's *"R. F. K. Must Die!"* and Aziz Shibab's *Sirhan*.[75] He wrote:

> "I'm gonna get convicted. It's gonna be very similar to Sirhan. Might as well flaunt the fucker. On second thought, fucing's too good for him [Sirhan].[76]

While on the Wallace stalk, as Bremer killed time in a bar, his thoughts again turned to Sirhan, a person whose crime he was very familiar with:

> Had 2 Manhatins. Drank 2 glasses of water. The drinks didn't bother me much at all. Except financialy. A buck each. Nice little bar. Good bar tender. I thought of Sirhan. He had 4 drinks & was, he claimed drunk when he did his thing.[77]

When doctors examined Bremer after his arrest, they observed his above average intellectual capacity and vocabulary, excellent perception, good conceptual ability, and absence of any organic brain damage.[78] The most intriguing of the results, however, was Bremer's extraordinary response to the Rorschach test. This procedure requires subjects to interpret what they see in ten ink blots that are presented on cards. The typical response rate is generally between twenty and forty-five interpretations per patient. Bremer recorded over eight hundred responses in his first test and over five hundred in his second.[79] It was the interpretation of this excessive response rate that seemed to provide the most tangible support for the defense's contention that Bremer was mentally ill; that he lacked the capacity to appreciate the criminality of his act or to conform his conduct to the law. Even on this point, however, the examining psychiatrists and clinical psychologists could not agree on whether such an extraordinary response rate revealed symptoms of mental illness.[80]

More important, however, was the fact — the significance of which was seemingly overlooked by the mental health witnesses — that Bremer had read Robert Blair Kaiser's book on Sirhan.[81] In that book, Kaiser describes the general confusion among forensic specialists at that trial who analyzed Sirhan's Rorschach test results. He also comments on what appeared to him to be the highly subjective nature of the scoring procedures. For example, Kaiser reports that some of the jurors administered the test to themselves and were surprised to learn that their responses were "startlingly similar to Sirhan's `paranoid' reactions."[82] Moreover, Kaiser devoted some ten additional pages to a discussion of the Rorschach test results and the scoring procedures; an appendix included reproductions of ten Rorschach cards with Sirhan's responses noted on them.[83]

Given Bremer's familiarity with the Sirhan case and the book, it seems reasonable to suspect, as the prosecution did, that this information might have been used by him to manipulate his test results to advance his own case for acquittal by reason of insanity. Having also had a college level course in psychology, he might have learned about the average response rate to this test. Moreover, it would not require an advanced degree in psychology to surmise that increasing one's responses ten—to twenty-fold over the average would be a relatively easy way to raise diagnostic eyebrows.

With psychiatrists deadlocked on either side of the sanity issue, jurors made their decisions largely on the basis of what Arthur Bremer had written, and not on what the doctors had to say about him or his diary. They found him guilty on all counts. Before sentencing, the judge asked Bremer if he had anything he would like to say. Bremer replied in the only statement he ever made that was faintly remorseful:

Well, Mr. Marshall [the prosecutor] mentioned that he would like society to be protected from someone like me. Looking back on my life I would have liked it if society had protected me from myself. That's all I have to say at this time.[84]

The judge wasn't moved. Arthur Bremer was sentenced to sixty-three years in the Maryland State Penitentiary.

Conclusions

There is some insight in that laconic statement. Bremer was a young man who grew up in an environment almost devoid of positive experiences. By the age of thirteen he had virtually given up hope of finding any contentment in life. It appears that the most meaningful relationship in his unhappy life was a fifteen-year-old girl he hardly knew. That relationship failed because Arthur simply did not know how — he had never learned, never been taught — to relate to anyone on a mature emotional level. Thus, despite the fact of his sound intelligence, pleasant appearance, and seemingly good intentions, he was an outcast who had no idea of how to conduct himself in social situations. The girlfriend's rejection and his symbolically shaved head, whether intended or not, confirmed the misfit status he had always known was his. That confirmation was later underscored by his humiliating experience at a New York massage parlor. But unfortunately Bremer never understood *why*. And his response to the disappointments of his life was simply to shut down emotionally.

Giuseppe Zangara was much the same: the loveless past, the resentment of a father who denied him a normal childhood by forcing him into child labor at the age of six. He, too, never felt part of anything, let alone society. He was, like Bremer, only its victim. Intelligent but emotionless except for the chronic anger and resentment festering beneath an indifferent facade, the description applies to both men.

Because Zangara did not have the extensive psychiatric examination that Bremer received, his case is more speculative, but the similarities are there. The persona of both was one of detachment, of dealing with life only on a cognitive level. As Type III would-be assassins, neither had a real political purpose — any prominent political leader would do, nor were their acts compensatory. Unlike Type II subjects there was no one who mattered any longer (or, perhaps, ever in Zangara's case) in their lonely, isolated lives. Neither one had learned to love and be loved because those experiences were missing from both their childhoods.

Nor were they insane in a legal sense as Type IV subjects. The usual symptoms of psychosis were absent: no intellectual impairment, no delusions, or hallucinations which account for their conduct. Other than their atrophied emotions, they resembled the psychotic Type IV assassins only in their social isolation. They did not imagine themselves to be divinely inspired, nor were their grievances imagined; there were real reasons for their anger. So they scoffed at society, denied its conventions, and, most importantly, rejected its morality. For these reasons, each concluded that the most meaningful comment on a meaningless society was to commit an atrocity; an act vile and reprehensible, planned and publicly executed so there could be no mistake of their perverse intent. But the real outrage, each realized, would come when society understood that the ultimate meaning and significance of their despicable acts was the absence of real meaning or purpose, like their own miserable lives. To paraphrase G. K. Chesterton, a Type III subject is not someone who has lost his reason; rather he is someone who has lost everything but his reason.

And so Arthur Bremer grows old in his cell in the Maryland State Penitentiary with little hope of ever leaving those walls alive. Ironically, however, Bremer has received in prison the respect and admiration that eluded him as a free man. In the predominantly black Maryland State Penitentiary, he is viewed as a hero, of sorts, by black inmates. To them, he is not a self-destructive and apolitical would-be assassin; rather Arthur Bremer is the "man," the man who brought down one the most racist politicians in recent American history.

Notes

1. *Documents, Giuseppe Zangara, Federal Bureau of Investigation,* File No. 6228219-1-61, February 16, 1933. Hereafter cited as *FBI Documents.*
2. Giuseppe Zangara, "Sworn Statement of Joseph Zangara, Miami Dade County, Florida, February 16, 1933, pp. 10–11. Hereafter cited as Sworn Statement.
3. Ibid, p. 9.
4. Ibid, p.22.
5. Ibid., pp. 13–14.
6. *FBI Documents,* February 16, 1933.
7. Ibid., February 18, 1933.
8. *Newark Evening News,* February 16, 1933, 1.
9. *Newark Evening News,* February 16, 1933, 2.
10. *FBI Documents,* March 18, 1933.
11. *Newark Evening News,* February 20, 1933, 1.
12. Ibid., February 21, 1933, 3.
13. Ibid.
14. Ibid.
15. Ibid.
16. Ibid., March 10, 1933, 1.
17. *Miami Herald,* March 21, 1933, 1.
18. Ibid., February 21, 1933, 8,14, 33.
19. Sworn Statement, pp. 6–7, 11–12, 14.

20. Ibid., 1, 7, 12.
21. F. Dostoyevsky, *Notes From Underground,* R.G. Durgy, ed. (New York: Thomas Y. Crowell, 1969).
22. Although Wallace would be eventually reelected governor of Alabama, his recovery from his wound was never complete. He died a broken man on September 13, 1998.
23. *State of Maryland v. Arthur Herman Bremer* , No. 1237612379, Circuit Court for Prince George's County, Maryland (1972), 205. Hereafter cited as *Trial Transcripts.*
24. *Trial Transcripts,* testimony of J. Schanno, pp. 380–381.
25. Ibid., p. 4.
26. *Annotated Code of Maryland,* Article 59, Section 25.
27. E. M. Agger, Case Report, *Trial Transcripts,* p. 831. Hereafter cited as Agger Report.
28. Ibid., pp. 566–567, 831–835.
29. *Milwaukee Journal,* May 21, 1972, 1.
30. Agger Report, p. 837.
31. Ibid.
32. Ibid. pp. 838–839.
33. Ibid., pp. 844.
34. *Trial Transcripts,* testimony of Eugene B. Brody, p. 637.
35. Ibid., p. 654.
36. Ibid., p. 708.
37. Bremer had registered a low average IQ in high school, probably because he did not care about the test. After his arrest, he was variously tested and compiled scores on the Weschsler Adult Intelligence Scale ranging from 114 to 120. These scores place him in the "bright-normal" to "superior" range of intelligence. Only 10 percent of the population score in this range.
38. Ibid., pp. 639–642.
39. Ibid., statements of K. Johannes and P. Holmes, and FBI reports, pp. 894–932.
40. Ibid., testimony of E.B. Brody, p. 641; statement of J. Johannes, pp. 934–937.
41. Ibid., testimony of E.B. Brody, p. 642.
42. Ibid., FBI interview of J.M. Pembrick, pp. 865–868.
43. Ibid., statement of J. Pembrick, pp. 870–871.
44. Ibid., statement of D. Lemberger, p. 887.
45. Ibid., statement of J. Pembrick, pp, 868–869.
46. This film, which was made after Bremer's diary was published, draws directly on some aspects of Bremer's personality in developing the fictional character, Travis Bickle, played by DeNiro. As the next chapter reveals, the film was subsequently linked in 1981 to the motives of President Reagan's attacker, John W. Hinckley, Jr.. Hinckley, who became infatuated with a teen-age actress in the film, began to imitate the persona of the Travis Bickle in a vain attempt to get the attention of the actress. In the film, Bickle expresses his love for the girl in an act of violence.
47. Ibid., statement of M. Pembrick, p. 877.
48. Ibid., FBI Report, p. 875.
49. Ibid., testimony of E.B. Brody, p. 644.

50. Ibid.
51. Ibid., testimony of W. Heely, pp. 897–899.
52. Ibid., testimony of J.E. Olsson, pp. 509–510; E.B. Brody, p. 645.
53. Ibid., testimony of E.B. Brody, pp. 645–646.
54. See, for example, G. Vidal, "Now for the Shooting of George Wallace," *New York Review of Books,* December 13, 1973, pp. 17–19; and J. McKinley, *Assassination in America* (New York: Harper & Row, 1977).
55. *Trial Transcripts,* testimony of J.E. Olsson, pp. 483–532; E.B. Brody, pp. 669–740; and E.C. Stammeyer, pp. 741–754.
56. *Trial Transcripts,* pp. 1006–1007. Bremer's *Diary* is quoted here from the trial transcripts rather than the published version. Hereafter cited as *Diary.*
57. Ibid., pp. 1009–1010.
58. Ibid., p. 994.
59. Ibid., p.1012.
60. Ibid., pp. 1019–1021.
61. Ibid., pp. 1023–1024.
62. Ibid., pp. 1024–1025.
63. Ibid., p. 1035.
64. Ibid., 1040.
65. *Trial Transcripts,* testimony of E.B. Brody, pp. 633, 656.
66. Ibid., testimony of J.E. Olsson, p. 482.
67. *Diary,* pp. 1034.
68. A. Camus, *The Stranger* (New York: Alfred A. Knopf, 1946).
69. *Diary,* p. 1026.
70. Ibid., p. 1008.
71. Ibid., p. 1036.
72. Ibid.
73. Ibid., p. 1042.
74. Ibid., p. 1027.
75. Ibid., pp. 952, 1027.
76. Ibid., p. 1037.
77. Ibid., p. 1045.
78. *Trial Transcripts,* testimony of J.E. Olsson, pp483–485; E.B. Brody, pp. 669–670; and E.C. Stammeyer, p. 754.
79. Ibid., testimony of J.E. Olsson, p. 514 and E.C. Stammeyer, p. 755.
80. Ibid., testimony of J.E. Olsson, p. 515 and E.B. Brody, p. 668.
81. Ibid., see, for example, the testimony of E.B. Brody, pp. 696–697.
82. R.B. Kaiser, *"RFK Must Die!" A History of the Robert Kennedy Assassination and Its Aftermath* (New York: Dutton, 1970), p. 512.
83. Ibid., pp. 412, 440, 447–478, 481, 492, 597–609.
84. Ibid., p. 1277.

7

Type III—Nihilism
John W. Hinckley, Jr. and
Francisco Martin Duran

> *"I can't begin to be happy . . . I plot revenge in the dark . . . I was desperate in some bold way to get attention."—John W. Hinckley, Jr.*

> *"Can you imagine a higher moral calling than to destroy someone's dreams with a bullet?"—Francisco Martin Duran*

It is their nihilism — the Dostoyevskian self-loathing that accompanies the hatred and contempt for society — that distinguishes Type III subjects Zangara, Bremer and, in this chapter, John W. Hinckley, Jr. and Francisco Martin Duran from other assassins and would-be assassins.

Hinckley and Duran are poles apart in a sociological sense. Hinckley is the son of a multimillionaire Texas oilman and a mother who was always there for him. He was a pampered child who grew up with material comfort, privilege, and boundless opportunity. Duran, in contrast, was the illegitimate Hispanic son of a welfare mother who never knew his father and was well acquainted with uncertainty and hardship most of his life. More is known, on the record, about Hinckley than about Duran, for Hinckley's parents wrote a book about their lives with a troubled son. Although less complete and detailed, there is sufficient information on Duran to conclude that psychologically both men were very similar; their motives as would-be assassins virtually the same — getting even. And neither was motivated by the politics of his intended victim — one a conservative Republican, the other a liberal Democrat.

* * *

JOHN W. HINCKLEY, JR. (1955–)

If it had not been for the quick and courageous actions of President Ronald Reagan's Secret Service detail, and the skill of emergency room surgeons, the president would have surely died on March 30, 1981. And John Hinckley would be known as an assassin rather than a would-be assassin. A young man who had never accomplished anything in his life, nearly succeeded in ending the life of the most powerful person in the world. For Hinckley that was pretty heady stuff.

Coming of Age in Dallas

What made John Hinckley unusual was his background. The soft cushion of family affluence and the comfortable material life it assured suggested little to be bitter about. But what made him a would-be assassin was his upbringing, comfortable — perhaps too comfortable — and well-intentioned though it was. He was not a marginal person in a sociological sense, not a person one would expect to be criminally inclined. His financially secure upbringing compares only to that of two other political assassins, John Wilkes Booth and Carl Weiss. Hinckley seemed to many to be a wealthy, spoiled child who never grew up, a young man who remained a mama's boy, whining and pouting for his mother's attention and resentful of a father who wanted him to become a man.

There is some truth in that, for John Hinckley was a marginal person psychologically — the creation of an anxious, indulgent mother and a well-meaning but demanding and busily distracted father. But like all of us, he was also a product of intangibles. How else could he differ so greatly from an older brother and sister raised in the same environment?

Some of those intangibles were cultural. John Hinckley was a product of the 1970s in America and, one might argue metaphorically without too much exaggeration, Dallas — both the city and the television series. The cultural context of that particular era, dominated as it was by the banalities and bogus sophistication of country club values and hollow solipsistic aspirations, is central to an understanding of John Hinckley. Surrounded all his life by wealthy people with what appeared to be very ordinary talents, John had two goals in life: to be rich like his father, and to be famous, unlike his father. The goals seemed reasonable at first. After all, his father had preached relentlessly to all his children — but especially to his timid, apprehensive younger son- that there were no limits to what a man could achieve in America if he was willing to apply himself and work. And, of course, Jack Hinckley was the self-satisfied, living example of his own tedious, repetitious sermons.

But nothing John ever did pleased his father — at least, he never heard his father say he was pleased. As a child John resented him; as he grew older that resentment turned to contempt if not outright hatred. That situation — that absence of a positive male figure in his life — was a major reason why, at the age of twenty-five, John Hinckley was trying still to decide *who* he was and, in the process, get back at the father he could never please.

Mom and Dad

John W. Hinckley, Jr., was born on May 29, 1955, in Ardmore, Oklahoma, the third and youngest child of his parents, Jack and Jo Ann. Like his older brother and sister, Scott and Diane, he entered the world healthy, attractive, and intelligent, delighting a solidly middle-class Midwestern family with traditional moral and religious values. There were loving grandparents, family vacations, pets to cuddle, new toys to look forward to every Christmas, and a mother who was *always* there. It seemed all the elements were present for little John Jr. to have a very pleasant, nurturing childhood. On the surface the Hinckleys seemed like one of those families in the television sitcoms that were popular at that time — shows like *Leave It to Beaver, Ozzie and Harriet,* or, more to the point of this chapter, *Father Knows Best.* But the television families solve their problems and leave everyone smiling within a half hour. In the Hinckleys' case, however, a problem developed and continued to grow over the years to tragic proportions.

Jo Ann Hinckley (until 1981 she was called Jodie by her family and friends) was the typical housewife of that era, baking cookies, washing and ironing, keeping the house spotless. Each chore was carefully planned and scheduled, just like the three meals she prepared for her family every day. And then, of course, she spent a good bit of time in the family station wagon, shopping and shuttling the kids around to dental appointments and keeping up with all their various carefully arranged activities. Everything had a time and place in a life of devotion structured around her husband and children. In the afternoons, when the kids were in school or out playing, she would have some time alone to watch the game shows she enjoyed. But even then she usually ironed. "How many shirts I pressed in thirty-four years of marriage," she said, looking back over those years, "and every one with pride."[1] She was exactly the kind of mother companies like Procter and Gamble and Lever Brothers wanted to portray in their commercials.

But her husband wasn't quite the traditional father — at least not in the mellow, approachable way fathers were portrayed in those television shows. Despite the best intentions, Jack was too busy to be the kind of father who came home on time for meals and spent his evenings with the family, smoking a pipe or puttering around with a hobby in the basement. Jack Hinckley was a driving, ambitious, self-made man, a man for whom time meant money, not refinishing antiques or showing his sons how to build bird houses as Fred MacMurray did in *My Three Sons*. It was quicker to buy those things. Time and money. Neither was meant to be squandered; that was one lesson he tried to teach his three children.

Jack Hinckley had always had goals and been in a rush to reach them. In 1942, a year before he was to graduate from high school, he was accepted into an accelerated naval officer training program at the University of Oklahoma. Within three years he had completed both high school and college, earning a degree in mechanical engineering and an ensign's commission. Even in an accelerated, academically demanding program he found time to earn spending money by playing drums in a dance band, was active in several honor societies, and managed to get himself elected vice president of his class. By the time he was twenty-one he had completed his education, served his country as a naval officer, gotten himself a job with Carter Oil Company when he was discharged, and, best of all, on Christmas Eve that same year, married a pretty blonde freshman who thought she was the luckiest young lady in the world when he proposed. It was 1946.[2]

Moving Up in the World

To get ahead, Jack believed, you had to be willing to move. And the Hinckleys did, from drilling site to drilling site, fourteen times in the first five years of their marriage. After Scott was born in 1950 they decided to settle down in Ardmore, Oklahoma, where they had lived for two years, to raise a family. Diane was born three years later, in 1953; John's birth followed in 1955. But it wasn't just the moves that put strains on the family, it was Jack's absences. "If hard work could provide our children with a good home and a decent education," he said, "they were going to have them."[3] But all that hard work took its toll as his children went to bed at night and got up in the morning too often without him. And it was hard on both him and Jo Ann. "Many months I'd see Jo Ann only occasionally, sleeping most nights in my car at a drilling site, longing to be with her. I was doing it all for Jo Ann, I believed, to earn the good life post-war America held out to those who were willing to work."[4]. By the time the Hinckleys moved to Dallas in 1958 Jack admitted that he had been so wrapped up in business and making money, he barely knew his three-year-old son.[5]

The move to Dallas proved to be more difficult for Jo Ann than anyone imagined it would be. She was terrified by the size, pace, and impersonality of the city. She hated the rented house they moved into but was afraid to leave it.[6] Jack wasn't very understanding about what he considered Jo Ann's "imaginary" problems. So she spent a lot of time just crying.[7] The children didn't understand, but Scott and Diane were in school and gone most of the day. It was the youngest, John, who was there alone with her all day long, absorbing her fears and anxieties — and resenting his father's disdain during those rare evenings when he was home.

The first year in Dallas was difficult, but everyone seemed to weather it all right, except John.[8] When he started school he seemed to be a fairly typical child — no special talents, no special problems — who played basketball and football in elementary school and had an ordinary range of friends and other activities. But John was too quiet. He rarely initiated conversations. If his birthday parties were boisterous, as his father remembered them, it was because of the other children. Jo Ann could hardly miss that he was uncomfortable away from home. She had to urge him to seek out his playmates or arrange meetings for him herself. If children came to see him, he played with them; if not, he was content to remain home, near his mother. He was very different from his more gregarious older brother and sister.[9]

When a boy approaches adolescence and such patterns of dependency don't begin to change, when he doesn't begin to venture out with friends his own age, it becomes a concern. And the Hinckleys *were* concerned, not only for John, but also for themselves: the strains that were always there in their marriage were exacerbated by John's continuing dependence on his mother.

Perhaps it was the onset of adolescence, when other children are beginning to assert their independence, that made him feel different, that made him feel he didn't fit in. It was all right when his mother planned his birthday parties and invited friends in to play. But he was too old to be thought of as a shy little boy now; his peers probably began to find such motherly intrusions odd and perhaps even offensive.

His withdrawal, although gradual, was completed within two years. He dropped out of sports, the primary source of his social activity up until that time. His move to the sidelines became a metaphor for the rest of his life. The first sign was his decision not to play; he wanted to be a "team manager" instead. Maybe it was the stiffer competition at that age. Disparities in ability become more noticeable in adolescence as some boys develop their coordination more quickly than others and performance is evaluated less benignly than it is among younger boys. The social pressures are no longer there to conceal disappointment in another's performance under a facade of uncaring good sportsmanship. Ridicule is more readily expressed in words and looks by everyone involved: players, coaches, and parents. Or it could have been the embarrassment of the showers and locker room vulgarity after the games. Whatever it was, after a year or so he dropped sports altogether.

There can be little doubt that moving again hastened his move to the sidelines of life. It was 1966 when Jack decided that it was time to relocate— this time merely across town, to a fancier neighborhood and a stately old house on Beverly Drive in Highland Park, a Dallas suburb a step or two above their University Park address. It was also a move into the country club society of Dallas, where, more than anything else, money and its adornments determine an individual's importance. It was that kind of respectability that Jack had worked all his life to attain.[10]

What the move meant for his eleven-year-old son was another matter: the loss of the few friends he had, a familiar school and way of life. After the move to Highland Park, John Hinckley rarely had a sustained conversation with anyone except his mother. When his few friends started to date, John was left out. He never dated in high school.[11] Most of the time he just stayed in his room, usually playing Beatles records. And because of Jack's growing resentment toward the son who was so unlike himself, John's cherished conversations with his mother had to be guarded, had to occur only when Jack wasn't around. It was sad, but the knowledge of the now furtive nature of their relationship made both John and his mother feel uncomfortable. It was as if they were doing something wrong, and John's resentment of his father deepened because of it.

That wasn't the only thing about his father's domineering presence that he resented. On those rare occasions when John did try to talk to his father, it always ended the same way: Jack talked and John listened to why *he* was wrong. There just had never been much communication between Jack and his youngest child. As they both grew older, the distance between them widened. John was just a little boy the last time his father hugged him, as far as Jack could remember. After that time not even a pat on the shoulder passed from father to son.[12]

Instead of spankings and reprimands there was ridicule — invidious comparisons between John and his favored older brother and sister — and disdain. In contrast to the accomplishments of Scott and Diane there was little that John Hinckley ever did that his father appreciated or approved . John's interest in music and poetry, for example, was dismissed as evidence of John's "lack of any concept of what it took to get ahead in the real world."[13]

His mother could see what was happening, and she felt sorry for her son. It was a dilemma. On the one hand, she wanted John to develop some initiative and direction in his life as badly as her husband did. But possibly because of Jack's scathing ridicule, the way he often belittled the boy, she had no choice but to defend him. She knew he had to change, but she could also empathize with his fears and timidity—and, recalling the difficult period he shared with her that first year in Dallas and the way she pampered him after that, she may have felt somewhat responsible.

But that didn't make the situation now any easier to contend with. Arguments occurred regularly; every meal together became a reason for anxiety. When the three of them sat down to eat, either the meal was silent or an argument developed before they were finished. When Jack accused her of pampering John, she knew it was true, but what else could she do in the face of Jack's overbearing manner and constant badgering? Why couldn't he see that his ridicule was undermining the very self-reliance he wanted John to develop? By this time, Jo Ann Hinckley was well aware that her husband considered their son an unwelcome intruder in the house, an annoying rival for her attention.

The Exile

By the time John Hinckley graduated from high school in 1973 his sulking dependence on his mother had become not only an embarrassment, especially to his father, but also the source of great strains on his parents' marriage. The Hinckleys were in their mid-forties, at a stage in their own lives when they were ready to put the responsibilities of child rearing behind them, to enjoy the freedom to pursue interests apart from their children. But John showed no evidence of having a plan to leave home. Jack was ashamed of him. In contrast to Scott and Diane, John was rarely mentioned to friends and even less often introduced to visitors.[14] Even his mother was becoming weary of his presence and the strains it caused.

Finally Jack couldn't take any more and he didn't mince words: He wanted John out of the house. Fortunately there was a nice antiseptic way to accomplish that purpose. He made it clear that John, like it or not, was going to college. Both Scott and Diane had done so, and there was no reason why he shouldn't as well. But John didn't want to go. As bored and as unhappy as he seemed to be moping around the house or sitting alone in his room, he didn't want to leave home or, more to the point, his mother.

After several meetings with a high school guidance counselor Jack decided that Texas Tech would be appropriate and that John would major in business.[15] As with most of his father's views, John didn't agree. But this time, for a change, he said so. He didn't see the need for college, he protested, adding that he didn't want to leave Dallas; moreover, he made it clear that he definitely did not want to study business. His interests were music and literature, he insisted.

It didn't matter. Jack, who had spent the last several years traveling back and forth to New York to borrow investment capital for the oil exploration company he had founded, scoffed at the thought. John, he maintained, needed to study something "realistic" that would prepare him to earn a living. "A liberal arts degree," he said, "wouldn't mean very much at a job interview."[16]

In September 1973, a month after they had packed their reluctant son off to Texas Tech in Lubbock, the Hinckleys moved to Evergreen, Colorado, a wealthy suburb in the Denver foothills. For their youngest child their move meant that on top of being separated from his mother, he no longer even had a home to return to in Dallas. It was exile, and John Hinckley resented it deeply.

The Road to Ruin

John Hinckley remained the same friendless person at Texas Tech in the fall of 1973 that he had been during high school. Emotionally he had relied completely on his mother. In Lubbock he no longer had her stabilizing influence to check his drifting existence. And drift he did, without social connections or control, trying to find himself. For the next seven years John Hinckley dropped in and out of school, moving from apartment to apartment, managing to complete only three years of credit by 1980 when he finally dropped out and, much to his parents' dismay, returned home to stay.

The whole time Hinckley had been in college he continued to demand their attention. He was never out of their minds. There were letters and phone calls, almost always about problems. There were two persistent themes, health and money. He complained about one ailment after another with symptoms like "pressure" in his throat or a "rocking" feeling in his head. Then his weight would balloon up, at one point to 230 pounds, making him look lumpy, ugly, and, somehow, small. Physical examinations would reveal no cause or explanation for his complaints. Drugs would be prescribed, usually tranquilizers like the Surmontil a Lubbock doctor prescribed, to calm his anxieties about his health. Away from home he continued, one way or another, to remind his parents—his mother especially—of what *they* were doing to him.

In April 1976, for example, John startled his parents with this note:

Dear Mom and Dad,
    By the time you receive this letter, I will no longer be in Lubbock. I have dropped out of school. I know you'll never understand, but I'm too miserable here to take it any longer. I honestly won't blame you if you get mad and cut me off.... I'm sorry I'm doing this to you.... I only hope someday I can make you proud of me.
    It was signed, "Love, John."[17]

A month went by before a Mother's Day card arrived with a Los Angeles postmark. In the letter be enclosed with it, John told his parents that he was in Hollywood "within easy walking distance of about 30 of the most famous music publishers in the world ... trying to sell some of my songs." He went on to say that he hoped they were not "too disappointed in me for dropping out of school," adding that "for the first time in years I am happy." In closing he said that he hoped his newfound happiness would make them "at least tolerant" of his actions.[18] John Hinckley had loved the Beatles from the moment he first heard their music in the early 1960s when he was eight years old. He had always wanted to write poetry and music like the Beatles. If he could have had one wish, it probably would have been to become someone like John Lennon.

But it wasn't to be. A couple of weeks later, his parents received another letter this one announcing that things had taken a sharp turn for the worse: he had been burglarized. The letter was oozing with self-pity expressed in passages like this: "Your son, for the past 2 1/2 weeks, has had to walk up to strangers and ask them for spare change, so I can eat. Although I am physically ravaged, my spirit has not yet been broken." Then he got to the point: "You don't know how grateful I would be if you could give me limited financial support and a great deal of moral support during this period." The message was sharpened in the next paragraph with "please send cash." Then he applied a rich layer of guilt as he closed: "On the other hand, if you feel that being robbed is just what I deserve for the way I've acted, I'll try to understand."

It worked, as it always had. After a couple of paragraphs of that, his mother was weeping and Jack had dashed off to wire money, concerned about his son, but less so than about the tears this troublesome boy had brought to his mother's eyes.[19] Throughout his stay in Los Angeles, his pleas brought in more money from his parents. "Please keep in mind," he wrote in one, "the only reason I'm out here in Hollywood is to try and attain some success with my music and this could be the golden opportunity I've been looking for."[20]

Then in July the worried parents received good news: John had a "contact" at United Artists which was looking at his music and, at long last, he had a girlfriend, an aspiring young actress named Lynn Collins whom he said he had met in a Hollywood laundromat. In letters and phone calls that followed he described restaurants where he and Lynn had dined and trips they had taken together to Malibu Beach. Her family, he hinted, was quite wealthy; "they're behind her all the way," he added meaningfully. "Write soon." And his encouraged parents did, with additional money accompanying virtually every letter.[21]

The whole story was a hoax, of course. It was concocted solely as a means to keep the dollars flowing west from Evergreen. He knew there were three things his parents wanted him to do more than anything: leave home, succeed at something, and find a girlfriend. So he strung the story out as long as he could. But by the end of the summer he had tired of L.A. and needed a reason to leave. His parents received the inevitable tale of woe in September when another letter arrived. It began with how he had been stuck in an elevator, then got worse as he moved through "severe eye sting attacks" that forced him to leave his job, being dumped by United Artists, a near mugging, and finally, worst of all, his breakup with Lynn. "Now if you'll excuse me," he concluded, "I think I'm going to go and kill myself. (Just kidding ... I think)."[22] His parents fell for it. A few days later he was back in Evergreen.

Finding a Job

It was to remain a familiar pattern. John was like a boomerang cast from his parents' home: Lubbock and back; Los Angeles and back; Dallas and back; the traveling not only continued, it accelerated as John Hinckley's search for himself became more frantic. As the stress continued to increase, so did his ailments. When he wasn't home there were more phone calls, more complaints about headaches, earaches, backaches, colds, chest pains, pains in his arms and legs, things caught in his throat, insomnia—anything, it seemed, to keep his parents off balance.

Jack was exasperated. During the periods when John was back in Evergreen Jack insisted that he look for work. He didn't want him lounging around the house or sulking in his room, listening to records and munching his mother's cookies, as he was inclined to do. When the suggestion was made, John countered with yet another problem: he was afraid to drive in Denver traffic. When Jo Ann quietly reminded her husband that their son was also afraid to drive at night, Jack just shook his head.[23]

Afraid to drive in traffic? And at night? It was hard to accept. What could any father say about a grown son like that? When Jack was John's age, he was serving as a naval officer — in a war! But much to her husband's dismay Jo Ann agreed to chauffeur her son back and forth — an hour each way — between Evergreen and Denver for job interviews.

Eventually someone hired this unimpressive young man whose mother waited outside during the interviews. The job was as a busboy at a nightclub. It wasn't much, but he had never worked at anything other than menial jobs, and never for very long. Since he was afraid to drive at night, his father insisted that he take a motel room across the street from the nightclub to spare Jo Ann — not to mention to get him out of the house. Even so, she dropped by regularly to keep her chubby son supplied in cookies and casseroles, feeling bad every time she looked at his only companion in the dingy room, a small black and white television.[24]

After five months of clearing tables and sweeping floors he quit, or was fired. It isn't certain which. It was the longest he had worked at any job and the closest he had ever come to supporting himself. He then managed to convince his parents that he deserved another chance with his music and a trip to Los Angeles to pursue it. Two weeks later he called collect from Los

Angeles to ask for plane fare back home. Then it was back to Texas Tech with a new major in liberal arts that his exasperated father himself had suggested.

Jodie

In reality it was not the fictitious Lynn who occupied John Hinckley's thoughts and imagination, although she was resurrected briefly in 1979 when he again needed money from his parents. It was a real young actress who had caught his eye on that trip to California in 1976. Jodie Foster played the role of Iris, a child prostitute in a film he saw there, *Taxi Driver*. Hinckley thought she was beautiful, the most attractive female he had ever seen. She became his fantasy and, ultimately, his obsession. He wrote songs and poems about her and to her. His thoughts were sweet and endearing, never lewd or explicitly sexual, as one might expect of fantasies about a prostitute. There was never more than a hint of sexuality in the words of this sexually repressed young man.[25]

Hinckley also found the main character in the film appealing, a cabdriver, Travis Bickle. Bickle, played by Robert DeNiro, is a lonely, angry man who tries to kill a political candidate and, in the final scenes of the film, becomes a mass killer as he rescues Iris from her pimps. In his search for identity Hinckley, like many younger children whose heroes change with age and the resonance of impressions made by certain screen or sports heroes, gradually began to shift from the Beatles to this fictional role model. Perhaps it was because of the disappointments in Hollywood and the realization that a career like John Lennon's was out of reach that his interests changed. As he began to share Travis Bickle's love for the underage prostitute, John Hinckley began to imitate other features of Bickle's life, including his tastes in clothing (an army fatigue jacket and jeans) as well as the handguns he fondled in his lonely room, staring blankly at a flickering television screen. In the summer of 1979 Hinckley bought his first handgun at the Galaxy Pawn Shop in Lubbock and began practicing with it.[26]

It was also at about this time that Hinckley's curiosity about desperate men with violent pasts and reputations came to full bloom.[27] He first began to read about the Nazi movement for that reason, but his interest soon focused on the lives of violent *individuals,* people who had been involved in spectacular crimes where weapons had played a part. Hijackers, kidnappers, serial killers, mass murderers, and assassins became his heroes as he collected books and articles about them, probably seeking some vicarious release from the frustration and anger that was building within himself.[28]

By September 1980 Hinckley had seen the movie *Taxi Driver* many of the fifteen times he claims that he ultimately saw it. It wasn't the violence in the film that intrigued him most, although he found it fascinating; it was Iris — a beautiful, sexy little girl. Her childlike vulnerability was irresistible to this immature young man whose emotional development had never progressed beyond adolescence. It was the compelling mix of sensuality and innocence that Iris conveyed on the screen that got him. She was everything he wanted.

But how could he meet her? For four years he had fantasized about Jodie Foster, the actress who played the part — not Iris — collecting photographs and magazine articles about her. It was in May 1980 that he read in *People* magazine that she would begin attending Yale University that September. For the rest of the summer he was consumed with thoughts about how he might use that opportunity to meet her. He knew that a date with Jodie Foster was a long shot, but he decided to try anyway. For once he would invoke some of the well-known Hinckley initiative and determination that his father had chided him for lacking for as long as he could remember. If old demanding, self-satisfied Jack only knew what he was up to now, he might have thought. What would his father and mother think if he were to bring a famous movie star home to meet the family? Would they be impressed? Would it be something that Scott — with his Vanderbilt, engineering degree, and all that — would ever come close to doing? Just the thought probably brought a smile to his lips. Sweet revenge.

But first he needed an excuse to get to New Haven. He couldn't just tell his parents he wanted to go there to meet Jodie Foster. He could imagine what his father would say about that. Even his mother would think he was crazy. As he house sat while his parents were in Europe that summer, he thought of a scheme. What if he said he wanted to study something at Yale? Jack might spring for that. He had recently relented on his insistence that John study business; nearly seven frustrating years had finally worn down his resolve. At this point in their troubled relationship John knew that his father didn't care what he studied — or did — as long as it was something, and away from home. Yale was away from home, but he would need to pry some money out of his parents. When they returned from a European vacation, he announced that he wanted to attend a writer's workshop that was being held at Yale University in September.

For some time Hinckley had resented the fact that his father had refused to let him have access to a trust account that Jack had established for each of the children. Scott and Diane had been given theirs, but Jack had withheld his, claiming correctly that John had not yet learned to manage money responsibly. Now John wanted his share to cover his expenses in New Haven. As further evidence of his willingness to do anything he could to help resolve his son's problems, Jack agreed. He gave John a check for $3,600 drawn from John's trust account to use in New Haven. The only condition was that when he completed the workshop at Yale he would then return to Texas Tech to complete his degree.²⁹ The writer's workshop ploy was yet another shrewd move on Hinckley's part to get what he wanted.

His mother was hopeful when John asked her to drive him into Denver to spend a day shopping together. He wanted her to help him select a new wardrobe for the trip. She saw nothing unusual in such a request from a young man of twenty-five, just as she saw nothing particularly odd about his fears of city traffic and driving after dark.³⁰

Hinckley, of course, had no intention of attending a workshop on writing or anything else at Yale. He arrived in New Haven on September 17, 1980, for the sole purpose of meeting Jodie Foster at her Yale dormitory. Within hours of arriving he called and talked briefly with her on the telephone. And he kept calling for the next three days. But after a few short phone conversations, she refused to talk to him.³¹ Frustrated, he went to the campus in an attempt to see her as she walked back and forth to classes. When he did, however, he found himself too apprehensive to approach her. "Just basically shyness," he explained later. "I mean she was a pretty famous movie star and there I was, Mr. Insignificant himself."³²

Hinckley was also sensitive to the looks and sneers that followed as male students began to notice him loitering around the women's dormitory. "Mr. Toxic Shock," they chuckled behind the back of this obviously out-of-place young man.

Jodie Foster and her roommate had at first treated him with polite indifference on the phone; after all, he wasn't the first young man at Yale to pester a pretty student. But both made it clear that Jodie wanted him to leave her alone, especially after the tone of the "love notes" he left for her at the dorm became a little too insistent. At about this time, too, the FBI had warned Foster of an anonymous kidnap threat they had received. John Hinckley, it was established later, had made the threat.³³

After three unrewarding days of courtship John called his mother to say that he didn't like the workshop (no explanation), New Haven (dirty, industrial, and too expensive), or the students (sloppy and unfriendly). He wanted to come home. Disgusted, his father didn't want to be there if he did. The next day Jack left for California.³⁴ Sensing the consternation at home, John remained in New Haven for another day skulking around the Yale campus, trying to sneak glimpses of Foster. On September 22 the phone rang in Evergreen. When his mother answered it, it was John calling to ask her to pick him up at the Denver airport. He told her that he was on his way back to Lubbock to close out his checking account there. He was depressed, he said, and he didn't want to go back to Texas Tech. He went on to say that he had also quit the writer's program and needed a couple of days of rest before flying on to Lubbock.

Jo Ann was in a familiar bind: not wanting to turn her son away, on the one hand, and on the other, worried about what would happen if Jack returned from California early to find him back home. After John spent one night at home, she told him he would have to spend the next night — the night before he was to fly back to Lubbock — at a motel in case Jack came home. John was crushed. Rejection: first Jodie, now the other Jodie in his life — his mother. "How am I going to get to the airport tomorrow?" he whined. Jo Ann hesitated, then softened, agreeing to return in the morning to take him.[35] When she did, the hurt still remained in his eyes.

It was not only hurt; beneath it there was anger — probably a decade's accumulation of anger. John Hinckley had decided that he was going to get even. But how? He couldn't bring himself to strike out at his parents directly, certainly not at his mother, and he couldn't hurt his father without hurting her. But he could embarrass them. He could make them regret the way they had treated him all these years. Guilt, that was it. He could make them feel responsible for some terrible thing he did. He had contemplated suicide for months, probably years, the thoughts expressed in the morbid, self-deprecating poems he had written. Instead he chose assassination — after considering mass murder — like many of the people he had read about after his exile to Lubbock.[36] It was an extraordinary act that no one — especially Jodie Foster and his parents — could ignore.

Assassination, Mass Murder, or Suicide?

When John Hinckley left New Haven the third week of September, he didn't fly directly home. Instead he took a train to Washington. When she found out, Jo Ann assumed that he had spent a couple of days "sightseeing." Actually Hinckley's trip to Washington marked the beginning of his presidential stalk. After his brief, melancholy sojourn in Evergreen with his mother, he flew to Lubbock, where he purchased two more .22 caliber handguns at Snidely Whiplash's gun shop, bringing his total to three.[37] He also bought three thousand dollars worth of traveler's checks. By this time Hinckley was tracking President Jimmy Carter's movements through articles he read, and often clipped, in the *New York Times*. On September 27 he again flew to Washington. The next day he flew to Columbus, Ohio, to await Carter's scheduled visit. But nothing happened. Two days later he took a bus to Dayton. On October 2 Hinckley was in Dayton, standing in a crowd of well-wishers when Carter arrived. Carter, smiling and waving, walked into the crowd to within a handshake of Hinckley. Claiming later that he was unarmed, Hinckley said he just wanted to see if he could get close enough to shoot.[38]

On October 6 Hinckley flew to Lincoln, Nebraska, in a futile attempt to interview a member of the American Nazi party. On October 7 he flew to

Nashville to prepare for Carter's visit there later in the week. On October 9, the day Carter was to arrive, he was arrested at the Nashville airport with three handguns in his suitcase. The guns were confiscated, and he was fined and released after being held four or five hours. Shaken, Hinckley then destroyed a diary that he had been keeping — in the manner of Arthur Bremer, whose published diary Hinckley had read — for fear that it would have been too incriminating had the authorities bothered to examine it after his arrest. Undoubtedly the diary contained references to his designs on Carter, much as Bremer's had on Nixon and Wallace.[39]

After his release the police dropped Hinckley off at the airport and he flew to New Haven. Then he phoned his sister in Dallas to ask if it would be convenient for him to stop by for a visit with his little nephew. Later the same day, October 11, he flew to Dallas. While in Dallas he went to Rocky's Police Equipment and purchased two .22 caliber pistols to replace two of the three guns the police had confiscated. On October 15 he flew back to New Haven; two days later he was in Washington; and two days after that he was back in Evergreen.[40] When he left Dallas, his sister wasn't sure whether he was going back to New Haven for "another seminar" or to Los Angeles, unaware that her brother had Jimmy Carter on his mind.[41]

Hinckley's choice of Carter had nothing to do with the president's personality, or Carter's politics; nor did it have anything to do with Hinckley's father's politics. Jack Hinckley was a staunch conservative, critical of Carter, and a strong supporter of the Republican nominee, Ronald Reagan. Hinckley decided to kill Carter simply because of his *prominence.* Jimmy Carter was the president, someone whose position — whatever his policies — would ensure notoriety for the person who killed him. Hinckley, like Bremer, understood that if he had the courage to do it, his name would be on the lips of every anchorman on network news, and it would be spelled out in the headlines of the nation's newspapers and news magazines. It would be an event Jack Hinckley could not ignore.

But by the middle of October all the polls were predicting that Carter would be defeated. Most suggested that it wouldn't even be close. Hinckley decided Carter had become an unworthy victim. He wasn't going to make the same mistake as Arthur Bremer. Bremer, he believed, had moved down "a few pegs" when, failing to get President Nixon, he shot candidate George Wallace instead.[42] He would wait for the next president. It wouldn't be a long wait. By the third week of October John was back in Evergreen with two frustrated and decidedly unhappy parents. Something had to change.[43]

Jo Ann suggested that they seek professional help for John. They had tried everything else. Jack agreed. Within days, John was seeing an Evergreen psychiatrist, but not before taking a valium overdose. It was an attention getter. "I think I might have taken too many," he volunteered sheepishly to his mother. He went on to say that he had been "throwing up all day." But he had waited until Jack was gone before he told her.[44] He was once more the object of everyone's attention. Jack couldn't take any more of his son's stunts. A few days after the overdose incident he left for Africa to work on a World Vision project, more worried now about how to salvage his badly listing marriage than about a son he could no longer bear to be around.[45] John, of course, was relieved his father was gone. Things were always easier, more relaxed, when Jack wasn't around.[46]

On November 30, the day before Jack returned from Africa, John left for Washington. He spent a good part of December stalking President-elect Reagan. The stalk was interrupted on December 8 when Beatles star, John Lennon, was murdered by Mark David Chapman outside his apartment house in New York. Hinckley was very distressed and left for New York immediately. He spent much of the next week standing vigil outside Lennon's apartment building with other mourners. He also had a sexual encounter — like Arthur Bremer's, his first — with a teenage prostitute.[47] Later that month when he returned home for the Christmas holidays, his first words to his father were, "Don't make any cracks about Lennon, Dad. I'm in deep mourning."[48] It was one of the very few occasions that he had ever "talked back" to his father.

Throughout this period Hinckley continued to make trips, wandering between Evergreen, Washington, New York, and New Haven, where he continued to make futile attempts to see Jodie Foster. In February he began to consider other possible victims who would pay the price for the frustration and anger gnawing at his insides. His reading had given Hinckley an informed grasp of the history of American violence. That month, following the lead of Oswald and Sirhan in his choice of victims, he waited in the corridor outside Senator Edward Kennedy's office on one occasion; on another he got as far as a metal detector leading into the U.S. Senate chamber before giving up the idea of a mass murder there, imitating the attack made by Puerto Rican nationalists in 1954. He browsed among the tourists on a White House tour with assassination on his mind. And on every disappointing trip to New Haven he continued to weigh the possibilities of a mass murder on the Yale campus in an attack much like the one made by Charles Whitman at the University of Texas in 1966 and the one Arthur Bremer considered in Milwaukee in 1972.[49]

He was also writing poetry, particularly morbid, self-debasing poetry that reflected another view of his growing anger, depression, and blossoming desire for revenge. In a poem he titled, "Regardless," he wrote:

> I remain the mortal enemy of Man
> I can't escape this torture chamber
> I can't begin to be happy

> I plot revenge in the dark
> I plot escape from this asylum
> I follow the example of perverts.[50]

In another entitled, "Pretend," his feelings of isolation and ulcerating self-contempt are expressed in these words:

> A solitary weed among carnations
> The last living shit on earth
> Dracula on a crowded beach
> A child without a home
> The loser of a one-man race.[51]

Throughout this period he continued to see the psychiatrist in Evergreen. But he was gone much of the time, traveling the circuit between New Haven and Washington with a stop along the way in New York, where he continued to seek out underage prostitutes. No one — neither the psychiatrist nor Hinckley's parents — was curious enough to inquire about where he was going and what he was doing on these mysterious jaunts.[52] They all knew that he made frequent trips to Washington, but no one ever inquired why. Also, in his many sessions with the psychiatrist Hinckley never revealed the violent crimes he was considering as his frustrations in New Haven and Evergreen continued to build, nor did he mention the extensive collection of articles on assassins and assassinations that he was accumulating in his room.

But he did mention his feelings of overwhelming isolation and estrangement when he was asked to write an autobiographical statement. "Because I have remained so inactive and reclusive over the past five years," he wrote, "I have managed to remove myself from the real world."[53] Hinckley also mentioned his attraction to Jodie Foster and his depression about John Lennon's death, but none of these issues was pursued during therapy. His psychiatrist was completely unaware, for example, that on January 21, 1981 — in the midst of his therapy John Hinckley had bought a Charter Arms .38 at Kawasaki West in Lakewood, Colorado.[54] It was just like the weapon Mark Chapman used to kill John Lennon six weeks before. But there was little that John Hinckley said throughout his therapy that enabled his psychiatrist to recognize that he was dealing with a very dangerous patient. Rather, it was what John Hinckley was *doing* — not saying — that his therapist missed in his diagnosis.

The Ultimatum

Perhaps that was why the prescribed treatment was so inappropriate — one of psychiatry's trendier cures at that time — biofeedback therapy. It seemed to help some patients, and Hinckley's psychiatrist prescribed it for most. The therapy was to accompany a behaviorally oriented program of self-discipline defined by a formal contractual agreement between John and his parents. Accordingly, John had to assume certain responsibilities by mutually agreed upon deadlines: by the end of February he was to have a full-time job; by March 30 he was to have his own place to live.[55] To John only the Marine Corps could have been worse. It was as if Jack had written the prescription himself.

On February 25 the Hinckleys flew to Phoenix for a stock holders' meeting followed by a few days to unwind at a guest ranch in Wickenburg, Arizona. When they returned on March 1, they found a note from John saying, "Your prodigal son has taken off again to exorcise some demons." As usual there was no hint as to where he had gone. Five days later the phone rang at 4:30 A.M. It was their son calling from New York with a familiar story: he was sick, hungry, and broke, and, of course, he wanted to come home. After much anguish over whether to send more money — against the therapist's advice — Jack bought an airline ticket for a flight to Denver which John was to pick up at the Newark airport. The next day John called again to say that he didn't have enough money for bus fare to the airport.[56]

It is little wonder that Jack Hinckley was disgusted on March 7, when John got off the plane in Denver. Jack had to get it off his chest as he ushered his musty-smelling, unshaven son to a vacant boarding area. "You've broken every promise you've made to your mother and me," he began. "Our part of the agreement [arranged by the therapist] was to provide you a home and an allowance while you worked at becoming independent. I don't know what you've been doing these past months, but it hasn't been that, and we've reached the end of our rope." Jack handed him two hundred dollars and suggested that he move into the YMCA. "From here on you're on your own," he said. "Do whatever you want to." Jack later recalled that John "looked at me like he couldn't believe his ears."[57]

In John Hinckley's unstated view his father had also broken the agreement. The agreement was that he had twenty-three more days before moving out. In this depressed, angry young man's mind it was another heartless, forced departure. The next time Jack Hinckley spoke to his son was on March 30, 1981. It was a phone call at 8:30 P.M. from a jail in Washington where his son was being held for shooting the president and three other persons.[58] After that Jack Hinckley couldn't get that look in his son's eyes out of his mind.[58] Sweet revenge.

Conclusions

Months later when a jury acquitted John W. Hinckley, Jr. outrage spilled out in newspapers and commentary across the nation. After weeks of listening to a bewildering and contradictory array of expert witnesses, jurors believed there was a "reasonable doubt" about Hinckley's mental state and decided he was not guilty by reason of insanity. Some whispered that a racially mixed jury that probably had no great affection for one of his victims, President Ronald Reagan, might have had something to do with the controversial verdict.

Whether or not John Hinckley was insane when he shot the president and three others is a question that still stirs spirited debate. The logic of his actions that fateful day suggests that he knew exactly what he was doing, was quite aware that it was wrong and — like the Type III personality that he is — simply didn't care. In any case, Hinckley has not known freedom. He remains confined as a patient in St. Elizabeths Hospital in Washington, not far from where he shot the president. In recent years, he has been granted opportunities to leave the hospital for supervised weekend visits with his parents. In December 2003, a federal district court judge concluded on appeal that Hinckley, now fifty-one years of age, was no longer "a danger to himself or others" and ruled that he would be allowed "unsupervised" visits with his parents in the Washington, DC area. The ruling was opposed by the Justice Department and the families of Hinckley's victims.[59]

* * *

FRANCISCO MARTIN DURAN (1968–)

Sunday, October 29, 1994 was cool, partly cloudy, and almost warm when the sun was out, a pleasant autumn day in Washington. Clusters of sightseers strolled along Pennsylvania Avenue in front of the White House, others sat across the street in Lafayette Square, some of them paying concessionaires to have themselves photographed beside life-size images of President Bill Clinton and his wife. At approximately 2:55 P.M., a man in a long, bulky, tan trench coat stood next to the wrought iron fence, gazing intently toward the White House. He had been standing there for nearly an hour when two young boys on a field trip ran to a spot near him, pointing excitedly toward a small group of men in dark suits strolling near the north portico of the White House. "That looks like Bill Clinton," one of them said. "Yeah it does," replied the other.

At that moment, the man near the fence, pushed the boys aside, slipped a semiautomatic assault rifle from beneath his coat, extended the folding stock and began firing at the person he mistakenly believed was President Clinton. Running back and forth along the fence as he fired, the shooter quickly emptied a clip of thirty rounds at his intended victim as bystanders scattered in panic, one of them leaving unattended an infant in a baby carriage. When he stopped to insert another thirty-round clip, a very courageous tourist,

Michael Rokosky, tackled him from behind. As they struggled on the sidewalk, two other courageous bystanders joined Rokosky, subduing the attacker before uniformed Secret Service officers arrived.[60] As he was being handcuffed, Francisco Martin Duran spoke for the first time: "I wish you had shot me," were his only words. Meanwhile, President Clinton was watching a televised football game on the opposite side of the White House, unaware until he was informed moments later by his Secret Service detail of what had happened.[61]

Something to Look Forward To

Francisco Martin Duran, or "Frankie" as his mother called him, was born on September 8, 1968 in the barrio Barelas of Albuquerque, New Mexico. Like its counterparts in other cities in the Great Southwest, the barrio is poor, often crime ridden, and it's mainly old women who show up regularly for Mass. Posters of the Virgin of Guadalupe announce religious observances that compete for space with gang graffiti on weathered stucco walls. Fiery "Evangelistico Cristiano" preachers come and go in storefront churches, offering "born again" salvation, and sometimes hot food, to people short on both. Discount liquor stores, seedy bars, a plasma clinic, pawn shops and the underfunded Barelas Community Center round out a neighborhood where half the residents, like the Durans, spoke Spanish much of the time and lived below the poverty line.[62]

Frankie was the youngest of Celia Duran's six sons, all born to different fathers. Frankie never knew his father; instead he knew only a succession of males who rotated in and out of his mother's life. How many? It was a question he couldn't, or wouldn't, answer. Unlucky in love, Celia tried to support her sons as best she could as a cleaning lady, supplementing her income with food stamps and whatever other assistance she could get from the government. She "scrubbed floors for a living," Frankie said bitterly years later.[63] Family life was bleak in the small apartment in a neglected public housing project where she struggled to raise six fatherless children alone. A sympathetic sister-in-law said, "[Celia] had to work hard, so hard, but she was a good and loving mother to those boys."[64]

Of the six boys, Frankie may have been closest to his mother. He was always a quiet, withdrawn child and his behavior didn't change as he grew older. Sometimes he went over to the community center to shoot pool. Adam Rodriquez, the director of the center, knew most of the boys who spent time there, but he had only vague recollections of Frankie. "When [Frankie] was growing up," a girl in the neighborhood said, "all his brothers, they'd hang around the community center, but Frankie, he wouldn't so much. He'd stay home with his Mom."[65]

By the time he graduated from high school in 1986, few of his classmates and teachers remembered much about him. Except for the updated photographs that appeared in the high school yearbook each year, it was as though he made no impression on anyone, one way or another. His one extracurricular activity, the high school Junior ROTC program, was duly noted, but it was, for him, much more important than that. The ROTC program with its military trappings and rituals provided status and a sense of belonging to something he could be proud of in a life where such satisfactions were scarce. Even so, his participation was unremarkable and, like most students who pass through large public high schools every year, his instructors remembered little about him. One of the few people outside of his family who did was an old woman with blurred tattoos on her hands, a neighbor. "Frankie was always a good boy," she recalled[66]

Most of the time. Albuquerque court records reveal that he had one relatively minor brush with the law when he was seventeen and a senior in high school. It was just a foolish prank, a "joy ride," on a front-end loader he managed to start at a construction site. He didn't intend to steal it. But he was quickly arrested and charged with attempted theft in the New Mexico Children's Court. For a while it seemed to Frankie and everyone else who knew the family that he was embarking upon a path of juvenile crime well-worn by his older brothers in world where there wasn't much to look forward to.

But his luck changed. The judge, noting that this was Frankie's first offense — and impressed that the defendant had graduated from high school and had participated in the Junior ROTC — offered him a deal: He would drop the charges, he said, if Frankie agreed to enlist in the Army. Frankie was quick to accept the offer and, in fact, welcomed the opportunity to serve in the military. Since he was underage, his mother had to give her approval, but that didn't require much persuasion. She was proud, happy, and probably relieved to do so. "The Army had been [Frankie's] only dream [since he was in] the eleventh grade," she said, "[so] I signed the papers." The Army was certainly better than seeing her youngest son serve months in juvenile detention as his older brother had. The Army, the judge explained to her and her son, would offer Frankie opportunities to pursue further education and economic advancement, not to mention the coveted status military service conveyed in the Hispanic community. By the time he left for basic training in the summer of 1986 Frankie was excited and optimistic about the future. A photograph after his successful completion of basic training reveals a young man in his "dress greens" with an expression of confidence and pride on his face, an American flag at his side. Later, when he was asked why he had joined the Army, Frankie replied, "I needed a job, and something to look forward to."[67]

Shattered Dreams

Despite the circumstances of his enlistment, good fortune continued as Frankie began what he hoped would be a military career. After basic training, he was pleased to learn that he had been selected for training as a medical specialist just as he had requested. More good fortune followed after his medical training was completed when he received his permanent duty assignment. It was every young soldier's dream — Hawaii, historic Schofield Barracks, only thirty minutes from Honolulu and the surf and sand of world famous Waikiki Beach. For the first time in his life, things seemed to be breaking Frankie's way. A career in the Army was developing as a very attractive possibility for this poor, fatherless kid from the barrio that only an optimist could have imagined. From what can be learned from military records, Frankie's tour of duty with the 25th Light Infantry Division in Hawaii was unremarkable, which is to say he performed as an average soldier, no better, no worse. One of his officers later described the young soldier as "a very good man when he was under me."[68] In Honolulu, he met a young woman, they fell in love, and in 1989 a son was born. Not long after they married. Again, unremarkable.

Until the evening of August 9, 1990, that is. On that evening, Frankie met a group of his army buddies at a bowling alley. It was a typical night on liberty for soldiers. Gallons of beer were consumed as they bowled, and by late in the evening everyone, including Frankie, was drunk. An argument developed between the soldiers and some civilian men and women who objected to their boisterous behavior. Tempers and decibel levels escalated and they were ordered out of the bowling alley. As the crowd spilled into the parking lot, Frankie got into his car and tried to leave, but a crowd of hostile civilians, shouting and cursing, blocked his path. He got out of the car, confronted one of them, then got back in his car and managed to drive off.

That should have been the end of it for Frankie, but it wasn't. It must have been something his antagonist said to him, because he turned his car around and drove back to the parking lot where the crowd was still milling around. In what must have been a drunken rage, Duran suddenly swerved his car and accelerated directly into the crowd of civilians, hitting and injuring a woman and scattering the rest before speeding away. He didn't get far before he was stopped by military police, dragged out of his car, and arrested.[69]

The charges were serious: drunken driving, felony assault, aggravated assault, and leaving the scene of an accident. At a general court martial, he was convicted on all charges. He tried to explain how sorry he was, that he really didn't mean to do what he had done. He wasn't a violent person, he insisted. This was his first offense. He was drunk, things got out of control, and he was truly remorseful.

It didn't matter to this military court. Frankie was stripped of his military rank, forfeiting all pay and allowances, and sentenced to five years hard labor at the U.S. Military Detention Center at Fort Leavenworth, Kansas.[70] Hard labor. Five years. At Leavenworth, the Army's most feared prison. It was devastating, especially for a first offense, or so it seemed to Francisco Martin Duran who now, like all convicts, would be known by his first, middle, and last names. There was no more "Frankie" in — and after — Leavenworth, and not much to look forward to either. His military career was finished. In disgrace.

Getting Even

Duran was released from Leavenworth in 1993 after serving two-and-half years of his five year sentence. But the dishonorable discharge he left with seemed like a life sentence to him. And, in fact, it was something a man must live with the rest of his life. It was the bitter end to a career he had cherished since joining the high school ROTC. While he was in prison, two of his brothers died, one of a drug overdose. His requests to attend their funerals were denied. He was just twenty-six years old. Now he was condemned to live the rest of his life in a dark shadow of disgrace and humiliation, decreed by the government he had tried his best to serve. At least that's the way Duran saw it; and that reality drained away much of the joy when he was reunited with his wife, Ingrid, and their five-year-old son.

They settled in a mobile home park in Widefield, Colorado, near Colorado Springs. The thought of returning to Albuquerque was too depressing. The only work he could find was as an upholsterer at the Broadmoor, a resort hotel in Colorado Springs. It wasn't much of a job for someone trained as a medical specialist, cleaning and repairing soiled and damaged upholstery. It quickly confirmed what he had feared all those months in prison. A dishonorable discharge meant dreary, low-paying, odd-hours jobs that no one else wants. His medical training meant nothing now. Scrubbing floors, cleaning rugs; it was his mother's life — the life he had tried to escape in the Army. The alienation that began with his court martial and deepened during his incarceration steadily evolved into an obsession with getting even.

But with whom? There is no evidence that Duran ever had any interest in politics. But that had changed in the grim daily routine at Fort Leavenworth. He hated government and the people who ran it. He didn't care who, or which party, was in office. A fellow worker at the Broadmoor Hotel recalled Duran's frequent complaints about "the government" and how he "really hated taxes" because the government was corrupt. "Time to take our country back" was a message he frequently scrawled on note pads and the business cards he distributed to selected acquaintants. As time wore on, his hostility became more focused. Another co-worker recalled him saying that "he didn't want to have any government official telling him what to do." A bumper sticker on his pickup truck denounced Attorney General Janet Reno and opposed gun control. He also began to tune into conservative radio and television talk shows that regularly railed against the evils of the federal government and, especially, President Clinton and his wife Hillary. During one of these talk shows the host urged his listeners to make their views known to their congressmen in Washington. Duran did. On August 23, 1994 he made what was later described as a threatening phone call to the office of Colorado senator Ben Nighthorse Campbell.[71]

But it was the president who, by this time, commanded Duran's attention. "He disliked the president," one male co-worker speculated, "because, I think, the way he saw it, he was the top guy. He told me one time that if there's anything to be done about it, you have to take out the top person."[72] "He hated President Clinton," a co-worker, Stacy Stallwood, recalled, adding that Duran said that "if he had the chance he would kill him."[73] But no one, neither Senator Campbell's staff nor his co-workers, took him seriously, and the repeated threats were never reported to authorities until after Duran proved he was not kidding.

Throughout this period, it was not only his anger that could be observed. The feelings of rejection that deepened his depression were also evident. At home he was impatient and angry much of the time, quarreling with his wife and paying little attention to his five-year-old son.[74] His struggle to contain the anger, disappointment, and profound sense of loss was being lost. His neighbors in Colorado Springs noticed that he almost always wore neatly pressed Army fatigues, as a matter of pride, unaware that he was mourning its loss.[75]

On September 13, 1994, the same day that President Clinton signed a crime bill banning assault weapons, and five days after his twenty-sixth birthday, Duran walked into a Colorado gun store and tried to purchase a handgun. The background security check required under the Brady Law revealed Duran's felony conviction and the purchase was denied. Duran was not deterred. He purchased instead at the same store a Chinese-made SKS 7.62 x 39mm semiautomatic assault rifle and 100 rounds of ammunition, a weapon he would not have been able to purchase the following day. Moreover, he had the weapon customized, adding a folding stock so it could be more easily concealed, and extra large — thirty round — military ammunition clips to ensure sustained firepower.[76] For the next two weeks, Duran continued his lethal preparations, buying another weapon, a shotgun, and additional ammunition for it and the assault rifle, and practicing at a firing range.

Duran continued to report to work through the month of September, but his wife suspected something was going on. He was moody, quarrelsome, and indifferent to her and their son. She knew he hated his job and was stressed about his low wages and their mounting debts. Especially troubling was his decision to shift some $6,000 in charges from his credit card to one they had taken out in her name. She said he told her not to worry, that "there would be money coming in soon. He said it would be big." The charges included those for the two weapons, an abundance of ammunition, a cellular phone, and a pager he had purchased. When she pressed him, he told her that he "wanted to be in the history books."[77] She claims she didn't understand. Not long afterward, he told a co-worker that he probably wouldn't be seeing him again. When asked why, he said Duran told him that "he figured he was going to be killed," but didn't elaborate.[78] No one took his threats seriously.

On September 30, Duran dropped off his wife at work. He told her that after depositing their little boy at a day care center, he was going to pick up some supplies for target practice. When he didn't pick up her or their son later that afternoon, as expected, or return that evening, she was perplexed and worried, having no idea where her husband had gone. The next day, she filed a missing person report with the El Paso County Sheriff's Office.[79] Apparently she said nothing about his threats and weapons purchases. By this time Duran was on the road, circling through New Mexico and Texas before heading east toward Washington. As he sped across the interstates, his pickup was loaded with weapons, ammunition, and other military paraphernalia, including a nerve gas antidote kit, and an order form for a book entitled *Hit Man.*[80]

When he arrived in Charlottesville, Virginia on October 10, he stopped at a gun store and purchased another thirty-round ammunition clip for the assault rifle. The next day he bought an oversized tan trench coat in Richmond that he would use to conceal his weapons and ammunition. Later he checked into a hotel in the same city. The next morning he drove into Washington. Duran moved around the district, staying in several hotels, including the Washington Hilton on Connecticut Avenue where John W. Hinckley, Jr. shot President Reagan in 1981. It was no coincidence. Like Hinckley, he also read the *Washington Post,* learning that President Clinton had left town three days earlier on a nine-state fund-raising trip and would not return to Washington for nearly two weeks. Duran realized that he had a lot of time on his hands.ABundant circumstantial evidence suggests that Duran was monitoring the president's schedule as it appeared in the *Washington Post* and the *Washington Times* from the time he arrived in the Washington area.

On October 15, he called his wife. It was the first she had heard from him. He was very agitated. She said that he told her that "he was preparing to do something drastic and that he would be killed in the assault that he was planning." When she asked where he was, he refused to tell her. Later she claimed that she had no idea what he was talking about, and guessed that he was somewhere in Texas. After worrying for two days, she called the FBI office in Colorado Springs and reported the call and his threat. The FBI later explained that since Ingrid Duran's call contained no reference to the president, or any other protectee for whom it was responsible, it was not reported to the Secret Service.[81]

Sometime after he made the call, Duran left downtown Washington and checked into the Embassy Suites hotel in the Virginia suburb of Tysons Corner.[82] While awaiting the president's return, he moved about the Washington area, spending some time with a woman whose personal ad in the *Post* he answered. At another hotel in the Virginia suburbs, he tried to date a second woman, whose tattoos he admired as they shared the hotel's hot tub. She declined.[83]

The president returned to Washington on October 22 and spent the next two days closeted with aides in the White House, preparing for an upcoming trip to the Middle East. He departed on that trip on October 24. By this time, Duran was running out of money, credit, and patience. On October 27, Washington newspapers carried the story of a disgruntled soldier who had shot and killed his executive officer and wounded eighteen others at Fort Bragg, North Carolina. Duran must have read this story, but it is not known whether this event, reflecting his own motives, had any influence on his behavior. No sooner had the president returned on October 28, when plans were announced that he would leave town again a day later on October 30 for a trip to Pennsylvania. That meant Duran's window of opportunity had closed to one day — Sunday, the 29th.

Duran arose early on that Sunday morning and checked out of his room at the Embassy Suites at 6 A.M. The drive into Washington was easy and quick with light weekend traffic. He found parking on 17th Street between D and E Streets not far from the White House. On the seat beside him he had a Washington telephone directory. At some point during his travels, he had torn a photograph of President Clinton from a San Antonio telephone directory, drawing a circle around the president with an "X" centered on Clinton's face. He had scrawled "Kill the Pres" on the cover of a Road Atlas. A letter he had written asked the question, "Can you imagine a higher moral calling than to destroy someone's dreams with a bullet?"[84]

Duran could not. Absent from all this evidence were political issues. His earlier complaints about gun control and high taxes were superficial and merely symptomatic of his deeper, all-encompassing contempt for the person who symbolized the government that had shattered his dreams.

His thoughts also included his wife and little boy. On the back of an order form for the *Hit Man* book, Duran composed what he titled his "Last Will and Words." Anticipating his own death, he wanted to make sure that his truck would be given to his wife and son and not be confiscated by the government. The will was left in the truck. He then composed a second note which he placed in his pocket. It began, "Hey Secret Service," and listed his wife's name and address and directions to where the he had parked the truck and left this request: "Please send my truck to my wife and son."[85] Recognizing the distance from the White House fence to the structure itself was beyond the range of his shotgun, he left it in the truck, loading instead the assault rifle with a thirty-round clip, carefully folding the stock down so that it could be concealed under his trench coat. He slipped an extra ammo clip into a coat pocket.[86] It was just a short walk to the spot on Pennsylvania Avenue where he stood waiting for what he considered the opportunity of a lifetime — getting even, destroying someone else's dreams.

The Verdict

After John Hinckley's controversial acquittal — not guilty by reason of insanity — for his nearly successful attempt on President Reagan's life in 1981, the standard of proof in such cases was changed. The burden of proof now rests on the defense, not the prosecution as it had when Hinckley was acquitted. It is the defense which must prove beyond a reasonable doubt that the defendant is insane. Bolstered by the testimony of three therapists, Duran's attorneys tried to convince a jury that he was legally insane — a "paranoid schizophrenic" — who was acting in the grip of a delusion when he fired all those bullets toward a man he thought was President Bill Clinton. He wasn't shooting at the president, they insisted. Instead it was an "evil controlling mist" that he imagined had enveloped the White House. The evening before the shooting, a psychiatrist testified, Duran claimed he saw a message appear at the bottom of a hotel television screen. It read, "Tomorrow will be the day action must be taken."[87] "What Mr. Duran did," his attorney subsequently argued, "was fire at the White House as a symbol . . . and at this force that was controlling the White House . . . but he didn't try to kill the President of the United States, and he didn't assault any Secret Service Officers."[88]

But there was just too much evidence that contradicted a claim that seemed flimsy and contrived: First, there were Duran's many threats and ominous statements and writings, all referring to the government, in general, or President Clinton, in particular, that anticipated his attack on the president; second, his purchase of weapons and ammunition that could be adapted to different situations he might encounter (e.g., the shotgun for short range accuracy and devastation, the assault rifle for a more distant target); third, his "Last Will and Words" reveal he clearly understood the personal consequences of what he was about to do; fourth, his purchase of an oversized trench coat to conceal his customized assault rifle and extra ammunition left little doubt that he understood the legal implications of his actions; and, finally, the patience and stealth he employed in positioning himself and waiting within range of the main entrance to the White House where he believed he would have the best opportunity to see his intended victim suggested he was in control of his actions. Taken together, all the evidence supported the prosecution's claim that Duran took "substantial steps" to kill the president, not protect him from an imaginary "evil mist" that threatened to envelope the White House. Prosecutors argued that Duran was feigning insanity to advance his case.

The jury agreed. It was also difficult for them to accept that Duran intended no harm to the president when a psychiatrist for the prosecution testified that Duran had related to him fantasies about not only killing the president with "his hands, very privately and intimately," but also Mrs. Clinton, and cannibalizing them both.[89] He added that Duran was consumed with self-loathing, describing himself as "hateful" and a "pervert," with recurring violent fantasies. According to expert testimony, Duran claimed that he wanted "to kill people in a way that might horrify others." Duran was described by another psychiatrist for the prosecution as "what we would characterize as not a very nice person . . . a person who essentially will do anything primarily for their own benefit." To support that claim, evidence that developed after his arrest revealed Duran's desire for notoriety. Rather than exhibiting shame or remorse, he told his wife to accept invitations to appear on tabloid television shows and to ask $5,000 per interview. He also suggested that she try to sell to collectors the many business cards he had embellished with handwritten anti-government statements and threats. The weight of the evidence, prosecution witnesses testified, supported their diagnosis that Duran had a "narcissistic" and "antisocial personality disorder," but he was not legally insane.[90]

On April 4, 1995 a jury in the Federal District Court of the District of Columbia rejected Francisco Martin Duran's insanity plea, and found him guilty of attempting to assassinate the president of the United States (18 *USC* 1751) and nine other related charges. On June 29, 1995, before U.S. District Judge Charles R. Richey handed his sentence, Duran's mind seemed clear enough. "My acts . . . were inexcusable and wrong," he said quietly. "I'm sorry that I've not only ruined my life and my future but that of my wife and son. . . . I wish no harm on anyone." The judge was not moved. Francisco Martin Duran was sentenced to forty-four years in prison without the possibility of parole.[91]

Conclusions

Devoid of political purpose, it is their nihilism — the pointlessness of their acts beyond revenge — that distinguishes Type III subjects from other assassins and would-be assassins. What set Francisco Martin Duran on his destructive course was a court martial and a sentence that he believed was unfair and excessive. The disgrace of a dishonorable discharge — especially for someone like Duran who attached so much value to his military service, who proudly wore his uniform, and contemplated a career in the army — is difficult to exaggerate. The humiliation that always accompanies a soldier's confinement and treatment in a military prison served to deepen Duran's depression and sense of injustice that remained after his release. His intended victim was a "symbol" as his defense attorney claimed. But it was not the "White House" or a "controlling mist" above it. For this disgraced former soldier, it was the *commander in chief* who lived there, a person who just happened to be Bill Clinton. Had he been reelected in 1992, George Bush might have been that symbol, for *any* person who happens to occupy the White House, regardless of his party affiliation, is fair game for the suicidal Type III would-be assassin. It was President Clinton's position and prominence — not his politics — that determined Duran's course of action; and, of course, his desire to end his own life in infamy — just like his Type III counterparts Zangara, Bremer, and Hinckley. It is perhaps ironic that because he like the others failed, Duran has achieved not infamy, but like them, has instead confirmed the ignominy they all sought to erase.

Notes

1. J.W. and J.A. Hinckley (with E. Sherrill), *Breaking Points* (Grand Rapids, MI: Chosen Books, 1985), p. 11.
2. Ibid., p. 39.
3. Ibid., p. 40.
4. Ibid.
5. Ibid., p. 58.
6. Ibid.
7. Ibid., p. 59.
8. Ibid.
9. Ibid., pp. 56, 60.
10. Ibid., pp. 60–61.
11. Ibid., p. 65.
12. Ibid., pp. 59, 134, 313.
13. Ibid., pp. 79, 66.
14. G. Getschow and B.R. Schlender, "Friends View Parents of Hinckley as Loving, Devoted to Children," *Wall Street Journal*, April 6, 1981, p. A1.
15. *Breaking Points,* p. 68.
16. Ibid., pp. 66, 80.
17. Ibid., p. 82.
18. Ibid., p. 84.
19. Ibid., pp. 86–87.
20. Ibid., pp. 92–93.

21. Ibid. p. 93.
22. Ibid., pp. 95–96.
23. Ibid., p. 100.
24. Ibid.
25. *United States v. John W. Hinckley, Jr.,)*, Cr. No. 81-3-306 (1981), testimony of T.C. Goldman, p. 4956. Hereafter cited as *Trial Transcripts.*
26. Federal Bureau of Investigation, "John W. Hinckley, Jr.," p. 965; and "Evidence from Evergreen, Colorado," File NO. 175–601 (1981). Hereafter cited as *FBI Files.*
27. *FBI Files* and *Trial Transcripts*, testimony of D. Bear, pp. 3847, 3878–3884; and P. Dietz, pp. 6546–6561, 6626–6627, 6629, and 6946.
28. Among the many books Hinckley collected and read were: *The Myth of the Six Million* (an anonymously written pro-Nazi book that argues that the Holocaust did not occur); *Welcome to Xanadu* (a fictional account of a kidnapper who eventually commits suicide); *The Fox Is Crazy Too* (a true story about a skyjacker); *The Fan* (a novel about a man who stalks and kills an actress); *Fade to Black* (a novel about a serial killer); *The Boston Strangler* (a true account of a serial killer); Priscilla McMillan s, *Marina and Lee* (a true story about the Oswalds); Robert Blair Kaiser's *R.F.K. Must Die!* (a true account of the trial of Sirhan Sirhan); *Starkweather* (a factual account of the murderous rampage of Charles Starkweather and his teenage girlfriend); and Arthur Bremer's *An Assassin's Diary.* Hinckley had also written a college term paper that he had plagiarized from *Starkweather.* Among the articles he had clipped were a number about the Wallace shooting: "Wallace Shot," *Dallas Morning News,* April 16, 1972, as well as articles from *Time* and *Life* published the week of the shooting. Several articles were about mass killer Charles Whitman. Hinckley also had a bibliography of published materials on President Kennedy's assassination.
29. *Breaking Points*, 127–128.
30. Ibid., pp. 100, 126.
31. *FBI Files*, p. 620.
32. *Trial Transcripts*, as quoted by P. Dietz, p. 6642.
33. Ibid., pp. 6631–6635; Defense Exhibit F-7; see, also, *Breaking Points*, pp. 297–299.
34. *Breaking Points*, p. 128.
35. Ibid., p. 129.
36. *FBI Files*, "Evidence from Evergreen, Colorado."
37. *FBI Files*, p. 968.
38. *Trial Transcripts*, testimony of S. Johnson, pp. 7487–7533.
39. *FBI Files*, "Evidence from Evergreen, Colorado;" testimony of P. Dietz, pp. 6623–6624.
40. *Trial Transcripts*, Government Exhibits 221a-221b (travel charts); see, also, testimony of S. Johnson, pp. 7487–7533..
41. *Breaking Points*, pp. 130–131.
42. *Trial Transcripts*, testimony of P. Dietz, pp. 6662–6896; and testimony of S. Johnson, pp. 7487–7533.
43. *Breaking Points*, pp. 131, 138–139.

44. Ibid., pp.139–140.
45. Ibid., p. 142.
46. Ibid., p. 141.
47. *Trial Transcripts,* testimony of T.C. Goldman, p. 5041.
48. *Breaking Points,* p. 146.
49. *Trial Transcripts,* testimony of T.C. Goldman, pp. 5242–5047; see, also, testimony of P. Dietz, pp. 7068–7078.
50. Quoted in *Breaking Points,* p. 195.
51. Ibid.
52. Ibid. p. 153.
53. *Trial Transcripts,* testimony of J.J. Hopper, p. 2556; *Breaking Points,* p. 291.
54. *FBI Files,* p. 970.
55. *Trial Transcripts,* pp. testimony of J.J. Hopper, pp. 2556, 2554.
56. *Trial Transcripts,* testimony of Jack Hinckley, pp. 2898–2899; *Breaking Points,* pp. 160–161.
57. Ibid.
58. *FBI Files,* "Arrest and Interview Log, John W. Hinckley, Jr," March 30, 1981.
59. M. Janofsky, "Man Who Shot Reagan Allowed To Visit Parents Unsupervised," *New York Times,* December 18, 2003, A1.
60. Another bystander coolly recorded the whole event on videotape.
61. The account is drawn is drawn from *White House Security Review Public Report: Francisco Martin Duran,* http://org/irp/agency/ustreas/usss/t1pubrpt.htm, p.1. Hereafter cited as *White House Security Report.*
62. A. Gottlieb, "Duran the Child Nobody Knew," *Denver Post* (November 6, 1994), p.1. *Denver Post* Archives at http://newslibrary.com/deliverdoc.asp. Hereafter cited as *Gottlieb Website.*
63. S. Rimer, "Few Knew of White House Suspects Turmoil," *New York Times,* November 7, 1994, A14
64. Ibid., p.3.
65. Ibid.
66. Ibid.
67. *Gottlieb Website,* November 6, 1994, C1; Rimer, "Few Knew of White House ...," A14.
68. *United States v. Francisco Martin Duran,* No. 95–3096, U.S. District Court, District of Columbia (1996). Website at http://www.Fed-Ct/Circuit/dc/optinions/95–3096a.html . Hereafter cited as *U.S. v Duran Website.*
69. *U.S v. Duran Website,* Flores testimony, March 27, 1995, p.41. See, also, Rimer, "Few Knew of White House ...," A14.
70. *U.S. v. Duran Website.*
71. L. Howard and C. Roehl, "Fair Warning?" *Newsweek,* November 28, 1994, p.6.
72. T. Locy, "Defense to Tell Its Side in White House Shooting," *Washington Post,* March 24, 1995.
73. *U.S. v. Duran Website,* S. Stallwood testimony, March 20–21, 1995, *pp. 14, 193.*
74. M. Janofsky, "Man Convicted of Trying to Assassinate President," *New York Times,* April 5, 1995.
75. H. Lucy and C. Roel, "Fair Warning?" *Newsweek,* November 28, 1994, p.6.

76. *White House Security Report.*
77. L. Howard and C. Roehl, "He Was Not Alone," *Newsweek,* December 19, 1994, p.6.
78. *U.S. v. Duran Website,* D. Millis testimony, March 21, 1995, p.18.
79. *FBI Report,* Colorado Springs, CO, October 17, 1994.
80. Ibid.
81. Statement of Richard Griffin, Secret Service Assistant Director for Protective Operations, the Secret Service had no file on Duran. None of his numerous threats had ever been reported.
82. Ibid.
83. T. Locy, "Defense to Tell Its Side."
84. Ibid.
85. *U.S. v. Duran Website,* March 22, 1995, pp.9, 161; Government Exhibits 155A1, 155A2.
86. *White House Security Website.*
87. *U.S. v. Duran Website,* testimony of N. Blumberg, March 27, 1995.
88. *U.S. v. Duran Website,* statement of A.J. Kramer, April 3, 1995.
89. *U.S. v. Duran Website,* P. Phillips testimony, March 29, 1995.
90. Ibid. See, also, T. Locy, "Duran Convicted of Trying to Kill President Clinton," *Washington Post,* April 5, 1995, p. D1.
91. *U.S. v. Duran Website,* June 29, 1995.

Part 4

Type IV and Atypical

8

Type IV—The Psychotics
Richard Lawrence, Charles J. Guiteau, and John Schrank

> *"It is for me, gentlemen, to pass upon you, and not you upon me."*—Richard Lawrence (to the jury)

> *"I presume the President was a Christian and that he will be happier in Paradise than here. It will be no worse for Mrs. Garfield, dear soul, to part with her husband this way than by natural death. He is liable to go at any time anyway."*—Charles J. Guiteau

> *"While writing a poem, someone tapped me on the shoulder and said: 'Let not a murderer take the presidential chair. Avenge my death.' I could clearly see Mr. McKinley's features."*—John Schrank

Of the twenty-one subjects selected for study, only four possess clear and undeniable symptoms of severe mental disorder. Although each represents a unique case, differing in interesting ways from the others, the symptoms of chronic cognitive distortion, hallucination, delusion, impaired reality contact, and, consequently, social isolation are evident in each. However, the previously applied label, paranoid schizophrenic, does not accurately describe even these four subjects, let alone all assassins and would-be assassins as some would have it.[1] Of the three psychotic assassins — Richard Lawrence, Charles Guiteau, and John Schrank — only Lawrence exhibited symptoms of the extreme and irrational suspicion, fear, and hostility that characterize the paranoid schizophrenic.[2] Although severely disordered, both Guiteau and Schrank had remarkably benign views of the world. Consider the evidence in each of these four cases.

* * *

RICHARD LAWRENCE (c.1800–1861)

On the cold, gray Friday of January 30, 1835, Richard Lawrence, armed with two pistols, attempted to take the life of President Andrew Jackson. Standing on the east portico of the Capitol, Lawrence calmly waited for Jackson to emerge from the funeral services of Congressman Warren R. Davis. As the elderly and stooped Jackson walked unsteadily from the rotunda, leaning heavily on the arm of Treasury Secretary Levi Woodbury, Lawrence stepped from the crowd, drew a pistol from beneath his cloak, took aim from a distance of no more than eight feet, and pulled the trigger. When the pistol misfired (only the cap exploded noisily but harmlessly), Lawrence pulled a second pistol from his pocket and fired again, and again with no effect. In both attempts, the exploding cap failed to detonate the powder which, from that range, should have fired a steel ball, probably ending the frail old man's life. Fortunately for Jackson, the powder and balls in both pistols had fallen out in the would-be assassin's pockets.

Lawrence was quickly subdued while the president himself, enraged by the event, struggled to get at his attacker as aides tried to restrain him. Waving his cane, the old man shouted, "Let me alone! Let me alone! I know where this came from." Jackson had immediately and incorrectly assumed that certain political opponents were behind the attack.[3]

The Attacker

Richard Lawrence was born in England — the date remains uncertain, but probably in 1800 or 1801 — and came to this country with his parents when he was about twelve years of age. The family settled in Virginia, near Washington, and Lawrence seems to have lived an uneventful life as a house painter until November 1832; that year he abruptly announced he was returning to England. Until then, Lawrence was described by relatives and acquaintances who testified at his trial as "a remarkably fine boy . . . ," as one put it, "reserved in his manner; but industrious and of good moral habits."[4]

After a month's absence when relatives and friends assumed he was in England, Lawrence returned to Washington in December, explaining that he had decided against the trip because the weather was too cold. His brother-in-law, a man whose last name was Redfern, testified that soon after

Lawrence left once again, explaining that he was going to England to study landscape painting. But soon after a brief stay en route in Philadelphia, he returned a second time, this time claiming that unnamed "people" prevented him from going on to England. The "government," he insisted, also opposed his trip. When he arrived in Philadelphia, he said that he found the newspapers so full of attacks on his character and plans that he had no choice but to return to Washington until he could hire his own ship and captain for the voyage.[5]

These incidents mark the first symptoms of Lawrence's advancing mental deterioration. At this point, he gave up his job and first described the delusion that was to lead to his attack on President Jackson. He explained to his perplexed sister and her husband, with whom he was living, that he had no need to work because he had huge financial claims on the United States government that were now pending before Congress. The claims were based on his belief that he was in fact King Richard III of England and, as royalty, the owner of two English estates, "Tregear and Kennany that were attached to the crown."[6]

A major political issue at the time was whether or not a national bank should be established in the United States. In his disordered mental state, Lawrence believed President Jackson's opposition to a national bank would prevent him from receiving a just settlement for his claims. He reasoned that with Jackson gone, the vice president would recognize the logic and merits of his case and permit Congress to make the proper reimbursement to him through a newly established national bank, enabling him to settle his estate claims in England.

While this seemed to be his primary delusion, there were also other symptoms of his worsening mental state.[7] During the same period, Lawrence, the once steady and reliable young man, suddenly became enamored with fashion. Cultivating a moustache and changing from one extravagant recently purchased costume to another three or four times a day, he would then stand mute in the doorway of his residence for hours, presumably to give passers-by the opportunity to gaze upon his sartorial splendor. When neighborhood children picked up on the fancy and addressed him as "King Richard," Lawrence was pleased, oblivious to the intended humor.

It was also at this time that he first expressed a keen interest in the opposite sex. The owner of a livery stable testified that Lawrence, dressed in extravagant and uncharacteristic clothing, would regularly hire two horses, one for himself and another with side-saddle for a young companion, a woman he described as being of "loose character." Together, the two would parade the Washington thoroughfares like royalty.[8]

In addition to these delusions of grandeur, those of persecution and a deepening paranoia that ultimately consumed Lawrence's senses became manifest during this period. Witnesses testified that this once pleasant, courteous young man suddenly became extremely hostile and suspicious. On one occasion, for example, he threatened to kill a black maid because he claimed, perhaps correctly, she was laughing at him; on another, he seized his sister by the shoulders, threatening to strike her with a paperweight because he imagined that she had been talking about him. Verbal and physical abuse describe his actions toward other family members, especially his sisters, during this period, in each instance claiming imagined grievances.[9]

Doctors and other witnesses testified, as well, to marked changes in Lawrence's physical appearance in the two years preceding his attack on the president. The effects of such changes could be observed at his trial. Dressed in a gray "shooting coat," black cravat, vest, and brown pantaloons, a strange look in his eyes, he made odd gestures or sat motionless, chin lifted, with the demeanor of royalty. Others testified to his periodic fits of laughter and cursing, his incoherent conversations with himself and a peculiar loping gait that would suddenly manifest itself as he walked. Perhaps most bizarre was and his insensitivity to cold while confined in his damp jail cell. Taken together all these symptoms describe the severity of his mental disorder.[10]

At one point during the trial, for example, he rose and, in the words of one observer, "addressed himself wildly" to the court. Ranting that the United States had owed him money since 1802 when he claimed his property had been confiscated, Lawrence, at once suddenly became calm, then announced with regal disdain, "You are under me, gentlemen." When a deputy marshal tried to seat him, an indignant Lawrence looked at him sternly and said, "Mr. Woodward, mind your own business or I shall treat you with severity." Then turning slowly back to the court with head held high, he intoned, "It is for me, gentlemen, to pass upon you, and not you upon me." When an attempt was made to pacify him with assurances that his rights would be protected, Lawrence replied, "Ay, but when?"; then suddenly with great aplomb he sat down, suddenly withdrawn, seemingly lost in thought, oblivious to his surroundings.[11]

In the weeks preceding his attack on the president, one observer reported that Lawrence would sit in his paint shop for hours, muttering to himself, "Damn him, he does not know his enemy; I will put a pistol.... Erect a gallows.... Damn General Jackson! Who's General Jackson?" When a bill was delivered, King Richard refused to accept it, shouting after the retreating postman, "Damn him! He don't know who he's dunning!"[12]

Lawrence refused to pay this and all other debts. On another occasion, his landlord approached him with a pleasant, "Lawrence, how do you do?" Lawrence replied angrily, "Go to hell! What's that to you?" When the startled landlord explained that his rent was overdue, Lawrence replied, "You mean to warrant me for it, I suppose? [Well] if you do, I will put a ball through your head."[13]

On the morning he attacked Jackson, he was seen sitting on a chest in his shop, holding a book and chuckling aloud to himself. Suddenly he dropped the book and left the shop with a smile on his face, muttering, "I'll be damned if I don't do it."[14]

Conclusions

Underscoring the abundant evidence of what would probably be diagnosed today as paranoid schizophrenia, Lawrence's family history also revealed a persistent pattern of mental illness. According to testimony, Lawrence's father had been treated for a mental disorder and an aunt had died in a mental institution.[15] The combined evidence, not to mention the defendant's bizarre courtroom behavior, was enough to convince the jury and even the prosecutor, the composer of the national anthem, Francis Scott Key, that Lawrence could not be held criminally responsible for his attempt on the president's life. He was subsequently acquitted by reason of insanity. He spent the rest of his life in the Government Hospital for the Insane in Washington. He died there on June 13, 1861. The name of the facility was later changed to St. Elizabeths Hospital.

* * *

CHARLES J. GUITEAU (1841–1882)

With the single exception of Richard Lawrence, there has been no American assassin more obviously deranged than Charles Guiteau. Unlike Lawrence, however, who could be reasonably described as a paranoid schizophrenic, Guiteau was not paranoid. Indeed, he possessed a rather benign view of the world until shortly before he was hanged. On the gallows, he did lash out at the injustice of his persecutors, but even then his anger was tempered by a sense of martyrdom, glories anticipated in the next world, and a dying man's belief that in the future a contrite nation would erect monuments in his honor. So it was delusions of *grandeur* rather than persecution that describe this bizarre little man's life.

That Lawrence was confined in mental hospitals for the remainder of his life and Guiteau hanged can be attributed primarily to two facts: President Jackson survived; President Garfield did not. For certainly the symptoms of severe mental disorder in Guiteau's case, although of a different sort, were as striking as in Lawrence's. As we will see, the convenient label and implied motive — "disappointed office-seeker" — that has been attached to Guiteau by some writers and historians confuses symptoms with causes.[16]

Religion, Law, and Politics

Charles Julius Guiteau was born on September 8, 1841 in Freeport, Illinois. His mother, a quiet, frail woman, died seven years and two deceased infants later of complications stemming from a mind-altering "brain fever," as doctors of the day described it, she had initially contracted during her pregnancy with Charles. In addition to Charles, she was survived by her husband, Luther, an intensely religious man and Charles' older brother and sister, John and Frances.[17]

From the beginning, people noticed that little Julius, as he was called (until he dropped the name in his late teens because "there was too much of the Negro about it"), was different.[18] Luther Guiteau soon became exasperated with his inability to discipline his unruly and annoying youngest son and, as a result, Julius was largely raised by his older sister and her husband, George Scoville.[19] Years later, in 1881, Scoville, an attorney, would be called to represent the accused assassin at his trial.

Although plagued by a speech impediment, for which he was whipped by his stern father, Julius was, in his fashion, a precocious youngster who learned to read quickly and write well. An annoying aversion to physical labor was observed early and remained with him the rest of his life. At the age of eighteen, he became interested in furthering his education and, against his father's will, used a small inheritance he had received from his grandfather to enroll at the University of Michigan.

His father, who was scornful of secular education, had urged his son to seek a scripture-based education at the utopian Oneida Community in New York. The curriculum there focused on study of the Bible. The elder Guiteau had hopes that his errant son might also acquire some self-discipline in a more authoritarian, God-fearing environment.[20]

After a couple of semesters at Ann Arbor, Charles, as he was now insisted on being called, decided to heed his father's advice and transfer to Oneida where, in addition to religious instruction, he had recently learned that free love was encouraged. With steamy sex and the Lord on his mind, he enthusiastically entered the New York commune in June 1860. Like his father, Charles now believed that Oneida was the first stage in establishing the Kingdom of God on Earth. He was delighted to be there.

Not long after his arrival, Charles came to believe that he had been divinely ordained to lead the community because, as he announced with what had become a typical lack of humility, he alone possessed the ability. Since no one else had received this revelation, Charles soon found himself at odds with the community leadership. Moreover, the Oneida leaders believed that Charles' vigorously protested need of longer periods for contemplative pursuits was merely evidence of the slothfulness his father had hoped they would correct.

Other tensions also began to build. Charles was becoming increasingly frustrated because the young women of the community were not responding to his amorous overtures. Convinced of his personal charm, this nervous, squirrel-like little man was annoyed because these objects' of his intended affection were so unresponsive. Adding insult to injury the young women he so avidly pursued soon began to refer to him laughingly as Charles "Gitout."[21]

As his credibility and respect within the community continued to erode, Charles's frustrations grew as he became increasingly isolated until, in April 1865, he left for New York City. He wrote to his father to explain his decision after arriving in Hoboken:

> DEAR FATHER:
> I have left the community. The cause of my leaving was because I could not conscientiously and heartily accept their views on the labor question. They wanted to make a hard-working businessman of me, but I could not consent to that, and therefore deemed it expedient to quietly withdraw, which I did last Monday . . . .
>
> I came to New York in obedience to what I believed to be the call of God for the purpose of pursuing an independent course of theological and historical investigation. With the Bible for my textbook and the Holy Ghost for my schoolmaster, I can pursue my studies without interference from human dictation. In the country [Oneida] my time was appropriated, but now it is at my own disposal, a very favorable change. I have procured a small room, well furnished, in Hoboken, opposite the city, and intend to fruitfully pursue my studies during the next three years.[22]

Then he announced a new scheme:

> And here it is proper to state that the energies of my life are now, and have been for months, pledged to God, to do all that within me lies to extend the sovereignty of Jesus Christ by placing at his disposal a powerful daily paper. I am persuaded that theocratic presses are destined, in due time, to supersede to a great extent pulpit oratory. There are hundreds of thousands of ministers in the world but not a single daily theocratic press. It appears to me that there is a splendid chance for some one to do a big thing for God, for humanity and for himself.[23]

With a new suit of clothes, a few books, and a hundred dollars in his pocket, he planned to publish his own religious newspaper that would, he was convinced, spearhead a national spiritual awakening.

In another lengthy letter to his father, Charles continued to detail his plans for the "Theocratic Daily" that would "entirely discard all muddy theology, brain philosophy and religious cant, and seek to turn the heart of men toward the living God." Buoyed with an ill-founded sense of well-being and enthusiasm, Charles went on euphorically: "I claim that I am in the employ of Jesus Christ and Co., the very ablest and strongest firm in the universe, and that what I can do is limited only by their power and purpose." And knowing full well that *he* would edit the paper, he announced confidently:

> Whoever edits such a paper as I intend to establish will doubtless occupy the position of Target General to the Press, Pulpit, and Bench of the civilized world; and if God intends me for that place, I fear not, for I know that He will be "a wall of fire around me," and keep me from all harm.[24]

Confidently expecting to promote the Kingdom of God without the restrictions of the Oneida Community and, not incidentally, also enjoy abundant wealth and fame in the process, Guiteau sought financial backing for the paper in New York City. In a flurry of optimistic salesmanship, he scurried about presenting his proposal to prospective subscribers and advertisers. They, as it turned out, were not impressed with this odd little entrepreneur or his religious views.[25] Soon finding himself short of money, tiring of a diet of dried beef, crackers, and lemonade that he ate in his dingy Hoboken room, Charles returned to Oneida after only three months in the big city, somewhat discouraged.

But he was not humbled. His return only confirmed his original reservations about the place, and he soon left again — this time more embittered by his experiences there than ever before. As always short on money, Charles wrote to the Community requesting a $9,000 reimbursement — $1,500 a year, compensation he claimed, for the six years he had misspent there. When the Community refused to pay, Charles sued, threatening to make public the alleged sexual, as well as financial, exploitation practiced by the Oneida leadership, especially its founder, John Humphrey Noyes.

Undoubtedly bitter about the rejection he had endured in this sexually permissive environment, Charles lashed out in an unintentionally amusing attack on both Noyes and the women of the Oneida community. Noyes lusted after little girls, Guiteau angrily told a reporter. "All the girls that were born in the Community were forced to cohabit with Noyes at such an early period it dwarfed them. The result was that most of the Oneida women were small and thin and homely."[26]

Obviously stung by such criticism, Noyes threatened to bring extortion charges against Guiteau. In a letter to Charles' father, who was mortified by his son's behavior, he advised that Charles had admitted to, among other sins, stealing money, frequenting brothels, and being treated for a venereal ailment. Noyes added that Charles had apparently also thrown in the towel, so to speak, in an uninspired struggle with masturbation. Such appraisals confirmed his father's sad suspicion that Charles' real purpose in going to Oneida was, as he put it, "the free exercise of his unbridled lust." Charles' "most shameful and wicked attack," he continued, and subsequent episodes convinced Luther Guiteau that his prodigal son was "absolutely insane." In despair, he wrote to his oldest son John that, unless someone or something intervened, Charles would become "a fit subject for the lunatic asylum."[27]

Having thus incurred his father's anger, and facing the prospect of a countersuit for extortion, Charles abandoned his legal claim and left New York for Chicago. There, given the standards of the day, he began to practice law, after a fashion. After only one memorably incoherent attempt to argue a case, his practice of law was reduced to collecting delinquent bills for clients. In 1869, he married an unfortunate young woman he had met at the Y.M.C.A., a Miss Annie Bunn. By 1874, the law practice and marriage had both failed, the latter the result of his adultery with what Charles admitted shamelessly was a "high toned" prostitute. The occasional beatings he used to discipline his beleaguered wife were also factors in the divorce.

When the marriage ended, Charles wandered back to New York. Continually borrowing small sums of money that he never repaid voluntarily, he soon found himself, once again, in trouble with creditors. Resentful of what he considered such unseemly harassment, he wrote an indignant letter to his brother John addressing him as "Dear Sir." This and other letters reveal the unfounded arrogance and unintentional humor of a man with an incomplete understanding of the reality of his situation:

> Your letter from Eaton . . . dated Nov. 8, '72, received. I got the $75 on my supposed responsibility as a Chicago lawyer. I was introduced to Eaton by a gentleman I met at the Young Men's Christian Association, and it was only incidentally that your name was mentioned.
>
> I wrote to Eaton several times while at Chicago, and he ought to have been satisfied, but he had the impertinence to write you and charge me with fraud, when he knew he let me have the money entirely upon my own name and position. Had he acted like a "white" man, I should have tried to pay it long ago. I hope you will drop him.
> Yours truly,
> CHARLES J. GUITEAU.[28]

A few days after this letter was written, Charles' exasperated brother himself became the target of an angry response when he requested a repayment of a small loan:

> J. W. GUITEAU: NEW YORK, March 13th, 1873
> Find $7 enclosed. Stick it up your bung-hole and wipe your nose on it, and that will remind you of the estimation in which you are held by
> CHARLES J. GUITEAU
> Sign and return the enclosed receipt and I will send you $7, but not before, and that, I hope, will end our acquaintance.[29]

Disdainful of the pettiness of such small lenders, Charles confidently launched another major venture in the publishing business: he wanted to purchase the Chicago *Inter-Ocean* newspaper. But businessmen and bankers, from whom he sought financial backing, were unimpressed and not a little skeptical about this seedy little man with a confidential manner. Frustrated but ever the undaunted optimist, Charles turned again to religion.[30]

He was immediately impressed with the bountiful collection plates he observed at the Chicago revival meetings of Dwight Moody where he served as an usher in the evening services. Charles decided to prepare himself for the ministry. After a short period of voracious reading in Chicago libraries, he soon had himself convinced that he alone had ascertained the "truth" on a number of pressing theological questions. With familiar enthusiasm, he launched his new career with pamphlets and newspaper advertisements. Adorned with a sandwich-board poster, Charles walked the streets inviting all who would listen to attend his sermons on such topics as the physical existence of hell, the Second Coming, and so forth. The self-promotion campaign was repeated in one town after another as he roamed between Milwaukee, Chicago, New York, and Boston.

In handbills, Charles proclaimed himself "the Eloquent Chicago Lawyer." His performances, in fact, followed a quite different pattern: a bombastic introduction that soon deteriorated into a series of incoherent non sequiturs, whereupon he would end inconclusively and abruptly dash from the building amid the jeers and laughter of his audiences — the whole episode lasting perhaps ten to fifteen minutes. With his dubious reputation as an evangelist growing, Charles darted from one town to another leaving in his path a growing accumulation of indignant audiences and unpaid bills. Often arrested, he was periodically jailed for short periods between 1877 and 1880 when he again turned his attention to politics.[31]

The Garfield Obsession

Describing himself as a "lawyer, theologian, and politician," in 1880 Guiteau threw himself into the Stalwart wing's intra-party fight for the Republican presidential nomination in New York. When a third term was denied President Ulysses S. Grant, the Stalwart's choice, the nomination went to a dark horse, James A. Garfield. Guiteau quickly jumped on the Garfield bandwagon. In New York, he began to hang out at party headquarters and, as he was to remind people later, he did work on the "canvass" for the candidate. In his view, his most noteworthy contribution to the campaign and Garfield's subsequent election, however, was an obscure speech he wrote (and may have delivered once in Troy, New York) entitled, "Garfield vs. Hancock." A few weeks before, the same speech had been entitled "Grant vs. Hancock." Undeterred by the change in candidates, the speech, Guiteau later claimed, first identified and developed the issue that won the election for Garfield. That issue, in brief, was the claim that if the Democrats gained the presidency it would mean a resumption of the Civil War because the Southern Democrats, who dominated the party, had only sectional, rather than national, loyalties. The only way to avoid war, Guiteau insisted, was to vote for Garfield. In a personal note, dated March 11, 1881, to the newly appointed secretary of state, James G. Blaine, Guiteau explained his claim:

> I think I have a right to claim your help on the strength of this speech. It was sent to our leading editors and orators in August. It was the first shot in the rebel war claim idea, and it was their idea that elected Garfield . . . . I will talk with you about this as soon as I can get a chance. There is nothing against me. I claim to be a gentleman and a Christian.[32]

Indeed, from the moment the election results were in, Guiteau began to press his claims in letters to Garfield and Blaine. He also became a familiar figure at the Republican Party headquarters in New York, confident that he would be rewarded for his efforts with a consulship; the only question remaining, he believed, was the location. Would it be Paris, Vienna, or some other post of prominence? With this in mind, he moved from New York to Washington on March 5, 1881, where he began to badger not only the president's staff but Blaine and the president himself in the corridors of the White House. Striking a posture of irritatingly unwarranted familiarity with those he encountered, he also let loose a flurry of "personal" notes written in the same annoying style. Typical is the following:

> [Private].
> GEN'L GARFIELD:
> From your looks yesterday I judge you did not quite understand what I meant by saying "I have not called for two or three weeks." I intended to express my sympathy for you on account of the pressure that has been on you since you came into office.

I think Mr. Blaine intends giving me the Paris consulship with your and Gen. Logan's approbation, and I am waiting for the break in the Senate.

I have practiced law in New York and Chicago, and presume I am well qualified for it. I have been here since March 5, and expect to remain some little time, or until I get my commission.

Very respectfully,
CHARLES GUITEAU.[33]
AP'L 8.

Shortly before he had written to the secretary of state to inquire whether President Hayes' appointments to foreign missions would expire in March 1881, as he expected. Learning that they would, Guiteau became more persistent in pressing his claim for an appointment to the missions of either Vienna, Paris, or possibly Liverpool. Earlier he had written again to Garfield, whom he had never met, to advise him of his plans to wed a "wealthy and cultured" woman (whose acquaintance, also, he had not at that time — or ever — made). Such unknowingly ludicrous acts were intended, in the bizarre judgment of Charles J. Guiteau, to enhance his already eminent qualifications for a foreign ministry.[34]

In the meantime, the newspapers were filled with the controversy that had developed between the new president and the boss-dominated Stalwart faction of the Republican Party over patronage appointments in New York. Finally, on May 13, 1881, the two most powerful of the Stalwart bosses, Roscoe Conkling and Tom "Me Too" Platt of New York, resigned their Senate seats in protest over the president's failure to follow their preferences in his patronage appointments. In so doing, they discounted the fact that Garfield had accepted their man, "Chet" Arthur, as his running mate and vice president. Angrily condemning the beleaguered Garfield's disloyalty and traitorous tactics, the resignations triggered numerous editorial attacks and denunciations of the president and his mentor Blaine, which were to continue until July 2, 1881.

On the same day the resignations were announced, Guiteau once again approached Blaine with his by now familiar appeals, only to have the exasperated secretary roar, "Never bother me again about the Paris consulship as long as you live!"[35] Still Guiteau persisted. A week later, on May 23, he wrote again to the president:

[Private]
General GARFIELD:

I have been trying to be your friend; I don't know whether you appreciate it or not, but I am moved to call your attention to the remarkable letter from Mr. Blaine which I have just noticed.

Type IV—The Psychotics 247

According to Mr. Farwell, of Chicago, Blaine is "a vindictive politician" and "an evil genius," and you will "have no peace till you get rid of him."

This letter shows Mr. Blaine is a wicked man, and you ought to demand his immediate resignation; otherwise you and the Republican party will come to grief. I will see you in the morning, if I can, and talk with you.
Very respectfully,
CHARLES GUITEAU[36]

If past behavior provides a clue to the future, at this point Guiteau would have begun to consider yet another occupational change, returning again, perhaps, with his typical enthusiastic optimism to theology or law. Previously, Guiteau had accepted failure with remarkable equanimity, sustained always by the exalted opinion he had of himself. As one scheme after another collapsed — his leadership aspirations at Oneida, his journalistic ventures, the law practice, and the evangelistic crusade — his bitterness and disappointment were short-lived as he moved on to other careers. His confidence in his own ability and the Horatio Alger-like opportunities that abounded in nineteenth-century America remained unshaken. Even his angry exchanges with the Oneida establishment possessed the tone of someone who enjoyed the battle as well as the spoils; certainly these exchanges reflected none of the desperation of the inveterate loser that he, in fact, was. In Guiteau's grand delusions, these frustrations were merely temporary setbacks in a career that was, he remained convinced, destined for wealth and fame.

Now, for the first time in his oddly chaotic life, Guiteau found himself sharing his outsider status with men of prominence he admired: Conkling and Platt and the other Stalwarts. And it was in this realization — not the denial of the various appointments he had sought — that his assassination scheme germinated.[37] Indeed, a month later, on June 16, he wrote in his "Address to the American People":

I conceived of the idea of removing the President four weeks ago. Not a soul knew of my purpose. I conceived the idea myself. I read the newspapers carefully, for and against the administration, and gradually the conviction settled on me that the President's removal was a political necessity, because he proved a traitor to the men who made him, and thereby imperiled the life of the Republic. At the late Presidential election, the Republican party carried every Northern State. Today, owing to the misconduct of the President and his Secretary of State, they could hardly carry ten Northern States. They certainly could not carry New York, and that is the pivotal State.

Ingratitude is the basest of crimes. That the President, under the ma-

nipulation of his Secretary of State, has been guilty of the basest ingratitude to the Stalwarts admits of no denial.... In the President's madness he has wrecked the once grand old Republican party; and for this he dies....
I had no ill-will to the President.
   This is not murder. It is a political necessity. It will make my friend Arthur President, and save the Republic. I have sacrificed only one. I shot the President as I would a rebel, if I saw him pulling down the American flag. I leave my justification to God and the American people.
   I expect President Arthur and Senator Conkling will give the nation the finest administration it has ever had. They are honest and have plenty of brains and experience.
[signed] Charles Guiteau[38] [Emphasis added.]

Later, on June 20, he added this even more bizarre postscript:

The President's nomination was an act of God. The President's election was an act of God. The President's removal is an act of God. I am clear in my purpose to remove the President. Two objects will be accomplished: It will unite the Republican party and save the Republic, and it will create a great demand for my book, "The Truth." This book was written to save souls and not for money, and the Lord wants to save souls by circulating the book.
                    Charles Guiteau[39]

   It is unlikely that Guiteau would have chosen the course of action he did without the sense that he was in good company — "a Stalwart of the Stalwarts," as he liked to describe himself. In his disordered mind, to "remove" the president, as he put it euphemistically, would provide the same status and recognition he had sought in a consulship appointment and every other hare-brained scheme he had botched since he first entered the Oneida Community to establish "the Kingdom of God on Earth." In this last grand delusion, his aspirations in theology, law, and politics were to culminate in a divinely inspired and just act "to unite the Republican party and save the Republic;" it was also intended to launch a new career for Charles Guiteau, not only as a lawyer, theologian, and politician, but as a national hero with presidential aspirations.[40]
   With this in mind, on June 8, Guiteau borrowed fifteen dollars and purchased a silver-mounted English revolver. He planned to have it, along with his papers, displayed after the assassination at the Library of the State Department or the Army Medical Museum. To prepare for the big event, he began target practice on the banks of the Potomac. After stalking the president for

several weeks and bypassing at least two opportunities to shoot him, Guiteau rose early on Saturday, July 2, 1881. He had rented a room a few days before at the Riggs House and, on this morning, began preparations to meet the president at the Baltimore and Potomac Railroad Station. The President was scheduled to leave that morning for a vacation trip. Downing a hearty breakfast, which he charged to his room, he pocketed the last of a series of bizarre explanations he had carefully written:

July 2, 1881
To the White House:
   The President's tragic death was a sad necessity, but it will unite the Republican party and save the Republic. Life is a fleeting dream, and it matters little when one goes. A human life is of small value. During the war thousands of brave boys went down without a tear. I presume the President was a Christian, and that he will be happier in Paradise than here.
   It will be no worse for Mrs. Garfield, dear soul, to part with her husband this way than by natural death. He is liable to go at any time anyway.
   I had no ill-will towards the President. His death was a political necessity. I am a lawyer, a theologian, a politician. I am a Stalwart of the Stalwarts. I was with General Grant and the rest of our men in New York during the canvass. I have some papers for the press, which I shall leave with Byron Andrews and his co-journalists at 1440 N.Y. Ave., where all the reporters can see them.
   I am going to jail.
   [signed] Charles Guiteau[41]

Guiteau then walked to the banks of the Potomac where, after taking a few final practice shots with his pistol, he proceeded to the railroad station to await the president's arrival. Once at the station, he used the men's room, had his shoes shined, and, after estimating that his assignment would be completed shortly before the president's train was scheduled to leave, he reserved a hackman for an anticipated 9:30 arrest and departure to the District Prison. He had already checked the prison's security, lest in the emotion of the moment he might be attacked by crowds who had not had time to realize what a great patriotic service he had just rendered. He was convinced that after his explanation was published the wisdom and justice of his act would be appreciated. Until such time, however, he had taken a further precaution of drafting a letter requesting that General Sherman see to his safekeeping in jail. The letter, which fell from his pocket during the scuffle that followed the shooting, read as follows:

TO GENERAL SHERMAN:
  I have just shot the President. I shot him several times, as I wished him to go as easily as possible. His death was a political necessity. I am a lawyer, theologian and politician. I am a Stalwart of the Stalwarts. I was with General Grant and the rest of our men in New York during the canvass. I am going to jail. Please order out your troops and take possession of the jail at once.
  Very respectfully,
  [signed] Charles Guiteau[42]

So it was with this completely distorted grasp of reality that Charles Guiteau fired two bullets into the president's back as he walked arm-in-arm with Secretary Blaine toward the waiting train. The president, failing to respond to treatment, lingered two and a half months before dying on September 19, 1881.

The Trial

Throughout his lengthy seventy-two-day trial, Guiteau's delusional state was apparent to anyone inclined to acknowledge it. His brother-in-law, George Scoville, represented him at the trial and entered a plea of not guilty by reason insanity. In Scoville's opening statement, he described in some detail the history of mental illness in the Guiteau family: at least two uncles, one aunt, and two cousins, not to mention Charles' mother who died of "brain fever." He went on to mention the highly eccentric behavior of Charles' father that, at least one physician thought, properly qualified him for this category.[43] Additionally, Guiteau's sister, Frances, the wife of George Scoville, behaved so strangely during her brother's trial that her probable mental condition was noted by at least one participating physician who had had occasion to observe her closely.[44] And indeed, her husband later had her declared insane and institutionalized in October 1882, after her brother's execution.

But this overwhelming evidence of a hereditary affliction was ignored or discounted by expert witnesses and finally the jury. Also discounted were the defendant's own unmistakable symptoms of mental disorder evident in the outlandish schemes, bizarre letters to prominent persons he had never met, and his wildly distorted conception of reality, which could be observed in his remarks throughout the trial and afterward to the day he was executed.

It didn't help that Scoville's line of defense was rejected by the defendant himself and greatly resented by John W. Guiteau, Charles' older brother. In a letter to Scoville, dated October 20, 1881, shortly after the trial began, John denied the history of family mental illness. Rather than heredity, he argued indignantly, most of the cases Scoville cited could be explained by self-induced factors such as insobriety and something he called "mesmerism"; the others, specifically his parents' symptoms, he categorically denied. Then, endorsing previous explanations of the causes of Charles' problems, most notably that of leaders of the Oneida Community, John Guiteau wrote, "I have no doubt that masturbation and self-abuse is at the bottom of his mental imbecility."[45]

As for Charles himself, thoroughly contemptuous of his brother-in-law's legal abilities, he drafted his own plea, which read as follows:

> I plead not guilty to the indictment and my defense is threefold:
> 1. Insanity, in that it was God's act and not mine. The Divine pressure on me to remove the President was so enormous that it destroyed my free agency, and therefore I am not legally responsible for my act.[46]

Throughout his trial, Guiteau would acknowledge only this interpretation of insanity: that is, he was insane only in the sense that he did something that was not his will but God's. He adamantly rejected the idea that he was in any way mentally ill. Typical of his remarks on this issue made throughout the trial is the following:

> 1 . . . the Lord interjected the idea [of the President's removal] into my brain and then let me work it out my own way. That is the way the Lord does. He doesn't employ fools to do his work; I am sure of that; he gets the best brains he can find.[47]

His plea continued, describing two rather novel circumstances that, he claimed, were the Lord's will just as the assassination was:

> 2. The President died from malpractice. About three weeks after he was shot his physicians, after careful examination, decided he would recover. Two months after this official announcement he died. Therefore, I say he was not fatally shot. If he had been well treated he would have recovered.[48]

This argument, as we know now, was not without merit. The third circumstance had to do with the court's jurisdiction:

> 3. The President died in New Jersey and, therefore, beyond the jurisdiction of this Court. This malpractice and the President's death in New Jersey are special providences, and I am bound to avail myself of them in my trial in justice to the Lord and myself.

He went on to elaborate:

I undertake to say that the Lord is managing my case with eminent ability, and that he had a special object in allowing the President to die in New Jersey. His management of this case is worthy of Him as the Deity, and I have entire confidence in His disposition to protect me, and to send me forth to the world a free and innocent man.[49]

The jury's guilty verdict not withstanding, it was clear that Guiteau had only the most tenuous and incomplete grasp of the reality of his situation. Almost to the last, he believed he would be acquitted, at which point, he planned to begin a lecture tour in Europe and later return to the United States in time to re-enter politics as a presidential contender in 1884. He was confident that the jury, like the great majority of Americans, would recognize that Garfield's "removal" was divinely ordained and that the Almighty himself was responsible. He was convinced they would accept his contention that he was only an instrument in the Master's hands.

Contrary to some assessments,[50] there was no evidence of paranoia in his behavior. Buoyed by a badly misplaced optimism, he mistook the crowds of curious on-lookers at the jail as evidence of respect and admiration; bogus checks for incredible sums of money and ludicrous marriage proposals that were sent to him by cranks were sincerely and gratefully acknowledged. At the same time promotional schemes evolved in his muddled mind to market his ridiculous books and pamphlets — all this while anticipating a run for the presidency in 1884! All the while, in high spirits, Charles ate heartily and slept well in a small cell located both literally and figuratively in the shadow of the gallows.

The Execution

When at the very last he realized that there was no hope for survival, his anger was tempered, much as it had been during his dispute with the Oneida Community. There were warnings, to be sure, of divine retribution awaiting the ungrateful new president, Chester Arthur, the unfair prosecuting attorneys, and the jury. But his anger lacked the intensity and desperation of someone facing what he believed was an unjust execution. As the execution date approached, Charles, confronting failure once again, simply set his sights elsewhere as he had on many previous occasions. Eschewing politics, the presidency, the Stalwarts, and the law that had failed him, the lawyer and politician once again became the theologian. Anticipating a position at the side of the Almighty in Heaven, Charles walked serenely to the gallows. Earlier he had given a last letter to the chaplain who stood by him at the end:

Washington, D.C.
June 29, 1882
TO THE REV. WILLIAM W. HICKS:

I, Charles Guiteau, of the City of Washington, in the District of Columbia, now under sentence of death, which is to be carried into effect between the hours of twelve and two o'clock on the 30th day of June, A.D., 1882, in the United States jail in the said District, do hereby give and grant to you my body after such execution; provided, however, it shall not be used for any mercenary purposes.

And I hereby, for good and sufficient considerations, give, deliver and transfer to said Hicks my book entitled "The Truth and Removal" and copyright thereof to be used by him in writing a truthful history of my life and execution.

And I direct that such history be entitled "The Life and Work of Charles Guiteau"; and I hereby solemnly proclaim and announce to all the world that no person or persons shall ever in any manner use my body for any mercenary purpose whatsoever.

And if at any time hereafter any person or persons shall desire to honor my remains, they can do it by erecting a monument whereon shall be inscribed these words: "Here lies the body of Charles Guiteau, Patriot and Christian. His soul is in glory."

[signed] Charles Guiteau[51]

Witnesses: Charles H. Reed
James Woodward

Before the noose was placed around his neck, he was given permission to read his "last dying prayer" to the crowd of faces gazing up at him from the prison yard below. Comparing his situation to that of Jesus Christ at Calvary, Guiteau condemned President Arthur's ingratitude "to the man that made him and saved his party and land," and warned of divine retribution that was certain to befall him.[52]

After completing his prayer, he again looked thoughtfully out over the crowd before announcing in a loud clear voice:

I am now going to read some verses which are intended to indicate my feelings at the moment of leaving this world. If set to music they may be rendered effective. The idea is that of a child babbling to his mamma and his papa. I wrote it this morning about 10 o'clock.

Then with childlike mournfulness, Guiteau read:

I am going to the Lordy. I am so glad.

> I am going to the Lordy. I am so glad.
> I am going to the Lordy. Glory, hallelujah; glory hallelujah.
> I am going to the Lordy;
> I love the Lordy with all my soul; glory, hallelujah.
> And that is the reason I am going to the Lord.
> Glory, hallelujah; glory, hallelujah. I am going to the Lord.
> I saved my party and my land; glory, hallelujah.
> But they have murdered me for it, and that is the reason
> I am going to the Lordy.
> Glory, hallelujah; glory, hallelujah. I am going to the Lordy.
> I wonder what I will do when I get to the Lordy;
> I guess that I will weep no more when I get to the Lordy.
> Glory, hallelujah!
> I wonder what I will see when I get to the Lordy,
> I expect to see most splendid things, beyond all earthly conception.

As he neared completion, he raised his voice to a high falsetto pitch and concluded with,

> When I am with the Lordy, glory, hallelujah! Glory, hallelujah!
> I am with the Lord.

Whereupon attendants strapped his legs, adjusted the noose, and placed a black hood over his head as Rev. Hicks prayed, "God the Father be with thee and give thee peace evermore." Guiteau, according to his own request, signaled the hangman by dropping a slip of paper from his fingers. As the trap sprung, Charles Guiteau slipped confidently into eternity with "Glory, Glory, Glory" on his lips.[53]

Conclusions

Although the debate on the true state of Guiteau's mental condition was to continue among physicians for some years afterward,[54] a brief article in the *Medical News* a day after the execution seems to have been representative of the prevailing view of the medical profession. While conceding that the neurologists who testified to the assassin's obvious mental disorder may have been correct, society would still be better, the editors reasoned, for having rid itself of such persons.[55] As a further practical matter, it is unlikely that in 1881 any jury in the country would have acquitted a presidential assassin whatever his mental condition.

Type IV—The Psychotics 255

* * *

JOHN SCHRANK (1876–1943)

The election of 1912 proved to be a volatile event in the history of the Republican Party. The Progressive wing had formally split from the badly divided party and chose the colorful former president Theodore Roosevelt as its candidate. Leading the Progressives, Roosevelt ran against the incumbent, formerly his old friend, William Howard Taft. Thus divided, the Republicans set the stage for the election of only the second Democratic president since the Civil War — Woodrow Wilson.

On the evening of October 14, 1912, Colonel Roosevelt, as he liked to be called, emerged from the Hotel Gilpatrick in Milwaukee and walked briskly toward a waiting car. He was on his way to the municipal auditorium where he was to speak to an audience of some nine thousand people. A large crowd had gathered in front of the hotel and around his car, hoping to catch a glimpse of the charismatic former president and hero of the Spanish American War. As Roosevelt climbed into the open touring car and was about to seat himself, a shot rang out. In almost the same instant, a short, stocky, and oddly pleasant-looking little man was knocked to the pavement unconscious, the pistol he fired kicked from his hand.

Roosevelt staggered briefly when the bullet struck him, pulled out a handkerchief, coughed into it, and observing no blood, called repeatedly to his aides who had grabbed the dazed assailant, "Do not kill him. Bring him here."[56] The crowd by this time was shouting "Lynch him, kill him," but Roosevelt shouted back that no one was to harm the man. He probably saved John Schrank's life as Schrank was dragged though the crowd and carried into the hotel kitchen where he was held until the police arrived.

As one of the Colonel's aides, Henry F. Cochems, stood at his side providing support, Roosevelt calmly observed, "He pinked me, Henry." He then turned to the crowd and shouted, "We are going to the hall; we are going to the hall; start the machine; go ahead; go on."[57] His aids protested to no avail, urging him to get medical attention. On the way to the speech, blood flowed steadily from the wound in his chest, staining his shirt, seeping down though his underclothing and puddling in and around his left shoe. His aides were terrified, but Roosevelt ignored their pleas, insisting that he be taken, as planned, to the auditorium to give the speech.

As he sat on stage waiting to be introduced, an aide issued the stunning announcement that Roosevelt had been shot. The audience gasped. When a heckler boisterously disputed the claim, Roosevelt, grinning defiantly, strode to the podium and with a flourish unbuttoned his vest to expose the blood-stained shirt. As expressions of shock and horror rippled through the auditorium, Roosevelt seized the moment. Drawing himself to full height, he announced:

> It takes more than one bullet to kill a Bull Moose. I'm all right, no occasion for any sympathy whatever, but I want to take this occasion within five minutes after having been shot to say some things to our people which I hope no one will question the profound sincerity of.[58]

Amid cheers from the audience, the Colonel proceeded with a typically bombastic campaign speech. At one point, Roosevelt appeared faint and a doctor rushed to his side pleading with him to stop and get the medical attention he needed. But Roosevelt refused. Then, turning dramatically to the audience he added, "If these doctors don't behave themselves I won't let them look at me at all." The crowd roared its approval. What a performance! They loved it. So did Roosevelt. "It takes more than one bullet to kill a Bull Moose," he repeated with obvious pride, triggering another roar from his admirers. A moment later, for all to hear, he again admonished the worried doctors, "Good gracious, if you saw me in the saddle at the head of my troops with a bullet in me you would not mind."[59] The old "rough rider" stayed around long enough to finish his speech and wring the last drop of political advantage from the circumstances. But it was more than politics; it was a statement about the kind of man's man Theodore Roosevelt was.

Later, after treatment at the hospital, doctors announced that the old Bull Moose would have been killed had it not been for the fifty-page speech that had been folded along with a spectacle case he had carried in his left breast pocket. These items and his heavy clothing absorbed the shock of the .38 caliber bullet and prevented it from penetrating the rib cage, thus sparing his life. After a brief period of recuperation, he resumed his vigorous campaign schedule.

The Assailant

Roosevelt's thirty-six-year-old assailant was a mild-mannered, but deeply troubled man who was offended and obsessed with the threat, he claimed, that the former president's bid for a third term in the White House posed to the nation's democratic institutions. In Schrank's mind, breaking the two-term tradition was the first step toward dictatorship. Although pleading guilty to the shooting, Schrank explained that he did not intend to kill "the citizen Roosevelt" but rather *only* "Theodore Roosevelt, the third termer." "I did not want to kill the candidate of the Progressive Party," he continued, "I shot Roosevelt as a warning to other third termers."[60]

Although Roosevelt's decision to compromise the "third term tradition" was what prompted Schrank's act, he said there were other grievances that provoked him as well. Prior to the campaign of 1912, Schrank had composed a curious essay on four unwritten laws of government, or as he called them, "The Four Pillars of Our Republic." In it, he discussed the crucial importance of denying a third term to presidents, denying the presidency to Roman Catholics, enforcing the Monroe Doctrine, and avoiding wars of conquest. The "Four Pillars," he reasoned, were fundamental to the nation's well-being.[61] The fact that Roosevelt was a nominal Protestant (whose concept of religion, he once confided, was based almost exclusively on the verse in St. James: "I will show my faith by my works"[62]) and a firm believer in the Monroe Doctrine did not compensate, in Schrank's mind, for his other deficiencies. In addition to the third-term bid, Schrank also resented what he called Roosevelt's "rough-rider masquerade" in Cuba during the Spanish American War. And there was another more personal issue: As a former saloon keeper in New York City, Schrank was angry about Roosevelt's vigorous enforcement of blue laws requiring the closing of bars on Sundays when Roosevelt had been city police commissioner.[63] That had cut into his income.

Who was this plump and seemingly comfortable little man with the rumpled appearance and courteous manner who wanted to kill the former president? John Flammang Schrank's short stature, drooping eyelids, and normally pleasant expression were reminiscent of "Dopey," the dull-witted but lovable dwarf who befriended "Snow White" in Walt Disney's film. Born in Bavaria in 1876, he came to live with his uncle and aunt in New York City when he was twelve in 1888. He was never close to his real parents who remained in Europe.

His foster parents operated a respectable and profitable neighborhood saloon at 370 East Tenth Street, a neighborhood crowded with immigrants like Schrank. His aunt and uncle were as good to their kind, well-mannered nephew as he was to them. They were close. John helped tend bar and did other chores associated with the family business.

Having had only five years of schooling in Bavaria, Schrank was eager to enroll in night classes after arriving in New York. There he learned English and became an avid reader of history, government, and the Bible. His English improved until he was considered quite proficient in his adopted language. At the age of fifteen or sixteen, John developed an interest in poetry and the writings of the liberal German-American political philosopher and reformer Carl Schutz.

He was deeply grieved when his aunt and uncle died within a year of each other in 1910 and 1911. He was alone. After their deaths, he learned that he had inherited the business and other real estate valued at some $25,000 — a significant sum for the time. He promptly sold the business and lived from that time until his arrest a year later simply and comfortably on that money.

He never married. Although always courteous and pleasant, Schrank became more withdrawn after the deaths of his aunt and uncle. He spent increasing amounts of his time in solitary strolls in the city parks, or just reading and jotting down his thoughts and composing odd poems. A representative sample of the latter is quoted below:

ELECTRIC LIFE
The law that rules electricity
Controls the human life:
The magnitude you possess
Will draw to you a wife.
For positive and negative
Are poles that never meet.
So be sure that she is negative
If you intend to lead.
All matrimonial troubles
Rise from the same defect
Because positive and positive
Are poles that don't connect
Your station and your influence
The number of friends you control,
Depends upon the power
Of your positive pole.
Your powerhouse is heaven,
The current is your soul,
Your spirit is the wire,
And God your positive Pull;
A sudden death-the failure of heart
Is in other words-a circuit short
But when you die at 90, about
We simply say your fuse burnt out.[64]

It was presumably with such thoughts running through his mind that he retired on the evening of September 15, 1901 — the day after President McKinley died, the victim of an assassin's bullet. At 1:30 A.M., Schrank claimed he was awakened by a vision that he described in a scrawled note:

September 15th, 1901
TO THE PEOPLE OF THE UNITED STATES:
  In a dream I saw President McKinley sit up in his coffin, pointing at a man in a monk's attire in whom I recognized as Theo. Roosevelt. The dead President said, "This is my murderer, avenge my death."[65]

Type IV—The Psychotics 259

It was during the period following this dream that Schrank had — or imagined he had — his first and only romance with a neighborhood girl, one Elsie Ziegler, to whom he claimed he had been engaged. But according to Miss Ziegler's brother, Edward, Schrank was never more than a "nodding acquaintance" to his sister. In any case, John recalled the relationship differently in a conversation with a newspaper reporter after his arrest. "I had a sweetheart once," he said. "I haven't any relatives, but I did have a sweetheart once. Her name was Elsie Ziegler. She was a pretty girl. I loved her."[66] He went on to explain that she had died in 1904 when a ferryboat burned and sank in New York harbor. He added that he never wanted a girlfriend after that.

Whether or not John's love affair with Elsie Ziegler was imagined, as her brother and others claimed, or real, other delusions and strange ideas were now beginning to dominate his thinking and loosen his grasp on reality. He also began to spend long hours alone at the gravesides of his aunt and uncle. He even moved to an apartment near the Brooklyn cemetery so that he could be closer to them.[67]

According to Schrank, on September 14, 1912, at 1:30 A.M. — almost eleven years to the minute after his first vision — he was once again visited by the spirit of William McKinley on the eve of the anniversary of his death. He wrote down a description of the experience:

September 14, 1912 1:30 A.M.
 While writing a poem, someone tapped me on the shoulder and said: "Let not a murderer take the presidential chair. Avenge my death." I could clearly see Mr. McKinley's features.
 Before the Almighty God, I swear that the above written is nothing but the truth.[68]

Already greatly distressed by what he considered Roosevelt's traitorous bid for a third term, this second visitation and explicit command from the dead president Roosevelt succeeded convinced Schrank that it was time to act. He bought a .38 caliber pistol for fourteen dollars and a steamship ticket to Charleston, South Carolina where Roosevelt was scheduled to campaign. On September 21, 1912, he embarked on his pursuit of the campaigning candidate, following a trail that would lead him eventually from Charleston to Augusta, Atlanta, Birmingham, Chattanooga, Nashville, Louisville, Evansville, Chicago, and Milwaukee before he finally got his chance.[69]

After his arrest, Schrank, denied that he was insane, citing the divinely inspired visions of Moses and Joan of Arc as comparable to his own. He explained that such experiences were common to a select few chosen to do God's bidding. Convinced that he now enjoyed such status, he sought to legitimize his claim by requesting that his pistol and the bullet that struck Roosevelt be given to the New York Historical Society for public display. When a sheriff's deputy explained that doctors had decided against removing the bullet from Roosevelt's rib cage, Schrank was furious:

> That is my bullet. In after years when I am regarded as a hero, the bullet will be valuable and I want it to go to the New York Historical Society. I want the gun to go with it also and I am putting that in my will.[70]

The Verdict and Aftermath

Statements such as this considered along with the McKinley visitations left little doubt that Schrank was psychotic. Further investigation also revealed a hereditary strain of mental disorder in his family: an aunt and possibly his father and grandfather had been afflicted. Thus, there was little controversy when a panel of alienists (as psychiatrists were called at the time) concluded that John Schrank was insane and was therefore exempt from criminal proceedings.

Although diagnosed as a paranoid by the panel,[71] except for the hostility Roosevelt's possible third term generated, Schrank appeared to possess a remarkably benign view of the world. There was no evidence of either physical or verbal aggression in his past. Witnesses recalled him as a quiet but pleasant man who didn't bother anyone. Indeed, until a few minutes before the shooting, he sat in Herman Rollfink's saloon talking pleasantly with the bartender Paul Thume. According to Thume:

> He . . . asked the bar musicians to play some song, something with stripes in it, and then he bought each one a drink.

Enjoying the company, Schrank danced merrily around as they played, perhaps feeling the effects of the beer he had been drinking. He then bought another jovial round of drinks and left. Schrank later chuckled openly as the bartender related the incident at a pre-trial hearing, recalling that the song with "stripes" was the popular patriotic march, "Stars and Stripes Forever." A few minutes later, he shot Roosevelt.[72]

During his confinement in the Milwaukee jail, his friendly ways and thoughtfulness soon made him a favorite with the other prisoners. A pleasant conversationalist on most topics except the shooting, which he would not discuss with anyone but authorities, he laughed and joked while he taught fellow inmates and guards the finer points of checkers.

Apparently the only thing offensive about John Schrank was his body odor — even by the lenient standards of that era. He did not like to bathe. After a week or so in confinement, the sheriff directed that he be required to wash. Schrank's smelly clothes were destroyed and new ones issued with the strict injunction that he bathe regularly. It remained something he did without enthusiasm.[73]

Later when the panel of doctors announced their insanity verdict, the agreeable Schrank, shaking hands and thanking each, informed them that while he disagreed with their diagnosis, he felt that they had done their best. Similarly, as he was being transferred from the jail for his trip to the state mental hospital, he thanked the sheriff and a jailer for their kindness adding, "I hope I haven't caused you much trouble." "Not a bit," the sheriff replied. "You've been the best prisoner we have had here since I have been in office."[74]

As the train rolled across the wooded Wisconsin countryside en route to the state mental hospital, he was asked whether he liked to hunt. "Only Bull Moose," he replied with a smile.[75]

Schrank lived the remainder of his years as a patient in the state hospital for the criminally insane at Waupon, Wisconsin, where he became known affectionately as "Uncle John." He was described as a model patient and a very kind person when he died at the age of sixty-seven on September 15, 1943 — the forty-second and thirty-first anniversaries of the two visions that had so influenced his life, if not the nation's history as he had intended.

John Schrank never received a card or visitor in over thirty years of confinement. When he died, unlike his heroes, the biblical Moses and St. Joan, there was no one to memorialize him or even claim his body. The kindly, old would-be assassin became just another cadaver at the Marquette University Medical School.

Conclusions

There can be little doubt that Richard Lawrence, Charles Guiteau, and John Schrank were legally insane. But even among these rather obvious cases of mental disorder there are differences. Lawrence was the most severely afflicted, a victim of profound emotional and cognitive confusion. He actually did not know who he was, nor was he fully aware of what he was doing. His behavior had assumed a random quality, unrelated to events and circumstances around him. He was even insensitive to the realities of his physical environment; he seemed impervious, for example, to the cold temperatures of his jail cell. For Lawrence, the world was a hostile place — he had no allies, everyone was out to get him. He alone seems to have possessed the all-consuming symptoms associated with paranoid schizophrenia.

Charles Guiteau and John Schrank were less severely afflicted than Lawrence. Although both suffered from delusions and markedly distorted perceptions of the world and their place in it, neither possessed the severe loss of contact with reality experienced by Lawrence. While both were motivated by grandiose delusions of their own importance, the darker side of that phenomenon — paranoia — was missing. Both acted in concert with remarkably benign views of society. They saw good not only in themselves but in almost everyone else. Indeed one of faulty perceptions of each was their expectation that, in time, society would view their actions sympathetically. Almost to the end, Guiteau felt the nation would come around to his point of view and, consequently, spare his life. His sense of injustice before his execution was simply a reflection of the disappointment of an optimist whose expectations no sane person would have entertained. And even then, he died believing he would be honored eventually by a repentant nation. And Schrank, living the rest of his life in confinement, without bitterness, became the kindly old "Uncle John" to hospital attendants that he probably had always been, making almost believable his belief that his aggression on that cool October evening in 1912 came not from within, but from above.

There is no evidence to support the contention commonly put forth that Guiteau and Schrank were motivated by delusions of personal persecution as was Lawrence. Mentally disordered, to be sure, but only in their grandiose delusions that each was convinced he had been selected by God to implement His will.

Notes

1. D. W. Hastings, "The Psychiatry of Presidential Assassination, Part I: Jackson and Lincoln," *Journal-Lancet* 85 (March 1965): 93–100; "The Psychiatry of Presidential Assassination, Part II: Garfield and McKinley," *Journal-Lancet* 85 (April 1965), 157–162; and "The Psychiatry of Presidential Assassination, Part III: The Roosevelts," *Journal-Lancet* 85 (May 1965): 189–192.
2. On July 24, 1998, Russell E. Weston, Jr. shot and killed two security officers inside the U.S. Capitol in an intended assault on the U.S. Congress. Weston, who was arrested at the scene, told authorities his act was in retaliation for the government spying on him. A psychiatric evaluation concluded that Weston was psychotic, a paranoid schizophrenic too delusional to be tried. Weston believes that the Central Intelligence Agency had placed listening devices in his teeth. He also claimed that his thoughts were being monitored by satellite dishes near his Montana residence which was surrounded with atomic weapons. Records on his case are sealed as he remains hospitalized at a government facility in Butner, North Carolina.
3. "Trial of Richard Lawrence," in *Assassination and Insanity: Guiteau's Case Examined and Compared with Analogous Cases from the Earlier to the Present Times,* ed. William R. Smith (Washington, D.C., 1881), pp. 26–80. Hereafter cited as *Cases.* See also *United States v. Richard Lawrence* (March 1835), Circuit

Type IV—The Psychotics 263

Court, District of Columbia, Case No. 15, 577; *Niles Register,* vol. 48, 1836; and *Criminal Appearances* 119 (March 1835), United States District Court of the District of Columbia, Record Group 21, National Archives.
4. *Cases,* p. 33.
5. Ibid., pp. 30–31.
6. Ibid., p. 31.
7. Ibid., p. 30.
8. Ibid., p. 35.
9. Ibid., p. 31.
10. Ibid., pp. 32, 34, 38.
11. Ibid., p. 30
12. Ibid., p. 32.
13. Ibid., p. 34.
14. Ibid., p. 32.
15. C. Jackson, "Another Time, Another Place-The Attempted Assassination of President Andrew Jackson," *Tennessee Historical Quarterly* 26 (Summer 1967): 188.
16. See, for example, J. McKinley, *Assassination in America* (New York: Harper & Row, 1977), p. 42; and S. E. Morison and H. S. Commager, *The Growth of the American Republic* (New York: Oxford University Press, 1950), 2:221.
17. *United States v. Charles J. Guiteau* (1882), Supreme Court of the District of Columbia, Criminal Case No. 14056 National Archives), statement of George Scoville, p. 294. Hereafter cited as *Trial Transcripts.*
18. *Trial Transcripts,* testimony of Charles J. Guiteau, p. 311.
19. *Trial Transcripts,* statement of George Scoville, pp. 294–295.
20. Ibid.
21. Ibid., pp. 297–298.
22. J.W. Guiteau, "Letters and Facts Not Heretofore Published, Touching the Mental Condition of Charles J. Guiteau Since 1865," Document submitted to the President of the United States by John W. Guiteau in the Matter of Application for a Commission De Lunatico Inquirendo, June 23, 1882, File No. 14056, National Archives, p. 11.
23. Ibid.: See also C. J. Guiteau, "The New York Theocrat," prospectus, File No. 14056, National Archives."
24. J.W. Guiteau, "Letters and Facts," p. 11.
25. C.J. Guiteau "The New York Theocrat."
26. C. E. Rosenberg, *The Trial of the Assassin Guiteau* (Chicago: The University of Chicago Press, 1968), p. 26.
27. J. Guiteau, "Letters and Facts," p. 23.
28. Ibid., p. 22.
29. Ibid.
30. *Trial Transcripts,* statement of George Scoville, pp. 2115–2116
31. Ibid., pp. 305–307, 2118–2119.
32. Letters of Charles J. Guiteau, File No. 14056, National Archives. Hereafter cited as Guiteau Letters.
33. Ibid.

34. Ibid.
35. *Trial Transcript*, p. 211.
36. C. J. Guiteau Letters.
37. *Trial Transcripts*, testimony of Charles J. Guiteau, pp. 56–57.
38. *Letters, Trial Transcripts*, Exhibit, p. 216.
39. Ibid.
40. *Trial Transcripts*, testimony of Charles J. Guiteau, p. 2206.
41. Guiteau Letters
42. Ibid.
43. C. F. Folsom, *Studies of Criminal Responsibility and Limited Responsibility* (Boston: Privately printed, 1909), p. 20; and *Trial Transcripts*, statement of George Scoville, pp. 291–293.
44. E. C. Spitzka, "A Contribution to the Question of the Mental Status of Guiteau and the History of His Trial," *Alienist and Neurologist* 4 (April 1883): 204.
45. J. W. Guiteau, "Letters and Facts," p. 2.
46. W. W. Godding, Two *Hard Cases: Sketches from a Physician's Port*folio (Boston: Houghton Mifflin, 1882), p. 46.
47. "The Trial of Charles J. Guiteau for the Murder of President Garfield, in *American State Trials,* ed. J. D. Lawson (St. Louis, MO: Thomas Law Book Co., 1923), 14, 68.
48. Godding, Two *Hard Cases, pp.* 46–47.
49. Ibid., p. 47.
50. Hastings, "The Psychiatry of Presidential Assassination, Part II."
51. Guiteau Letters.
52. Lawson, "The Trial of Charles J. Guiteau," pp. 156–157.
53. Ibid., p. 157.
54. J. P. Gray, "The United States vs. Charles J. Guiteau," *American Journal of Insanity* 38 (January 1882): 303–448; Spitzka, "A Contribution"; A. M. Hamilton, "The Case of Guiteau," *Boston Medical and Surgical Journal* 106 (March 9, 1882): 235–238; S. Mitchell, "The Man Who Murdered Garfield," *Proceedings of the Massachusetts Historical Society* 68 (1941–1944): 452–489; and Rosenberg, *The Trial of the Assassin Guiteau.*
55. "Guiteau-Finis," *Medical News* 41 (July 1882): 12.
56. O. E. Remy et al., *The Attempted Assassination of Ex-President Theodore Roosevelt* (Milwaukee: The Progressive Publishing Co., 1912), p. 147.
57. Ibid., p. 148.
58. Ibid., p. 20.
59. Ibid., pp. 42, 45.
60. Ibid., pp. 101–102.
61. Ibid., pp. 224–234.
62. G. E. Mowry, *The Era of Theodore Roosevelt and the Birth of Modern America* (New York: Harper & Row, 1958), p. 48, citing E. E. Morison, ed., *The Letters of Theodore Roosevelt,* 8 vols. (Cambridge, MA: Harvard University Press, 1951), 3: xvi.
63. *Milwaukee Journal,* October 15, 1912, 1–2.
64. Ibid., November 13, 1912, 1–2.

Type IV—The Psychotics   265

65. A. MacDonald, "The Would-Be Assassin of Theodore Roosevelt," *Medical Times* 62 (April 1914): 100.
66. *Milwaukee Journal,* October 15, 1912, 1.
67. Ibid., October 16, 1912, 1, 4.
68. MacDonald, "The Would-Be Assassin," p. 100.
69. Remy et al., *The Attempted Assassination, p.* 202.
70. *Milwaukee Journal,* October 18, 1912, 1.
71. MacDonald, "The Would-Be Assassin," p. 101.
72. Remy et al., *The Attempted Assassination, pp.* 108–109.
73. *Milwaukee Journal,* October 18, 1912, 1.
74. Ibid., October 17, 1912, 1–2; November 25, 1912, 1; Remy et al., *The Attempted Assassination, p. 111.*
75. *Chicago Tribune,* November 26, 1912, 1.

9

The Atypicals—Family and Money
Carl Austin Weiss and James Earl Ray

> *"[H]ow could he have left the wife and baby that he loved above everything?—A relative of Carl Austin Weiss, 1935*
>
> *"If he done it there had to be a lot of money involved because he wouldn't do it for hatred or just because he didn't like somebody, because that is not his line of work."—Jerry Ray, 1968*

In my analysis of assassins and would-be assassins, only two defy classification, and these two atypical subjects are as different from each other as they are from the others. Carl Austin Weiss was the most unlikely of all American assassins. Happily married, a doting parent, and a prosperous, respected physician, no one could have predicted that he would kill the flamboyant United States senator and presidential aspirant, Huey P. Long in 1935. At the opposite end of the sociological spectrum, we find the other atypical case, James Earl Ray, the convicted slayer of civil rights leader Martin Luther King, Jr. Unlike Weiss, Ray was notably unsuccessful, even compared to other assassins. Born into poverty and crime, Ray had spent most of his life in prison for clumsily executed robberies. His whole life can be understood, in one sense, as a futile attempt to reach the height of material comfort and respectability that Carl Weiss acquired at birth.

Just as their lives differed, so did their motives: Weiss killed in order to remove what he considered to be an eminent threat to the family he loved; Ray killed for the basest of reasons — money. It is important to note in the following accounts how far each of these cases depart from the assassin stereotype.

* * *
CARL AUSTIN WEISS (1905–1935)

Senator Huey P. Long was shot on the evening of September 8, 1935 in a corridor of the capitol building in Baton Rouge Louisiana. His assassin was killed immediately by his bodyguards; Long died shortly after, on September 10. So unlikely was his assassin, that to this day there are those who question whether he actually did shoot Long, in spite of the scores of persons who witnessed the incident in the crowded corridor. And even among those who accept that he did, no one is completely sure why. Carl Austin Weiss remains, without question, the most improbable of American political assassins.

Although the life of his colorful victim has been the subject of numerous books, among them Robert Penn Warren's fictionalized treatment, *All The King's Men*[1] (which later became an Oscar-winning movie) and T. Harry Williams' biography *Huey* Long[2] — both of which won Pulitzer Prizes — comparatively little is known or remembered about his assassin.[3] Few official records were kept; only the most perfunctory of inquests were held in both deaths.

The first detailed accounts of the actual assassination were published coincidentally in 1963 in two books: David Zinman's *The Day Huey Long Was Shot*,[4] and Hermann B. Deutsch's *The Huey Long Murder Cases*.[5] Both books attempt to reconstruct the assassination and possess the authenticity of primary sources. Deutsch's book is based on his notes and recollections of the event and its aftermath as a New Orleans newspaperman who knew Long and many of his associates personally. Zinman's book is the first and only account based on extensive interviews in the early sixties with the families of the slain assassin and his wife.

It is indicative of the improbable qualities of the event that both of these carefully researched books arrive at different conclusions: Deutsch ends convinced that Weiss undoubtedly shot Long on that warm Sunday evening in 1935 for personal reasons, Whereas Zinman believes, along with Weiss's family, that Long was shot accidentally by his own trigger-happy bodyguards after he was accosted by Weiss. T. Harry Williams, in his biography of Long, relies heavily on the work of both Deutsch and Zinman, agreeing with Deutsch that Weiss did kill Long, but differing in that Williams believed it was for political rather than personal reasons. The conflicting conclusions of these factually consistent books can be traced directly to the mysterious motives of Dr. Carl Austin Weiss. The purpose of my account is to draw together, for the first time, important facts presented separately by Deutsch, Zinman, and Williams that provide a more plausible and complete explanation for Long's death.

A Good Life

On December 18, 1905, Viola Maine Weiss gave birth to her first child, a son they named Carl Austin, in Baton Rouge, Louisiana. Her husband, Carl Adam Weiss, was a young physician who had just started a practice in Baton Rouge. Two years and another child, Olga Marie, later, the family moved to New Orleans where Dr. Weiss had decided to return to medical school to specialize in eye, ear, nose, and throat medicine. After completing his studies in 1916, he and his family returned to Baton Rouge where he began what was to become a successful medical practice. In 1917, their third and last child was born, another son, Thomas Edward.

The Weiss family settled into a comfortable but unpretentious life in leafy, warm, and very southern, Baton Rouge. Strict German Catholics, the family attended church regularly and took their religion seriously. The elder Weiss was a demanding, stern, but loving father who attended Mass daily at 5:15 A.M. and imposed a strong belief in punctuality on all the activities of his family.

His oldest son, Carl Austin, appeared to be his favorite. A quiet, obedient, and highly intelligent youngster, he developed an early interest in mechanics, electricity, and music. He would spend long hours alone playing with erector sets and radios, and eventually learned to play the piano, clarinet, and saxophone. At the age of eight, he disassembled and repaired a family heirloom clock without assistance. Later he was to impress his chums by surreptitiously running electricity from a streetcar stop into their clubhouse. At the age of twelve or thirteen, he wired his grand aunt's house. His competence was later verified by a qualified electrician he agreed to have check his work.

Carl was a curious youngster, interested in many things. An early and avid reader, he damaged his eyes as a result of his refusal to stop reading while he had the measles. He made sketches, dabbled in photography and woodcarving, played tennis, and fished. He also liked guns, although he never hunted, preferring instead to test his skill on targets rather than living creatures.[6]

Carl's very obvious talents enabled him to graduate from St. Vincent's Academy as valedictorian at the age of fifteen in 1921. He entered Louisiana State University at the end of that summer to major in engineering. At the end of two years, he had a B-plus average, but decided he would switch from engineering to medicine like his father. Since Louisiana State had no premedical program, the change meant that he would have to transfer down the river to Tulane.

As a child, Carl had always been quiet, somewhat introverted. Invariably polite and courteous, he seemed to be more comfortable puttering with things rather than socializing. During college, however, he became more sociable. A wry sense of humor, musical ability, and knowledge about a wide variety of subjects made him a popular person with his fraternity brothers. Despite his retiring manner, he was, nonetheless, elected secretary-treasurer of the Sigma medical fraternity. He was also quietly public spirited and regularly gave up his evenings to play the organ for songfests that were held in a nearby old folks home.[7]

Graduating with a bachelor of science degree in 1925, Carl continued on with his medical training at Tulane winning an internship in pathology at the Touro Infirmary in New Orleans. In 1927, at the early age of twenty-one, he received his M.D. He was invited to remain on another year at the infirmary. In 1928, the impressive young physician was awarded a prestigious internship to study at the American Hospital in Paris. On September 19, 1928, Carl sailed from Hoboken, bound for France on the *George Washington.* While in Europe, he also studied briefly in Vienna and found time to tour Italy, Hungary, and Yugoslavia, where he witnessed the first ripples of the Fascist tide that was to sweep over Europe in the next decade. But in Europe, he was much more interested in art, music, architecture, and professional matters than he was in politics. As his brother recalled later:

> He felt that politics, as he saw it, was an awful lot of wheels spinning and it really didn't get you very far. He always seemed to have more interesting things to talk about. . . . In fact, I never recall he ever had any strong political philosophy. Just right and wrong. And that was it.[8]

After his return to the states in May 1930, Weiss accepted an internship at Bellevue Hospital in New York where, following his father's lead, he specialized in eye, ear, nose, and throat medicine. At Bellevue, this talented young surgeon from Baton Rouge impressed virtually everyone. Describing Weiss as "really a brilliant man," one of his colleagues there reported that he also had a way with his patients:

> He did some of the most constructive work ever performed in Bellevue clinic. Strong-willed, or even hot-headed, as some might call it, he had a certain charm of manner with troublesome patients. I remember that several times patients were turned over to him when nobody else could handle them. He did.[9]

His colleagues at Bellevue also recalled that he had firm political opinions, but they agreed that politics was not a central concern with him. When asked about the controversial Huey Long, Weiss made it clear that he didn't care for Senator Long, and would never vote for him, but his feelings were not intense; instead they were like those of any number of other professional people in Louisiana who found the senator's politics and coarseness embarrassing, more offensive to their taste than a threat to their interests.[10]

The Atypicals—Family and Money   271

In 1932, Carl decided to return to Baton Rouge and practice with his father. Even though the state capital, Baton Rouge at that time remained a small, southern town with a population of only about thirty thousand — a far cry from New York, but the quieter small-town life appealed to Carl and, besides, he was very close to his parents. When he arrived, the town gave one of its favorite sons an enthusiastic welcome. An article in the Baton Rouge *Morning Advocate* reported:

> Dr. Weiss has always wanted to practice in Baton Rouge, his birthplace, and on his return two weeks ago went into the office with his father Dr. C. A. Weiss. He jokingly declared that a few gray hairs would aid him immeasurably. However, his large, capable hands, his serious eyes, and friendly smile inspire confidence.
>
> When asked whether the girls in Baton Rouge and America compared favorably with foreign girls, he answered: "Well, I could hardly be called an expert on that subject. But you see didn't bring any back with me."[11]

The young doctor went through the jitters sometimes experienced by professionals who decide to practice in their home towns. The need to establish a professional identity that would gently replace the more familiar boy-next-door image was expressed in growing a moustache, shaving it, aging his satchel through deliberate abuse, joining the Kiwanis Club, and, in general, attempting to appear older and more mature. But it was a smooth transition. His regular church attendance, his father's well-established practice and reputation — he was elected president of the Louisiana Medical Society in 1933 — and his own professional skill soon made the handsome, young doctor one of the most respected members of the community and, perhaps, the most eligible bachelor in Baton Rouge.

One of those who shared that assessment was a young woman named Louise Yvonne Pavy. Yvonne — she preferred her middle name — was born and raised across the Mississippi and down U.S. 190 west through the pine and cypress swamps in the little town of Opelousas. She was one of seven children of Judge Benjamin Pavy. The Pavys lived in the quiet elegance of prosperous French Louisianans. The judge presided over the Thirteenth Judicial District composed of St. Landry and Evangeline Parishes. It was Cajun country and he was popular with his constituents. He campaigned in French, won the judgeship in 1910 and in every election after that. The Pavy's were powerful. One of the judge's brothers was a member of the state legislature. But the judge was too independent and popular for Long's liking. The "Kingfish" considered him a troublesome rival.

Yvonne was an attractive dark-haired young woman who graduated from Tulane's Newcomb College for Women in 1929 with a degree in French.

After graduation, she taught school briefly before applying for and being awarded a scholarship to study at the Sorbonne in 1931, after Carl, unknown to her at the time, had returned to the United States.[12] Following a truly memorable year in Paris Yvonne returned home in 1932 without the advanced degree she had sought. She promptly applied for graduate work at Louisiana State in Baton Rouge, determined to make up for the misspent year abroad.

Yvonne's commitment to her studies was real. Not long after her return, she walked into the Weiss and Weiss office suite on the seventh floor of the Reymond Building for treatment of eyestrain. The elder Weiss, impressed with his attractive patient, inquired about her studies and brightened when she told him she had spent a year at the Sorbonne. Seizing upon the common experience, he promptly introduced her to his bachelor son.[13]

Carl was impressed, but he didn't like to rush into things. It was nearly four months later before he sent his patient an Easter egg and asked her for a date. After a very traditional courtship of evening strolls, porch-swing conversations, and Sunday dinners after Mass, they were engaged in the summer of 1933. Their families were delighted. A more attractive couple was difficult to imagine. Two days after Christmas that same year they were married in the St. Landry Parish Catholic Church in Opelousas. An elaborate and joyous reception, complete with Cajun music, followed.[14]

It was to be a close and loving relationship that began with a Florida honeymoon and grew with first year happiness in a cozy apartment near the capitol. When Yvonne became pregnant the following September, they moved to an attractive three-bedroom house at 527 Lakeland Drive to await happily the birth of their child. The house was conveniently located only a few blocks from Our Lady of the Lake Hospital where Carl did most of his surgery and only a short walk from St. Joseph's Church where the young couple attended Mass every Sunday. It was also less than two blocks from the capitol.

According to Yvonne, Carl was more than a doting father to the son born in June 1935. He adored the child and insisted on participating in every aspect of the little boy's care. Not content with the traditional role of his own father, Carl prepared and gave bottles at all hours, changed diapers, pushed the carriage on contented strolls through the tree-shaded neighborhood, and recorded his happiness with numerous photographs.[15] Not even the hot, humid Louisiana summer that had enveloped Baton Rouge could dampen the happiness of the little family that summer as they planned optimistically for the future.

But apparently Huey Pierce Long could. The senator, who was by this time the unquestioned political boss of Louisiana, had long been at odds with Yvonne's father. Old Ben Pavy, secure in the loyalty of the Cajun voters of

Louisiana's Thirteenth Judicial District, was a man the Long organization could not control. Long associates in St. Landry and Evangeline Parishes had convinced the senator that Pavy had to go, one way or another. It seemed clear that he could not be beaten in an honest election. During the summer of 1935 Long ordered his cronies in the state legislature to draft a bill that would effectively dilute the judge's electoral strength by redrawing the boundaries of the Thirteenth District. Irritated by Judge Pavy's quiet contempt and self-confidence, it was widely rumored that Long, not content with just the gerrymander, would also "tar brush" the judge with a racial smear dredged up from the judge's distant political past.[16] The slur, simply stated, was that there was black ancestry in the Pavy family. Although this old rumor had not worked against the judge in the past — he hadn't lost an election in nearly thirty years — the fact remains that the charge had never been invoked by anyone approaching the political skill and influence of Huey Long. Although Long associates have denied their leader's plan to smear Pavy in this underhanded way, there can be no doubt that there was ample precedent for such tactics in Longs political repertoire.[17]

Since virtually all Louisiana newspapers opposed Long, he created his own weekly, the *Louisiana Progress,* to set forth his views and attack his opponents. It was widely read, and the use of racial innuendo was common. For example, he always referred to a New Orleans political opponent as "Kinky," a nickname Huey had coined to convey his view of the man's black lineage. The term "shinola" was also regularly used for the same purpose.[18] And he publicly criticized another opponent, Dudley LeBlanc, because he employed blacks as fellow officers in his burial insurance company.[19]

The Pavy family, accustomed to the rough and tumble of Louisiana politics, reported that they were not unduly disturbed by the rumor.[20] The judge had survived many a campaign. The judge's brother, still a member of the Long-dominated legislature, acknowledged that the issue had been discussed in the family but that it had been taken "lightly rather than otherwise."[21]

Carl Weiss, however, was not a political person himself, nor was he especially interested in the state politics. But he had a devout Catholic's concern about right and wrong and good and evil, and certain of Long's actions during that summer of 1935 left little doubt about the powerful and devious Senator's contempt for the Pavys. The gerrymander bill, for example, had been introduced on September 7 in a special session of the legislature. This followed in the wake of the Long organization's recent and abrupt termination of the contracts of Paul Pavy, Yvonne's uncle, who was principal of the high school in Opelousas, and Yvonne's sister, Marie, an elementary school teacher there. Long's people claimed that neither had been properly certified by the Long-controlled state board of education.[22]

The Victim

On Sunday, September 8, 1935, Huey P. Long was one of the most powerful, loved, and feared men in the United States. His rise from obscure beginnings in Winn Parish, Louisiana, through the State Railroad Commission in 1918, the governor's mansion in 1928, and on to the United States Senate in 1932 remains one of the more colorful tales of political success in America. According to his biographer, T. Harry Williams, he was probably the most powerful political boss in American history.[23] A southern populist with a way with words, he was a William Jennings Bryan with brains. Long launched his political career by attacking the big corporate special interests that controlled the state and struck a responsive cord with the people when he followed through with positive action on his campaign promises: the "Kingfish," as he referred to himself, delivered. He demanded and got legislation and appropriations to pave roads, build bridges, improve hospital services, supply free textbooks to the public schools, expand educational opportunities for adults, and abolish the poll tax. More significant, perhaps, he made the Depression-weary plain folks of Louisiana feel that they were important. And they mourned his death for it surely removed one of the most powerful and effective spokesmen for the poor in American history. It also assured Franklin Roosevelt an extended tenure in the White House. With Long dead, the only effective challenge from the political left ended.

President Roosevelt was worried about Long. It was clear that the outspoken and irreverent senator was staking out a position from which to challenge FDR in the 1936 presidential election.[24] A secret poll commissioned by the president revealed that Long could attract as—many as six million votes; moreover, his appeal was not restricted to the South. And the politically astute Long had not yet even begun to campaign.[25]

There was no doubt that the Kingfish had his eye on the White House. As early as 1933, the year Roosevelt took office, he began to develop his claim as the only candidate of "the people." The populist appeal that had worked so successfully for him in Louisiana would be broadened and projected on to the national scene. Quoting the Bible and damning privilege, Long had the name of his weekly newspaper changed from the *Louisiana Progress* to the *American Progress*. In 1933, he published his autobiography, *Every Man a King*, which, in a self-congratulatory manner, detailed his campaign against special interests and his accomplishments in behalf of common people. In a well-publicized public letter, he demanded that his name be removed from the Washington *Social Register*. In February 1934, he announced the establishment of local chapters for a "Share the Wealth" campaign around the country and commissioned rabble-rousing evangelist Gerald L. K. Smith as his chief organizer. Long was now clearly directing his appeals beyond the rural South to the depression-ravaged centers of discontent in the urban Northeast and Midwest. Advocating a four-million-dollar limit on personal fortunes and stiff corporate income taxes, Long promised to convert the excess into a home, an automobile, a radio, and two thousand dollars a year for every poor family in America.[26] He got the attention of millions of hollow-eyed victims of the Depression who found the promise heartening.

In the spring of 1935, Long dictated a second book entitled *My First Days in the White House*.[27] In it, he outlined with greater specificity how he intended to implement his share-of-the-wealth philosophy once in the White House. In addition to the programs already mentioned, he promised a ten billion-dollar public works program to build roads and eliminate slums, to promote national health care, and to establish tuition-free college education for all children with requisite ability. Moreover, he announced that he would nationalize corporations that did not operate in the public interest. And in a dig at the president, he also promised to appoint a highly qualified cabinet that would include FDR — as secretary of the navy.[28]

Long was aware that his outspoken and often heavy-handed political style had created many bitter enemies. So more than any of his peers, he was concerned about his safety and always had himself accompanied by a loyal cadre of heavily armed bodyguards. On August 9, 1935, only a month before his death, he rose in the U.S. Senate to announce that a conspiracy to kill him had been uncovered in Louisiana; he referred to what has become known as the "Desoto plot." The plot supposedly unfolded in a meeting of anti-Long forces that had met in mid-July at the Desoto Hotel in New Orleans. Although the actual murderous intent of this meeting has been disputed, there can be no doubt that Long's removal from public life one way or another was a frequent and continuing topic at meetings of Long opponents.[29]

In the minds of many, especially corporate America, Huey Long posed a direct threat to the nation's political and economic establishment; compared to him, the patrician-reformer in the White House — by way of Groton, Harvard, and Hyde Park — was clearly preferable. There is also every reason to think that when Long died on September 10, 1935 there was probably a collective sigh of relief in the White House as well as on Wall Street. But at no time was evidence ever substantiated that the senator died as a result of a conspiracy of his opponents.[30]

Possible Explanations

Why then did Carl Weiss, a successful physician — a man with seemingly nothing to gain and everything to lose — kill Huey Long? The number of different answers to this question are listed below:

1. Long died as a result of a conspiracy in which Weiss had been selected through a drawing of straws as the shooter.
2. Weiss, alone, killed Long to end the career of a politically dangerous demagogue. He was in this sense a zealot and a willing martyr for a political ideal.
3. Weiss did not kill Long. He had no sufficient motive. Rather, Long was killed by his own bodyguards in the melee that followed after Weiss struck the senator in the mouth.
4. Long's death was an impulsive, unpremeditated case of homicide. Weiss was angry about Long's treatment of his wife's family but did not intend to kill the senator.
5. Weiss killed Long in a willful, premeditated manner in retaliation for his actions, real and anticipated, against his wife's family.

Briefly consider each of these explanations:

The conspiracy explanation simply has not been substantiated. There has been no evidence to show that Weiss attended the Desoto Hotel meeting in spite of rumors to the contrary. Weiss's office records and patients, as well as family testimony, confirm that on the days of the New Orleans conference he was in Baton Rouge and Opelousas, not New Orleans.[31]

Foremost among the proponents of the second explanation that Weiss killed Long for patriotic reasons is the historian T. Harry Williams. Suggesting that the young doctor and his family were unaware of the rumored racial slur, Williams concluded that Long died because "Carl Weiss was a sincere and idealistic young man who agonized over the evils that he believed Huey Long was inflicting on his class and his state."[32] Similarly, *Playboy* author James McKinley also concluded that "it could only have been the impulse of idealism, a hatred and fear of oppression, of Long's fascism [that motivated Weiss]."[33] Both of these views are consistent with the explanation offered by the perplexed family spokesman, Dr. Octave Pavy, who told the press immediately after the tragedy:

> Our only explanation for his action is that this [Long's] suppressive type of rule preyed on his mind until it unhinged, and he suddenly felt himself a martyr, giving his life to the people of Louisiana. He must have felt that way, else how could he have left the wife and baby that he loved *above everything*?[34]

The family later changed its view, insisting that Weiss did not kill Long. Rather, they contended that he was killed along with the senator by Long's bodyguards. Weiss did confront Long and punched him in the month, they said. But that was all he did. But his assault precipitated a wild shooting spree by Long's bodyguards that left Long mortally wounded and Weiss dead. This is the explanation embraced by Zinman, but it doesn't quite bear the weight of conflicting evidence.[35]

According to the family spokesman, they were not unduly upset about Long's actions against them. The Sunday morning newspaper the day of the shooting, which most of the family had read, described the bill that had been introduced the evening before. While acknowledging that the gerrymander was discussed during a pleasant Sunday dinner that afternoon, it was almost in a joking manner; although Carl's wife did recall that he told her, "You know Long is out to get your father. Your father is going to be gerrymandered out of office."[36] The family claimed, however, that they were not aware of the rumor about the racial slur until after the assassination — a statement consistent with one made by Long's associates.[37] In any case, according to his family, Weiss was probably unaware of the slur since he had not mentioned it to anyone.

Family members also pointed to a number of inconsistencies to support their claim that Weiss did not shoot Long: First, the bullet that killed Long was never recovered, raising suspicions that it had been shot from the gun of one of his over-zealous bodyguards. Second, an autopsy that could have provided more information on this point was not performed; rather, the senator's body was viewed from across the room by a quickly appointed coroner's jury who, from the distance of approximately twelve feet, were given a very brief view of the tiny exit wound in his back.[38] Indeed, except for a very brief and superficial inquest, an official investigation into the assassination was never conducted. Third, no convincing explanation was ever given for the cut on Long's mouth, which he reportedly explained to a nurse as, "That's where he hit me." The failure to address this issue, they claimed, suggests that Weiss did strike the senator rather than shooting him as Long's associates claimed.[39]

These and other bits of circumstantial inconsistencies in the official version of the events, underscore the family's central claim that Carl Weiss lacked motive for doing what the state concluded he did. According to his own words and actions prior to the shooting, there was every reason to conclude that Carl Weiss did not anticipate his own death. He appeared on September 8, 1935 to be a happy, content young man looking forward to the future.

With that in mind, consider the following: On the day of the shooting, he attended Mass as usual with his wife. After a pleasant Sunday dinner with his parents, the two couples drove to the family retreat, a cottage on the river, where they spent the remainder of the warm afternoon swimming, playing with the baby, and in easy conversation on the screened porch overlooking the water. Driving back to Baton Rouge that evening, Carl and Yvonne bid goodbye to Carl's parents and went home, where Carl ate heartily — a couple of sandwiches washed down with two glasses of milk — while his wife bathed their son and got him ready for bed. He then fed the dog, called an anesthetist who was to assist him in a tonsillectomy the *next* morning to confirm the arrangements; then as his wife read the Sunday comics, he showered. Later he emerged in the white linen suit and accessories he had worn that morning to Mass. After some light banter about whether they would rock the baby to sleep as usual or let him cry, Carl told Yvonne he had a call to make but would return shortly. He kissed his wife and son and left at about 9 P.M. Although his activities beyond this point remain obscure, it appears that he drove across town to Baton Rouge General Hospital where he was to operate the next morning. A nurse reported having a brief conversation with him there that evening, but there was some confusion concerning the time.[40]

Earlier that week, Weiss had gone with his wife to Kornmeyer's furniture store and purchased a new dining room suite. He also planned to purchase a new gas furnace for the house. He told his mother, who had questioned the wisdom of investing money in a small house he would probably want to leave as his family grew, that he and Yvonne planned to remain there "for ten years at least."[41] There was not a single clue in the words or behavior of the young doctor that he was planning to shoot — or even confront — Huey P. Long.

A number of commentators on the Long case have concluded that Weiss must have killed for personal rather than political reasons and differ only on whether or not the act was premeditated.[42] Of this group, most are somewhat skeptical that the shooting was premeditated because both the Weiss and Pavy families had denied a major concern over Long's vendetta against the Pavys. When asked about whether the vendetta might have motivated Weiss, Dr. Octave Pavy, speaking for the family, replied: "In the first place, none of us would kill anyone over such a matter as the loss of a public office."[43] Years later when Yvonne was asked how her family responded to news of the gerrymander, she replied:

> Mother was delighted because Papa didn't make much money as a judge. He had wonderful connections and my brother was practicing law. My mother was elated. The ambition of her life was to get him out of that judgeship. Get him off the bench. So there was no great grief. Nobody was complaining. Judge Pavy himself, never felt an injustice was being done to him personally. It was just the fact that it wasn't legally right. He didn't feel that he was personally suffering from it.[44]

Thus, to a politically seasoned family such as the Pavys, politics was not taken personally: if one wanted to pursue a political career, it was just part of the game — something one expected, and accepted — especially in Louisiana. But unlike the Pavys — and the Longs — Carl Weiss was not capable of such detachment. But Carl's world was defined by moral principles and personal concerns, not political expedience.

The Motive

Running through the substance of these various theories is a thread of facts and circumstances that provides the most plausible explanation for the young doctor's behavior. Although most commentators on the killings have focused on a single explanation for Weiss's motives or lack of them, it is almost certain that he was driven by a combination of factors. Let me explain.

First, it is true that Weiss and people of his class did not like the coarseness and demagogy of Huey Long. But, as we have seen, Weiss was no political zealot; therefore political ideology alone could not have triggered the events of that day.

Second, given Weiss's quiet, intense personality and his strict Catholic sense of right and wrong, it is reasonable to suggest that Long's well-publicized intent to gerrymander his wife's father out of office, following on the heels of the Long-inspired dismissal of her uncle and sister, angered him more than he let on. For example, his seemingly impatient and somewhat condescending remark on the matter to his wife at the dinner table hints of such anger. But it doesn't seem reasonable that the gerrymander and the loss of a couple of relative's jobs would be sufficient to propel Weiss toward his self-destructive act. Carl Weiss had too much to live for.

Furthermore, there was an undeniably impulsive quality about the doctor's behavior when he left home that evening. His actions that Sunday evening could not have been anticipated by what is known about what preceded them — a relaxed day with his family, his preparations for surgery the next morning, his assurance to his wife that he would return shortly after a quick stop at the hospital. Also Long's appearance in the legislative chambers of the capital that Sunday evening was unplanned and could not have been anticipated; the special session of the legislature had been called only the day before, providing little time for a carefully premeditated assassination. Something must have happened *after* the doctor left home that evening that precipitated his fateful rendezvous with Long at the Capitol.

Third, most observers who discounted the importance of the alleged racial slur are unaware that on Sunday afternoon Long had telephoned his New Orleans printer, Joe David, that he would be sending down an important story on Judge Pavy for the *American Progress*.[45] This was probably the story containing the racial slur. "Tar brushing," as such racial slurs were called, was a familiar weapon in the arsenal of Southern politics. Weiss may have heard of Long's intentions on his car radio or from some other unidentified source after leaving home that evening, but this cannot be documented. Since he normally carried a pistol in his car for night calls, the fact that he was armed was not unusual. What Huey Long didn't realize as he joked with his protégés in the legislature as Weiss changed direction and drove toward the Capitol parking lot, was the very subjective limits of political propriety. His systematic attacks on the Pavy family — which were politics as usual for Long and even the Pavys — had now extended into an area of vital concern to an intense and now deadly serious young husband and father. The Kingfish, always concerned about his personal safety, had no idea that he would be killed by a man with whom, as far as he knew, he had no quarrel.

This is what probably happened: Distressed after hearing of a breaking story on his wife's father, Weiss suspected that the content of that story involved the racial slur. He would be well aware that such actions were a familiar tactic in Long's repertoire of dirty tricks. Weiss quickly considered his options. Given Long's recent attacks on the Pavys, he would have no reason to doubt the story. He would realize that he had little time, that he had to act at once to prevent Long from publicizing a charge throughout the state that would jeopardize the future of a wife and son he loved literally, as he would momentarily demonstrate, more than life. And if Long had already released the story, there would at least be the satisfaction of sweet revenge. Honor, in Weiss's mind, demanded as much.

To appreciate the immediacy and salience of this threat, one must consider the virulent form of racism that existed throughout the South in the 1930s. Lynchings, for example, a long-established Southern custom, rose sharply that decade as the hardships of the Depression aggravated racial tensions. To be black in the South of the 1930s meant relegation to an existence of unrelenting discrimination, oppression, and vulnerability undeserving of any human being.[46] Weiss, who probably shared in the racial prejudices of his fellow white Southerners, recognized that even the suspicion of black ancestry was enough to ruin the lives of his wife and son. Another time-honored tradition of the Old South was *honor* among males. For a Southerner to ignore an insult to his family was unthinkable. Long had to be stopped; honor demanded no less.

The Event

Driving to the capitol from the hospital, Weiss entered the building with a .32 caliber pistol he had purchased in Europe concealed under his coat.[47] In the capitol corridor, Weiss spoke pleasantly to a young woman who happened by, patted the former patient on the head, and walked quickly toward the corridor outside the governor's office.[48] Once there, he stood quietly in a tiny alcove opposite the double doors that led into the governor's anteroom.[49]

Moments later, Long and his entourage entered the corridor after a quick walk from the legislative chamber. Long planned to use Governor O. K. Allen's office to issue a press release blaming President Roosevelt for the deaths of Civilian Conservation Corps youths in a Florida hurricane.[50] Coat unbuttoned, elbows swinging, and belly bouncing, Long was bellowing over his shoulder to aides as his bodyguards scrambled to keep up with him, when a slight figure in a white linen suit appeared. Long's eyes bulged in fear, and as he began to recoil, Carl Weiss, without a word, fired from a distance of a few feet. Long screamed, clutching his abdomen, and ran hysterically from the corridor moments before bedlam broke loose. It was during those moments that he may have been struck in the mouth by those trying to assist him, for witnesses said that Weiss never got close enough to strike Long with his fist as some claimed.

As aides grappled with Weiss knocking him to the floor, he fired again at his assailants. Then the corridor exploded in gunfire and smoke as Weiss, who had regained his feet, crouched facing the onslaught before being slammed to the floor under the impact of the .44 and .45 caliber hollow-point bullets that tore through his face, neck, and torso.[51] Seemingly crazed with frustration and anger, Long's bodyguards continued to fire into the lifeless body causing it to lurch and roll across the marble floor as it was torn apart by some thirty-two to sixty bullets fired at point-blank range.[52]

Long raced down a stairway to the ground floor where, on the verge of collapse, he met an aide who flagged down an unknown car in the parking lot and escorted the wounded Senator to Our Lady of the Lake Hospital. Dr. Arthur Vidrine, a political appointee and friend of Long's who had been at the special session, arrived soon after and decided to operate. Vidrine, who had little training in surgery, failed to perform the standard pre-operative diagnosis of the wound and, as a result, the surgery failed to reveal a hemorrhaging kidney. Doctors arriving after the surgery had been completed quickly observed Vidrine's fatal error, but there was nothing to be done; Long was too weak to survive a second operation. He died some thirty odd hours later on Tuesday, September 10, 1925.[53] A few days later, Huey Long was buried in front of the skyscraper capitol he had built after the largest funeral in Louisiana history.

Carl Weiss was given a Roman Catholic burial the day after he died in the church he had attended most of his life. His funeral, the largest of any assassin in American history, was attended by several hundred friends, former patients, civic leaders, a former governor, a congressman, the district attorney, and virtually the entire Baton Rouge medical profession. Thousands more stood in a pouring rain at Roselawn Cemetery during the internment. Most of the mourners could not believe that he had killed Long; many of those who did, considered him a martyr.[54]

Conclusions

The most improbable of American assassins, Carl Weiss bore no resemblance to the stereotyped, mentally ill assassin so often mistakenly characterized in the literature of such events. Those who would label him a zealot who killed for political purposes have ignored the apolitical qualities of his life. He was a highly individualistic person. He was not drawn to, nor was he motivated by, political causes. Carl Weiss killed Huey Long somewhat impulsively when he learned that Long threatened direct harm to those he loved as a matter of *honor*.

The only case that resembles this one, and then only in some respects, is the 1978 murders of Mayor George Moscone and Supervisor Harvey Milk of San Francisco. Like Long, Moscone and Milk did not realize that their decision to deny Dan White's seat on the city Board of Supervisors meant much more to White than merely losing a political office. For White, it was not merely "the breaks" in a rough and tumble world of Bay Area politics, it meant everything — his future, his family, and his self-respect. Like Carl Weiss, he was not temperamentally suited for politics. He was too intense, without the emotional slack to handle defeat, especially when he considered it unfair and humiliating. There was also no real separation of political and personal for White either. He did not have the emotional resiliency and moral flexibility to handle politics as usual. Just as the politically seasoned and sophisticated Pavy family could not imagine killing Long for what he did, or was threatening to do, to them, most Bay Area politicians could not understand why Dan White would do what he did. But the Carl Weisses and Dan Whites of the world are wired too tightly for the stresses of political life. And in each case that wire of constraint snapped at the personal level with tragic and completely unanticipated consequences.

A wheeling and dealing style in political life always involves risks, and overcoming those risks makes winning even more satisfying; it's like a political aphrodisiac for many practitioners. But unfortunately, tough successful politicians like Huey Long, George Moscone, and Harvey Milk fail to realize that the stakes of the game can reach intolerably high limits with unanticipated rapidity for those who are not emotionally prepared to play such a high-stakes game. It is the unpredictable risks represented by improbable killers such as Carl Weiss and Dan White that define a thin, white-hot thread of emotion that marks the sometimes too subtle and fatal boundary between political and personal life.

* * *
JAMES EARL RAY (1928–1998)

Unlike the now relatively unknown Carl Weiss, much has been written about James Earl Ray, the convicted killer of Dr. Martin Luther King, Jr. Ray was arrested at Heathrow Airport in London on June 8, 1968, some sixty-five days and an international manhunt after Dr. King was fatally shot in Memphis, Tennessee. Except for John Wilkes Booth, Ray is the only other subject who had planned and implemented an elaborate escape.

After a succession of lawyers and much controversy surrounding deals to market the James Earl Ray story, an anti-climatic guilty plea was entered, and Ray was sentenced to ninety-nine years imprisonment. The plea was unexpected because Ray had the nationally known criminal attorney Percy Foreman representing him, and the expectation was that there would be a well-publicized trial rather than a brief ceremony in which Ray admitted his guilt and was sentenced.

The case against Ray was overwhelming: evidence that he had been stalking King; that he had purchased the murder weapon; that he had rented a room adjacent to the bathroom from which the fatal shot was fired; that witnesses saw a person matching Ray's description fleeing the scene; and that Ray's fingerprints were the only ones found on the rifle and personal belongings dropped in a doorway near the scene of the crime. The only thing that could have strengthened the case against him, it seemed, was a witness who actually saw him pull the trigger. Everything else was there.[55] But the fact that there was no trial, combined with Ray's subsequent claim that he was not the killer, as he had admitted, have contributed to the strong suspicion that Ray did not act alone.

Two of Ray's better known biographies are William Bradford Huie's *He Slew the Dreamer*[56] and George McMillan's *The Making of an Assassin*.[57] Huie's book is based largely on written statements that Ray gave to him as well as his own investigation of Ray's story. McMillan's book relies heavily on Huie's research, supplemented with information obtained through interviews with members of Ray's family, especially his brothers John and Jerry. Both writers conclude that Ray acted alone and disagree only in their interpretation of his motive. Huie believed Dr. King was killed to enable Ray to achieve notoriety, a familiar overworked explanation for a number of assassins and would-be assassins.[58] Imposing a rather strained psychoanalytic interpretation without much evidence to support it, McMillan concluded that Ray killed the civil rights leader to satisfy an obsessive racist hatred of blacks which had somehow become tangled up with the unresolved oedipal conflicts Ray had with his father. According to McMillan, Dr. King had become a father figure to Ray and had died as a result.[59] Both books have drawn criticism and lawsuits from Ray and outright denials of accuracy by Ray's brothers. Jerry Ray also acknowledged that he had deliberately lied to McMillan and referred to the book as "a joke."[60]

Although there are obvious risks in writing books based on paid interviews with known criminals, taken together, the two books provide an intriguing view of the man James Earl Ray up to the time of his escape from Missouri State Penitentiary on April 23, 1967. Other sources provide a more complete and convincing account of activities from that time to his arrest and conviction for the King assassination. What follows is an attempt to present a revealing collage of James Earl Ray's background selectively drawn from these primary, if controversial, accounts.

A Hard Life

James Earl Ray was born on March 10, 1928 to poor parents in Alton, Illinois. He was the first of the nine children of George and Lucille Ray. Drab river towns and hard-clay farms with deteriorating, unpainted buildings marked the boundaries of their existence on the Missouri-Illinois border. The Rays were the poorest of the poor. In fact, the Crash of 1929 and the Depression that followed did not substantially change their life for the worse as it did for many people of that era. The failures of George Ray, or "Speedy," as he was called, were complete before the Depression. Speedy was the kind of person who wanted to farm but actually spent a good part of his time just trying to keep one dilapidated truck after another running. He had the appearance of someone who had spent a good part of his life under vehicles in need of repair. His wife had the drawn, hollow-eyed appearance of a woman who was having too many children too fast with too little help and money to support them. Even more than her husband, she was being overwhelmed by the harsh realities of what she saw happening, but was unprepared to handle. Before long she would turn to drink.

Many who grew up during those times can remember someone like James Earl Ray in grade school. In a roomful of shabbily, hand-me-down dressed schoolchildren, his clothes were the most colorless. The shoes on his feet were "clodhoppers"– cheap, sturdy, ankle-high shoes that kids who could not afford rubber galoshes for snow and slush in the winter wore year round. Children like this seemed to have constantly running noses that, because they rarely had handkerchiefs, were wiped on sleeves or on the backs of their hands. The damp, musky smell of urine announced their presence, regardless of personal habits, because in many cases they slept in the same beds with younger brothers and sisters. It didn't matter to teachers, however, who held them responsible and expressed their contempt in low grades in "health" or "citizenship," not to mention unsubtle remarks to the class about personal hygiene.

Confronted with such obstacles, it is little wonder that many of these children became withdrawn, just as the six-year-old James did. Missing a lot of school and possessing none of the endearing social graces middle-class teachers prefer, he flunked the first grade in spite of his normal I.Q. of 105 to 108.

The old farm in Ewing where the Ray's lived was the rural equivalent of the wrong side of the tracks. It was the place anyone in Ewing could contemplate and feel a little bit better about his or her lot in life. Living under such a stigma saddens children and sometimes makes them bitter. Little boys become tough — not bullies usually — but kids who do not back down from a fight, and, once engaged, battle with a ferocity and abandon that, regardless of skill, is likely to cause alarm among better dressed, sweeter smelling rivals. James was no exception.

Often children in these circumstances don't have a lot of close friends the way middle-class children do. Friendships are less intimate because there is so little in the home environment to share with friends; few outsiders want to share adversity. Paradoxically, however, the same adversity often seems to meld a common bond between siblings, particularly those closest in age and experience. James was always closer to his family than to anyone else. In spite of his loner ways, he would remain in regular contact with his brothers, John and Jerry, and also his sister, Carol, throughout his life.[61]

James also got along well with his parents in spite of the hardships that would eventually destroy the family. He liked to sit by his dad as they clattered along in a succession of old trucks. He also watched with pride as Speedy defeated opponents at the local pool hall and listened carefully as his hero taught him to play the game.[62]

His mother, too, loved and cared for this shy little boy as best she could with all the other younger children. But in family situations such as the Ray's, it was tough to get all the attention you needed, — not for lack of love — but simply because there was no time or energy; attention spans were constrained by necessity. There was a quiet, non-conflictive resignation to the bad hand they had been dealt as a family, interrupted occasionally only by some additional crisis — like a little daughter dying from household burns, or James breaking his leg in the schoolyard.

But the hardships were eventually too great to endure, and the family collapsed when James was in the eighth grade. He quit school and went to live with his grandmother, eventually winding up in the town of his birth, Alton, Illinois. The three youngest children were placed in the Catholic Children's Home in Alton, and his mother took the older ones with her to Quincy, Illinois. Speedy took up with another woman.

286   Defining Danger

The Rays provide a classic example of the sociological conception of a family that accepted culturally defined goals of success but was denied the socially structured means of achieving it. It would run a convulsively destructive course of desertion, neglect, despair, alcoholism, and crime, with only a daughter, Carol, managing to cling tenaciously to a remnant of stability and respectability. The rest would be destined for mental hospitals, prisons, and premature graves.

There was a point when James tried to make it in a conventional sense. At the age of sixteen, in 1944, he got a job at a tannery in Hartford, Illinois. He was a good, reliable worker who saved his money for almost two years before he was laid off in January 1946. Six weeks later, he joined the Army and, after basic training, was sent to serve with the occupation forces in Germany. But Army life did not agree with him. Soon after his arrival in Bremerhaven, his main pursuits became drinking, fighting, whoring around, and financing most of it through the black market sale of cigarettes. These were hardly the activities of "a young political idealist," as George McMillan describes him, looking for ideological answers in bombed-out Germany.[63]

The fact is there is little evidence of Ray's political concerns during this period beyond a friendship with an alleged crypto-Nazi he worked with at the Hartford tannery and questionable hearsay evidence of rather ordinary racist remarks attributed to him.[64] Such remarks could have been made by any number of white Americans in 1946, not to mention whites on the lower rungs of society such as Ray.

Although Ray could be considered a tough young man, he was not a bully, and his subsequent criminal record reveals no tendency toward personal violence.[65] Rather, that record, which begins after his honorable discharge from the Army and continues consistently to his arrest for the King slaying, is a record of bungled and ludicrously inept robberies and burglaries during which no one was ever hurt or seriously threatened with bodily harm.

For example, he served time for stealing a typewriter in Los Angeles in 1949, robbing a Chicago cab driver in 1952, stealing money orders in Hannibal, Missouri and cashing them on a carefree trip to Florida in 1955, and robbing a St. Louis supermarket in 1959. The $120 he lifted from the Kroger's cash register got him twenty years in the Missouri State Penitentiary in Jefferson City. After two unsuccessful escape attempts in 1960 and 1966, he finally made it through the gates concealed in a bread truck on April 23, 1967.

There is not much in the record to suggest that after the age of twenty-one James Earl Ray ever thought of going straight. Prison authorities considered him a habitual criminal with only a marginal chance of changing.[66] He wanted success — to experience the American Dream. But he was also smart enough to see that the reality of success in America was defined in dollars, the magnitude of which was far beyond the potential offered through the kind of honest hard work available to men like him. For James Earl Ray, money was everything.

The Alleged Racist Motive

The five years and few months Ray spent in the Missouri State Penitentiary figure importantly in some attempts to explain his subsequent behavior. George McMillan, for example, claims Ray's motive for killing Dr. King was an obsessive racist hatred and describes events in Ray's prison experience to support his claim. Ray, for example, supposedly declined a desirable opportunity for transfer to a prison farm because it was racially integrated. Ray denied that, claiming he declined the transfer to avoid the possibility of trouble, which could jeopardize his chances for parole, due to the extensive drug dealing among the farm inmates.[67] Other accounts refer to the verbal rages Ray allegedly went into when Dr. King appeared on the prison television screens.[68] Such behavior is attributed to the Nazi sympathies Ray supposedly acquired in his youth. Both Ray and his family have denied these allegations, and their denials have been essentially substantiated. In fact, the prison warden reported that Ray and other inmates did not have access to television.[69]

Other examples of the depths of Ray's acknowledged racism have also been questioned. After his escape from prison, Ray left on an odyssey of sorts that carried him from Chicago to Puerto Vallarta, Mexico with stops in Montreal and Birmingham, Alabama before arriving in Los Angeles on November 19, 1967. Authors Huie and McMillan have cited a number of events during his travels to underscore their contention that Ray was aggressively hostile toward blacks.[70]

In Montreal, for example, Ray had a brief affair with a young and very attractive Canadian woman. In the course of their relationship, Ray was described as having made racist remarks to her about "niggers." But the woman later denied that she had ever said that. To the contrary, she said, "He never mentioned the name Martin Luther King and never indicated any hatred toward Negroes."[71]

Two racially motivated altercations at bars also have been attributed to Ray. The first of these occurred in Puerto Vallarta sometime in October or November 1967, when Ray allegedly tried to provoke a fight with some black sailors who were celebrating at a nearby table. According to Ray's companion, a prostitute, Ray did no such thing. What actually happened was that a drunken black sailor, who had gotten up to leave, stumbled and fell into Ray's table and, in the process, grabbed the prostitute by the shoulders in a vain attempt to prevent his fall. Ray became angry, swore at the sailor — "son-of-a-bitch" — and later showed the prostitute a pistol he intended to use if they were bothered again. When she explained the incident later, however, his companion claimed that Ray's anger was over the intrusion and not because the drunken sailor was black.[72]

The second incident occurred later, after Ray had traveled to Los Angeles from Mexico. During his stay there from November 19, 1967 to March 18, 1968, he frequented a couple of bars. The incident in question occurred at one of these during a discussion in which Ray argued that a white person would not be safe in the Watts section of Los Angeles. According to an FBI report,[73] Ray became angry when his statement was challenged and attempted to drag a female participant in the discussion out of the bar, supposedly to drop her off in Watts. The story has been questioned, and although the FBI agent still claims its accuracy, a bartender who witnessed the discussion claims, in a signed statement, that the FBI report distorts what actually happened. According to bartender, a discussion did occur involving a number of people at the bar — including blacks who were *regular* patrons — but it was not a heated discussion, nor did Ray accost, or attempt to drag, anyone from the bar; nor was he subsequently attacked by a black in the parking lot. Rather the evening ended without incident.[74]

Also of note in this context is the fact that the two bars Ray favored in Los Angeles — the Rabbit's Foot and the Sultan Room — were racially integrated. It was estimated that approximately half the regular clientele of the Rabbit's Foot and a third of the Sultan Room's customers were black. If this bothered Ray, it was not to a degree sufficient to cause him to select another from the countless bars in the Los Angeles area. Moreover, a woman who knew Ray during his stay in Los Angeles revealed that, for a period, he dated a black woman he met in the Sultan Room and gave no overt indication of any racism in his conduct toward her.[75]

Although these accounts do not deny Ray's basic racism, they do raise doubts about its alleged intensity. And in so doing, one must question whether an obsessive racist rage provides a convincing explanation of his assassination of Dr. King.[76] As a lower-class white male from the Southern culture of rural Missouri, it is not surprising that Ray held racist views. But it is doubtful that Ray's racism alone was the force that caused him to leave Los Angeles on March 18, 1968 to begin a single-minded and deadly journey that would eventually lead some eleven weeks later to a cracked and grimy bathroom window in a seedy rooming house in Memphis, Tennessee.[77]

As we will see, his racism did, however, alter his view of the *seriousness* of his crime and, to that degree, his assessment of his ability to get away with it. In other words, it was not James Earl Ray's white, lower-class resentment of what Martin Luther King, Jr. represented — a prominent national leader, a recipient of a Nobel Peace Prize, and a person who was invited to counsel with presidents — that drove him obsessively to the assassination. Rather,

Dr. King was killed, in part, because he was *merely* a "nigger" to James Earl Ray. Ray understood that, at that time, no white man had been convicted in a Southern state for killing either a black person or a civil rights worker. Killing a nigger in the South was an act a man could get away with, even if caught: it was, therefore, worth doing if the *price* was right

The Family Connection

With a single significant qualification — his family — Ray's relationships with other people were invariably brief and superficial; he was a loner. Over the years, however, he faithfully maintained contact with his brothers John and Jerry, and his sister Carol. It was a curious bond, probably formed by the adversity they shared as children, nurtured in adulthood by a common knowledge that life was unfair and there were precious few people they could count on except each other. "James would do anything for us and we for him," his brother John said. "But he wasn't particularly sociable with strangers."[78]

Other than the mysterious alleged accomplice "Raoul," who, according to Ray's alibi, suddenly appeared after Ray's escape from Missouri State Penitentiary in April 1967 and simply vanished — literally without a trace — after the King slaying, Ray had no sustained relationships with anyone but his two brothers and sister. For example, Jerry and John were the only persons who visited James Earl in prison. And he corresponded only with them and their sister Carol.[79]

There is an overwhelming amount of evidence that documents the interaction between the Ray brothers during the critical period preceding the assassination. Moreover, the coincidental nature of these interactions and those attributed by Ray to the puzzling Raoul is revealing. Consider the following chronology of Ray's activities from the time of his prison escape until a few days before King's death:[80]

- *April 22, 1967. Brother* John visits James on the day before his escape on April 23, 1967, and this suggests a strong probability that he assisted his brother in the escape.[81]
- *April 30 to July 13, 1967.* The *brothers* remain in contact after the escape and possibly discuss some joint illicit enterprises during Ray's stay in the Chicago area.[82]
- *July 13, 1967.* Ray almost certainly participates with *one or both brothers* in the $27,000 robbery of the Bank of Alton, Illinois. From this point on, Ray appears to have plenty of money.[83]
- *July 14 to August 21, 1967.* After the robbery, Ray travels to Montreal, where he remains. He maintains contact with his *brothers* while in Canada. Ray tells a girlfriend there that he is working for his *brother.*[84]

- *August 21 to August 30, 1967.* Returning to the states, Ray meets with *brother* Jerry in Chicago en route to Birmingham, Alabama. During this period, Ray receives three payments totaling $4,500 — almost certainly money from the Alton bank heist — from someone, almost certainly his brothers — he claims Raoul.
- *October 7 to November 18, 1967.* Ray travels to Mexico in a white Ford Mustang he purchased in Birmingham. It is not clear what the purpose of this trip was. It has been suggested that he hoped to get started in the pornography business with newly purchased photography equipment and the availability of cheap Mexican prostitutes.[85] He may have also been exploring the possibilities of a burgeoning marijuana market, although this has been denied.[86]
- *November 19, 1967.* Ray arrives in Los Angeles and soon establishes contact with one or both of his *brothers* by mail and telephone.
- *December 14 or 15, 1967.* Ray cancels an appointment with a psychologist, explaining that he has to *meet his brother* in New Orleans about a job. Ray calls *brother* Jerry twice on his way to New Orleans. He then receives a payment of five hundred dollars from someone in New Orleans — almost certainly Jerry — he claims it was Raoul.
- *December 1967.* After returning to Los Angeles on December 21, Ray makes a $364 payment for dancing lessons and casually mentions to the instructor that he had just returned from visiting his *brother* in Louisiana. An anonymous witness later testified that Jerry Ray had told him that he had been in New Orleans with his *brother* the third week of December 1967.[87]
- *February 1968.* Sometime this month someone — almost certainly *brother* Jerry — writes or calls Ray in Los Angeles and instructs him to return to New Orleans in March. Ray then calls New Orleans for more complete information. Ray claims his contact was Raoul.
- *March 2 to March 19, 1968.* Ray casually mentions to someone in the bartending school he was attending that he was going to Birmingham to see his *brother*. He repeats this story when he declines a bartending job on March 9. Then on March 17, Ray leaves Los Angeles, indicating his ultimate destination on a postal change-of-address form as Atlanta — Dr. King's home and headquarters — not New Orleans, as he later claims.[88]
- *March 20–28, 1968.* Arriving in New Orleans on March 20, Ray receives a message instructing him to meet *brother* Jerry — he claims Raoul — in Birmingham. Ray leaves for Birmingham the next day but takes a suspiciously roundabout route through Selma, Alabama, where he spends the night of March 22. Dr. King had just left the area

the day before. That morning Ray drives to Birmingham where he meets *brother* Jerry — he claims Raoul — before driving on together to Atlanta on March 23. During this time, Ray is armed only with a .38 caliber pistol. After a day together, Ray's *accomplice* — he alleges Raoul — leaves and did not return until March 28 or 29. During his stay in Atlanta, Ray circled the areas of Dr. King's home, office, and church on an Atlanta map.[89]

- March 29–30, 1968. Sometime during this period, Ray and his accomplice, *brother* Jerry, decide it would be easier and safer to kill Dr. King with a long-range rifle rather than a pistol. On March 29, Ray receives $750 from his *accomplice* — he alleges Raoul. That same day, according to attorney Percy Foreman, Ray *and his brother Jerry* drive to Birmingham together where Ray purchases a .243 Remington rifle at Aeromarine Supply Company. Later that day, Ray calls the Aeromarine salesman to say that his *brother* had convinced him that he needed a larger caliber rifle. The next day, the exchange is made, and Ray leaves with a Remington 30.06 — the murder weapon.[90] From this point until the assassination Ray is alone.

Following the rifle purchase, Ray returns to Atlanta on his stalk of Dr. King. On March 31, he pays his room rent, and on April 1, he drops off some clothing at the Piedmont Laundry. Ray later denied making this trip back to Atlanta since it would provide strong circumstantial evidence that he was, in fact, stalking Dr. King. He stated flatly before the House Select Committee on Assassinations: "If I did return to Atlanta on those dates, I will just take responsibility for the King case here on TV." The committee then presented the laundry receipt as undeniable evidence that his purpose in Atlanta was to kill Dr. King.[91]

After reading in the Atlanta papers of Dr. King's plan to be in Memphis on April 3 and 4, Ray leaves Atlanta on April 2 and drives to Memphis, arriving on April 3 when he checks into the New Rebel Motel. Then reading in the Memphis *Commercial Appeal* that Dr. King is staying at the Lorraine Motel, Ray leaves his motel and rents another room in Bessie Brewer's rooming house only a short distance and an unobstructed view across a back alley from King's room.[92]

There can be little doubt that throughout the period extending from his prison escape until he shot Dr. King, James Earl Ray's only consistent contacts were with his brothers — especially Jerry — unless one accepts the concocted Raoul story. His own testimony and written statements, the testimony of others he happened to talk with (for example, the woman in Canada), acquaintances in Los Angeles, the policeman who guarded him after his arrest in England, his attorneys, author William Bradford Huie, *Playboy* magazine, and Dan Rather of CBS News substantiate the enduring pattern and exclusivity of this brotherly association in crime.[93]

Moreover, not one shred of evidence has ever been produced to verify the existence of the fictitious "Raoul" — not a fingerprint, witness, telephone call, or even a reasonable circumstantial clue. Beyond this, there is reason to believe that contact was maintained between the brothers *after* the assassination. For example, it is probable that John Ray knew his brother was in London *before* his arrest and planned to join him there.[94] James Earl Ray remained close and protective of his family until his death.

There is a considerable amount of circumstantial evidence indicating that James Earl Ray killed Martin Luther King, Jr. with the probable knowledge and assistance of his two brothers. But why? There is no evidence to support earlier claims that Ray was motivated either by a desire for notoriety or racism. What motivated James Earl Ray was what had always motivated him throughout his criminal career — money.

The Contract

Two days before Ray was arrested at London's Heathrow Airport on his way to a sanctuary in some colonial African nation, a companion asked his brother Jerry if he thought his brother had actually killed Dr. King. "If I was in his position," he recalled, "and had 18 years to serve and someone offered me a lot of money to kill someone I didn't like anyhow, and get me out of the country, I'd do it." Was there money involved, he was asked. ". . . if he done it there had to be a lot of money involved," he replied, "because he wouldn't do it for hatred, or just because he didn't like somebody, because that is not his line of work."[95] Brother John expressed the same view in a June 9, 1968 interview with the *St. Louis Post-Dispatch*.[96]

Given this acknowledged history of James Earl Ray's past motives and behavior, consider the outline of a probable conspiracy that was not revealed for some ten years — and a curiously conducted FBI investigation — after Dr. King's death.

Sometime early in 1967, a St. Louis underworld figure, Russell G. Byers, was approached by an acquaintance, John Kauffmann, and asked if he was interested in making fifty thousand dollars.[97] John Kauffmann, a jowly-faced, bald, paunchy man in his early sixties, was well-known among people operating outside of the law in the St. Louis area. Kauffmann, a sometime stockbroker, actually ran a fencing operation for stolen cars and other goods out of a motel he owned in Barnard, Missouri, near St. Louis.[98] His main activity, however, was drug dealing through a licensed drug company he owned. Kauffman would purchase drugs wholesale and then market them illegally, making a considerable profit on the mark-up. As a result of these activities, he came into contact with many known criminals and ex-convicts in St. Louis.[99]

One of Kauffmann's more interesting associates was Hugh Maxey, a physician at Missouri State Prison where James Earl Ray and Russell Byers' brother-in-law, John Paul Spica,[100] knew each other as fellow inmates.[101] Spica also worked as an orderly in the prison hospital with Dr. Maxey. It is probable drug trafficking within the prison defined the association between John Kauffmann and Dr. Maxey.[102] This was one segment of a pattern of associations that existed when John Kauffmann approached Russell Byers about a fifty-thousand-dollar assignment.

During this same period, Carol Ray Pepper, the Ray brothers' sister, owned the Grapevine Tavern in St. Louis. The tavern was managed by her brother John. A fairly rough bar in the rundown south side of the city, it was, as its name suggests, a place where one could go for information and contacts with the St. Louis underworld. John Kauffmann used to drop by the tavern occasionally for that reason.[103] It was also a distribution point for Alabama governor and presidential candidate George Wallace's 1968 American Independent party campaign literature, located as it was, just across the street from the Wallace campaign headquarters in that section of the city.[104]

Outside of St. Louis in a rural area near Imperial, Missouri lived a wealthy distinguished-looking man with carefully barbered snow-white hair. John Sutherland was born in Virginia in 1905. In 1926 he graduated from the Virginia Military Institute with a degree in engineering. After military service, Sutherland went on to earn both a bachelor's and a master's degree in law before establishing a successful practice as a patent attorney in St. Louis. Active in social, fraternal, and professional associations and activities in the area, Sutherland was proud of a Southern family heritage he traced back to the early colonists. He was also a racist. Sutherland was the chief organizer and sponsor of a segregationist White Citizens' Council and an avid supporter of Governor George Wallace's presidential campaign in 1968. Sutherland alone paid the six-hundred-dollar-a-month salary for the state chairman of the Alabama governor's American Independent Party.[105]

Sutherland's right-wing affiliations extended to the ultraconservative Southern States Industrial Council and its president, Thurman Sensing, with whom he shared concerns, friendship, correspondence, and many telephone conversations in 1968.[106] The Southern States Industrial Council was one of the most powerful and vigorous opponents of civil rights reform in the nation. Less than two weeks after Dr. King's death, Thurman Sensing addressed the Daughters of the American Revolution in a remarkably tasteless speech in which he said, "It is not too much to say, in fact, that Martin Luther King, Jr., brought this crime [his assassination] on himself." Sensing did not stop there.

He went on to speculate sympathetically that Dr. King's assassin may have reasoned: "I think Martin Luther King should be killed. I realize there is a law against murder, but in this case, I think the law is unjust."[107] One of those who responded favorably to his remarks was his friend, FBI Director J. Edgar Hoover.[108]

Back in the St. Louis suburbs, another of Sensing's racist friends, John Sutherland, lived in what could be described as a fantasy world of the Old South he loved so dearly. When John Kauffmann led Russell Byers into Sutherland's richly furnished den on that evening in early 1967, they took an almost farcical step back in time. As they walked across a rug replica of the Confederate flag amid swords, pistols, and other trappings and memorabilia of the South, the War Between the States, and an era now a century old, the wealthy attorney greeted them in the gray uniform of a Confederate soldier, adorned with medals, his unsmiling eyes shadowed beneath the wide brim of a cavalry officer's Stetson.[109] One can only wonder what crossed the minds of Kauffmann and Byers who were more accustomed to the illuminated Clydesdales, pickled eggs, and calendar nudes of places like the Grapevine.

After some somewhat awkward pleasantries, Sutherland addressed the purpose of the gathering: Would Byers arrange the murder of Martin Luther King, Jr. for fifty thousand dollars? Byers claimed he was stunned, completely unprepared for the proposal. After some hesitation he asked where the money was going to come from. "A secret Southern organization," Sutherland replied.[110] After declining the offer, Byers later testified that he was never approached again about the matter and did not think much about it until the assassination.[111] Concerned at that time that he might be implicated, he related the incident to two of his attorneys who advised him just to remain quiet. Then sometime during late 1973, some five and a half years after the assassination, Byers happened to mention the incident unknowingly to an FBI informant. The informant related the story to agents in the St. Louis FBI office a few months later in March 1974. For strange and mysterious reasons, this important information was not investigated by the Bureau. Byers, for example, was never questioned despite the fact that he was a known criminal. It was not until March 13, 1978 — four years after receiving the information — that it was finally reported to the House Select Committee on Assassinations. The FBI claimed this breakdown in an important investigation was nothing more than an administrative error.[112]

The probable route of communication between Sutherland and Kauffmann and members of the Ray family is fairly direct: word that a murder contract was out on the black civil rights leader need not have depended on chance and rumor. The link between Kauffmann and Dr. Maxey extended to Russell Byers' brother-in-law John Spica, the inmate acquaintance of James Earl Ray; Spica was also an associate of one Robert Regazzi whose ex-wife,

Naomi, was employed as a barmaid by Carol Ray at the Grapevine Tavern. Recall that the tavern was a watering hole for Wallace campaign workers who were headquartered just across the street. And Wallace's American Independent party in St. Louis was bankrolled in part, as we have seen, by John Sutherland and the White Citizens Council he founded.[113]

Although it is unlikely that a Southern gentleman with aristocratic pretensions like John Sutherland ever bellied-up to the bar at the Grapevine to discuss anything directly with its sleazy clientele, it is known that John Kauffmann and his associates did from time to time. His underworld activities required that he make the kind of contacts available in a place like the Grapevine where criminal transactions were a well-known topic of conversation and pattern of activity.[114] Another of Mr. Sutherland's friends, Glen Shrum, a Wallace organizer, enjoyed the ambience of the Grapevine and regularly crossed the street for a drink or two and some congenial conversation. A member of the John Birch Society and the radical Minutemen, there was no question about where Glen Shrum stood on the race issue. There is also no doubt that John Sutherland liked men like that, men ready to use whatever means available to save the Republic from the evils of civil rights and race mixing. Sipping their Buds amid the Wallace bumper stickers, campaign pamphlets, and stale bar odors of the Grapevine, there were no doubts in the minds of these angry racists about the threat posed by the articulate black minister from Atlanta.[115]

About this time — the middle of March 1968 — James Earl Ray received word from one of his brothers (he falsely claimed it was Raoul) about the contract on King's life. He left on his long drive to New Orleans to seal the deal. After the meeting in New Orleans, James Earl Ray began his systematic stalk of Dr. King, following his movements and plans in newspaper accounts that recorded his activities in and out of his Atlanta headquarters. The hunt would end on the balcony of the Lorraine Motel in Memphis on April 4.[116]

Escape and Arrest

Ray's reasonably well-planned and successful getaway after the assassination, however, was marred by the same sort of blunders that haunted him throughout his criminal career and, once again, led to his capture. As he ran from Bessie Brewer's rooming house after firing the fatal shot, he spotted a police car. Ray panicked, impulsively discarding the murder weapon and a number of personal belongings he had wrapped in a bedspread in the doorway of Canipes Amusement Company.[117] It was a fatal mistake. The fingerprints on these articles eventually led to his arrest on the morning of June 8, 1968 as he was preparing to board a Brussels-bound jet at London's Heathrow Airport. Except for this incriminating evidence, it is unlikely that authorities could have pieced together other clues in time to prevent him from making good an ingenious escape through Canada and England to some anticipated sanctuary in Angola, Rhodesia, or South Africa.[118]

A second major blunder of Ray and those who conspired with him was the way they bungled and lost the payoff. Operating under the assumption that once King was dead and he was safely out of the country the bounty could be claimed, Ray and his accomplices, in typical Ray fashion, failed to work out the details. It is interesting to note that after his arrest, neither John nor Jerry Ray attempted to deny their brother's guilt. Instead they stated simply that if he had killed Dr. King, he had done it for money[119] — a hint, perhaps, to those now silent partners of the contract that it was time to pay up.

The bumbling, inept Ray brothers were victims of a double-cross. Acting on the presumption that the fifty-thousand-dollar payoff would be made after Dr. King's death, they failed to realize that they were dealing with dishonest men like themselves, except they were more intelligent. Once King was dead and Ray arrested, there was no reason to make the payoff and risk exposure. Since John and Jerry had less at stake in the murder, the two brothers, whom defense attorney Percy Foreman referred to as "a couple of morons," had only to be kept quiet.[120] And that was easy to do, since both had everything to lose and nothing to gain from talking. Almost immediately after Ray's arrest, Jerry was quickly befriended and employed by Ku Klux Klan attorney J. B. Stoner[121] who also offered to represent James Earl Ray free of charge.[122]

The problem for those now silent co-conspirators, however, was that James Earl Ray, facing murder charges with overwhelming evidence of his guilt, might be inclined to talk to investigators. For that reason, two curious and related events occurred that strongly suggest a strategy to avoid trial and further investigation of a wealth of evidence pointing to other conspirators.

First, Ray dismissed segregationist attorney Arthur Hanes, a man of dubious legal skill who had volunteered to represent him, when the internationally known criminal defense attorney, Percy Foreman, volunteered his services. After the surprise move by Foreman, many expected to see the kind of colorful, well-publicized trial the high-profile Houston attorney preferred. But that didn't happen. Foreman, whose considerable reputation was based on his shrewd, entertaining, and successful courtroom performances on very difficult cases, advised Ray to enter a guilty plea. He acted quickly after a reportedly very casual — some believed superficial — examination of the evidence. Foreman said that he explained to the shaken defendant that if he didn't accept the plea and the ninety-nine-year sentence that went with it, he would probably die in Tennessee's electric chair.[123]

Second, Foreman then moved quickly to convince author William Bradford Huie, to whom Ray had sold his story, that Ray acted *alone*. Foreman told Huie that Ray killed King for the all-too-familiar reasons attributed to assassins — fame and notoriety. Foreman was persuasive; Huie bought it and didn't even consider the possibility of a conspiracy. One can reasonably assume that those persons who put out the contract on King were greatly relieved as a result of Foreman's timely and skillful maneuvers that precluded a trial and established a false, but credible, motive for the "lone assassin." Foreman added that Ray had "mistakenly" believed that if he was part of a conspiracy, he could not be convicted of murder.[124]

Until that point, James Earl Ray had it figured differently. Ray was aware that there had not been a single conviction in a Southern state court for any of those responsible for the deaths of civil rights volunteers during this turbulent period of Southern history. Ray also believed that the combined seventy-percent Nixon-Wallace vote in Shelby County, Tennessee and the numerous letters of support he received nationwide would translate into a very favorable jury verdict.[125] Killing King was a crime, he thought he could get away with, even if arrested and tried.

Foreman surely was aware of this as well. For example, to cite just a few instances of Southern justice: the trial of Mississippi civil rights leader Medgar Evers' accused killer, Byron de la Beckwith, ended in a hung jury in 1964. The accused killers of civil rights worker Viola Liuzzo were convicted only on federal conspiracy charges and received ten-year sentences. Of the eighteen accused participants in the 1964 abduction and slaying of civil rights workers James Chaney, Andrew Goodman, and Michael Schwerner, only seven were convicted and, again, only on federal conspiracy charges — not murder. And many other known murderers of blacks were never brought to trial. For decades since the Civil War, white-on-black violence was not a punishable crime in the South. Fewer than one percent of those responsible for thousands of lynchings were ever arrested and convicted.[126]

But Ray would not be so fortunate. Instead he accepted a ninety-nine-year sentence only to protest feebly and in vain after he was sentenced that there was *more* to it. Three days later he wrote the judge, angrily denouncing "that famous Houston attorney Percy Fourflusher" for having deceived and pressured him into the guilty plea.[127] Only an attorney with Foreman's reputation could have closed this explosively controversial case so quickly and skillfully without a trial. Is that the reason he took the case? No one is sure. In any case, Ray had been had, and he knew it. He had to be careful about his protests, however, because a slip could mean the arrest of his brothers who had been involved, the facts suggest, in everything but the actual shooting.

But without them, he soon realized, there was no tangible evidence of conspiracy. Ray resolved the dilemma concerning his brothers by doing the only thing he could, inventing a surrogate — the mysterious, enigmatic, and fictitious Raoul, whose alleged movements, as we have seen, so closely paralleled those of his brother Jerry.[128]

A Curious Investigation

When James Earl Ray was arrested, a considerable amount of circumstantial evidence suggested that other persons were involved in a conspiracy to kill Martin Luther King, Jr. Yet the intense and very thorough FBI investigation that led to Ray's arrest curiously failed to pursue the most obvious clues leading back from the bathroom in the Memphis rooming house on April 4, 1968 to a mysterious February message to the convicted killer in Los Angeles and the killer's return to New Orleans to discuss the feasibility of the contract murder of the nation's most prominent black leader. Ray, had been casting about since his prison escape, looking for an opportunity to gain the respectability and material comforts that had eluded him all his life. For example, he had embarked on a number of self-improvement schemes with that objective in mind: Self-confidence counseling, a correspondence course, bartenders' school, dancing lessons, even a nose job, were part of the effort to move in that direction. But the bottom line was money. In Ray's world money bought respectability. So it was the lure of money — big money — that caused him to drop everything and leave for New Orleans on March 17.

Although the identity of the "Secret Southern Organization" that put out the contract cannot be proven, it seems highly probable that the source was in Nashville and a pattern of telephone communication led from there up the Mississippi to the comfortable, flag-adorned sanctuary of attorney John Sutherland in Imperial, Missouri. John Kauffmann, as we know, picked it up and that point and the details of the contract eventually reached the dingy confines of the Grapevine Tavern, where John and Jerry Ray relayed a proposal to their brother in Los Angeles. The obvious point of departure for such an investigation was the Ray family. But once the arrest was made, the FBI chose to ignore all conspiracy leads despite a clear, persistent and documented pattern of interaction between the Ray brothers that was known to the Bureau.[129]

Even the March 19, 1974 FBI memorandum detailing Russell Byers' revelation to one of their informants remained buried for four years in the Bureau's St. Louis files. By the time it was revealed, both the main suspects, Sutherland and Kauffmann, were dead.[130] Also dead were the number one and two men at the FBI who had directed the investigation of King's assassination. Director J. Edgar Hoover and his associate director and companion, Clyde A. Tolson. Others of the Bureau's top leadership in 1968 were also either dead or retired by 1978.[131]

It is perhaps only coincidental that the Bureau's failure to pursue this obvious line of investigation occurred in the wake of its illegal counter intelligence program (COINTELPRO) designed to harass and discredit Dr. King and the civil rights movement.[132] But even J. Edgar Hoover's well-docu-

The Atypicals—Family and Money   299

mented and virtually pathological hatred and harassment of Dr. King — which is outlined in the Justice Department's 1977 investigation of the Bureau's activities (and also presented in some detail during the 1978 assassination hearings) — are not enough to explain the breakdown in the investigation.[133]

Although it is unlikely that there was direct collusion between the FBI and those persons who instigated the King assassination, there was — without doubt — a common perception shared by those persons and the FBI of the threat posed by the civil rights movement and its leader. Few people hated Dr. King more than J. Edgar Hoover. Also, Hoover's admiration for the values espoused by individuals such as Thurman Sensing, John Sutherland, and groups such as the Southern States Industrial Council is a matter of record.[134]

Given these facts, it is reasonable to assume that J. Edgar Hoover probably had mixed feelings when he heard the news of King's death. On the one hand, he no longer had to worry about what he falsely believed was the Communist threat posed by his black adversary [135] — a man he had labeled a "sexual degenerate" and "the most notorious liar in the country."[136] On the other hand, however, given his well-publicized disputes with Dr. King, it was imperative that the FBI get the killer before existing awareness about the FBI's vendetta could lead to suspicions of the Bureau's involvement in the assassination.[137] But as soon as Ray was apprehended, the Bureau essentially concluded its investigation. Hoover chose not to follow a well-defined path of evidence when he was gravely concerned about where that investigation might lead. He did not want to know, nor, in his fashion, did he think it would be in the national interest for the country to know who put out the contract on King's life. Percy Foreman made sure of that by avoiding a trial. King was dead, his silenced killer in prison; the case was, to Hoover's relief, closed.

Conclusions

James Earl Ray possessed few of the characteristics of other assassins. A career criminal and a contract killer, he eludes classification as a typical assassin. Except for the pre-eminence of his victim, Ray might have still gotten away with the crime, just as had the accused killers of civil rights activists Medgar Evers, James Chaney, Andrew Goodman, Michael Schwerner, Viola Liuzzo, and scores of nameless black persons over the years. Given that record in the southern courts and the $50,000 bounty, it seemed like a reasonable venture to Ray. The risks were well within the range of acceptability for a man who, in the past, would gamble twenty years of his life for the contents of a supermarket cash register. What he did not know that might have changed his mind was that, paradoxically, Dr. King's well-placed enemies would insist that his assassin, who had so well served their purposes, be railroaded by a skillful attorney into a plea that would avoid the damaging revelations of a trial.

Meanwhile, the contract money was never paid and James Earl Ray spent the rest of his life languishing in a Tennessee prison, betrayed by the ineptitude he shares with his slow-witted brothers. They remain free thanks to their older brother's loyalty and J. Edgar Hoover's refusal to pursue further a potentially damaging investigation. James Earl Ray died of kidney failure on April 23, 1998 after a lengthy illness. To the end, Ray refused to acknowledge his guilt for the crime he certainly committed. Near the end of his life, in a bizarre turn of events, the family of his victim rallied to his cause. In 1997, Dr. King's son, Dexter, met with Ray. "I just want to ask you, for the record, did you kill my father," he asked. Ray stammered, as he often did in these circumstances, "No, no I didn't, no." But then he was more equivocal, adding, "But like I say, sometimes these questions are difficult to answer, and you have to make a personal evaluation."[138]

What accounts for such ambivalence, especially in a man who knew he was dying? History and experimental research have shown that persons who kill or harm others "on command" do not accept *personal responsibility* for their actions. Instead they are "just following orders," as defendants famously claimed at Nuremberg after World War II and at virtually every war crimes trial since. In the minds of the perpetrator, the responsibility for what he did falls on the person or persons who gave the order or, in this case, the person or persons who put out the contract on King's life. And so it was probably for James Earl Ray.[139]

In June 2000, the Department of Justice concluded an exhaustive re-examination of evidence in the case with these words:

> Finally, while we conducted no original investigation directed at determining whether James Earl Ray killed Dr. King, we found no credible evidence to disturb past judicial determinations that he did... At this time, we are aware of no information to warrant further investigation of the assassination of Dr. Martin Luther King, Jr.[140]

Notes

1. R.P. Warren, *All the King's Men* (New York: Harcourt, Brace & Co., 1946).
2. T. H. Williams, *Huey Long* (New York: Bantam Books, 1969).
3. Other interesting accounts of the Long era would include C. Beals, *The Story of Huey Long* (New York: Lippincott, 1935); H. Kane, *Louisiana Hayride* (New York: Morrow, 1941); A. P. Sindler, *Huey Long's Louisiana* (Baltimore, MD: Johns Hopkins, 1956); S. Opotowsky, *The Long's of Louisiana* (New York: Dutton, 1960); A. M. Schlesinger, Jr., *The Politics of Upheaval*, vol. 3 (Boston:

The Atypicals—Family and Money   301

  Houghton Mifflin, 1960); and V. O. Key, *Southern Politics in State and Nation* (New York: Alfred A. Knopf, 1949).
4. D.H. Zinman, *The Day Huey Long Was Shot* (New York: Ivan Oblensky, Inc., 1963).
5. H. B. Deutsch, *The Huey Long Murder Case* (Garden City, NY: Doubleday & Co., 1963).
6. Zinman, *The Day,* pp. 55–57.
7. Ibid., p. 60.
8. Ibid., pp. 64–65.
9. Ibid., pp. 66–67.
10. Ibid., p. 66.
11. Ibid., quoted on p. 71.
12. Ibid., p. 77.
13. Ibid., p. 76.
14. Ibid., pp. 78, 81.
15. Ibid., p. 83.
16. Deutsch, *The Long Murder Case,* p. 129.
17. Williams, *Huey Long,* p. 913.
18. Zinman, *The Day,* p. 280.
19. Deutsch, *The Long Murder Case,* p. 164.
20. Ibid., p. 128.
21. Ibid., pp. 128, 162.
22. Ibid., p. 71.
23. Williams, *Huey Long,* p. 896.
24. Ibid., p. 886.
25. Ibid., p. 887.
26. R. H. Luthin, *American Demagogues* (Boston: The Beacon Press, 1954), pp. 263–267.
27. H. P. Long, *My First Days in the White House* (Harrisburg, PA, 1935); published posthumously.
28. Williams, *Huey Long,* p. 888.
29. Deutsch, *The Long Murder Case,* pp. 161–162; Williams, *Huey Long,* pp. 880883, 900-901.
30. For a detailed discussion of the rumors circulating at the time, see Deutsch, *The Long Murder Case,* and Williams, *Huey Long.*
31. Zinman, *The Day,* pp. 234–235; Williams, *Huey Long,* p. 915.
32. Williams, *Huey Long,* p. 915.
33. J. McKinley, *Assassination in America* (New York H 1977), p. 97.
34. Deutsch, *The Long Murder Case,* p. 128.
35. Zinman, *The Day.*
36. Deutsch, *The Long Murder Case,* p. 162.
37. Zinman, *The Day,* pp. 85–86, 279-280.
38. Deutsch, *The Long Murder Case,* pp. 132–133.
39. Zinman, *The Day,* p. 284.
40. Ibid., pp. 85–92; Deutsch, *The Long Murder Case,* pp. 82–83.
41. Zinman, *The Day,* pp. 83-84.

42. H. G. Fields, *The Life of Huey Pierce Long* (Farmerville, LA: Fields Publishing Agency, 1944); Luthin, *American Demagogues;* Deutsch, *The Long Murder Case;* J. Pearl, *The Dangerous Assassins* (Derby, CT: Monarch Books, 1964); M. C. Havens et al., *The Politics of Assassination* Englewood Cliffs, NJ: Prentice-Hall, Inc., 1970); L. Paine, *The Assassins' World* (New York: Taplinger Publishing Co., 1975); and S. Lesberg, *Assassinations in Our Time* (London: Peebles Press International and Bobbs-Merrill, 1976).
43. Deutsch, *The Long Murder Case,* p. 128.
44. Zinman, *The Day,* p. 155.
45. Williams, *Huey Long,* p. 905.
46. Recall that the legal basis for the "separate but equal" doctrine of racial segregation was established by the Supreme Court in its ruling in a Louisiana case, *Plessy v. Ferguson* (1896). The *Plessy* decision upheld the Louisiana law which specified that a person with even one thirty-second of black lineage was considered black and was therefore forbidden to use "white only" facilities. *Plessy* remained the law of the land until it was overturned in 1954 in the famous *Brown* decision.
47. For various immediate newspaper descriptions and interpretations of the event, see the following papers for September and October 1935: Baton Rouge *Morning Advocate* and *State-Times,* and the New Orleans *States Item* and *Times-Picayune.*
48. Zinman, *The Day,* p. 112.
49. Deutsch, *The Long Murder Case,* p. 89.
50. Williams, *Huey Long,* p. 906.
51. Deutsch, *The Long Murder Case,* p. 151.
52. Williams, *Huey Long,* p. 908.
53. Zinman, *The Day,* pp. 148–154; Deutsch, *The Long Murder Case,* pp. 108–110, 120-121.
54. Zinman, *The Day,* p. 158.
55. U.S. Congress, House, Select Committee on Assassinations, *Hearings on the Investigation of the Assassination of Martin Luther King, Jr.,* 95th Cong., 2d Sess., 1978, vols. 1–12, pp. 346–351. Hereafter cited as *Hearings.*
56. W.B.Huie, *He Slew the Dreamer* (New York: Delacorte Press, 1970).
57. G. McMillan, *The Making of an Assassin* (Boston: Little, Brown, 1976).
58. Huie, *The Dreamer,* p. 173.
59. McMillan, *Assassin,* pp. 70, 246–247.
60. *Hearings,* testimony of Jerry Ray, vol. 7, pp. 395, 400, 436–437, 499–500, 520–521.
61. *Hearings,* statement of J. Wolf, vol. 8, pp. 1–13, 33.
62. McMillan, *Assassin,* pp. 69–71.
63. Ibid., p. 106.
64. *Hearings,* testimony of Jerry Ray, vol. 7, p. 500.
65. Ibid., vol. 4, p. 195.
66. Huie, *The Dreamer,* p. 11.
67. *Hearings,* statement of G. R. Blakey, vol. 4, pp. 112, 132, 147–149.

The Atypicals—Family and Money 303

68. McMillan, *Assassin,* pp. 206–207.
69. *Hearings,* testimony of James Earl Ray, vol. 1, pp. 230, 329–330, 334; statement of G. R. Blakey, vol. 4, p. 112; testimony of Jerry Ray, vol. 7, pp. 500, 520–521.
70. *Hearings,* testimony of James Earl Ray, vol. 4, pp. 112–113.
71. *Hearings,* statement of G. R. Blakey, vol. 4, pp. 117–121.
72. *Hearings,* Exhibit F-172, vol. 4, pp. 155, 158; Exhibit F-166, vol. 4, pp. 171–175.
73. *Hearings,* Exhibit F-171, vol. 4, pp. 144–145.
74. *Hearings,* statement of G. R. Blakey, p. 124; Exhibit F170, vol.4, pp. 130–134.
75. *Hearings,* Exhibit F-166, vol. 4, pp. 148–154.
76. McMillan, *Assassin,* pp. 221–227.
77. *Hearings,* statement of G. R. Blakey, vol. 4, pp. 112–113, 194.
78. *St. Louis Post-Dispatch,* June 9, 1968, A31; see also Hearings: testimony of John Larry Ray, vol. 8, pp. 589, 600.
79. *Hearings,* testimony of Jerry Ray, vol. 7, pp. 338–340; narration of James Wolf, vol. 8, p. 3; testimony of John Larry Ray, p. 57. See also *Report of the Department of Justice Task Force to Review the FBI Martin Luther King, Jr. Security and Assassination Investigations* (Washington, DC: U.S. Department of Justice, January 11, 1977); hereafter cited as *Justice Report.*
80. Contradictions in Ray's various accounts of his activities are detailed in U.S. Congress, House, Select Committee on Assassinations, *Compilation of the Statements of James Earl Ray,* 9Sth Cong., 2d Sess., August 18, 1978.
81. *Hearings,* testimony of John Larry Ray, vol. 8, pp. 57–66.
82. *Hearings,* testimony of James Earl Ray, vol. 3, pp. 169–174; *Justice Report,* pp. 101–103.
83. *Hearings,* testimonies of James Earl Ray, vol. 2, pp. 486–487; Jerry Ray, vol. 7, p. 520; narration of J. Wolf, vol. 8, pp. 9–12.
84. *Hearings,* statement of G. R. Blakey vol 4 118–120 and vol. 7, p. 313.
85. Ibid., vol. 4, pp. 156–157, 182.
86. Ibid., p. 176.
87. *Hearings,* testimony of James Earl Ray, vol. 3, p. 203; statement of G. R. Blakey, vol. 7, pp. 315, 317.
88. *Hearings,* statement of G. R. Blakey, vol. 7, pp. 315, 317; testimony of James Earl Ray, vol. 1, p. 303, and vol. 2, pp. 48–53.
89. *Hearings,* testimony of James Earl Ray, vol. 3, pp. 213–214; statement of G. R. Blakey, vol. 7, pp. 316–318.
90. *Hearings,* testimony of James Earl Ray, vol. 1, pp. 100-101, and vol. 3, pp. 215–222; statement of G. R. Blakey, vol. 4, p. 8; vol. 5, pp. 219–220, 331; and vol. 7, pp. 316, 318; testimony of Jerry Ray, vol. 7, p. 440.
91. *Hearings,* testimony of James Earl Ray, vol. 2, p. 61 (see also pp. 62–67, 70–95); statement of A.E. Peters, vol. 3, pp. 302–512.
92. *Hearings,* testimony of James Earl Ray, vol. 2, pp. 96–101, and vol. 1, pp. 76–82.
93. Ibid., vol. 1, pp. 87–112, 2S8, 333; vol. 2, pp. 26–27, 44; vol. 3, p. 271; vol. 4,

introduction, p. 6; statement of G. R. Blakey, pp. 21, 118–120; testimony of P. Foreman, vol. 5, pp. 101–103, 116, 206, 219, 326, 330–332; statement of G. R. Blakey, vol. 7, pp. 313–317; testimony of Jerry Ray, vol. 7, pp. 338–340, 396–401, 439–444;statement of James Wolf, vol. 8, pp. 3, 31; testimony of John Larry Ray, vol. 8, pp. 57–66, 600–604; and vols. 9, 10, 11, and 12, which contain eight interviews with James Earl Ray in 1977 and his "20,000 word" handwritten statement.

94. *Hearings,* testimony of John Larry Ray, vol. 8, p. 601.
95. *Hearings,* testimony of Jerry Ray, vol. 7, p. 462.
96. *Hearings,* testimony of John Larry Ray, vol. 8, pp. 589, 599.
97. *Hearings,* testimony of R.G Byers, vol. 7, p. 181.
98. Ibid., p. 187.
99. Ibid.
100. Spica was killed after his release from prison in a car bombing on November 7, 1979.
101. Ibid., pp. 194, 294.
102. Ibid., pp. 194, 198; statement of E. Evans, vol. 7, pp. 250, 294–295.
103. Ibid., vol. 7, p. 310.
104. Ibid., p. 297.
105. Ibid.
106. Ibid., pp. 250–251.
107. Ibid., p. 263.
108. Ibid., pp. 252–253.
109. Ibid., p. 249.
110. *Hearings,* testimony of R.G. Byers, vol. 7, pp. 181–183, 188–189, 245–246.
111. Ibid., p. 191.
112. Ibid., p. 199; statement of E. Evans, vol. 7, pp. 247–248, 305.
113. Ibid., vol. 7, p. 293.
114. Ibid., p. 310.
115. Ibid., pp. 293–302; Hearings: testimony of John Larry Ray, vol. 8, pp. 586–593.
116. *Hearings,* testimony of James Earl Ray, vol. 2, pp. 45–102.
117. *Hearings,* statement of G. Johnson, vol. 1, p. 84; testimony of James Earl Ray, vol. 3, p. 274; testimony of A. Eist, vol. 4, p. 22.
118. *Hearings,* testimony of James Earl Ray, vol. 3, pp. 239–253; statement of G. R. Blakey, vol. 4, pp. 113–116.
119. *Hearings,* statement of G. R. Blakey, vol. 4, p. 195; testimony of Jerry Ray, vol. 7, p. 462; Exhibit F-642, vol. 8, p. 589.
120. *Hearings,* testimony of P. Foreman, vol. 5, p. 208.
121. In 1980, J.B. Stoner was convicted and sentenced to ten years in prison for his role in the 1963 bombing of a black Baptist church in Birmingham, Alabama that claimed the lives of four little girls.
122. *Hearings,* testimony of Jerry Ray, vol. 7, pp. 328–329.
123. *Hearings,* D. Rather interview of James Earl Ray quoted in vol. 1, p. 343; testimony of P. Foreman, vol. 5, pp. 300–302, Exhibit 47, p. 303.
124. *Hearings,* deposition of P. Foreman, vol. 5, pp. 200–203; testimony of P. Foreman, vol. 5, pp. 323, 329; Huie, *The Dreamer,* p. 170.

125. *Hearings,* statement of A. Eist, vol. 3, pp. 274–275; testimony of A. Eist, vol. 4, pp. 22–23; deposition of P. Foreman, vol. 5, pp. 94–95; Huie, *The Dreamer,* pp. 207–212.
126. *Congressional Quarterly,* "Revolution in Civil Rights, 1945–1968," June 1968, pp. 11–12; J. W. Clarke and J. W. Soule, "Southern Children's Reaction to King's Death," *Trans-Action* 5 (October 1968): 35–40; J. W. Clarke, "Without Fear or Shame: Lynching, Capital Punishment, and the Subculture of Violence in the American South," *British Journal of Political Science,* 28 (April 1998), 269–289.
127. *Hearings,* D. Rather interview, vol. 1, pp. 283–291; Huie, *The Dreamer,* pp. 198–199.
128. *Hearings,* Exhibit F-607, vol. 7, pp. 313–316.
129. *Justice Report,* pp. *101–110.*
130. John Sutherland died in 1970 and John Kauffmann in 1974, both from natural causes.
131. *Hearings,* testimony of A. L. Murtagh, vol. 6, p. 112.
132. *Justice Report,* p. 115.
133. Ibid., pp. 115–120, 125–142; *Hearings,* statement of G. R.Blakey, vol. 6, pp. 59–80; testimony of A. L. Murtagh, vol. 6, pp. 91–105.
134. *Hearings,* statement of E. Evans, vol. 7, p. 251; Exhibit F-578, pp. 252–268; Exhibit F-578A, vol. 7, pp. 269–292; statement of E. Evans, vol. 7, p. 293.
135. The director's concerns about King's alleged communist leanings were purely imaginary, according to a Justice Department investigation. See, *Report of the Department of Justice Task Force to Review the FBI Martin Luther King, Jr., Security and Assassination Investigations* (January 11, 1977), pp.123–125.
136. *Justice Report,* pp. 123–126.
137. Concerns about the FBI's purposes in the South during this period were not unfounded. In 1978, for example, Gary Thomas Rowe, a paid FBI informant, was finally indicted for the 1965 murder of civil rights worker Viola Liuzzo. But, as a result of an earlier immunity agreement, a federal appeals court ruled that Rowe could not be brought to trial.
138. "King Killer James Earl Ray Dies; Widow Calls Passing a 'Tragedy," *Arizona Daily Star,* April 24, 1998, A2.
139. See, for example, H. Arendt, *Eichmann in Jerusalem: A Report on the Banality of Evil* (New York: Viking Press, 1965); C.R. Browning, *Ordinary Men: Reserve Police Battalion 101 and the Final Solution in Poland* (New York: Harper Collins, 1992); S. Milgram, *Obedience to Authority: An Experimental View* (New York: Harper & Row, 1974).
140. *United States Department of Justice Investigation of Recent Allegations Regarding the Assassination of Dr. Martin Luther King, Jr.* (June 2000) at http:www.usdoj.gov/crt/crim/mlk/part1.htm.

Part 5

Domestic Terrorists

10

Industrial Society: Theodore John Kaczynski

> *"My God! I'm thinking, what incredible shit we put up with most of our lives — the domestic routine, the stupid and useless and degrading jobs, the insufferable arrogance of elected officials, the crafty cheating and the slimy advertising of the businessmen, the tedious wars in which we kill our buddies instead of our real enemies back home in the capital ... what intolerable garbage and what utterly useless crap we bury ourselves in day by day.... The degree of personal freedom that exists in a society is determined more by the economic and technological structure of society than by its laws or its form of government.... In order to get our message before the public with some chance of making a lasting impression, we've had to kill people."—Theodore Kaczynski*[1]

As *domestic* terrorists, Theodore Kaczynski, Timothy McVeigh, and Eric Rudolph represent a more recent variation of political violence in America. Rather than presidents and presidential candidates, they selected civilian targets which symbolize government policies. Perhaps that change is the consequence of the extraordinary security measures that were put into place for presidents and other Secret Service protectees following John Hinckley's attack on President Reagan. It is now almost impossible to get close enough to harm a president so other less secure, more accessible symbols of government authority are selected instead.

This is not to imply that domestic terrorism originated with them. America has a long history of homegrown terrorism that traces its origins to the strife between the early colonists and settlers, on the one hand and, on the other, the Native Americans whose ancestral lands they claimed. During the same period, slavery in America was a form of institutionalized terror. And the system of Jim Crow that replaced it gave rise to lynching and other countless acts of terrorism carried out against black men, women and children by white supremacist groups like the Ku Klux Klan. As did the labor strife of the late nineteenth and early twentieth centuries which recorded many instances of terrorism. Perhaps the best known of that bloody era was the bombing at Haymarket Square in Chicago on May 4, 1886. In the 1970s, members of the Symbionese Liberation Army murdered, kidnapped, and robbed banks in the Bay Area before six of them were killed in a shootout with Los Angeles police in 1974.[2] What made Kaczynski, McVeigh, and Rudolph different was that, unlike other terrorists — both domestic and international — they acted *alone*[3] to advance their political agendas, apart from organized groups that shared their views.

From 1978 until his arrest in 1996, Dr. Theodore Kaczynski, brilliant mathematician and former university professor, elevated the anxieties of the nation as a political *serial killer*. His homemade bombs killed three and injured twenty-three in sixteen separate incidents. Although he considered targeting political figures, all his victims were, instead, people who Kaczynski believed represented a more insidious evil. They were scientists, academics, and businessmen scattered across the country, but all in one way or another connected to American technology. As such, they symbolized, in his mind, the worst and most threatening force in American society and the world, a world where human values and the quality of life were being destroyed by industrialization and needless, self-serving, technological advancement.

Ted Kaczynski cannot be neatly classified in the original typology. His is a more complex story, reflecting dimensions of both Type I and Type II subjects and, in the view of some — not all — examining psychiatrists, also the symptoms of the mentally disordered Type IV. Kaczynski is a unique, atypical actor in the annals of political violence in America. Additionally, his method of attack — *serial* violence that focused on civilian victims — which McVeigh might have embraced had he not been arrested after the Oklahoma City bombing, and Rudolph later adopted, sets him and them apart from the other subjects in this book.

* * *

THEODORE JOHN KACZYNSKI (1942–)

On May 25, 1978, a package was found in a campus parking lot at the University of Illinois, Chicago Circle. The package was addressed to Professor E.J. Smith of Rensselaer Polytechnic Institute in Troy, New York. The return address was that of Professor Buckley Crist of Northwestern University in Evanston, Illinois. When the package was returned to Crist, who had not sent it, he was suspicious and contacted the Illinois Department of Public Safety. A public safety officer sustained minor injuries when he opened the package and it exploded. This was the first documented bombing attributed to a serial bomber/killer soon to be named the "Unabomber," by the FBI. Other bombings would follow in a campaign of terror that lasted nearly eighteen years:

- May 9, 1979, a package explodes in the Civil Engineering Department at Northwestern University, injuring a graduate student.
- November 15, 1979, a bomb explodes in the baggage compartment of an American Airlines Boeing 727, forcing an emergency landing in Dallas.
- June 10, 1980, the president of United Airlines is seriously injured when a book he was sent explodes in his hands.
- October 8, 1981, a package bomb sent to the University of Utah is defused by a police bomb squad.
- May 5, 1982, a secretary is badly burned at Vanderbilt University, when a package intended for a professor of electrical engineering listed on the return address explodes.
- July 2, 1982, another engineering professor is seriously injured at the University of California, Berkeley, when he tries to lift what appears to be a piece of engineering equipment and it explodes in the faculty lounge.
- May 5, 1985, a second explosion occurs in the same location at UC, Berkeley, causing serious injury to a graduate student.
- June 13, 1985, a bomb is defused at a Boeing plant in Auburn, Washington.
- November 15, 1985, a psychology professor and a graduate student are injured at the University of Michigan when a package allegedly containing a manuscript explodes.
- December 11, 1985, Kaczynski's first murder occurs when the owner of a computer store in Sacramento is killed when he picks up a package left in the parking lot.
- February 20, 1987, the vice-president of a Salt Lake City technology firm is seriously injured when a bomb explodes in the firm's parking lot.
- June 22, 1993, a geneticist at the University of California Medical School in San Francisco opens a package sent to his home which explodes, tearing away several fingers and breaking his arm.

- June 23, 1993, a mail bomb explodes in the hands of a computer science professor at Yale University, blinding him in one eye, destroying hearing in one ear, and tearing away part of one hand.
- December 10, 1994, a package bomb explodes in the hands of a North Caldwell, New Jersey, advertising executive, making him Kacyznski's second murder victim.
- April 24, 1995, the president of the California Forestry Association, a timber industry lobbyist, is killed when a package bomb explodes in his face, making him Kacyznski's third and final murder victim. The bomb was intended, however, for the victim's predecessor.

Kacyznski's victims fell into four categories, although there is some overlap: nine were associated with universities, seven with the computer industry, three with airlines, and two with public relations or lobbying related to technology.[4]

Childhood and Identity

In 1990 when Ted Kaczynski learned that his father, Theodore "Turk" Kaczynski had died of a self-inflicted gunshot wound to the head, he expressed no sorrow or sympathy for his father or for other members of the family, and chose not to attend the funeral. That event and his response to it conveyed much about the seeds of anger and resentment toward his family that took root early in Kaczynski's childhood and grew into the flowering rage of his adult years. There appears to have been no time in his life that Ted Kaczynski was happy, for he never felt loved and accepted for who he was. Instead, love and acceptance were always conditional, based on his achieving goals set out for him — first by his parents and, later, by a society whose standards of success he met, but then angrily rejected. He might have killed his family, as some mass murderers do in similar circumstances, but Kaczynski focused instead on symbols of the "industrial society," whose values and emphasis on success his parents embraced so enthusiastically.

Ted Kaczynski was an exceptional first child born on May 22, 1942 to ordinary parents. His father and mother, Turk and Wanda, struggled through the Great Depression of the 1930s with hard work and thrifty living in various blue-collar neighborhoods in Chicago. There was only a brief interlude in Iowa before moving back to Chicago where they remained. Turk worked as a sausage maker in a meat-packing business owned by relatives. He changed jobs a few times, looking to move up. By the time Ted was ten, they had made it to Evergreen Park, a middle-class Chicago suburb. But the fact is, Turk never really got beyond paying the bills and providing "adequately" for his wife and son and, later, a second son, David, born in 1949. He expected more.⁵ That's why his gifted oldest son, from early childhood, came to figure prominently in Turk's dogged pursuit of the American Dream.

According to his mother, Ted was born an exceptionally intelligent and seemingly contented baby. "I used to pick him up out of the crib," she recalled, "and he would be bouncing around and he would nuzzle his head in my neck and chortle and gurgle and pull my hair. And he was a bundle of joy."⁶ But the joyful little boy changed when he was nine months old. At that time he was hospitalized for several days due to an allergic reaction. His mother insists that the trauma of being separated from her during that hospitalization left him withdrawn and less responsive to her and other family members. "In those days," she explained,

> they did not allow you to stay with the child. I would remember how he'd grab the bars of the crib in this hospital and he'd scream and hold out his arms and I'd have to go out the door. When I finally came back to take him home, what they handed to me was not this bouncing, joyous baby, but a little rag doll that didn't look at me, that was slumped over, was completely limp.... He became a very sober sort of child⁷

A child whose feelings were easily hurt. When they were — or if he feared they *might be* — he went off by himself, spending long hours alone upstairs in his room. Uncomfortable around other children and adults, neighbors reported no memories of ever seeing him smile. He was aloof, his mother agreed, yet there was nothing "gross" about his behavior. "He wasn't violent," she said:

> He was a good kid, no problems with delinquency. How do you tell people he's easily hurt and goes off by himself, you know? The teachers liked him because he was such a good student.⁸

By the time he was in the fourth grade, he had few friends and sought none. A superior student with an IQ in the 160 to 170 "genius" range, he was often the object of ridicule for that reason and also because his small physical size made him an inviting target. He had little in common with fellow students who he said "bordered on delinquency." As a consequence, Turk moved the family to Evergreen Park, a better neighborhood with better schools. Aware of his son's natural talent and enormous potential, Turk sought to encourage it as much as possible because it reflected on him, or so Ted believed. Report cards were always closely scrutinized and critiqued, but there was also abundant encouragement. For example, the family subscribed to *Scientific American* and kept him supplied with countless books until Ted left home to attend college. But much as some fathers pressure their sons to succeed in athletics as a means of enhancing their own self-image, Turk's pressure on Ted to excel academically was relentless. Nothing the boy did was ever good enough. Ted became convinced that academic success was a condition of his parents' love and acceptance. It added to this lonely youngster's growing insecurities and deepened the resentment that accompanied them.

But excel he did. After an impressive year at Evergreen Park Central Elementary School he was permitted to skip the sixth grade. Turk was delighted. For Ted it was a disaster. He didn't fit in with his older classmates and they made sure there was no doubt in his mind about that. The ridicule and verbal abuse that was heaped on this small, socially inept, and sensitive boy by older students that year made every day an excruciating test of his endurance. The searing experience of that year, he said, was a "pivotal event" which left permanent scars.[9] Still he continued to excel in the classroom, eventually skipping the eleventh grade, and graduating from high school two years early at the age of sixteen. But a sad case, a gifted student who had never attended a dance or dated — because he had never learned how to dance or even make friends.

Instead of conversations with other children, Ted read. Constantly. In part, it was escapism; the subject matter is revealing: " . . . I read about *other* ways of life," he recalled years later,

> in particular that of primitive peoples. When I was about eleven I remember going to the little local library in Evergreen Park, Illinois. They had a series of books published by the Smithsonian Institute that addressed various areas of science. Among other things, I read about anthropology in a book on human prehistory. I found it fascinating. After reading a few more books on the subject of Neanderthal man and so forth, I had this itch to read more. I started asking myself why and I came to the realization that what I really wanted was not to read another book, but I just wanted to live that way. . . .
>
> I used to read books like, for example, Ernest Thompson's Seton's *Lives of Game Animals* to learn about animal behavior. But after a certain point, after living in the woods for a while, I developed an aversion to reading any scientific accounts. In some sense reading what the professional biologists said about wildlife ruined or contaminated it for me. What began to matter to me was the knowledge I acquired about wildlife through personal experience.[10]

Away from his tormentors, he might have added.

Instead of playing with friends, Ted played with gadgets. Alone. In a letter accompanying his application to Harvard in 1958, his mother wrote:

Industrial Society   315

Much of his time is spent at home reading and contriving numerous gadgets made up of wood, string, wire, tape, lenses, gears, wheels, etc.; that test out various principals in physics. His table and desk are always a mess of test tubes, chemicals, batteries, ground coal, etc. He will miss greatly, I think, this browsing and puttering in his messy makeshift lab.[11]

But this benign view of his solitary activities contrasts with Ted's own description of what it was like. He spent much time alone, he said, because he had been so pressured by his parents to excel academically that he was denied the opportunity to interact and mature normally with children his own age. Instead, after skipping the sixth grade, he found himself in a peer environment where he had to face an "increasing amount of hostility . . . from the other kids. By the time I left high school," he recalled, "I was definitely regarded as a freak by a large segment of the student body." As his frustrations grew with daily humiliations and his resentments deepened toward his parents and fellow students, they were, he said, "given outlet through snotty behavior in the classroom which often took a sarcastic or crudely humorous turn." It was at this point in his life — high school — that he began to develop a rationale for "hating" people, although he lacked the courage to express it openly.[12]

> I would therefore indulge in fantasies of revenge. However, I never attempted to put any such fantasies into effect because I was too strongly conditioned . . . against any defiance of authority. To be more precise, I could not have committed a crime of revenge, even a relatively minor crime, because my fear of being caught and punished was all out of proportion to the actual danger of being caught.[13]

Still, there was some ambivalence about the anger he felt welling up inside or, perhaps, it was denial. In an autobiography written in 1959 when he was seventeen years of age and in college, an unremarkable childhood is described by this lonely unhappy boy. Playing the trombone in the school band and his coin collection are presented as if to balance the trauma involved in skipping grades, having no friends, and no involvement with girls, not to mention being an object of ridicule to his older classmates. The friction with his parents is downplayed and attributed to his own rebellious ways and his mother's "artist's temperament." Except to say that he respected her more than his father, Turk is described mildly as "an extrovert" with "a number of community interests." He describes his parents as being "in some respects generous and unselfish." There is no mention of the antagonism between them and himself, except to acknowledge that he was "probably a very difficult person to live with," implying that the problems were his own fault.[14]

Harvard, Michigan, and Berkeley

The autobiography was written during his freshman year at Harvard University where his failure to fit in with classmates who were two years older and, one must assume, more mature and better prepared to handle campus life than he was. For four years, he lived what was described as "a very isolated existence," with but a few fleeting and superficial friendships and virtually no social life.[15]

Kaczynski's years at Harvard extended the bitter social experiences of his childhood and youth that he had, by this time, come to expect. But his classes were intellectually stimulating and Ted took full advantage of that. A brilliant student of mathematics and a thoughtful writer with wide-ranging interests in science, natural history and psychology, he found himself in a near perfect environment to indulge those interests.

Much has been made of the Harvard curriculum and its possible impact on Ted's evolving views and behavior. During his time there, 1958 to 1962, students were required to take general education courses that reflected a clash of ideas. On the one side were courses based on *humanism* that examined and, presumably, extolled Judeo-Christian values and ethics as safeguards against the evils that afflict mankind; on the other were courses that emphasized *positivism*, the belief that only "value free" science based on empirically verifiable evidence could be trusted as a guide to human progress. The conflict between these two perspectives, Alston Chase contends, created a "culture of despair" among the privileged students at Harvard, Ted Kaczynski among them. "From the humanists we learned that science threatens civilization," Chase writes. "From the scientists we learned that science cannot be stopped."[16]

Literally adding insult to injury, Chase argues, Kaczynski was drafted to become part of a questionable experimental project. It was conducted by psychology professor Henry A. Murray, a man, Chase implies, of dubious ethics. Murray's "Multiform Assessments of Personality Development Among Gifted College Men," as the experiment was called, was not concerned with the subjects' philosophies of life as they were led to believe. Rather, according to Chase, "these experiments focused on stressful dyadic relations. The naive subjects were placed in highly confrontational situations with a skilled interrogator, whose purpose it was to challenge, badger, and humiliate them as much as possible to determine how each handled extreme stress. Chase assumes that it was probably an alienating experience that may have set Kaczynski on his violent course of action.[17]

If it did, Ted did not embark on the course quickly. Instead, after compiling a brilliant academic record at Harvard, he was an easy choice for admission to the graduate program in Mathematics at the University of Michigan.

There, from 1962 to the time he received his doctorate in 1967, Ted handled the rigors of a challenging graduate program as handily as he had handled Harvard's as an underage undergraduate. Evidence of his brilliance was apparent to all who observed him. Even his work as a graduate teaching assistant brought very positive appraisals from hard-to-please undergraduates during those years of political turmoil on the Ann Arbor campus. Despite manifest opportunities for involvement, there is no evidence that Kaczynski was drawn to the student protests of the sixties. Organizations like Students for Democratic Society, a force on the Michigan campus, were ignored. Apart from mathematics, what appeared to be consuming most of Kaczynski's thoughts throughout this period was not civil rights, not the Vietnam War, or even the evils of science and technology. Rather it was his own sexuality and his inability to establish any satisfying relationships with women.

It must have been especially frustrating for this involuntary celibate during these awakening years of sexual liberation among women, especially those on university campuses. But his many attempts to remedy the problem were unsuccessful. He couldn't understand why and wanted answers. For a while, he blamed malicious gossip, but that couldn't explain all those lonely years. Women, what do they want? he may have wondered.

Perhaps in an attempt to answer that familiar question, he began to imagine what it would be like to be a woman. To his surprise he found his fantasies highly erotic, the stimulation overwhelming, yet as a man he was unable to satisfy those longings. Perhaps he should have been a woman, he wondered. With that in mind, he made an appointment with a psychiatrist to discuss the possibility of having a sex-change operation. The decision underscores just how desperately lonely and unhappy he was at this point in his life. But as he sat in the waiting room, reflecting on the implications of such surgery, he realized he couldn't go through with it. Instead, he lied to the psychiatrist, telling him that he was depressed about the possibility of being drafted.[18] Kaczynski's response to this unsettling event reveals the coping pattern he would follow from that point on. For others in this situation, their thoughts might have turned to suicide, but not Ted's. His disgust with himself was redirected toward the psychiatrist he had deceived, a person who had done nothing except offer help. "As I walked away from the building afterwards," he said,

> I felt disgusted about what my uncontrolled sexual cravings had almost led me to do and I felt — humiliated, and I violently hated the psychiatrist. Just then there came a major turning point in my life. Like a Phoenix, I burst from the ashes of my despair to a glorious new hope. I thought I wanted to kill that psychiatrist because the future looked so utterly empty to me. I felt I wouldn't care if I died. And so I said to myself why not

really kill the psychiatrist and anyone else whom I hate. What is important is not the words that ran through my mind but the way I felt about them. What was entirely new was the fact that I felt I could kill someone. My very hopelessness had liberated me because I no longer cared about death. I no longer cared about consequences and I said to myself that I really could break out of my rut in life and do things that were daring, irresponsible or criminal.[19]

For the first time in his unhappy life, Kaczynski realized that he "had the courage to behave irresponsibly" — to hurt *others*. There is a strange Dostoyevskian quality to his logic. Reminiscent of the narrator in *Notes from Underground* or, perhaps, Raskolnikov in *Crime and Punishment,* he began to fantasize about various ways to harm people he didn't like, people who had, in his view, in some way treated him unfairly. It was during this time, for example, that he considered attacking and disfiguring a woman he hardly knew who had once rejected his advances. He also began to formulate plans to kill a scientist, a stranger who was merely a symbol of the technological society that now was to bear, along with his parents, the blame for his personal difficulties.[20]

Unlike Type II and Type III subjects, however, he did *not* displace or redirect his anger from the personal to the political; he recognized *both* as sources his unhappiness: He blamed the "technophiles," the "power-holding elite," for creating and advancing an oppressive system whose values he rejected; but he also blamed his parents for the relentless pressure they put on him to become a cog in that system. Although his hostility was directed at both, it was only representatives of the "system" who were targeted with violence. He could not find it within himself to harm his parents, at least in a physical sense. Furthermore, he was not overtly suicidal and never considered dying with his victims as is the case with some Type II and all Type III subjects. Instead, he would take his revenge from some remote location where the risk of discovery was slight; and, with sweet revenge, he would use *technology* to do it.

But before striking out on this destructive course, he decided to make one last attempt to find peace of mind apart from revenge. Instead he would escape, withdrawing as far as possible from the society he didn't fit into. The remote Canadian wilderness would become his haven where he could live *naturally,* apart from the world in a state of nature, the way he had fantasized as a child. It was not a novel idea. "Dropping out" and "alternative lifestyles" had became common among his generation. "If it doesn't work," he reasoned, "and if I can get back to civilization before I starve, then I will come back here and kill someone I hate." But first he needed some money to buy the land that would become his refuge. That meant finishing his doctorate and acquiring an academic position just long enough to save the money. He accomplished that by completing his doctoral dissertation in 1967 and accepting an assistant professorship in mathematics at the University of California at Berkeley — a prestigious institution that paid generous salaries to its distinguished faculty.[21]

As was the case at Ann Arbor, Kaczynski had minimal involvement in the tumultuous political events on the Berkeley campus and in the Bay Area generally during the two years he was there — 1967 to 1969. He consciously avoided politics at Berkeley, even reading newspapers, he explained, to avoid "build[ing] up too much tense and frustrated anger against politicians, dictators, businessmen, scientists, communists, and others in the world who were doing things that endangered me or changed the world in ways I resented."[22] He also was contemptuous of the "oversocialized" leftist radicals who dominated the Berkeley campus and community at that time. In Kaczynski's view, they were phonies, pretending to care about the oppressed merely as a way "to express their own hostility and frustrated need for power . . . [all the while] secretly embracing conventional attitudes of our society while pretending to be against it."[23] Instead of politics, he remained consumed by his quest for female companionship which continued, without success, in the personal columns of Bay Area "singles" publications.

With tenure and a successful academic career virtually assured after just two years, Kaczynski surprised his colleagues at Berkeley when he resigned at the end of the spring semester in 1969. With enough money saved, he packed up his few belongings and traveled east to meet his brother, David, in Wyoming. Together they drove north to British Columbia to look for land to purchase. After making a bid to purchase property near Prince George, the brothers returned to their parents' home in Lombard, Illinois, to await approval by the Canadian government. Some six months later, he received word that his bid had been rejected. According to David, Ted was very angry and depressed, barely speaking to anyone. Except for brief exits to eat or mail angry letters to newspaper editors about how technology infringes on individual freedom, he sulked in his room. Conflicts quickly resumed and intensified with his parents and everyone knew it was time for him to leave.[24]

In the late summer of 1970, Ted traveled to Great Falls, Montana, where his brother, David, was living and working. Together the two brothers drove to the tiny community of Lincoln, Montana, where they paid $2100 for 1.4 wooded acres on Canyon Creek, some four miles on gravel road south of town.[25] Ted, alone, then bought lumber and supplies and built a tiny one-room cabin on the site. He lived there until late 1972 or early 1973 when he moved to Salt Lake City where he worked a short time as a carpenter's helper. In June 1973, he returned to Montana where, except for brief travels elsewhere, he remained until May 1978.

Paradise Lost

By that time, he realized that his withdrawal to the wilderness was not going to work. Technology could not be escaped even in the tall timber and pristine alpine meadows of Montana. Timber companies were ravaging the mountain slopes and valleys with "clear-cutting" operations that were decimating huge areas of the forested landscape in the Northern Rockies. Vast areas of the Bitterroot National Forest, for example, were hard hit by this most virulent form of corporate greed and environmental insensitivity. The Lewis and Clark National Forest, which surrounds Lincoln, was another target of these destructive operations.

In 1969, Dale Burk, a reporter for the *Missoulian* in Missoula, Montana, wrote a series of articles describing the devastation — the mosaic of rutted roads, clear streams that now ran thick with mud, the slash and rubble left behind in place of trees that had thrived there for centuries.[26] So devastating was this conquest of America's western forests that in 1970, Arnold Bolle, dean of the Forestry School at the University of Montana, was moved to write a blunt expose. In it Bolle described the impact of the mismanagement of national forests resulting from policies dictated from the corporate boardrooms of large timber companies. In 1972, Congressional hearings were held to examine the issue. Despite the passage of major legislation in 1976, the "timber frenzy" continued into the 1980s.

The racket of chainsaws and heavy machinery, and the logging trucks that rumbled down the road near his cabin, were a daily reminder that he could not escape the "system," even at a remote cabin in Montana. He had tried, but withdrawal had failed as a solution for the anger that was, by this time, all-consuming. It was at this point that he decided on a new course of action — serial murder. Stealth would be the key to inflicting damage from afar on those he held responsible for what was happening to him and a world dominated by "technophiles" like those "milling" beautiful trees into plywood peels before his own eyes. And probably with some satisfaction, he would turn technology against them in the form of lethal, technically sophisticated bombs.

Sometime in May, Kaczynski left Montana, traveling by bus to his parent's home in Lombard, Illinois. He was low on money and his father had promised him a job with Foam Cutting Engineers, a company he was managing at the time in Addison, Illinois. Brother David also worked as a managerial assistant at the same firm. But Ted had more than a job and some needed extra money on his mind during this trip home. Shortly after arriving in Chicago, he placed his first bomb-laden package in the campus parking lot near the Engineering Building at the University of Illinois, Chicago Circle.

A month later, on June 26, Ted began work and, at first, things seemed to go extremely well. He met a female employee, a friendship developed, and he invited her to dinner. He was elated. A second date followed, after which, the woman told him she was no longer interested in dating him. It was humiliating. He was devastated. A relationship might have altered the course of action he had chosen. At first, he thought about suicide, then the depression spilled into rage. He briefly considered killing her. But he took his revenge, instead, by writing sexually suggestive limericks about her, leaving them around the plant where they could be read by other employees, humiliating her, he hoped, as she had him. His brother confronted him about it, an argument ensued, and on August 23, 1978, David fired him in the presence of the woman he had offended.

Despite this humiliating experience, Ted continued to live with his parents, working sporadically as a menial laborer at another company until the summer of 1979 when he returned to Montana. Before returning, however, he left a second bomb at Northwestern University. It exploded on May 9, injuring a graduate student. From this time until his arrest in 1996, Kaczynski remained at his retreat in Montana, leaving periodically to mail or plant fourteen more bombs.

Montana

No one in Lincoln, Montana thought much about the scruffy little guy who rode his bicycle to town to pick up mail or check out books at the tiny Lincoln Public Library. "We'd see him around. He didn't seem unusual to us. We see lots of people like him in these parts," a U.S. Forest Service employee said of Kaczynski. "Live to themselves. Want to be left alone. And we try to do that."[27]

It would be easy for someone accustomed to urban living of the type familiar on the east and west coasts to believe that anyone who lived like Ted Kaczynski was "crazy." The isolation, the absence of modern conveniences, no television to entertain or inform, no car to drive, the struggle with the elements — to choose that kind of life would be unthinkable to many. But rural Montana has a fair number of reclusive people who look and act like Ted Kaczynski, who live there because they like it. They don't make bombs, but like him, they view the lives of mainstream urban Americans as an odd way to live: Hours wasted in daily commutes, fifty- and sixty-hour work weeks, only to make money that is drained away with exorbitant rents and costly mortgages, all the while rarely seeing the stars, breathing polluted air, and bathing in water that is not fit to drink — all that seems pretty crazy to them.

Rural Montanans tend to be hardy, proudly independent men and women, some of whom, like Kaczynski, hold deep resentments about the intrusive nature of the federal government in their lives. Some think of themselves as "survivalists" and all tend to mind their own business, and that's probably a big reason why Ted was comfortable there. "Butch" Gehring, for example, his nearest neighbor, didn't pry, never asked personal questions. Probably because Gehring didn't find Kaczynski's lifestyle unusual or much different from his own, living in a small cabin on a steep hillside, scratching out a living with a small sawmill, a large hog roaming the property providing security when he was gone. Conversations over the years, yes, but no questions; neither man had ever been inside the other's cabin.

As far as is known, the only person to have seen the inside of Kaczynski's cabin before his arrest was his brother David on a brief visit in 1986. The windowless cabin was only ten by twelve feet, built completely of wood, the exterior protected with a redwood stain. Tar paper covered the roof. The only furnishings were a plank bed with a foam pad, a small table, and a chair — all made by Ted himself. There was no electricity, running water, or indoor plumbing. Ted used candles with metal reflectors for light and he relieved himself outside except when it was too cold. On those occasions he defecated on newspaper which he burned in the wood stove he used for heat. His water supply came from the creek or melted snow. He washed clothing and himself in a water bucket. He had few clothes, wearing the same clothes daily; but he did set aside jeans and shirts that were more presentable for his trips to town and elsewhere. He cut his own hair short and when he wore a beard, he kept it trimmed.[28]

The cabin was cluttered as one might expect such a small space to be after twenty-five years: More than 200 books; a Samsonite briefcase containing his Masters and Doctoral degrees; three typewriters, boxes of papers, including diaries, letters, bus schedules, newspaper clippings; hand tools and seed packets; and dozens of jars and boxes with screws, nails, wire, twine, cooking utensils, and other assorted household junk. Then there was the incriminating material: batteries, pipes, explosives, triggering devices, maps, and addresses of former and potential corporate and academic victims.[29]

Except for purchases of staples such as cooking oil, flour, sugar and coffee, Kaczynski lived off the land. He had a small garden where he grew potatoes, onions, parsnips and carrots which, along with an abundance of wild plants he gathered, were stored in a small root cellar he had dug near the cabin. He was very proud of the root cellar which one entered by lifting a wooden hatch at ground level. The inside was carefully finished with wood. He supplied the protein he needed in his diet with small game that he hunted with a bolt-action .22–caliber rifle or the .25 caliber handgun he kept. He also kept a Remington 30.06 in the cabin, so he may have poached an occasional deer. Squirrels, rabbits and grouse were the preferred diet. But he was selective. He once told his brother that he never shot any squirrels within a mile radius of his cabin because he considered them "neighbors." He liked squirrels, found their chatter and antics amusing. According to his brother, whenever he shot one, he practiced an American Indian custom of expressing his gratitude with the words, "Thank you, Grandfather Squirrel."[30] In some respects, he lived like a twentieth-century Henry David Thoreau.

According to a handful of people in Lincoln who became acquainted with him, Kaczynski was not the complete loner who has been described in the popular media. They considered him a friend, a person they looked forward to seeing. Not one of them thought he was "insane."[31] One of those is Sherri Wood, the librarian at the Lincoln Public Library. Kaczynski was a familiar face at the library which he visited every week or two, sometimes more. He introduced himself soon after the visits began. "Hi, my name is Ted Kaczynski," Sherri recalled the introduction. For the first couple of years their conversations were strictly functional, about ordering books she "never heard of" from the main branch in Helena and elsewhere. She could tell right away from his "astounding vocabulary" and choices of books and periodicals that he was very intelligent, but he never mentioned his educational background. Sherri credits him for helping justify her efforts to diversify the library's holdings which at that time consisted mainly of romance novels and westerns.

Aside from him often smelling like wood smoke, she recalled, there was nothing offensive about him; he was always courteous and invariably grateful for whatever help she and her part-time assistants — Lucille Sullivan and Mary Sperling — gave him. He also helped them inventory and move books and furniture when they rearranged the library. His only other annoying quality, she said, was when he spread out his reading material and began to read and write for hours, taking up a complete table and leaving no room for others. They assumed that with his army surplus clothing and the old bicycle he always rode that he was just a "little hermit-type guy," probably a Vietnam vet who needed his solitude. And they respected that. They also joked among themselves that he might be a "Jesse James type" who was hiding out from the law.[32]

It took a couple of years of visits, however, before the conversations got beyond the books he wanted to read. The ice was broken, so to speak, one "awful, cold, snow-coming-in-sideways, winter day," Sherri recalled, when Ted walked in, the snow still clinging to his beard and clothes. "You surely didn't ride your bike in this weather, did you?" she asked. He laughed and invited her outside. "That's how," he smiled, pointing to the chains he had rigged up on the bicycle tires. "We both had a good laugh," she said, smiling with the memory, and after that we started to visit more when he came in. We never asked any questions about his personal life and he never volunteered any, except to say that he had a brother and his parents lived in Illinois. But we talked about the usual stuff: the weather, politics, you know — he was a big environmentalist, but nice about it, always respectful of our opinions. If he didn't agree with something, he never made you feel stupid. He'd just say things like, "That's an interesting viewpoint," and let it go. You could tell that he didn't like politicians, although he never said anything bad about Marc Racicot [Governor of Montana], but his views were no more extreme than a lot of people's, even some of mine. I don't condone what he did, but the Ted we knew was probably the most non-violent man I've ever met. I know he couldn't have ever hurt anyone up close and personal. It just wasn't in him.[33]

On June 24, 1995, two months after his third and final victim died, Kaczynski mailed copies of a manuscript entitled, "Industrial Society and Its Future" to the *New York Times,* the *Washington Post,* and *Penthouse* magazine. Taking the "publish or perish" standard he found so offensive in academe to another level, he made an offer in the accompanying letters: If it was published, he would stop the bombings. On September 19, 1995, the "Unabomber Manifesto," as it was called by the media, was published nationwide. The manuscript lays out in a very organized and academic fashion, Kaczynski's critique of how American technology and scientific advancements have combined to produce an "industrial system" that is destructive of "human" and "wild" nature. The manuscript was presented as a first step toward destroying the system by creating public awareness of what he believes is at stake.[34] "If we had never done anything violent," he explains, "and submitted the present writings to a publisher, they probably would not have been accepted."[35] Few could disagree with that.

David Kaczynski recognized his brother's ideas and writing and, after much agonizing, reported him to the FBI. Ted Kaczynski was arrested at his Montana cabin on April 3, 1996.

Paranoid Schizophrenia?

Opinions differ about Ted Kaczynski's state of mind during his eighteen-year campaign of terror against representatives of the technological society. The complex mix of motives and the unprecedented nature of his violent actions set him apart from other assassins and would-be assassins. Government psychiatrists concluded that he was psychotic, but there is abundant evidence that challenges that conclusion.

According to the government's psychiatric evaluation of Ted Kaczynski, he suffers from a serious mental disorder: "Schizophrenia, Paranoid Type, Episodic with Interepisode Residual Symptoms." The key symptoms of his illness, it concluded, are "significant social and occupational dysfunction" and "delusional" thinking, the latter defined as "a false belief based on incorrect inference about external reality that is firmly sustained despite of what almost everyone else believes, and despite what constitutes inconvertible and obvious proof or evidence to the contrary." Kaczynski had two "delusions," the report suggests: One being that he was "being controlled by technology;" the other that his difficulties with women stemmed from "the extreme psychological verbal abuse by his parents" endured during his childhood and youth.[36] Depending on the legal standard used, Kaczynski could be considered *legally* insane, only if he did not know what he was doing and/or did not understand that it was wrong (M'Naghten), or if his crimes were a direct result of his mental illness (diminished capacity). If correct, this diagnosis would, in the language of the present research, place him in the Type IV classification of mental disorder.

But a number of issues can be raised about whether Ted Kaczynski was legally insane, as government psychiatrists and his family claimed.[37] Clearly he fails to meet the M'Naghten standard of insanity. There is no doubt that he knew what he was doing; and that he knew his actions were criminal (although morally justifiable in his view). Eighteen years of shrewd and elusive behavior and his manifesto, "Industrial Society and Its Future," itself provide sufficient evidence for that conclusion.

The diminished capacity standard is more problematic: Was he mentally ill? And was that mental illness the reason for his crimes? The conclusions about his mental state rest on the presumption that beliefs that are different from what "almost everyone else believes" are symptomatic of paranoid schizophrenia. But if this is true, one must wonder, for example, about those who insist that extraterrestrials visit this planet, and others who readily embrace a variety of "conspiracy" theories about historic events that most reject. Are they also paranoid schizophrenics? Kaczynski's views about modern technology and the troubled society he claims it has created are extreme, to be sure, but are they "delusions" without any factual basis? Probably not, when there are so many other people who embrace them, among them well-known writers like Edward Abbey and Kurt Vonnegut, intellectuals like Jacques Ellul, organizations like Earth First! in America and the Green Anarchists in Great Britain, not to mention worldwide concerns about the consequences of genetic engineering and global warming. More than 59,000 websites have been created about the "Unabomber," many with favorable views of Kaczynski and his assessment of modern society as set forth in his widely-read manifesto. Furthermore, questions can be raised about the "incontrovertible and obvious proof" that the issues he addresses are imaginary or "delusional."

Especially when those who disagree with the official diagnosis of his mental state, like Kaczynski himself, might point to "incontrovertible evidence" and "obvious proof" of the ravages of clear-cutting, for example, that he and so many others observed and opposed in Montana — not to mention global warming, species extinction, false pharmaceutical claims, intrusive telemarketing, and corporate corruption that support or confirm the validity of Kaczynski's central concerns.

Historically, mental health professionals (and the media) have portrayed Type I assassins — John Wilkes Booth, Leon Czolgosz, Oscar Collazo, Griselio Torresola, and Sirhan Sirhan — as being mentally deranged. The single exception is Timothy McVeigh. Familiar with that history and anticipating that the label would be applied to him, Kaczynski wrote his manifesto, where he painstakingly and logically makes his case: "Our society tends to regard as a 'sickness' any mode of thought or behavior that is inconvenient for the system...," he writes.[38] As if to confirm this observation, psychiatrists described his non-conforming ways as "significant social and occupational dysfunction" and symptomatic of paranoid schizophrenia. Other symptoms, they claimed, were his rejection of their diagnosis and refusal to enter an insanity plea as his attorneys urged. Thus Kaczynski found himself in the curious catch-22 situation of either accepting the diagnosis of paranoid schizophrenia to prove that he was not; or rejecting it, which would, in the doctors' view, support their claim that he was.

Sherri Wood, the librarian at the Lincoln Public Library, probably knew Ted Kaczynski better than anyone except his family. "Was he mentally ill like the psychiatrists said?" a visitor asked. "No way," she replied immediately. "I know that's what they said, but I grew up with a close relative who was a clinically diagnosed and medicated paranoid schizophrenic. When he wasn't on medication, you knew it. I know what that is all about. Ted wasn't like most people, that's true. He was shy and quiet, yes, but just someone who wanted to live his own life. He was not a paranoid schizophrenic"[39]

Notoriety?

In addition to paranoid schizophrenia, the government report on Kaczynski's mental state also concluded that he possessed features of several personality disorders that were observed in Type III subjects Guiseppe Zangara, Arthur Bremer, John W. Hinckley, Jr., and Francisco Martin Duran. "Paranoid Personality Disorder with Avoidant and Antisocial Features" allegedly was the cause of Kaczynski's "delusional" fears, his social inhibitions, as well as his disregard for social norms, lawful behavior, and his absence of remorse for wrongdoing.[40] Taken together the latter characteristics describe what is commonly called a "sociopath." But by this standard all political terrorists and extremists are sociopaths. The conflicts in Northern Ireland and the Middle East have shown that one person's sociopathic terrorist is another person's hero; whether one is defined as a terrorist or a hero depends on which side of a political conflict is making the assessment. Type III subjects seek notoriety; they are nihilists, sociopaths *without* any political agenda. Kaczynski, in contrast, cherished his anonymity and had a very explicit political agenda.

Elsewhere in the government report, Kaczynski is described in language suggestive of the Type II classification, that is, as someone whose intimate personal problems are blamed on the political system and whose violence is rationalized as being in the public interest.[41] Suicide and notoriety are the primary goals Type II males hope to accomplish with their violent acts.

But Kaczynski recognizes and readily acknowledges the association between his personal experiences and his political perspective. The connection between the two was made in 1966 during graduate school. This occurred after the visit to a psychiatrist to discuss his sexual identity problem. At that time, he rejected the idea that he was mentally ill, that his difficulties were "internally generated." Instead, at this "turning point" in his life, as he described it, he said that he realized that his problems were a direct result of his unusual upbringing *and* a technological system he was being educated to advance, and whose values he rejected.[42] Kaczynski did not see the issue as being an either-or proposition between personal and political. In his view *both* aspects of his experience were causes of his unhappiness. In other words, he was not projecting blame from one to the other; both were equally responsible. He makes this point in a journal entry:

> True, I would not fit into the present society in any case [due to his inadequate socialization as a child and youth], but that is not an intolerable situation. What makes a situation intolerable is the fact that in all probability, the values that I detest will soon be achieved through science, an utterly complete and permanent victory throughout the whole world, with a total extrication of everything I value... there will be no place for a rebellious person to hide and my kind of people will vanish forever from the earth. It is not merely the fact that I cannot fit into society that has induced me to rebel as violently as I have, it is the fact that I can see society made possible by science inexorably imposing on me.[43]

Elsewhere, in a second autobiography written in 1979 twenty years and many disappointments after the first reasonably benign one, there is no need to read between the lines to identify the strains in the Kaczynski household. Ted's enduring hostility toward his parents is explicitly set out in great detail. His parents are excoriated for pushing him as a youngster into situations that he was unprepared to handle, causing him lacerating embarrassments and unhappiness, offering no understanding or support, and "ruining" his life. Expressing these thoughts in a letter to his mother, he wrote,

> ... So generally, if I experienced any failure or showed any weakness, I found that I couldn't come to you for sympathy.... You were simply using me as a defenseless butt on which to take out your frustrations. I was supposed to be your perfect little genius.... The rejection I experienced at home and at school even affected me physically. In case you wonder why Dave [his brother] is three inches taller than I, I have read of two different studies that purport to show that rejection during adolescence tends to stunt growth.[44]

He returns to this same issue in his manifesto where he writes revealingly,

> The system HAS TO force people to behave in ways that are increasingly remote from the natural pattern of human behavior. For example, the system needs scientists, mathematicians, and engineers. It can't function without them. So heavy pressure is put on children [like me, he might have said] to excel in these fields. It isn't natural for an adolescent human being to spend the bulk of his time sitting at a desk absorbed in study. A normal adolescent wants to spend his time in active contact with the real world. Among the primitive peoples the things that children are trained to do are in natural harmony with human impulses. Among the American Indians, for example, boys were trained in active outdoor pursuits — just the sort of things that boys like. But in our society children are pushed into studying technical subjects, which most do grudgingly.
>
> Because of the constant pressure that the system exerts to modify human behavior, there is a gradual increase in the number of people who cannot or will not adjust to society's requirements: [among them] anti-government rebels, radical environmentalist saboteurs, dropouts and resisters of all kinds.[45]

Kaczynski's family had no doubts about his feelings toward them. His hostility toward his parents is confirmed and described by his brother David as something he observed as long as he could remember. It was usually expressed bluntly. For example, he recalls Ted writing to one of them, "I can't wait until you die so I can spit on your corpse." On other occasions, his anger was expressed by refusing to speak or even acknowledge their presence.[46] By the mid–1980s he had broken off all contact with both parents and his brother — and he made sure they knew why. After his arrest, his contempt for them deepened.

Additionally, what sets Kaczynski apart from other Type II males, Lee Harvey Oswald and Samuel Byck, is that there is no self-serving or self-sacrificial purposes in his behavior; he sought to create awareness of his ideas, not seek notoriety for himself; nor was he self-destructive as they were. Ted Kaczynski did not intend to be identified or caught, providing further proof that he was not trying to get back at his family, like Oswald and Byck, by making them feel responsible for what he had done. He never intended for them to know that he was the "Unabomber." If not for his brother's observant reading of the "manifesto" and subsequent report to the FBI, the bombing would have probably stopped as agreed, no one would have known the identity of the "Unabomber," and Ted Kaczynski would probably still be living quietly, still estranged from his family, with his secret in Montana.

Politics?

If Kaczynski was not paranoid and delusional as are mentally disordered Type IV assassins, and was not suicidal and seeking notoriety in death as emotionally disturbed Types II and III, what was the source of his anger and extremism? Whether or not the Harvard experience deserves as much blame for his violent career as Alston Chase gives it, there can be no doubt that this thoughtful, shrewd, highly intelligent, serial killer's actions were based on an intellectual rationale which he laid out in meticulous detail in his manifesto.[47] The important question from the theoretical perspective of this book is whether that political defense contains the words of a Type I political zealot, or is, instead, an elaborate rationalization of personal rejection and disappointments — in his case, worthy of a genius — that characterize Type II subjects.

Kaczynski, himself, offers his own explanation for his actions, a somewhat different perspective from Chase's Harvard thesis. Instead of Harvard, Kaczynski insists that it was experiences in the backwoods of Montana and things he read there that consolidated his thinking, turned him against "runaway utilitarian science . . . [that] reduces people to gears in a machine; [that] takes away our autonomy and our freedom," and set him on his destructive course.[48] As he explained,

> Back in the sixties there had been some critiques of technology, but as far as I knew there weren't people who were against the technological system as such . . . It wasn't until 1971 or 72, shortly after I moved to Montana, that I read Jacques Ellul's book, *The Technological Society*. The book is a masterpiece. I was very enthusiastic when I read it. I thought, look, this guy is saying things I have been wanting to say all along. . . . I read Edward Abbey in the mid-eighties and that was one of the things that gave me the idea that, yeah, there are other people out there that have the same attitudes that I do. I read *The Monkeywrench Gang*, I think it was. But

what first motivated me wasn't anything I read. I just got mad *seeing* machines ripping up the woods and so forth . . .

The honest truth is that I am not really politically oriented. I would have rather just be living out in the woods. If nobody had started cutting roads through there and cutting trees down and come buzzing around in helicopters and snowmobiles I would still just be living there [in Montana] and the rest of the world could just take care of itself. I got involved in political issues because I was driven to it, so to speak. I'm not really inclined in that direction.[49]

Unless Kaczynski is lying or deluding himself, the reinforcing influence of writers like Jacques Ellul was absorbed in the 1970s, long *after* Harvard. And there is never any mention of the Murray experiment as a factor in his behavior. Also, Edward Abbey's advocacy of "monkey-wrenching" in his novel about eco-terrorists who blow up the Glen Canyon Dam, which Kaczynski says he read in the mid–1980s, followed six bombs he had planted in the years before that. During that same period, Kaczynski admitted doing some monkey-wrenching of his own near Lincoln. There he "clothes-lined" snowmobile tracks, vandalized logging equipment and a vacation home or two that were being built in pristine natural areas, and sometimes fired his rifle at low-flying helicopters.[50] But Abbey, like Ellul, probably confirmed and reinforced the appropriateness of his views and actions, as he claims — especially after his first victim died on December 11, 1985. In any case, Kaczynski's views, if not his extreme actions, are shared by significant numbers of other environmentalists in this country and abroad.

Conclusions

Regardless of whether one agrees with it or not, the "Unabomber Manifesto," cannot be read without recognizing Kaczynski's intelligence. His is a political perspective that many in this country and Europe find persuasive, especially at the dawn of a new century when an epidemic of corporate greed and growing environmental concerns feature prominently in the world news. Nor can there be any doubt about his sincerity; Kaczynski did not seek fame or notoriety as is the case with Type II and III subjects like Lee Harvey Oswald, Samuel Byck, Arthur Bremer, John Hinckley and Francisco Martin Duran. His purpose was to arouse public awareness. Taken together his views and actions suggest a Type I rational political extremist.

Perhaps the best evidence that supports a Type I classification is this: Although he sought professional counseling for stress and depression on different occasions throughout his adult life, Kaczynski adamantly rejected the contention that mental illness was the cause of his criminal behavior.

Even facing a possible death sentence, he refused to enter an insanity plea that would have provided an opportunity for acquittal. To do so, he understood, would represent a denial of the political values he sought to advance. Instead he pled guilty to the charges and was sentenced to Life Without Parole. As John Wilkes Booth, Leon Czolgosz, Oscar Collazo, Sirhan Sirhan, and Timothy McVeigh have shown, Type I subjects do not recant on their political principles under any circumstances.

Still, Kaczynski was *different* from that group as well. The extraordinary personal sources of his discontent cannot be denied, and that sets him apart from the other Type I subjects. Like Leon Czolgosz, but unlike the others, he was a so-called "loner" all of his life. Being a loner may be a solution to problems, if one wants to be alone, as Czolgosz apparently did. Kaczynski did *not*, and the evidence of his futile search for companionship to relieve the loneliness and the depression that are usually its companions is distributed across the years. Kaczynski sought help from mental health professionals a number of times concerning "the issue of establishing relationships with women." Only once in his life, when he was fifteen years of age, was he ever complimented on his appearance. He never forgot it.[51]

Desperately lonely people often form premature attachments and exaggerate the significance of ordinary relationships. In 1991, for example, in the midst of an extended depression, Kaczynski sought help for stress-related heart palpitations and insomnia from a female physician in Missoula, Montana. Even this physician's professional concern for him — she reassured him and prescribed low-dosage sleeping pills for the insomnia — was misread by this desperately lonely man. Not long after a visit, he wrote to ask her out for dinner. She ignored the invitation.[52] Given the painful nature of his experiences with women throughout his life, it is not surprising that he so greatly valued the attention and friendship extended by the ladies at the Lincoln Public Library.

It is doubtful that without the searing personal frustrations and lacerating disappointments that began in childhood and continued into his adult life, anything Ted Kaczynski read would have set him on the course he took. Two things might have altered that course: If, unlike other Type I subjects, he had been able to savor the company of women — to have been able to love and be loved, in other words — Ted Kaczynski probably would have just made speeches and written articles about the evils of technology. Failing that, if he had been able to find the sanctuary he sought in the Montana wilderness, insulated from the society he didn't fit into, he might have remained there, just a lonely, eccentric man, living a Walden-like existence in a state of nature. But places like that no longer exist. So Ted Kaczynski will pay for his crimes by spending the rest of his life in a small cell in a maximum-security Federal prison, as far from nature as one can imagine.

Notes

1. "Interview with Ted Kaczynski," at www.spiritoffreedom.org.uk/tedinterview.htm, p. 1. Hereafter cited as *Green Anarchist Interview;* and "Industrial Society and Its Future," at www.time.com/time/reports/unabomber/wholemanifesto.html, p. 31. Hereafter cited as *Unabomber Manifesto.*
2. In recent years, there have been a growing number of cases of eco-terrorism and terrorist acts carried out by animal-rights activists associated with shadowy groups fringe groups like Earth First, Earth Liberation Front and Animal Liberation Front. Often using incendiary devices, these terrorists have attacked power lines, housing and resort developments, medical laboratories where animal experiments are conducted, slaughterhouses, and U.S. Forest Service facilities, mostly in western states. In addition to their group affiliations, what sets these terrorists apart from the subjects included of this book is that the focus of their attacks has been property rather than people and, for that reason, they have been excluded.
3. Except for McVeigh. Although without any group affiliation, he had the assistance of Terry Nichols who helped him acquire and load explosives into the truck McVeigh used in the attack. Nichols was sentenced to life imprisonment. Another defendant, Michael Fortier, a friend of McVeigh's who knew about the attack, but warned no one, was released from prison in 2006 after serving just over ten years of a twelve-year sentence.
4. Affidavit of FBI Agent T.D. Turchie, April 3, 1996, pp. 5–30, 36 at http://www.unabombertrial.com/documents/turchie_affidavit.html Hereafter cited as *Turchie Affidavit.*
5. Background material on the Kaczynski family is drawn primarily from the forensic evaluation of Theordore John Kaczynski, dated January 16, 1998, prepared by Dr. Sally C. Johnson, at courttv.com/casefiles/unabomber/documents/psychological. html. Hereafter cited as *Johnson Report.*
6. Wanda Kaczynski Interview, "60 Minutes," at http://web.lexus-nexus.com/univers Hereafter cited as *60 Minutes.*
7. *60 Minutes.*
8. Ibid.
9. *Johnson Report*, p. 9.
10. *Green Anarchist Interview*, pp. 2–3.
11. Quoted in *Turchie Affidavit*, p. 58.
12. *Johnson Report*, p. 18.
13. Ibid, p. 19.
14. Ibid., pp. 15, 18.
15. Ibid., p. 18.
16. A. Chase, "Harvard and the Making of the Unabomber," *The Atlantic Online*, June 2000 at http://www.theatlantic.com/issues/2000/06/chase.htm.
17. Ibid., Parts 2–3.
18. *Johnson Report*, pp. 21–22.
19. Ibid., p. 22.
20. Ibid., p. 26.
21. Ibid., p. 23.

22. Ibid., p. 23.
23. *Unabomber Manifesto,* pp. 7, 9.
24. *Turchie Affidavit,* pp. 48–49.
25. *Turchie Affidavit,* p.39.
26. Kaczynski read current and back issues of the *Missoulian,* the Helena *Independent Record,* and the Great Falls *Tribune.* Sherri Wood Interview, FBI, April 2, 1996.
27. Anonymous, author's interview, July 15, 2002.
28. David Kaczynski Interview, FBI, February 24–25, 1996, p. 1 at http://unabombertrial.com/documents/david022496.htmil. Hereafter cited as David Kaczynski Interview.
29. *Turchie Affidavit,* pp. 63–66.
30. David Kaczynski interview, pp. 2–3.
31. D.S. Jackson, "He's Not Crazy, He's Our Neighbor," *Time Magazine* November 3, 1997.
32. Sherri Wood, author's interview, July 15, 2002. Hereafter cited as Sherri Wood Interview.
33. Ibid.
34. *Unabomber Manifesto,* pp.59, 73.
35. Ibid., p. 31.
36. *Johnson Report,* pp. 55–56, 60 (emphasis added).
37. Concern about the possibility of a death sentence may have been a factor influencing the opinion of family members.
38. *Unabomber Manifesto,* p. 54.
39. Sherri Wood Interview.
40. *Johnson Report,* pp. 57–58.
41. Ibid., p. 37.
42. Ibid., especially pp. 37, 59–60.
43. Quoted in *Johnson Report,* pp. 23–24.
44. Quoted in *60 Minutes.*
45. *Unabomber Manifesto,* pp. 37–38.
46. David Kaczynski Interview.
47. *Unabomber Manifesto.*
48. *Green Anarchist Interview.*
49. Ibid., p. 2 (emphasis added).
50. Sherri Wood Interview.
51. *Johnson Report,* pp. 12, 19–20, 40.
52. Carolyn Goren Interview, FBI, March 6, 1996 at www.unabombertrial.com/documents/goren030696.html.

11

Ruby Ridge, Waco, and Roe v. Wade Timothy James McVeigh and Eric Robert Rudolph

> *"When violent action thus became an option, I considered, among other things, a campaign of individual assassination, with "eligible" targets to include: Federal Judge Walter Smith (Waco trial); Lon Horiuchi (FBI sniper at Ruby Ridge); and [Attorney General] Janet Reno (making her accept "full responsibility" in deed, not just word).... What the U.S. government did at Waco and Ruby Ridge was dirty, and I gave dirty back to them at Oklahoma City."*—Timothy McVeigh[1]

> *"Perhaps I should have found a peaceful outlet for my opposition to the government in Washington: maybe I should have been a lawyer and fought [for] decency in the face of this rotten system; perhaps I could have taken up teaching and sought to inculcate a healthy outlook in a decidedly unhealthy society. But I didn't do any of these things, and I resorted to force to have my voice heard. However wrongheaded my tactical decision to resort to violence may have been, morally speaking my actions were justified."*[2]—Eric Robert Rudolph's letter to his mother[3]

Timothy McVeigh, an intelligent young man and a decorated war hero, chose *mass murder* as the means to convey his estrangement from an American government that had, he insisted, betrayed its founding principles. After considering political assassination in the serial pattern initiated first by Kaczynski, McVeigh decided on a terrorist act that on April 19, 1995 would take the lives of 168 men, women and children who occupied a government office building in Oklahoma City. Until September 11, 2001, it remained in scope and devastation the worst act of terrorism on American soil.

Eric Rudolph, two years younger than McVeigh, but also highly intelligent and a former soldier, was obsessed with the abortion issue. It was primarily for that reason that he carried out a series of bombings that killed two and injured hundreds to dramatize his opposition to the federal government's support of legalized abortion. He also was strongly opposed to any attempt to advance or legitimize homosexuality as an acceptable lifestyle. Except for the methods they used and the targets they selected, McVeigh and Rudolph fit the profile of the politically motivated Type I assassin.

* * *

TIMOTHY JAMES MC VEIGH (1968 –2001)

As the sun came up in a clear blue, nearly cloudless, sky on April 19, 1995, a figure rose to peer out of the cab of a yellow Ryder rental truck that had been parked outside a cheap motel on Highway 77 north of Oklahoma City. Timothy McVeigh opened the door and climbed out to stretch, his lanky body, stiff from the chill and the hours he slept curled on the seat. He checked his watch, a little after six. Right on schedule for what was going to be the second biggest day of his life; McVeigh was excited and anxious to get on with it. He opened a military "MRE" — meal-ready-to-eat — he had stashed under the seat and wolfed down a breakfast of cold spaghetti. Unappetizing, but he didn't care; it was just the "carbos" he was going to need to get through the morning. It was about 7 A.M. when he drove carefully out of the lot and turned south for the two-or-so hour drive remaining. The truck sagged low on its springs from the seven thousand pounds of explosives it carried toward its destination, the Alfred P. Murrah Federal Building in downtown Oklahoma City.[4]

It was almost 9 A.M., when just blocks from his objective, he pulled to the side of NW 5th Street and stopped just long enough to light the first of two fuses that a few minutes later would detonate the explosives. A second fuse was lit as he sat waiting for a stoplight to change. Timing was critical; he didn't have any slack with the fuses burning. McVeigh planned to live, but he was willing to die, if necessary, to accomplish his mission. A security camera in the Murrah Building recorded the truck as it pulled to stop in the loading zone adjacent to its north entrance. Unseen by the camera and others who noticed McVeigh get out of the truck and walk away were the fuses that smoked and sputtered toward their lethal destination in the bed of the truck. Less than a minute later, at 9:02 A.M., the ground shook as a deafening explosion tore away the north face of the nine-story building, ripping out its interior as it collapsed in an avalanche of twisted steel and broken concrete. Men, women, and children died — 168 in all — some instantly, others in horrible, lingering deaths, entombed in the smoking rubble. Hundreds more lay injured, sirens wailing as rescue workers raced to the scene and struggled to find and extricate them from the tangled wreckage. It was a nightmare of destruction.

Meanwhile, Tim McVeigh had walked calmly, but at a brisk pace, to a battered 1977 Mercury Grand Marquis, the getaway car he left parked in a vacant lot several blocks from the crime scene a few days before. The bomb exploded just as he approached the car; its force lifted him from the ground. Sweet revenge, he thought. It was so satisfying.

As he drove away, he worried, not about capture, not about the license plate he had forgotten to put on the car, but about the "body count"; that, he knew, was the key to just how successful his mission had been, for it would determine the weight of its "psychological impact" on the nation. His motive was retribution; his purpose was to strike back at federal agencies for the men, women and children they killed at Ruby Ridge and Waco.[5]

About seventy-five minutes and as many miles north of Oklahoma City, McVeigh was stopped by an Oklahoma state trooper for speeding. He was arrested when the trooper observed that he not only had no license plate, but also no registration and no car insurance; nor did he have a valid permit for the .45 caliber Glock pistol he carried in the shoulder holster he wore. Odd mistakes for someone who had planned the details of this crime so carefully for weeks.

Odd, also, was McVeigh's conspicuously political attire. He was wearing a T-shirt with an image of Abraham Lincoln that covered his chest. Beneath were the words shouted by John Wilkes Booth after he fired the fatal shot into the president's head — *"sic semper tyrannis"* — "Thus ever to tyrants." On the back of the shirt a familiar quote from Thomas Jefferson was displayed: "The tree of liberty must be refreshed from time to time with the blood of patriots and tyrants."

Speeding with no license plate or car registration and that t-shirt adorned with a shoulder holster, it was almost as if Timothy McVeigh wanted to be caught. Still, as the radio in the patrol car crackled with activity related to the explosion in Oklahoma City, the trooper had no idea that he had just taken the bomber into custody.[6]

Who was Timothy McVeigh, the cold-blooded, remorseless mass killer of

168 innocent people? The most complete account of McVeigh's life is the book, *American Terrorist: Timothy McVeigh and the Oklahoma City Bombing* by Lou Michel and Dan Herbeck.[7] The authors, who had McVeigh's cooperation and access to his family throughout his incarceration, were able to piece together details of his life that can be found nowhere else. For that reason, their important biography, combined with court documents and the trial transcripts are the primary sources drawn upon in this analysis of McVeigh. It will show that McVeigh was a Type I subject whose victim or victims could have been one or more prominent political figures rather than the ordinary people he ultimately decided to kill in Oklahoma City. President Bill Clinton and especially Attorney General Janet Reno, were often in his thoughts, as was Lon Horiuchi, the ATF Agent who shot and killed Vicki Weaver in the federal siege at Ruby Ridge, Idaho. McVeigh, for example, had cards printed with Horiuchi's name and address which he made available at gun shows, leaving no doubt about their purpose.[8]

There were at least four defining experiences in McVeigh's life that together set him on his destructive course: the breakup of his parents' marriage, the disillusionment that followed his military service, and the actions of federal authorities first at Ruby Ridge, Idaho and later at Waco, Texas. Absent any one of these it is reasonable to suggest that the Murrah Building might still be standing and few would have heard of, or be interested in, Timothy McVeigh.

Formative Years

Timothy McVeigh was born in Pendleton, New York on April 23, 1968 in unremarkable circumstances. He was the second of three children, but the only son born to his parents, Bill and Mickey. The McVeighs, a pair of mismatched high school sweethearts who married young, were a typical blue-collar American family. Bill McVeigh was a big, handsome, quiet fellow, who worked at Harrison Radiator in nearby Lockport, a company that built radiators for General Motors. Bill was a man who liked routines; shifts and assembly line work didn't bother him a bit, and he liked the extra money he made on overtime. Routines, which he followed with little variation, structured his life. When he wasn't working, he liked to bowl during the long winters and, when the weather warmed up, he played in a local softball league in the evenings, enjoying a few beers with the boys afterwards. Bill with his quiet, unassuming ways, was a "solid citizen," as someone said, a fairly non-reflective, very ordinary guy content with life.

His wife, Mickey, was different. Outgoing, vivacious, impulsive, she yearned for excitement and change. Routines bored her and so, after a while, did Bill. When they first met in high school, Mickey was a strikingly pretty, flirtatious girl who easily got all the attention she wanted from boys. Romance, yes, but marriage and motherhood seemed far from her mind. She wanted to become a flight attendant. Independence, travel, and the adventure of new experiences were the things she valued. So when Bill began a two-year hitch in the Army, she moved to Hartford to begin training as a flight attendant. But in the early sixties, people married young and raised children. That's what Bill and her good Roman Catholic parents wanted for her. By the time Bill was discharged, she had reluctantly given up the idea of an airline career, deciding to marry and raise a family like almost everyone else they knew.[9]

Mickey tried hard, but after the births of three children at regular intervals, she realized that motherhood just didn't appeal to her. She was bored with homemaking, the kids, and, most of all, her husband. By the time she had her third child in 1974, she decided to make a change, something more exciting than Bill, the three kids, and the Monday night bingo ritual she had fallen into with her mother. Working for a travel agency was as close as she could come, at that point, to the airline career she had given up with profound regret to become a wife and a mother. Timmy, as she called him, was just six when she struck out on her new career. Until that time, she had been there, trying hard to be a good "mom" — making cookies, reading stories, putting together photo albums and diaries, recording her little boy's birthdays, cute expressions, and mishaps, making everyone happy but herself. Then she was gone.

Mickey's work exacerbated the growing strains in the marriage; strains that were evident to her young son for as long as he could remember. It seemed to him that his mother cared more about her work and the new friends she liked to party with than she did about him. As his parents' arguments escalated in frequency and volume, and rumors of his mother's partying, wild holiday trips, and alleged infidelities began to circulate, he began to withdraw from them both. It wasn't a complete social withdrawal, however. He had friends and he dearly loved his paternal grandfather, Ed McVeigh. But when he was home, he kept to himself, asking — and expecting — little from either his father or mother.

By the time his parents separated when he was eleven years old, he had become a very independent child for his age. Comic book super-heroes fueled his fantasies and may have provided the first impulse in the compulsive self-sufficiency that described the rest of his life. Such behavior is often observed in children with *attachment disorders* brought on by parental neglect.[10] There was a theme to his fantasies and play that would endure: It was Tim McVeigh — alone — struggling against the forces of evil. "He entertained himself throughout his childhood by creating fantasy monsters of various kinds," a psychiatrist who examined him years later explained. "He was the warrior hero who always fought these monsters." As evidence of his preoccupation (and, perhaps, of his withdrawal), McVeigh spent more than a thousand dollars, most of which he earned himself, on comic books of this sort during this troubled period of his life.[11]

By the time his parents divorced in 1986, the year he graduated from high school, it was anti-climatic, but McVeigh would confide to a friend that his mother was nothing but a "whore" and a "bitch" for leaving his father and breaking up the family.[12] He felt sorry for his father, but they were never close. Tim, it seems, found him no more interesting than his mother did. As he explained later,

> When I came home from school, I looked for something to do. Years ago, there [would have been] a mom there who said, "Do the dishes," or "Let's talk about what happened at school." Maybe even there was a dad there. Maybe the mom said, "Well your dad will be home in two hours. If you're having trouble with bullies [which McVeigh did as a youngster], why don't you talk to your dad?"[13]

Still, although he claimed that he didn't blame his parents for not being there for him, the claim is not convincing. "I don't know why I go off on that," he told his biographers, "but I do say that I have very few memories of interactions with my parents." Sadly, the *only* person he said he ever truly loved was his grandfather. If given a choice of being with the family or alone, Tim chose the latter. It was during this period of his youth that he became obsessed with "survival," consuming stories about people who had — alone — overcome great adversity through careful preparation for the worst, and unyielding determination. You can't count on anyone but yourself was the message of the survivalist subculture he found so reassuring. That idea was especially appealing to a youngster watching helplessly as his parents' marriage unraveled. One of McVeigh's favorite television shows was *Little House on the Prairie,* a series about an idyllic pioneer family, struggling together to survive on the Western frontier. His favorite films — *Red Dawn, The Omega Man, Logan's Run,* and *Planet of the Apes* — all dealt with the same theme, of people surviving on their own in the face of great adversity.[14]

Another theme that appealed to McVeigh was revenge, little people getting even with the evil monsters that threatened their existence. That was especially satisfying, and excited him like nothing else, as it did after his triumph in Oklahoma City. "Tim is really immature," a psychiatrist who examined him after the bombing observed. "He's almost childlike in some ways, boylike.... But there's a certain gleefulness, a certain excitement that came from Tim when I examined him, about pulling this prank off downtown, as if it were a childish prank."[15]

Guns and Uniforms

When McVeigh graduated from high school he, like many high school graduates, had no clear idea of what he wanted to do. A very bright, but unchallenged, student with an IQ of 126, he had been awarded a five hundred-dollar-a-year college scholarship at graduation. Not wanting to waste that, he enrolled in a two-year business college with the intention of studying computer programming. His score on the math aptitude test was near perfect, the highest in the school's history. But he was unhappy that he had to take courses in addition to computer programming to graduate. Not long into the semester, he dropped out, preferring instead to work at a Burger King so he could earn some money, even at minimum wage. The idea of having to depend on his father for money bothered him. He wanted to be on his own.[16]

Out of school with an exceedingly boring job for someone with his intelligence, McVeigh began to fill his spare time reading about another subject that had always fascinated him — firearms. He had learned to shoot and handle guns as a youngster at his grandfather's side. The sense of power and independence a weapon in his hands provided were compelling emotions that remained with him all his life. As he grew older, his interests gradually shifted from comic books to gun and adventure magazines. It was not long before he became an avid reader of *Soldier of Fortune,* a magazine devoted to weapons and the interesting people who used them to fight evil.[17] McVeigh consumed every issue. It is not an exaggeration to suggest that a big part of his fantasy world seemed to revolve around living — on his own — an exciting, dangerous life as a soldier of fortune. What he needed, however, was an enemy — an evil force — to focus his anger. He wanted someone or something to fight, something real to take the place of the imaginary comic book monsters that had occupied his thoughts as a child. There was a childish immaturity to his zeal — his search for monsters to fight — that remained with him all his short life.

The "monster" began to take form after McVeigh read *The Turner Diaries,* a racist, anti-Semitic novel, written by an American Nazi. It was a story about one man's fight to resist the efforts of the United States government to take away his rights — most notably his right to own weapons of self-defense. Without a gun, the story suggests, one is defenseless against the nefarious designs of Jews and blacks who control America, and the federal government which does their bidding. Federal gun control laws, the author insists, are the first step in rendering the typical white American defenseless. Tim believed it. In the book, the main character fights back by detonating a truck bomb which destroys the headquarters of the FBI in Washington. The book resonated with McVeigh, focused his anger. He underlined passages, took notes, studied it like a textbook, like Islamic zealots study the Koran. By the time he finished reading it, he was obsessed with the issue, just as he had been with the comic book villains of his childhood.[18] It was also gratifying to know that his concerns were widely shared by powerful organizations like the National Rifle Association and other ordinary men and women who follow the gun show circuit and wear camouflaged uniforms on weekend retreats.

Tim McVeigh was less than a month away from his thirteenth birthday when President Reagan was nearly assassinated in 1981. There is no evidence that the event had any great influence on him, but the push for gun control legislation that followed it clearly did. *The Turner Diaries* confirmed his worst fears about the ulterior motives of Congress in seeking to pass such laws, and the federal authorities — specifically, the FBI and the Bureau of Alcohol, Tobacco and Firearms — that would enforce them.

Tim's response was to begin collecting guns. He wanted to build a stockpile. Guns, lots of them, became a source of security for this troubled young man. He was eighteen when he sold his comic book collection to raise money for the purchases. He also applied for the gun permit he would need to get a job as a security guard. By the time he was nineteen, he had quit the job at Burger King and was working for Burke Armored Car in Buffalo. It was to be the first time in his life that he spent any significant time outside his familiar haunts in Pendleton and Lockport. The extra money was nice, better than flipping burgers for minimum wage. But what he liked most about the job was carrying a weapon. There was also an exciting sense of strangeness and danger in a large, racially mixed city like Buffalo that appealed to this small-town white boy who found black people unattractive and threatening.[19]

With additional income at his disposal, he decided to buy a new car — a sporty Chevrolet Geo Spectrum — and more guns. He also purchased, with a friend, a ten-acre parcel of forested land near Pendleton that briefly became his retreat, a place where he could store food, water, fuel and ammunition for an impending crisis he would have welcomed. It was also a sanctuary where he could fire his guns and do as he pleased without having to deal with nosey neighbors. Lots of guns and his own private compound — a virtual bunker for this young survivalist with the vivid fantasy life about epoch conflicts between good and evil. But the satisfactions were fleeting and he soon became restless and bored with the job and his life.

Tim was no ladies man. He never had much luck with girls, probably because of his immaturity. His fascination with guns and apocalyptic visions of the future limited the range of conversation anyone could have with him, especially young women. And his self-absorption prevented him from understanding why the young women he did meet, those who were able to tolerate the warrior mentality, didn't respond the way he hoped to his conversational overtures laden, as they usually were, with adolescent sexual innuendo. Women and romance were something he either didn't understand or, perhaps, just wasn't willing to expend the time on.

A friend suggested that he join the military where he would be paid to do what he most liked to do, handle all sorts of weaponry. Tim took the advice. On May 24, 1988, Tim McVeigh joined the army. It wasn't until the day before he left that he told his father what he had done.[20] Bill McVeigh, who had served in the army himself, was proud of his son and told him so.

In one sense, it was an odd decision for someone who, by this time, had become such a strident critic of the U.S. government. But the idea of guns, uniforms, the possibility of adventure in strange places and, perhaps, the "soldier of fortune" mystique were so compelling that he put those reservations aside. For a while.

Going to War

The army and Private Timothy McVeigh were a perfect match. McVeigh thrived on the challenges of basic training at Fort Benning, Georgia, and he loved the military subculture. It offered everything he had been looking for — structure, the absence of ambiguity, the uniform, and all the trappings of belonging to something he admired. And it showed. He quickly developed into an outstanding young soldier, excelling in every aspect of his training, registering the maximum overall test score for army recruits. But, most of all, he loved the weaponry — his new "toys," as he described them. Often when his friends were out on liberty, McVeigh would remain in the barracks reading weapons manuals and war stories in paperbacks, or in magazines like *Soldier of Fortune*. For the first two years of his enlistment, McVeigh gave every appearance of becoming a "lifer," a career soldier.[21] That would have pleased the army. Tim McVeigh was the kind of young man the army needs, and his rapid advancement to the rank of sergeant over the course of his enlistment proved it.

Following more training at Fort Riley, Kansas, McVeigh was assigned to a mechanized infantry company. His technical mastery of weapons was exceptional, as was his skill in using them. For that reason, he was elevated to the position of "gunner" on a Bradley troop carrier. It was in that position that he arrived in Saudi Arabia in January 1991 as the Gulf War began. A month later, he was in Iraq as part of his nation's "Desert Storm" offensive. He was excited. At last he would have the opportunity to battle a real enemy, something he had been looking for most of his life, not the imaginary monsters in the comic books he loved as a child, or the enemies, real and fictional, others had faced in the books and magazines he had read all his life. But it was one experience, in particular, during that brief but devastatingly effective invasion that left a lasting mark on Timothy McVeigh.

His company was on the front lines during an assault on Iraqi infantry positions when they were targeted by enemy machine guns. After the source of the incoming fire was located, McVeigh focused his .25mm canon on the target, nearly two thousand yards distant. At that moment an Iraqi soldier suddenly stood up, waving his arms. McVeigh squeezed off a single round. "His head just disappeared . . . ," he recalled, describing its effect. "I saw everything above the shoulders disappear, like in a red mist." Another soldier who witnessed the event recalled that he saw "[the Iraqi] just vaporize before my eyes. . . . Tim hit this guy dead-on with the first shot. That's unheard of." Another Iraqi standing near the first was also killed by the same shot. Thirty others quickly surrendered.[22]

It was a remarkable demonstration of military skill, but was it courage, was it really necessary? Was this poor soldier frightened, about to surrender in the face of overwhelming force as so many others had? Those were the questions that immediately began to bother McVeigh. Nobody else saw it that way. He was decorated for his actions with the Army Commendation Medal. But for McVeigh it was not a pleasant occasion. From the moment he saw the "red mist" he was remorseful and depressed about what he had done. As he explained later,

> What made me feel bad was, number one, I didn't kill them in self-defense. When I took a human life, it taught me these were human beings, even though they speak a different language and have different customs. The truth is, we all have the same dreams, the same desires, the same care for our children and our family. These people were human beings, like me, at the core. . . . I killed a man who didn't want to fight us, but was forced to.[23]

Surprising thoughts and emotions for a young man who would a few years hence destroy 168 innocent victims in a heartless act of terrorism. But Timothy McVeigh's disillusionment with the military began with that experience, and it was reinforced by the tragic scenes he witnessed after that in Iraq — terrified mothers and children begging for food, the mangled bodies of soldiers mutilated by overwhelming military might. It made him depressed. For McVeigh, Iraq wasn't a worthy opponent. The campaign was a mismatch, more like a slaughter than a war. He felt used.

So it was with mixed feelings he could not have anticipated a few months before that McVeigh received orders in March 1991 to report to the Special Forces Selection and Assessment Center at Fort Bragg, North Carolina. It was a huge honor, an invitation not made to many soldiers to become part of an elite military organization, probably the world's best. He had seen the movies, read the books and articles; before Desert Storm it was his dream to become a Green Beret, a member of the army's highly trained, combat-ready Special Forces. Now he wasn't sure.

Within two days at Fort Bragg, he finally acknowledged what he had been feeling for weeks: a military career was something he no longer wanted. Like many soldiers returning from Persian Gulf, he arrived in the States weakened by the experience. After only two days of grueling physical challenges, blistered, sore, and bone-weary, McVeigh withdrew from the program. But it wasn't the sore feet, aching muscles, and burning lungs that changed his mind; he knew he could get through that. The problem was much deeper: the desire was no longer there. He wanted out. So after forty-three months of exceptional military service, Sergeant Timothy McVeigh left the army, a decorated veteran, arriving back home in Pendleton, deeply troubled and depressed, without a clue as to what he would do with the rest of his life.

Depression and Anger

In 1899, Émile Durkheim, the eminent French sociologist, published a classic study of suicide. Suicide, Durkheim suggested, is most likely to occur when a person feels disconnected from society, not knowing what standards to follow, or to whom to turn for guidance; a condition he described as *anomie*.[24] Those circumstances describe Timothy McVeigh during the year following his discharge from the Army. His dreams of a military career shattered by the disillusionment that followed his Desert Storm experience, McVeigh felt cut off, alone, disconnected; his life had suddenly become meaningless, without purpose. No longer a decorated war hero, he was suddenly, once again, a nobody, broke, looking for a job in the middle of a recession, sleeping on a couch in his father's living room.

The best job he could find was with Burns Security, once again a security guard working shifts with other uninspired people like himself at the Buffalo Zoo. At least he got to carry a gun, he reasoned, but it wasn't enough. Unable to relate to his father, and still unlucky with women, McVeigh was swept under by a deepening depression that within a few months of his discharge left him suicidal.[25]

It was during this darkest period of his depression, in early 1992, that he began to express the anger that probably was at its core, once more projecting his darkest thoughts on a familiar adversary, the United States government. For weeks he had been withdrawn, without words, often close to tears. Then he slowly came out of it, began writing letters to newspapers and public officials, complaining about various government policies, the erosion of the "American Dream," corrupt politicians who were enriching themselves at the public's expense, and a nation that was "in serious decline." In one such letter to the Lockport [NY] *Union Sun & Journal,* he asked, "What is it going to take to open the eyes of our elected officials? . . . Do we have to shed blood to reform the current system? I hope it doesn't come to that, but it might."[26]

But McVeigh's anger seemed excessive, far out of proportion to what might have been expected in response to the political issues he was raising. The urgency of his language alone hinted that its real source was probably his deep disappointment in his life and himself. It was as though McVeigh's anger was therapeutic, transforming and alleviating his depression, providing once again a sense of purpose. Adults often respond to the frustrations of life in the same way they learned to deal with frustrations as children. For Timothy McVeigh, the child and now the remarkably immature adult, he needed a "monster," an evil force, toward which to redirect and focus his anger. The government in Washington — a monster that was consuming the resources and compromising the freedoms of its citizens — fulfilled that need.

Ruby Ridge and Waco

If there were ever any lingering doubts in his mind about the evil intentions he attributed to the federal government, they were removed on August 21, 1992. On that day, a heavily armed "Special Operations Group" of some one hundred federal agents laid siege to the cabin of Randy Weaver at Ruby Ridge, Idaho. Weaver, a former Green Beret, had moved with his wife and three young children to property he had purchased in rural Idaho to live "off the land." When Weaver declined the invitation to serve as an "informer" in a federal investigation of the so-called Aryan Nations located in the area, he was told he would be arrested for a relatively minor federal firearms violation that had been prearranged to ensure his cooperation. Outraged by what he considered a case of federal entrapment and blackmail, Weaver refused to be arrested. He, along with his wife and three young children, and a young man who lived with them, barricaded themselves on their property and refused to leave.

One did not have to be a government hater to conclude that Ruby Ridge was a remarkable display of governmental hubris, incompetence, and brutality. As the siege began, federal agents killed one of their own men in a misdirected burst of machine gun fire. By the time it ended more than a week later, federal agents had shot and killed Weaver's fourteen-year-old son and his dog — both shot in the back. Under fire, Randy Weaver dragged his son's body to a shed. When he tried to make it back to the house, he also was shot in the back. Badly wounded, Weaver was crawling toward the house when his wife, Vicki, was shot and killed as she stood holding a door open for him. Their infant daughter dropped from her arms.[27]

McVeigh was horrified, beside himself with anger when he learned what had happened — Randy Weaver was a guy like himself who just wanted to be left alone. In January 1993, he quit his job, thanked his father for room and board, said goodbye, and drove to Florida where he found a construction job.

The following month, near Waco, Texas, the same federal agencies — the FBI and Bureau of Alcohol, Tobacco, and Firearms (ATF) surrounded the compound of Branch Davidian cult leader David Koresh and his followers. Like Randy Weaver, Koresh was wanted for alleged federal firearms violations. Also, like Weaver, Koresh refused arrest and barricaded himself, with his followers, inside a walled compound they called Mt. Carmel. On February 28, 1993, when federal agents approached the compound to arrest Koresh, gunfire erupted and a bitter fire fight began. At the end of the day four federal agents and six Branch Davidians lay dead from gunshot wounds. Others were wounded. A weeks-long federal siege began, pitting heavily armed ATF and FBI agents against American citizens — just like Timothy McVeigh — who believed they had a Constitutional right to live as they please and own as many guns as they wanted.

When the Waco story broke, McVeigh abruptly left Florida and drove directly to Waco to witness personally the unfolding story. By this time, he had acquired a carload of anti-gun control bumper stickers that he intended to sell. He was photographed and interviewed in Waco amid these stickers as he sat on the hood of his car parked as close to the compound as federal agents would allow. His interviewer, a student covering the story for the Southern Methodist University student newspaper, asked for this thoughts. McVeigh's dual preoccupations with his personal freedom and fears of government control couldn't be missed. "The government is afraid of the guns people have," he replied,

> because they have to control people at all times. Once you take away the guns, you can do anything to the people. You give them an inch and they take a mile. I believe we are slowly turning into a socialist government. The government is continually growing bigger and more powerful, and the people need to prepare to defend themselves against government control.[28]

After a few days, McVeigh left Waco. His preoccupation — by then an obsession — with intrusive government controls was from that point reflected in a restless, transient existence, roaming about the country from one gun show to another, buying and selling weapons and distributing anti-government propaganda, but mostly talking with people with views like his own. The gun show subculture provided the dynamic for confirming and acting out his obsessions. Without it, he was lost, drifting rudderless in the swells of anger and depression. Texas, Oklahoma, Missouri, Arkansas, Arizona, Michigan, and points in between, you name it, if there was a gun show somewhere, he tried to be there, no matter how far the drive. After Waco and throughout much of 1993, he wandered back and forth across the country, following the gun show circuit, but making periodic stops in Arizona and Michigan where two old army buddies lived.

One of those friends, Michael Fortier, lived with his wife, Lori and their infant daughter in a mobile home in Kingman, Arizona. Fortier shared the right-wing survivalist perspective with McVeigh — evident in the bumper stickers on his pickup and a "Don't Tread On Me" flag along with Old Glory fluttering in the wind outside his mobile home — but, unlike McVeigh, that wasn't the *only* thing on his mind. Of the three men who were involved in the plot — McVeigh, Terry Nichols, and Fortier — Fortier was the easiest to be around. He wasn't angry and obsessed with a sense of victimization like McVeigh and Nichols. He loved his pregnant wife and child and was reasonably content working as a clerk in a hardware store, and doing a fair amount of drugs. According to Fortier, Tim could often be a boring guest, for his conversations rarely strayed from the same topics — a government that was out to enslave its people and, of course, endless conversations about scenarios he would spin out of *The Turner Diaries*, a book McVeigh had been talking about since they first met years before in the army. That's probably why Fortier tried to turn him off — and on to — drugs.

But drugs had little appeal to McVeigh. He just didn't like mind-altering experiences that diminished his sense of self-control. It didn't matter whether it was the beer blasts he had disdained during his army days, or the marijuana and crystal methamphetamine Fortier and his wife, Lori, offered him in Kingman.[29] That cherished sense of personal independence, that freedom that comes from not having to depend on anyone, was something he couldn't compromise. It was what Timothy McVeigh was all about since his mother walked out of his life when he was a little boy. His survivalist compulsions reflected that dynamic, as did his hatred for a government that he believed threatened it.

The Plot

McVeigh's other regular stop was in Decker, Michigan where he stayed with another old army buddy, Terry Nichols. Like the connection with Fortier, he and Nichols had met during basic training at Fort Benning and then were transferred together to Fort Riley, Kansas. Nichols never made it to Iraq, but he and McVeigh stayed in contact. Nichols lived with his family on a farm he shared with his brother James. Terry and James Nichols were government haters. It was a family tradition. Going back at least a generation, the Nichols were a family of right-wing fanatics, well-know in and around Decker and that part of Michigan for their extreme views and challenges to government authority. Terry and James, for example, tried to refuse payment of their mounting debts by claiming in court that U.S. currency had no value because it was no longer backed by gold.[30]

At least James farmed. Terry Nichols was a loser. He never succeeded at anything anyone could remember. He was bright enough, but dropped out of college and joined the army. But that short career ended with a hardship discharge. In civilian life he couldn't seem to hold a steady job. When his first wife left him, he married a seventeen-year-old mail-order bride from the Philippines who was already pregnant when they first met. She and his infant stepson later joined him on the farm in Michigan. Some people considered Terry and the rest of the Nichols clan a little strange. But McVeigh liked their politics and, as he soon discovered, also Terry's petite, dark-haired mail-order bride, Marife, with whom he had a brief affair.[31]

James Nichols liked to experiment with explosives and construct homemade bombs, so the two brothers and McVeigh talked bombs, guns and politics endlessly. Another topic was the ongoing standoff between "the feds" and the Branch Davidians in Waco. At some point, however, McVeigh convinced Terry that they had talked enough, that it was time to do something to help David Koresh and his people who were surrounded by tanks and heavily armed men in helmets and flak jackets. In April the two decided to drive down to Waco to help, possibly organize a mass protest against the government's actions. They were preparing to leave on April 19, 1993, when a special report flashed on CNN. The scene, broadcast live from the Branch Davidian compound, was unbelievable. Federal agents had attacked with tanks and tear gas. There had been an explosion and wind-whipped flames were licking up the sides buildings and exploding through roofs as plumes of dense black smoke billowed skyward. Viewers across America, like McVeigh and the Nichols brothers, realized that men, women and children were trapped inside the inferno. Fifty-three adults and twenty-one children died that day in Waco. It was appalling. With his eyes stinging, McVeigh vowed to get even. Nichols agreed to help. They decided to bomb a federal facility somewhere, just as the protagonist in *The Turner Diaries* had.

In the months following Waco, the plan for revenge evolved. By the end of summer 1994, McVeigh and Nichols were ready to implement it by acquiring explosives needed to build a bomb. By this time, Terry Nichols and his family had moved from Michigan to a new job in Herington, Kansas, not far from Fort Riley. McVeigh was enraged again on September 13, 1994 when President Clinton signed a crime bill banning assault weapons. "I just snapped," he said, now more determined than ever to strike back.[32]

On September 22, McVeigh rented a storage bin in Herington where materials needed to make the bomb could be stored. A week later, Nichols bought forty fifty-pound bags of ammonium nitrate at a fertilizer store in McPherson, Kansas. The next day, McVeigh and Nichols stole explosives from a quarry near Marion, Kansas. Two weeks later, Nichols rented a second storage bin in Council Grove, Kansas as their stockpile of explosives grew.[33]

In October McVeigh interrupted his preparations to race back to Pendleton after learning from Michael Fortier of his grandfather's death. He missed the funeral since neither his father nor his sister Jennifer knew where he was or how to reach him. It was a sad visit for Tim. He said at the time, and since, that he was closer to his grandfather than anyone else in his life.

But this period of reflection didn't alter his plans. He confided to his sister Jennifer that he was going to do something "big" to get back at the government for the atrocities committed at Ruby Ridge and Waco. During one of their visits, he asked if he could create a file on her personal computer. He labeled the file "ATF Read," leaving no doubt that it was meant for agents of the Bureau of Alcohol, Tobacco, and Firearms to read *after* the big "event" he was planning. His message said in part,

> All you tyrannical motherfuckers will swing in the wind one day for your treasonous actions against the Constitution and the United States. . . . Die, you spineless, cowardice [sic] bastards.[34]

Sometime in early November, Nichols drove to Royal, Arkansas. There on November 5, at McVeigh's urging, he robbed a gun collector who had befriended McVeigh. That friendship had ended during one of McVeigh's visits there and he later planned the robbery which Nichols carried out. After the robbery, Nichols turned over part of the stolen weapons to McVeigh and returned with the others to his family in Herington. After altering serial numbers, McVeigh began to sell and trade the stolen weapons at various gun shows to raise the money they needed to carry forward their planned terrorist attack.

In December, McVeigh arrived back at the Fortier's in Kingman, Arizona.[35] Except for jaunts here and there to gun shows, he stayed with them, or in nearby rentals like the Uptown Motel, from the end of December 1994 through March of 1995. Fortier knew about McVeigh's and Nichols's plot to bomb a federal facility but not its location. McVeigh told Fortier that he was considering several locations in as many states. By this time, assassination had been ruled out — at least for the time being. McVeigh wanted to duplicate as close as possible the fictional bombing described in *The Turner Diaries*.

On December 16, 1994, McVeigh and Fortier drove from Kingman to Oklahoma City to case the Murrah Building. The trip reinforced McVeigh's opinion that it was the best site for what he wanted to accomplish. It housed the offices of the federal agencies he hated, but it also had a conveniently vulnerable glass front, and good camera angles for the dramatic media coverage, McVeigh was anticipating, that would follow the explosion. But most importantly, he was convinced that the orders for the Waco raid came from the ATF office located in that building.

The plan was too much for Fortier. After they returned to Arizona, and he realized that McVeigh was truly serious, that he was intent on going ahead with a terrorist-style bombing, he told McVeigh that he wanted no part in it. Yet he did keep the confidence McVeigh had placed in him.[36]

In early April, McVeigh left Kingman and drove back to Kansas where he met with Terry Nichols to resume with grim determination the final preparations for the attack. When Nichols got cold feet and tried to back out, McVeigh contacted Michael Fortier and again tried to persuade him to join in. Fortier again refused. McVeigh then really pressured Nichols and he reluctantly agreed to cooperate.[37] The date was set. There could be no doubt about that — April 19, 1995 — the second anniversary of the cataclysm at Waco. McVeigh wanted to make it very clear that this was about revenge.

On April 14, he bought the 1977 Mercury Marquis he would use as his getaway car, at a Firestone Tire dealership in Junction City, Kansas. By this time, he and Nichols had acquired all the materials they needed for the bomb — ammonium nitrate, nitromethane, blasting caps, fuses, the works, some 7,000 pounds of destruction. On April 15, McVeigh rented the Ryder truck in Junction City, using a fake South Dakota driver's license, and checked into the Dreamland Motel. On April 18, the day before the bombing, Terry Nichols met McVeigh at Geary Lake State Park near Nichols's home in Herington. There they mixed the explosives, filling each of thirteen barrels with a lethal mixture of ammonium nitrate and nitromethane, and wired the truck for its deadly mission. The two men struggled to arrange the heavy barrels in a T-shaped configuration that, McVeigh had calculated, would provide the maximum blast and destruction. Later that afternoon, McVeigh alone drove south on Route 77 toward Oklahoma City, anxiously anticipating the horrific blast that would soon rock Oklahoma City and the nation.[38]

Conclusions

As a potential assassin and domestic terrorist, Timothy McVeigh reflects the motive and characteristics of the politically motivated Type I assassin that the nation has seen before. He made it very clear that he seriously considered assassination before deciding on an act of terrorism. After his arrest, McVeigh told his biographers that had he read a book about a fictional assassination plot, *Unintended Consequences*, by John Ross, he probably would have chosen that mode of revenge instead of a bombing. A sniper campaign against government officials, like Ross describes, assassinating them one by one, probably would have been more satisfying, McVeigh concluded.[39]

Like the Type I subjects who preceded him, McVeigh was not suicidal or mentally disordered, but he was willing to die to achieve his objective. He planned to escape, but as he told his biographers, he didn't care whether he was caught. His actions confirm that. Surely he understood that investigators would, in time, track him down, given the trail of evidence he left behind. And, it is reasonable, given the circumstances that led to his arrest, to suspect that he wanted to take "credit" for what he had done. In any case, the evidence against him was overwhelming, and he never denied any of it. He was tried, convicted, and, on June 13, 1997, sentenced to death by lethal injection.

As the automatic appeals that accompany a death sentence dragged on, McVeigh became impatient to get it over with. In December 1999, he asked that all appeals be waived on his impending May 16 execution. Only weeks before the execution date, however, the FBI acknowledged that it had failed to turn over some 4,400 pages of documents to McVeigh's attorneys, opening the door for further appeals and delay. But after six years in prison with four of them on death row, McVeigh was ready to die; he, again, requested that all appeals be dropped. His attorneys reluctantly agreed to honor his wishes.[40]

His behavior on death row and the way he died provide the most compelling evidence supporting his Type I classification: Like his Type I counterparts — John Wilkes Booth, Leon Czolgosz, Oscar Collazo, Sirhan Sirhan and Ted Kaczynski — McVeigh never apologized, never asked forgiveness, or ever recanted on his principles. For example, in 1998, McVeigh published an essay in *Media Bypass* in which he compared the Oklahoma City bombing to U.S. bombing raids in Iraq:

> The [Bush] administration has admitted to knowledge of the presence of children in or near Iraqi government buildings, yet they still proceed with their plans to bomb — saying that they cannot be held responsible if children die. There is no such proof, however, that knowledge of the presence of children existed in relation to the Oklahoma City bombing.... Who are the true barbarians?... [Americans] approve of bombing government employees [in Iraq] because ... they are Iraqi government employees. In regard to the bombing in Oklahoma City, however, such logic is condemned.... Do people think that government workers in Iraq are less human than those in Oklahoma City? Do they think that Iraqis don't have families who will grieve and mourn the loss of their loved ones? In this context, do people come to believe that the killing of foreigners is somehow different than the killing of Americans?[41]

Six weeks before his execution, McVeigh wrote the following letter to Fox News correspondent Rita Cosby:

I explain herein why I bombed the Murrah Federal Building in Oklahoma City. I explain this not for publicity, nor seeking to win an argument of right or wrong. I explain so that the record is clear as to my thinking and motivations in bombing a government installation.

I chose to bomb a federal building because such an action served more purposes than other options. Foremost, the bombing was a retaliatory strike; a counter attack, for the cumulative raids (and subsequent violence and damage) that federal agents had participated in over the preceding years (including, but not limited to, Waco.) ... [F]ederal agencies during the '80s, culminating in the Waco incident ... grew increasingly militaristic and violent, to the point where at Waco, our government — like the Chinese [at Tienaman Square] — was deploying tanks against its own citizens ... Bombing the Murrah Federal building was morally and strategically equivalent to the U.S. hitting a government building in Serbia, Iraq, or other nations ... my mindset was and is one of ... clinical detachment ... not personal, no more than when Air Force, Army, Navy, or Marine personnel bomb or launch cruise missiles against government installations and their personnel.... Many foreign nations and peoples hate Americans for the very reasons most Americans loathe me. Think about that.[42]

Still, sometimes when he reflected on what he had done in Oklahoma City, it was as though he was reliving the imaginary exploits of the comic book heroes of his childhood. As if there were no consequences. Throughout his adult life, Timothy McVeigh remained remarkably immature. It was as though he never really grew out of his teen years. He obviously took pride in describing how he had accomplished his objective, as if the "collateral damage" was nothing to dwell on. In interviews, the gravity of that horrific explosion often seemed to elude him, as if it were nothing more than a grand adventure, or even a "gotcha" prank played on the federal authorities he hated. There was an irritating smugness to his demeanor, the smart-aleck posturing of someone who seemed proud of what he done, that trivialized the lives of his victims.

That ended on June 11, 2001 — the biggest day of his life, the nation's attention focused on him — the day Timothy James McVeigh was executed at the Federal Prison in Terre Haute, Indiana as members of his victims' families watched on closed-circuit television. Witnesses said that when the camera switched on, they had a close-up view of his face as he lay on the gurney. As the lethal drugs began to drain through the needle into a vein in his right leg, he lifted his head slightly and stared for a moment directly into the camera. He said nothing. Then his head eased back. He died with his eyes open, starring at the ceiling. Defiant to the end, McVeigh did allow, however, that he might have chosen a different target had he known there was a day-care center in the Murrah Building. "That's a large amount of collateral damage," he said, referring to the children he killed. At one point, he considered having his ashes scattered at the memorial that had been built at the site of the bombing, but then recanted. "That would be too vengeful, too raw, cold. It's not in me," he wrote in a letter.[43] That's as close as he ever came to remorse.

* * *

ERIC ROBERT RUDOLPH (1966–)

Fifteen months after Ted Kaczynski and Timothy McVeigh killed their last victims with bombs in California and Oklahoma, another terrorist bomber struck. The bomber, Eric Robert Rudolph, a young white man from rural North Carolina, closely follows the Type I pattern of remorseless political extremism of Timothy McVeigh and, with some qualifications already discussed, Theodore Kaczynski.

July 27, 1996 was a bright, warm morning at the Summer Olympics in Atlanta, Georgia. A large crowd had gathered for a concert at Centennial Olympic Park when Rudolph called the 911 number of the Atlanta Police Department and said, "There's a bomb in Centennial Park; you have thirty minutes." Police were unable to locate the bomb before it exploded with a deafening blast, killing one woman and injuring more than 100 others. Despite the warning, there was no doubt the bomb was designed to harm people, not simply destroy property. It contained thirty-four pounds of smokeless gunpowder and six pounds of flesh-shredding masonry nails.[44]

At first, FBI investigators mistakenly suspected the bomber was a security guard who worked at the park. Months later, on January 16, 1997, growing doubts about the original suspect's guilt were elevated even more when another bomb exploded at an abortion clinic in the Atlanta suburb of Sandy Springs. No one was injured in the first blast, but then a second bomb, timed to detonate when police and rescue workers were on the scene, exploded. Five were badly injured in the second blast. Both bombs were set off by timing devices and contained dynamite and more than three pounds of flooring nails to inflict maximum human injury.[45]

Suspicions that both the Olympic Park and Sandy Springs bombs were planted by the same person or persons — not the original suspect — were strengthened five weeks later, on February 21, 1997, when bombs exploded at an Atlanta nightclub, The Otherside Lounge, that catered to lesbians. The pattern was the same: Not long after the first bomb exploded, injuring patrons at the bar, investigators at the scene found and disarmed a second bomb, intended for them, before it exploded. Like the Sandy Springs bombs, both contained dynamite and more than six pounds of wire nails. In the aftermath,

Rudolph wrote letters to four news organizations claiming responsibility. He described himself as being part of an "Army of God," and threatened to carry out more bombings so long as the federal government protected abortionists, who he considered murderers, and tolerated public displays of homosexuality, which he considered decadent.[46]

After that Rudolph laid low for nearly a year. Then on January 29, 1998, a fourth bombing occurred at another abortion clinic, the New Woman All Women Health Care Clinic, in Birmingham, Alabama. The bomb was hidden in shrubbery outside the clinic but, unlike the three previous attacks in Atlanta, which were set off by timing devices, Rudolph was on the scene to detonate these bombs himself. He could see his victims fall, a security guard who died at the scene and a nurse who was critically injured. It was an exhilarating experience for him. Once again, he wrote "Army of God" letters to the same Atlanta news organizations, claiming responsibility and warning of more bombings to come.[47]

Rudolph's identity might have remained unknown except for a witness at the scene who noticed that while others rushed to help the injured, one man walked away. Moments later, he saw the same man pull off a wig and get into a pickup truck. He noted the license number and notified authorities. The truck was traced to Rudolph. It was the first big break in the case. Investigators quickly pieced together a chain of evidence from the Atlanta and Birmingham bombings that was linked to Rudolph. He was placed on the FBI's "Ten Most Wanted" list with a million dollar reward for information leading to his arrest.

Rudolph made good his escape to the territory he knew best, the mountains of North Carolina. There he eluded his pursuers for five years, living off the land in the Appalachian backcountry. He moved from campsite to campsite, never remaining long in one place, sleeping on mattresses fashioned out plastic sheeting he filled with leaves. He slept and spent much time under rock ledges and deadfall to avoid not only the rain and snow but, also, the heat detectors, infra-red scanners, and other high-tech devices used in flyovers by government agents in their futile search to find him. Drinking water was no problem. There were plenty of streams and ponds.

Food was another matter. At first, he hunted with a .223 caliber rifle and ate native plants he gathered. But he soon discovered it was easier to make night raids into the nearby towns of Andrews and Murphy where he would forage for food in trash containers and, in season, neighborhood gardens. He also bagged soy beans and corn that he stole from grain silos. Three of his favorite sources for food were the dumpsters behind a McDonald's restaurant in Anderson and a Taco Bell in Murphy; the other was a container behind the Civic Cinema where he sometimes found discarded popcorn. At the same locations, he said he often found "two or three" newspapers a week which he took back to his various campsites to read and keep up to date on current events, especially the status of the manhunt for him. Authorities found the book, *Incident at Big Sky: The True Story of Johnny France and the Capture of the Mountain Men,* at one campsite. A special pleasure, he said, were the "half smoked" Marlboro Lights he found behind Gibson's Furniture Store.[48] Rumors still persist that Rudolph was probably given food and other assistance by sympathetic residents of the area, but that has never been proven.

Eventually, after five years of battling the elements and scavenging for food, his luck ran out. He got careless and was arrested late at night on May 31, 2003 by a security guard as he was looking for food in a dumpster behind a Sav-A-Lot store in Murphy. He was unarmed and did not resist arrest. Hungry and tired, but in good physical condition, he seemed, to some, relieved that his sojourn in the wild had ended. Rudolph denied that.

His Confession

As of this writing Rudolph has granted no interviews and has challenged much that has been written about him. His only public thoughts about his crimes are contained in the statement he made admitting his guilt as part of a plea agreement on April 13, 2005.[49] As part of the plea agreement, he also revealed the location of more than 200 pounds of explosives he had hidden for use in future attacks. In return, he was sentenced to consecutive life terms without the possibility of parole.

Admitting his responsibility, sometimes offering qualified apologies, but expressing no remorse, Rudolph justified his actions in these defiant words:

> The fact that I have entered an agreement with the government is purely a tactical choice on my part and in no way legitimates the moral authority of the government to judge this matter or impute guilt. . . . [As a consequence of entering a plea] I have deprived the government of its goal of sentencing me to death. . . . Abortion is murder. And when the regime in Washington legalized, sanctioned and legitimized this practice, they forfeited their legitimacy and moral authority to govern. . . . There is no more fundamental duty for a moral citizen than to protect the innocent from assault. This is inherent in the values of all higher civilizations. [I had] the right, the responsibility and the duty to come to the defense of the innocent when the innocent are under assault. . . . I am not an anarchist. I have nothing against the government or law enforcement in general. It is solely for the reason that this [government] has legalized the murder of children that I have no allegiance to . . . this particular government in Washington.[50]

Unlike McVeigh and Kaczynski, Rudolph did express some regret for his actions, but not much, especially for the senseless bombing at the Olympics' Centennial Park. His purpose for planting a bomb at a public event which had nothing to do with abortion or gay rights, he explains, was not to injure innocent civilians. Rather it was to

> confound, anger and embarrass the Washington government in the eyes of the world for its abominable sanctioning of abortion on demand [by forcing] cancellation of the Games, or at least [to] create a state of insecurity to empty the streets around the venues and thereby eat into the vast amounts of money invested.[51]

But why the six pounds of flesh-shredding masonry nails if he did not intend to harm innocent civilians? He does not explain. Instead he offers a flimsy excuse, claiming he tried to make two more warning calls. The first call, he insists, was ignored by the 911 operator. In near panic as he watched his watch ticking toward an unfolding disaster, he claims he tried to make a second warning call from a motel phone booth. But he abruptly terminated it when he sensed that he was being watched:

> I was eyeballed closely by two individuals. This caused me to leave off the last sentence which indicated the exact location of the device. The result of all this was to produce a disaster — a disaster of my making and for which I do apologize to the victims and their families.[52]

In similar, unconvincing fashion, he explains his reasons for attacking the innocent patrons at a gay bar as not an attack on them, but on the federal government for its tolerance of "the practice of homosexuality." Until his younger brother told the family he was gay, Rudolph's hostility to homosexuals was unqualified. He described them as "faggots," "Sodomites," and worse. After his brother's admission, his views became more tolerant of those he described as "suffering from this condition." He explains that "consenting adults," like his brother, who engage in such behavior in private should not be "hassled" by the government or anyone else. Private sexual behavior "is not a threat to society," he writes. "But when the attempt is made," he continues,

> to drag this practice out of the closet and into the public square in an "in your face" attempt to force society to accept and recognize this behavior as being just as legitimate and normal as the natural man/woman relationship, every effort should be made, including force if necessary, to halt this effort.[53]

In defending his bombing of the Birmingham abortion clinic, he explains that his primary target was the "doctor-killer," but when a security guard discovered the device, he said "it had to be detonated" prematurely. "I had nothing personal against [the security guard who was killed and a nurse who was badly injured]," he said.... They were targeted for what they did, not who they were as individuals."[54]

Rudolph did acknowledge that the security guard was just a person trying to make a living. In different circumstances, he might have been working at a bank or an athletic event. Like a lot of people, he probably didn't think much about abortion one way or another. "He may have been a good guy," he writes. But, for Rudolph, that did not matter:

> Every employee is a knowing participant in this gruesome trade. He chose to wield a weapon in defense of [abortionists] ... that makes him as culpable as the murderers themselves. I have no regrets or remorse for my actions that day in January, and consider what happened morally justified.[55]

Rudolph's eleven-page statement reveals an intelligent man who is at once defiant, some would say arrogant, at times apologetic, but utterly remorseless. Like his predecessors Kaczynski and McVeigh, and terrorists elsewhere, he is an absolutist, a killer without any reservations about the morality of his actions.

A Quest for Absolutes

Eric Robert Rudolph was born on September 19, 1966 in Merritt Island, Florida, one of six children — five boys and a girl — born to Robert and Patricia Murphy Rudolph.*[56] Not much is known about his father or the Florida years. When Bob Rudolph died of cancer when Eric was fifteen, the family moved from Florida to the rural community of Topton, North Carolina. After her husband's death, Pat Rudolph raised her six children alone in a rustic homestead on eight-and-a-half acres in the foothills adjacent to the Nantahala National Forest. She never remarried. A strong, self-sufficient, and opinionated woman, she encouraged those same qualities in her children. Her former daughter-in-law, Deborah Rudolph, described her as a "really intelligent and sociable and artistic woman," who was educated in a Catholic convent until she left to marry and raise a family.[57] Their house, described as clean and comfortable, was heated with a woodstove. A gasoline generator was set up to supply electricity in the event of emergencies, and they drank spring water, rather than the fluoridated water available from the tap. Eric and his brothers grew up in the outdoors. The woods and streams of the Appalachians were their playground. Hunting, fishing and exploring the backwoods were more satisfying to him than city parks and the Little League he pitched in. The survival skills he used so well during his five years as a fugitive were honed in that environment. In many respects, Rudolph's background seems unremarkable, at least in terms of the influences that might have set him on his destructive course. But there was something odd about this family's intolerance and search for absolutes.

Pat Rudolph and her late husband had always encouraged their children to read and think critically about the political and moral issues that were frequent topics of family discussions. These were informed discussions, not simply rants. You were expected to know what you were talking about and able to defend your ideas. And Eric, among others, could. He was described as being "very well read" and a vigorous debater. The living room of the Rudolph home was lined with "wall-to-wall bookshelves" that sagged under the weight of books on philosophy, religion, history and politics. Nietzsche, Orwell, Dostoyevsky and many books on European and American history shared shelf space with the Bible and stacks of off-beat religious publications like *Thunderbolt*, a white supremacist magazine published in Marietta, Georgia. Rather than accepting the dogma of Roman Catholicism or any other religion, Pat encouraged her children to interpret the Bible themselves, perhaps as she did when she decided to leave the convent. As she told an interviewer after her son's arrest, "You can find a scripture in there to suit anything."[58] She also encouraged her children's curiosity about the world. Despite limited resources, she and two of her sons, Eric and Joel, toured Western Europe. Well read and cultured in a perhaps eccentric way, this was not a family of unsophisticated Southern hillbillies. But it was also a family that embraced the Southern legacy of racial intolerance and religious bigotry.

Questioning authority was a basic presumption in the frequent family discussions, especially, it seems, what they considered the intrusive authority of the federal government. If there were any reservations about that perspective, they were probably removed when Bob Rudolph was diagnosed with terminal skin cancer. The family believed laetrile, a substance derived from apricot pits, was an effective treatment that could have saved his life. Banned by the Federal Drug Administration, the family tried unsuccessfully to acquire it. When Bob Rudolph died in 1981, it was a sad and, also, a bitter event. Close family friends who shared the Rudolph's resentment of the federal government included a neighbor, Tom Branham. Branham was a frequent visitor and a steadfast source of support for the family during the difficult adjustment that followed Bob Rudolph's death. Branham thought the federal government was "oppressive" and a source of "tyranny and despotism." His friend Bob Rudolph's untimely and, perhaps, unnecessary death was further proof of that. There is no question that as an impressionable teenager, Eric looked up to Branham, his own political views mirroring those of the older man.

According to Deborah Rudolph, Branham was a strange, authoritarian man who lived in a black-and-white world of good and evil. Life for him was a daily struggle against the encroachments of the federal government and the minorities and liberals whose interests it advanced. At his expense. He was a character like those featured in survivalist magazines, living as if in a state of siege, depending on no one, but welcoming other's, like the Rudolph's, reliance on him. Food, fuel, water, weapons and ammunition were stored in a house he built out of reinforced steel and concrete. When he was falsely arrested on a federal weapons violation for having a submachine gun and explosives in his possession, the Rudolphs rallied to his defense. Pat Rudolph returned his generosity and many kindnesses to the family by co-signing his bond.[59] His conviction was later overturned.

Other reports have linked Pat Rudolph and her family to a racist and anti-Semitic religious sect called "Christian Identity." Its leader, Dan Gayman, was a charismatic minister well-known for his racism and bigotry. Pat Rudolph was drawn to that message and spent several months with Eric and a younger brother at a Christian Identity compound in Schell City, Missouri before she apparently lost interest. Eric was 18 at the time. It is not known what influence Gayman may have had on Eric Rudolph's thinking, but his sister-in-law claimed he "idolized" Gayman and saw him as a father figure.[60] Rudolph denied that. In any event, Christian Identity appears to have been one of any number of fringe religious sects that drew Pat Rudolph's attention and interest before she moved on to something else in her search for the Truth. That search, however, always seems to have led her and her children in one direction, to the angry, vengeful, self-righteous margins of society, to groups that hated blacks, Jews, gays, and abortionists, and the federal government that did their bidding. It was a familiar pattern of behavior, according to Deborah Rudolph:

> They [the family] called it "Pat's search for *the* church." It became a joke after a while because she'd find this little group and she'd get pissed off at them, just like she got pissed off at Dan Gayman, and then she'd leave.[61]

"I don't think that Christian Identity was the whole thing for [Eric]," Deborah Rudolph replied when asked about the sect. "Eric's not a follower . . . he developed his own thoughts on things." But it was difficult to distinguish his political views from Dan Gayman's and Tom Branham's. Although Eric did not formally belong to any sect that she was aware of, she said that he, like his brothers, nevertheless, did share with those groups their siege mentality as well as their strong and enduring racist and anti-Semitic views.

And it appears to have been a life-long preoccupation. For example, Eric's former school principal reported that when Eric was in grade school, he wrote a paper, arguing that the Holocaust was Jewish propaganda and had never occurred. According to Deborah Rudolph, the whole Rudolph family shared that belief:

> This was Eric's, Joel's [her former husband] and the whole family's deal. I mean they had it down to numbers. Okay, there were X amount of Jews before the Holocaust and then after the Holocaust there were this many Jews, so how the hell could Hitler have killed 6 million Jews?[62]

Other evidence suggests that Rudolph's political extremism sometimes got in the way of his relationships with others. Although there is nothing to suggest that loneliness and relationships with women were problems for Rudolph as they had been for his predecessors, McVeigh and, most famously, Kaczynski. His good looks, intelligence, and the good manners his mother expected of all her children virtually assured that. That he was accustomed to the attention of women was suggested when, after his capture, he told a detention officer that he had been in the mountains without a woman for so long that even "the bears started looking good."[63]

"He was a high school sweetheart of mine," a former girlfriend recalled of the freshman year they dated:

> I knew the guy when he was 14, 15 years old. . . . He was a really well-mannered guy. . . . It's hard for me to think of him in a bad way. I have memories of what he was. . . . [Back then] was like in the 'Urban Cowboy'[64] days and people were following the whole country music thing. I thought he was that type of persona. He assumed the whole country-boy thing. I never thought [of him as] a redneck or skinhead type of guy. I was attracted to him because he was quiet and shy. He had the southern accent. He spoke like a country boy. I remember him being a smoker, or chewing tobacco. He introduced me to chewing tobacco.[65]

But there was one thing about this nice, country boy that really bothered her, and it wasn't that he chewed tobacco. She said Eric always referred to blacks as "niggers." Easily, without embarrassment.

> I was totally caught off guard. It was something I didn't expect to come out of his mouth. . . . He had some pretty radical views regarding race. . . . He was quiet and shy and respectful of me, but that was one of the things we had a really big difference of opinion on. . . . I was not comfortable with that.[66]

Drifting

After his father's death, Eric seemed adrift. Despite strong academic skills, he dropped out of school in the ninth grade, a year after the family moved to North Carolina. He found work with an older brother as a carpenter. And he was pretty good at it, earning a reputation as "a meticulous, talented craftsman." But he soon lost interest in carpentry. Not long afterward, in 1985, he had no trouble getting the GED he needed to gain admission to Western Carolina University in Cullowhee. But college lasted only two semesters before he became bored and quit. For the next year or so, it appears that he was unemployed, and probably supported himself by growing and selling marijuana. According to Deborah Rudolph, he grew the high-quality pot hydroponically in a shed at the Topton homestead. That was after his mother had moved to the nearby town of Sylva, and he and a brother purchased the property from her.

He also was in the habit of smoking pot regularly himself as he lay around the house, often reading European and American military history, and maybe wondering what to do with his life. At some point, he also became a regular reader of the magazine *Soldier of Fortune,* and found appealing its articles on weaponry, survivalism, and killing as solace for frustrated, angry males with military aspirations and revenge on their minds. In 1986, at the age of twenty, he decided to pursue the life he enjoyed reading about and joined the Army. It seemed like a logical thing to do. Why not become a part of that glorious history, he might have thought. Like Timothy McVeigh, he had his sights set high when he joined the elite 101st Airborne. His ultimate goal was Special Forces. He welcomed the challenge and had no difficulty handling the rigorous training. Rules and regulations proved to be another matter. After completing basic training at Fort Benning, Georgia, he was assigned to Air Assault School at Fort Campbell, Kentucky. It may have been there that he learned to design and build bombs like the ones he would use later to kill innocent civilians. Or he may have learned how from the "how to" military manuals and *The Little Black Book of Explosives* a friend reported that Rudolph read on his own.

The same friend said that Rudolph was quiet, unassuming and often kept to himself, preferring to remain in the barracks in the evenings to read rather than socializing with other soldiers. He read military magazines and probably books of that genre, some with titles like *The SAS Survival Manual, The Black Book of Revenge, The Poor Man's James Bond,* and *Survival, Evasion & Escape* that are published by Delta Press. He was also an avid reader of *High Times,* a magazine devoted to marijuana cultivation and processing. On weekends, he often would make the one-hour trip from Fort Campbell to Nashville where he would hang out with his brother, Joel, and his wife

Deborah. According to Deborah, Eric's typical weekend there consisted of lying around, getting high and philosophizing, eating pizza, watching old movies, and sometimes visiting Civil War battlefields in the vicinity.[67]

But like everything else he had tried, army life did not suit Rudolph either. Eighteen months into his enlistment, he received an early discharge for reasons that remain unclear. Some have reported that it was for smoking pot. Others claim his marijuana use was just part of a larger problem of insubordination. In either case, the problem was that Eric Rudolph had a mind of his own and did not accept authority easily. Despite his natural ability, he never rose above the rank of private. He was discharged from the army about the same time Timothy McVeigh entered it.

After returning to the homestead in Topton in 1989, Rudolph apparently resumed his marijuana business to support himself, because there is no record of other steady employment after that. In 1996, he and his brother sold the house in Topton for $65,000 and his share of the profits probably eased whatever financial concerns he may have had. After that he lived in rental housing. His last known address was a mobile home.

It was a restless, pointless and, probably, isolated existence. For example, there is no evidence of close friendships beyond his own family. Such were the circumstances of his life when, at thirty years of age, and utterly without direction in his life, he decided to launch a campaign of terror to provide purpose and fill that void.

In some respects, Eric Rudolph's aimless existence reminds one of Timothy McVeigh's before he focused on a federal building in Oklahoma City. The major difference between these two domestic terrorists is McVeigh's estrangement from his family. Rudolph was close to his, and remains so. But the similarities invite comment. Both these young men were intelligent, but bored with school and conventional education. In both cases, they were drawn by the allure of military adventurism and might that fill the pages of magazines like *Soldier of Fortune*. But for different reasons, the attraction of military life lost its appeal as a way to provide meaning to their drifting, uncertain lives. For whatever reason, it appears that sometime after his discharge, Rudolph's views, like McVeigh's after his unhappy departure from the army, began to focus intensely on the alleged abuses of federal authority. From that point on, hate and a quest for retribution filled the void in both their lives.

Conclusions

Some mental health professionals who analyzed Rudolph's confession described him as "suffering from delusions of grandeur, paranoia and [being] a classic anti-social personality." In other words, Rudolph was thought by these experts to display the symptoms of a severely disordered Type IV subject. One of them is quoted as saying, "This is black-and-white thinking. It's making mountains out of molehills. It's projecting his hostility to the government onto a big screen in which he *imagines* the government and everyone in it is hostile to him."[68]

But is it not questionable to so easily assume that Rudolph — with a million-dollar bounty on his head and his photo on the FBI's "Ten Most Wanted" list, and the target of an intense manhunt that lasted for five years — had to "imagine" anything about the government's dead-or-alive desire to bring him to justice? That is hardly paranoia, as these experts suggest. Rather it's a very realistic assessment of his situation. Similarly, to describe Rudolph as an "anti-social personality" is to imply that all political terrorists are sociopaths, no different than serial killers and child molesters. To do so hardly advances an understanding of political terrorism in this country, or the world.

The defining characteristic of the clinical "anti-social personality" is the absence of conscience and empathy for others. Such a person is unconcerned about anyone but themselves and will do anything they can get away with to advance their own self-interest. In contrast, a Type I terrorist or assassin is conscience driven, justifying his actions on moral principles rather than the laws of society he believes are flawed. If Rudolph was an anti-social personality, he would have been utterly indifferent to issues that did not affect him like, as he claims, the Supreme Court's "sanctioning of infanticide and by that act consign[ing] 50 million unborn children to their graves."[69]

Furthermore, Rudolph's views on the Supreme Court's *Roe v. Wade* decision and abortion were widely shared in the South, a fact he mentions in his confession. Many, if not most, southerners opposed abortion and a woman's right to choose. Many also sympathized with Rudolph and identified with him. As one woman said after his capture:

> Rudolph's a Christian and I'm a Christian and he dedicated his life to fighting abortion. Those are our values. These are our woods. I don't see what he did as a terrorist act.[70]

During the manhunt for Rudolph, there was a lively market in Murphy and other small towns in the Appalachian foothills for T-shirts and bumper stickers that read, "Eric Rudolph the Hide and Seek Champion of the World," and "Run Rudolph Run."

At the same time Rudolph was viewed sympathetically by many residents of the area, federal agents seeking him were viewed with a certain degree of contempt. "We thought it was kind of funny when the feds rolled in here all arrogant," one man told a reporter. "Nobody around here condones murder, but I think a lot of people weren't sure which side to be on."[71]

Whether the arrogance and defiance reflected in his words can be described as "delusions of grandeur" is a bit more problematic. For example, he concludes his statement melodramatically with these words:

> And now after the [plea] agreement has been signed, the talking heads on the news opine that I am 'finished,' that I will 'languish broken and unloved in the bowels of some supermax [prison] . . . but I say to you that by the grace of God I am still here — a little bloodied, but emphatically unbowed.[72]

Self-serving, to be sure, even offensive, but surely such thoughts might flow from sources other than delusions of grandeur. Attempts to portray Rudolph as a mentally deranged person are reminiscent of how John Wilkes Booth in the nineteenth century and Sirhan Sirhan in the twentieth were similarly described by the media and some members of the mental health community. But as earlier chapters have demonstrated, they were wrong then about Booth and Sirhan as they are in the twenty-first century about Rudolph. Still, it does seem that Eric Rudolph's outrage and political extremism were about more than just the lost lives of aborted babies and the alleged threat to nature and western civilization posed by emboldened homosexuals, as important as those issues were to him. There was a consistent pattern of religious and political extremism that ran through the Rudolph family history. From his mother's entrance and departure from a convent as a young girl through her continuing, life-long search for "the" church, that path always seem to lead to the fringes of society where intolerance, hatred and resentment were preached, and draconian solutions embraced. Never the Golden Rule, it was white supremacy and anti-Semitism, as well as anti-abortion and anti-government radicalism that describe that fringe.

In addition to Eric Rudolph's remorseless campaign of violence, the behavior such extremism inspired in other family members was sometimes bizarre. To the point, at least in one instance, that mental derangement may be the only explanation. In March 1998, for example, not long after federal authorities identified his brother as a terrorist bomber, Dan Rudolph cut off his left hand with a power saw in protest. "This is for the FBI and the media," he spoke to a video camera he had set up to record the event.[73] This was not simply an impulsive act that he, at once, regretted. In his view, self-mutilation was an act of love and concern for his brother.

Coming from that kind of background, it may be easy to understand why Eric Rudolph found so appealing the exploits of characters he read about in *Soldier of Fortune* magazine, men like him who were driven by a quest for power and destructive obsessions with right and wrong. Rudolph's fevered opposition to abortion and homosexuality provided both meaning and purpose in a rudderless, drifting life without either. Those issues focused his anger on the federal government, just as the sieges at Waco and Ruby Ridge did for Timothy McVeigh.

Like McVeigh, Rudolph fits the profile of the politically-motivated Type I assassin. He had a clear understanding of what he was doing and the consequences, and he refused to recant on the principles that motivated him. He did not seek personal notoriety, as Type II and Type III subjects — indeed he tried to avoid capture and keep his identity secret — and, to date, has refused to be interviewed. Nor did he exhibit the consuming personal problems that fueled the frustration and anger of Types II and III subjects.

In a letter to his mother, written in a prison cell where he will spend the rest of his life, he wrote,

> Despite my many flaws, I still hope that you can find it in your loving, selfless heart to forgive me.... And even though I cannot apologize for being who I am and expressing myself in the way that I did, it troubles me greatly that you had to experience any hardships because of my deeds.[74]

In another century, another political extremist, who was described as suffering from paranoia and delusions of grandeur, wrote these words after he killed a president: "God, try and forgive me, and bless my mother.... [But] I do not," John Wilkes Booth continued, "repent the blow I struck."[75] These words, like Rudolph's, are the words of a dangerous and uncompromising political zealot, not the words of a sociopath or a psychotic person suffering from paranoia and delusions of persecution and grandeur.

Notes

1. Timothy McVeigh's letter to Fox News (April 27, 2001) at wtsuwtg://4http://foxnews.com/story/0,2933,17500,00.html; and abcnews.go.com/sections/primetime/..../PRIMETIME_010329_mcveigh_feature.htm 2/29/01.
2. Morrison, "Special Report."
3. Statement of Eric Robert Rudolph, April 13, 2005 at http://www.tallahassee.com/mld/tallahassee/news/local/11386671
4. *United States v. Timothy James McVeigh*, CR No. 96–CR–68 (1997) lectlaw.com/bomb.html. Hereafter cited as *Court Documents;* and http://more.abcnews.go.com/sections/us/oklahoma/transcripts.html. Hereafter cited as *Trial Transcripts*.
5. *Trial Transcripts,* Statement of J. Hartzler, April 24, 1997.
6. *Court Documents; Trial Transcripts*, Testimony of Charles Hanger, April 28, 1997.
7. L. Michael and D. Herbeck, *American Terrorist: Timothy McVeigh and the Oklahoma City Bombing* (New York: HarperCollins/Regan Books, 2001).

Ruby Ridge, Waco, and Roe v. Wade 367

8. McVeigh letter to Fox News, April 27, 2001; *American Terrorist,* p. 137.
9. *American Terrorist,* pp. 8–12.
10. See, for example, M.S. Ainsworth, M.C. Blehar, E. Waters, and S. Wall, *Patterns of Attachment* (Hillsdale, NJ: Lawrence Erlbaum Associates, 1978).
11. Dr. J. Smith quoted at: http://www.abcnews.go.com/sections/primetime/ ... PRIMETIME_010329_mcveigh_feature_htm 3/29/01; see, also, *American Terrorist,* p. 41.
12. *American Terrorist,* p. 106.
13. Ibid., p. 21.
14. Ibid., pp. 23, 25.
15. Remarks of Dr. J. Smith; abcnews.go.com/sections/primetime_010329_mcveigh_feature.htm 3/29/01
16. *American Terrorist,* pp. 37–38.
17. Ibid., pp. 38–39.
18. *Trial Transcripts,* Statement of J. Hartzler, April 24, 1997; Testimony of M. Fortier, May 12, 1997.
19. *American Terrorist,* pp. 43–44.
20. Ibid., pp. 45–48.
21. Ibid., pp. 49–56.
22. Ibid., pp. 73–74.
23. Ibid., p. 76.
24. Emile Durkheim, *Suicide: A Study in Sociology.* Translated by J.A. Spaulding and G. Simpson (Glencoe, ILL: Free Press, 1951; orig., 1899).
25. *American Terrorist,* pp. 95–102.
26. McVeigh letter of February 11, 1992 quoted in *American Terrorist,* pp. 98–99.
27. For a concise description of this event, see the account of Colonel James "Bo" Gritz, in the Foreword to *The Federal Siege at Ruby Ridge* by Randy and Sara Weaver (Marion, MT: Ruby Ridge, Inc., 1998), xi-xiv.
28. http://dailycampus.smu.edu/HTMLPages/spring96/DC.04–23–96DC.04–23–96–news.html; see, also, *American Terrorist,* p.120.
29. *American Terrorist,* pp. 122–123,
30. abcnews.go.com/sectons/us/oklahoma/nichols.html.
31. abcnews.go.com/sections/us/oklahoma/nichols.html; see, also, *American Terrorist,* 161–162, 290.
32. abcnews.go.com/sections/primetime_010329_mcveigh_feature.htm
33. abcnews.go.com/sections/us/oklahoma/oklahoma_timeline.html.
34. *Trial Transcripts,* quoted in statement of J. Hartzler, April 27, 1997.
35. abcnews.go.com/sections/us/oklahoma/oklahoma_timeline.html.
36. *Trial Transcript,* Testimony of Michael Fortier, May 12, 1997; courttv.com/casefiles/oklahoma/documents/grandjury_123098.html; and abcnews.go.com/sections/primetime_010329_mcveigh_feature.htm.
37. courttv.com/casefiles/oklahoma/documents/grandjury_123098.htmil.
38. http://more.abcnews.go.com/sections/us/oklahoma/oklahoma_timeline.html.
39. *American Terrorist,* p. 304.

40. cnn.com/2001/LAW/06/11mcveigh.01/
41. Timothy McVeigh, *Media Bypass* (June 1998); reproduced at kwtv.com/news/bombing/mcveigh-essay.htm
42. foxnews.com/story/0,2933,17500,00.html
43. cnn.com/2001/LAW06/11/mcveigh.01/
44. *United States of America v. Eric Robert Rudolph*, Criminal Indictment No. 1:00–CR-805, November 15, 2000 at www.Findlaw.com. Hereafter cited as Criminal Indictment.
45. Criminal Indictment.
46. The news organizations in Atlanta were Reuters America News Tip, A.J.A.C. News Tip, NBC News Bureau, and WSB Television.
47. Criminal Indictment.
48. B. Morrison, "Eric Rudolph Tells How He Eluded FBI," *USA TODAY,* July 5, 2005 at www.usatoday.com/news/nation/2005-07-05 .
49. *United States v. Eric Robert Rudolph*, Guilty Plea and Plea Agreement, CR 00-S-0422-S (2005).
50. "Full text of Eric Rudolph's written statement, which was handed out ... " at www.tallahassee.com/mld/tallahassee/news/local. Hereafter cited as Rudolph statement.
51. Rudolph statement.
52. Rudolph statement.
53. Rudolph statement.
54. Rudolph statement.
55. Rudolph statement.
56. Because Rudolph did not go to trial, less is known of the details of his background than is known of his predecessors, Kaczynski and McVeigh. To date, Rudolph has refused to discuss his past. He has also contested much of what others have written about him. Apart from his mother, who claims not to understand her son's behavior, as of this writing, Rudolph's former sister-in-law, Deborah Rudolph, appears to be the best informed and most balanced source of background information on him. She was interviewed by the Southern Poverty Law Center before his arrest. Much of the background information presented here is drawn from that interview.
57. Southern Poverty Law Center Intelligence Report, "Running with Rudolph," at www.splcenter.org/intelreport/article. Other accounts drawn from this interview include: Q. Ellison, "Eric Rudolph Background," Asheville (NC) *Citizen-Times*, May 31, 2003 at www.orig.citizen-times.com/cache/article/news/ ; M.E. Ross, "Eric Rudolph's Rage was a Long Time Brewing," April 13, 2005 at www.msnbc.msn.com/id/ .
58. As quoted in B. Morrison, "Special Report: Eric Rudolph Writes Home," at www.usatoday.com/news/nation/2005-07-05 .
59. Southern Poverty Law Center, "Intelligence Report."
60. M.E. Ross, "Eric Rudolph's Rage Was a Long Time Brewing," at www.msnbc.msn.com/id.
61. Southern Poverty Law Center, "Intelligence Report."

62. Ibid.
63. As quoted in A. Campo-Flores and C. Skipp, "Eric Robert Rudolph Says Solitude in Woods Got to Him," *Newsweek,* June 16, 2005 at www.prnewswire.com.
64. Urban Cowboy was a popular Hollywood film of the period, starring John Travolta and Deborah Winger, about a romance between a construction worker and a city girl set against a backdrop of cowboy bars and country western music in Houston, Texas.
65. As quoted in M.E. Ross, "Eric Rudolph's Rage Was a Long Time Brewing," MSNBC, April 13, 2005 at www.msnbc.msn.com.
66. As quoted in Ross, "Eric Rudolph's Rage."
67. Southern Poverty Law Center, "Intelligence Report;" and H. Shuster and C. Stone, "High Times," February 28, 2005 at www.cnn.law.printthis.clicability.com.
68. Associated Press, "Manifesto Shows How Rudolph's Mind Works, *Arizona Daily Star,* April 17, 2005, A9.
69. Rudolph statement.
70. J. Gettleman and D.M. Halbfinger, "Suspect in '96 Olympic Bombing And 3 Other Attacks Is Caught," *New York Times*, June 1, 2003, A1.
71. Gettleman and Halbfinger, "Suspect in '96 Olympic Bombing."
72. Rudolph statement.
73. Southern Poverty Law Center, "Intelligence Report."
74. Morrison, "Special Report."
75. Diary of John Wilkes Booth, Attorney General's Papers, Lincoln Assassination, Record Group No. 60, National Archives.

Part 6

Conclusion

12

Criminal Responsibility and Risk

This book began with an account of John Hinckley's nearly fatal attack on President Reagan on March 30, 1981. Since then, no president has been harmed by a would-be assassin. Except for seriously tightened security and good fortune, other incidents might have added to the list of subjects and their victims included in these accounts.

For example, in September 1994 a pilot died when his small plane crashed on the South Lawn of the White House grounds. Was this a first attempt on President Clinton's life, borrowing an idea from the tapes of Sam Byck? No one is sure. A month later, Francisco Martin Duran, emptied two clips of ammunition from the barrel of his assault rifle, aiming at a person he believed was Bill Clinton. Seven months after that, in May 1995, uniformed Secret Service officers shot and wounded a man climbing over the White House fence. The pistol he carried was unloaded. During the summer of 1998, a severely deranged gunman, Russell Weston, shot and killed two security guards on his way into the U.S. Capitol to assassinate members of Congress. Weston appears to be a latter day Richard Lawrence, a paranoid schizophrenic too delusional even to stand trial. In February 2001, uniformed Secret Service officers shot and wounded a clinically depressed man who waved a pistol and fired shots in the air on a street bordering the White House. Robert Pickett intended to harm no one, hoping only that the Secret Service would end his unhappy life and troubles with the Internal Revenue Service. Except for authorities, no one knows how many other plots probably were thwarted by tight security and/or preemptive arrests before anything happened. So, it is clear that eternal vigilance remains not only the price of liberty, but also of presidential security as the nation moves into a new century.

What changed, however, in the last decade of the twentieth century was that ordinary citizens became the targets of political violence. Timothy

McVeigh's Oklahoma City bombing on April 19, 1995, just five days before another bomb blast killed Ted Kaczynski's last victim in California both represent significant new terrorist dimensions of political violence in America. The following year at the Summer Olympics in Atlanta, Eric Rudolph exploded the first in a series of bombs he would use over the next several years in his personal campaign against the Federal government and, in particular, the abortion clinics sanctioned by Federal law. Was their choice of targets a response to the greatly enhanced security since the Reagan assassination attempt that now protects nationally prominent political figures? No one is sure. In any case, the perpetrators themselves reflect the familiar motivational patterns set forth in the typology presented in chapter 1. With McVeigh and Rudolph the profile is clearly that of a Type I political extremist set in the mold of John Wilkes Booth, Leon Czolgosz, Oscar Collazo, Griselio Torresola, and Sirhan Sirhan. But Ted Kaczynski's profile is a bit more problematic, although the political purpose laid out in his manifesto and implemented in terrorist acts that extended over nearly eighteen years — and expressed after his arrest and conviction — cannot be denied. But, unlike Type I subjects, Kaczynski's violent political agenda might have been altered by a change in his personal situation, that is, if he had found the female companionship he had sought unsuccessfully for so many years. With that single qualification, the lives and personalities of Type I subjects are varied and, with the exception of Sirhan Sirhan, unremarkable.

But emotionally troubled Type II and Type III subjects — for whom politics is a secondary or non-existent consideration — continue to pose the greatest threat to American presidents and presidential candidates. Such persons account for nearly half (eight of twenty) of all attacks and seven of ten of those that occurred in the modern era since 1963.[1] Type II and Type III subjects are consumed with overwhelming and unmet needs for affection and approval that, in most cases, can be traced back to anxious, unhappy childhoods where parental love was conditional or absent. Confronted with the often lethal combination of failed relationships and careers, they turn to violence, scapegoating prominent political figures whose deaths will assure them the attention and notoriety that has eluded them all their lives. Lynette Fromme's and Sara Jane Moore's highly personal motives were different in that each of them acted to demonstrate their affection for, and loyalty to, significant others in their lives. In Fromme's case, it was Charles Manson, for whom she sought a new trial; in Moore's, it was the Bay Area radicals she had, with enormous regret, betrayed. But, like their male counterparts, media attention was central to the motives of both. The predominance of Type II and Type III assailants in the modern era reflect the unprecedented changes in media and communication that have defined that era. Giuseppe Zangara, Franklin D. Roosevelt's would-be assassin in 1933, is the single exception.

Why? Abundant evidence points to the profound effect of the unprecedented televised media coverage of President Kennedy's assassination in 1963 — and his assassin, Lee Harvey Oswald. That assured notoriety, as we have seen, figured prominently in the motives of his counterparts who followed: Arthur Bremer, Samuel Byck, Lynette Fromme, Sara Jane Moore, John Hinckley, and Francisco Duran.

Type IV subjects like Richard Lawrence, Charles Guiteau, and John Schrank, who are truly mentally impaired, are the easiest to identify and apprehend before they act. That is probably why John Schrank's attempt to assassinate Theodore Roosevelt in 1912 is the last time someone in that mental state has seriously threatened the life of a president or presidential candidate.[2] The delusions that drove Lawrence, Guiteau, Schrank seemed to emerge from a documented history of hereditary mental illness in their families. Unable to reason clearly, they were driven to their extreme acts by totally illusory (Lawrence) or the most absurd (Guiteau and Schrank) political circumstances.

Only three subjects, Carl Austin Weiss, James Earl Ray, and Theodore Kaczynski cannot be classified within the typology. Weiss and Kaczynski were poles apart in socialization and background from James Earl Ray. Moreover, the life experiences of all three were significantly different from the other subjects. Weiss, the successful physician, loving husband and doting father; Kaczynski, a Ph.D. and brilliant mathematician; and Ray, a dregs-of-society career criminal, represent extremes in any sociological ranking of American assassins and domestic terrorists. And each killed for reasons associated with the values of these extremes: Weiss killed impulsively, probably out of a profound feeling of responsibility and protectiveness for his wife and infant son; Ray killed for money in the calculating manner of a hardened criminal and hit man; Kaczynski killed in serial fashion in his personal war against those who advanced and profited from American technology.

A central issue in this book has been *criminal responsibility,* and how that is assessed. The perspective advanced is that persons who are aware of what they are doing, and/or understand that their actions are wrong, can be held accountable for their crimes. Following this standard, only the three Type IV subjects — Richard Lawrence, Charles Guiteau, and John Schrank — were considered legally insane. Courts recognized that in the Lawrence and Shrank cases where their victims survived. Charles Guiteau, whose disordered mental state seems beyond dispute, was executed, probably because President Garfield died and the memory of Lincoln's assassination was still fresh in the public's mind. John Hinckley, who meets this more stringent standard of criminal responsibility, was, nonetheless, found not guilty by reason of insanity. Hinckley's controversial acquittal had less to do with medical science than it did with the District of Columbia's more lenient "diminished capacity" standard of criminal responsibility, the racial composition of the jury, and President Reagan's unpopularity among blacks.

Connecting Dots

An equally import issue is how potential assassins and domestic terrorists can be identified before they strike. Identification of suspects usually occurs as a result of suspicious behavior (e.g., inappropriate attire or conduct in proximity to a protectee), weapons possession, threats, or tips from informants. Assessing the *risk,* or the danger, posed by suspects, once identified, is one of the most difficult challenges mental health professionals and authorities face. The subjects of this book differ from ordinary street killers. Actuarial studies reveal that the best predictors of ordinary violent crime are, in descending order of importance, these:

1. Previous history of violence
2. Age (18–25)
3. Gender (male)
4. Race (disproportionately black)
5. Social class (lower)
6. Intelligence (below average)
7. Substance abuse
8. Skills/education (high school dropouts)
9. Unemployed
10. Peer influence

Few of these characteristics describe the subjects of this book. For example, only James Earl Ray and Francisco Martin Duran (one offense) had a previous history of violence. Only six of twenty-one (Torresola, Oswald, Sirhan Bremer, Hinckley, and Duran) are included in the crime-prone eighteen to twenty-five age group. Gender fits, except for the two females. Race does not, without a single incident involving a black assailant. Only four (Oswald, Ray, Bremer, and Duran) can be described as lower class. None could be described as below average in intelligence. None were substance abusers. Only four (Lawrence, Torresola, Oswald, Ray, and Rudolph) were school dropouts. Unemployment does describe most except Booth, Weiss, Collazo, and Duran. Peer influence was a factor in the actions only of the two women.

Clinical assessments are also problematic in assessing dangerousness, for wrongdoers lie. Mental health professionals are no better prepared than experienced law enforcement officers to determine when a suspect is lying and when he/she is not.[3] As one can see from the relative diversity of these subjects, there is no valid single profile that describes assassins, would-be assassins and domestic terrorists.

But once a suspect has come to the attention of authorities, there may be identifiable patterns in their *behavior* that provide situational clues to their dangerousness. As we have seen, *anger* and *depression* are the two key driving emotions in the actions of assassins, would-be assassins, and domestic terrorists. The anger and depression experienced by suspects who are truly dangerous is reflected in what is going on in their lives and what they are *doing*.

Anger and potential aggression toward a political figure are often reflected in what I will call *engagement* indicators. These include ideological intensity, interest in an intended victim, an unusual interest in earlier assassins and/or other violent persons, and stalking. Consider, for example, how these indicators are reflected in the lives of recent subjects, that is, those twelve subjects, including James Earl Ray, whose crimes were committed in the modern era since the Kennedy assassination in 1963 when unprecedented media exposure, for the first time, altered the dynamics of assassinations in America.

Anger-Engagement Indicators

- *Ideological intensity.* Angry suspects often have in their possession an unusual amount of political material: books, newspaper and magazine articles, campaign literature, and the like. This material is often carried with them or was found in living quarters and vehicles. Evidence of this sort was found in the possession of six of the twelve subjects (Oswald, Sirhan, Byck, Fromme, Moore, McVeigh, and Kaczynski); all can be described as having had strong ideological perspectives. What may seem odd is that nearly half (Ray, Bremer, Hinckley, and Duran) did not. The rational basis of those perspectives varied, however, from the political extremism of Type I's like Sirhan, McVeigh, Kaczynski, and Rudolph through the compensatory rationalizations of Type II's like Byck. But rationality per se doesn't matter in assessing the potential significance of such evidence.
- *Interest in an intended victim.* Victim interest can be distinguished from ideological intensity, although the two may be related since the sources are often the same. Possession of books and articles, for example, about a president's or a candidate's personal life are one important bit of information, as are clipped newspaper, magazine, and postcard photographs. Evidence of this sort was found in the possession of six of the twelve subjects –Oswald, Sirhan, Bremer, Byck, Hinckley, and Duran even though Bremer, Hinckley and Duran had no discernable political perspective.
- *Interest in prior assassinations or violent crimes.* As time goes on and assassination attempts continue, it has become common for those con-

templating such acts to read about their predecessors or persons who have committed comparable, high-profile, violent crimes. Books, articles, videos about such persons are usually found among the subject's possessions or, in some cases, such as Oswald and Sirhan, for example, in the form of well-used library cards. Eight of the twelve subjects were so inclined. Oswald read about Huey Long's assassination; Sirhan read about Oswald and European assassins; Bremer read about Oswald and, especially, Sirhan; Byck read about Oswald and Sirhan, as well as other Palestinian terrorists, and followed with great interest the story of rooftop sniper Jimmy Essex; Hinckley had a consuming interest in violent criminals like serial killer, Ted Bundy and earlier assassins but, most famously, Arthur Bremer and the film taxi Driver, which was drawn, in part, from Bremer's diary. Duran was enthralled with the book, *Hit Man*; McVeigh and Rudolph read widely in the magazine, *Soldier of Fortune,* and elsewhere about assassins and terrorists; Kaczynski read widely, but appeared less drawn to such topics and, indeed, did not appear to look for violent role models, but he did read Graham's and Gurr's, *The History of Violence in America.*

- *Stalking.* Bus and airline ticket stubs, motel and credit card receipts, newspaper clippings from different places and, most obviously, copies of presidential or campaign schedules probably provide the best clues to this behavior. Although observing the same person at different rallies separated by time and distance, as security personnel did with Arthur Bremer, is significant in this regard. Six of the twelve subjects stalked their intended victims — Sirhan, Ray, Bremer, Hinckley and, probably, Duran and Rudolph. Sam Byck did not stalk President Nixon, but he did check out presidnetial security at the Capital before Nixon's second inaugruration. James Earl Ray was the most calculating stalker of them all.

Depression-Disengagement Indicators

Depression in potentially dangerous suspects may likewise be reflected in what I will call *disengagement* indicators that suggest something about the isolation and withdrawal from ordinary social constraints that often precede violent acts. These indicators — occupational instability, transience, family estrangement, attention-seeking behavior, and suicidal tendencies describe circumstances and patterns of behavior that often precede assassination attempts. They are reflective of the interpersonal difficulties and situational stress that characterize the lives, especially Type II and Type III subjects. Note in the following that none of these indicators is dependent on self-reported information; all can be ascertained by other means when a suspect comes to the attention of authorities.

- *Occupational instability.* Unemployment or marginal employment is one thing, beyond being disproportionately male, that assassins, would-be assassins, and domestic terrorists share with ordinary street criminals. All twelve of the modern subjects fit this characterization.
- *Transience.* Restlessness, moving about, changing addresses, and traveling are linked to both occupational difficulties and emotional instability. Transience should not be confused with stalking, although the same evidence applies: transportation, credit card, and motel receipts found in the subject's possession. The salient difference being transience and stalking is that the travels of the transient do not coincide with the appearances of a political figure. Eight of the twelve modern subjects meet this criterion. Sirhan Sirhan, Francisco Duran, and Ted Kaczynski are the only exceptions. John Hinckley and Timothy McVeigh stand out in this regard in their restless wanderings back and forth across the country.
- *Family estrangement.* This very important indicator, which characterizes ten of the twelve modern subjects, is also a bit more difficult to assess. An attempt to locate next of kin is a standard part of most criminal investigations. If none can be identified, that in itself may be important information; if persons are identified, a phone call or two may be revealing, as it would have been when John Hinckley was arrested in Nashville. Ordinary family members provide constraints on one another's behavior as Timothy McVeigh's grandfather seemingly did on his grandson's behavior until he died. Without those constraints, estrangement of this sort is often a precursor of violent behavior as it was in all but two of these subjects, Sirhan and Rudolph.
- *Attention-seeking behavior.* This attribute is observed in nine of the twelve modern subjects. The only exceptions are Sirhan Sirhan and the stealthy James Earl Ray. The object and purpose of that attention-seeking varies, however. Some seek the *intimate* attention of loved ones who have rejected them; some also seek *public* attention; some seek both. Additionally, some seek to focus attention on *themselves*; others attempt to focus it on their *ideas*. Attention-seeking behavior of Type II and Type III subjects is observed at all levels — spouses, parents, significant others, and the public. Recall: Lee Harvey Oswald's futile attempts gain the attention of his wife and his picketing and media activities on behalf of his bogus Fair Play for Cuba organization, not to mention the threat made to the FBI; Arthur Bremer's bizarre dress and behavior at Wallace rallies; Sam Byck's futile at-

tempts to reconcile with his wife and see his children, his letter writing, and his picketing in front of the White House; Lynette Fromme's many, and varied, efforts to attract media attention to Charles Manson's plight; Sara Jane Moore's not so subtle threat to authorities that she intended to test "presidential security;" John Hinckley's harassment of his parents and his failed attempts to get the attention of actress Jodie Foster; Francisco Martin Duran's calls to talk shows, and a U.S. senator, and his strident behavior at home and on the job; Timothy McVeigh's t-shirts, bumper stickers, and activities at gun shows and during the stand-off in Waco. Even the reclusive Ted Kaczynski sought to publicize his grievances in letters to newspapers and, failing there, resorted to the bargain he struck with the *New York Times* and the *Washington Post* to publish his notorious publish or perish "manifesto." As Kaczynski explained, "In order to get our message before the public with some chance of making a lasting impression, we've had to kill people." Such behavior at these various levels of personal and public is most significant in the assessment of risk posed by suspects.

- *Suicidal tendencies.* Suicide or suicidal gestures are often a form of attention-seeking behavior. Five of the twelve modern subjects — Oswald, Bremer, Byck, Hinckley, and Duran — displayed moderate to strong suicidal tendencies. Indeed the assassination attempts of Bremer, Byck, Hinckley and Duran can be considered suicidal acts because all intended to die. One can only speculate about whether McVeigh and Kaczynski might have contemplated suicide during their periods of deepest depression. Kaczynski's suicide attempt after his arrest was of a different sort, that is, an alternative to spending the rest of his life in prison. Information of this type is difficult to obtain on suspects. Police and medical records or the reports of family members or friends are the only sources of such evidence. Oswald, Bremer, and Hinckley also stated their intentions in diaries; Byck did the same on tape.

9/11

Obviously, none of these indicators taken alone is very revealing of anything, let alone a suspect's potential for harming others or themselves. Countless numbers of Americans possess many of these characteristics and are not dangerous. It is an unknown combination and occurrence of these circumstances in a person's life that form a volatile and potentially lethal mass that may signal danger, or so it seems for the dangerous subjects of this book. There are several limitations of this approach that critics will be quick to point out: First, the relatively small number of subjects and the absence of a control group. Certainly the relatively small number of only twenty-one subjects contrasts sharply with the thousands of suspects who probably have been investigated by the Secret Service, and the unknown number, drawn from that total, who at any one time are considered dangerous and placed on a "watch list" for protective surveillance. But these twenty-one indivduals are more significant than any of the rest because they *acted.* There is also no control group. But, how does one define a valid control group for such a diverse lot? No one knows. Finally, the risk of false-positive errors (i.e., concluding a suspect is dangerous, when he or she is not) is significant. But the possibility of mistakenly detaining a suspect for up to seventy-two hours, has to be weighed against the false-negative assessments of the past that, as we have seen, enabled Lee Harvey Oswald, Arthur Bremer, Samuel Byck, Lynette Fromme, Sara Jane Moore, and John Hinckley — all of whom were known to authorities at some level — to strike. In a small way, this book is simply an attempt to connect what might be some potentially significant dots.

Overshadowing these sad events in American history, however, are the Islamic terrorist attacks on the World Trade Center, the Pentagon, and probably the U.S. Capitol on September 11, 2001, which claimed nearly 3,000 lives. Since that date, attacks like those described in these pages have lost some resonance in the array of things Americans are concerned about — even the Murrah Building explosion and the reasons for it, Waco and Ruby Ridge. As I write these words, controversy continues over how and why "9/11" happened. Reports of "intelligence failures" — authorities who ignored sometimes subtle, sometimes powerful clues of the unfolding terrorist plot have been exposed in Phoenix and Minneapolis; there were other lapses among those who, as congressional critics claim, were unable to "connect the dots" that would have defined the looming tragedy that was about to occur. Such criticism continues amid a growing public demand for evidence that, at this writing, the Bush administration seems hesitant to release. Assessing risk is an exceedingly difficult, multifaceted enterprise based on access to information, the ability to process and interpret it, science, intuition, and luck. Now the reality of so-called "sleeper cells" of Islamic terrorists — both foreign—and native-born — on American soil heighten the danger. And there are no perfect methodologies to assist in the daunting task of identifying and apprehending them, for even experts disagree.

But when we try to comprehend the consuming hatred that motivated the nineteen Middle Eastern young men who killed themselves in those attacks, it may be useful to reflect on another young Arab's words, "Kennedy, you sonofabitch," as Sirhan Sirhan pressed the barrel of a pistol into the senator's ear more than thirty years before. The central issue was the same — United States foreign policy in the Middle East. When we marvel at the satanic ingenuity of those devastating attacks, it may be useful to remember that the idea originated with an American on February 22, 1974, when Sam Byck failed in his attempt to crash-dive a Delta jetliner into the White House. There was no defense then either, maybe because we believed that no one was that crazy. Now we know better. So what might the motives and crimes of Timothy McVeigh and Ted Kaczynski reveal now, for example, about the future of political violence in America? Maybe nothing, but no one can be sure.

Scholars have distinguished between political terror and other forms of random terror; and between group-initiated acts and terror initiated by individuals.[4] But such distinctions have now become less useful in the American context. The essence of terror, whatever its origins, is random acts of violence that may occur without warning, anytime and anywhere. The purpose of terrorist attacks is to instill fear with their randomness and to immobilize potential victims with a profound sense of vulnerability. In these circumstances, Who's next? is a question never far from one's thoughts, affecting every aspect of a person's life. Knowing that question is being asked provides the terrorist with an exhilarating sense of power; the violent act itself ensures the satisfying notoriety that is the companion of such power, whether it is a terrorist group like the Ku Klux Klan in decades past, striking fear in the hearts of Southern blacks as it lynched thousands; or a serial killer like Daniel Yates, who for years terrorized women in Spokane, claiming the lives of thirteen before he was finally arrested; or the two serial snipers, John Mohammad and Lee Malvo, who for three weeks in 2002 randomly shot and killed ten strangers, wounding three others, terrorizing the suburbs of the nation's capitol.

The distinction between personal and political has become blurred in America, for as Lee Harvey Oswald wrote in his diary decades ago, "There is no borderline between one's personal world and the world in general." Although Oswald could not have known, he was — with those words — anticipating the modern era of American assassinations that began on November 22, 1963. The unprecedented number of Type II and Type III assassins and would-be assassins who followed in his footsteps underscore his point.

Now confronted with the unprecedented security that protects presidents and other nationally prominent political figures, it appears that such persons — primarily motivated by personal issues rather than politics, but *not* necessarily suicidal — may follow the lead of Ted Kaczynski, Timothy McVeigh, and Eric Rudolph, choosing as victims more accessible ordinary men, women and children instead of prominent political figures. Recall that Type III subjects of the past considered mass murder before choosing assassination and, also, that McVeigh considered assassinating Attorney General Jane Reno, among others, before choosing mass murder. And no one knows who Rudolph planned to attack with the more than two hundred pounds of explosives he had when he was captured. But unlike their earlier counterparts who were suicidal and intended to die with their victims, there is now the added danger that this new breed of killer — like Kaczynski, McVeigh, and Rudolph — tries to avoid death or capture to savor the notoriety and fear his crimes have generated, despite the personal anonymity required to ensure their continuation.

Notes

1. This excludes the assassination of Martin Luther King, Jr. by James Earl Ray, a contract killer.
2. One partial exception is Russell Weston's shooting spree in the Capitol in 1998. But it is not clear who Weston's intended victims were. Records and evidence in Weston's case remain sealed by the Court.
3. See, for example, J. Monahan, "Predicting Violent Behavior: A Review and Critique of Clinical Prediction Studies," in J. Takeuchi, F. Solomon, and W. W. Menninger (eds.), *Behavioral Science and the Secret Service* (Washington, DC: National Academy Press, 1981), 129–132.
4. See, for example, I.L. Horowitz, "The Texture of Terrorism: Socialization, Routinization, and Integration," in R.S. Siegel (ed.) *Political Learning in Adulthood: A Sourcebook of Theory and Research* (Chicago: University of Chicago Press, 1989), 386–414.

Epilogue

It was mid-morning on January 8, 2011, a bright sunny day in Tucson, Arizona, and I had just returned home after a walk with my dog. I picked up the grocery list my wife had left on the table and was about to drive the short distance to the local Safeway when I heard sirens and helicopters. Then I noticed traffic was backed up on the road leading to the store. I assumed it was a bad wreck and decided to wait. I turned on the radio and that's when I heard a news report that there had been a mass shooting in Tucson where Congresswoman Gabrielle Giffords and others had been gunned down as she met with constituents outside the Safeway store I was about to visit.

Early reports that Giffords had been killed were wrong. She survived, but in critical condition with a bullet that pierced her left forehead and passed through her brain. She faces a long and challenging recovery. I have never met Giffords, but I have voted for her, seen her more than once as she met with constituents outside that Safeway, and was aware of the vitriol directed at her during her recent re-election campaign. For someone who has spent a career writing about such events, the proximity of this incident was particularly poignant.

Giffords, the primary target, was shot first. But as the shooter turned his attention and his 9 mm Glock pistol toward others, six others were killed, including a little nine-year-old girl, one of Giffords' aides, and a federal judge. Thirty-one rounds were fired, wounding thirteen more people before two bystanders wrestled the shooter to the ground as he attempted to reload with another extended thirty-one round magazine.

The shooter, Jared Lee Loughner, was a twenty-three-year-old college dropout with a troubled past reminiscent of Type III nihilists, such as Arthur Bremer and John Hinckley. When police arrived and took him into custody, he said, "I plead the Fifth." A photo, which appeared nationwide in newspapers and on the Internet, was taken as he was booked into the Pima County jail; it shows a young man, head shaved, with a smirk below eyes radiating weirdness and what looks like satisfaction. On May 25, following weeks of clinical evaluation, Christina Pietz, a psychologist appointed by the prosecution, and Matthew Carroll, a psychiatrist appointed by Federal District Court Judge Larry A. Burns, both agreed that Loughner was schizophrenic and not mentally competent to stand trial. The judge ordered Loughner to undergo treatment for at least four months at a federal psychiatric facility in Springfield, Missouri, to determine whether he can be rendered competent to stand trial.[1]

Defining Danger

Whatever is ultimately decided about Loughner's mental state and thus his accountability, one of the tragedies of this case is that there was abundant evidence of his mental deterioration prior to the incident. His advancing dangerousness was ignored by authorities and everyone who had contact with him in the months preceding the shooting.

In the previous chapter, four anger-engagement indicators were identified that, combined with five depression-disengagement indicators, define the danger represented by an individual who, as a result of his or her conduct, comes to the attention of authorities—as Loughner did repeatedly in the months preceding the shooting. Although police and court records remain sealed at this writing, some tentative conclusions can be drawn. Perhaps the most egregious failure can be attributed to authorities at Pima Community College where Loughner had five contacts with campus police for classroom disruptions, threats, and an eerie video he made late at night, while wandering through the campus, during which he claimed the college was committing "genocide." Loughner was ultimately dismissed and barred from classes with a stipulation that he undergo a mental evaluation showing he was not a danger to himself or others before he could be considered for readmission. But no further action was taken, no evaluation occurred, and no treatment was sought for him.[2] What were his parents thinking? Had someone been concerned enough to address this angry young man's disturbing behavior, they would have discovered that Loughner had passed the superficial state background check and had purchased a deadly 9 mm Glock semi-automatic, two high-capacity thirty-one round magazines, two fifteen round magazines, and enough ammunition to load them. And, in Arizona, Loughner could legally carry a concealed weapon anywhere without a permit.

After viewing Loughner's troubling on-campus video, it doesn't require much imagination to believe that he probably considered a mass shooting on the Pima Community College campus, similar to those which occurred at Columbine or Virginia Tech, before he turned his attention to Gabrielle Giffords. Recall that both Type IIIs, Arthur Bremer and John Hinckley, considered mass murder before focusing on their ultimate political victims. Consider the following indicators of dangerousness as they relate to Jared Lee Loughner:

Anger-Engagement Indicators

- Ideological intensity. There is indisputable evidence here. A persistent anti-government refrain characterizes Loughner's otherwise incoherent political views displayed in numerous Internet postings. A believer in conspiracy theories, on YouTube he posted bizarre rants about his desire to establish a new currency because he believed "Government Officials" were involved in a conspiracy to manipulate money to defraud him and an illiterate public through "mind control and brain wash methods." He asked a staff member at the YMCA where he worked out "about the government taking over."[3] He believed a majority of people who resided in his congressional district were illiterate. Elsewhere, he blamed the Army for judging him unfit for service when he tried to enlist. At one point, he warned, "I'm ready to kill a police officer."[4] Perhaps the most vivid evidence of his hostility toward the government was a YouTube video showing a figure, presumably himself, cloaked in a black hooded robe, burning an American flag, accompanied by the lyrics, "Let the bodies hit the floor" playing in the background. Another MySpace posting shows a photo of a 9 mm Glock pistol—presumably the murder weapon—superimposed on a document entitled "United States History."

- Interest in an intended victim. There is clear evidence here. Loughner was a registered Independent voter in Giffords' district, had voted in 2006 and 2008, but not 2010,[5] and had attended at least one of her earlier gatherings with constituents. At that gathering, he asked Giffords a question and was unhappy with her response. Later, he received a form letter from her, as did everyone who registered at these gatherings, thanking him for his interest. The letter, which he considered unresponsive to his concerns, angered him. When FBI investigators searched Loughner's home after the shooting, they found an envelope containing handwritten notes with these words, "I planned ahead," "My assassination," "die bitch," "assassination plans have been made," and "Giffords."[6]
- Interest in prior assassinations or violent crimes. There is compelling evidence here. In the days and weeks before the assassination attempt, investigators found that Loughner had surfed the Internet to view sites on political assassins, the death penalty, solitary confinement, and the process of lethal injection, to inform himself about the history and consequences of what he was planning to do.[7]
- Stalking. There is no evidence that Loughner stalked Giffords prior to the shooting, although it is not known what he may have had in mind when he attended her earlier Congress on the Corner gathering.

Depression-Disengagement Indicators

- Occupational Instability. There is clear evidence of this. After he dropped out of school, Loughner was never able to hold a job and seemingly gave up looking for work. He was fired from his job at a Quiznos restaurant. Later he was asked to leave a county animal shelter where he had volunteered because he wouldn't follow instructions.[8]
- Transience. This was not a factor. Except for one very brief period in an apartment, he lived at home with his parents.
- Family estrangement. This seems to have been the case. Although Loughner lived at home, those who knew him said his relationship with his parents was distant and troubled. Friends said it was characterized by shouting matches, strange absences, and runaway attempts.[9] A young

woman, who had befriended Loughner in high school said, "I know he had a difficult relationship with his parents. They would never let me come in the house, and I couldn't understand why they wouldn't let me come in. ... I honestly think he had some sort of definite dysfunction in his family, like his parents were just there but lacked [a] parental role in [his] life." [10] Neighbors described the parents as reclusive. No one really knew them. One neighbor said Loughner's father seemed "angry," and was unfriendly. But another called him a good neighbor "who doesn't talk to you and doesn't borrow." Another described the Loughner home as "an elaborate cage" concealed by a wooden barricade that blocked views of the front door and windows. Windows in the garage were covered and a block wall enclosed the back yard.[11]

- Attention-seeking behavior. There is indisputable evidence of this. Loughner's many YouTube and MySpace postings were pleas for attention. According to fellow students at Pima Community College, he repeatedly disrupted classes with bizarre outbursts and attempts to draw attention to himself.[12] One of his instructors said, "I was getting concerned about the safety of the students and the school. I was afraid he was going to pull out a weapon." A student in one of his classes emailed, "We do have one student in the class who was disruptive today, I'm not certain yet if he was on drugs (as one person surmised) or disturbed. He scares me a bit. ... The teacher tried to throw him out and he refused to go, so I talked to the teacher afterward. Hopefully, he will be out of class soon, and not come back with an automatic weapon."[13] A friend of Loughner's reported that he liked to provoke people. "I think the reason he did it was just to create chaos. He wanted the media to freak out about this whole thing. He wanted exactly what's happening [attention]."[14] Within a month prior to the shooting, Loughner posted this statement on MySpace: "WOW! I'm glad i didn't kill myself. I'll see you on National T.v.! This is a foreshadow. ... why doesn't anyone talk to me?"[15]

- Suicidal tendencies. There is strong evidence of this. Loughner probably expected to die in his attack. He had no plan or means to flee. Just hours before his attack, Loughner left a cell phone message for a friend: "Hey Bryce, it's Jared. We had some good times together. Peace out." About the same time, he typed a farewell message, including a photo of himself, on his MySpace page: "Goodbye, friends."[16]

Thus on an index of dangerousness, Jared Loughner's positives on seven of the nine indicators suggest a very dangerous person indeed. Yet, despite all the warning signs, Loughner was evaluated and treated only once by mental health professionals, and that was when he showed up intoxicated at his high school some six years before. After that, this angry, paranoid, extremely volatile person was never evaluated or treated and—with no difficulty—was able to purchase the deadly semi-automatic weapon and extended magazines that he used to kill six people and wound thirteen others in one final spasm of anger. Or was it craziness?

Criminal Responsibility

At this writing, Loughner is undergoing psychiatric treatment. A determination of his fitness to stand trial is not known. Whether he was psychotic or not, few could disagree that Loughner was a very disturbed individual when he opened fire at the Safeway.

Insanity was an issue in the trials of Richard Lawrence, Charles Guiteau, John Schrank, Ted Kaczynski, Arthur Bremer, and John Hinckley, Jr. Whether or not Jared Loughner is held responsible for his actions and executed as was Charles Guiteau; sentenced to years or life in prison as were Arthur Bremer and Ted Kaczynski; or acquitted by reason of insanity, as were Richard Lawrence, John Schrank and John Hinckley, and confined to a mental hospital for years and, perhaps, the rest of his life, remains to be seen.

Loughner's fate depends largely on the standard being used to make that judgment. Loughner would almost certainly be considered criminally responsible using the traditional M'Naghten standard: Did the defendant know what he was doing at the time the crime was committed? And did he know that his actions were unlawful? But a conviction is problematic under the more lenient diminished capacity standard that holds a person cannot be held accountable for his actions if at the time of such conduct, he lacks substantial capacity either to appreciate the criminality of his conduct or to conform his conduct to the requirements of the law. In the foregoing analysis, the evidence is beyond doubt that Loughner's actions were premeditated. He intended to kill and he understood the consequences. That conclusion is also supported by the evidence of his actions in the hours leading up to the shooting: [17]

- At 11:35 p.m., on the night before the shooting, he dropped off a roll of 35 mm film to be developed at Walgreens.
- Sometime after that, he stopped at a Circle K convenience store and then checked into a Motel 6 where, it appears, he never returned.
- At 1:45 a.m., he returned to his parents home where he presumably made a call leaving a final cell phone message for an old friend: "Hey Bryce, it's Jared. We had some good times together. Peace out."
- At 2:19 a.m., he returned to Walgreens, picked up his photos, and then stopped to make other purchases at a convenience store.
- At 4:12 a.m., at an unknown location, Loughner typed the message "Goodbye friends" on his MySpace page and included a photo he had just had developed.
- At 6:12 a.m., he stopped at a Walmart near his home and tried to buy ammunition, but was told ammunition could be sold only after 7 a.m.
- At 7:04 a.m., he returned to the store but did not make a purchase. Instead, he drove five miles in his 1969 Chevy Nova to another Walmart superstore where he purchased 9 mm ammunition and a black backpack style bag.

- At 7:30 a.m., he was stopped and given a warning for running a red light.
- Around 8 a.m., he returned home, had a brief argument with his father, and then ran off and disappeared in the desert behind the house. Ultimately, he made his way back to the Circle K he had visited earlier. There he called a cab.
- At 9:41 a.m., the cab picked him up and took him to the Safeway.
- At the Safeway, he entered the store and got change for a twenty dollar bill to pay the cabdriver, who then drove away.

A witness to the attack said that when Loughner came out of the Safeway he got in a line of people waiting to greet Giffords near the entryway. Loughner asked a Giffords volunteer, "Can I talk to the congresswoman?" He was told it would be about twenty minutes, and to wait in the line. When Giffords appeared, Loughner left the back of the line, walked to within a few feet of her, raised the pistol to her face, and pulled the trigger. "He was intent when he came back," the witness said, and had "a pretty stone-cold glance and glare. ... I didn't see his gun, but it was clear who he was going for. He was going for the congresswoman."[18]

Loughner was wearing earplugs and had $93 in cash in a plastic bag, a Visa card, a four-inch buck knife, and extra ammunition in his pocket when he was arrested.[19] He had contemplated his actions, wore earplugs to protect his ears, paid the driver, and sent the cab away. He did not intend to flee.

So was Jared Lee Loughner mad when he attacked Gabrielle Giffords and others on January 8, 2011, or was he merely angry? Loughner differs from his Type III predecessors who were focused only on their intended victims—although others were injured—such as Bremer on Governor Wallace and Hinckley on President Reagan. It is true that, like Bremer and Hinckley, Loughner was seeking notoriety but, unlike them, attempting to kill the politician he hated was not enough for Loughner. After shooting Giffords in the face, he turned his weapon on innocent bystanders, including a little girl. His actions were without purpose or remorse. In this, they recall Timothy McVeigh's remorseless antigovernment rage and mass murder of innocent men, women, and children in Oklahoma City.

Two unchallenged diagnoses of Loughner by mental health experts concluded that he suffers from paranoid schizophrenia characterized by bizarre behavior and delusions of persecution and grandeur. But how is it that this killer whose illness renders him incompetent to stand trial—unable to participate in his own defense—was still able to premeditate, plan, and willfully harm so many innocent victims as he did on January 8, 2011?

That said, it seems certain that Loughner got what he wanted, what Type III assassins seek—notoriety. As he predicted on MySpace, "I'll see you on National T.v." He was right: that happened, and not only on national television. His notorious photo lit up the Internet and appeared on the front pages of newspapers around the world. But it also seems certain that whatever the final determination of his mental state, Jared Lee Loughner will probably be permanently removed from society. It may be in a prison cell, or a mental institution for the criminally insane, or on a gurney with a needle in his arm but, if justice is served, he will harm no one again.

Notes

1. M. Lacey, "Loughner Ruled Incompetent For Trial in Tucson Shootings," New York Times, May 26, 2011, A1.
2. T. Steller, "Dupnik: suspect is mentally unstable," Arizona Daily Star, January 9, 2011, A5; "Suspect faced no legal barrier to buying a gun at local store," Arizona Daily Star, January 10, 2011, A2; Associated Press, "PCC officials were told to watch for Loughner," Arizona Daily Star, February 16, 2011, A1.
3. K. Johnson, S. F. Kovaleski, D. Frosch, and E. Lipton, "Alarm Grew at Suspect's Disturbing Behavior," New York Times, January 10, 2011, A1.
4. Ibid.
5. T. Steller, "Dupnik suspect."
6. M. Lacey, "Congresswoman's Condition Is Critical," New York Times, January 10, 2011, A1; http:www.cnn.com/2011/CRIME/01/12/arizona.shooting.suspect/; K. Smith, "Judge orders Loughner to undergo psych exam," Arizona Daily Star, March 10, 2011, A1.
7. J. Goldstein and M. Lacey, "Man Charged in Tucson Shootings Had Researched Assassins, Official Says," New York Times, January 27, 2011, A14; http://washingtonpost.com/wp-dyn/content/article/2011/01/26/AR2011012603159.ht . . .
8. G. Strauss, P. Eisler, J. Gillum, W. M. Welch, http://tucsoncitizen.com/usa-today-news/2011/01/10/friends-co-workers-loughner-had-curious-dark-change.
9. R. Anglen, "Portrait of Jared Loughner's parents emerges," http://www.azcentral.com/arizonarepublic/news/articles/2011/01/22/20110122gabrielle-giffords.
10. J. Waldman, http://www.kgun9.com/Global/story.asp?S=13834898.
11. K. Johnson et al., "Alarm Grew." http://www.dailymail.co.uk/news/article-1358735/Arizona-shooting-suspect-Jared-Loughner.
12. Ibid.
13. K. Johnson, et al, "Alarm Grew."
14. N. Baumann, http://motherjones.com/politics/2011/01jared-lee-loughner-friend-voicemail-phone-messag . .
15. J. Pritchard and M. R. Blood, www.huffingtonpost.com/2011/01/15/jared-loughners-chaotic-i_n_809525.html.
16. Ibid.
17. J. Prtichard and M. R. Blood, http://huffingtonpost.com/2011/01/15/jared-loughners-chaotic-i_n_809525.html.
18. P. Finley, "'It was clear who (gunman) was going for,' witness says," Arizona Daily Star, Janurary 9, 2011, A5.
19. K. Smith, "Judge orders Loughner to undergo psych exam," Arizona Daily Star, March 10, 2011, A1.

Selected Bibliography

General

Books and Articles

Clarke, J.W. 1982. American Assassins: The Darker Side of Politics. Princeton, NJ: Princeton University Press.

Clarke, J.W. 1990. On Being Mad Or Merely Angry: John W. Hinckley, Jr. And Other Dangerous People. Princeton, NJ: Princeton University Press.

Dollard, J.; Doob, L.; Miller, N.; Mowrer, O.; and Sears, R. 1939. Frustration and Aggression. New Haven: Yale University Press.

Donovan, R. J. 1952. The Assassins. New York: Harper & Brothers.

Freedman, L.Z. 1965. "Assassination: Psychopathology and Social Pathology." Post graduate Medicine 37 (June): 650–658.

Hassel, C.V. 1974. "The Political Assassin." Journal of Police Science and Administration 4 (December): 399–403.

Hastings, D.W. 1965. "The Psychiatry of Presidential Assassination, Part I: Jackson and Lincoln." The Journal-Lancet 85 (March): 93–100.

Hastings, D.W. 1965. "The Psychiatry of Presidential Assassination, Part II: Garfield and McKinley." The Journal-Lancet 85 (April): 157–162.

Hastings, D.W. 1965. "The Psychiatry of Presidential Assassination, Part III: The Roosevelts." The Journal-Lancet 85 (May): 189–192.

Hastings, D.W. 1965. "The Psychiatry of Presidential Assassination, Part IV: Truman and Kennedy." The Journal-Lancet 85 (July): 294–301.

Horowitz, I.L. 1989. "The Texture of Terrorism: Socialization, Routinization, and Integration," in R.S. Siegel (Ed.). Political Learning in Adulthood: A Sourcebook of Theory and Research. Chicago: University of Chicago Press.

Lasswell, H. D. 1948. Power and Personality. New York: The Viking Press.

Slomich, S.J. and R.E. Kantor. 1969. "Social Psychopathology of Political Assassination." Bulletin of Atomic Scientists 25 (March): 9–17.

Weisz, A.E. and R.L. Taylor. 1969. "American Presidential Assassinations." Diseases of the Nervous System. 30 (October): 658–659.

Government Publications

Fein, R.A. and B. Vossekuil. 1998. Protective Intelligence and Threat Assessment Investigations: A Guide for State and Local Law Enforcement Officials. Washington, DC: U.S. Department of Justice Office of Justice Programs (July).

Institute of Medicine. 1984. Research and Training for the Secret Service: Behavioral Science and Mental Health Perspectives. Washington, DC: National Academy Press (February).

Kirkham, J.F., S.G. Levy, and W.J. Crotty. 1970. Assassination and Political Violence: A Report to the National Commission on the Causes and Prevention of Violence. New York: Praeger and the New York Times.

Takeuchi, J., F. Solomon, and W.W. Menninger (Eds.). 1981. Behavioral Science and the Secret Service: Toward the Prevention of Assassination. Washington, DC: Institute of Medicine/National Academy Press.

Statutes and Court Cases

Daniel M'Naghten's Case (1843). 10 Clark and Fin. 200, 8 Eng. Rep. 718.
Model Penal Code (1962). American Law Institutue, P.O.D.

John Wilkes Booth

Books and Articles

Beard, C. A., and Beard, M. R. 1927. The Rise of American Civilization. New York: Macmillan & Co.

Brock, W.R. 1973. Conflict and Transformation: The United States, 18441877. New York: Penguin Books.

Clarke, A.B. 1882. The Elder and the Younger Booth. Boston: James R. Osgood & Co.

Clarke, A.B. 1938 [orig., 1888]. The Unlocked Book. New York: G. P. Putnam's Sons.

Cottrell, J. 1966. Anatomy o f an Assassination. London: Frederick Muller

Davis, J. 1881. The Rise and Fall of the Confederate Government. Reprint 1958. 2 vols. South Brunswick, N.J.: Thomas Yoseloff.

Donald, D. 1961. Lincoln Reconsidered. New York: Vintage Books.

Dusinbeere, W. 1965. Civil War Issues in Pennsylvania. Philadelphia: University of Pennsylvania Press.

Eisenschiml, O. 1937. Why Was Lincoln Murdered? Boston: Little, Brown.

Headley, J. 1873. The Great Riots of New York, 1712 to 1873. Reprint 1971. New York: Dover.

Hyams, E. 1969. Killing No Murder. Camden, N.J.: Thomas Nelson & Sons.

Kimmel, S. 1940. The Mad Booths o f Maryland. Reprint 1969. New York: Dover.

Mahoney, E. V. 1925. Sketches of Tudor Hall and the Booth Family. Belair, Md.: Ella V. Mahoney.

Morris, C. 1901. Life on the Stage. New York: McClure, Phillips & Co.

Pitman, B. 1865. *The Assassination of President Lincoln and the Trial of the Conspirators: The Courtroom Testimony.* Reprint 1954. New York: Funk & Wagnalls.
Randall, J.G. 1937. *The Civil War and Reconstruction.* Boston and New York: D. C. Heath.
Randall, J.G. 1947. *Lincoln the Liberal Statesman.* New York: Dodd, Mead & Co.
Royster, C. 1991. *The Destructive War.* New York: Alfred A. Knopf.
Weichmann, L, J. 1865. *A True History of the Assassination of Abraham Lincoln and the Conspiracy of 1865.* Reprint 1975. F. E. Risvold (ed.). New York: Vintage Books.
Weissman, P. 1958. "Why Booth Shot Lincoln." In Psychoanalysis and the Social Sciences, vol. 5. New York: International Universities Press: 99–115..
Williams, T. H. 1941. Lincoln and the Radicals. Madison: University of Wisconsin Press.
Wilson, F. 1929. John Wilkes Booth. Reprint 1972. New York: Benjamin Bloom, Inc.
Wilson, G. W. 1940. "John Wilkes Booth: Father Murderer." The American IMAGO 1 (June): 49–60.

Government Documents and Publications

Diary of John Wilkes Booth. Attorney General's Papers, Lincoln Assassination, National Archives: RG No. 60.
"Investigation and Trial Papers Relating to the Assassination of President Lincoln." National Archives: Microfilm No. 599.
Letters of John Wilkes Booth. Attorney General's Papers, Lincoln Assassination, National Archives: RG No. 60.

Newpapers

Chicago Times 1865. (March).
Daily National Intelligencer. 1865.
New Orleans Times. 1865 (March).
Washington Evening Star. 1865 (April).

Leon F. Czolgosz

Books and Articles

Adler, S. 1963. "The Operation on President McKinley." Scientific American 208 (March): 118–130.
Bell, T. 1941. Out of the Furnace. 1941. Reprint 1976. Pittsburgh: University of Pittsburgh Press.
Briggs, L. V. 1921. The Manner of Man that Kills. Boston: The Gorham Press.
Bruce, R. V. 1959. 1877: Year of Violence. Chicago: Quadrangle Books.
Charming, W. 1902. "The Mental State of Czolgosz, the Assassin of President McKinley." The American Journal of Insanity 59 (October): 233–278.

David, H. 1958. The History of the Haymarket Affair. 2d ed. New York: Russell & Russell.
Donovan, R. J. 1952. The Assassins. New York: Harper & Brothers.
Drinnon, R. 1961. Rebel in Paradise: A Biography of Emma Goldman. Chicago: The University of Chicago Press.
Fine, S. 1955. "Anarchism and the Assassination of McKinley." American Historical Review 60 (July): 777–799.
Foner, P.S. 1977. The Great Labor Uprising of 1877. New York: Monad Press.
Goldman, E. 1906. "The Tragedy at Buffalo." Mother Earth 1 (October): 11–16.
Goldman, E. 1931. Living My Life. Garden City, N.Y.: Garden City Publishing Co.
Greene, V.R. 1968. The Slavic Community on Strike. Notre Dame, Ind.: University of Notre Dame Press.
Hamilton, A. M. 1916. Recollections of an Alienist. New York: George H. Dolan.
Hastings, D. W. 1965. "The Psychiatry of Presidential Assassination, Part II: Garfield and McKinley." The Journal-Lancet 85 (April): 157–162.
Hughes, C. H. 1902. "Medical Aspects of the Czolgosz Case." Alienist and Neurologist 23 (January): 40–52.
Johns, A. W. 1970. The Man Who Shot McKinley. South Brunswick and New York: A. S. Barnes.
Key, V. O. 1955. "A Theory of Critical Elections." The Journal of Politics 17 (February): 3–18.
Leech, M. 1959. In the Days of McKinley. New York: Harper & Row.
Lindsey, A. 1942. The Pullman Strike. Chicago: The University of Chicago Press.
MacDonald, C.F. 1902. "The Trial, Execution, Autopsy and Mental Status of Leon F. Czolgosz, Alias Fred Nieman, the Assassin of President McKinley." The American Journal of Insanity 58 (January): 369–386.
McKinley, J. 1977. Assassination in America. New York: Harper & Row.
Novak, M. 1978. The Guns of Lattimer. New York: Basic Books.
Rayback, J.G. 1959. A History of American Labor. New York: The Free Press.
Spitzka, E.A. 1902. "The Post-Mortem Examination of Leon F. Czolgosz, the Assassin of President McKinley." American Journal of Insanity 58 (January): 386–388.

Government Documents and Publications

Fowler, J., F.S. Crego, and J.W. Putnam. 1901. "Official Report of the Experts for the People in the Case of the People v. Leon F. Czolgosz." Reprint 1923. J.D. Lawson (ed.), American State Trials, vol. 14. St. Louis: Thomas Law Book Co.: 195–199.
"Report of Dr. Carlos F. MacDonald and Dr. Arthur Hurd, Experts for the Prisoner" (1901). Reprint 1923. J.D. Lawson (ed.) American State Trials, vol. 14. St. Louis: Thomas Law Book Co.: 196–203.

Court Case

People v. Leon F. Czolgosz (1901). Courthouse Archives, Erie County, Buffalo, New York. Reprinted 1923. J. D. Lawson (ed.), American State Trials, vol. 14. St. Louis: Thomas Law Book Co: 159–231.

Newspaper

Cleveland Plain Dealer. 1901 (May).

Oscar Collazo and Griselio Torresola

Government Documents and Publications

"Incidents Preceding November 1,1950, Attempted Assassination of President Truman." Federal Bureau of Investigation, File No. 62–7721–1695.
"Nationalist Party of Puerto Rico." Federal Bureau of Investigation, File No. 100–7689.
"Origin of Nationalist Party of Puerto Rico (NPPR), Including the Rise of Pedro Albizu Campos." Federal Bureau of Investigation, Document 9450590–2.
Puerto Rican Nationalists, Oscar Collazo. Federal Bureau of Investigation, File No. 3–36-A, November-December 1950.

Court Case

United States v. Oscar Collazo (1951). United States District Court for the District of Columbia.

Newspapers

Chicago Daily News. 1950 (November).
New York Times. 1979 (September, December).

Sirhan Bishara Sirhan

Books and Articles

Jansen, G. 1970. Why Robert Kennedy Was Killed. New York: The Third Press.
Kaiser, R. B. 1970. "RFK Must Die!" A History of the Robert Kennedy Assassination and its Aftermath. New York: Dutton, 1970.
McKinley, J. 1978. "Inside Sirhan." Playboy (April).
Rovere, R.H. 1960. Senator Joe McCarthy. New York: World Publishing.

Court Case

The People of the State of California v. Sirhan Bishara Sirhan (1969). Superior Court, Crim. Case No. 14026.

Newspapers

Arizona Daily Star. 1980 (September).
New York Times. 1970 (September).

Tucson Daily Citizen. 1981 (February).
Washington Post. 1979 (August).

Lee Harvey Oswald

Books

Lasswell, H. D. Power and Personality. 1948. Reprint 1962.. New York: The Viking Press.
McMillan, P. J. 1977. Marina and Lee. 1977. Reprint 1978. New York: Bantam.
Posner, G. 1993. Case Closed. New York: Random House.
Schorr, D. 1977. Clearing the Air. Boston: Houghton Mifflin.

Government Documents and Publications

President's Commission on the Assassination of President Kennedy. Hearings on the Investigation of the Assassination of President John F. Kennedy. 1964. vols. 1–26. Washington, D.C.: U.S. Government Printing Office.
Report of the President's Commission on the Assassination of President John F. Kennedy. 1964. Washington, D.C.: U.S. Government Printing Office.
U.S. Congress, House, Select Committee on Assassinations. Hearings on the Investigation of the Assassination of President John F. Kennedy. 1978. vols. 1–12. 95th Cong., 2d Sess.
U.S. Congress, House, Select Committee on Assassinations. Report on Findings and Recommendations. 1979. HR 95–1828, part 2. 95th Cong., 2d Sess.
U.S. Congress, House, Subcommittee on Civil and Constitutional Rights of the Committee on the Judiciary. Hearings on Federal Bureau of Investigation Oversight. 1975–1976. Serial No. 2, pt. 3. 94th Cong., 1st and 2d Sess.

Newspaper

New Orleans Times-Picayune. 1963 (August-September).

Samuel Joseph Byck

Government Documents and Publications

Byck, S. 1974. Recorded Tapes. Federal Bureau of Investigation.
Byck, S. 1974. Department of Transportation, Federal Aviation Administration, Security Summary (SE–1600–20) ASE–74–4.
Byck, S. 1974. Federal Bureau of Investigation, File No. BA 164–170.
Byck, S. 1973. Federal Communications Commission, File Nos. 8310–100, C6–1833.
Byck, S. 1973. File. National Park Service, National Capital Parks.
Byck, S. 1974. File. Office of Pardon Attorney, U.S. Department of Justice (January 9).
Byck, S. 1973. File. Small Business Administration.
Byck, S. 1972–1974. File. United States Secret Service.

Newspapers

New York Times. 1974. (February-March).
Philadelphia Inquirer. 1974 (February).
Washington Post. 1974. (February-March).
Washington Star. 1974. (February-March).

Lynette Alice Fromme

Book

Bugliosi, V., with C. Gentry. 1974. Helter Skelter. New York: W. W. Norton & Co.

Court Case

United States v. Lynette Alice Fromme (1975). United States District Court for the Eastern District of California, CR. No. 575–451, vols. 1–10.

Unpublished Document

Fromme, L. Untitled Manuscript.

Newspaper

Sacramento Bee. 1975 (September).

Sara Jane Moore

Article

Moore, S. J. 1976. "Playboy Interview." Playboy (June).

Newspapers and Periodicals

Charleston (West Virginia) Gazette. 1975. (September).
Los Angeles Times. 1975. (September).
Newsweek. 1975 (September).

Giuseppe Zangara

Government Documents

Zangara. G. 1933. Federal Bureau of Investigation, File No. 6228219–1–61.
Zangara, G. 1933. Sworn Statement of Joseph Zangara. Federal Bureau of Investigation. Miami, Dade County, Florida (February 16).

Newspapers

Miami Herald. 1933. (February-March).
Newark Evening News. 1933. (February-March).

Arthur Herman Bremer

Books and Articles

Bremer, A.H. 1972. An Assassin's Diary. New York: Harper & Row.
Camus, A. 1946. The Stranger. New York: Alfred A. Knopf.
Dostoyevsky, F. 1969. *Notes From Underground*. R. G. Durgy. (ed.). New York: Thomas Y. Crowell.
Kaiser, R. B. 1970. "RFK Must Die!": A History of the Robert Kennedy *Assassination and its Aftermath*. New York: Dutton.
Vidal, G. 1973. "Now for the Shooting of George Wallace." *New York Review of Books* 20 (December 13,): 17–19.

Court Case

State of Maryland v. Arthur Herman Bremer (1972). Circuit Court for Prince George's County, Maryland, Crim. Tr. Nos. 12376–12379.

Statute

Annotated Code of Maryland.

Newspaper

Milwaukee Journal. 1972 (May).

John W. Hinckley, Jr.

Books and Articles

Hinckley, J.W. and J.A. Hinckley (with E. Sherrill). 1985. Breaking Points. Grand Rapids, MI: Chosen Books.

Court Case

United States v. John W. Hinckley, Jr. (1981). Cr. No. 81-3-306.

Government Documents and Publications

Hinckley, J.W., Jr. 1981. "Evidence from Evergreen, CO." Federal Bureau of Investigation, File No. 175-601.

Hinckley, J.W., Jr. 1981. "Arrest and Interview Log." Federal Bureau of Investigation, File No. 175–601.

Newspaper

Wall Street Journal. 1981 (April).

Francisco Martin Duran

Court Case

United States v. Francisco Martin Duran. 1996. Cr. No. 95–3096. U.S. District Court, District of Columbia, at *http://www.Fed-Ct/Circuit/dc/optinions/95–3096a.html*.

Government Documents and Publications

Duran, F.M. 1994. Federal Bureau of Investigation Report (October 17).
White House Security Report: Francisco Martin Duran. 1994. at *http://org/irp/agency/ustreas/usss/t1pubrpt.htm*.

Newspapers and Periodicals

Denver Post. 1994 (November).
Newsweek. 1994 (November—December).
New York Times. 1994 (November); 1995 (April).
Washington Post. 1995 (March).

Richard Lawrence

Articles and Chapters

Hastings, D. W. 1965. "The Psychiatry of Presidential Assassination, Part I: Jackson and Lincoln." The Journal-Lancet 85 (March): 93–100.
Jackson, C. 1967. "Another Time, Another Place – The Attempted Assassination of President Andrew Jackson." Tennessee Historical Quarterly 26 (Summer): 184–190.
Smith, W. R. (Ed.). 1881. "Trial of Richard Lawrence." In Assassination and Insanity: Guiteau's Case Examined and Compared with Analogous Cases from the Earlier to the Present Times. Washington, D.C.: 26–80.

Court Documents

United States v. Richard Lawrence 1835). Circuit Court, District of Columbia, Case No. 15,577; also, Niles Register. 1936. vol. 48.
Lawrence, Richard. Criminal Appearances 119. 1835. (March). United States District Court of the District of Columbia. National Archives, Record Group 21.

Newspaper

Daily National Intelligencer. 1835. (January, April).

Charles Julius Guiteau

Books and Articles

Folsom, C. F. 1909. Studies of Criminal Responsibility and Limited Responsibility. Boston: Privately printed.
Godding, W. W. 1882. Two Hard Cases: Sketcbes from a Physician's Portfolio. Boston: Houghton Mifflin.
Gray, J. P. 1882. "The United States vs. Charles J. Guiteau." American Journal of Insanity 38 (January): 303–448.
"Guiteau-Finis." 1882. Medical News 41 (July): 12.
Hamilton, A. M. 1882. "The Case of Guiteau." Boston Medical and Surgical journal 106 (March 9): 235–238.
Hamilton, A.M. 1916. Recollections of an Alienist. New York: George H. Doran.
Hastings, D. W. 1965. "The Psychiatry of Presidential Assassination, Part II: Garfield and McKinley." The Journal-Lancet 85 (April): 157–162.
Lawson, J. D., Ed. 1923. "The Trial of Charles J. Guiteau for the Murder of President Garfield." *In American State Trials.* Vol. 14. St. Louis: Thomas Law Book Co.
Mitchell, S. 1941–1944. "The Man Who Murdered Garfield." Proceedings of the Massachusetts Historical Society 68: 452–489.
Rosenberg, C. E. 1968. The Trial o f the Assassin Guiteau. Chicago: The University of Chicago Press.
Smith, W.R. 1881. Assassination and Insanity: Guiteau's Case Examined and Compared witb Analogous Cases from the Earlier to the Present Times. Washington, D.C.
Spitzka, E. C. 1883. "A Contribution to the Question of the Mental Status of Guiteau and the History of His Trial." Alienist and Neurologist 4 (April): 201–220.

Government Documents and Publications

Guiteau, Charles J. "The New York Theocrat" (prospectus). National Archives, File No. 14056.
Guiteau, J. W. "Letters and Facts Not Heretofore Published, Touching the Mental Condition of Charles J. Guiteau Since 1865. Document submitted to the President of the United States by John W. Guiteau in the Matter of Application for a Commission De Lunatico Inquirendo, June 23, 1882." National Archives, File No. 14056.
Guiteau, Charles J., Letters. National Archives, File No. 14056.

Court Case

United States v. Charles J. Guiteau (1882). Criminal Case No. 14056. Supreme Court of the District of Columbia. National Archives.

John Schrank

Books and Articles

Hastings, D. W. 1965. "The Psychiatry of Presidential Assassination, Part III: The Roosevelts." The Journal-Lancet 85 (May): 189–192.
MacDonald, A. 1914. "The Would-Be Assassin of Theodore Roosevelt." Medical Times 62 (April): 97–101.
Morison, E. E. (Ed.). 1951. The Letters of Theodore Roosevelt. Vol. 3. Cambridge, MA: Harvard University Press.
Mowry, G. E. 1958. The Era of Theodore Roosevelt and the Birth of Modern America. New York: Harper & Row.
Remy, O. E., H.F. Cochems, and W.P. Bloodgood. 1912. The Attempted Assassination of Ex-President Theodore Roosevelt. Milwaukee: The Progressive Publishing Co.

Newspapers

Chicago Tribune. 1912 (November).
Milwaukee Journal. 1912 (October-November).

Carl Austin Weiss

Books

Beals, C. 1935. The Story of Huey Long. New York: Lippincott.
Deutsch, H. B. 1963. The Huey Long Murder Case. Garden City, NY: Doubleday & Co.
Fields, H. 1944. The Life of Huey Pierce Long. Farmerville, La.: Fields Publishing Agency.
Havens, M. C., C. Leiden, and K.M. Schmitt. 1970. *The Politics of Assassination.* Englewood Cliffs, N.J.: Prentice-Hall, Inc.
Kane, H. 1941. Louisiana Hayride. New York: Morrow.
Key, V. O. 1949. Southern Politics in State and Nation. New York: Alfred A. Knopf.
Lesberg, S. 1976. Assassinations in Our Time. London: Peebles Press International and Bobbs-Merrill.
Luthin, R. H. 1954. American Demagogues. Boston: The Beacon Press.
Optowsky, S. 1960. The Longs of Louisiana. New York: Dutton.
Paine, L. 1975. The Assassins' World. New York: Taplinger Publishing Co.
Pearl, J.. The Dangerous Assassins. Derby, CT: Monarch Books.
Schlesinger, A. M., Jr. 1960. The Politics o f Upheaval. Vol. 3. Boston: Houghton Mifflin.
Sindler, A. P. 1956. Huey Longs Louisiana. Baltimore: Johns Hopkins University Press.
Warren, R. Penn. 1946. All The King's Men. New York: Harcourt, Brace & Co.
Williams, T. H. 1969. Huey Long. New York: Bantam Books.

Zinman, D. H. 1963. The Day Huey Long Was Shot. New York: Ivan Obolensky, Inc.

Newspapers

Baton Rouge Morning Advocate. 1935 (September-October).
Baton Rouge State-Times. 1935. (September-October).
New Orleans States Item. 1935. (September-October).
New Orleans Times-Picayune. 1935. (September-October).

James Earl Ray

Books and Articles

Arendt, H. 1965. Eichmann in Jerusalem: A Report on the Banality of Evil. New York: Viking Press.
Browning, C.R. 1992. Ordinary Men: Reserve Police Battalion 101 and the Final Solution in Poland. New York: Harper Collins.
Clarke, J.W. 1998. "Without Fear or Shame: Lynching, Capital Punishment, and the Subculture of Violence in the American South." British Journal of Political Science 28 (April): 269–289.
Clarke, J.W., and J.W. Soule. 1968. "Southern Children's Reactions to King's Death." Trans-Action 5 (October): 35–40.
Huie, W.B. 1970. He Slew the Dreamer. New York: Delacorte Press.
McMillan, G. 1976. The Making of an Assassin. Boston: Little Brown.
Milgram, S. 1974. Obedience to Authority: An Experimental View. New York: Harper & Row.

Government Documents and Publications

Congressional Quarterly. 1968. 4th ed. "Revolution in Civil Rights, 1945–1968." (June).
Report of the Department of Justice Task Force to Review the FBI Martin Luther King, Jr. Security and Assassination Investigations. 1977. Washington, D.C.: U.S. Department of Justice, (January 11).
U.S. Congress, House Select Committee on Assassinations. 1978. Hearings on the Investigation of the Assassination of Martin Luther King, Jr., vols. 1–12. 95th Cong., 2d Sess.
U.S. Congress, House, Select Committee on Assassinations. 1978. Compilation of the Statements of James Earl Ray. 95th Cong., 2d Sess. (August 18).
U.S. Congress, House Select Committee on Assassinations. 1979. Final Report of the Select Committee on Assassinations. 95th Cong., 2d Sess. (January 2).
U.S. Department of Justice Investigation of Recent Allegations Regarding the Assassination of Dr. Martin Luther King, Jr. 2000 (June) at http:www.usdoj.gov/crt/crim/mlk/part1.htm.

Newspaper

Arizona Daily Star. 1998 (April).
St. Louis Post-Dispatch. 1968. (June).

Theodore John Kaczynski

Articles

Chase, A. 2000. "Harvard and the Making of the Unabomber," The Atlantic Online (June) at *http://www.theatlantic.com/issues/2000/06/chase.htm.*
Kaczynski, T. 1995. Industrial Society and Its Future at *www.time.com/time/reports/unabomber/wholemanifesto.html.*

Government Documents and Publications

Affidavit of FBI Agent T.D. Turchie. 1996. (April 3) at *http://www.unabombertrial.com/documents/turchie_affidavit.html.*
Johnson, S. 1998. Psychological Evaluation of Theodore Kaczynski. at courttv.com/casefiles/unabomber/documents/psychological.html.
Goren, C. FBI Interview. 1996. (March 6) at *www.unabombertrial.com/documents/goren030696.html.*
Kaczynski, D. FBI Interview. 1996. (February 24–25) at *http://unabombertrial.com/documents/david022496.html.*
Wood, S. FBI Interview. 1996. (April 2) at *http://www.unabombertrial.com/documents/sherri.html.*

Periodicals

"Interview with Ted Kaczynski.". 2001. Green Anarchist (July) at *www.spiritoffreedom.org.uk/tedinterview.htm.*
Jackson, D.S. 1997. "He's Not Crazy, He's Our Neighbor." Time (November 3).

News Media

"Wanda Kaczynski Interview." 1996. 60 Minutes (March 26) at *http://web.lexusnexus.com/univers.*

Timothy James McVeigh

Books and Articles

Ainsworth, M.S., M.C. Blehar, E. Waters, and S. Wall. 1978. Patterns of Attachment. Hillsdale, NJ: L. Erbaum Associates.
Durkheim, E. 1951 [orig. 1899]. Suicide: A Study in Sociology. Glencoe, ILL: Free Press.

Michael, L. and D. Herbeck. 2001. American Terrorist: Timothy McVeigh and the Oklahoma City Bombing. New York: HarperCollins/Regan Books.

Weaver, R. and S. Weaver. 1998. The Federal Siege at Ruby Ridge. Marion, MT: Ruby Ridge, Inc.

Government Documents and Publications

Final Report of the Grand Jury. 1998 (December 30) at http://www.courttv.com/casefiles/oklahoma/documents/grandjury_123098.html.

United States v. Timothy James McVeigh (1997). CR. NO. 96-CR–78 at lectlaw.com/bomb.html; and http://more.abcnews.go.com/sections/us/oklahoma/transcripts.html.

News Media

abcnews.com [mcveigh/bombing/oklahoma city]
cnn.com [mcveigh/bombing/oklahoma city]
courttv.com [mcveigh/bombing/oklahoma city]

McVeigh, T. 1998 (June). "Essay." Media Bypass at kwtv.com/news/bombing/mcveigh-essay.htm.

McVeigh, T. 2001. "Letter to Fox News." (April 27) at wysiwyg://4http://foxnews.com/story/0,2933,17500,00.html.

Smith, J. "Inside McVeigh's Mind." 2001 (March 29). ABC News: Prime Time at sysiwyg://15http://more.abcnews.go...e_010329_mcveigh/smith_feature.html.

Eric Robert Rudolph

News Media

Associated Press. 2005. "Manifesto Shows How Rudolph's Mind Works," *Arizona Daily Star* (April 17), A9.

Campo-Flores, A. and C. Skipp. 2005. "Eric Robert Rudolph Says Solitude in Woods Got to Him," *Newsweek* (June 16) at *www.prnewswire.com/2005–06–16* .

Ellison, Q. 2003. "Eric Rudolph Background," Asheville (NC) *Citizen-Times* (May 31) at *www.orig.citizen-times.com/article/news/2003–05–31* .

Gettleman, J. and D.M. Halbfinger. 2005. "Suspect in '96 Olympic Bombing And 3 Other Attacks Is Caught," *New York Times* (June 1), A1.

Morrison, B. 2005. "Eric Rudolph Tells How He Eluded FBI," *USA TODAY* (July 5) at *www.usatoday.com/news/nation/2005–07–05*

———. 2005. "Special Report: Eric Rudolph Writes Home," *USA TODAY* at *www.usatoday.com/news/nation/2005–07–05* .

Ross, M. E. 2005. "Eric Rudolph's Rage Was a Long Time Brewing" (April 13) at *www.msnbc.msn.com/id/2005–04–13* .

Shuster, H. and C. Stone. 2005. "High Times," at *www.cnn.law.printthis. clickability.com/pt/cpt?action=cpt&title=CNN.com+-+High+Times*

Southern Poverty Law Center, Intelligence Report, "Running with Rudolph" at *www.splcenter.org/intelreport/article.jsp?aid=161&printable=1*

Government Documents

United States of America v. Eric Robert Rudolph, Criminal Indictment, November 15, 2000 at *www.Findlaw.com.*
United States v. Eric Robert Rudolph, Guilty Plea and Plea Agreement, CR 00-S–04–422-S (2005).
Eric Rudolph's Statement, April 13, 2005 at *www.tallahassee.com/mldtallahassee/news/local/2005–04–13.*

Index

Aaron, Benjamin, xiii
Abbey, Edward, 329, 330
Abel, Rudolph, 89
abortion, public opposition to, 364–365
abortion clinics, bombings of, 354, 355, 358, 374
African Americans. *See* black Americans; racism as factor in political violence
airplanes. *See* hijackings
All the King's Men, 268
Ambassador Hotel, 70–71, 85–86
American Civil Liberties Union, 119
American Independent Party, 293, 295
American Indians, 33
American Journal of Insanity, 30–31
American Law Institute, 3
American Railway Union, 38
American Terrorist: Timothy McVeigh and the Oklahoma City Bombing, 338
anarchist movement
    Czolgosz's sympathies for, 32, 37, 39, 42, 43–45
    martyrs of, 35
    reactions to McKinley assassination, 32, 49
Ancient Mystical Order of the Rosae Crucis, 78–79, 85
anger-engagement indicators, 377–378, 380–381
    See also specific engagement indicators
anomie, 345
anonymity of domestic terrorists, 383
    Kaczynski, 318, 320, 327, 329
    McVeigh, 351
    Rudolph, 355, 366
    See also publicity, shunning of
anti-semitism, 78, 341, 360–361, 365
    See also Arab-Israeli conflict
anti-social personality, 363–364

anti-war movement (American Civil War), 17–18, 20
Appomattox Campaign, 12, 19, 20, 25
Arab-Israeli conflict
    Byck's interest in, 130, 138
    as central to Sirhan's political views, 71–73, 74, 77–79, 82–84
    dismissed as motive in Sirhan's trial, 70, 89–90
    Robert Kennedy's position on, 76, 79, 83–84
Army of God, 355
    See also Rudolph, Eric Robert
Arnold, Samuel, 24
Arthur, Chester, 246, 248, 252, 253
Aryan Nations, 346
assassinations, 1–2, 2f
    See also political violence
assassinations/violent crime, subject interest in. *See* violent crime/prior assassinations, subject interest in
assassins. *See entries for individual subjects*
ATF (Bureau of Alcohol, Tobacco, and Firearms), 342, 346, 347, 350, 351
    See also FBI (Federal Bureau of Investigation)
attention-seeking behaviors
    Bremer, 181, 183, 185, 186
    Byck, 128, 130–131, 379–380
    Duran, 224, 225–226, 380
    Fromme, 145, 149, 151–154, 375, 380
    Hinckley, xv, 208–210, 211–214, 215–216, 218
    Kaczynski, 319, 324
    McVeigh, 337, 345–346, 347, 350
    Moore, 164–165, 374, 375, 380
    Oswald, 112, 114, 115, 120, 122
    overview, 4–5, 374–375, 379–380
    See also notoriety as motivation; publicity, shunning of

Atypical subjects
    Kaczynski as, 310
    overview, 5–6, 6f, 375
    Ray as, 267, 299–300
    Weiss as, 267, 282
Atzerodt, George, 24, 26, 29
authorities prior knowledge of subjects
    Bremer, 181, 381
    Byck, 128, 129, 130–131, 381
    Duran, 226
    Fromme, 146, 151–152, 381
    Hinckley, 215, 381
    Moore, 146, 161, 162, 163–165, 381
    Oswald, 113, 119–120, 123, 381
    overview, 376, 381
    Ray, 286
Azcue, Eusebio, 117

Bandowski, Frank, 37
Bay Area radicals, 160–163, 164
Beckwith, Byron de la, 297
behavioral patterns, 377–381
    See also motivational patterns
behaviors, suspicious, 119, 130–131, 151–152, 181, 376
Bellamy, Edward, 37
Berkman, Alexander, 36
Berman, Emile Zola, 70, 91
Bickle, Travis, 185, 211
Bidstrup, Hans, 85
Birdzell, Donald T., 66, 68
black Americans
    Booth's views on, 22–23
    Byck's identification with, 127–129, 131
    legal emancipation of, 18–19
    status after emancipation, 33–34, 310
    See also Essex, Mark "Jimmy";
        King, Martin Luther, Jr.; racism as factor in political violence
Black Liberation Army, 127
Blaine, James G., 245–247, 250
Blair House, 64–65, 66, 69
Bolle, Arnold, 320
bombings
    abortion clinics, 354, 355, 358, 374
    carried out by Kaczynski, 310–312, 320, 321, 324, 330
    Federal Building in Oklahoma City, 336–337, 350–351, 353–354

    gay nightclub, 354–355, 357
    Haymarket Square, 35
    Olympics in Atlanta, 354, 357, 374
Booth, John Wilkes, 11–12
    assassination of Lincoln, 25–26
    career as actor, 12, 14–17, 20
    childhood and youth, 13–14
    compared to Rudolph, 366
    death, 28–29
    escape attempted by, 26, 27–28
    hatred of Lincoln, 20, 22, 27–28
    health, physical, 12, 16
    motivations, political, 20, 21–24, 27–28, 29–30
    personal relationships, 16
    plot to abduct president, 20–21, 24–25, 27
    violent crime predictors compared to, 376
    See also Lincoln, Abraham
Boro, Harold, 148
Brady, Jim, xii, xiii
Brady Law, 224
Branch Davidians, 347, 349
Branham, Tom, 359–360
Bremer, Arthur Herman, 380
    assassination attempt on Wallace, 179, 180–181
    childhood and youth, 181–184
    interest in prior assassinations/violent crimes, 187, 194, 195, 378
    interest in victims, 179, 187, 190, 192, 377
    nihilism/perversity, 172, 187, 188–189, 191–192, 197
    notoriety sought by, 186–187, 189, 190–192, 197
    personal relationships, 184–186, 190, 196
    stalking of Nixon, 179, 188–190
    stalking of Wallace, 181, 190–191, 193–194, 378
    trial, 181, 187–188, 192–193, 195–196
    as Type III subject, 171–172, 196–197, 374–375
    violent crime predictors compared to, 376
Bresci, Gaetano, 43
Briggs, L. Vernon, 30, 31–32

Brown, Jerry, 154
Brown, John, 22–23
Brownley, William, xvii
Brussel, James A., 88
Bryan, William Jennings, 38
Bryant, William Cullen, 19
Bugliosi, Vincent, 154
Bundy, Ted, 378
Bunn, Annie, 243
Bureau of Alcohol, Tobacco, and Firearms (ATF), 342, 346, 347, 350, 351
    See also FBI (Federal Bureau of Investigation)
Burk, Dale, 320
Butler, Benjamin, 19
Byck, Samuel Joseph, 380, 381
    assassination attempt on Nixon, 125–126, 131–132
    attention-seeking behaviors, 128, 130–131, 379–380
    childhood and youth, 126
    family estrangement, 128, 130, 131, 132–133
    ideological intensity, 128–129, 131, 139, 377
    interest in Nixon, 128–129, 130, 131, 377
    interest in prior assassinations/violent crimes, 128–129, 131, 133, 378
    marriage, 126–127
    mental health, 104, 127, 128, 129, 132
    motivations, political, 127–131, 132, 137–139
    as precursor for later attacks, 373, 382
    stalking activities, 129, 378
    suicidal tendencies, 128, 129, 131, 133–136
    as Type II subject, 103–104, 139
Byers, Russell G., 292, 293, 294, 298

Campbell, Ben Nighthorse, 224
Campos, Pedro Albizu, 58, 59, 60–61, 66
Cancel-Miranda, Rafael, 67, 68
Capitol, U.S., 1, 67, 216, 373, 378
careers. See occupational instability/marginalization
Carter, Jimmy, 67, 214–215
A Case Book of a Crime Psychiatrist, 88
Castro, Fidel, 111–112, 115–116

Cermak, Anton, 173, 177, 178
Chaney, James, 297
Channing, Walter, 30–31
Chase, Alston, 316, 329
Chase, Salmon P., 19, 24–25
Cheyney, Kathleen, xiii
childhood factors, 103, 374
    See also entries for individual subjects
Chmiel, George, xvii
Choate, Raymond, 151
Christian Identity, 360
Christieson, Sanderson, 32
Civil Air Patrol (CAP), 116
civil rights movement. See King, Martin Luther, Jr.
Civil War, American
    military successes against Confederacy, 12, 19, 20, 25
    reelection of Lincoln, 12–13, 19–20, 21, 22
    unpopularity of Lincoln, 12–13, 17–20, 30
    unpopularity of war, 17–18, 19–20, 27
    See also Confederacy (American Civil War)
Clark, Alvin, 82, 90
Clarke, John Sleeper, 21
class and region subjects. See Booth, John Wilkes; Czolgosz, Leon
Cleveland, Grover, 38
clinical assessments. See criminal responsibility of subjects; insanity defense, use of
Clinton, Bill, 219–220, 224, 226–227, 349, 373
    See also Duran, Francisco Martin
Cochems, Henry F., 255
Coffelt, Leslie, 66, 67
Cohn, Roy, 74
COINTELPRO, 298
Collazo, Oscar
    assassination attempt on Truman, 64–66
    childhood and youth, 58
    involvement in Nationalist Party, 58–59, 60
    motivations, political, 61–63, 65, 67, 68–69
    relationship with wife/children, 59, 60, 63, 64, 69

412   Defining Danger

stalking activities, 64–66
trial and sentencing, 66–68
as Type I subject, 57, 67, 69
violent crime predictors compared to, 376
Collins, E.C., 177
Colo, Steve, xvii
Communist Party, 82, 117, 119
compensatory motives. *See* vengeance as motivation
Confederacy (American Civil War)
    Booth's support for, 20, 21–24, 25
    hopes of independence, 19–20, 23
    Jefferson Davis and, 25, 27, 30
    plot to abduct president, 20–21, 24–25, 27
    successful campaigns against, 12, 19, 20, 25
    See also Civil War, American
Congress, U.S., 1, 67, 216, 373
Conkling, Roscoe, 246, 247, 248
Connally, John, 105, 124
Cordero, Humphrey, 85
Crime and Punishment, 318
crime predictors, violent, 376
criminal responsibility of subjects
    Booth, 29–30, 366
    Bremer, 172, 179–180, 187–188, 192–194, 196–197
    Byck, 104, 132
    Collazo and Torresola, 67, 69
    Czolgosz, 30–32, 41–42, 48, 49–50, 51
    diminished capacity standard, 3, 70, 181, 325, 375–376
    Duran, 227–228
    Fromme, 145–146, 156–157
    Guiteau, 250–252, 261–262
    Hinckley, 219
    Kaczynski, 310, 324–327, 330–331
    Lawrence, 237–239, 261–262
    McVeigh, 352
    M'Naghten Rule, 2, 3, 70, 325
    Moore, 166
    Osward, 104
    Ray, 300
    Rudolph, 363–364, 365–366
    Schrank, 260, 261–262
    Sirhan, 57–58, 69–70, 80–81, 86–87, 91–94
    Weiss, 282

Zangara, 172, 177, 178–179, 196
See also insanity defense, use of
Crist, Buckley, 311
Crowe, Walter, 82, 83
Cuba-U.S. relations, 112, 115–116
Czolgosz, Leon
    anarchist movement and, 32, 43–45, 49
    assassination of McKinley, 30, 46–47
    childhood and youth, 30–31, 32–33, 34–37
    employment, 34–35, 36–37, 42, 78
    motivations, political, 30, 35, 41, 43–45, 48–51
    motivations erroneously ascribed to, 30–32, 45, 49–50, 51
    personality, 37, 42–43
    relationship with family, 33, 39, 41–42, 43, 44
    trial and execution, 30, 47–49
    as Type I subject, 11–12, 49–51
    See also industrial revolution, American

danger assessments, 7, 376, 377–381
Davis, Jefferson, 25, 27, 30
The Day Huey Long Was Shot, 268
Deaver, Michael, xii
Debs, Eugene, 37, 38
Deir Yassin, 72–73
Delahanty, Tom, xii, xiii
delusions as motivations. *See* Type IV subjects (psychotics)
delusions of grandeur
    Guiteau, 239, 247–248, 249–250, 252, 253
    Lawrence, 237, 238
    Rudolph signs of, 365
    Schrank, 259–260
dementia praecox. *See* paranoid schizophrenia
depression-disengagement indicators, 377, 378–381
    See also specific engagement indicators
Desoto plot, 275, 276
Deutsch, Hermann B., 268
Diamond, Bernard L., 70, 89
diminished capacity standard, 3, 70, 325, 375–376

See also criminal responsibility of subjects; insanity defense, use of discrimination. *See* ethnic discrimination; racism as factor in political violence
District of Columbia, Washington, 375–376
Dolores, Carmen, 60, 64
domestic terrorists, 2, 5, 309–310, 373–374, 382–383
   See also anarchist movement; Kacynski, Theodore John; McVeigh, Timothy James; Rudolph, Eric Robert; Symbionese Liberation Army
Dostoyevsky, Fyodor, 171, 179–180, 201, 318
Downs, Joseph H., 66
Duran, Francisco Martin, 380
   assassination attempt on Clinton, 219–220, 226–227
   attention-seeking behaviors, 224, 225–226, 380
   childhood and youth, 201, 220–221
   hatred of Clinton/government, 223–224, 226, 228, 377
   interest in prior assassinations/ violent crimes, 225, 378
   military career, 221–223
   motivations, compensatory, 223–225, 227, 228–229
   relationship with wife/children, 222, 224, 225–226
   stalking activities, 225–226, 378
   trial and sentencing, 227–228
   as Type III subject, 201, 228–229
   violent crime predictors compared to, 376
Durkheim, Émile, 345

Eastern European immigrants. *See* immigrants, Slavic
Ellul, Jacques, 329, 330
Emancipation Proclamation, 18, 19
emotional patterns, 377–381
   See also motivational patterns
emotionally troubled subjects. *See* Type II subjects (political personalities); Type III subjects (nihilists)
employment. *See* occupational instability/marginalization

engagement indicators, 377–381
Engel, George, 35
environmentalist concerns
   Fromme, 150, 151
   Kaczynski, 320, 324, 325–326, 329–330
Essex, Mark "Jimmy", 128–129, 131, 172, 378
ethnic discrimination, 33, 35–36, 39–40, 41
   See also racism as factor in political violence
Evers, Medgar, 297
Every Man a King, 274

Failure Analysis Associates, 124
Fair Play for Cuba, 115–117, 379
family estrangement
   Bremer, 184
   Byck, 128, 130, 131, 132–133
   Czolgosz, 39, 41–42, 43, 44
   Duran, 224, 225–226
   Fromme, 146, 148
   Guiteau, 243–244
   Hinckley, 216, 218
   Kaczynski, 312, 327–328
   McVeigh, 340, 350, 379
   Moore, 159
   Oswald, 110, 120, 122
   overview, 103, 172, 379
   Zangara, 175, 176
FBI (Federal Bureau of Investigation)
   failure to investigate plot to kill King, 294
   harassment of King, 298
   investigation of King's assassination, 294, 298–299, 300
   McVeigh's hatred of, 335, 338, 341–342, 347, 350–351
   monitoring of Oswald, 113, 119–121, 123, 381
   Moore's involvement with, 161, 162, 163–164
   prior knowledge about Duran, 226
   Ruby Ridge assault by, 346
   search for Rudolph, 355, 364
   Waco seige by, 347, 349
   warning Jodie Foster of kidnap threat, 213
   See also Secret Service
Federal Communications Commission, 130, 131

Federal Drug Administration, 359
female subjects, 145–146, 374
   See also Fromme, Lynette Alice; Moore, Sara Jane
Fenner, Nancy Lee, 120
Ferrie, David, 116
Figuero-Cordero, Andres, 67, 68
financial motivations. *See* Ray, James Earl
Fischer, Adolph, 35
Fitts, David, 90
Flores-Rodriguez, Irving, 67
Ford, Gerald
   assassination attempt by Fromme, 146, 154–155, 156
   assassination attempt by Moore, 157, 165
   Byck's grievance against, 130
   security during presidency, 154, 157
Ford's Theater, 15, 25, 26
foreign policy, U.S.
   in Middle East, 79, 82, 84
   towards Cuba, 112, 115–116
   towards Puerto Rico, 59, 61, 62–63, 65, 68
Foreman, Percy, 283, 296–297, 299
Fortier, Michael, 348, 350–351
Foster, Jodie, xv, 211–213, 216, 217, 381
Foster, Marcus, 162
Free Society, 45, 51
Fremont, John C., 19
Frick, Henry Clay, 36
Fromme, Lynette Alice, 377, 381
   assassination attempt on Ford, 154–155, 156
   attention-seeking behaviors, 145, 149, 151–154, 375, 380
   childhood and youth, 146, 147–148
   Manson as Christ, 145–146, 149, 152, 153, 156–157
   Manson as father figure, 146–147, 148
   political/personal motivations, 145–146, 149–152, 153–155, 156–157
   trial and sentencing, 147, 155–156
   as Type II subject, 145–146, 156–157, 374
   violent crime predictors compared to, 376

Garfield, James, 245–246, 248–250, 375
   See also Guiteau, Charles J.
Garry, Charles, 163
gay nightclub, bombing of, 354–355, 357
Gayman, Dan, 360
Gehring, Butch, 322
George Washington University Hospital, xii–xiii
Giardano, Joseph M., xiii
Goldman, Emma
   impression made on Czolgosz by, 43, 44
   views on Czolgosz, 33, 45, 49
   writings on Haymarket Square martyrs, 35
Good, Sandra, 149, 150, 151–152, 154
Goodman, Andrew, 297
Grant, Ulysses S.
   denied third term in presidency, 245
   as military commander, 18, 19, 20
   planned assassination of, 25, 26
   refusal for prisoner exchange, 21
Grapevine Tavern, 293, 295, 298
Greeley, Horace, 19
Guiteau, Charles J.
   assassination of Garfield, 249–250
   childhood and youth, 240–241
   conflicting opinions about, 31, 250–252
   employment schemes/ventures, 241–242, 243, 244–247
   execution, 239, 252–254, 375
   involvement with Oneida Community, 240–241, 242–243, 251
   motivations, delusional, 247–248, 249–250, 251
   stalking activities, 248–249
   trial, 250–252
   as Type IV subject, 235–236, 254, 261–262, 375
gun control laws, 360
   Clinton's ban on assault weapons, 224, 349
   David Koresh's opposition to, 347, 349
   Duran's opposition to, 224, 226
   McVeigh's opposition to, 341–342, 347, 349

Hamilton, Allan McLane, 31
Hanes, Arthur, 296
Hanna, Marcus, 38–39
Harris, William and Emily, 163
hatred of society/self. *See* nihilism as motivation
Haymarket Square affair, 35, 44
He Slew the Dreamer, 283–284
Hearst, Patty, 151, 160, 162, 163, 164
Helter Skelter, 151, 154
Herbeck, David, 338
Herold, David, 24, 26, 27, 28, 29
High Times, 362
hijackings, 125–126, 132, 373, 381–382
Hinckley, John W., Jr., 380, 381
   arrest, xvi–xvii, 218
   assassination attempt on Reagan, xi–xii, xiii–xvi, 202
   attention-seeking behaviors, xv, 208–210, 211–214, 215–216, 218
   childhood and youth, 201, 202, 203–207
   education, college, 207–208, 210, 211
   interest in intended victims, xiv, 215, 216, 377
   interest in prior assassinations/ violent crimes, xiv, 211–212, 215, 216, 378
   motivations, compensatory, 201, 203, 212, 214, 218
   nihilism, 201, 214, 216–217
   notoriety sought by, xiv, xvii, 202, 215
   psychiatric treatment, 215–216, 217–218
   stalking activities, 214–215, 216, 217, 378
   transience, 208, 209–211, 216, 217, 379
   trial and acquittal, xvii–xviii, 3, 218–219, 375–376
   as Type III subject, 201, 219, 380
   violent crime predictors compared to, 376
The History of Violence in America, 378
Hit Man, 225, 226, 378
Hoffa, James, 75
Homestead strike, 36
homosexuality, attacks on, 354–355, 357
Hoover, Herbert, 173, 177
Hoover, J. Edgar, 190, 294, 298–299
   See also FBI (Federal Bureau of Investigation)
Horiuchi, Lon, 335, 338
Hosty, James, 119–120, 123
Howard, John E., 91
Huberty, James, 172
Huey Long, 268
The Huey Long Murder Cases, 268
Huie, William Bradford, 283–284, 292, 296–297
humanism, 316
Humbert I (king), 43, 44
Humphrey, Hubert, 79

identification of suspects
   overview, 376, 381
   suspicious behavior, 119, 130–131, 151–152, 181
   threats, 120, 128, 146, 151, 164–165
   tips from informants, 164–165, 226
   weapons possession, 215
   See also authorities prior knowledge of subjects
ideological intensity of subjects
   Booth, 20, 21–24, 27–28
   Byck, 128–129, 131, 139, 377
   Collazo and Torresola, 58–61, 64
   Czolgosz, 37, 39, 42, 43–45
   Fromme, 148–149, 152, 153–154, 156, 377
   Kaczynski, 309, 322, 324, 329–330, 377
   McVeigh, 337, 338, 341–342, 347, 377
   Moore, 162, 163–164, 166, 377
   Oswald, 107, 115, 377
   overview, 377
   Rudolph, 335, 356–358, 360–361, 365–366, 377
   Sirhan, 77–78, 79, 82–83, 377
immigrants, Slavic, 33, 34, 35–36, 39–40, 41
Indians, American, 33
industrial revolution, American
   economic depression during, 34, 37

ethnic discrimination, 35–36, 39–40, 41
Haymarket Square martyrs, 35, 44
labor strikes, 34, 36, 37–38, 40–41
mainstream society, views of, 38–39, 46
overview, 33–34, 50–51
Industrial Society and Its Future. *See* Unabomber Manifesto
industrial society as target. *See* Kaczynski, Theodore John
Insanity Defense Reform Act, 3
insanity defense, use of
   in Bremer's trial, 181, 187–188, 191, 193–194, 195–196
   diminished capacity standard, 3, 70, 181, 325, 375–376
   in Duran's trial, 227–228
   in Guiteau's trial, 250–252, 254, 375
   in Hinckley trial, xvii–xviii, 3, 218–219, 375–376
   in Lawrence's trial, 238, 239, 375
   M'Naghten Rule, 2, 3, 70, 325
   Schrank's exemption from trial, 260, 375
   in Sirhan's trial, 69–70, 80–81, 87–91
   See also criminal responsibility of subjects
Irgun terrorists, 72, 138
Isaak, Abe, 45, 51
Islamic terrorists, 381–382
   See also Arab-Israeli conflict; Sirhan Bishara Sirhan
Israeli-Arab conflict. *See* Arab-Israeli conflict

Jackson, "Popeye", 160, 161, 164
John Birch Society, 295
Johnson, Andrew, 25, 26, 236
Johnson, Lyndon B., 75, 79, 179
Johnston, Joe, 25
Jones, Boney, 129, 132–133, 134, 136

Kaczynski, Theodore John, 377, 379
   arrest, 324, 329
   attention-seeking behaviors, 319, 324, 380, 383
   as atypical subject, 310, 375
   bombings carried out by, 310–312, 320, 321, 324, 330
   childhood and youth, 312–315
   education, college, 316–317, 318–319
   employment, 319, 320–321
   interest in prior assassinations/violent crimes, 378
   mental illness, conflicting opinions about, 310, 324–327, 330–331
   motivations, personal, 315, 317–318, 320, 327–328, 331
   motivations, political, 309–310, 318, 320, 324, 327–331
   as new breed of killer, 2, 309–310, 374, 382–383
   personal relationship, search for, 317, 319, 321, 331, 374
   trial, 331
   woods, life in, 314, 319–320, 321–324
Kahn, Olaf, 158, 159
Kaiser, Robert Blair, 70, 83, 88, 89, 93
Kauffmann, John, 292–293, 294, 295, 298
Keating, Kenneth, 75
Kennedy, Edward, xiv, 91, 92, 216
Kennedy, John F.
   assassination of, 104–105, 124
   media coverage of assassination, 375
   policies toward Cuba, 112, 115–116
   Robert Kennedy's affiliation with, 75
   scheduled visit to Dallas, 121
   See also Oswald, Lee Harvey
Kennedy, Joseph P., 75
Kennedy, Robert, 124
   advocacy for Israeli interests, 74, 76, 79, 83–84
   assassination of, 70–71, 85–86
   presidential campaign, 79, 84–85
   senatorial campaign, 75–76
   support of McCarthy, 74–75
   See also Sirhan Bishara Sirhan
Key, Francis Scott, 239
Kimmel, Stanley, 12
King, Martin Luther, Jr., 1
   conspiracy to assassinate, 292–295, 296–297, 298, 299
   harassment by FBI, 298–299
   investigation of assassination, 294, 298–299, 300

Ray's perception of, 288
Sirhan's interest in, 82
See also Ray, James Earl
Koresh, David, 347, 349
Ku Klux Klan, 296, 382

labor movement, American
martyrs of, 35
strikes, 34, 36, 37–38, 40–41
weakening of, 39
Lasswell, Harold, 103, 145, 146
Lattimer mines massacre, 40–41
law enforcement officers, 151, 164–165, 376
See also FBI (Federal Bureau of Investigation); Secret Service
Lawrence, David, 84
Lawrence, Richard
assassination attempt on Jackson, 236
latter day comparison to, 373
motivations, delusional, 237, 238, 239, 375
as Type IV subject, 235–236, 239, 261–262, 375
violent crime predictors compared to, 376
LeBlanc, Dudley, 273
Lebron, Lolita, 67
Lee, O.H., 119, 120
Lee, Robert E., 20, 25
Lennon, John, xiv, 209, 216, 217
Lincoln, Abraham, 11
assassination of, 25–26
knowledge of Booth, 15
plot to abduct, 20–21, 24–25, 27
public reaction to assassination, 27–28, 29, 30
reelection of, 12–13, 19–20, 21, 22
unpopularity of, 12–13, 17–20, 30
See also Booth, John Wilkes
The Little Black Book of Explosives, 362
Liuzzo, Viola, 297
Long, Huey P.
assassination of, 268, 280–281
political maneuverings of, 271, 272–273, 274–275, 279–280
See also Weiss, Carl Austin
Looking Backward 2000-1887, 37
Lopez, Manuel, 62

Loughner, Jared Lee, 385-391
Anger-engagement, 386-387
Anti-government views, 386-387
Assassination attempt on Giffords, 385
Criminal responsibility, 389-391
Depression-disengagement, 387-388
Education, 385
Mass murder victims, 385, 388, 390
Nihilism of, 385, 390
Notoriety sought, 390
Parents, 387-388
loyalty/affection as motivation, 146, 374
See also Fromme, Lynette Alice; Moore, Sara Jane

The Mad Booths of Maryland, 12
The Making of an Assassin, 283–284
Malcolm X, 1
Malvo, Lee, 382
The Manner of Man that Kills, 31
Manson, Charles, 158
as Christ figure for Fromme, 145–146, 149, 152, 153, 156–157
as father figure for Fromme, 146–147, 148
Marxist theory, 82–83, 110–111
Maryland, 181
Matthews, John, 25
Maxey, Hugh, 293, 294
McBride, Thomas J., 155
McBroom, Marcus, 71
McCarthy, Eugene, 75, 79
McCarthy, Joseph R., 74–75, 107
McCarthy, Tim, xi, xii, xiii
McClellan, George, 19
McGovern, George, 128, 130, 179, 192
McKinley, James, 276
McKinley, William, 11, 30, 38–39, 46–47, 51
See also Czolgosz, Leon; industrial revolution, American
McMillan, George, 283–284
McMillan, Priscilla Johnson, 110
McVeigh, Timothy James, 377
arrest, 337
attention-seeking behaviors, 337, 345–346, 347, 350, 380

418 Defining Danger

bombing of Murrah Building, 336–337, 350–351, 353–354
childhood and youth, 338–340
comparison to Rudolph, 363, 366
family estrangement, 340, 350, 379
interest in prior assassinations/violent crimes, 341–342, 343, 378
military experience, 343–345
motivations, political, 341–342, 345–347, 348, 349–351, 352–353
as new breed of killer, 2, 309–310, 373–374, 382–383
personal relationships, 342–343, 348–349
transience, 347–348, 379
trial and execution, 352, 353–354
as Type I subject, 335–336, 338, 351–354, 374
media, influence of, 375, 377
  See also attention-seeking behaviors; notoriety as motivation; publicity, shunning of
Melcher, William, 156
mental health assessments. *See* criminal responsibility of subjects; insanity defense, use of
mentally impaired subjects. *See* Type IV subjects (psychotics)
Mercado, Rosa, 60, 63, 64
Meyers, Eddie, xvi–xvii
Michel, Lou, 338
Middle East, U.S. policy towards, 79, 82, 84
  See also Arab-Israeli conflict
Milk, Harvey, 93, 282
mind control, 78–79, 80–81, 90, 91
Minutemen, 295
M'Naghten Rule, 2, 3, 70, 325
  See also criminal responsibility of subjects; insanity defense, use of
Model Penal Code, 3, 70, 325, 375–376
  See also criminal responsibility of subjects; insanity defense, use of
modern era, political violence in, 1–2, 373–374, 377, 382–383
Mohammad, John, 382
The Monkeywrench Gang, 329, 330
Monroe Doctrine, 257
Moore, Sara Jane, 377
  attempted assassination of Ford, 157, 165
  attention-seeking behaviors, 164–165, 374, 375, 380
  Bay Area radicals and, 160–163, 164
  childhood and youth, 157–158
  FBI interactions with, 161, 162, 163–164
  marriages, 159–160
  political/personal motivations, 146, 161–162, 163–164, 165–166
  trial and sentencing, 166
  as Type II subject, 145, 146, 165–166, 374
  violent crime predictors compared to, 376
Moscone, George, 93, 282
motivational patterns, 3–7, 4f, 6f, 374–375
  See also behavioral patterns
Mroz, Vincent P., 66
Murphy, Susan, 149–150
Murrah Federal Building, 336–337, 350–351, 353–354
Murray, Henry A., 316
My First Days in the White House, 275

Nasser, Gamal Abdel, 78
National Rifle Association, 342
nationalism as motivation. *See* Collazo, Oscar; Sirhan Bishara Sirhan; Torresola, Griselio
Nationalist Party of Puerto Rico
  Campos rise to leadership in, 59
  insurrection by, 58, 60–62, 66
  subsequent attacks on U.S. by, 67, 68
  Torresola and Collazo involvement in, 58–59, 60–61
  See also Puerto Rico, U.S. policy towards
Native Americans, 33
New York Times, 71, 324, 380
Nichols, Terry, 348–349, 350, 351
Nieman, Fred C., 37, 45, 50
nihilism as motivation
  Bremer, 172, 187, 188–189, 191–192, 197
  Duran, 201, 228–229
  Hinckley, 201, 214, 216–217
  overview, 5, 171–172, 197
  Zangara, 172, 178, 179, 197

Nixon, Richard M., 79
  Bremer's stalking of, 179,
    188–190
  Byck's assassination attempt on,
    125–126, 132–133
  Fromme's hatred of, 146, 149,
    152–153, 154–155
  Oswald's bluffed threat against,
    114
  reelection and inauguration, 128,
    129, 179, 180
  resignation, 139
  small business loan program, 127
  Watergate investigation, 128, 131,
    132
  See also Byck, Samuel Joseph
Notes from the Underground, 171,
  179–180, 318
notoriety as motivation
  allegedly sought by Ray, 283–284,
    296–297
  Bremer, 186–187, 189, 190–192,
    197
  Byck, 131, 132, 136
  Duran, 225, 228, 229
  Hinckley, xiv, xvii, 202, 215
  McVeigh, 352, 383
  overview, 4–5, 374–375, 382, 383
  See also attention-seeking behaviors;
    publicity, shunning of
Nowak, Walter, 43
Noyes, John Humphrey, 242–243

occult, 78, 158
occupational instability/marginalization
  Bremer, 184, 186
  Byck, 126–127
  Collazo, 59, 60
  Czolgosz refusal to work, 31, 41, 42
  Duran, 223, 224–225
  Guiteau, 241–242, 243, 244–246,
    247
  Hinckley, 210
  Kaczynski, 319, 320–321
  Lawrence, 237
  McVeigh, 341, 342, 345, 347
  Moore, 158, 159, 160
  Oswald, 109, 110, 113, 115, 118
  overview, 379
  as prevalent in Types II/III, 4, 103,
    123, 374
  Ray, 286–287

  Rudolph, 362–363
  Sirhan, 77, 78
  Torresola, 60
  Zangara, 174, 175, 176–177
Odio, Silvia, 116
oedipal conflict as legal defense, 87,
  89, 91
Oklahoma City bombing, 336–337,
  350–351, 353–354
Olney, Richard, 38
Olympics in Atlanta, bombing of, 354,
  357, 374
Oneida Community, 240–241,
  242–243, 251
Organization of Arab Students, 78, 82
Oswald, Lee Harvey, 375, 377, 382
  arrest, 105, 123
  assassination attempt on Walker,
    112–114, 123
  assassination of Kennedy,
    104–105, 124
  authorities prior knowledge of,
    113, 119–120, 381
  childhood and youth, 105–107
  Cuban-alternative, 111–112, 114,
    115–117, 121, 123
  military career, 107–108, 115, 124
  move to Soviet Union, 108–109
  relationship with wife, 110, 114,
    118–119, 120–121, 122
  return to United States, 109–111
  subject of interest by other assassins,
    187, 378
  as Type II subject, 103–104,
    123–124, 379
  violent crime predictors compared
    to, 376

Paine, Ruth, 116, 120
Palestinian conflict. *See* Arab-Israeli
  conflict
Pan-American Exposition, 46
paranoid schizophrenia, 3, 373
  Czolgosz incorrectly labelled as,
    31–32, 49–50
  Duran incorrectly labelled as,
    227–228
  Kaczynski incorrectly labelled as,
    324–326
  Lawrence as, 235–236, 261–262
  Sirhan incorrectly labelled as,
    69–70, 80–81, 87, 90–91

See also insanity defense, use of; Type IV subjects (psychotics)
Parr, Jerry, xi–xiii
Parson, Russell E., 87, 88
Parsons, Albert, 35
Patrusky, Martin, 86
Pavy, Louise Yvonne, 271
Pavy, Octave, 276, 278
Payne, Lewis, 24, 26, 29
Pembrick, Joan, 184–185, 186
Pentagon, attack on, 381
Penthouse, 324
People in Need (PIN), 160, 161
Pepper, Carol Ray, 293
Perez, Jesus, 86
Pickett, Robert, 373
Placentia, Art, 71
Platt, Tom, 246, 247
political extremism. *See* Type I subjects (political extremists)
political personality, 5, 103–104, 145, 146
    See also Type II subjects (political personalities)
political violence, 1–2, 2f, 7, 382
    See also engagement indicators; motivational patterns
politics, American, 1–2, 2f, 33, 38–39, 46
    See also foreign policy, U.S.
Pollack, Seymour, 90
Populist party, 38, 274–275
positivism, 316
Posner, Gerald, 124
Powers, Francis Gary, 89
presidential security
    Ford administration, 154, 157
    Lincoln administration, 21, 24
    McKinley administration, 46, 47
    Nixon administration, 129, 378
    Reagan administration, xi–xii
    tightening of, 309, 373, 374, 375, 382
    Truman administration, 65
    See also Secret Service
presidents/presidential candidates, U.S., 1–2, 2f, 5, 374, 375
    See also specific political figures
psychiatric evaluations. *See* criminal responsibility of subjects; insanity defense, use of
psychotics. *See* Type IV subjects (psychotics)

public, attacks on. *See* domestic terrorists
publicity, shunning of
    Booth, 28–29
    Collazo, 69
    Czolgosz, 50
    Kaczynski, 328–329
    overview, 4
    Rudolph, 356, 366
    Sirhan, 69, 93
    See also attention-seeking behaviors; notoriety as motivation
Puerto Rican nationalism. *See* Nationalist Party of Puerto Rico
Puerto Rico, U.S. policy towards, 59, 61, 62–63, 65, 68
Pullman, George, 38
Pullman strike, 37–38

Rabago, Enrique, 85–86
racism as factor in political violence
    anti-government radicalism, 341–342, 346, 359, 360, 361
    Huey Long assassination, 273, 276, 277, 279–280
    James Earl Ray, alleged motive for, 283–284, 286, 287–289
    Jim Crow system, 33–34, 310
    Lincoln assassination, 18–19, 22–23
    Manson family beliefs about, 149
    Martin Luther King Jr. assassination, 293–295, 297, 298, 299
    Oswald's motivations and, 112
    racial riots of 1960's, 147
    Sam Byck's motivations and, 127–129, 131
    as terrorism, 310, 382
    See also ethnic discrimination
Raoul, 289–292, 297
Rather, Dan, 292
Ray, James Earl
    arrest, 283, 295–296
    as atypical subject, 267, 299, 375, 377, 379
    brothers as accomplices, 289–292
    childhood and youth, 284–286
    conspiracy, evidence of, 292–295, 296–297, 298
    criminal activities, 286–287
    family relations, 285, 289
    motivations, financial, 292, 294–295, 296, 298, 299–300

racism, alleged, 283–284, 286, 287–289
stalking activities, 283, 291, 295, 378
trial, 283, 291, 296–297
violent crime predictors compared to, 376
Reagan, Ronald, 373
assassination attempt on, xi–xii, xiii–xvi, 202
Hinckley stalking of, 216, 217
hospitalization of, xii–xiii
See also Hinckley, John W., Jr.
region and class subjects. See Booth, John Wilkes; Czolgosz, Leon
rejection. See Byck, Samuel Joseph; Oswald, Lee Harvey
Reno, Janet, 224, 335, 338
repentance, lack of
Booth, 27, 28, 29
Collazo, 67, 68–69
Czolgosz, 30, 48
Kaczynski, 330–331
McVeigh, 352–353, 354
overview, 4
Rudolph, 356–358, 366
Sirhan, 86, 91, 92–93
revenge as motivation. See vengeance as motivation
R.F.K. Must Die! A History of the Robert Kennedy Assassination and Its Aftermath, 70
Richey, Charles R., 228
Rio Piedras riots, 59, 62
risk assessments, 7, 376, 377–381
Roe v. Wade, public opposition to, 364–365
See also abortion clinics, bombings of
Roesch, William, 150
Rokosky, Michael, 220
Roosevelt, Franklin D., 39, 173, 274, 275
See also Zangara, Giuseppe
Roosevelt, Theodore, 255–256, 375
See also Schrank, John
Rosecrucian Society, 78–79, 85
Rosenberg case, 107
Ross, John, 351
Rossie, Charles, 152–154
Ruby, Jack, 105, 124
Ruby Ridge, 338, 346–347

Rudolph, Eric Robert, 377
arrest, 356
bombings carried out by, 336, 354–355
childhood and youth, 358–362
escape and hide out, 355–356, 383
interest in prior assassinations/violent crimes, 356, 362, 363, 378
military career, 362–363
motivations, political, 335, 356–358, 359–362, 365–366
as new breed of killer, 2, 309–310, 374, 382–383
relationship with family, 358–359, 363, 366
trial and sentencing, 356
as Type I subject, 336, 354, 364, 365–366, 374
violent crime predictors compared to, 376

sacrificial themes of Type I subjects
Booth, 23, 24, 27, 28–29
Collazo/Torresola, 63, 64, 65, 69
Czolgosz, 48, 49
McVeigh, 336, 352
overview, 4
Rudolph, 365
See also suicidal tendencies of subjects
Schilling, Emil, 43–44
Schorr, Martin M., 87, 88
Schrank, John
assassination attempt on Roosevelt, 255–256, 375
childhood and youth, 257–258
motivations, delusional, 256–257, 258, 259–260
personality and habits of, 257, 258, 260–261
as Type IV subject, 235–236, 261–262, 375
Schutz, Carl, 257
Schwerner, Michael, 297
Scoville, George, 240, 252–254
Secret Service
defense of White House, 373
protection of Ford, 154, 157
protection of Ronald Reagan, xi–xii
protection of Wallace, 180

questioning of Byck, 128, 129, 130, 381
questioning of Moore, 164–165
See also FBI (Federal Bureau of Investigation); presidential security
Sensing, Thurman, 293–294
September 11 attacks, 381-382
Seward, William H., 25, 26
Seymour, Horatio, 18
Share the Wealth, 274, 275
Sherman, William Tecumseh, 19, 20, 25, 249–250
Shrum, Glen, 295
Sirhan Bishara Sirhan, 377, 379
   arrest, 86–87
   assassination of Kennedy, 70–71, 85–86
   childhood and youth, 71–73, 76–77
   family, 71–72, 73, 74, 76, 77
   insanity defense in trial, 69–70, 80–81, 87–91
   interest in prior assassinations/violent crimes, 78, 378
   motivations, political, 71, 77–79, 81, 82–84, 89
   as precursor of Islamic terrorist attacks, 93–94, 381–382
   stalking activities, 84, 85, 378
   subject of interest by other assassins, 187, 194, 378
   trial, 69–70, 89–91
   as Type I subject, 57–58, 91–94
   violent crime predictors compared to, 376
   See also Kennedy, Robert
slavery issue in American Civil War, 18–19, 22–23, 310
   See also racism as factor in political violence
Slavic immigrants, 33, 34, 35–36, 39–40, 41
Small Business Administration, 127, 130, 131, 139
Smith, Gerald L.K., 274
Smith, Walter, 335
socialist movement, 37, 38
socialization. *See* depression-disengagement indicators
sociopaths, 326–327
Soldier of Fortune, 341, 362, 363, 365, 378

Soliah, Kathy, 161
Soliah, Steve, 164
Southern States Industrial Council, 293
Soviet government, 108–109, 117, 119, 120
Spahn, George, 148
Spica, John Paul, 293, 294–295
Spies, August, 35
stalking activities of subjects
   Bremer's stalking of Nixon, 179, 188–190
   Bremer's stalking of Wallace, 181, 190–191, 193–194, 378
   Byck, 129, 378
   Collazo and Torresola, 64–66
   Duran, 225–226, 378
   Hinckley, 214–215, 216, 217, 378
   Oswald, 112–113, 119
   overview, 378, 379
   Ray, 283, 291, 295, 378
   Sirhan, 84, 85, 378
Stalwarts, 244–245, 246, 247, 248, 249
Stoner, J.B., 296
strikes, labor (industrial revolution), 34, 36, 37–38, 40–41
suicidal tendencies of subjects
   Bremer, 179–180, 183, 186–187, 189–190, 194
   Byck, 128, 129, 131, 133–136
   Duran, 225, 226, 229
   Hinckley, xv, 210, 214
   Kaczynski, 321
   McVeigh, 345
   Oswald, 108–109, 113–114, 121, 123
   overview, 4, 5, 380, 383
   Zangara, 177–178, 179
   See also sacrificial themes of Type I subjects
Surratt, John, 24, 29
Surratt, Mary, 29
suspicious behaviors, 119, 130–131, 151–152, 181, 376
Sutherland, John, 293, 294, 295, 298
Symbionese Liberation Army, 310
   arrest of Patty Hearst, 164
   kidnap of Patty Hearst, 151, 160, 162, 163
   political views, 151, 161

Taft, William Howard, 255
Tate-LaBianca murders, 149, 150, 151, 152, 156

Taxi Driver (movie), xv, 185, 211–212, 378
The Technological Society, 329
technology as target. *See* Kaczynski, Theodore John
terrorism, political, 1–2, 2f, 7, 382
    See also engagement indicators; motivational patterns
Texas School Book Depository, 105, 118, 121
Thompson, Ely O., 178
threats
    made by Byck, 128
    made by Fromme, 146, 151, 154
    made by Moore, 146, 164–165
    made by Oswald, 120
    overview, 376
Thume, Paul, 260
Thunderbolt, 358–359
Tilton, Theodore, 19
Tippit, J.D., 105, 123
tips from informants, 164–165, 226, 376
Tolson, Clyde A., 298
Torresola, Griselio
    assassination attempt on Truman, 64–66
    childhood and youth, 58
    death, 66
    involvement in Nationalist Party, 58–59, 60–61
    motivations, political, 61–63, 65, 69
    relationship with wife/children, 59, 60, 63, 64, 69
    stalking activities, 64–66
    as Type I subject, 57, 69
    violent crime predictors compared to, 376
    See also Collazo, Oscar
trances, self-induced, 89–90
    See also mind control
transience of subjects
    Czolgosz, 44–45
    Guiteau, 243, 244
    Hinckley, 208, 209–211, 216, 217, 379
    Lawrence, 236–237
    McVeigh, 347–348, 379
    Oswald, 110, 118, 119
    overview, 379
    Rudolph, 362, 363

Troyer, Charles, 125, 126
Truman, Harry S., 57, 64–66, 67
    See also Collazo, Oscar; Torresola, Griselio
The Turner Diaries, 341–342, 348, 349, 350
Type I subjects (political extremists)
    Booth as, 11–12, 29–30
    Collazo as, 57, 67, 69
    context as critical to, 7, 11–12, 29–30, 50–51, 57–58
    Czolgosz as, 11–12, 49–51
    Fromme's similarities to, 156–157
    Kaczynski's similarities/differences, 310, 326, 328–331, 374
    McVeigh as, 335–336, 338, 351–354, 374
    Moore's similarities to, 146
    Oswald contrasted with, 123–124
    overview, 4, 4f, 374
    Rudolph as, 336, 354, 364, 365–366, 374
    Sirhan as, 57–58, 91–94
    Torresola as, 57, 69
    Type III, contrasted with, 172, 178, 196
Type II subjects (political personalities)
    Bremer contrasted with, 196
    Byck as, 103–104, 139
    female subjects as variation on, 145–146, 374
    Fromme as, 145–146, 156–157, 374
    Kaczynski contrasted with, 310, 318, 327–329, 330
    Moore as, 145, 146, 165–166, 374
    Oswald as, 103–104, 123–124, 379
    overview, 4–5, 4f, 103–104, 374–375, 378–379
    as predominant threat to political figures, 374–375, 382
    Type I, contrasted with, 69, 104, 123
    Zangara contrasted with, 178, 196
Type III subjects (nihilists)
    Bremer as, 171–172, 196–197, 374–375
    Duran as, 201, 228–229
    Hinckley as, 201, 219, 380
    Kaczynski contrasted with, 318, 326–327, 330

424   **Defining Danger**

overview, 4*f*, 5, 171–172, 374–375, 378–379
    as predominant threat to political figures, 374–375, 382
    Type I, contrasted with, 69, 172, 178, 196
    Zangara as, 171–172, 178–179, 196–197, 374
Type IV subjects (psychotics)
    Collazo/Torresola contrasted with, 69
    Guiteau as, 235–236, 254, 261–262
    Kaczynski contrasted with, 310, 324–326
    Lawrence as, 235–236, 239, 261–262
    overview, 4*f*, 5–6, 235, 261–262, 375
    Rudolph contrasted with, 363–364, 365
    Schrank as, 235–236, 261–262
    Type II, contrasted with, 104, 157
    Type III, contrasted with, 172, 196–197
typology, motivational, 3–7, 4*f*, 6*f*, 374–375
    See also behavioral patterns

Umm Kulthum, 76–77
Unabomber Manifesto
    as evidence of Kaczynski's sanity, 324, 325, 326
    political ideas expressed in, 324, 328, 330
    publication of, 324, 329, 380
    See also Kaczynski, Theodore John
unemployment. *See* occupational instability/marginalization
Unintended Consequences, 351
Union (American Civil War), 17–19
    See also Civil War, American
Unrue, Drew, xii
Unruh, Jesse, 71, 86
U.S. Capitol, 1, 67, 216, 373, 378
U.S. politics, 1–2, 2*f*, 33, 38–39, 46
    See also foreign policy, U.S.
U.S. presidents. *See* presidents/presidential candidates, U.S.

Vallandigham, Clement L., 19

Vandervort, Edward, 150
vengeance as motivation
    Bremer, 172, 186–187, 191–192, 196, 197
    Byck, 103–104, 128–129, 130, 131–133, 139
    Duran, 223–225, 227, 228–229
    Hinckley, 201, 203, 212, 214, 218
    Moore, 164, 165–166
    Oswald, 103–104, 120, 121, 123
    Zangara, 172, 174–175, 177, 178–179, 197
victim, subject interest in
    Booth, 20, 22, 27–28
    Bremer, 179, 187, 190, 192, 377
    Byck, 128–129, 130, 131, 377
    Duran, 224, 225, 226, 377
    Fromme, 154–155
    Guiteau, 247–248, 249–250, 251–252
    Hinckley, xiv, 215, 216, 377
    Kaczynski, 310, 311–312, 318, 320, 322
    Lawrence, 237, 238, 239
    McVeigh, 335, 338, 351, 352–353
    Moore, 164, 166
    Oswald, 115, 117, 121, 377
    overview, 377
    Rudolph, 357–358
    Schrank, 256–257, 258, 259
    Sirhan, 71, 79, 81, 82–84, 377
    Zangara, 173, 177
Victor Emmanuel III (king), 175
Vidrine, Arthur, 275
violence, political, 1–2, 2*f*, 7, 382
    See also engagement indicators; motivational patterns
violent crime predictors, 376
violent crime/prior assassinations, subject interest in
    Bremer, 187, 194, 195, 378
    Byck, 128–129, 131, 133, 378
    Czolgosz, 43, 44
    Duran, 225, 378
    Hinckley, xiv, 211–212, 215, 216, 378
    Kaczynski, 378
    McVeigh, 341–342, 343, 378
    Oswald, 378
    overview, 377–378
    Rudolph, 356, 362, 363, 378
    Sirhan, 78, 378

Waco seige, 347, 349
Walker, Edwin A., 112, 113, 114, 119, 123
Wallace, George
　assassination attempt on, 179, 180–181
　Bremer's stalking of, 181, 190–191, 193–194, 378
　racist affiliations of, 180, 293–294, 295, 297
　See also Bremer, Arthur Herman
Warren, Robert Penn, 268
Warren Commission, 124
Washington, D.C., 375–376
Washington Post, 324, 380
Watergate investigation, 128, 131, 132
Watson, Tom, 38
Watson, Van, 158
weapons possession, 215, 376
Weaver, Randy, 346–347
W.E.B. DuBois Club, 82
Weicker, Lowell, 130
Weidner, John, 78
Weiss, Carl Austin
　as apolitical, 270, 273, 279, 282
　assassination of Long, 268, 280–281
　as atypical subject, 267, 282, 375
　career, 270, 271, 375
　childhood and youth, 269–270
　marriage and family, 271–272, 276, 277–278
　motivation, protection of family as, 279–280, 282
　motives, conflicting theories on, 268, 275–279
　violent crime predictors compared to, 376

Weston, Russell, 373
White, Dan, 282
White, Travis, 71
White Citizens' Council, 293, 295
White House, 130–131, 132, 226–227, 373, 382
　See also Secret Service
white supremacy groups, 293–294, 295, 298, 346, 360
Whitman, Charles, 172, 187
Williams, T. Harry, 268, 274, 276
Wilson, Woodrow, 255
Wood, Sherri, 323–324, 326
Woodbury, Levi, 236
working class conditions (industrial revolution), 34, 35, 36, 38, 40
　See also labor movement, American
World Trade Center, attacks on, 381–382

Yates, Daniel, 382
Yoshimura, Wendy, 164

Zangara, Giuseppe
　attempted assassination of Roosevelt, 173
　childhood and youth, 173–174
　employment/financial activities, 174, 175, 176–177
　motivations, 172, 174, 175, 177–178, 179
　trial and execution, 177–178
　as Type III subject, 171–172, 178–179, 196–197, 374
Ziegler, Elsie, 259
Zinman, David, 268
Zionist movement, 72, 73, 78
　See also Arab-Israeli conflict

CPSIA information can be obtained at www.ICGtesting.com
Printed in the USA
BVOW011716190612

293125BV00003B/4/P